Frommer's®
Switzerland

Our Switzerland

by Darwin Porter & Danforth Prince

PERHAPS THE MOST FAMOUS QUOTE ABOUT SWITZERLAND WAS uttered in the 1949 film noir classic, *The Third Man*. The cynical character Harry Lime, played by troubled genius Orson Welles, claimed that after 500 years of peace and democracy, the sum total of Switzerland's achievement was the cuckoo clock. Welles had a point—it's easy to caricature the country as the home of watches, bankers (derisively called "the gnomes of Zurich"), great chocolate, greater cheese, and the world's best pocketknives.

But Switzerland is so much more. We have returned, time and again, because we find this the world's most beautiful country. Blue lakes, flowing rivers, towering alpine peaks, and lush valleys—it's a picture postcard come to life. The cities feel at once aged and exuberantly modern—particularly Zurich, with its 11th-century cathedral serving as backdrop for the annual Street Parade, an anything-goes dance party that celebrates love, peace, and tolerance. And there's a tradition of diversity here, with French, German, Italian, and Romansh the four official languages spoken.

Switzerland's innkeepers have raised hospitality to a fine art, but it comes at a cost—this is not the most affordable European country to visit. But watching the sun set over the Alps for the first time is a priceless memory. Read on and discover some of our favorite Swiss things.

© VISUM Foto GmbH/Alamy

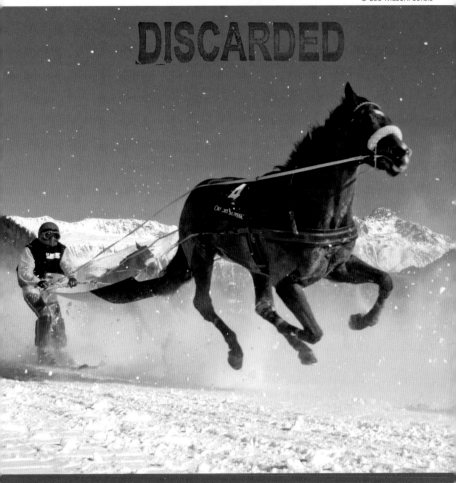

DISCARDED

The capital city of Bern is home to the world's second most famous time-piece (next to London's Big Ben). At four minutes before every hour, the **ZYTGLOGGETURM (left)** puts on a delightful show of revolving mechanical bear cubs, jesters, and a crowing cock, among other figures—and has done so since 1530. For centuries all clocks in the land were synchronized to this timepiece.

At the ritzy ski resort St. Moritz, in the upper Engadine, adventurers brave the alpine air to go **SKIJÖRING (above)**, where a studly horse, trained to run on ice, pulls a flamboyantly attired skier across untrammeled snowfields or frozen lakes. This 100-year-old sport has been compared to horse-drawn waterskiing; competitive races are staged, and skiers sometimes harness reindeer or dogs as well.

At 2,463m (8,079 ft), **MT. SÄNTIS** is the highest peak in the Alpstein massif in northeastern Switzerland, a mere tiddler when compared to other Swiss mountains such as the Matterhorn. We prefer the nail-biting, cable-car ascent to the jagged peak. From the observatory, you can see the Grisons, the Bernese Alps, the Voralberg mountains, Lake Constance, Lake Zurich, and, on a clear day, Swabia in southern Germany.

The Swiss love their cows, and at the end of every summer, farmers lead a procession of **COWS IN FANCY HEADDRESS (right)** from alpine meadows down to all their villages. But Swiss cows are not all stereotypically placid cud-chewers. In the Valais region, Combat de Reines (or cowfights) are staged like bullfights; cows charge, lock horns, and push each other back. The winner is declared "queen of the cows."

This **MATTERHORN,** at 4,410m (14,465 ft.), evokes Switzerland itself, much like the Eiffel Tower evokes Paris. Locals say this snaggle-toothed mountain "blinds the sun"; so far, the snowy rock has yet to succumb to global warming. In 1865, the English explorer, Edward Whymper, along with his guides, scaled the mountain, a feat once thought impossible.

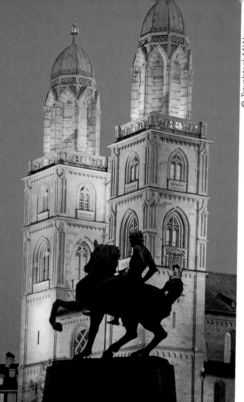

Long the symbol of Zurich, the **GROSSMÜNSTER (left; "great church")** was erected between the 11th and 13th centuries on the foundation of a church said to have been founded by Charlemagne. The women of Switzerland's smallest canton, Appenzell, still wear their **TRADITIONAL COSTUMES (below).** with embroidered "necklaces" and elaborate headdresses, but only on special occasions such as the Alpfahrten, when the cows are herded down the mountain from their summer meadows. From fondue pots to the raclette held over an open fire to soften, cheese remains a way of life in Switzerland, especially for **ALPINE CHEESE-MAKERS (right)** such as this one. Lucerne's **KAPELLBRÜCKE (below right),** or Chapel Bridge, spans the Reuss River and has been called the most romantic bridge in the world. Constructed in 1333 but damaged by fire in 1993, it has been restored to its original style. The 122 paintings that hang inside, from its arched roof, illustrate the daily life of the town.

The **LAUTERBRUNNEN VALLEY,** in the Bernese Oberland, stretches for 18km (11 miles) between the mountain resorts of Wengen and Mürren. Aficionados call it Europe's most beautiful valley, and rightly so; it has 72 waterfalls plummeting down its towering rock walls, hence its name (*Lauterbrunnen* means "loud springs"). The valley inspired both Goethe, who put it to poetry, and Franz Schubert, who put it to music.

Frommer's®
Switzerland

14th Edition

by Darwin Porter & Danforth Prince

WILEY

Wiley Publishing, Inc.

Published by:

WILEY PUBLISHING, INC.

111 River St.
Hoboken, NJ 07030-5774

ISBN 978-0-470-54125-8

Editors: William Travis with Jennifer Polland
Production Editor: Michael Brumitt
Cartographer: Guy Ruggierro
Photo Editor: Richard H. Fox
Production by Wiley Indianapolis Composition Services

Front cover photo: Graubunden, Engadine, Guarda village ©SIME / eStock Photo
Back cover photo: Zermatt, Valais: colorful mountain chalet in the shadow of the Matterhorn ©John Warburton-Lee / DanitaDelimont.com

For information on our other products and services or to obtain technical support, please contact our Customer Care Department within the U.S. at 877/762-2974, outside the U.S. at 317/572-3993 or fax 317/572-4002.

Wiley also publishes its books in a variety of electronic formats. Some content that appears in print may not be available in electronic formats.

Manufactured in the United States of America

5 4 3 2 1

CONTENTS

LIST OF MAPS

ABOUT THE AUTHORS

As a team of veteran travel writers, **Darwin Porter** and **Danforth Prince** have produced numerous titles for Frommer's, which have included Italy, France, the Caribbean, Spain, England, Scotland, and Germany. A film critic, columnist, and broadcaster, Porter is also a Hollywood biographer. Recent releases by Darwin include *Merv Griffin: A Life in the Closet,* documenting the private life of the richest and most notorious man in television, and *Paul Newman, The Man Behind the Baby Blues.* Prince was formerly employed by the Paris bureau of the *New York Times* and is today the president of Blood Moon Productions and other media-related firms.

HOW TO CONTACT US

In researching this book, we discovered many wonderful places—hotels, restaurants, shops, and more. We're sure you'll find others. Please tell us about them, so we can share the information with your fellow travelers in upcoming editions. If you were disappointed with a recommendation, we'd love to know that, too. Please write to:

Frommer's Switzerland, 14th Edition
Wiley Publishing, Inc. • 111 River St. • Hoboken, NJ 07030-5774

AN ADDITIONAL NOTE

Please be advised that travel information is subject to change at any time—and this is especially true of prices. We therefore suggest that you write or call ahead for confirmation when making your travel plans. The authors, editors, and publisher cannot be held responsible for the experiences of readers while traveling. Your safety is important to us, however, so we encourage you to stay alert and be aware of your surroundings. Keep a close eye on cameras, purses, and wallets, all favorite targets of thieves and pickpockets.

FROMMER'S STAR RATINGS, ICONS & ABBREVIATIONS

Every hotel, restaurant, and attraction listing in this guide has been ranked for quality, value, service, amenities, and special features using a **star-rating system.** In country, state, and regional guides, we also rate towns and regions to help you narrow down your choices and budget your time accordingly. Hotels and restaurants are rated on a scale of zero (recommended) to three stars (exceptional). Attractions, shopping, nightlife, towns, and regions are rated according to the following scale: zero stars (recommended), one star (highly recommended), two stars (very highly recommended), and three stars (must-see).

In addition to the star-rating system, we also use **seven feature icons** that point you to the great deals, in-the-know advice, and unique experiences that separate travelers from tourists. Throughout the book, look for:

(**Finds**)	Special finds—those places only insiders know about
(**Fun Facts**)	Fun facts—details that make travelers more informed and their trips more fun
(**Kids**)	Best bets for kids, and advice for the whole family
(**Moments**)	Special moments—those experiences that memories are made of
(**Overrated**)	Places or experiences not worth your time or money
(**Tips**)	Insider tips—great ways to save time and money
(**Value**)	Great values—where to get the best deals

The following **abbreviations** are used for credit cards:

AE	American Express	**DISC**	Discover	**V**	Visa
DC	Diners Club	**MC**	MasterCard		

TRAVEL RESOURCES AT FROMMERS.COM

Frommer's travel resources don't end with this guide. Frommer's website, **www.frommers. com**, has travel information on more than 4,000 destinations. We update features regularly, giving you access to the most current trip-planning information and the best airfare, lodging, and car-rental bargains. You can also listen to podcasts, connect with other Frommers.com members through our active-reader forums, share your travel photos, read blogs from guidebook editors and fellow travelers, and much more.

The Best of Switzerland

Presumably you're visiting Switzerland to relax and have a good time, and you don't want to waste precious vacation hours searching for the best deals and experiences. So take us along and we'll do the work for you. Throughout our years traveling in Switzerland, we've walked the best lakeshores, reviewed countless restaurants, inspected hotels ranging from remote alpine inns to luxurious city palaces, and sampled the best skiing, mountain climbing, and hiking. We've even learned where to get away from it all when you want to escape the crowds. The following is a very personal, opinionated list of what we consider to be the best Switzerland has to offer.

1 THE BEST TRAVEL EXPERIENCES

- **Hiking the Swiss Mountains:** From the time the snows melt in spring until late autumn when winds blow too powerfully, visitors head for the country's alpine chain to hike its beautiful expanses. Well-trodden footpaths through the valleys and up the mountains are found in all the resorts of Switzerland. Hiking is especially enjoyable in the Ticino and the Engadine, but quite wonderful almost anywhere in the country. You'll find fewer visitors in some of the less inhabited valleys, such as those in the Valais. Every major tourist office in Switzerland has a free list of the best trails in their area. If you go to one of the area's local bookstores, you can purchase topographical maps of wilderness trails.

- **Viewing Castles & Cathedrals:** There is so much emphasis on outdoor sports in Switzerland that many visitors forget that it's rich in history and filled with landmarks from the Middle Ages. Explore at random. Visit the castle at Chillon where Lord Byron wrote *The Prisoner of Chillon.* Or Gruyères, which everyone knows for the cheese, but is also the most craggy castle village of Switzerland, complete

with dungeon and spectacular panoramic views. Both Bern and Basel have historic Münsters of cathedrals—the one in Bern dates from the 14th century. Among the great cathedrals, St. Nicholas's Cathedral, in the ancient city of Fribourg near Bern, dominates the medieval quarter, and Schloss Thun, on Lake Thun in the Bernese Oberland, was built by the dukes of Zähtingen at the end of the 12th century.

- **Joining the Revelers at Fasnacht (Basel):** Believe it or not, Switzerland has its own safe and very appealing version of Carnival, which dates back to the Middle Ages. It begins the Monday after Ash Wednesday (usually in late Feb or early Mar). The aesthetic is heathen (or pagan), with a touch of existentialist absurdity. The horse-drawn and motorized parades are appropriately flamboyant, and the cacophonous music that accompanies the spectacle includes the sounds of fifes, drums, trumpets, and trombones. As many as 20,000 people participate in the raucous festivities, which may change your image of strait-laced Switzerland. See "Basel" in chapter 7.

- **Summiting Mount Pilatus:** The steepest cogwheel train in the world—with a 48-degree gradient—takes you to the top of Mount Pilatus, a 2,100m (6,888-ft.) summit overlooking Lucerne. Once at the top you'll have a panoramic sweep that stretches all the way to Italy. Until the 1600s it was forbidden to climb this mountain because locals feared that Pontius Pilate's angry ghost would cause trouble. According to the legend, his body was brought here by the devil. Queen Victoria made the trip in 1868 and did much to dispel this long-held myth. You can follow in the queen's footsteps. See "Lucerne" in chapter 13.

- **Discovering the Lakes of Central Switzerland:** Experience the country's sparkling lakes with a tour through central Switzerland on the William Tell Express. Begin in Lucerne on a historic paddle-wheel steamer that chugs across the lake while you have lunch. Before the tour is over, you'll have boarded a train on the lake's most distant shore, traversed one of the most forbidding mountain ranges in central Europe (through the relative safety of the St. Gotthard Tunnel), and descended into the lush lowlands of the Italian-speaking Ticino district. See chapter 13.

- **Wandering the Waterfront Promenades:** One of the greatest summer pleasures of Switzerland is wandering the palm-lined promenades in the Ticino, the Italian-speaking southern section of the country. The best resorts—and the best promenades—are found at Ascona, Locarno, and Lugano. You'll have both lake scenery and the rugged Italian Alps as a backdrop on your stroll. Of course, you can do more than just walk: You'll have the opportunity for swimming, boating, cafe sitting, people-watching, and even shopping. At night, when the harbor lights shine, you can join the Ticinese in their evening stroll. See chapter 16.

2 THE BEST SCENIC DRIVES

- **The Road over the Great St. Bernard Pass:** Of the many mountain passes of alpine Europe, this is the most famous. Since the days of the Roman Empire, much of the commerce between northern Italy and the rest of Europe has navigated this low point in one of the most forbidding mountain ridges in the world. Modern-day pilgrims follow in the steps of Napoleon and his armies, who traversed the perilous pass in 1800 to invade Italy. Since 1964, a tunnel beneath the mountains has allowed traffic to move unhindered for at least half of every year. The Swiss section of the pass road begins in French-speaking Martigny and ends in Italian-speaking San Bernardino, 56km (35 miles) away, but most motorists use the pass road as a slow but scenic midsummer diversion with long drives that begin near Basel or Zurich and end in the Italian cities of Aosta or Milan. See "Verbier" in chapter 10.

- **The Road over the Furka Pass:** Traveling in a southwest-to-northeast line for only 32km (20 miles), from the hamlet of Gletsch, northeast of Brig, to the mountain resort of Andermatt, the road follows the high-altitude frontier between German-speaking and Italian-speaking Switzerland. En route you'll see the frozen mass of the glacier that feeds the Rhône and scenery that's absolutely magnificent. Any number of scenic highlights radiate out from here. See "Andermatt" in chapter 13.

- **St. Gotthard Pass Road:** One of the most vital roads in Europe stretches for

64km (40 miles) between German-speaking Andermatt and the Italian-speaking village of Biasca. It shares many characteristics of the above-mentioned St. Bernard Pass, which lies about 40 almost-impassable kilometers (25 miles) to the east. Some historians have suggested that the tolls collected since the 1300s along this road helped finance the continued independence of Switzerland itself. Since 1980, a 16km (10-mile) tunnel has allowed motorists to travel the route year-round. Traffic on the high road, however, remains clogged with summer vacationers who come for the stunning views. The landscape is mournful and bleak throughout much of this adventure, a testimony to the savage climactic conditions that exist at these high altitudes. See "Andermatt" in chapter 13.

- **The Road over the Bernina Pass:** During the Middle Ages, merchants led horse- and donkey-drawn caravans over this pass, risking their lives to carry supplies between what are now the German-speaking and Italian-speaking regions of Switzerland. Frostbite was commonplace, and many died in the snows en route. Today cars can navigate the pass as part of a 2-hour, 55km (34-mile) drive between St. Moritz and Tirano. Be warned: This drive is never

problem-free. The road is winding, and ice patches have a way of surfacing even in summertime. Snow usually closes the pass completely between mid-October and late April, although trains can usually get through except during the worst midwinter blizzards. But the views are truly spectacular. See "Pontresina" in chapter 15.

- **The Simplon Pass Road:** Unlike the St. Gotthard Pass Road, which is interspersed with artfully engineered bridges, hairpin turns, and retaining walls, the Simplon Pass Road gracefully conforms to the natural topography of some of the most scenic mountainsides in Europe. It stretches about 64km (40 miles), from German-speaking Brig over the Italian border to Domodossola. Napoleon demanded a low-altitude pass for his artillery, and the present road follows the 1805 plan designs. Napoleon's grip on power, ironically, crumbled before his armies could ever use the pass. Despite the best efforts of the Swiss Department of Highways, the road is often closed between December and early May, with automobiles diverted onto flatbed trains instead. These are rather awkwardly carried through one of the longest railway tunnels in the world, the Simplon Tunnel. See chapter 16.

3 THE BEST TRAIN TRIPS

- **The Glacier Express:** It's advertised as the slowest express train in the world, requiring more than 7½ hours to pass through southeastern Switzerland. Despite that, its 274km (170 miles) of track are an awesome triumph of engineering (of which Switzerland is justifiably proud). Beginning every day in Zermatt, in southwest Switzerland, and ending in St. Moritz, in Switzerland's

east, it crosses more than 291 bridges and goes through 91 tunnels, traversing some of the country's most inaccessible mountains with an ease that medieval pilgrims would have considered an act of God. You can also take the train from St. Moritz to Zermatt. Naturally, the scenery is breathtaking. The windows are large enough to allow clear views, and a dining car serves lunch with civilized efficiency. Advance reservations are required; for more information, call **Rail Europe** (℡ **877/272-RAIL** [272-7245]). See chapters 10 and 15.

- **The Palm Express:** This 2-day itinerary of bus and rail routes takes travelers from St. Moritz (in the rugged Engadine district, near Switzerland's eastern frontier) to either Brig or (for a supplemental fee) Zermatt, in Switzerland's southwest. More leisurely than either of the two rail routes described here, it includes a hotel night en route. The scenery is spectacular. For more information, call **Rail Europe** (℡ **877/272-RAIL** [272-7245]). See chapter 15.

- The **Bernina Express:** Like the Glacier Express, this railway excursion offers sweeping views of otherwise inaccessible alpine landscapes. A 4-hour trip (each way), it begins in the German-speaking capital of Zurich, traverses isolated regions where the native tongue is the ancient Romansh language, and ends in Italian-speaking Lugano. The rugged, high-altitude landscapes near Chur give way to the verdant, palm-lined lake districts near Tirano. It's the only train route in Switzerland that crosses the Alps without the benefit of tunnels en route. (It also travels some of the steepest railway lines in the world, negotiated without the benefit of racks and pinions.) Consider extending this trip with bus connections from Tirano—the end of the rail line—to the resort town of Lugano. For more information, call **Rail Europe** (℡ **877/272-RAIL** [272-7245]). See chapter 16.

4 THE BEST WALKS

- **Mount Säntis:** At 2,463m (8,079 ft.), Säntis is the northern outpost of the Alps and the most towering peak in the Alpstein massif. The quaint village of Appenzell is a good place to base yourself. The walk itself begins in the village of Wasserrauen, which is linked to Appenzell by hourly trains. After 8.9km (5½ miles)—4½ to 5½ hours, depending on your stamina—it ends at the village of Schwägalp, from which you can take a cable car to the viewing platform overlooking the summit of Säntis. Schwägalp is the terminus of the roads coming in from Urnäsch and Neu-St-Johann. See "Appenzell" in chapter 6.

- **Grosse Scheidegg:** This popular walk ("the Great Watershed" in English) takes you through some of the most dramatic scenery in the Jungfrau region of central Switzerland, known for stunning white glaciers and soaring summits. One of the highlights of the walk is the awesome beauty of the Wetterhorn's massive gray rock walls. Setting out from the village of Meiringen, the walk ends 21km (13 miles) away (6½–9 hr.) in the resort of Grindelwald. If you get tired, take advantage of the bus stops along the way. See "Grindelwald" in chapter 9 for more details.

- **The Upper Engadine Lakes:** The four highland lakes of the Upper Engadine are 1,771m (5,809 ft.) above sea level, but as you walk along, it's like traversing the floor of a valley. Craggy ranges and scenic lake vistas greet you at every turn as you make your way along the 14km (8½-mile), 3- to 3½-hour walk from Maloja to the resort of Silvaplana. You'll pass through the enchanting village of Segl-Maria, one of the most charming of the Romanesque-style villages in eastern Switzerland, eventually arriving at the western edge of Lej da Silvaplana, a lake of unsurpassed beauty. See chapter 15.

- **Around the Katzensee:** If you're in Zurich on a hot summer day and you're longing for the perfect place to swim, try cycling from Seebach station through the shaded woods to Katzenruti (picnic spot) and then on to the Katzensee, a lake with a beach and Waldhaus restaurant. Return via Affoltern. Duration: 1½ hours, 13km (8 miles). See "Attractions" in chapter 5.

- **Around the Lake of Murten:** Start out at the small medieval town of Murten (stroll down the main street and visit the castle). Carry on to Faoug, Salavaux, Bellerive (a perfect lookout point), and Vully. Duration: 4 hours, 40km (25 miles). See "Murten" in chapter 7.

- **In the Rhône Valley, Lower Valais:** Cyclists on this route through the Valais set off from Martigny station then cross the Rhône River to the villages of Fully, Chataigner, Mazembroz, and Saillon. The cable-car ride to Iserables from the terminus of Riddes is well worth the trip. Duration: 1½ hours, 20km (12 miles). See chapter 10.

- **Through the Lake Geneva Vineyards:** Before leaving from the station at Morges, take a look at the castle (military museum). The route then leads up to Lully and, via Bussy and Ballens, to Biere. Continuing down a small valley to Begnins and Fechy (a scenic lookout point), you'll find yourself in Aubonne. Finally, take the second-class road, via Lavigny, Villars-sous-Yens, and Lully, back to Morges. Duration: 5½ hours, 56km (35 miles). See "Attractions" in chapter 12.

- **Along the Shore of Lake Lucerne:** This trip can last a whole day, as there are so many spots worth stopping at along the way. Set off from Lucerne station and head for St. Niklausen and Kastanienbaum in the direction of Tribschen (location of the Richard Wagner Museum). The most beautiful stretch is along the lake to Winkel-Horw Beach. Return to Lucerne. Duration: 1½ hours, 13km (8 miles). See "Lucerne" in chapter 13.

- **Lugano's Hinterland:** To discover the small villages around Lugano, set off from the station for the nature reserve at Origlio Lake, and then proceed to Ponte Capriasca (a parish church with a well-preserved copy of Leonardo da Vinci's *The Last Supper*). Continue to Tesserete and Colla, along the left valley side of Cassarate, through the woods to Sonvico, and then on to Dino, Ponte di Valle, and Lugano. Duration: 4 hours, 37km (23 miles). See "Lugano" in chapter 16.

6 THE BEST SMALL TOWNS & VILLAGES

- **Appenzell:** Nowhere is folkloric Switzerland as well preserved as at the base of the green foothills of the Alpstein, where this old-fashioned country town still has cowmen in yellow breeches and scarlet waistcoats walking its streets. People in other parts of Switzerland tend to call the locals "hillbillies," and for many Americans attracted to the quirky and the quaint, it evokes the Ozarks. As you wander its centuries-old streets, sampling pear bread and honey cakes while in pursuit of local embroidery, you'll know why Appenzell is called the most authentic of Swiss villages. See "Appenzell" in chapter 6.

- **Wengen:** On a sheltered terrace high above the Lauterbrunnen Valley, this ski resort is one of the gems of the Bernese Oberland. No cars are allowed in this idyllic village, and from its streets (cleared of snow even in winter) and hotel windows, magnificent panoramic views greet you at every turn. The sunsets—over crags and waterfalls—are the most memorable we've ever seen in Switzerland. The village is best known for hosting the Ski World Cup, with the longest and most dangerous downhill race staged every January. See "Wengen" in chapter 9.

- **Sion:** Although it's the small capital of the Valais, this old Roman town with a French-speaking population is often neglected by those rushing to sample the pleasures of Zermatt and Verbier. But sleepy Sion has its own rewards. The town is dominated by the castles of Valère and Tourbillon, and, in its greater days, Sion's bishops were big players on the medieval stage. The moody, melancholy look of the town has inspired such luminaries as Rilke, Goethe, and Rousseau. See "Sion" in chapter 10.

- **Andermatt:** At the crossroads of the Alps, in the Urseren Valley, this picture-postcard town lies at the junction of two alpine roads—the St. Gotthard highway and the road to Oberalp and Furka. From the top of Gemstock, reached by cable car, you can see 600 alpine peaks. Hikers, cross-country skiers, and mountain bikers are attracted to this little backwater. The life of the town is centered on the main street, some sections of which are still paved with granite stones. See "Andermatt" in chapter 13.

- **Morcote:** At the southernmost tip of the Ceresio peninsula, 11km (7 miles) south of Lugano, stands Switzerland's most idyllic village. Built in the Lombard style familiar to those who have toured Milan, Morcote's arcaded houses, often clay-colored, open directly on the water, with everything set against a backdrop of vineyards and cypresses. For the best view of this cliché of Ticino charm, climb the 400 steps to the Chiesa di Madonna del Sasso, which dates from the 13th century. See "Morcote" in chapter 16.

7 THE BEST ROMANTIC GETAWAYS

- **Mürren:** It's so isolated that you can only get here by cog railway or cable car. Set on a rocky, high-altitude ledge hundreds of feet above the Lauterbrunnen Valley, Mürren has a handful of chalet-style hotels, excellent ski and hiking trails, and sweeping views over the mountains of the Bernese Oberland. It's as picture-perfect a Swiss village as you'll find. See "Mürren" in chapter 9.

- **Gstaad:** Lying at the junction of four alpine valleys midway between the Bernese Oberland and the Vaud Alps, Gstaad is a winter capital of the European glitterati. You can't get any more

stylish, and the skiing is good, too. Regardless of their price range, all the hotels seem to have cozy bedrooms, blazing fireplaces, and enough schnapps to set the mood. See "Gstaad" in chapter 9.

- **Verbier:** It lies at the bottom of an enormous alpine bowl ringed with spectacular ski slopes. Although many British travelers appreciate Verbier's charms, the language and atmosphere of the resort are unpretentious and very, very French. You can have a lot of fun in Verbier, and if you didn't happen to import your own romance, you're likely to find some here. See "Verbier" in chapter 10.

- **Arosa:** One of the highest (1,800m/5,904 ft.) ski resorts in Switzerland, Arosa is less expensive and less forbiddingly elegant than its nearest competitor, St. Moritz. Although the skiing here is excellent, you may consider a romantic getaway in midsummer, when a network of hiking trails leads to lush forests and small lakes. When you tire of these, cable cars can carry you and your companion to alpine heights and sublime vistas. See "Arosa" in chapter 14.

8 THE BEST SKIING

The jagged borders of Switzerland contain dozens of worthwhile ski resorts; the most popular are described in detail in the chapters that follow. But before heading off to the mountains for a bit of downhill racing, ask yourself some important questions: Do you prefer to schuss down a Swiss mountainside in relative isolation or accompanied by many other skiers? How chic and how expensive do you want your vacation to be? Do you pursue sports other than skiing (perhaps hang gliding, curling, ice-skating, or tobogganing)? And after a day in the great outdoors, do you prefer to retire early to a simple mountain hut with a view of the stars, or do you yearn for late nights with the glittering demimonde of Europe?

- **Grindelwald:** This is one of the few resorts in the Bernese Oberland that occasionally mistakes itself for a genuine city rather than an artificial tourist creation. It offers a healthy dose of restaurants, bars, discos, and, unfortunately, traffic. There are a lot of affordable accommodations here—it's not nearly as snobby as some of the other resorts. Many skiers use it as a base camp for long-haul excursions to the slopes of First, Männlichen, and Kleine Scheidegg. From Grindelwald, the resorts of Wengen and Mürren are accessible by cog railway and/or cable car (no traffic!). See "Grindelwald" in chapter 9.
- **Gstaad/Saanenland:** Gstaad is the most elegant pearl in the larger ski region of Saanenland, on the western edge of the Bernese Oberland. Although you can find a few inexpensive lodgings if you're lucky, don't count on it. The jet set comes here to see and be seen, and there's a lot to do off the slopes, such as music festivals, shopping, and people-watching. The architecture is stubbornly alpine, and the interior decorations range from baronial and woodsy in the most expensive hotels to kitschy in the cheaper ones. Opportunities for skiing are widespread, but the slopes are hardly the most difficult in Switzerland. Skiing is best for beginners and intermediates. See "Gstaad" in chapter 9.
- **Mürren:** One of the most oddly positioned resorts in Switzerland, Mürren sits on a rock ledge high above the Lauterbrunnen Valley of the Bernese Oberland. Accessible only by cable car, it's among the most picture-perfect resorts, full of chalet-style architecture and completely free of traffic. Though its isolation makes it charming, it also makes the cost of staying here somewhat higher. Mürren is closer than any other resort to the demanding slopes of the Schilthorn, where experienced skiers are offered nearly 32km (20 miles) of some of the finest powder in Europe—and eagle-eyed panoramas over some of the most dramatically beautiful landscapes. See "Mürren" in chapter 9.
- **Verbier:** This is the premier ski resort of French-speaking Switzerland, with an unpretentious panache and a fun-filled atmosphere. Its restaurants serve some

of the finest creative cuisine in the region; others make do with simple alpine fare for hearty appetites. If you don't speak French, you won't feel uncomfortable—many of the resort's nightlife options cater to Brits. (Throughout the town, English-style pubs compete cheerfully with French cafes.) Verbier lies at the heart of a sprawling, high-tech network of cable cars and gondolas that will connect you to such relatively unknown satellite resorts as Veysonnaz and La Tzoumaz. The resort is favored by world-class athletes for the difficulty of many of its slopes. See "Verbier" in chapter 10.

- **Zermatt:** It's the most southwesterly of the great Swiss ski resorts, occupying a high-altitude plateau at the foot of Switzerland's highest and most photographed mountain, the Matterhorn. Much of the resort's charm derives from its strict building codes—you'll rarely see a modern-looking building here—and its almost complete lack of traffic. Access from the valley below is via cog railway only. Known for over a century as the party town of the Alps, Zermatt has always been a place where the beer-drinking and hedonistic—sometimes raunchy—revelry last into the early morning hours. The skiing, incidentally, is superb. A complicated network of chairlifts, cog railways, and gondolas carries skiers to such peaks as Stockhorn, Rothorn, Riffelberg, Trockner Steg, and Testa Grigia. See "Zermatt & the Matterhorn" in chapter 10.

- **Arosa:** One of the most isolated of eastern Switzerland's resorts, Arosa is a relative newcomer to the country's ski scene. Drawing a young crowd, it's filled with contemporary buildings rather than traditional, chalet-inspired architecture. Ample annual snowfall, vast alpine meadows, and only one steeply inclined road into town make Arosa ideal for escapists and nature

lovers. Families with children usually like the place too. Not as stratospherically expensive or pretentious as St. Moritz, Arosa offers lots of runs for intermediate skiers. Some of the resort's most dramatic slopes, which drop more than 1,000m (3,280 ft.) from beginning to end, are only for very experienced athletes. See "Arosa" in chapter 14.

- **Davos:** It's larger, with many more hotels, restaurants, après-ski bars, and discos than its neighbor, Klosters (see below), with which it shares access to a sweeping network of ski lifts and slopes. Davos attracts a sometimes-curious mixture of the very wealthy and the more modest. It has slopes that appeal to advanced skiers, intermediates, and beginners. One of the most challenging runs descends from Weissflühgipfel at 2,622m (8,600 ft.) to Küblis at 810m (2,657 ft.). See "Davos" in chapter 14.

- **Klosters:** Named after a 13th-century cloister founded on the site, this resort is smaller, more intimate, and less urban than its nearest major competitor, Davos (see above). A favorite of the royal families of both Sweden and Britain, it offers at least two easily accessible ski zones, the snowfields of the Gotschna-Parsenn and the Madrisa. There's a wide range of trails and facilities, offering challenges to all skill levels. See "Klosters" in chapter 14.

- **St. Moritz:** The premier ski and social resort of eastern Switzerland, St. Moritz draws a lot of folks familiar with the art of conspicuous consumption; this is as close as you'll get to Hollywood in Switzerland. It's more distinctly Austrian than French in its flavor. Although only one or two authentic buildings remain from the town's medieval origins, vast amounts of money have been spent installing folkloric fixtures, carved paneling, and accents of local granite in the public and private areas of most hotels. Skiing in the region is divided into

Impressions

A Swiss artist living in the south of France said it: "Switzerland does not exist." This made some Swiss upset. Though Switzerland doesn't exist, every Swiss citizen has his assault rifle at home (with ammo). Of course they very rarely use their rifle to attack a bank or to hurt their wives. The Swiss used to be mercenaries, but today they don't want to get involved in other countries' feuds. Although they use migrant workers, they don't like foreigners (tourists are okay). Switzerland is this Disneyland of order and social harmony. It is a secure and peaceful place. It is not part of Europe. It might not even really be part of the world. This, I guess, should be good for the banking business.

—Olivier Mosset, 1994

distinct areas, the most popular of which is Corviglia, on the mountains above St. Moritz. Adventurers seeking diversion farther afield head for the slopes above the satellite resort of Sils Maria (Corvatsch) and the slopes above the nearby village of Pontresina (Diavolezza). There are plenty of difficult slopes in the region if you seek them out, but intermediate-level skiers enjoy taking a cable car from St. Moritz-Dorf to the top of Piz Corvatsch, almost 3,401m (11,155 ft.) above sea level. From here, with only one cable-car connection en route, you can ski a network of intermediate-level trails all the way back down to the resort's lake. St. Moritz boasts some of the most dependable annual snowfalls in Switzerland. See "St. Moritz" in chapter 15.

9 THE BEST FESTIVALS

- **L'Escalade:** Way back on December 11, 1602, the city of Geneva was attacked by Savoyard soldiers trying to scale its ramparts. The duke of Savoy had lost his former possession and wanted it back. Alas, it was not to be. The denizens of Geneva valiantly held out, and one brave Amazon, Mère Royaume, scaled the ramparts and poured a pot of hot soup on the head of a Savoyard soldier. For 3 days and nights beginning December 11, normally staid Geneva becomes virtually Rabelaisian, staging torchlight marches, country markets, and fife-and-drum parades, as a festive crowd in period costumes marches through the streets of the old city. Many present-day Mère Royaumes—armed with soup pots, of course—can be seen. See "When to Go" in chapter 3.

- **Vogel Gryff Volksfest:** This colorful tradition has a griffin, a lion, and a "wild man of the woods" floating down the Rhine, followed by dancing in the streets. It occurs alternately on January 13, 20, or 27 (changes every year). On a wintry day in January, a raft floats down the Rhine, laden with two drummers, two men with large flags, and two cannoneers who repeatedly fire gun salutes. The principal figure is a savage masked man carrying an uprooted pine tree. At Mittlerebrücke (the middle bridge), he's met by a lion and a bird with an awesome beak. At noon the three figures dance on the bridge to the sound of drums. The Wilder Mann (savage man), the Leu (lion), and the Vogel Gryff (griffin) are old symbols for three Basel societies that could be called neighborhoods today. Throughout the afternoon and evening, street dancing in Basel honors the occasion, which originated in the 16th century. The purpose of all this madness? Ostensibly, to strengthen community ties. See "Basel" in chapter 7.

- **Celebrating the Onion:** If your favorite sandwich consists of only bread, mayonnaise, and onions, or your idea of humor is to poke fun at buffoons disguised as onions, you'll love the Swiss capital's celebration of Zibelemärit, held annually on the fourth Monday of November.

During the festival, huge sections of the city's historic center are filled with vegetable stalls featuring plaited strings of onions (more than 100 tons may be sold in a day here) and other winter vegetables. The barrels of confetti thrown by competing camps of high-spirited students offer endless photo ops. Facetiously dressed jesters appear in bars and restaurants to poke fun (usually in Swiss-German) at the sometimes-pompous political posturing of their governmental elders. See the introduction to chapter 8 for more information.

10 THE BEST MUSEUMS

- **Museum Rietberg (Zurich):** Some of Europe's most interesting collections were amassed by gifted amateurs with enough money to pursue their hobbies. This museum honors the acquisitive skill of Baron von der Heydt, who donated his collection to the city of Zurich in 1952. It includes sculptures and artworks from the Americas and North and South Asia, archaic Buddhist art, carpets from Armenia, and masks from Africa and Oceania. See p. 116.

- **Landesmuseum (Swiss National Museum, Zurich):** This museum traces the growth and development of Swiss civilization from prehistory to the modern age. The collections include prehistoric artifacts, mementos from the Roman and Carolingian empires, and artworks from Romanesque, Gothic, and Renaissance periods. There are also unusual collections of Swiss clocks, Swiss armor and weapons, and folkloric costumes and artifacts from each of the country's cantons. See p. 115.

- **The Paul Klee Collection (Bern):** Lying 3 miles east of Bern's Altstadt, more than 4,000 works of the great artist Paul Klee, born here in 1879, have been assembled under one roof. Today his magnificent art has been brought

together as the finest example of "a Bern son who made good." See p. 203.

- **Kunstmuseum (Fine Arts Museum, Bern):** This museum showcases the great art that the capital of Switzerland acquired up until the end of the 1800s, beginning with a collection of medieval Italian primitives. The museum also has a collection of the leading Swiss artists of today, but focuses on old masters from Cézanne to Matisse. See p. 134.

- **Musée d'Art et d'Histoire (Art and History Museum, Geneva):** Geneva's premier museum devotes equal space to exhibits on the history of civilization, the civic history of Geneva, archaeology, and world-class painting—everything from medieval to modern art. See p. 336.

- **Verkehrshaus der Schweiz (Swiss Transport Museum, Lucerne):** One of Switzerland's newer museums, founded in 1959, this collection pays homage to the railway, auto, and airplane industries that helped propel Europe into the modern age. It contains more than 60 historic locomotives, 40 automobiles, 50 motorcycles, and dozens of other conveyances. Other exhibitions are devoted to cable cars, steamships, and spaceships. There's even a planetarium. See p. 365.

- **Baur au Lac** (Zurich; ✆ 044/220-50-20; www.bauraulac.ch): Prestigious and historic, it's one of the country's grandest hotels, welcoming prosperous guests since 1844. Richard Wagner, Franz Liszt, and John Lennon are some of the artists who have experienced its charms. Today the international business community considers it a favorite. See p. 94.

- **Widder Hotel** (Zurich; ✆ 044/224-25-26; www.widderhotel.ch): In the heart of the city's Old Town, 10 historic buildings dating from the 15th century have been transformed into an intimate luxury inn. Massive wooden beams and 16th-century frescoes still exist from the days when these buildings were part of the butchers' guild, but now they're juxtaposed with glass elevators and stainless-steel furniture. It's an offbeat, fun choice in a staid city, made especially inviting because of the live jazz in the bar. See p. 95.

- **Hotel Drei Könige** (Basel; ✆ 061/260-50-50; www.drei-koenige-basel.ch): Claiming to be the oldest hotel in Europe, the Hotel Drei Könige has operated continuously as an inn since 1026. It was the site of a meeting between two Holy Roman emperors and a Burgundian king that eventually established the southwestern borders of present-day Switzerland. Voltaire, Queen Victoria, and Kaiser Wilhelm II were only a few of this hotel's famous guests. Today there's live jazz in the bar and a cosmopolitanism that permeates every part of this very comfortable hotel. See p. 168.

- **Allegro Bern** (Bern; ✆ 031/339-55-00; www.allegro-hotel.ch): This is the hippest, most savvy, and most sophisticated hotel in the Swiss capital. Set just across the river from the town's historic core, the hotel offers great service, grand comfort, and a lot of style and charm. See p. 194.

- **Palace Hotel Gstaad** (Gstaad; ✆ 800/223-6800 or 033/748-50-50; www.palace.ch): Every winter this becomes one of the most sought-after hotels in the world, attracting the chic and fabulous who create what's been called the most amusing and expensive annual house party in Europe. Built in 1912, the hotel sits on a promontory above Gstaad (not exactly a village unfamiliar with luxury). Everything is very, very luxurious. See p. 245.

- **Beau-Rivage Palace** (Lausanne; ✆ 800/223-6800 or 021/613-33-33; www.brp.ch): This is the most prestigious hotel in Lausanne. Undeniably beautiful, it's a Beaux Arts masterpiece richly associated with the city's cultural and social elite. Service is impeccable. Although it has long catered to wealthy and conservative French-speaking Swiss, it has made great efforts in recent years to attract a younger, more international clientele. See p. 286.

- **Le Richemond** (Geneva; ✆ 022/715-70-00; www.lerichemond.com): Built in 1875 in the style of a neoclassical palace, the newly restored Le Richemond drips with Gobelin tapestries, French antiques, and a sophisticated, hardworking staff for whom absolutely nothing is a surprise. It also has the most fascinating bar in town; but if you decide to have a drink here, don't even think of showing up in torn jeans. See p. 319.

- **Kulm Hotel** (St. Moritz; ✆ 800/223-1230 or 081/836-80-00; www.kulm hotel-stmoritz.ch): This is the great bastion of luxury of the Engadine, rivaling even Suvretta House and Badrutt's Palace Hotel for supremacy. The greats and near-greats of the world have found refuge from the snows here in this trio of buildings, the oldest of which dates from 1760. See p. 427.

12 THE MOST CHARMING SMALL HOTELS

- **Hotel Romantik Florhof** (Zurich; ✆ 044/250-26-26; www.florhof.ch): The most charming of the little boutique hotels of Zurich, this was originally the home of a wealthy 15th-century merchant before its transformation. At the edge of Old Town, the hotel represents superb value. See p. 97.
- **Hotel Appenzell** (Appenzell; ✆ 071/788-15-15; www.hotel-appenzell.ch): Set on the main square of the most folkloric town in Switzerland, this hotel is outfitted in a rustic country-Swiss theme with touches of marble and walnut in the bedrooms. Check out the elaborate antique paneling in one of the dining rooms, rescued from a much older building just before it was demolished. See p. 147.
- **Hotel-Restaurant Adler** (Stein-am-Rhein; ✆ 052/742-61-61; www.adler steinamrhein.ch): Although its bedrooms are comfortable and clean, the location, in one of the most colorful cities on the Rhine, is what gets our vote. We love the hotel's frescoed facade, which depicts characters and plots derived from medieval Rhenish legends. See p. 155.
- **Hotel Krafft** (Basel; ✆ 061/690-91-30; www.hotelkrafft.ch): It's inexpensive and conveniently located a short walk from the historic core of the city. Its outdoor terrace overlooks the river, the town hall, and the cathedral. The bedrooms have the kind of worn but decent early-20th-century furnishings that remind us of these old-fashioned family-run pensions of postwar Europe. See p. 170.

- **Hostellerie des Chevaliers** (Gruyères; ✆ 026/921-19-33; www.gruyeres-hotels.ch): This atmospheric inn stands conveniently aloof from the overrun tourist center but offers the same panoramic views as the châteaux at Gruyères. The decor is the warmest and most old-fashioned in town, rich with antiques, woodwork, and ceramic stoves. See p. 185.
- **Belle Epoque** (Bern; ✆ 031/311-43-36; www.belle-epoque.ch): The most sophisticated small-scale hotel in the Swiss capital was created out of two historic town houses from the Middle Ages. The hotel celebrates Jugendstil or a Teutonic Art Nouveau. The place is a jewel. See p. 194.
- **Hotel Olden** (Gstaad; ✆ 033/748-49-50; www.hotelolden.ch): Set on the town's main thoroughfare, the Olden is a great deal compared to other Gstaad hotels. It enjoys a solid reputation, especially among the many skiers and mountain guides who patronize the restaurant and cafe on the hotel's ground floor. The rooms are cozy and a bit cramped, but comfortable—perfect if you're planning to spend your time out and about. See p. 245.
- **Hotel Antika** (Zermatt; ✆ 027/967-21-51; www.antika.ch): It's one of the few hotels in Zermatt that won't gobble up most of your travel budget. You wouldn't really guess that it's an affordable option at first glance: Each room has its own covered loggia, and the lobby is carefully paneled with weathered planks. This is a good choice for exploring the most famous resort town of Switzerland's Valais district. See p. 272.

- **The Hotel** (Lucerne; 🕾 041/226-86-86; www.the-hotel.ch): This is central Switzerland's most charming boutique hotel. Designed by Jean Nouvel, France's most famous architect, it is exclusive and elegant, luxury personified yet artfully simple at the same time. See p. 368.
- **Hotel Drei Könige und Post** (Andermatt; 🕾 041/887-00-01; www.3 koenige.ch): Located directly north of the St. Gotthard Pass at 2,109m (6,918 ft.), this hotel was built on the site of an inn that has been showing wayfarers hospitality since 1234. Even Goethe spent a night

at this family-run place in 1775. Some of the rooms open onto balconies, and the hotel's regional Swiss cuisine attracts both locals and visitors. See p. 389.
- **Hotel Drei Könige** (Chur; 🕾 081/354-90-90; www.dreikoenige.ch): Its foundations were laid in the 1300s, and the same hardworking family has owned and managed the place since 1911. It provides a note of cheer in an industrialized, high-altitude town where the temperatures can sometimes plummet. Of special note is its restaurant, one of the most consistently popular in town. See p. 394.

13 THE BEST RESTAURANTS

- **Kronenhalle** (Zurich; 🕾 044/262-99-00; www.kronenhalle.com): It has a hearty, rustic alpine theme, but a glance at its menu, its clientele, and its artwork will quickly convince you that this is a supremely distinctive restaurant. Enjoy paintings by such luminaries as Kandinsky, Matisse, Klee, and Braque as you dine. See p. 105.
- **Petermann's Kunststuben** (Küsnacht; 🕾 044/910-07-15; www.kunststuben. com): Come here for the sublime cuisine of chef Horst Petermann. Since he opened this acclaimed restaurant south of Zurich, demanding diners have been heading here to partake of the constantly changing specialties. After you've sampled his herby Tuscan dove with pine nuts or his lobster with artichoke and almond oil, you'll know that this is as good as it gets in the Zurich area. See p. 108.
- **Restaurant Stucki Bruderholz** (Basel; 🕾 061/361-82-22; www.stucki-bruderholz.ch): There are a garden, a collection of upscale antique furniture, a clientele speaking every conceivable European language, and some of the best cuisine in northwestern Switzerland, all

based on modern interpretations of French and German recipes. See p. 173.
- **Le Restaurant Pierroz** (Verbier; 🕾 027/771-63-23): You'd never know that the simple chalet-style facade of this place shelters one of the most legendary restaurants in the Valais. One of the finest meals we've ever had in Switzerland was served here on a snowy night. It included a platter of sea bass with sea urchins, followed by couscous of crayfish and pigeon with truffles. Gourmets and epicures will cross any number of national borders to sample the creative cuisine of Roland Pierroz. See p. 255.
- **Hotel de Ville** (Crissier; 🕾 021/634-05-05; www.philippe-rochat.ch): Philippe Rochat is the chef of the moment in Switzerland, having taken over from Alfred (Frédy) Girardet, who some hailed as the world's greatest chef. That left some chef's toque for Rochat to try and fill, but he successfully retained the international acclaim that Girardet enjoyed. Occupying a building originally designed as the town hall of a village outside Lausanne, the master continues to please the hundreds of devoted gastronomes who often travel

great distances at great expense to dine here. See p. 291.

- **Le Pont de Brent** (Brent; ✆ 021/964-52-30; www.lepontdebrent.com): No one had even heard of Brent until this restaurant opened in a late-19th-century house in the heart of the village. Today, the restaurant has put the village on the map, in part because of the excellence of such dishes as mussel-and-leek soup and roast rabbit with mustard sauce. See p. 305.

- **Le Chat-Botté** (Geneva; ✆ 022/716-69-20): Richly sheathed with tapestries and accented with the kind of art and accessories that would have made Louis XVI feel right at home, this restaurant attracts some of the wealthiest and most jaded clients in the world. Everything works smoothly, with nary a glitch, but you can only imagine how hard the staff labors to maintain its position as one of the best restaurants in Switzerland. See p. 323.

- **La Favola** (Geneva; ✆ 022/311-74-37; www.lafavola.com): This is the best Italian restaurant in Geneva, and possibly the city's best restaurant of any kind. The chefs' tender pillows of tortellini would be hard to find this side of Bologna. The cuisine has authentic flavor, the service is skilled and smooth, and only the freshest ingredients go into the kitchen's skillets and stew pots. See p. 329.

- **Chesa Grischuna** (Klosters; ✆ 081/422-22-22; www.chesagrischuna.ch): Every evening this restaurant succeeds at creating a genuine sense of unpretentious, old-fashioned warmth. Over the years it has hosted such showbiz and political types of yesterday as Truman Capote and Audrey Hepburn. The food is hearty and nourishing—perfect for the cold-weather climate of Klosters. See p. 405.

- **Chadafo Grill, in the Chesa Veglia** (St Moritz; ✆ 081/837-28-00): Built in 1658, this business is located in what's said to be the only authentic Engadine-style house that remains in all of St. Moritz. It contains three different dining rooms, one of which is an informal pizzeria. The other two are rustically elegant hideaways, redolent with warmth and comfort, which cater to an international and very prosperous clientele. See p. 430.

- **Jöhri's Talvo** (St. Moritz; ✆ 081/833-44-55; www.talvo.ch): It's hailed by many food critics as the best restaurant in the Engadine. Located in Europe's ritziest resort, in the satellite village of Champfèr, it attracts some of the most discerning palates in the world to its refined take on a French and regional cuisine. See p. 430.

Switzerland in Depth

Switzerland has a rich cultural life, with many fine museums, theaters, and world-renowned orchestras, but most people visit the country for its superb scenery—alpine peaks, mountain lakes, and lofty pastures. As important as Geneva, Zurich, St. Moritz, and other obvious tourist centers are, they do not convey the full splendors of Switzerland. To experience these, you must venture deep into William Tell country, into the heart of Switzerland.

The Federal Republic of Switzerland covers 41,287 sq. km (15,941 sq. miles). It has four recognized national languages—German, French, Italian, and Romansh, a romance dialect. Many of its people, however, speak English, especially in the major tourist regions. You will find the Swiss hospitable, restrained, and peace loving. Switzerland's neutrality allowed it to avoid the wars that devastated its neighbors twice in the past century. It also enabled it to achieve financial stability and prosperity.

Switzerland occupies a position on the "rooftop" of the continent of Europe, with the drainage of its mammoth alpine glaciers serving as the source of such powerful rivers as the Rhine and the Rhône. The appellation "crossroads of Europe" is fitting, as all rail lines, road passes, and mountain tunnels seem to lead to Switzerland. From the time when the Romans crossed the Alps and traversed Helvetia (the ancient name for part of today's Switzerland) on their way to conquests in the north, the major route connecting northern and southern Europe has been through Switzerland. The country's ancient roads and paths were eventually developed into modern highways and railroad lines.

The main European route for east-west travel also passes through Switzerland, between Lake Constance and Geneva, and intercontinental airports connect the country with cities all over the world. London and Paris, for instance, are less than 2 hours away by air. The tourist industry as we know it started in Switzerland, and the tradition of welcoming visitors is firmly entrenched in Swiss life. The first modern tourists, the British, began to arrive "on holiday" in the 19th century, and other Europeans, as well as a scattering of North Americans, followed suit.

Today, the "nation of hotel keepers" hosts some 20 million visitors every year. Swiss catering, based on many years of experience, has gained a worldwide reputation, and the entire country is known for its efficiency and its cleanliness.

Don't be misled. A visit to Switzerland is not tantamount to a visit to paradise. Even in the well-ordered and immaculate city of Zurich, there are drug addicts and the homeless wander its streets, although not in the vast numbers found in most of the world's capitals.

Readers often comment on the reserve of the Swiss. The locals don't necessarily rush to embrace you, as they are, for the most part, a conservative people. Even if they don't have the spontaneity more associated with their southern neighbor, Italy, they will most often welcome you politely and provide you with a good bed and a good meal for the night—for which they'll charge a good price! Few people return from Switzerland commenting on how cheap it is. However, good value is to be found there by those who seek it out, and the Swiss probably have fewer "tourist traps" than most of the top 10 major tourist destinations of the world.

Did You Know?

- More than 3½% of the working population of Switzerland is employed in the banking industry.
- As a financial center, Switzerland ranks in importance behind only New York, London, and Tokyo.
- Since the late 18th and early 19th centuries, there has been no foreign invasion of Swiss territory, despite the devastating conflagrations that surrounded it.
- Until the early 19th century, Switzerland was the most industrialized country in Europe.
- Famous for its neutrality, Switzerland once was equally known for providing mercenaries to fight in foreign armies. (The practice was ended by the constitution of 1874, with the exception of the Vatican's Swiss papal guard, dating from 1505.)
- Switzerland drafts all able-bodied male citizens between the ages of 20 and 50 (55 for officers). These soldiers, who continue to live at home, form a reserve defense corps that (in theory) can be called to active duty at any time.
- With its four major language groups, Switzerland effectively contradicts the axiom that a national identity cannot exist without a common language.

1 SWITZERLAND TODAY

Don't be fooled by Switzerland's cookie-cutter folklore, its photogenic villages, and an image that its tourist officials widely promote—that of a well-oiled machine ticking efficiently from within the safety of an alpine landscape. The changes that the country has experienced lately have been as painful as anything since World War II, and have shattered long-cherished myths that were zealously taught to Swiss schoolchildren for years. Here's a simplified version of a situation that's noteworthy for its murky complexity.

In what is now widely conceived as a major political blunder, President Harry Truman a half-century ago decided not to force Switzerland to disgorge millions in Nazi gold or to expose its half-hearted role in supporting the German war effort. During the late 1940s, Truman was more interested in fighting Communism and rebuilding Europe than in putting pressure on Switzerland. Just when the issue seemed buried forever, it resurfaced passionately during the late 1990s. The ensuing hue and cry caused Switzerland its most horrendous publicity ever, sparked a worldwide controversy, and threatened forever the country's much-vaunted myth of political neutrality.

As one Swiss banker told the press, "The Swiss are shocked by this banking affair, because they are not used to seeing themselves on CNN. In our view, we are the victims of a plot to take our quiet little country away, to drag us back into history."

The evidence is now in: Swiss bankers and businessmen, with the tacit approval of government officials, stored Nazi gold bars, often with swastikas emblazoned on them. That gold was then used to buy war materials, which no doubt extended World War II. Swiss officials also provided warehouses for property looted by Nazis from other countries, barred Jewish refugees from coming into their land, and even charged the Swiss Jewish community a tax for every single Jew living within its borders. Swiss bankers have also been less than forthright in helping Holocaust survivors track family assets. In recent years, the veil covering the face of Swiss banking has been lifted somewhat, but much of the behind-the-scenes activities remain impenetrable. There is suspicion that Swiss bankers, acting in their own best interests, continue to cover up many banking scandals.

The Jewish Chronicle of London reported in September 1996 that even Adolf Hitler himself was among the prewar customers of Swiss banks, hiding his royalties from *Mein Kampf* in the country's biggest bank. Around the same time the British Foreign Office reported that only one-tenth of the war loot stored in Switzerland had been returned to the Allies at the end of the war.

After months of pressure from American Jewish groups to atone for wartime dealings, the Swiss government, banks, and some big business interests agreed to establish a Holocaust memorial fund.

The Swiss argue that what they did was for survival reasons during the war. Critics claim that what was done was based on opportunism and amorality and should be paid for in both moral and financial terms. On the defensive, many citizens now view the actions of many of their critics as "Swiss bashing."

Others take a more enlightened view as expressed by Rolf Bloch, the leader of the main umbrella group representing Switzerland's 18,000 Jews. He claimed that the Swiss should be having a national dialogue among themselves to define anew what the country stands for. "People still feel they are moral paragons," he said, "but if we can conclude that we're just normal people—not angels, not devils—then we will have made a breakthrough."

Although the debate over the Swiss role in modern history is likely to continue long past the millennium, there is other trouble in paradise.

To the rest of the world Switzerland is perceived as a very rich country—and it is. The magic economy has brought watch making, chocolate making, civil engineering, and tourism to high levels of accomplishments. But the high value of the cherished Swiss franc has cut deeply into the profitability of the country's exports and into its tourism.

Many Swiss citizens don't want to join the European Union, even though the country's present nonmember status is severely affecting the Swiss economy. As the E.U. grows bigger, more and more markets become expensive for Swiss products, such as chocolate. An example occurred when Sweden, Austria, and Finland joined the E.U.; several Swiss exports were suddenly tagged with tariff barriers in those heretofore lucrative markets.

Trade protections from the E.U. aren't the only thing blocking Swiss exports. The cruelly high value of the Swiss franc continues to threaten exports as well. Swiss goods, even if they weren't before, have suddenly become luxury items, and correspondingly expensive.

Even Swiss manufacturers are deserting their own country and going elsewhere where labor is cheaper and taxes are lower. For example, that Swiss chocolate bar you're eating might have actually been made in Spain or Greece.

Impressions

In Switzerland they had brotherly love—they had 500 years of democracy and peace, and what did that produce? The cuckoo clock!

—Orson Welles, *The Third Man*, 1949

Impressions

Switzerland is simply a large, humpy solid rock, with a thin skin of grass stretched over it.
—Mark Twain, *A Tramp Abroad,* 1880

Though warned that failure to stay out of the European Union would mean trouble for their economy, Swiss voters in 1992 narrowly chose to remain outside the free-trade zone. As a result of that highly contested vote, the E.U. continues to impose the same trade barriers and protections against Switzerland that it does against Japan and the United States.

As an industrious people, the Swiss are taking steps to stay "lean and mean" with their manufacturing. For example, the august Swiss Parliament voted in 1995 to allow chocolate producers to use vegetable oils rather than cocoa butter in chocolate bars. In some parts of Switzerland this provoked a massive outcry. Chocolate makers have slimmed down their workforces, becoming more mechanized and needing fewer workers who traditionally earn extremely high wages when stacked up against much of the Western world.

Discontented rumblings and differing opinions have been heard from various linguistic factions within Switzerland as well. The French-speaking section tends to be more cosmopolitan, more liberal, and more socialist than voters in the German-speaking hamlets of the country's staunchly conservative center. (Residents of Italian-speaking Switzerland are, surprisingly enough, viewed as only a bit less conservative than their German-speaking compatriots, and in some cases, much less liberal than their French-speaking counterparts.) Interestingly, Zurich has been viewed as more fiscally stable and growth oriented than Geneva, reversing a trend. As for the European Union, Swiss women, young voters, and the country's French-speaking western tier tend to favor membership,

Zurich remains divided, and the German-speaking hamlets of the country's center overwhelmingly are steadfastly opposed.

Switzerland remains one of the safest countries in the world to visit, but even its image of peace and tranquillity is being shattered by "tourist criminals." Some of the most publicized of these have involved refugees from the traumatized Balkans and what used to be Yugoslavia. Many are people entering Switzerland with 3-month tourist visas who, with cameras, a bagful of Swiss handicrafts, and, in some cases, a guidebook in hand, have burglarized houses or mugged passersby in small towns that until recently had never experienced even a whiff of crime. Ironically, the vocabulary used by the Swiss to describe this unheard-of phenomenon often evokes lawless Chicago-style 1920s gangs from the era of Al Capone.

In spite of gnawing problems, there's a lot to be proud of in Switzerland today. A proposal to increase the price of a university education in Switzerland was voted down by an assembly of town councils, a fact that makes a college degree for their children a distinct possibility for most Swiss families even today.

The country continues its impressive advances in technical training for high-skilled engineers and financiers, but artists still have a stony road to travel in their struggle to survive. Despite that, growing communities of counterculture photographers, painters, writers, and sculptors, as well as large numbers of gay people, continue to congregate in the inner cores of such cities as Zurich, Basel, and Geneva.

As mirrored in urban centers throughout the rest of Europe, victims of AIDS and other diseases, as well as heroin

Impressions

No money, no Swiss.

—Jean Racine, *Les Plaideurs (The Litigants),* 1668

addicts, continue to find greater options in the country's large cities than in small towns, and their migration from small towns toward Switzerland's large cities continues. Although Switzerland is medically very advanced in the technology of providing substitutes (such as methodone) for heroin to deeply entrenched addicts, the use of such legalized, carefully controlled substitutes remains a hotly contested issue during virtually every election.

What most Swiss finally admit is that they've entered the real world whether they like it or not, and can never be viewed again as heirs to a nation of cuckoo clocks, contented cud-chewing cows, and Heidi's great-uncle.

2 LOOKING BACK AT SWITZERLAND

AT THE CROSSROADS OF EUROPE

Despite its neutral image, Switzerland has a fascinating history of external and internal conflicts. Its strategic location at the crossroads of Europe made it an irresistible object to empires since Roman times. There's even evidence that prehistoric tribes struggled to hold tiny settlements along the great Rhône and Rhine rivers.

The first identifiable occupants were the Celts, who entered the alpine regions from the west. The Helvetii, a Celtic tribe, inhabited a portion of the country that became known as Helvetia. The tribe was defeated by Julius Caesar when it tried to move into southern France in 58 B.C. The Romans conquered the resident tribes in 15 B.C., and peaceful colonization continued until A.D. 455 when the barbarians invaded, followed later by the Christians. Charlemagne (742–814) conquered the small states, or cantons, that occupied the area now known as Switzerland and incorporated them into his realm, which later became the Holy Roman Empire. In later years, Switzerland became a battleground for some of the major ruling families of Europe, especially the Houses of Savoy, the Habsburgs, and the Zähringen.

BIRTH OF THE CONFEDERATION

The Swiss have always guarded their territory jealously. In 1291 an association of three cantons formed the Perpetual Alliance—the nucleus of today's Swiss Confederation. To be rid of the grasping Habsburgs, the Confederation broke free of the Holy Roman Empire in 1439. It later signed a treaty with France, a rival power, agreeing to provide France with mercenary troops. This led to Swiss fighting Swiss in the early 16th century. The agreement was ended around 1515, and in 1516 the confederates declared their complete neutrality.

THE REFORMATION

The Protestant Reformation created bitter conflicts in Switzerland between those cantons defending papal Catholicism and those embracing the new creed of Protestantism. Ulrich Zwingli, who like Martin Luther had converted from the Catholic faith, led the Swiss Reformation, beginning in 1519. He translated the Bible into

A Loose Confederation of Cantons

Switzerland is a confederation of 3,029 communes, each largely responsible for its own public affairs, including school systems, taxation, road construction, water supply, and town planning. The international sign CH, found on Swiss motor vehicles, stands for *Confoederatio Helvetica* (Swiss Confederation). Over the centuries, neighboring communes have bonded together in a confederation of 23 cantons, each with its own constitution, laws, and government. They have surrendered only certain aspects of their authority to the Federal Parliament, such as foreign policy, national defense, and general economic policy.

The Federal Parliament of Switzerland consists of a 200-member National Council, elected by the people, and a 46-member Council of States, in which each canton has two representatives. The two chambers constitute Switzerland's legislative authority. The executive body, the Federal Council, is composed of seven members, who make decisions jointly, although each councilor is responsible for a different department. The president of the Federal Council, who serves a 1-year term, leads the Confederation as *primus inter pares* (first among equals).

All Swiss citizens, in general, become eligible to vote on federal matters at the age of 20. Surprisingly, it wasn't until 1971 that Swiss women were granted the right to vote.

Despite its neutrality, Switzerland has compulsory military service. The army, however, is devoted solely to the defense of the homeland. Swiss soldiers are always ready to fight—they keep military gear at home, including a gas mask, rifle, and ammunition. Annual shooting practice is mandatory.

Swiss-German and reorganized church rituals. The Protestant movement was spurred by the 1536 arrival in Geneva of John Calvin, who was fleeing Catholic reprisals in France.

Geneva became one of the most rigidly puritanical strongholds of Protestantism in Europe, fervently committed to its self-perceived role as the New Jerusalem. The spread of Calvinism led to the coining of the French term "Huguenot," a corruption of the Swiss word Eidgenosse (confederate).

After Zwingli died in a religiously motivated battle in 1531, the Swiss spirit of compromise came into play and a peace treaty was signed, allowing each region the right to practice its own faith. Today 55% of the Swiss define themselves as Protestant,

43% as Roman Catholic, and 2% as members of other faiths.

Despite the deep divisions within the confederation created by the Reformation, the confederates managed to stay together by adopting a pragmatic approach to their religious and political differences. Such an approach to national issues, based on compromise, remains one of the cornerstones of the Swiss political system. Later, during the Thirty Years' War (1618–48), the Swiss remained neutral while civil wars flared around them.

INDUSTRIALIZATION & POLITICAL CRISES

Turning to economic development, 18th-century Switzerland became the most industrialized nation in Europe. But a rapid population growth created social problems, widening the division between the new class of wealth and the rest of the population. Uprisings occurred, but it was only after the French Revolution that they had an effect, causing the Swiss Confederation to collapse in 1798.

Under French guardianship, progressives moved to centralize the constitution of the Swiss Republic. This pull toward centralization clashed with the federalist traditions of the semi-independent cantons. In 1803 Napoleon Bonaparte established a confederation with 19 cantons, but when he fell from power, Swiss conservatives revived the old order. Much of the social progress resulting from the Napoleonic period was reversed and the aristocrats had their former privileges restored to them.

Current Swiss boundaries were fixed at the Congress of Vienna in 1814. In 1848, a federal constitution was adopted and Bern established as the capital.

The federal state, by centralizing responsibility for such matters as Customs and the minting of coins, created conditions favorable to economic progress. The construction of a railway network and the establishment of a banking system also contributed to Switzerland's development. Both facilitated the country's export industry, consisting chiefly of textiles, pharmaceuticals, and machinery.

A Nation of Four Languages

Because the country is a patchwork of ethnic and religious groups, Swiss citizens tend to have a natural tolerance of others and an equally strong intolerance for bureaucracy and autocracy. Perhaps as a result, they are polite but reserved.

Three-quarters of Switzerland's people reside in the central lowlands between the Alps and the Jura; more than two-fifths live in cities and towns of more than 10,000 residents. There are some 400 inhabitants per square mile.

The bulk of Switzerland's income derives from industry, crafts, and tourism, which together employ more than a million people. Only about 7% of the Swiss are engaged in agriculture and forestry, although the country produces about half of its food supply. Switzerland exports engineering, chemical, and pharmaceutical products, as well as world-famous clocks and watches.

The Swiss have a vastly diverse culture. There are four major linguistic and ethnic groups which overlap each other—German, French, Italian, and Romansh. Despite these variations, however, the Swiss have formed a strong national identity.

About 70% of the people speak Swiss-German, or Schwyzerdütsch (*Schweizerdeutsch* in standard German); about 20% speak French; and about 9% speak Italian, mostly in the southern Ticino region. Approximately 1% speak Romansh, a Rhaeto-Romanic dialect that contains a pre-Roman vocabulary and a substratum of Latin elements; it is believed to be the language of old Helvetia and is spoken mainly by people in the Grisons. Most Swiss speak more than one of the four languages. Many also speak English.

NEUTRALITY THROUGH TWO WORLD WARS

During World War I (1914–18), Switzerland maintained its neutrality from the general European conflict but experienced serious social problems at home. As purchasing power fell and unemployment rose dramatically, civil unrest grew. One cause of bitterness was that Swiss men conscripted into the army automatically lost their jobs. In 1918, workers, dissatisfied with their conditions, called a general strike, the first and only one in Switzerland's history. The strike led to the introduction of proportional representation in elections. In the 1920s a 48-hour workweek was introduced and unemployment insurance was improved.

In 1920 Switzerland joined the League of Nations and provided space for the organization's headquarters at Geneva. As a neutral member, however, it exempted itself from any military action that the League might take.

In August 1939, on the eve of World War II (1939–45), Switzerland, fearing an invasion, ordered a mobilization of its defense forces. But an invasion never came, even though Switzerland was surrounded by Germany and its allies. It proved convenient to all the belligerents to have, in the middle of a continent in conflict, a neutral nation through which they could deal with each other. It also indicated to Hitler that it was determined to defend itself, and convinced Nazi Germany that any invader would pay in blood for every foot of ground gained in Switzerland.

The sense of neutrality remains so strong that even as recently as 1986, the Swiss voted, in a national referendum, against membership in the United Nations. Switzerland, however, did join the United Nations Educational, Scientific, and Cultural Organization, contributing to its Third World development funds.

Switzerland's political isolationism of the postwar years coincided with a period of unprecedented financial and industrial growth. Many social-welfare programs were introduced, unemployment was virtually wiped out, and the country moved into an enviable position of wealth and prosperity.

INTO THE FUTURE

In 1992 the Swiss rejected the opportunities offered by the economic integration of Europe, preferring their traditional isolation and neutrality. A referendum in December 1992 vetoed the government's attempt to seek full membership in the E.U. But the vote was close: 50.3% against and 49.7% in favor.

All six French-speaking cantons backed the plan, while all but one of the German-speaking cantons opposed it. This revealed a rather dangerous split in a multicultural country's aspirations and political hopes. The plan for European integration was favored not only by the government but also by bankers, labor leaders, intellectuals, and most industrialists. However, it was overwhelmingly rejected by the small rural communities that form much of the Swiss landscape.

Fear of a flood of refugees might have made the final decision for many Swiss, who watched in horror as an onslaught of workers from abroad poured into Germany and created disharmony.

In 1996 and 1997, headlines proclaimed Switzerland a banker for Nazi gold. In July 1997, teams from three major U.S. accounting firms moved into 10 Swiss banks to begin an independent inquiry into funds that may have belonged to Holocaust victims.

The Clinton administration accused Switzerland of prolonging World War II by acting as banker to Nazi Germany. But authorities in Bern quickly rejected the accusation as "unsupported" and termed

Washington's assessment "one-sided." Reeling from these charges, Switzerland faced new accusations that its wartime weapons industry profited from—and favored—Hitler's Germany in arms trading worth millions of dollars.

The Swiss government ordered its banks to preserve any remaining records of their dealings with Nazi Germany. But in January 1997, a Swiss security guard at the Union Bank of Switzerland halted the destruction of documents from the wartime era, including some that appeared to deal with the forced auctions of property in Berlin during the 1930s.

In 1998 three Swiss banks agreed to pay $1.25 billion to Holocaust survivors, hoping to settle the claims of thousands of survivors whose families lost assets in World War II.

In May 2000 Swiss voters, by a 67% majority, broke with their long-held isolationism and approved agreements with the E.U. that will link this tiny alpine nation more closely with its neighbors. The government hoped that the accords will be a first step toward eventual Swiss membership in the union.

In March 2002, by a slender margin, neutral Switzerland agreed in a country-wide vote to leave behind decades of isolationism and become a member of the United Nations. The referendum passed by a ratio of 54.6% for it and 45.4% against it. The government lobbied hard for Switzerland to shed its go-it-alone stance and become the 190th member of the global body.

Neutral, peace-loving Switzerland a base for Al Qaeda? Impossible, you say. In 2004 the attorney general of Switzerland, Valentin Roschacher, announced that his country has been used as a financial and logistical base by associates of Al Qaeda for plotting terror against the West. Thirteen suspects were arrested, each involved in Islamic "charity" work.

Switzerland celebrated the 50th anniversary of the first voting rights for women in 2007. To show how far women have come since they got the vote, for the first time in Swiss history the country elected a female president, Micheline Calmy-Rey, and a woman speaker of Parliament, Christine Egerszegi-Obrist.

On February 10, 2008, Zurich made unwanted headlines when three men wearing ski masks pulled off one of the largest and most audacious art robberies of all time. It was the second multimillion-dollar art heist in Switzerland in less than a week.

The thieves grabbed four 19th-century masterpieces—a Cézanne, a Degas, a van Gogh, and a Monet. The quartet of art was worth an estimated $163 million.

Only 7 days earlier, thieves in the nearby town of Pfäffikon stole two Picassos worth an estimated $4.4 million.

On February 19, two of the stolen Impressionist paintings were found unharmed in the parking lot of a mental hospital just a few hundred yards from the scene of the crime. In the back seat of an unlocked car a painting by Monet and one by van Gogh were recovered. The other two paintings remain missing.

The most valuable painting owned by the museum, Cézanne's *Boy in a Red Vest*, remains missing. It is worth $91 million. It is one of the most famous Impressionist paintings in the world and would be difficult to sell except to a rich private collector who wanted to enjoy it in secret.

In the spring of 2009, a relatively obscure Swiss architect, Peter Zumthor, won the Pritzker Prize, the highest recognition for architects. He had toiled quietly for some 3 decades in a remote village in the Swiss mountains. The project most closely associated with Zumthor is the spa he completed in 1996 for the Hotel Therma in Vals, an alpine village. In this dramatic structure, he used slabs of quartzite evoking stacks of Roman bricks.

3 SWITZERLAND'S ART & ARCHITECTURE

ART

Switzerland's museums and art collections are known throughout the world. Among them are the Public Art Collection in Basel and the Oskar Reinhart Foundation in Winterthur. Also major are the art museums of Zurich, Bern (including the Klee Foundation), and Geneva, as well as the Avegg Foundation in Bern (Riggisberg) and the Foundation Martin Bodmer (Geneva-Cologny). The Swiss National Museum in Zurich contains valuable exhibits on history and archaeology. There are also museums of church treasures and ethnological displays.

Before about the mid–1700s, the Swiss, a sober and matter-of-fact people, did not regard art with the passion that some of their neighbors did. As a consequence, Swiss painters were not as prominent as those of Italy and France. Sculpture and painting were secondary to architecture, useful only as embellishments to the major work of art, the building itself.

Among the major Swiss artists are Salomon Gessner (1730–88), who painted landscapes and mythological scenes, and Anton Graff (1736–1813), a portraitist. Johann Heinrich Füssl (1741–1825) studied in England, where he became known as Henry Fuseli; he later was appointed keeper of the Royal Academy in London. He is best remembered for his visionary painting *The Nightmare*.

Angelica Kauffmann (1741–1807) became the country's most acclaimed neoclassical painter, depicting allegorical, religious, and mythological themes.

Arnold Böcklin (1827–1901) also became widely known in his time. The subjects of his paintings were either extremely light, even frivolous, or else morbidly depressing, as exemplified by his *Island of the Dead*.

Ferdinand Hodler (1853–1918) was one of the first really significant people to emerge within the world of Swiss art. Some critics have suggested that he "liberated" Swiss painting, making effective use of color and rhythmic tension. His works are displayed in such museums as the National Museum in Zurich and the Museum of Art and History in Geneva. His gargantuan murals, one of which depicts the *Retreat of the Swiss Following the Battle of Marignano*, remain among his best-known works.

During World War I, Zurich was the setting for the launching of Dadaism. This nihilistic movement, which lasted from about 1916 to 1922, was influenced by the absurdities and carnage of the war. It was based on deliberate irrationality and the rejection of laws of social organization and beauty.

The most famous artist to come out of Switzerland was Paul Klee (1879–1940). He became a member of the Blaue Reiter, the German expressionist movement, and worked at the Bauhaus in Weimar. His work is characterized by fantasy forms in line and light-toned colors. Klee also combined abstract elements with recognizable images. Among his better-known works are *Mask of Fear, Man on a Tightrope, Pastorale,* and *The Twittering Machine.*

The most distinguished sculptor to emerge from Switzerland was Alberto Giacometti (1901–66). His metal figures, as lean and elongated as figures from an El Greco painting, can be seen in museums throughout the world. After 1930, Giacometti became closely associated with the surrealist movement. His sculpture, exemplified by *L'Homme qui marche (Man Walking),* is said to represent "naked vulnerability."

Another eminent sculptor, Jean Tinguely (b. 1925), became known for his kinetic sculptures, which he called "machine sculptures" or "metamechanisms." Some of these works, including *Heureka,* are displayed in Zurichhorn Park in Zurich. One of Tinguely's most controversial creations is *La Vittoria,* a golden phallus 7.8m long (26 ft.).

Graphic art is another area in which Swiss have distinguished themselves. Today Switzerland is a center of commercial art and advertising.

ARCHITECTURE

Switzerland's architecture has been remarkably well preserved. The country offers superb examples of Roman ruins as well as of medieval churches, monasteries, and castles.

The architecture of Switzerland has always been greatly influenced by the aesthetic development of its neighbors. As a result, it does not have a distinctive "national" style—except in its rural buildings, and perhaps its wood-sided chalets, which have been copied in mountain settings throughout the world.

Much of the country's earliest architecture was built by the Romans. The ruins at Avenches (Helvetia's chief town), with its once-formidable 6.4km (4-mile) circuit of walls and 10,000-seat theater, date from the 1st and 2nd centuries A.D.

Many buildings were created during the Carolingian period, including the Augustinian abbey of St. Maurice in the Valais. Considered the most ancient monastic house in Switzerland, it dates from the early 6th century. The Benedictine abbey on the island of Reichenau was launched around 725, and from the early medieval period until the 11th century it was the

- **1920** Switzerland joins the League of Nations, offering space for a headquarters at Geneva.
- **1939** Fearing an invasion by Nazi Germany, the country orders a total mobilization of its air and ground forces.
- **1939–45** Remaining neutral, despite its laundering of Nazi gold, Switzerland becomes a haven for escaping prisoners of war and avoids direct conflicts.

- **1948** Switzerland introduces broad-based social reforms, including the funding of old-age pensions.
- **1986** The Swiss electorate votes against membership in the United Nations.
- **1992** By a close vote, the Swiss reject ties to an economically integrated Europe.
- **1996–97** Critics around the world attack Switzerland's role as a World War II banker for the Nazi war effort.

- **1998** Three Swiss banks agree to a $1.25-billion fund to be distributed among Holocaust victims.
- **2000** Swiss voters agree to closer E.U. link.
- **2002** Swiss abandon isolation to join UN.
- **2004** Switzerland called a "terror way station" for Al Qaeda suspects who used the country as a base.
- **2007** Swiss celebrates 50th anniversary of voting rights for women.

Impressions

[Switzerland is] the land of wooden houses, innocent cakes, thin butter soup, and spotless little inn bedrooms with a family likeness to dairies.

—Charles Dickens

major cultural and educational center in the country.

Two of Switzerland's finest examples of Romanesque architecture are the Benedictine Abbey of All Saints, at Schaffhausen (1087–1150), and the Church of St. Pierre de Clages (11th–12th c.). The style of these buildings was followed by the Romanesque-Gothic transitional style of the 12th and 13th centuries, as exemplified by the Cathedral of Chur or by the imposing, five-aisle Minster of Basel.

In the 15th century, Switzerland adopted the Gothic style, as seen in the Cathedral of Notre-Dame at Lausanne and the Cathedral of St. Pierre in Geneva. In 1421 the Minster of Bern was constructed in the late Gothic style, with a three-aisled, pillared basilica; no transepts were added.

With the coming of the Renaissance, there was an increased emphasis on secular buildings. The best town for viewing the architecture of this period is Murten (Morat), with its circuit of walls, fountains, and towers. During the baroque era, no mammoth public buildings were erected. Instead, domestic buildings were adorned with the ornate curves developed in Austria, Italy, and Germany. Many of the elegant

town houses that give Bern its distinctive appearance were constructed during this era.

In the 19th century, impressive mansions were built in the neoclassical style. They were mostly those of prosperous merchants eager to evince their wealth.

In the 20th century, Switzerland produced a major architect, Le Corbusier (1887–1965), whose influence extended around the world. Known for his functional approach to architecture and city planning, Le Corbusier believed in adapting a building to the climate and to the convenience of both its construction and its intended use. The majority of his most significant works were erected abroad, in Berlin, Paris, Bordeaux, and Marseille, among other cities.

The principle of functionalism is evident in Switzerland's rural houses. Each region evolved its own style as it sought to build houses especially suited for retaining heat in the inhospitable, high-altitude Swiss climate. For example, in Appenzell, where it rains a lot, farm buildings were grouped into a single complex. And in the Emmental district, a large roof reached down to the first floor on all sides of the building.

4 THE LAY OF THE LAND

This mountainous, landlocked alpine country is surrounded by Austria, France, Italy, and Germany, and is one of the smallest countries in Europe, stretching only 220km (137 miles) north to south and 350km (217 miles) east to west.

Zurich and Geneva are its leading cities, and much of the northern border with Germany follows the course of the Rhine River. In the east, Lake Constance forms a border with both Germany and Austria. In

Impressions

[Switzerland is] small, and like everything within it, so clean that you can hardly breathe for hygiene, and oppressive precisely because everything is right, fitting, and respectable. . . . Everything in this country is of an oppressive adequacy.

—Max Frisch

the southwest, Switzerland shares a border with France that cuts across Lake Geneva.

The little country is divided in a trio of regions, including the Swiss Alps, the Swiss plateau, and the Jura. Most residents live on the plains and rolling hills of the plateau. The Alps are the biggest tourist attraction, reaching their highest peak at Dufourspitze at 4,634m (15,200 ft.) near the Italian-Swiss border. The highest mountain, the Dom at 4,545m (14,908 ft.) lies entirely within the boundaries of Switzerland. The Alps cover 65% of the surface of the country.

Skiing and other winter sports provide a large slice of the Swiss economy. The major resorts for this type of fun in the snow lie in the Valais, Bernese Oberland, and the Grisons. Many villages, such as Zermatt, are free of vehicular traffic, and most of these main regions can be reached within 3 hours of Switzerland's main cities.

The more populated Swiss plateau runs from Lake Geneva on the French border, cutting across central Switzerland to Lake Constance, which, as mentioned, is shared with Germany and Austria.

Most of the large lakes, including Lake Geneva, are located in the plateau. The only large lake that lies entirely within Switzerland is Lake Neuchâtel, at 218 sq. km (85 sq. miles). Three great rivers—the Rhône, Rhine, and Aar cross this great plateau, which occupies about one-third of the landmass of Switzerland.

Accounting for 12% of the landmass, the Jura is a limestone range running from Lake Geneva to the Rhine River. The name "Jurassic" comes from this region, because many fossils and dinosaur tracks have been found here.

In hydrography, Switzerland has 6% of all freshwater reserves in Europe, and is the source of several major rivers such as the Rhine and Aar that flow into the North Sea. The Rhône empties into the Mediterranean.

In general, about one-fourth of Switzerland is mountains, lakes, or rivers, with farming taking up around 35% of the land.

In all, 50,000 plant and animal species call Switzerland home. Once there were more. Because of city and agricultural growth in the plateau, and the elimination of many habitats, many species here are now endangered. To prevent further erosion, Switzerland is setting aside protected natural areas.

5 SWITZERLAND IN POPULAR CULTURE: BOOKS, FILMS & MUSIC

BOOKS

Read a few of the books below to get a feel for Switzerland—its people, atmosphere, and history—before you visit.

- *The Apple and the Arrow* (Conrad Buff) is told from the point of view of William Tell's young son Walter, and recounts the 1291 Swiss struggle for freedom.

From Carl Jung to Paul Klee, Switzerland's Famous People

Ernest Ansermet (1883–1969)   This Swiss conductor achieved fame with Diaghilev's Ballet Russe in 1915. In 1918, Ansermet founded what was to become one of Switzerland's most respected orchestras, the Orchestre de la Suisse Romande, in Geneva, and introduced many new works that later became famous. He frequently conducted musical tours of the United States.

Arnold Böcklin (1827–1901)   His paintings of mythical scenes and landscapes are displayed in galleries throughout Europe. Among his most famous works are *The Elysian Fields, The Sacred Grove,* and *The Island of the Dead.* Böcklin used color imaginatively and developed his mythological portrays with great originality.

Le Corbusier (1887–1965)   This Swiss architect helped revolutionize international concepts in city planning and functional architecture. Le Corbusier designed his first house at 18 and later became famous for his buildings in Berlin, Marseille, and other cities. In 1950, he contributed to the design of the United Nations Secretariat Building in New York. He also was in charge of the design of the Visual Art Center at Harvard University. Although famous primarily for his work as an architect (he was reputedly a master at the unusual applications of molded concrete), Le Corbusier was also well known as an abstract painter.

Jean Henri Dunant (1828–1910)   Co-winner of the first Nobel Peace Prize, in 1901, this Swiss humanitarian was the founder of the Red Cross. Greatly affected by his role in caring for the injured soldiers at the Battle of Solferino (Italy, 1859), he later wrote *A Souvenir of Solferino.* In it he called for an international organization, without political ties, to aid the wounded in future conflicts. His proposal eventually led to the Geneva Convention governing the treatment of combatants and to the establishment of the International Red Cross.

Friedrich Dürrenmatt (1921–90)   This Swiss playwright is best known for his grotesque farce *The Visit,* which was filmed with Ingrid Bergman and Anthony Quinn. *The Physicists,* a mordant satire, was also acclaimed. In it, Dürrenmatt chose as his theme the danger posed by one person's possession of nuclear and nuclear-related technology.

- *Arms and the Man* (George Bernard Shaw), a play first produced in 1894, takes place during the 1885 Serbo-Bulgarian War. It features a Swiss voluntary soldier who carries chocolates instead of pistol cartridges. Oscar Straus based his 1909 *The Chocolate Soldier* operetta on this play.

- *Daisy Miller* (Henry James), a novella, probes the emotional complications of a rich American traveling in Switzerland. Published in 1878, the novella became one of James's all-time big successes.

- *Heidi* (Johanna Spyri), a world classic, is the best-known book set in Switzerland.

Leonard Euler (1707–83)   One of the originators of pure mathematics, Eurler, who was born in Basel, was invited by Catherine the Great to study and teach in Russia. He discovered the law of quadratic reciprocity (1772) in the theory of numbers. His study of the lines of curvature (1760) led to the new branch of differential geometry. Euler conducted massive research in algebra, trigonometry, calculus, and geometry and made discoveries in astronomy, hydrodynamics, and optics.

Alberto Giacometti (1901–66)   This Swiss sculptor's works are characterized by surrealistically elongated forms and are filled with what critics have called "hallucinatory moods." During his early career, Giacometti worked as a painter; in later life he returned to painting, but his works reflected a sculptural quality, according to critics.

Carl Jung (1875–1961)   This Swiss psychologist and psychiatrist became the founder of analytic psychology. An early associate of Freud, Jung developed concepts of extrovert and introvert personalities and of the collective unconscious. Greatly influenced by artistic and archetypal themes held in common by many primitive societies, he stressed an active role for an analyst during the therapeutic process.

Paul Klee (1879–1940)   Swiss modernist painter, he was one of the most influential artists of the 20th century. Combining abstract elements with recognizable images, Klee painted in a style characterized by fantasy figures in line and light colors. His works are displayed in galleries of modern art all over the world. He was also an accomplished musician.

Ulrich Zwingli (1484–1531)   A Swiss religious reformer, Zwingli was a Catholic priest before becoming a Protestant minister. Enraged by the values of the 16th-century popes, he led the Protestant Reformation in Switzerland from 1519 until his death. The movement was later bolstered by the arrival of John Calvin in 1536. Zwingl translated the Bible into Swiss German and wrote a testament of Protestant teachings, *On the True and False Religion.* His influence helped transform Geneva into central Europe's most stalwart bastion of 16th-century Protestantism. Zwingli died in Kappel, near Zurich, in a religious war between Catholics and Protestants.

Charming readers of every generation since its publication in 1880, it's the story of a young orphan sent to live with her grumpy grandfather in the Swiss Alps. Calling Shirley Temple now that we need her.

- *Hotel du Lac* (Anita Brookner) is the story of a romance author who has been banished by her friends to a stately hotel in Switzerland, where she hears fascinating tales of the guests she befriends there.

- *The Magic Mountain* (Thomas Mann) is a classic, one of the most celebrated novels of the 20th century, and it's set in an alpine sanatorium in the resort of Davos-Platz. Mann tells the story of Hans

Impressions

The more one sees of Switzerland, the more one is pleased with the country, and the less one is pleased with the inhabitants.

—Henry Matthews, *Diary of an Invalid,* 1820

Castorp, a "modern everyman," who spends 7 years in the alpine sanatorium for TB patients before leaving to become a soldier in World War I.

- *Scrambles Amongst the Alps* (Edward Whymper) is the latest reprint of this classic mountaineer's account of his conquest of the Matterhorn.
- For some light reading, *Ticking Along with the Swiss* (Dianne Dicks) is an amusing collection of personal tales from travelers to Switzerland.
- *A Tramp Abroad* (Mark Twain) is the eternal tongue-in-cheek travelogue for "Innocents Abroad" touring the Swiss Alps.
- *Walking Switzerland—The Swiss Way* (Marcia and Philip Lieberman) is a useful guide for those who want to walk through the tiny country.
- *Why Switzerland?* (Jonathan Steinberg) provides the best look at Swiss society, culture, and history.
- *Wilhelm Tell* (Friedrich von Schiller), a play, is one of the Harvard Classics. It's based on the legendary Swiss hero who resisted Austrian domination. He was consequently forced to use a bow and arrow to shoot an apple placed on the head of his son. Rossini based his famous opera on this play.

FILMS

Switzerland is no Hollywood, not even a Bollywood. But the dramatic geography of the country itself has often made it a locale for filmmakers from all over the world. Of course, the all-time Swiss classic is *Heidi,* shot in 1937 and starring Shirley Temple as Heidi (who else?). This movie continues to win new fans—young ones, that is—every year.

One of the best of all James Bond films, *Goldfinger* (1964), uses Switzerland in some of its backdrop scenes with star Sean Connery. Secret Agent 007 returned to Switzerland for more background scenes in the 1969 *On Her Majesty's Secret Service* and the 1995 *Goldeneye.* The 1994 version of Mary Shelley's *Frankenstein,* directed by Kenneth Branagh, also used dramatic Swiss backdrops.

Trois couleurs: Rouge (Three Colors Red) in 1994, the last film in director Krzysztof Kieslowski's trilogy, used scenes in Geneva's Old Town as a backdrop, and director Peter Greenaway also used the city in his *Stairs 1 Geneva* (1995).

Director Blake Edwards used Gstaad and its swanky Palace Hotel for *The Return of the Pink Panther* (1975). The Bernese Oberland is showcased, perhaps as never before, in Clint Eastwood's *The Eiger Sanction* (1975). Even people who didn't enjoy this espionage spy thriller were charmed by the scenery. A Zurich bank figures into the plot of *The Bourne Identity* (2002), starring Matt Damon. The thriller is based very loosely on Robert Ludlum's novel.

MUSIC

For most of its history, religious and folk music has dominated this art form in Switzerland. Traditional instruments included the hammered dulcimer, the fife, the bagpipe, the cittern, the shawm, and the hurdy-gurdy.

Beginning in 1836, the accordion swept the country. The Swiss quickly incorporated this instrument into their folk music.

As more and more Swiss moved to the cities, folk music from rural areas was mixed with jazz and the foxtrot, with the saxophone coming into great prominence.

By the 1960s, trios of two accordions and a double bass ruled the night.

The rural Appenzell region in northeastern Switzerland remains the major center for folk music today.

Pop and rock invaded Switzerland in the 1960s, much to the horror of traditionalists. Swiss musicians like Les Aiglons or Les Faux Frères became major recording artists.

Swiss rock began to die out in the late '60s, replaced by more progressive music such as jazz and blues.

Hard rock appeared by the end of the '70s, and a rock band called Krokus became the most popular recording group in the history of Swiss music.

Metal bands dominated music in the 1980s, with a Swiss band, Celtic Frost, the leader of the pack. Swiss new-wave bands began to branch out and become internationally known. Fame came to such bands as Kleenex/LiliPUT and Yello.

Rappers and DJs arrived on the scene in the '90s, including Black Tiger from Basel, the first one to rap in a Swiss-German dialect. Birthed in the 1990s, the band Gotthard survived the millennium to become the leading Swiss rock group and one of the most acclaimed bands in western Europe.

---

6 A TASTE OF SWITZERLAND

Swiss cuisine is a flavorful blend of German, French, and Italian influences. In most restaurants and hotel dining rooms today, menus will list a wide array of international dishes, but you should make an effort to sample some of the local fare.

CHEESE

Cheese making is part of the Swiss heritage. Cattle breeding and dairy farming, concentrated in the alpine areas of the country, have been associated with the region for 2,000 years, since the Romans ate *caseus Helveticus* (Helvetian cheese). In fact, the St. Gotthard Pass was a well-known cattle route to the south as far back as the 13th century. The Swiss, who helped develop the American dairy industry, have exported cheese, cattle, and their expertise to the entire world.

Today, more than 100 different varieties of cheese are produced in Switzerland. The cheeses, however, are not mass produced—they're made in hundreds of small, strictly controlled dairies, each under the direction of a master cheese maker with a federal degree, to ensure that the product is

made according to manufacturing standards and is properly cured to produce its own natural, protective rind.

The cheese with the holes, known as Switzerland Swiss or Emmentaler, has been widely copied, since nobody ever thought to protect the name for use only on cheeses produced in the Emme Valley until it was too late. Other cheeses of Switzerland, many of which have also had their names plagiarized, are Gruyère, appenzeller, raclette, royalp, and sapsago. The names of several mountain cheeses have also been copied, including sbrinz and spalen, closely related to the *caseus Helveticus* of Roman times.

Fondue

Cheese fondue, which consists of cheese (Emmentaler and natural Gruyère used separately, together, or with special local cheeses) melted in white wine flavored with a soupçon of garlic and lemon juice, is the national dish of Switzerland. Freshly ground pepper, nutmeg, paprika, and Swiss kirsch are among the traditional seasonings. Guests surround a bubbling

The Literary Tradition of Switzerland

Many 19th-century English writers went to Switzerland for inspiration. Prominent among them were Mary Wollstonecraft Shelley (who wrote *Frankenstein* beside Lake Geneva), Lord Byron, Robert Browning, Henry Wadsworth Longfellow, and Charles Dickens. In the 20th century, Thomas Mann, James Joyce, Hermann Hesse, and Vladimir Nabokov were some of the major writers who gravitated to Switzerland.

Of course, Switzerland has fine literature of its own. Because of the country's different languages, much of Swiss literature has had strong connections with literary traditions and styles in Germany and Austria, in France, and in Italy. Literature produced solely in Switzerland, with few international influences, is usually written in the Rhaeto-Romanic group of local dialects, among them Romansh.

It wasn't until the 18th century that Swiss literature became defined as such. The most important works—except for those by the Geneva-born Rousseau—were written in German. Among them the most famous is the *Codex Manesse*, first published in 1732 (the manuscript is preserved in Heidelberg). It is a collection of the works of 30 different poets, known collectively as the Minnesingers. In the 19th century, Switzerland's national man of letters, Gottfried Keller, made the Codex the subject of one of his Zurich novellas.

Writers who emerged in the 18th century include Albrecht von Haller (1708–77), who wrote voluminous works on physiology and other scientific subjects, and Johannes von Müller (1752–1809), whose *History of the Swiss Confederation* inspired Schiller to write *William Tell*.

In the 1800s, two Swiss works were translated around the world. They were *Heidi* (1880), by Johanna Spryri, and *The Swiss Family Robinson* (1813), by Johann David Wyss.

---

caquelon (an earthenware pipkin or small pot) and use long forks to dunk cubes of bread into the hot mixture. Other dunkables are apples, pears, grapes, cocktail wieners, cubes of boiled ham, shrimp, pitted olives, and tiny boiled potatoes.

Raclette

This cheese specialty is almost as famous as fondue. Popular for many centuries, its origin is lost in antiquity, but the word "raclette" comes from the French word *racler*, meaning "to scrape off." Although raclette originally was the name of the dish made from the special mountain cheese of the Valais, today it describes not only the dish itself but also the cheese varieties suitable for melting at an open fire or in an oven.

A piece of cheese (traditionally half to a quarter of a wheel of raclette) is held in front of an open fire. As it starts to soften, it is scraped off onto one's plate with a special knife. The unique flavor of the cheese is most delicious when the cheese is hottest. The classic accompaniment is fresh, crusty, homemade dark bread, but the cheese may also be eaten together with potatoes boiled in their skins, pickled

Jacob Christoph Burckhardt (1818–97), one of the preeminent historians of the 19th century, is known for his great classic *The Civilization of the Renaissance in Italy* (1860). Burckhardt's emphasis on the cultural interpretation of history influenced the German philosopher Friedrich Nietzsche.

Gottfried Keller (1819–90), novelist, poet, and short-story writer, reigned supreme over Swiss literature in the latter part of the 19th century. His works, particularly *Der grüne Heinrich (Green Henry)* and *People of Seldwyla,* are still popular throughout the German-speaking world.

The last German-language poet of international reputation born in Switzerland was Carl Spitteler (1845–1924), whose major allegorical work, *Olympischer Frühling (Olympian Spring),* published before World War I, argued for the need of ethics in the modern world. Spitteler was awarded the Nobel Prize for literature in 1919.

French-Swiss literature is dominated by two towering figures, Jean-Jacques Rousseau (1712–78), the father of Continental Romanticism and author of *The Social Contract* and the autobiographical *Confessions,* and Germaine (Madame) de Staël (1766–1817), who conducted a famous salon in Paris. During the French Revolution, de Staël sought refuge at the family estate at Coppet, on the shore of Lake Geneva. Her principal work, *De l'Allemagne (On Germany,* 1810), was an encomium of German romanticism. In 1811 she was exiled from France by Napoleon, who objected to the book; she found comfort in her marriage to a young Swiss officer more than 20 years her junior.

In the 20th century, two Swiss literary figures have gained an international following. One is Friedrich Dürrenmatt (1921–90), who is known mainly for his plays *The Visit* and *The Physicists.* The other is Max Frisch (1911–91), who has achieved a place in contemporary German literature with his plays, among them *Andorra* and *The Firebugs,* and his novels. His most famous novel is *I'm Not Stiller,* a trenchant critique of Swiss smugness and isolationism.

onions, cucumbers, or small corncobs. You usually eat raclette with a fork, but sometimes you may need a knife as well.

OTHER REGIONAL SPECIALTIES

The country's ubiquitous vegetable dish is *röchti* or *rösti* (hash-brown potatoes). It's excellent when popped into the oven coated with cheese, which melts and turns a golden brown. *Spätzli* (Swiss dumplings) often appear on the menu.

Lake fish is a specialty in Switzerland, with *ombre* (a grayling) and *ombre chevalier*

(char) heading the list—the latter a delectable but expensive treat. Tasty alpine lake fish include trout and fried filets of tiny perch.

Country-cured sausages can be found at open markets around the country. The best known is called *bündnerfleisch,* a specialty in the Grisons. The meat, however, is not cured, but dried in the crisp, dry alpine air. Before modern refrigeration, this was the Swiss way of preparing meat for winter consumption. Now *bündnerfleisch* is most often offered as an appetizer.

The *Bernerplatte* is the classic provincial dish of Bern. For gargantuan appetites, it's a

From Yodeling to Raclette Parties

Swiss towns of even modest size usually have a resident symphony orchestra and a municipal theater. The theater and concert season runs from September through May. In summer, music and film festivals and folklore displays are presented.

It has often been said that there is really no such thing as Swiss music per se, just music in Switzerland performed by Swiss musicians. There is some validity to this view. Except for its alpine melodies and dance music, Switzerland has made only a modest contribution to the world's repertoire.

Yet, Switzerland has several excellent orchestras and opera companies. The **Zurich Opera** specializes in German-language productions and the **Grand Théatre de Genéve,** the country's leading opera house, has a predominantly French-language repertoire. The **Orchestre de la Suisse Romande** is the country's best-known orchestra, and the respected **Tonhalle Orchester of Zurich** has a loyal following.

Local cultural entertainment is highlighted by the folk music and dancing of the alpine regions, which you can also see and hear in the big cities. These include *Kuhreigen* (round dances), yodeling performances, and a style of dance tunes known as *Ländler,* performed by small orchestras, whose members usually appear in regional costumes.

Switzerland's cities offer a variety of evening entertainment. In Zurich, the traditional stamping grounds for night owls lie around the Niederdorf, a neighborhood within Old Town known for its strip joints, bars, and music halls. There's even a red-light district. Most nightclubs, however, close at 2am, and many of them seem sterile and a bit boring. Geneva, too, despite its Calvinist traditions, has a sophisticated nightlife.

It might be more interesting, especially if you're a first-time visitor, to patronize some of the local folkloric places, where you can see and hear yodeling and dancing to alpine music. Major Swiss cities also have their international-style bars and discos as well.

Theater presentations tend to be in German or French, so unless you speak either language, these shows may not be for you.

Throughout the winter, the après-ski life in Switzerland's high-altitude resorts might best be described as vigorous, with raclette parties, beer drinking in rustic taverns, sleigh rides, and lots of music, much of it brought in by live groups from Great Britain, France, and Germany or from the United States.

Many after-dark rendezvous joints close down in summer. The Swiss prefer to drink outside, under the summer sky, perhaps in some beer garden, rather than being cooped up inside a deliberately darkened disco.

version of the Alsatian *choucroûte garnie.* If you order this typical farmer's plate, you'll be confronted with a mammoth pile of sauerkraut or French beans, topped with pigs' feet, sausages, ham, bacon, or pork chops.

In addition to cheese fondue, you may enjoy *fondue bourguignonne,* a dish that has become popular around the world. It consists of chunks of meat spitted on wooden sticks and broiled in oil or butter, seasoned according to choice. Also, many establishments offer *fondue chinoise,* made with thin slices of beef and Oriental sauces. At the finish, you sip the broth in which the meat was cooked.

Typical Ticino specialties include risotto with mushrooms and a mixed grill known as *fritto misto.* Polenta, made with cornmeal, is popular as a side dish. Ticino also has lake and river fish, such as trout and pike. Pizza and pasta have spread to all provinces of Switzerland; if you're watching your centimes, either one is often the most economical dish on the menu.

Salads often combine both fresh lettuce and cooked vegetables, such as beets. For a unique dish, ask for a *zwiebelsalat* (cooked onion salad). In spring, the Swiss adore fresh asparagus. In fact, police have been forced to increase their night patrols in parts of the country to keep thieves out of the asparagus fields.

The glory of Swiss cuisine is its patisseries, little cakes and confections served all over the country in tearooms and cafes. The most common delicacy is *gugelhupf,* a big cake shaped like a bun and traditionally filled with whipped cream.

DRINKS

White wine is the invariable choice of beverage with fondue; if you don't like white wine, you might get by with kirsch or tea.

There are almost no restrictions on the sale of alcohol in Switzerland, but prices of bourbon, gin, and scotch are usually much higher than in the United States, and portions can be skimpy.

Wine

Swiss wines are superb. Unlike French wines, they are best when new. Many wines, such as those from the Lake Geneva region, are produced for local consumption. Ask your headwaiter for advice on which local wine to try.

Most of the wines produced in Switzerland are white, but there are also good rosés and fragrant red wines. Most exported wines are produced in the Valais, Lake Geneva, Ticino, and Seeland. However, more than 300 small winegrowing areas are spread over the rest of the country, especially where German dialects are spoken.

In the French-speaking part of Switzerland, two of the best wines are the fruity Fendant and the slightly stronger Johannisberg. In the German-speaking part, you might want to sample one of the dry and light reds, which include Stammheimer, Klevner, and Hallauer. In the Italian-speaking Ticino, red merlot is a fruity, ruby-red wine with a pleasant bouquet.

Beer

Swiss beer is an excellent brew; it's the preferred drink in the German-speaking part of the country. The beer varies in quality. *Helles* is light beer; *Dunkles* is dark beer.

Liqueur

Swiss liqueurs are tasty and highly potent. The most popular are kirsch (the national hard drink, made from the juice of cherry pits), and *Pflümli* (made from plums). *Williamine* is made from fragrant Williams pears. *Träsch* is another form of brandy, made from cider pears. In the Ticino, most locals are fond of the fiery *Grappa* brandy, which is distilled from the dregs of the grape-pressing process.

Chocolate Superpower

Cocoa beans (which look rather unappetizingly like shriveled almonds) are chocolate's raw ingredients. First publicized in Europe by Columbus, who noticed them growing on trees in Nicaragua in 1502, they were traded as currency by the conquistadores in the New World, who viewed them as an elixir of physical strength. (Cortés, oppressor of Mexico, believed that a foot soldier could march for many hours with renewed energy after consuming some of the beans.) Back in Spain, royal cooks mixed the pulverized beans with sugar and hot water and served them with great success to the royal family. The Spanish-born Anne of Austria introduced it to the French court at her dinner parties after her marriage to Louis XIII. And in a kind of chain reaction to the bean's original "discovery," London's first chocolate shop was established by a Frenchman in 1657.

Nineteenth-century attitudes about chocolate (as perceived in North America and in Europe) were widely different. In 1825, the leading culinarian of the French-speaking world (Brillat-Savarin) declared that chocolate was one of the most effective restoratives of physical and intellectual powers known to man. In contrast, Harriet Beecher Stowe, the American-born moral crusader and woman of letters, declared chocolate unfit for proper American tables, and—in a burst of prudishness—commented suspiciously on its French and Spanish origins.

Despite Ms. Stowe's invectives, the market for chocolate continued to grow, as consumers searched for inexpensive alternatives to their bland, homegrown diets. This fact was immediately noticed by the canny Swiss from their politically neutral bastion in the Alps.

From the early 1800s the Swiss began investing heavily in what they perceived as a long-range moneymaker. Pioneers of the industry opened the country's first chocolate factory in 1819 at Corsier, near Vevey. What's now a massive multinational concern, Suchard, was established near Neuchâtel in 1824. In 1875, Swiss-born Daniel Peter invented milk chocolate by adding condensed milk to his brew of pulverized cocoa and sugar. In 1879, the first chocolate bar was created (the Lindt Surfin bar). In 1899, the Sprungli and Lindt empires merged into a Zurich-based chocolate-making dynasty whose success has been likened by Swiss patriots to that of Henry Ford and the Wright brothers. The Tobler and Nestlé organizations were founded shortly afterward, just before a host of new inventions followed in relentless succession. (One of the most spectacular of these included liqueur-filled chocolate cups whose manufacturing process is considered an engineering marvel.) Ironically, improvements in dentistry have always paralleled the increased proficiency of the chocolate industry's blending and marketing techniques.

Technical advances since the 1970s have produced better-tasting, better-packaged chocolates. In 1980 and 1982, respectively, Katharine Hepburn and Mimi Sheraton (food critic for the *New York Times*) wholeheartedly endorsed chocolate as something wonderful. (In Sheraton's case, the endorsement specifically mentioned "Lindt's big flat extra bitter bittersweet bar.") Sales of Swiss chocolate in the United States soared, despite Harriet Beecher Stowe's injunctions.

Switzerland today is the largest chocolate superpower in the world, leading the globe in production. Both secrecy and precision have always been cited as Swiss virtues, and both of these qualities are required during a complicated blending process that transforms the raw ingredients into the final product. The allure is aesthetic as well as gastronomic: Swiss consumers expect new artwork on their chocolate wrappers at frequent intervals, and an army of commercial artists labors at yearly intervals to comply. The Swiss eat and drink more chocolate per capita than any other nation in the world, fueling their bodies for the bone-chilling temperatures of the alpine climate. (No self-respecting mountain climber ever embarks without the requisite chocolate bars.)

Swiss factories maintain "chocolate breaks" for sugar-induced bursts of energy. Swiss housewives usually don't buy less than a kilo of chocolate at a time, and a fortune is almost guaranteed to anyone who can invent transparent and translucent chocolate. (The challenge of producing white chocolate was already conquered—in Switzerland—many years ago.)

Planning Your Trip to Switzerland

This chapter is devoted to the where, when, and how of your trip—the advance planning required to get it together and take it on the road. Browse through this section before you hit the road to ensure you've covered all the bases.

For additional help in planning your trip and for more on-the-ground resources in Switzerland, please see "Fast Facts: Switzerland," on p. 480.

1 WHEN TO GO

Low-season airfares are usually offered from November 1 to December 14 and from December 25 to March 31. Fares are slightly higher during shoulder season (during Apr and May, and from Sept 16 to the end of Oct). High-season fares apply the rest of the year (June–Sept 15), presumably when Switzerland and its landscapes are at their most hospitable and most beautiful.

Keep in mind that it's most expensive to visit Swiss ski resorts in winter, and slightly less so during the rest of the year. Conversely, it's cheaper to visit lakeside towns and the Ticino in winter. Cities such as Geneva, Zurich, and Bern don't depend on tourism as a major source of capital, so prices in these cities tend to remain the same all year.

THE WEATHER

The temperature range is about the same as in the northern United States, but without the extremes of hot and cold. Summer temperatures seldom rise above 80°F (26°C) in the cities, and humidity is low. Because of clear air and lack of wind in the high alpine regions, sunbathing is sometimes possible even in winter. In southern Switzerland the temperature remains mild year-round, allowing subtropical vegetation to grow.

Switzerland's Average Temperatures (°F/°C)

	Jan	Feb	Mar	Apr	May	June	July	Aug	Sept	Oct	Nov	Dec
Geneva												
High	40/4	43/6	50/10	59/15	67/19	74/23	77/25	76/24	70/21	58/14	47/8	40/4
Low	29/–2	31/–1	36/2	41/5	49/9	56/13	59/15	58/14	54/12	45/7	38/3	32/0
Lugano												
High	43/6	49/9	56/13	63/17	70/21	77/25	81/27	81/27	74/23	61/16	52/11	45/7
Low	29/–2	31/–1	38/3	45/7	50/10	58/14	61/16	59/15	56/13	47/8	38/3	32/0
Zermatt												
High	26/–3	26/–3	27/–3	36/2	46/7	52/11	58/14	53/12	52/11	38/3	33/1	26/–3
Low	20/–7	19/–7	19/–7	28/–2	36/2	42/6	48/9	44/7	42/6	32/0	27/–3	20/–7
Zurich												
High	36/2	41/4	50/10	59/15	67/19	74/23	77/25	76/24	68/20	58/14	45/7	38/3
Low	27/–3	2/–29	34/1	40/4	47/8	54/12	58/14	56/13	52/11	43/61	36/2	29/–2

SWITZERLAND CALENDAR OF EVENTS

The festivals mentioned in this section, unless otherwise specified, fall on different dates every year. Inquire at the Swiss National Tourist Office or local tourist offices for an updated calendar. See "The Best Festivals" in chapter 1 for more information. For an exhaustive list of events beyond those listed here, check http://events.frommers.com, where you'll find a searchable, up-to-the-minute roster of what's happening in cities all over the world.

JANUARY

Vogel Gryff Festival (The Feast of the Griffin), Basel. The "Wild Man of the Woods" appears on a boat, followed by a mummers' parade. For more information, call 🕾 **061/268-68-68.** Mid-January.

FEBRUARY

Basler Fasnacht, Basel. Called "the wildest of carnivals," with a parade of "cliques" (clubs and associations). For more information, call 🕾 **061/268-68-68** (www.fasnacht.ch). First Monday after Ash Wednesday.

MARCH

Hornussen ("Meeting on the Snow"), Maloja. A traditional sport of rural Switzerland. For information, call 🕾 **081/824-31-81.** For a description of the sport, see the box *"Hornussen, Schwingen & Waffenlaufen,"* later in this chapter. Mid-March.

APRIL

Primavera Concertistica, Locarno. April marks the beginning of a festival of music concerts that lasts through October. For information, call 🕾 **091/791-00-91.** Mid-April.

Sechseläuten (Six O'Clock Chimes), Zurich. Members of all the guilds dress in costumes and celebrate the arrival of spring, which is climaxed by the burning of Böögg, a straw figure symbolizing winter. There are also children's parades. The **Zurich Tourist Office** (🕾 **044/215-40-00;** www.zuerich.com) shows the parade route on a map. (Böögg is burned at 6pm on Sechseläutenplatz, near Bellevueplatz.) Third Monday of April.

MAY

Corpus Christi. Solemn processions in the Roman Catholic regions and towns of Switzerland. End of May.

JUNE

Fête de Lausanne, Lausanne. Beginning of an international festival, showcasing weeks of music and ballet. For information, call 🕾 **021/315-22-14** (www.lausanne.ch). End of June.

William Tell Festival, Interlaken. Performances of the famous play by Schiller. For more information, call 🕾 **033/822-37-32** (www.tellspiele.ch). End of June through early September.

JULY

Montreux International Jazz Festival, Montreux. More than jazz, this festival features everything from reggae bands to African tribal chanters. Monster dance fests also break out nightly. The festival concludes with a 12-hour marathon of world music. For more information, call 🕾 **021/966-44-44** (www.montreuxjazz.com). Lasts 2 weeks and is held in the beginning of July.

Züri Fäscht, Zurich. This summertime citywide festival takes over Zurich with fairground revelry. Held every 3 years in early July; the next one will take place in 2010.

AUGUST

Fêtes de Genève, Geneva. Highlights are flower parades, fireworks, and live music all over the city. For more information, call 🕾 **022/909-70-70** (www.fetes-de-geneve.ch). Early August.

Lucerne Festival, Lucerne. Concerts, theater, art exhibitions, and street musicians. For more information, call © **041/226-44-80** (www.lucernefestival.ch). Mid-August through mid-September.

Zurich Street Parade. Visitors flock to Zurich for a daylong techno/dance party and parade that takes over the entire city. You'll either want to book a hotel far in advance, or avoid this at all costs. Visit www.streetparade.ch. See the detailed box on p. 111. Early to mid-August.

OCTOBER

Autumn Festival, Lugano. A parade and other festivities mark harvest time. Little girls throw flowers from blossom-covered floats and oxen pull festooned wagons in a colorful procession. For information, call © **091/913-32-32.** Early October.

Aelplerchilbi, Kerns and other villages of the Unterwalden Canton. Dairymen and pasture owners join villagers in a traditional festival to mark the end of an alpine summer. For more information, contact the **Sarnen Tourismus,**

Hofstrasse 2 (© **041/666-50-40;** www.sarnen-tourism.ch). Late September or October.

NOVEMBER

Zibelemärit, Bern. The famous "onion market" fair. Call © **031/328-12-12** for more information. Fourth Monday in November.

DECEMBER

Christmas Festivities. Ancient St. Nicholas parades and traditional markets are staged throughout the country to mark the beginning of Christmas observances, with the major one at Fribourg. Mid-December.

L'Escalade, Geneva. A festival commemorating the failure of the duke of Savoy's armies to take Geneva by surprise on the night of December 11, 1602. Brigades on horseback in period costumes, country markets, and folk music are interspersed with Rabelaisian banquets, fife-and-drum parades, and torchlit marches. Geneva's Old Town provides the best vantage point. Call © **022/909-70-11** for more information. Three days and nights (nonstop) in early December.

2 ENTRY REQUIREMENTS

PASSPORTS

Every traveler entering Switzerland must have a valid passport, although it's not necessary for North Americans to have a visa if they don't stay longer than 3 continuous months. For information on permanent residence in Switzerland and work permits, contact the nearest Swiss consulate.

For information on how to get a passport, go to the "Fast Facts: Switzerland" section of chapter 18—the websites listed provide downloadable passport applications as well as the current fees for processing passport applications. For an up-to-date country-by-country listing of

passport requirements around the world, go to the "Foreign Entry Requirement" Web page of the U.S. State Department at **http://travel.state.gov**.

CUSTOMS
What You Can Bring into Switzerland

You can take personal effects into Switzerland such as clothing, toilet articles, sports gear, photographic and amateur movie or video cameras (including film), musical instruments, and camping equipment. Medicine must be for your personal use only. You can also take 2 liters of alcohol

> ## (Tips) Passport Savvy
>
> Allow plenty of time before your trip to apply for a passport. And keep in mind that if you need a passport in a hurry, you'll pay a higher processing fee. When traveling, safeguard your passport in an inconspicuous, inaccessible place like a money belt and keep a copy of the critical pages with your passport number in a separate place. If you lose your passport, visit the nearest consulate of your native country as soon as possible for a replacement.

up to 15% proof or 1 liter of more than 15% proof. You are allowed 400 cigarettes, 100 cigars, or 500 grams of tobacco if you're flying in from outside Europe. Those entering from other European countries are allowed 200 cigarettes, 50 cigars, or 250 grams of tobacco.

What You Can Take Home from Switzerland

For information on what you're allowed to bring home, contact one of the following agencies:

U.S. Citizens: U.S. Customs & Border Protection (CBP), 1300 Pennsylvania Ave. NW, Washington, DC 20229 (© 877/287-8667; www.cbp.gov).

Canadian Citizens: Canada Border Services Agency (© 800/461-9999 in Canada, or 204/983-3500; www.cbsa-asfc.gc.ca).

U.K. Citizens: HM Customs & Excise (© 0845/010-9000, or from outside the U.K., 020/8929-0152; www.hmce.gov.uk).

Australian Citizens: Australian Customs Service (© 1300/363-263; www.customs.gov.au).

New Zealand Citizens: New Zealand Customs, the Customhouse, 17–21 Whitmore St., Box 2218, Wellington (© 04/473-6099 or 0800/428-786; www.customs.govt.nz).

MEDICAL REQUIREMENTS

Unless you're arriving from an area known to be suffering from an epidemic (particularly cholera or yellow fever), inoculations or vaccinations are not required for entry into the Switzerland.

3 GETTING THERE & GETTING AROUND

GETTING TO SWITZERLAND
By Plane

Switzerland is situated at the center of Europe and thus is a focal point for international air traffic. The busy intercontinental airports of Zurich and Geneva can be reached in about 8 hours from the east coast of North America and in less than 2 hours from London or Paris. The country is also the crossroads of Europe—all rail lines, road passes, and mountain tunnels

lead to it. Similarly, the main European route for east-west travel passes through Switzerland, between Lake Constance and Geneva.

From North America

From New York, it takes about 7 hours to fly to either Geneva or Zurich; from Chicago, about 10 hours; and from the West Coast, about 14 hours.

Swiss International Air Lines Ltd. (simply called **Swiss**) has taken over as the major carrier for Switzerland in the wake of the famous Swissair going belly up. For information, contact Swiss at ℂ **877/FLY-SWISS** (359-7947) in the U.S., 0848/700-700 in Switzerland, or 0845/601-09-56 in London. Or else search out www.swiss.com.

From North America, the most popular Swiss routes are daily flights from New York's JFK Airport to either Zurich or Geneva. There is also a daily Newark, New Jersey–Zurich flight, as well as a daily flight from Boston, Los Angeles, Miami, Chicago, and Dallas (in partnership with American Airlines).

From Montreal, Swiss flies to Zurich daily; from London, there are two daily Swiss flights to Basel, five to Geneva, and 14 to Zurich.

American Airlines (ℂ **800/433-7300;** www.aa.com) makes one daily nonstop flight to Zurich from both Dallas/Fort Worth (DFW) and JFK. There is one nonstop flight from DFW through Newark and one nonstop flight from DFW through Miami.

Delta Airlines (ℂ **800/221-1212;** www.delta.com) has one daily nonstop to Zurich from Atlanta and a daily flight from Portland, Oregon, with a stopover in Atlanta.

Air Canada (ℂ **888/247-2262;** www.aircanada.com) flies nonstop daily from Toronto to Zurich. Flight time from Toronto is about 8 hours.

From Britain

From London's Heathrow Airport, **British Airways (BA;** ℂ **0844/493-0787;** www.britishairways.com) offers six daily nonstop flights to Zurich; on Saturday there are five flights. The airline also provides eight daily flights from Heathrow to Geneva. From Gatwick, BA offers at least one daily nonstop to Geneva.

You can also check for flights by **Aer Lingus** (ℂ **0870/876-5000;** www.aerlingus.com) from Dublin, and flights from London on **easyJet** (ℂ **0870/600-0000;** www.easyjet.com).

British newspapers are always full of classified advertisements touting bargain airfares. Although competition is fierce, one well-recommended company that consolidates bulk ticket purchases and then passes the savings on to its consumers is **Trailfinders** (ℂ **0845/058-5858** in London; www.trailfinders.com), which offers discounted tickets on major airlines.

To find out which airlines travel to Switzerland, please see "Airline, Hotel & Car-Rental Websites," p. 484.

By Car

Situated in the middle of the Continent, Switzerland has a network of express highways linking it to other European countries. You can drive all the way from Britain to Switzerland by taking a northerly route through Belgium or the Netherlands and then Germany. British motorists tend to prefer this express auto route, which is free, to going through France and paying expensive toll charges.

The route through France is also much slower. It begins a few miles south of Calais and leads directly to the Périphérique (the ring road around Paris), where you can pick up the Autoroute du Soleil to Switzerland. In Britain the best connection for a road link across France is from Portsmouth to Le Havre.

From the south of Germany, Autobahn E35 leads directly into Basel. From Basel, head east to Zurich on E60.

Flying for Less: Tips for Getting the Best Airfare

- Passengers who can book their ticket either **long in advance or at the last minute,** or who **fly midweek** or **at less-trafficked hours** may pay a fraction of the full fare. If your schedule is flexible, say so, and ask if you can secure a cheaper fare by changing your flight plans.
- Search **the Internet** for cheap fares. The most popular online travel agencies are

Travelocity.com; Expedia.com; and **Orbitz.com.** In the U.K., go to **Travelsupermarket** (☎ **0845/345-5708;** www.travelsupermarket.com), a flight search engine that offers flight comparisons for the budget airlines whose seats often end up in bucket-shop sales. Other websites for booking airline tickets online include **Cheapflights.com, SmarterTravel.com, Priceline.com,** and **Opodo** (www.opodo.com). Meta search sites (which find and then direct you to airline and hotel websites for booking) include **Sidestep.com** and **Kayak.com**—the latter includes fares for budget carriers like JetBlue and Spirit as well as the major airlines. **last minute.com** is a great source for last-minute flights and getaways. In addition, most **airlines** offer online-only fares that even their phone agents know nothing about. British travelers should check **Flights International** (☎ **0800/018-7050;** www.flights-international.com) for deals on flights all over the world.

- Keep an eye on local newspapers for **promotional specials** or **fare wars,** when airlines lower prices on their most popular routes.
- **Consolidators,** also known as bucket shops, are wholesale brokers in the airline-ticket game. Consolidators buy deeply discounted tickets ("distressed" inventories of unsold seats) from airlines and sell them to online ticket agencies, travel agents, tour operators, corporations, and, to a lesser degree, the general public. Consolidators advertise in Sunday newspaper travel sections (often in small ads with tiny type), both in the U.S. and the U.K. They can be great sources for cheap international tickets. On the down side, bucket shop tickets are often rigged with restrictions, such as stiff cancellation penalties (as high as 50%–75% of the ticket

price). And keep in mind that most of what you see advertised is of limited availability. Several reliable consolidators are worldwide and available online. **STA Travel** (www.statravel.com) has been the world's leading consolidator for students since purchasing Council Travel, but their fares are competitive for travelers of all ages. **Flights.com** (☎ **201/541-3826;** www.flights.com) has excellent fares worldwide, particularly to Europe. They also have "local" websites in 12 countries. **Air Tickets Direct** (☎ **888/858-8884;** www.air ticketsdirect.com) is based in Montreal and leverages the currently weak Canadian dollar for low fares; they also book trips to places that U.S. travel agents won't touch, such as Cuba.

- Join **frequent-flier clubs.** Frequent-flier membership doesn't cost a cent, but it does entitle you to free tickets or upgrades when you amass the airline's required number of frequent-flier points. You don't even have to fly to earn points; **frequent-flier credit cards** can earn you thousands of miles for doing your everyday shopping. But keep in mind that award seats are limited, seats on popular routes are hard to snag, and more and more major airlines are cutting their expiration periods for mileage points—so check your airline's frequent-flier program so you don't lose your miles before you use them. *Inside tip:* Award seats are offered almost a year in advance, but seats also open up at the last minute, so if your travel plans are flexible, you may strike gold. To play the frequent-flier game to your best advantage, consult the community bulletin boards on **FlyerTalk** (www.flyer talk.com) or go to Randy Petersen's **Inside Flyer** (www.insideflyer.com). Petersen and friends review all the programs in detail and post regular updates on changes in policies and trends.

By Train
From Paris

One of the busiest rail links in Europe stretches from Paris to Geneva and Lausanne. Almost as busy are the rail routes between Paris and Zurich. Most of the trains assigned to these routes are part of Europe's network of high-speed trains (the French refer to them as *trains à grande vitesse,* or TGV). From Paris's Gare de Lyon, about four trains a day depart for both Geneva and Lausanne. Travel time to Geneva is about 4 hours; travel time to Lausanne is about 4½ hours.

Trains from Paris to Zurich depart three times a day from Paris's Gare de l'Est. Ironically, kilometers traveled by train within Switzerland are proportionately more expensive than equivalent distances within France, so ongoing fares from Zurich or Geneva to other points within Switzerland may come as an unpleasant surprise. Travelers who anticipate lots of rail travel are well advised to consider the purchase of any of Rail Europe's passes, or one of the Swiss Passes.

Schedules, prices, departure times, and confirmed reservations can be arranged before you leave North America through **Rail Europe** (© **877/272-RAIL** [272-7245]; www.raileurope.com).

From London

Rail links are also convenient between London and Switzerland. Both the following routes are easy, but the route through France is considerably more scenic (plus, you'll get the thrill of crossing the Chunnel—one of the world's engineering marvels).

VIA THE HOOK OF HOLLAND The standard EuroCity express route sets out from London's Liverpool Street Station, sails from Harwick to the Hook of Holland, and then proceeds by train via Cologne, Germany, to either Basel or Zurich. Once here, it's easy to find rail links to the rest of Switzerland.

ACROSS OR UNDER THE CHANNEL THROUGH PARIS It's also possible to take the rail link from London across or under the English Channel to Paris, where you can make ongoing rail connections to Switzerland. If you depart London at 10am, you can arrive in Geneva or Lausanne before 10pm the same day.

One of the most convenient ways to reach Paris from London is the Citylink rail-hovercraft-rail service. English trains originate at London's Victoria Station and chug through the English countryside to the port of Folkestone. Passengers disembark and board a hovercraft or, in some cases, a conventional ferryboat, and continue across the channel to the French port of Boulogne. Once you reach the Continent, you'll proceed south on a waiting train through France into Paris's Gare du Nord. In Paris passengers must travel by taxi or Metro (subway) across town to either the Gare de Lyon, for ongoing transfers to Geneva and Lausanne, or the Gare de l'Est, for Basel and Zurich. Trains then depart for Switzerland at regular intervals.

For information, timetables, and confirmed reservations (which are required on certain segments of these routes), contact **Rail Europe** (© **877/272-RAIL** [272-7245]).

In 1994 the Eurostar Express began twice-daily passenger service between London and both Paris and Brussels. The Channel tunnel, one of the great engineering feats of all time, is the first link between Britain and the Continent since the Ice Age. The 50km (31-mile) journey between Great Britain and France takes 35 minutes, although actual Chunnel time is only 19 minutes.

Eurostar offers a round-trip first-class fare between London and Paris that costs $570, $450 in regular second class. You can make reservations for **Eurostar** at © **0870/584-8848** in the United Kingdom;

in France at ☎ **01-55-31-54-54;** in the United States at ☎ **800/EUROSTAR** (387-6782); or online at www.eurostar.com.

Chunnel train traffic is roughly competitive with air travel, if you calculate door-to-door travel time. Trains leave from London's Waterloo Station and arrive in Paris at Gare du Nord, where fast rail connections can be made to whatever Swiss city you want.

The tunnel trains also accommodate passenger cars, charter buses, taxis, and motorcycles under the English Channel from Folkestone, England, to Calais, France. They operate 24 hours a day, 365 days a year, running every 15 minutes during peak travel times and at least once hourly at night. Tickets may be purchased at the tollbooth. With Le Shuttle, gone are weather-related delays, seasickness, and a need for reservations.

You'll drive onto a half-mile-long train and travel through an impermeable underground tunnel.

Before boarding Le Shuttle, you must stop at a tollbooth and pass through Immigration for both countries at one time. During the ride you'll stay in bright, air-conditioned carriages, remaining inside your car or stepping outside to stretch your legs. When the trip is completed, simply drive off toward your destination—in our case, heading southeast to Switzerland.

By Bus

Because of its location at the crossroads of Europe, Switzerland is on several important bus routes. **Eurolines, Ltd.,** 52 Grosvenor Gardens, London SW1W 0AU, UK (☎ **0870/514-32-19** or 020/7730-8235; www.eurolines.com), offers routes into Switzerland from several major European cities, including London. Departing from London's Victoria Coach Station, buses have toilets, air-conditioning, and reclining seats, and maintain a strict nonsmoking policy. They stop about every 4 hours for a brief rest and refreshments. Other buses depart 2 nights a week for Zurich at 8pm, arriving the next day at 1:15pm. Fares from London to Zurich go for £77 to £84 one-way and £126 round-trip. Persons 25 and under pay £77 each way and £118 round-trip.

GETTING AROUND
By Plane
Switzerland does not have an abundance of airports, partly because of the alpine terrain and partly due to the Swiss peoples' own resistance to having planes disturb their peace and quiet. To compensate, Switzerland has one of Europe's best railway systems, linking every major city in the country. This is particularly advantageous for cities such as Bern, the capital; it relies almost exclusively on rail transport to Zurich, Geneva, and Basel for air connections to the rest of the world.

If you want to fly within Switzerland, or from Switzerland to one of about 30 regional cities in Austria, Italy, Germany, or France, **Swiss** (☎ **0848/700-700;** www.swiss.com), a domestic airline, schedules flights from and to Basel and Amsterdam, Geneva and London, and Lugano and Geneva.

By Car
Switzerland has excellent roads and superhighways, all marked by clear road signs. Alpine passes are not difficult to cross, except in snowstorms, when they may shut down suddenly. Special rail facilities are provided for drivers wishing to transport their cars through the alpine tunnels of the Albula, Furka, Lotschberg, and Simplon. A timetable highlighting the various rates is available from the Swiss National Tourist Office.

CAR RENTALS Several American companies operate in Switzerland. One of the most reliable firms is **Budget** (☎ **800/472-3325;** www.budget.com); its prices are competitive with those offered by **Avis**

(© 800/331-1084; www.avis.com) and **Hertz** (© 800/654-3001; www.hertz.com). Under certain circumstances, the companies offer a discount if you prepay your rental 21 days or more in advance. Budget offers one-way rentals between any two of its more than 20 Swiss offices with no extra drop-off charge. **Kemwel Drive Group** (© 877/820-0668; www.kemwel.com) offers an alternative to more traditional car-rental companies, such as Budget, Hertz, and Avis, that actually own their automobiles outright. Kemwel leases blocks of cars a year in advance at locations throughout Switzerland, then rents them to qualified customers who prepay the entire rental.

Auto Europe (© 888/223-5555; www.autoeurope.com) is an equivalent company that leases cars, on an as-needed basis, from larger car-rental companies throughout Europe.

Note that there is a 6.5% government tax on car rentals in Switzerland, in addition to a tax of 12% of the total cost usually imposed for rentals at many of the country's airports, including Zurich. With this in mind, you might choose to skip getting a car at the airport and pick up a vehicle at one of the hundreds of downtown rental agencies run by Budget, Hertz, and Avis.

AUTOMOBILE PERMIT Apart from the auto and train tunnel trips mentioned above and a toll on the road through the Great St. Bernard Tunnel, there are no toll roads in the country. Instead of tolls, Switzerland levies a single annual fee of 40F per car, or 80F for trailers, motor homes, and RVs, for use of the nation's superhighways; when the fee has been paid, a permit sticker is affixed to the car. Drivers of cars without the permit sticker face a fine of more than twice the permit's cost. Most rental cars come equipped with this certificate. Otherwise, the appropriate permits may be purchased at any post office in Switzerland, at the Customs office at any Swiss border, or from one of the automobile associations.

If you didn't rent your car in Switzerland, you'll probably have to purchase the permit. Permits are available at border crossings and are valid for multiple reentries into Switzerland within the licensed period. To avoid long lines at border crossings, you can buy the permit sticker in advance at the Swiss National Tourist Office in Italy, Austria, or Germany (it is not sold in France). *Note:* If you drive into Switzerland on a secondary road, you don't need a permit sticker, but if you drive on a Swiss superhighway without one, you risk facing that heavy fine.

GAS The cost varies across the country. Gas stations are usually open daily from 8am to 10pm. U.S. gasoline credit cards generally are not accepted for payment. At stations along Swiss autobahns, gas prices are higher than along secondary roads. Autobahn stations usually give 24-hour service, and electronic machines accept 10- and 20-franc Swiss notes.

DRIVER'S LICENSE U.S. and Canadian driver's licenses are valid in Switzerland, but if you're at least 18 and touring Europe by car, you may want to invest in an international driver's license. Although you may not actually need one, many travelers like the added security blanket of having one, as they are recognized worldwide whereas your local driver's license isn't. In case of an accident, an international driver's license is easier to read among parties who may not understand your local license. In the United States you can apply for one at any local branch of the **American Automobile Association** (AAA; © 800/AAA-HELP [222-4357] or 407/444-4300; www.aaa.com). Include two 2×2-inch photographs, a $15 fee, and a photocopy of your state driver's license. Canadians can get the address of the nearest branch of the **Canadian Automobile Club** by phoning its national office (© 613/247-0117; www.caa.ca).

Note that your international driver's license is valid only if accompanied by your home state or provincial driver's license.

In Switzerland, as elsewhere in Europe, to drive a car legally, you must have in your possession an international insurance certificate, known as a **Green Card (Carte Verte).** Your car-rental agency will provide one as part of your rental contract.

DRIVING RULES The legal minimum age for driving in Switzerland is 18. Note, however, that car-rental companies often set their own minimum age, usually 20 or 21.

Drive on the right side of the road and observe the speed limit for passenger vehicles; it's 120kmph (about 75 mph) on superhighways, 80kmph (about 50 mph) on other highways, and 50kmph (about 30 mph) in cities, towns, and villages, unless otherwise posted. Non-Swiss drivers who exceed the speed limit by 50kmph (about 30 mph) or more are fined 1,200F on the spot. Swiss citizens similarly caught have their driver's licenses revoked.

When driving through tunnels, be sure to turn on and dim your headlights, as required by law. Never pass another car from the right, even on superhighways. Always wear your seat belt. Don't permit children 11 or under to ride in the front seat. And, needless to say, don't drink and drive; driving while under the influence of alcohol is a serious offense in Switzerland.

BREAKDOWNS & ASSISTANCE The Automobile Club of Switzerland and its branch offices will assist motorists at all times. For help, contact **Automobil Club der Schweiz,** Wassergasse 39, CH-3000 Bern 13 (✆ **031/328-31-11;** www.acs.ch), or **Touring Club Suisse,** 9, rue Pierre-Fatio, CH-1211 Geneva 3 (✆ **022/417-22-20;** www.tcs.ch). The Automobile Club der Schweiz offers 24-hour breakdown service. Motorists in need of help can call ✆ **0844/888-111.** Most mountain roads have emergency call boxes.

MAPS Towns, cities, and resorts in Switzerland will provide you with detailed maps of their town plans which will pinpoint walks and locations of museums and monuments. Most of these offices also have touring maps of their immediate regions and will suggest scenic drives or hiking possibilities in their area.

Before going to Switzerland, you can get detailed maps of the country itself. Distances are generally short because the country is small. You can drive from one end to the other in just a matter of hours, but who would want to? There is so much wonder to discover along the way.

The best maps for touring are published by **Rand McNally.** Call ✆ **800/333-0136** for the address of the outlet nearest to you, especially if you live in such cities as New York, Chicago, or San Francisco. If you live in more remote areas, you can download mail order forms by logging onto www.randmcnallystore.com.

Michelin maps are also good and are sold all over Switzerland, in nearly all bookstores and at certain newsstand kiosks. Especially good is *Michelin 427 Switzerland.* Another excellent map for those who plan extensive touring in Switzerland is published by **Hallwag.**

By Train

The Swiss Federal Railway is noted for its comfort and cleanliness. Most of the electrically operated trains have first- and second-class compartments. International trains link Swiss cities with other European centers. Intercity trains coming from Holland, Scandinavia, and Germany require a change at Basel's station, where a connection is usually available on the same platform. Most intercity trains offer the fastest connections, and since trains leave the Basel station hourly, there's never too long a wait.

You should purchase European train tickets before leaving home, especially when your itinerary is specific and complicated. All tickets are available through your travel agent.

SWISS PASS/SWISS FLEXIPASS The most practical and convenient ticket for your trip to Switzerland is the **Swiss Pass,** which entitles you to unlimited travel on the entire network of the Swiss Federal Railways, as well as on lake steamers and most postal motorcoaches linking Swiss cities and resorts. The Swiss Pass is good for a predetermined number of consecutive days.

A 4-day pass goes for $398 for first class and $226 in second class; an 8-day pass $489 in first class or $327 in second class; a 15-day pass $591 in first class or $394 in second class; a 22-day pass $682 in first class and $455 in second class; and a 1-month pass $751 in first class or $500 in second class. The Swiss Pass is issued at half price for children ages 6 to 15 (free ages 5 and under).

A variation of the Swiss Pass is the **Swiss Flexipass,** good for a predetermined number of days to be used anytime during a 30-day period of time. A 3-day pass goes for $324 in first class or $216 in second class; a 4-day pass $392 in first class or $262 in second class; a 5-day pass $454 in first class or $303 in second class; and a 6-day pass $516 in first class or $345 in second class. The **Swiss Family Card** is just for families traveling together. This card allows children 15 and under to travel free when accompanied by a parent. It's valid when traveling on a Swiss Pass or a Swiss Flexipass. Probably the best part of all about the Swiss Family Card is that it is free. Just request it when you purchase your Swiss Pass from Rail Europe.

An economical alternative is the **Swiss Saverpass,** which offers five consecutive-day durations to choose from, including 4, 8, 15, or 22 days unlimited travel or 1 month unlimited travel. This pass requires a minimum of two people traveling together at all times and offers the choice

of first- or second-class train travel. An individual traveling in first class for 4 days costs $287; 8 days, $416; 15 days, $503; 22 days, $508; or 1 month, $639. The cost in second class is 4 days for $192; 8 days, $279; 15 days, $335; 22 days, $388; or 1 month, $426.

Those under the age of 26 might consider the **Swiss Youth Pass,** which is a discounted version of the Swiss Pass. This pass also offers 5 consecutive day durations to choose from, including 4, 8, 15, or 22 days unlimited travel or 1 month unlimited travel. A 4-day pass goes for $254 for first class or $170 for second class; 8 days for $367 in first class or $245 in second class; 15 days for $444 in first class or $296 in second class; 22 days for $513 in first class or $342 in second class; or 1 month for $563 in first class or $376 in second class.

SWISS REGIONAL RAIL PASSES One of the country's most unusual transportation bargains is offered in the form of regional passes that divide Switzerland into about half a dozen districts. Passes, most of which are good for 5 days of unrestricted rail travel, are offered for the Lake Geneva region, the Graubunden (Grisons), the Ticino, central Switzerland, and the Bernese Oberland. If you plan to devote a block of days to exploring one of these specific regions, you might find one of these passes great savings.

One of the most popular of these passes is the **Bernese Oberland Regional Pass (Regional Pass für das Berner Oberland),** which comes in variations of 3 travel days out of 7 calendar days, and 5 travel days out of 15 calendar days. They're available from any railway station in the Bernese Oberland and are sold in Swiss francs. The 3-day option sells for 279F in first class or 230F in second class; the 5-day option sells for 332F in first class or 277F in second class. Either variation allows free transport during the appropriate time frames on all but a handful of the cog railways, buses, cable cars, ferryboats, and SBB trains within the region. Note to holders of either the Swiss Pass or the Swiss Card: If you present either of those documents at the time of purchase, you'll get a 50% discount off the above-mentioned prices.

SWISS CARD   This pass, which, like the Eurailpasses, must be purchased before you leave home, is valid for 1 month, entitling the holder to a free transfer from any Swiss airport or border point to any destination within Switzerland, and a second free transfer from any destination in Switzerland to any Swiss airport or border point. Each transfer has to be completed within 1 day. Additionally, the Swiss Card gives the holder unlimited half-fare trips on the entire Swiss travel system, including trains, postal coaches, lake steamers, and most (not all) excursions to mountaintops. The pass costs $222 for first class and $159 for second class. Children are charged half price.

For more information on Swiss railway passes, call **Switzerland Tourism** at ⓒ 212/757-5944.

EURAIL PASSES   The **Eurail Global Pass** allows you unlimited travel in 18 Eurail-affiliated countries. You can travel on any of the days within the validity period which is available for 15 days, 21 days, 1 month, 2 months, 3 months, and some other possibilities as well. Prices for first-class adult travel are $449 for 15 days, $579 for 21 days, $719 for 1 month, $1,019 for 2 months, and $1,259 for 3 months. Children 4 to 11 pay half fare; those 3 and under travel for free.

A **Eurail Global Pass Saver,** also valid for first-class travel in 18 countries, offers a special deal for two or more people traveling together. This pass costs $585 for 15 days, $759 for 21 days, $939 for 1 month, $1,329 for 2 months, and $1,649 for 3 months.

A **Eurail Global Youth Pass** for those 12 to 25 allows second-class travel in 18 countries. This pass costs $449 for 15 days, $579 for 21 days, $719 for 1 month, $1,019 for 2 months, and $1,259 for 3 months.

A **Eurail Selectpass** offers unlimited travel on the national rail networks of any three, four, or five bordering countries out of the 22 Eurail nations linked by train or ship. Two or more passengers can travel together for big discounts, getting 5, 6, 8, 10, or 15 days of rail travel within any 2-month period on the national rail networks of any three, four, or five adjoining Eurail countries linked by train or ship. A sample fare: for 5 days in 2 months you pay $439 for three countries.

Other passes include **Eurail Global Pass Flexi,** allowing you to choose either 10 or 15 days of unlimited travel in 21 European countries, including Switzerland, within a 2-month period. In first class, $811 gets you 10 days of travel in 2 months, rising to $1,066 for 15 days in 2 months. Children 4 to 11 pay half the adult fare.

If you're 25 and under, you can avail yourself of a **Eurail Global Pass Youth Flexi.** In second class, you get 10 days of travel in 2 months for $529, or 15 days in 2 months for $695. For that you get to travel in 18 European countries, including Switzerland.

For Switzerland only, there is a **Swiss Saver Flexipass,** granting you 3 days of travel in 1 month for $276 in first class or $184 in second class. This pass is also available for 4, 5, 6, or 8 days of travel in 1 month. These prices are based on two or more passengers traveling together. Under such an arrangement, children 14 and under ride for free.

WHERE TO BUY RAIL PASSES   Travel agents in all towns and railway agents in major North American cities sell all these tickets, but the biggest supplier is **Rail**

> ## (Tips) Rail Bargains
>
> In Switzerland children 16 and under—if accompanied by at least one adult—travel free on national rail lines. This family travel plan is valid for the purchase of Swiss Passes, Swiss Flexi Passes, Swiss Cards, and point-to-point tickets (see "By Train" in "Getting Around," above).

Europe (© 877/272-RAIL [272-7245]); www.raileurope.com), which can also give you informational brochures.

Many different rail passes are available in the United Kingdom for travel in Britain and continental Europe. Stop in at the **International Rail Centre,** Victoria Station, London SWIV 1JY (© **0870/5848-848** in the U.K.). Some of the most popular passes, including InterRail and Euro Youth, are offered only to travelers 25 years of age and under; these allow unlimited second-class travel through most European countries.

INTERRAIL European travelers can travel throughout Europe for up to 1 month by train with the InterRail ticket. In your home country you get a 50% reduction on the normal price. Only supplements, reservations, and special trains like the Eurostar cost extra. The ticket is sold at all European travel agents. All you need is a passport and the fee, of course.

By Bus

The extremely dense network covered by the Swiss postal buses is useful for trips into the mountains. Hopping on one of the popular yellow buses is a much safer and more comfortable way of seeing the Alps than trying to do your own driving in those regions.

By Boat

In the summer, passenger boats sail on Switzerland's major lakes and rivers. More than 100 boats, with accommodations for 60,000 passengers, operate on the lakes and along stretches of the Rhine and the Aare; most of them have dining. Evening trips, with music and dancing, are also quite popular. The old paddle-steamers on the lakes of Brienz, Geneva, Lucerne, and Zurich, dating from before World War I, are particularly attractive and romantic.

Remember that your Swiss Pass or Swiss Card (half-fare travel card) entitles you to unlimited travel on lake steamers.

4 MONEY & COSTS

The Value of Swiss Franc vs. Other Popular Currencies

F	US$	Can$	UK£	Euro (€)	Aus$	NZ$
1.00	$0.94	C$1.00	£0.57	€0.66	A$1.15	NZ$0.70

Frommer's lists exact prices in the local currency. The currency conversions quoted above were correct at press time. However, rates fluctuate, so before departing consult a currency exchange website such as **www.oanda.com/convert/classic** to check up-to-the-minute rates.

The basic unit of Swiss currency is the Swiss franc (F), which is made up of 100 centimes. Bank notes are issued in denominations of 10, 20, 50, 100, 500, and 1,000 francs, and coins are minted as 5, 10, 20, and 50 centimes, and 1, 2, and 5 francs.

ATMS

The easiest and best way to get cash away from home is from an ATM (automated teller machine), sometimes referred to as a "cash machine," or a "cashpoint." The **Cirrus** (© 800/424-7787; www.mastercard.com) and **PLUS** (© 800/843-7587; www.visa.com) networks span the globe. Go to your bank card's website to find ATM locations at your destination. Be sure you know your personal identification number (PIN) and your daily withdrawal limit before you depart. *Note:* Many banks impose a fee every time you use a card at another bank's ATM, and that fee can be higher for international transactions (up to $5 or more) than for domestic ones (where they're rarely more than $2). In addition, the bank from which you withdraw cash may charge its own fee. For international withdrawal fees, ask your bank.

Note: Banks that are members of the **Global ATM Alliance** charge no transaction fees for cash withdrawals at other Alliance member ATMs; these include Bank of America, Scotiabank (Canada, Caribbean, and Mexico), Barclays (U.K. and parts of Africa), Deutsche Bank (Germany, Poland, Spain, and Italy), and BNP Paribas (France). In Switzerland ATMs are plentiful in both cities and small towns as well as train stations, petrol or gasoline stations, and even department stores.

CREDIT CARDS

Credit cards are another safe way to carry money. They provide a convenient record of all your expenses, and they generally offer relatively good exchange rates. You can usually withdraw cash advances from your credit cards at banks or ATMs, provided you know your PIN. Keep in mind that you'll pay interest from the moment of your withdrawal, even if you pay your monthly bills on time. Also, note that many banks now assess a 1% to 3% "transaction fee" on *all* charges you incur abroad (whether you're using the local currency or your native currency).

Chip and PIN represents a change in the way that credit and debit cards are used. The program is designed to cut down on the fraudulent use of credit cards. More banks are issuing customers Chip and PIN versions of their debit or credit cards, and more vendors are asking for a four-digit personal identification number, which must be entered into a keypad near the cash register. In some cases, a waiter will bring a hand-held model to your table to verify your credit card.

Warning: Some establishments in Switzerland might not accept your credit card unless you have a computer chip imbedded in it. The reason? To cut down on credit card fraud. More and more places in Switzerland are moving from the magnetic strip credit card to the new system of Chip and PIN.

In the changeover in technology, some retailers have falsely concluded that they can no longer take swipe cards, or can't take signature cards that don't have PINs anymore.

For the time being, both the new and old cards are accepted in shops, hotels, and restaurants regardless of whether they have the new Chip and PIN machines installed.

In the interim between traditional swipe credit cards and those with an embedded computer chip, here's what you can do to protect yourself:

- Get a four-digit PIN from your credit card's issuing bank before leaving home, or call the number on the back of each card and ask for a four-digit PIN.
- Keep an eye out for the right logo displayed in a retailer's window. You want

What Things Cost in Switzerland

The prices in Switzerland are often higher than those found in the United States and Canada. Nevertheless, this book will try to help you stretch your national currency. There are many good-value hotels and restaurants, but don't expect to find them in the expensive cities of Zurich and Geneva or in such chic resorts as St. Moritz and Arosa. If you're watching your budget, try to stay in small villages, such as Klosters, on the periphery of celebrated resorts.

• Taxi from the airport to city center	55F
• Train service from airport to city	6F
• Average bus fare within city	4F
• Double room at Baur au Lac (very expensive)	820F
• Double room at Hotel du Theatre (moderate)	195F
• Double room at X-Tra Hotel Limmat (inexpensive)	166F
• Lunch for one, without wine, at Toscano (moderate)	30F
• Lunch for one, without wine, at Reithalle (inexpensive)	20F
• Dinner for one, without wine, at Cantinetta Antinori (expensive)	40F–65F
• Dinner for one, without wine, at Mère Catherine (moderate)	24F–45F
• Dinner for one, without wine, at Zeughauskeller (inexpensive)	26F
• Glass of beer	6.50F
• Coca-Cola in a restaurant	5F
• Cup of coffee in a cafe	4.50F
• Admission to Swiss National Museum	10F
• Movie ticket	16F
• Theater ticket	23F

Visa or MasterCard, not Maestro, Visa Electron, or Carte Bleue.

• Know that your Amex card will work where an Amex logo is displayed, but

the card is not as widely accepted as Visa and MasterCard.

• As a last resort, make sure you have enough cash to cover your purchase.

5 HEALTH

STAYING HEALTHY

Medical care and health facilities in Switzerland are among the best in the world. As a result, no endemic contagious diseases exist. Swiss authorities, however, require immunization against contagious diseases if you have been in an infected area during the 14-day period immediately preceding your arrival in Switzerland. Take along an adequate supply of any prescription drugs that you'll need, as well as a written prescription that uses the generic name—rather than the brand name—of the drugs (in general, French and German, not U.S., drugs are available in Switzerland). You may want to include some motion-sickness medicine as well. Be sure to carry your vital medicines and drugs in your carry-on luggage, in case your checked luggage is lost.

COMMON AILMENTS

ALTITUDE SICKNESS Switzerland may be one of the healthiest countries in the world, but because of its lofty position "at the top of Europe," some concerns might arise if you're planning strenuous activities at higher altitudes. All of us, of course, are affected by a lack of oxygen at altitudes more than 2,500m (8,200 ft.). Symptoms of altitude sickness include a severe headache, a feeling of nausea, dizziness, loss of appetite, and lack of sleep.

In a nutshell, high altitude sickness most often occurs when you go too high too fast. The body needs time to acclimatize itself as you climb to higher regions. This is an extremely complicated subject, and if you plan to climb Switzerland's highest peaks, read the study made by Princeton University at www.Princeton. edu/~oa/safety/altitude.html.

FROSTBITE In winter, higher elevations might also cause frostbite. Wet clothes, wind chill factor, and extreme cold can cause frostbite. Some people with poor circulation, such as those who suffer from diabetes, are particularly vulnerable. Precautions are advised—no smoking, no drinking, good food, and rest. As you proceed higher and higher, wear multiple layers of clothing, especially waterproof synthetics. Survive Outdoors Inc. has frostbite prevention advice on its website at www.surviveoutdoors.com/reference/frostbite.asp.

SNOW BLINDNESS Snow blindness is caused by the exposure of your unprotected eyes to the ultraviolet rays of the sun. This often happens in Switzerland in conditions of great snow or ice, mostly at higher altitudes. It is usually prevented by wearing dark-lensed "glacier glasses" which are of the wraparound, side-shielded variety. Wear these glasses even if the sky is overcast, as ultraviolet rays can pass through masses of cloud formations.

WHAT TO DO IF YOU GET SICK AWAY FROM HOME

Any foreign consulate can provide a list of area doctors who speak English. If you get sick, consider asking your hotel concierge to recommend a local doctor—even his or her own. You can also try the emergency room at a local hospital. Many hospitals also have walk-in clinics for emergency cases that are not life-threatening; you may not get immediate attention, but you won't pay the high price of an emergency-room visit. We list hospital and emergency contact numbers under "Fast Facts" in chapter 18 and in chapters 5, 8, and 12.

If you suffer from a chronic illness, consult your doctor before your departure. For conditions like epilepsy, diabetes, or heart problems, wear a **MedicAlert Identification Tag** (✆ 888/633-4298; www.medicalert.org), which will immediately alert doctors to your condition and give them access to your records through Medic Alert's 24-hour hot line.

Pack **prescription medications** in your carry-on luggage, and carry prescription medications in their original containers, with pharmacy labels—otherwise they won't make it through airport security. Also bring copies of your prescriptions in case you lose your pills or run out. Don't forget an extra pair of contact lenses or prescription glasses. Carry the generic name of prescription medicines, in case a local pharmacist is unfamiliar with the brand name.

Contact the **International Association for Medical Assistance to Travellers** (IAMAT; ✆ 716/754-4883 or 416/652-0137; www.iamat.org) for tips on travel and health concerns in the countries you're visiting, and lists of local, English-speaking doctors. The United States **Centers for Disease Control and Prevention** (✆ 800/232-4636; www.cdc.gov) provides up-to-date information on necessary vaccines and health hazards by region or country.

Travel Health Online (www.tripprep. com), sponsored by a consortium of travel medicine practitioners, may also offer helpful advice on traveling abroad. You can find listings of reliable medical clinics overseas at the **International Society of Travel Medicine** (www.istm.org). We list additional **emergency numbers** in chapter 18's "Fast Facts: Switzerland," p. 480.

6 SAFETY

The potential for specific threats or acts of violence involving American citizens in Switzerland is remote; nonetheless, travelers should always review their security practices and be alert to their surroundings. The Consular Agencies in Zurich and Geneva may close periodically to assess their security situations. Americans are encouraged to check the Consular Affairs home page for updated travel and security information.

Switzerland has a low rate of violent crime. However, pickpocketing and purse snatching do occur in the vicinity of train and bus stations, airports, and some public parks, especially during peak tourist periods (such as summer and Christmas) and when conferences, shows, or exhibits are scheduled in major cities. Liechtenstein has a low crime rate. Travelers may wish to exercise caution on trains, especially on overnight trains to neighboring countries. Even locked sleeping compartments can be entered by thieves, who steal from passengers while they sleep. The loss or theft abroad of a U.S. passport should be reported immediately to the local police and the nearest U.S. embassy or consulate. U.S. citizens may refer to the Department of State's pamphlet *A Safe Trip Abroad.* The pamphlet is available from the Superintendent of Documents, U.S. Government Printing Office, Washington, DC 20402, and via the Internet at www. gpoaccess.gov or via the Bureau of Consular Affairs home page at http://travel. state.gov.

If you are a victim of a crime overseas, in addition to reporting to local police, contact the nearest U.S. embassy or consulate for assistance. The embassy/consulate staff can, for example, assist you in finding appropriate medical care, contact family members or friends, and explain how funds could be transferred. Although the investigation and prosecution of a crime is solely the responsibility of local authorities, consular officers can help you to understand the local criminal process and to find an attorney if needed.

7 SPECIALIZED TRAVEL RESOURCES

In addition to the destination-specific resources listed below, please visit Frommers.com for additional specialized travel resources.

GAY & LESBIAN TRAVELERS

Basel, Zurich, and Geneva are the centers of gay life in Switzerland, although such chic resorts as Gstaad, St. Moritz, and Arosa are also popular destinations for gay and lesbian travelers (mostly in winter). The national organization for gays in Switzerland is **Pink Cross,** Zinggstrasse 16, P.O. Box 7512, 3001 Bern (© **031/372-33-00;** www.pinkcross.ch).

A city such as Zurich actively pursues the gay and lesbian market, even publishing brochures with two male lovers walking along a quay with one guy's hand on the other's butt. But away from such sophisticated meccas, it should be noted that rural Switzerland remains conservative, and open displays of homosexuality may be frowned upon. Use discretion when traveling in the more remote areas.

Incidentally, the age of consent in Switzerland is sweet 16. That pertains to boys and girls.

Except for Zurich, French-speaking Switzerland, especially Geneva, seems much more sophisticated about gaydom than the German sector. **Dialogai** at 11–13, rue de la Navigation in Geneva (℗ **022/906-40-40;** www.dialogai.org), offers information about gay and lesbian travel in this sector of the country.

Even before traveling to Switzerland, you might want to pick up a copy of *Spartacus: International Gay Guide,* published by Bruno Gmunder Verlag. Check www.spartacusworld.com/gay guide.

TRAVELERS WITH DISABILITIES

A fact sheet and special hotel guide for persons with disabilities is available from the Swiss National Tourist Office. On Swiss trains, wheelchair passengers travel in a special section of the passenger car. Certain trains cannot accommodate them there, in which case they travel in a specified area of the luggage car.

Because of Switzerland's many hills and endless mountains, visitors with disabilities may have difficulty getting around the country, but conditions are slowly improving. Newer hotels are more sensitive to the needs of those with disabilities, and the more expensive restaurants, in general, are wheelchair accessible. However, because most places have limited, if any, facilities for people with disabilities, you may want to consider taking an organized tour specifically designed to accommodate travelers with disabilities.

Many travel agencies offer customized tours and itineraries for travelers with disabilities. **Flying Wheels Travel** (℗ **507/451-5005;** www.flyingwheels travel.com) offers escorted tours and cruises that emphasize sports and private tours in minivans with lifts. **Access-Able Travel Source** (℗ **303/232-2979;** www. access-able.com) offers extensive access information and advice for traveling around the world with disabilities. **Accessible Journeys** (℗ **800/846-4537** or **610/521-0339;** www.disabilitytravel.com) caters specifically to slow walkers and wheelchair travelers and their families and friends.

For very specific information within Switzerland itself, contact **Mobility International Schweiz,** Frogurbstrausse 4, CH-4600 Olten (℗ **062/206-88-35;** www.mis-infothek.ch).

For traveling cross country in Switzerland, train travel is the preferred mode for transport for travelers with disabilities. The Swiss Federal Railways offer wheelchair access for most of its rail cars, and Inter-City and long-distance express rail cars have built-in wheelchair compartments.

Many or even most trains come with specially built toilets catering to those with disabilities. If given a choice, try for an IC or EC train, although some regional trains are also designed for those with various handicaps.

Motorists who have disabilities should rent from Avis, Hertz, or National. Each of these car-rental companies features hand-controlled vehicles.

When making a reservation at a Swiss hotel, always discuss your disability beforehand in case some extra preparation will be needed by the staff. It is also prudent to call a Swiss restaurant or museum you'd like to visit to see if they can accommodate you.

FAMILY TRAVEL

Family travel can be immensely rewarding, giving you new ways of seeing the world through smaller pairs of eyes.

On Swiss airlines, you must request a special menu for children at least 24 hours in advance. If baby food is required, however, bring your own and ask a flight attendant to warm it to the right temperature.

Arrange ahead of time for such necessities as a crib, bottle warmer, and a car seat (in Switzerland, car seats are legally required for children 7 or younger).

To locate accommodations, restaurants, and attractions that are particularly kid-friendly, refer to the "Kids" icon throughout this guide.

Should you be traveling with a baby 2 years old or under, it is recommended that you avoid taking the baby on excursions in Switzerland that will take you 6,500 feet above sea level. You can, of course, confirm this with your pediatrician before setting out on your jaunt. Of course, even a mama or papa with a heart condition should avoid excursions at this altitude.

SENIOR TRAVEL

Discounts are sometimes available for seniors in Switzerland but may not be evident at first—you'll have to ask. To qualify, women must be 62 and over, men 65 and over. You will need some proof of your age, however. Certain hotels, restaurants, or even tourist attractions offer senior discounts. Of course, these establishments prefer you to pay full price unless you speak up and specifically request a senior discount. Time and time again you might be denied such a discount, and then, on one day of travel, you might be granted two or three discounts in a row. It's such a mixed bag.

When visiting one of the Swiss National Tourist Offices, ask if the staff has an up-to-date guide for seniors traveling in Switzerland. These are issued periodically and might be available at the time of your visit.

VEGETARIAN TRAVELERS

If you follow Heidi's diet in Switzerland—that is, cheese in the morning, cheese at noon, and cheese at dinner—you'll surely die of cholesterol before the trip is over. Of course, Swiss cuisine has undergone a radical transformation since Heidi's days. In most cases, only the big cities have vegetarian restaurants, but don't despair if

---

Getting Carded

Check out the **International Student Travel Confederation (ISTC;** www.istc. org) website for comprehensive travel services information and details on how to get an **International Student Identity Card (ISIC),** which qualifies students for substantial savings on rail passes, plane tickets, entrance fees, and more. It also provides students with basic health and life insurance and a 24-hour help line. The card is valid for a maximum of 18 months. You can apply for the card online or in person at **STA Travel** (𝒞 **800/781-4040** in North America; 𝒞 132-782 in Australia; 𝒞 087/1230-0040 in the U.K.; www.statravel.com), the biggest student travel agency in the world; check out the website to locate STA Travel offices worldwide. If you're no longer a student but are still under 26, you can get an **International Youth Travel Card (IYTC)** from the same people, which entitles you to some discounts. **Travel CUTS** (𝒞 **800/592-2887;** www.travel cuts.com) offers similar services for both Canadians and U.S. residents. Irish students may prefer to turn to **USIT** (𝒞 **01/602-1906;** www.usit.ie), an Ireland-based specialist in student, youth, and independent travel.

you're traveling in smaller towns and villages. Nearly all Swiss restaurants, aware of the ever-growing number of vegetarians in the world, offer one or possibly two vegetarian specials a day.

Many restaurants now feature a section of the menu to be enjoyed by vegetarians. Of course, you can always sample such classic cheese dishes as fondue and raclette. Other dishes to order—available almost anywhere—are omelets or *rösti* (the Swiss version of hash browns). Salads and meatless pastas, available in most restaurants, are another choice for the vegetarian. If you're dining at a Swiss hotel and/or booked in on a half- or full-board arrangement, you can always request meatless dishes. Most independent restaurants will also serve you meatless dishes on request. So, never fear you'll be facing a bloody slab of Swiss beef.

8 SUSTAINABLE TOURISM

Switzerland has been promoting green travel since 1291. Perhaps more so than any other people in the world, the Swiss have been sensitive to protecting their environment. In addition to the oldest and wildest national park of Europe, many newly opened regional nature parks are being set aside for future generations.

Believe it or not, Switzerland even has volunteer "mountain cleaners," who sweep the landscape looking for garbage that careless tourists have left behind.

The country is also looking to the future, and many hotels plan to follow the example set by the Hotel Europa in St. Moritz. At this establishment the largest solar plant of any hotel in Switzerland was inaugurated. The solar energy collected on the hotel's roof feeds both the hot water and heating systems as well as the pool. Not only are high energy costs counteracted, but so are CO_2 emissions.

City tourist offices are even issuing "greenie points." Take Zurich tourist officials, for example. They are recommending that visitors take the train from London via Paris instead of flying to Zurich. It is estimated that this travel by train will save 176 kilograms of CO_2 emissions per person for the 966km (600-mile) journey.

Eco-tourism is the buzzword of the day, and more and more Swiss environmentalists are talking about keeping their splendid alpine peaks pristine. They need the words of critic John Ruskin, who said, "Mountains are the beginning and end of all natural scenery."

Swiss ecologists must guard against the impact of unbridled ski-lift development and exhaust fumes from motorized traffic, especially transalpine trucking.

The Swiss also fear the spread of vacation apartments springing up like a tourist housing sprawl, such as around Pontresina. The sprawl also plagues such neighboring resorts as St. Moritz and other vacation centers in the Upper Engadine.

In Davos, one of the most famous of all ski resorts, visitors are urged not to drive cars into town, but take one of the fleet of buses moving skiers in winter or hikers in summer to the mountains.

For a true eco-friendly holiday, consider a stay on a Swiss farm, getting close to nature. Prices are lower than at most hotels, and you even have the option of working in the fields. For this type of holiday, check with the **Schweizerischer Bauernverband (Swiss Farmers Association)** at Laurstrasse 10, CH-5200 Brugg (© **056/462-25-1110**), or **Verein Ferien auf dem Bauernhof (Swiss Holiday Farms Association)** at Feierlenhof, CH-8595 Altnau (© **071/695-23-72;** www.bauernhof-ferien.ch).

You can find eco-friendly travel tips, statistics, and touring companies and associations—listed by destination under "Your

3

General Resources for Green Travel

In addition to the resources for Switzerland listed above, the following web-sites provide valuable wide-ranging information on sustainable travel. For a list of even more sustainable resources, as well as tips and explanations on how to travel greener, visit www.frommers.com/planning.

- **Responsible Travel** (www.responsibletravel.com) is a great source of sustainable travel ideas; the site is run by a spokesperson for ethical tourism in the travel industry. **Sustainable Travel International** (www.sustainable travelinternational.org) promotes ethical tourism practices, and manages an extensive directory of sustainable properties and tour operators around the world.
- In the U.K., **Tourism Concern** (www.tourismconcern.org.uk) works to reduce social and environmental problems connected to tourism. The **Association of Independent Tour Operators** (AITO; www.aito.co.uk) is a group of specialist operators leading the field in making holidays sustainable.
- In Canada, **www.greenlivingonline.com** offers extensive content on how to travel sustainably, including a travel and transport section and profiles of the best green shops and services in Toronto, Vancouver, and Calgary.
- In Australia, the national body which sets guidelines and standards for eco-tourism is **Ecotourism Australia** (www.ecotourism.org.au). **The Green Directory** (www.thegreendirectory.com.au), **Green Pages** (www.thegreen pages.com.au), and **EcoDirectory** (www.ecodirectory.com.au) offer sustainable travel tips and directories of green businesses.
- **Carbonfund** (www.carbonfund.org), **TerraPass** (www.terrapass.org), and **Carbon Neutral** (www.carbonneutral.org) provide info on "carbon offsetting," or offsetting the greenhouse gas emitted during flights.
- **Greenhotels** (www.greenhotels.com) recommends green-rated member hotels around the world that fulfill the company's stringent environmental requirements. **Environmentally Friendly Hotels** (www.environmentally friendlyhotels.com) offers more green accommodations ratings. The **Hotel Association of Canada** (www.hacgreenhotels.com) has a Green Key Eco-Rating Program, which audits the environmental performance of Canadian hotels, motels, and resorts.
- **Sustain Lane** (www.sustainlane.com) lists sustainable eating and drinking choices around the U.S.; also visit **www.eatwellguide.org** for tips on eating sustainably in the U.S. and Canada.
- For information on animal-friendly issues throughout the world, visit **Tread Lightly** (www.treadlightly.org). For information about the ethics of swimming with dolphins, visit the **Whale and Dolphin Conservation Society** (www.wdcs.org).
- **Volunteer International** (www.volunteerinternational.org) has a list of questions to help you determine the intentions and the nature of a volunteer program. For general info on volunteer travel, visit **www.volunteer abroad.org** and **www.idealist.org**.

Travel Choice"—at the TIES website, www. ecotourism.org. Also check out **Conservation International** (www.conservation. org)—which, with *National Geographic Traveler,* annually presents **World Legacy Awards** to those travel tour operators, businesses, organizations, and places that have made a significant contribution to sustainable tourism. **Ecotravel.com** is part online magazine and part eco-directory that lets you search for touring companies in several categories (water based, land based, spiritually oriented, and so on).

The **Association of British Travel Agents** (**ABTA;** www.abta.com) acts as a focal point for the U.K. travel industry and is one of the leading groups spearheading responsible tourism.

9 SPECIAL-INTEREST TRIPS & ESCORTED GENERAL-INTEREST TOURS

SPECIAL-INTEREST TRIPS

The destination chapters in this book are full of specific details on local ski trails, hiking trails, boating, fishing, and more. But here we've assembled a roundup of sports highlights—some of the very best ways to get outdoors and enjoy Switzerland's magnificent scenery. Most activities can be enjoyed independently, but if you like to have someone else sweat the details, we've also listed some of the region's best outfitters.

BALLOONING Balloon rides over Switzerland are even more spectacular than those in France. Contact **Buddy Bombard's Europe** (© **800/862-8537** or 561/ 837-6610; www.buddybombard.com).

BIKING Biking is a great way to see the Swiss countryside. You can rent a bike for a small fee at one railroad station and return it at another. In addition, bikes can be transported on passenger trains for a nominal fee. You should reserve your bike a day or so in advance at the station from which you plan to start.

Touring Club Swiss (TCS) maintains 10 cycling centers that rent bicycles and offer brochures and maps of nearby bike routes. The club will direct you along the least congested routes, taking you through villages and past castles and manor houses that you would not otherwise discover. Even in remote areas, you can usually find someone who speaks English to help you if you have a problem or get lost. The central information office of the touring club is in a suburb of Geneva at 4, rue Blandonnet, 1214 Vernier (© **022/417-22-20;** www.tcs.ch).

Erickson Cycle Tours, 1667 SW 176, Seattle, WA 98116 (© **888/972-0140** or 206/524-7731; www.ecycletours.com), offers some of the best bike tours in Switzerland, through the Alps, past lakes and valleys, for groups limited in size to some 20 riders. Included are the mountain venues of Zermatt, Grindelwald, Bernina, and the San Bernardino passes.

CURLING & SKATING Curling is currently a hot team sport in Switzerland, particularly popular in Davos, Villars, Gstaad, and Zermatt. Curling, of course, is a game played by sliding a large, smooth stone along the ice at a mark (called the tee) 35m (115 ft.) away.

Ice-skating is one of the leading winter sports of Switzerland, and nearly all major resorts have natural ice rinks. Also, there are dozens of artificial ones, of which Davos has the best.

FISHING In this relatively small country, there are at least 32,000km (20,000 miles) of rivers and streams, as well as 1,349 sq. km (526 sq. miles) of lakes.

These waters are situated at heights between 210m and 1,965m (689–6,445 ft.) above sea level, and vary in configuration and fauna as much as in altitude. Such a wide choice of conditions certainly puts anglers on their mettle, for they're presented with a fascinating range of challenges. For those who know how to adapt themselves, there is excellent sport in store. Angling techniques and bait must be suited to the particular water one happens to be fishing. With few exceptions, fly-fishing, spinning, and ground fishing, with natural or artificial bait, are permitted in most waters. Trout can be found in most waters up to altitudes of 1,800m (5,904 ft.), and lake trout have been known to weigh up to 10 kilograms (22 lb.). You need a license to fish, but they're easily acquired through municipal authorities, beginning at 50F per day. Regulations vary from place to place, so to be sure you're legal; inquire at a hotel or local tourist office.

GOLF   There are more than 30 golf courses in Switzerland, 24 of them with 18 holes. Not a lot for a whole country, you may think, but they're located so strategically that, wherever you happen to be in Switzerland, you're likely to find a course nearby—and one within a wide range of altitudes: The lowest course is in Ascona, which lies a mere 210m (689 ft.) above sea level; among the highest are St. Moritz, at 1,692m (5,550 ft.), and Riederalp, at 1,920m (6,297 ft.). All the local clubs cater to visitors, who have the advantage of being able to play on weekdays while the locals earn their daily bread. If you left your clubs at home, a set can be rented locally. Should you want to improve your swing, "pros" are available, too.

For more information, contact the **Swiss Golf Association,** 19, place de la Croix-Blanche, CH-1066, Epalinges VD, Switzerland (© **021/785-70-00;** www. asg.ch). Another tool for computer-savvy golfers is the Swiss Golf Network (www.swissgolfnetwork.ch), which includes information on all major golf courses in Switzerland.

Some of the top courses include **Golf Club Davos** at Davos Dorf (© **081/416-56-34;** www.golfdavos.ch), **Golf Club de Verbier,** Verbier (© **027/771-53-14;** www. verbiergolf.com), and **Golf Club Interlaken-Unterseen** at Interlaken (© **033/823-60-16;** www.interlakengolf.ch).

HIKING   With 48,000km (29,760 miles) of well-marked and well-maintained walking paths, Switzerland is a Valhalla for hikers. The paths lead through alpine valleys, over lowlands, up hills to meadows, and into the heart of the Alps. Whether you choose a gentle walk or a rigorous trek, you're sure to see miles and miles of unspoiled beauty.

Many hotels offer walking or hiking excursions, with a serious hiking tour possibly entailing 4 to 7 hours of hiking each day.

Topographic maps, hiking maps, and books can be ordered from such outlets as Amazon.com and various bookstores. These include *Walking Switzerland—The Swiss Way,* which describes numerous hikes and a selection of inn-to-inn tours in the mountain areas. Also of interest is *100 Hikes in the Alps,* containing an interesting section on Switzerland. *Walking Easy in the Swiss Alps* is a 192-page book featuring day walks in six alpine villages, including Zermatt, Saas-Fee, Champex, Kandersteg, Lauterbrunnen, and Samedan/St. Moritz.

A specialist in walking and hiking tours is **Mountain Travel Sobek,** 1266 66th St., Ste. 4, Emeryville, CA 94608 (© **888/687-6235;** www.mtsobek.com). You can wander with this adventure company across the full landscape of Switzerland, from alpine mountains of the Bernese Oberland to lakeside vistas in Mediterranean-like Ticino. Most nights are spent in old-fashioned hotels or hikers' lodges, and at least 1 night is in an alpine refuge. Hikes are ranked as easy, moderate, or strenuous; one of the most challenging tours, the "Mount Blanc Circuit," is a 12-day hike that covers parts of Switzerland along with areas of Italy and France. The company will provide complete details about all tours.

MOUNTAINEERING Recognizing the allures (and the very real dangers) of climbing up the rocky crags that dot the surface of Switzerland, the 86,000-member Swiss Alpine Club (SAC), founded in 1863, promotes mountaineering and ski tours in the high Alps. Although its primary function is to organize alpine rescue services, it also lobbies politically to protect the alpine ecology. Working closely with equivalent associations in Austria, Germany, France, and Italy, the club has built mountain huts at strategic spots throughout the country, often hauling in building supplies by helicopter during the short summer season when construction is possible. The huts are modest, with bunk rooms sleeping 10 to 20 people. The average rate for a night's lodging (without food) for members of the club is from 26F per person per night. You can write the club and reserve space.

Applicants for membership in the club must be at least 10 years of age and should mail their applications, along with a passport-size photo and a check covering membership fees, to whatever branch of the club interests them the most. (Membership in any regional club grants the right to discounted accommodations at huts throughout the country.) To learn of branch offices, contact the organization's headquarters in Bern: the **Swiss Alpine Club,** Mombionstrasse 61, P.O. Box 3000, Bern, Switzerland 23 (📞 **031/370-18-18;** www.sac-cas.ch). If you're looking for a particularly active regional branch, consider joining the group in Zermatt. Their address is Swiss Alpine Club, Sektion Zermatt, c/o Herr Kreiger, Haus Dolomit, CH-3920 Zermatt, Switzerland (📞 **027/967-26-10**). Membership fees range from 75F to 130F, depending on the individual branch you join. Checks should be drawn on a Swiss bank. Membership includes a subscription to the organization's German- or French-language magazine, *Die Alpen,* and the above-mentioned discounted accommodations at the mountain shelters maintained by the club.

The organization is affiliated with mountain-climbing schools throughout the country, including branches in Andermatt, Champéry, Crans, Davos, Les Diablerets, Fiesch, La Fouly, Glarus, Grindelwald, Kandersteg, Klosters, Meiringen, Pontresina, Riederalp, Saas-Fee, Saas-Grund, Schwende, Tasch, Zermatt, and Zinal. Guides that are accredited by the Swiss Alpine Club are available at many other resorts as well, and usually remain in close contact with the staffs at the local tourist offices.

SKIING Skiing in Switzerland, a tradition that goes back 2 centuries, is big business—an estimated 40% of the tourist dollar is spent on it. There are more than 1,700 mountain railways and ski lifts, and ski schools, ski instructors, and the best ski equipment in the world are available throughout the country.

Switzerland, which faces heavy competition from Austria (for a complete guide to resorts in that country, see *Frommer's Austria*), has been called Europe's winter playground. What were once simple alpine farming villages have been transformed into bustling ski resorts, and there are more than 200 throughout the country. Nearly all of them have ski-rental shops.

All the cantons have skiing centers, but most are in the Bernese Oberland, the Grisons, and the Valais. The ideal ski season is from January to late March. At the very highest resorts, the season begins around mid-December. Even at some of the resorts at lower elevations, there is a ski season that begins before Christmas if there are suitable weather conditions and snow is adequate. February is the peak month, in which reservations are most difficult to come by. Skiing in some areas of the country continues until late April or, in other areas such as Zermatt, throughout the summer around the Klein Matterhorn.

Most slopes are nothing short of spectacular in Switzerland, as are the facilities, which cater to every type of skier from the beginner to the Olympic champion.

Europeans have always sought out family-oriented villages for inexpensive ski vacations, whereas Americans have traditionally preferred the more famous meccas such as St. Moritz and Gstaad. Happily, that is changing now, and many Americans (and Canadians) are choosing ski packages in the smaller alpine villages.

At the tourist offices of most resorts, ask for an area map depicting the various slopes. These maps also grade the ski trails for difficulty. Be sure to familiarize yourself with the resort's signs before hitting the slopes. Obviously, avalanche zones are particularly important to learn.

At more than 50 resorts in Switzerland, the Swiss Rent-a-Ski program prevails. This service allows you to rent skis (either downhill or cross-country), poles, and boots on a weekly basis.

Founded in 1863, the **Swiss Alpine Club** promotes ski tours and mountaineering at lofty alpine altitudes. For more details about membership, see "Mountaineering," above.

Swiss Ski School is the most famous such institution in Europe. Federally run, it provides on-site instruction for beginners as well as advanced skiers. The majority of instructors speak English. Most of these ski schools—found at all major resorts—reduce their charges for five half-day classes. However, all-day classes are usually recommended.

Warning: Always carry plenty of sunscreen, even in winter. The reflection of sunlight off the snow is intense.

Summer skiing, or glacier skiing, takes place on glaciers that retain their snow

throughout July and August, and ski schools and lifts are open all summer. Locals say that glacier skiing is best before lunch, especially during the early morning hours. The best glacier ski resorts are Zermatt, St. Moritz, Engelberg, Saas-Fee, Gstaad, and Pontresina.

Experienced skiers may wish to take a popular spring ski tour, the Haute Route, which crosses the French Alps into Switzerland; it's a weeklong tour that is usually offered between March and May. Led by a professional guide, skiers stop overnight and for noon rests at cabins maintained by the Swiss Alpine Club (see "Mountaineering," above, for more information on this club).

Cross-country skiing, or *langlauf,* is the fastest-growing sport in Europe, especially at St. Moritz, Pontresina, and Montana. You go at your own speed and are not at the whim of slope conditions. There are no age limits or charges for use of the well-marked cross-country trails.

From mid-December through March, you can get information on conditions in major Swiss ski areas by linking up with the Switzerland Tourism Office's **snow report** at **www.myswitzerlandtourism.com**.

The best resort for families is **Arosa** (see chapter 14). It's very family-oriented and offers runs suitable for every level of skier, especially beginners. Most of the runs, however, are intermediate.

Expert skiers head for the resort of **Zermatt** (see chapter 10). In just minutes skiers can be more than 3,600m (11,800 ft.) up on the Klein Matterhorn. Zermatt claims that it can guarantee a skier a vertical drop of some 2,700m (8,850 ft.), regardless of the snowfall.

Beginning skiers, often those with families, find the resort of **Grindelwald** (see chapter 9) ideal, the best base for skiing the Jungfrau area. It offers cable cars, lifts, funicular railways, and more than 160km (100 miles) of downhill runs.

A great center for intermediates is the resort of **Davos** (see chapter 14) along with

Spa Vacations

Switzerland has 22 resorts with natural curative springs. Most of these spas, which have been approved by the Association of Swiss Health Spas and the Swiss Society of Balneology and Bioclimatology, include a medical examination, along with thermal baths and excursions, in their package plans for visitors. Many of them are open all year. All the spas offer various treatments, along with Turkish baths, mud baths, whirlpools, exercise/weight-loss programs, anti-stress programs, massages, and diets. You can request information from **Switzerland Tourism,** Tours Dept., 608 Fifth Ave., New York, NY 10020 (ⓒ **877/794-8037**). For very specific data about individual spas, phone **Great Spas of the World** (ⓒ **800/SPA-TIME** [772-8463] or 212/889-8170; www.greatspas.com).

For a spa vacation in Switzerland, one resort towers over all the rest—chic **St. Moritz** in the Engadine. Its thermal springs were known 3,000 years ago. St. Moritz-Bad was the original spa resort lying at the base of the lake, although modern housing has spoiled much of its former character. For more details, see "Spas" under "St. Moritz," in chapter 15.

its twin resort of **Klosters.** The ski terrain at Davos extends for some 35km (22 miles) in a relatively sheltered valley floor. Of course, these resorts have peaks for the more daring expert skier but offer miles of easy terrain for the intermediate as well.

The chic resort of **St. Moritz** in the Engadine (see chapter 15) has more nightlife possibilities than any resort in Switzerland. All the major ski resorts have an active après-ski life, but St. Moritz offers more diversity, from pubbing to high casino action.

In a virtual ski valley, **Verbier** (see chapter 10) is ideal for early or late-season skiing. Its upper ski area, which culminates at Mont-Fort at 3,255m (10,676 ft.), is filled with a widely varied set of *pistes*. The snow falls early and lingers late into the spring.

FOR THE NONSKIER The number of nonskiers at ski resorts is growing. It's estimated that at such fashionable resorts as Gstaad, Pontresina, Arosa, and Davos, one out of two guests is a nonskier. Most resorts offer a host of other activities, such as sunbathing on mountain terraces, day hikes in the forest, sleigh rides, sightseeing excursions, and, of course, partying in the local bars and clubs. So if some of your family

members ski and others don't, everyone will still be happy and entertained.

SNOWBOARDING All the resorts mentioned under skiing offer snowboarding. The best centers are Celerina, Grindelwald, Gstaad, Kandersteg, St. Moritz, Wengen, and Zermatt. However, the top snowboard resort of Europe is Davos, which offers ideal slope conditions, snowboard schools, and a snowboard hotel. The resort also hosts national and international snowboarding events. Snowboarders will find a wide range of equipment to hire in all the resorts mentioned, with the largest concentration of sports shops in Davos.

ESCORTED GENERAL-INTEREST TOURS

Escorted tours are structured group tours, with a group leader. The price usually includes everything: airfare, hotels, meals, tours, admission costs, and local transportation.

There are many escorted-tour companies to choose from, each offering transportation to and within Switzerland, prearranged hotel space, and such extras as bilingual tour guides and lectures.

U.S. TOUR OPERATORS There are many different tour operators eager for a share of your business, but one of the most unusual is **Abercrombie & Kent International, Inc.,** 1520 Kensington Rd., Oak Brook, IL 60521 (② **800/554-7016;** www.abercrombiekent.com), a Chicago-based company established more than 30 years ago. It specializes in deluxe 10-day train tours of Switzerland, which, despite all the extras they offer, still cost less than any personally arranged tour.

Other well-recommended tour operators include outfits endorsed and approved by two of North America's largest airlines. These are **Delta Vacations** (② **800/654-6559;** www.deltavacations.com) and **American Airlines Vacations** (② **800/321-2121;** www.aavacations.com). Both outfits factor inexpensive airfare into land or hotel packages that can save substantial amounts of money over what you'd have paid if you'd booked the arrangements yourself.

Consider contacting one of the world's largest travel organizers, **American Express Vacations** (② **800/297-2977;** www.americanexpress.com). Favored treatment and special discounts are usually offered to holders of gold or platinum American Express cards (if you have one of these, call ② **800/443-7672**), but a wide array of interesting and unusual tours are offered to the general public as well.

Other organizations that offer both escorted and package tours are **Trafalgar Tours** (② **800/854-0103;** www.trafalgar tours.com); **Globus & Cosmos** (② **800/276-1241;** www.globusandcosmos.com); **Grand Circle Travel** (② **800/959-0405;** www.gct.com); **Switzerland Tours** (www.switzerlandtours.net); and **Connection Tours** (② **877/449-4652** in the U.S. or 416/449-4652; www.connectiontours.com).

For river cruises (also barge tours), the most reliable agency, for both Switzerland and Germany, is **KD River Cruises of Europe** (② **973/605-2442**).

BRITISH TOUR OPERATORS **HF Holidays,** Imperial House, Edgware Road, Colindale, London NW9 5AL (② **020/8905-9556;** www.hfholidays.co.uk for a brochure), offers a range of 1- to 2-week packages to Switzerland and an array of some 150 special-interest offerings throughout Europe.

For more information on escorted general-interest tours, including questions to ask before booking your trip, see www.frommers.com/planning.

OUTFITTERS

Be it rafting, canoeing, sea kayaking, sailing, biking, hiking, paragliding, or horse-and-wagon trips, **Eurotrek,** Dörflistrasse 30, CH-8057 Zurich (② **044/316-10-00;** www.eurotrek.ch), has a tour for you. All ages, tastes, and levels of fitness participate in these tours, from absolute beginners to experienced athletes. The outfit uses skilled travel guides, instructors, skippers, and coach drivers. Rafting adventures, for example, are arranged in the Bernese Oberland or on the Lütschine, the wild river at the foot of the Eiger and Jungfrau. Sailing trips are arranged on both Lake Thun and Lake Maggiore, and horse-and-wagon treks explore both the Emmental and the Jura in covered wagons. You can bungee jump in the alpine regions around Davos, or book a 3-day bike tour through the Ticino.

10 STAYING CONNECTED

TELEPHONES

The telephone system is entirely automatic and connects the entire country. **Helpful** **numbers** to know are ② 111 for directory assistance, ② 120 for tourist information and snow reports, ② 140 for help on the

(Fun Facts) Hornussen, Schwingen & Waffenlaufen

For the majority of the Swiss, the sport of choice is walking, followed by swimming, and, only then, skiing. The Swiss are fond of some uniquely Swiss sports as well: *Hornussen, Schwingen,* and *Waffenlaufen.* And while these sports may not be seen in the Olympics, they do call for a certain amount of athletic prowess.

One of Switzerland's greatest writers, Jeremias Gotthelf, praised Hornuss in 1840. He wrote, "There is not any game which calls for as much strength, agility, and coordination between hand, foot, and eye as 'Hornuss.'" The sport was first practiced in the 17th century and stems from war games that had the objective of avoiding projectiles sent flying in the air. Today, Hornuss can be most accurately described as a cross between lacrosse and cricket. The whistling sound the disk makes as it flies through the air is similar to the sound of a hornet. The German word for hornet is *Hornuss,* hence the name of the game. The opposing team must try to stop the flying disk as quickly as possible with heavy wooden bats.

In the wrestling game Schwingen, strength counts above all. Two wrestlers, or Schwingers, face each other in the middle of a pit with the goal of grabbing the adversary's oversize shorts, to unbalance him, and bringing both his shoulders down to touch the ground. This sport of attack and defense was once a training technique for soldiers preparing for war.

One sport that exists exclusively in Switzerland is called Waffenlaufen. Runners in military uniform must carry a mountain rucksack to which a rifle is fixed. Together, the rucksack and rifle must not weigh less than 7.5 kilograms (17 lb.). Thus equipped, thousands of Swiss race along courses ranging from 26 to 28km (16–17 miles) each year.

road, ☎ **162** for weather forecasts, and ☎ **163** for up-to-the-minute information on road conditions. Hotels add substantial service charges for calls made from your room; it's considerably less expensive to make calls from a public phone booth.

To use an old-fashioned **coin-operated telephone,** lift the receiver and insert 40 centimes to get a dial tone. Be sure to have enough coins on hand, as you must insert more for each message unit over your initial deposit. If you insert more coins than necessary, the excess amounts will be returned. A pay phone will accept up to 5F.

To make a local call, dial directly after you hear the dial tone (no area code needed); for other places in Switzerland, dial the area code and then the number. To call a foreign country, dial the code of the country first, then the area code, and then the number.

To call Switzerland:
1. Dial the international access code: 011 from the U.S.; 00 from the U.K., Ireland, or New Zealand; or 0011 from Australia.
2. Dial the country code: 41.
3. Dial the city code, dropping the zero, and then the number.

To make international calls: To make international calls from Switzerland, first dial 00 and then the country code (U.S. or Canada 1, U.K. 44, Ireland 353, Australia

61, New Zealand 64). Next you dial the area code and number. For example, if you wanted to call the British Embassy in Washington, D.C., you would dial 00-1-202-588-7800.

For directory assistance: Dial 111 if you're looking for a number inside Switzerland country, and dial 1159 for numbers to all other countries.

For operator assistance: If you need operator assistance in making a call, dial 111.

Toll-free numbers: Numbers beginning with 0800 within Switzerland are toll-free, but calling a 1-800 number in the States from Switzerland is not toll-free. In fact, it costs the same as an overseas call.

CELLPHONES

The three letters that define much of the world's wireless capabilities are **GSM** (Global System for Mobile Communications), a big, seamless network that makes for easy cross-border cellphone use throughout Europe and dozens of other countries worldwide. In the U.S., T-Mobile, and AT&T Wireless use this quasi-universal system; in Canada, Microcell and some Rogers customers are GSM, and most Australians use GSM. GSM phones function with a removable plastic SIM card, encoded with your phone number and account information. If your cellphone is on a GSM system, and you have a world-capable multiband phone such as many Sony Ericsson, Motorola, or Samsung models, you can make and receive calls across civilized areas around much of the globe. Just call your wireless operator and ask for "international roaming" to be activated on your account. Unfortunately, per-minute charges can be high—usually $1 to $1.50 in western Europe and up to $5 in places like Russia and Indonesia.

For many, **renting** a phone is a good idea. While you can rent a phone from any number of overseas sites, including kiosks at airports and at car-rental agencies, we

suggest renting the phone before you leave home. North Americans can rent one before leaving home from **InTouch USA** (✆ **800/872-7626;** www.intouchglobal.com) or **RoadPost** (✆ **888/290-1616** or 905/272-5665; www.roadpost.com). InTouch will also, for free, advise you on whether your existing phone will work overseas. The major gateways to Switzerland are either Geneva or Zurich. At the airport in either city, you can rent cellphones from **Rent@phone,** whose desks are clearly indicated with signs. To contact Rent@phone in Geneva, call ✆ **022/717-82-63;** in Zurich, ✆ 043/816-50-63. You can also log onto www.rentaphone.ch.

Buying a phone can be economically attractive, as many nations have cheap prepaid phone systems. Once you arrive at your destination, stop by a local cellphone shop and get the cheapest package; you'll probably pay less than $100 for a phone and a starter calling card. Local calls may be as low as 10¢ per minute, and in many countries, including Switzerland and Liechtenstein, incoming calls are free.

VOICE-OVER INTERNET PROTOCOL (VOIP)

If you have Web access while traveling, you might consider a broadband-based telephone service (in technical terms, **Voice over Internet Protocol,** or **VoIP**) such as Skype (www.skype.com) or Vonage (www.vonage.com), which allows you to make free international calls if you use their services from your laptop or in a cybercafe; check the sites for details.

INTERNET/E-MAIL
Without Your Own Computer

To find cybercafes in your destination, check **www.cybercaptive.com** and **www.cybercafe.com.**

Most major airports have **Internet kiosks** that provide basic Web access for a per-minute fee that's usually higher than cybercafe prices. Check out copy shops

Online Traveler's Toolbox

Veteran travelers usually carry some essential items to make their trips easier. Following is a selection of handy online tools to bookmark and use.

- **Airplane Food** (www.airlinemeals.net)
- **Airplane Seating** (www.seatguru.com and www.airlinequality.com)
- **Foreign Languages for Travelers** (www.travlang.com)
- **Maps** (www.mapquest.com)
- **Subway Navigator** (http://people.reed.edu/nreyn/transport.html)
- **Time and Date** (www.timeanddate.com)
- **Travel Warnings** (http://travel.state.gov, www.fco.gov.uk/travel, www.voyage. gc.ca, or www.dfat.gov.au/consular/advice)
- **Universal Currency Converter** (www.xe.com/ucc)
- **Visa ATM Locator** (www.visa.com), **MasterCard ATM Locator** (www.master card.com)
- **Weather** (www.intellicast.com and www.weather.com)

like **FedEx Office** (http://fedex.kinkos. com/fpfk/index.php), which offers computer stations with fully loaded software (as well as Wi-Fi).

With Your Own Computer

More and more hotels, resorts, airports, cafes, and retailers are going **Wi-Fi** (wireless fidelity), becoming "hot spots" that offer free high-speed Wi-Fi access or charge a small fee for usage. Most laptops sold today have built-in wireless capability. To find public Wi-Fi hot spots at your destination, go to **www.jiwire.com**; its Wi-Fi Finder holds one of the world's largest directories of public wireless hot spots.

For dial-up access, most business-class hotels throughout the world offer dataports for laptop modems, and a few thousand hotels in Europe now offer free high-speed Internet access.

Wherever you go, bring a **connection kit** of the right power and phone adapters, a spare phone cord, and a spare Ethernet network cable—or find out whether your hotel supplies them to guests.

11 TIPS ON ACCOMMODATIONS

HOTELS

Most hotels in Switzerland are clean, comfortable, and efficiently run. Many in the luxury category are among the finest in the world (two in Zurich, in fact, are regarded as the best in Europe). After all, César Ritz came from Switzerland.

There are several categories of hotels. An *alkoholfrei* hotel is one that doesn't serve liquor. A hotel *garni* is one that serves breakfast and beverages but no other meals. You can judge a hotel and its prices by its stars (as judged by Swiss travel authorities): Five stars signify deluxe; four stars, first class; three stars, superior; and two stars, standard. One star indicates minimum. A minimum hotel, with the most limited of facilities, can nevertheless be clean and reasonably comfortable, and standard hotels are among the country's best travel values.

Impressions

The Swiss managed to build a lovely country around their hotels.
—George Mikes, *Down with Everybody*, 1951

Reservations can be made directly with the hotel, through any recognized travel agency, or through various reservations systems that have toll-free numbers. The hotel is entitled to request a deposit when you make your reservation; the amount will vary from hotel to hotel.

If you want a total deluxe-hotel-chain trip, you'll find the Hilton with more choices, each ideally located. These include the Basel Hilton and Le Palace Hilton Geneva, which is one of the finest chain hotels in Switzerland. The latter hotel occupies an entire city block.

The chains do not dominate the hotel scene in Switzerland as they do in some countries. The InterContinental weighs in with such heavy-duty choices as the Royal Plaza Montreux, but we find this one often filled with convention people as the convention center is just next door.

If you're looking for a chain bargain, and your tastes aren't too demanding, you can book into any Novotel (there's one at the Zurich airport, for example).

Among the leading German chains, with minor but choice representation in Switzerland, is the German-owned Steigenberger. Hotels in this chain include the Steigenberger Belvedere at Davos Platz and the chic Steigenberger Gstaad-Saanen outside Gstaad.

All accommodations listed in this guide have private bathrooms unless otherwise noted.

To cut costs, you may consider a package tour (or book land arrangements with your air ticket). You'll often pay 30% less than individual rack rates (off-the-street, independent bookings). Also, be sure to ask about winter discounts. Some hotels won't grant them, but many will, especially if bookings that week are light. The price you'll pay in inexpensive hotels depends on the plumbing. Rooms with only showers are much cheaper than those with private bathrooms. Even cheaper is a room with only a sink and a *cabinette de toilet* (toilet and bidet).

When you check in, remember to ask if there's a surcharge on local or long-distance telephone calls (these can be lethal, up to 40%).

ALTERNATIVES TO HOTELS

BED & BREAKFASTS The Swiss concept of a bed-and-breakfast is different from that in the United States and Canada. In Switzerland, many bed-and-breakfast places are more like small, cozy hotels than private homes. Called "E + G Hotels"—a chain of 220 guesthouses—they can be found throughout the country. A folder listing addresses and phone numbers of E & Gs is available from the Swiss National Tourist Office.

PRIVATE HOMES In Swiss mountain and rural areas, a list of private accommodations can be obtained from most local tourist offices. Look for the following signs advertising such an accommodations (generally, a single room): ZIMMER FREI in German, CHAMBRE A LOUER in French, and AFFITASI CAMERA in Italian.

CHALET, HOUSE & APARTMENT RENTALS For a list of U.S. agencies handling such rentals, contact the Swiss National Tourist Office. Local tourist offices in Switzerland also provide listings of apartments and chalets to rent. The Swiss prefer to do business in writing rather than on the phone, so it's strongly recommended that you write to the home owners directly; allow about 20 days for a reply.

The best agency for arranging vacation homes in Switzerland is a Swiss-based company called **INTERHOME,** which represents some 20,000 properties throughout Europe—some 4,000 of these in Switzerland. Travelers have easy access to chalets and condos in all the major resort areas, from modest studio apartments at budget prices to luxurious chalets with all the modern amenities. The U.S. branch of INTERHOME, Inc., is at 131 S. State Rd. 7, Fort Lauderdale, FL 33317 (🄯 **800/882-6864;** fax 954/791-8522; www.interhome.us). Contact them for a catalog of vacation homes outlining some 4,000 listings in almost 200 locations.

In addition, **Hometours International, Inc.,** 1108 Scottie Lane, Knoxville, TN 37919 (🄯 **866/367-4668** or 865/690-8484), offers chalet apartments and apartment hotels in Zermatt overlooking the Matterhorn. Hometours also rents chalet apartments in the center of the resort in Interlaken and the Alps.

FARM VACATIONS A unique way to get to know Switzerland, this program lets you experience firsthand the working world and home life of a Swiss farming family. A brochure called *Swiss Farm Holidays* tells exactly how it can be done; it's available from the Swiss National Tourist Office.

YOUTH HOSTELS About 60 youth hostels exist in Switzerland, open to single people, families, or both. Fees range from 26F to 40F per person including bed linens and breakfast, depending on the hostel. There is no upper age limit, but in peak season travelers 25 and younger have priority. For more information, contact **Hostelling International USA,** 8401 Colesville Rd., Ste. 600, Silver Springs, MD 20910 (🄯 **301/495-1240;** fax 301/495-6697; www.hiusa.org).

Frommers.com: The Complete Travel Resource

Planning a trip or just returned? Head to **Frommers.com,** voted Best Travel Site by *PC Magazine.* We think you'll find our site indispensable before, during, and after your travels—with expert advice and tips; independent reviews of hotels, restaurants, attractions, and preferred shopping and nightlife venues; vacation giveaways; and an online booking tool. We publish the complete contents of over 135 travel guides in our **Destinations** section, covering over 4,000 places worldwide. Each weekday, we publish original articles that report on **Deals and News** via our free **Frommers.com Newsletters.** What's more, **Arthur Frommer** himself blogs 5 days a week, with cutting opinions about the state of travel in the modern world. We're betting you'll find our **Events** listings an invaluable resource; it's an up-to-the-minute roster of what's happening in cities everywhere—including concerts, festivals, lectures, and more. We've also added weekly **podcasts, interactive maps,** and hundreds of new images across the site. Finally, don't forget to visit our **Message Boards,** where you can join in conversations with thousands of fellow Frommer's travelers and post your trip report once you return.

Suggested Switzerland Itineraries

If you have unlimited time, one of Europe's greatest pleasures is getting lost in the Swiss Alps, wandering about at random, making new discoveries off the beaten path, and finding untrampled villages deep in the mountains.

But few of us have such a generous amount of time in the speeded-up 21st century. Vacations are getting shorter, and a "lean-and-mean" schedule is called for if you want to experience the best of any country in a short amount of time.

If you're pressed for time, the first two itineraries in this chapter ("Switzerland in 1 Week" and "Switzerland in 2 Weeks") may be most helpful for skimming the highlights. If you've been to Switzerland before—exploring such well-trodden tourist meccas as Zurich, Bern, Geneva, and Lucerne—you may want to discover a different area of the country this time. Consider our itinerary for "The Grisons, the Engadine & Ticino." We also suggest an itinerary for families.

If you stick to the main highways, Switzerland offers some of the best-maintained roads in Europe. But when you wander off the main roads—in particular heading up to the mountains—you'll find your driving skills tested. And though Switzerland is one alpine-high country, it also has miles upon miles of rolling meadowland, often filled with grazing cows.

Switzerland is blessed with one of the world's most efficient rail systems. Zurich and Geneva are the main hubs, and you can get to nearly anywhere from either one. The itineraries here take you to major attractions such as Bern and Lausanne, but also direct you to more secluded beauty spots and lesser known resorts such as Silvaplana and Morcote.

The pace may be a bit breathless for some visitors, so skip a town or sight occasionally to have some chill-out time—after all, you're on a holiday.

1 THE REGIONS IN BRIEF

The Swiss landscape was shaped by glaciers, which hollowed out the valleys and led to the creation of a multitude of magnificent lakes, a large part of Switzerland's beautiful scenery.

The Swiss plateau, set between the Jura and Alps mountain chains and extending from Lake Geneva in the southwest to Lake Constance in the northeast, represents about 30% of the country's surface area. The main cities and industries are concentrated on this plateau, making Switzerland one of the world's most densely populated countries. Most of the Swiss live in this zone, with half the population based in the urban areas of Geneva, Lausanne, Basel, Bern, Olten, Aarau, Zurich, and Baden. The plateau is also the country's center of agricultural production.

Within its borders Switzerland has nearly every variety of landscape, vegetation, and climatic condition known in Europe. Only a few dozen miles, as the crow flies, separate the lowest point in Switzerland, the shores of Lake Maggiore (where palm trees thrive in a Mediterranean climate), from the highest, the Dufourspitze (where the climate is one of eternal snow and ice).

Of course, the Alps are the main tourist attraction of Switzerland, with about 100 peaks above 3,600m (12,000 ft.). Some 1,800 glaciers offer the sight of an awesome and sometimes-savage nature. The view south from the Jungfraujoch, the highest rail station in Europe, is one of wind-swept rock and ice, majestic and dramatic.

The Swiss Alps form the centerpiece of Europe's alpine range. They're broken by the great valleys of the Rhône in the canton of the Valais and the Rhine in the canton of the Graubünden, as well as by many lateral valleys. (A canton is a division similar to a U.S. state.) To the north, the chain ends in the Bernese Alps (Finsteraarhorn); to the south in the Valais Alps (the Monte Rosa range); and to the east the Alps end at Piz Bernina. In the canton of Ticino, which on the map looks like a triangular section of northern Italy, Switzerland possesses part of the southern face of the Alps.

ZURICH   Close to the northern border of Switzerland, Zurich is not only the country's largest city, but also one of the most scenic capitals of the world, famous for its lakeside promenades set against a backdrop of towering mountains. The lakeside quays lead to the Alstadt or Old Town, presided over by the city's two most historic churches, Fraumünster and Grossmünster. For a view of the Alps, visitors head for Uetliberg. Two of Europe's greatest museums call Zurich home: the Rietberg with its magnificent non-European art collection, and the Bührle with its array of modern art.

THE BERNESE OBERLAND   Switzerland's best-known alpine region is named after its largest city, Bern, the Swiss capital. Known for the beauty of its mountains, it includes many famous resorts, the largest of which is Interlaken, popular mainly in the summer. At its higher altitudes, where the snowfall is more consistent, are such chic ski resorts as Gstaad, Grindelwald, Kandersteg, Mürren, and Wengen.

NORTHEASTERN SWITZERLAND   Relatively neglected by tourists, this region is separated from southern Germany and Austria by the waters of the Rhine and Lake Constance. Its highlights include St. Gallen, a lace-making center and the economic center of the region, certain sections of the Rhine valley, and the Rhine Falls, near Neuhausen.

BASEL & THE JURA   In northwestern Switzerland, Basel, the capital of the region, is an ancient university town and trading center on the Rhine, set midway between French Alsace and the Jura canton in Switzerland. The Jura is a range of "folded" limestone ridges between two great rivers, the Rhône and the Rhine.

THE VALAIS   This rugged valley of the upper Rhône offers such geographic attractions as the Matterhorn and the Great St. Bernard Pass. Equally divided between French- and German-speaking residents, it's rich in alpine folklore. Its most frequented ski resort is Zermatt.

LAUSANNE & THE SHORES OF LAKE GENEVA   Called Lac Léman by the Swiss, Lake Geneva is the largest freshwater body in central Europe, covering some 583 sq. km (225 sq. miles). It's partially fed by the alpine waters of the Rhône and is emptied by a continuation of the same river, which eventually pours into the Mediterranean. Lausanne, the cultural center of the area, is the second-largest city on Lake Geneva and the fifth largest in Switzerland.

GENEVA   Geneva, Switzerland's second-largest city, is distinctly different from the rest of Switzerland and culturally more attuned to France. It's built on the Rhône, at the

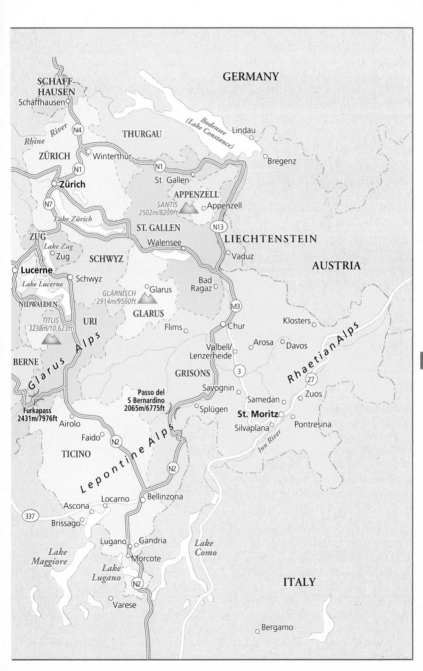

lower end of Lake Geneva, and is bordered on three sides by French territory. This center of world banking and commerce—and the site of many world organizations, such as the Red Cross—is celebrated for its prosperity, elegance, and sophistication.

LUCERNE & CENTRAL SWITZERLAND   The heartland of Switzerland, this region takes in four different cantons: Lucerne, Uri, Unterwalden, and Schwyz, from which the country's name is derived. The region's only major city is Lucerne, a medieval town made famous as a resort in the 19th century. It sits at the northern edge of the lake that bears its name. Despite Switzerland's wealth of attractions, Lucerne is the Swiss city that most North Americans prefer to visit.

THE GRISONS & THE ENGADINE   This area is the largest and most easterly of the cantons of Switzerland. It's also one of the least populated, taking in about 363 sq. km (140 sq. miles) of glaciers and legions of jagged, wind-swept mountain peaks. Its capital is Chur, the oldest town in Switzerland, but most visitors bypass it en route to the ski resorts of Arosa, Klosters, and Davos. The Engadine stretches for 97km (60 miles), from the Maloja Plateau to Finstermünz. The region's chief attraction is the glamorous winter resort of St. Moritz.

THE TICINO   The Italian-speaking part of Switzerland, the Ticino is the most southerly—and warmest—region of the country. Not surprisingly, it's the retirement dream for many residents in the northern cantons. The region includes the major cities of Lugano and Locarno, which share, respectively, the lakes of Lugano and Maggiore with Italy. The Italian influence is most strongly felt in the region's relaxed tempo.

---

2 SWITZERLAND IN 1 WEEK

The very title of this tour is a misnomer. No one can see all of Switzerland in 1 week—it's time enough merely for a few of its highlights. But you can have a memorable vacation in Switzerland in 1 week if you budget your time carefully. Because of its great highways and rail connections, you can virtually cross the country from one end to another in 1 day. Of course, that wouldn't leave much time for sightseeing.

One week, however, provides just enough time, although barely, to introduce yourself to the most visited cities in the country, which include Zurich, Lucerne (our favorite), Bern (next on our list), Lausanne, and Geneva. If you're on an even more rushed schedule, and you have to choose between Geneva and Zurich, make it Geneva, which is far more scenic and grand.

Days ❶ & ❷: Zurich: Gateway to Switzerland ★★★

Because of its superior transportation connections, chances are you'll arrive in Zurich, especially if you're winding your way across the Alps. If you can, hit the town as early in the morning as possible to get in a full round of the city's attractions. After checking into a hotel, take our **walking tour of Bahnhofstrasse** (p. 118), which is lined with some of the world's most elegant shops. Even if you can't afford to purchase anything, it's fun to just look at the luxury merchandise, especially the Swiss watches and jewelry. Follow this with a **boat trip along Lake Zurich,** departing from the lake end of Bahnhofstrasse. Depending on your time, tours last from 1½ to 4 hours. In the afternoon, take the city's best walk by promenading along

Days 1 & 2
1 Zurich

Days 3 & 4
2 Lucerne

Day 5
3 Bern

Day 6
4 Lausanne

Day 7
5 Geneva

the quays of Zurich, such as the finest and most famous, **Limmatquai** (p. 114). As the afternoon fades, check out the stained-glass windows at the church, **Fraumünster** (p. 114). That night, dine at Zurich's most famous beer hall, **Bierhalle Kropf** (p. 103) or at the **Zeughauskeller** (p. 104), a formal arsenal dating from 1487.

Begin **Day 2** with a **walking tour of Zurich's Altstadt** (**Old Town;** p. 120). Check out the Romanesque and Gothic cathedral of **Grossmünster** (p. 114) as you continue the walk. Before lunch, head for **Landesmuseum** (**Swiss National Museum;** p. 115), which is a virtual case history of the culture of the Swiss people.

After lunch, head in the afternoon to the **Kunsthaus Zürich** (fine art museum; p. 115), with one of the greatest art collections in Europe. With time remaining in the afternoon, take another tour, this one by boat and aerial cableway to **Felsenegg** at 795m (2,608 ft.; p. 138). You can view one of the greatest panoramas in this part of Switzerland here: a fit ending for your last day of Zurich sightseeing.

Days ❸ & ❹: Lucerne: Mountain Magic ★★★

Either by rented car or train, head 50km (31 miles) south of Zurich to the city most favored by American visitors, lying on the western edge of Lake Lucerne. Check in to a hotel for 2 nights. In the late morning take our **walking tour of Lucerne** (p. 360), which will not only be a beautiful experience but will also give you an orientation of the area. After lunch, visit the **Verkehrshaus der Schweiz (Swiss Transport Museum;** p. 365), one of the finest museums of its kind in the world. With time remaining, you can take in one or two of the minor sites that interest you, such as the **Picasso Museum** (p. 365), the **Gletschergarten (Glacier Garden;** p. 364), or the **Neues Kunstmuseum (Modern Art Museum;** p. 364). For atmosphere and good food, dine that night at the **Old Swiss House** (p. 373).

While based in Lucerne, **Day 4** can be devoted to two mountain excursions, each among the most important attractions in all of Switzerland. First, head to **Mount Pilatus** (p. 378), 15km (9 miles) south of Lucerne. The best way to go is to take a steamer from Lucerne to Alpnachstad, where you transfer to a cog railway. With careful planning, you can also visit **Rigi** (p. 379), 24km (15 miles) east of Lucerne. Rigi (1,680m/5,510 ft.) is the most famous mountain view in Switzerland. Even Mark Twain climbed it. Return to Lucerne for a final night.

Day ⑤: Bern: The Great Medieval Capital ★★★

On **Day 5** leave Lucerne early and travel by train or car 111km (69 miles) west to Bern, the capital of Switzerland. Trains leave every 30 minutes during the day, and the trip takes 1½ hours. Check in to a hotel for the night and set out to discover a city declared a World Heritage Site by UNESCO in 1983 because of its medieval architecture. To see the highlights, take our **2-hour walking tour** of the historic **Altstadt (Old Town;** p. 120), finishing at the Swiss Parliament (Bundeshaus). Sample a typical lunch like bratwurst and *rösti* (see p. 196 for dining options), then head

for **Mount Gurten** (p. 204) at 844m (2,768 ft.), for the grandest panoramic vista in the area. In the afternoon, visit the **Kunstmuseum (Fine Arts Museum;** p. 164) to see the capital's largest collection of paintings by European masters. No visit to Bern is complete without a stop at the famous **Bärengraben (Bear Pits;** p. 202). Spend the better part of the evening enjoying the regional food and plenty of wine at **Klötzlikeller** (p. 211), the oldest wine tavern in Bern.

Day ⑥: Lausanne: Gateway to Lake Geneva ★★★

From Bern, travel 101km (63 miles) southwest to the lakeside city of Lausanne, where you can not only enjoy boat trips but also wander the medieval labyrinth of its **Vieille Ville (Old Town).** Enjoying a great heyday under the Romans, the town has long been a favorite of expats and a choice watering hole for literati—everybody from Dickens to Thackeray; T. S. Eliot even wrote *The Wasteland* here. After checking in to a hotel for the night, wander for 2 hours or so around **Haute Ville** (p. 278), the Upper Town, visiting the **Cathedral of Lausanne** (p. 282) and other sights before lunch. Spend the afternoon exploring **Ouchy** (p. 280), the port and resort area of Lausanne, opening onto Lake Geneva. You can enjoy 2 or 3 leisurely hours exploring the quay-side flower gardens, which stretch for half a mile. The lakeside promenades of **quai de Belgique** and **quai d'Ouchy** are of particular interest. You can also rent *pédolas* (pedal boats) for fun in the lake itself.

Day ⑦: Geneva: A Summer Garden ★★★

Just 60km (37 miles) away, reachable by car or train in as little as 50 minutes, Geneva is very different from Lausanne. Straddling the Rhône River as it opens onto Lac Léman (Lake Geneva), the city itself will easily fill up one very busy day of sightseeing, so arrive as early in the day as you can. Spend the morning exploring **Vieille Ville (Old Town);** the highlight is the **Cathédrale de St. Pierre** (p. 338). For a fast preview, take our **2-hour walking tour of Geneva's quays and Old Town** (p. 341), viewing the famous fountain, **Jet d'Eau,** and the **Flower Clock** in the Jardin Anglais. At some point

before the afternoon fades, consider one of the **boat tours** (p. 345) of Lac Léman. Stay overnight in Geneva, which is one of the major transportation hubs of Switzerland. In Geneva you can usually link up by train or plane to where you're going next in Europe. It can also be a link in your journey homeward.

3 SWITZERLAND IN 2 WEEKS

With 2 weeks to explore Switzerland, you have a bit more breathing time, and you can take in some of the more esoteric destinations, such as Gruyères (of cheese fame) and Appenzell (capital of folkloric religion). The second week will also allow you to visit not only the cities previewed above, but also less touristy centers such as Basel.

Days ❶ & ❷: Geneva: Your Entry into Switzerland ★★★

On this trip we enter Switzerland from its French-speaking western frontier, the international city of Geneva. If you arrive early enough, take our morning **walking tour** (p. 341), which will allow you to see the highlights of the quays and the Old Town, including such attractions as the famous fountain, Jet d'Eau, trademark of the city. You can also explore Old Town landmarks like Place di Bourge-de-Four. In the afternoon visit **Musée Ariana** (p. 336), one of Europe's top pottery and glass museums (allow less than an hour), and the **Musée d'Art et d'Histoire (Museum of Art and History;** p. 336), with a fabulous collection covering everything from Swiss timepieces to Picasso. Allow an hour for a visit here. If time allows, duck into the **Palais des Nations** (p. 338), former seat of the League of Nations. Overnight in Geneva.

On **Day 2,** while still based in Geneva, take a **full-day tour of Lac Léman (Lake Geneva;** p. 345 for full details). Departures are at 9am daily, with a return at 8:45pm. You'll be back in Geneva in time for a late dinner.

Day ❸: Montreux: Chief Resort of the Swiss Riviera ★★

It's best to rent a car when you leave Geneva for this exploration of Switzerland. Drive 100km (62 miles) east from Geneva and you'll arrive at this chic resort on Lac Léman. Expect a balmy climate as you explore **Château of Chillon** (p. 302), which Lord Byron wrote about in *The Prisoner of Chillon.* The château will be the man-made highlight of your visit. After lunch head for **Rochers-de-Naye** (p. 302), at 2,042m (6,698 ft.), reached by cogwheel train from Montreux. One of the greatest vistas in all of western Switzerland unfolds at the top. That night, if you're a gambler, you can descend on **Casino de Montreux** (p. 306).

Days ❹ & ❺: Vevey ★ & Lausanne ★★

In the morning, drive 6km (4 miles) northwest of Montreux, arriving in Vevey, the home of Nestlé chocolate. Many famous artists have lived here, and Charlie Chaplin chose it as his final residence. Start your exploration at **Grand-Place** (p. 297), the large market square and town nerve center. All of the museums are minor, but if you have time for one, make it **Musée historique de Vevey** (p. 298), viewing its section on winemaker relics. Have lunch at **Café de La Clef** (p. 297), where Jean Jacques Rousseau stayed in 1730, before continuing to Lausanne, which lies 18km (11 miles) to the west. Check in to a hotel in Lausanne for 2 nights.

In the afternoon explore **Ouchy** (p. 280), the port area along the lakefront, especially the promenades, **Quai de Belgique** and **Quai d'Ouchy.** Filled with tropical plants, these gardens stretch for half a mile.

On the morning of **Day 5,** explore Lausanne's **Haute Ville** or Upper Town (p. 278). Allow 45 minutes for a visit. You will still have time for a visit to the **Château de Beaulieu et Musée de l'Art Brut** (p. 283), a château from 1756 with a museum of paintings by the criminally insane. For a change of pace, take one of the lake steamers leaving every hour in summer, heading for **Evian-les-Bains** (p. 281), one of the leading resorts of Lake Geneva (which lies across the French border). Along the way you can take in the beauty of the lake (Lac Léman is French). Once at Evian, you can walk its fashionable lakeside promenade before returning to your hotel in Lausanne for the night.

Day ➏: Gruyères ★★ & Fribourg ★★

Leave Lausanne in the morning and head 56km (35 miles) northeast to the small town of Gruyères, seat of the counts of Gruyères and known for its château and its famous cheese. The highlight of a visit here is the **Château Gruyères** (p. 184), which is filled with art and antiques. Allow 1 hour for a visit. Allow another hour to visit the **Fromagerie de Démonstration** (p. 184), a model dairy where the famed cheese is made. If you find yourself in Gruyères for lunch, and you're into cheese, order raclette. This traditional Swiss specialty is served all over town.

After lunch, continue on to **Fribourg** for the night, 35km (22 miles) north of

Gruyères. You can stroll around this university city, set between lakes and mountains, and visit its major attraction, **St. Nicholas's Cathedral** (p. 179). Allow 30 minutes. If time remains, duck into its **Eglise des Cordeliers** (p. 180), a historic Franciscan church. Overnight in Fribourg.

Days ➐ & ➑: Murten ★★ & Bern ★★★

Leave Fribourg in the morning and drive 18km (11 miles) north to Murten. Allow an hour for a walk along its medieval ramparts (p. 186), plus another 40 minutes to stroll its main street, **Hauptgasse** (p. 186). You can also pay a 45-minute visit to the **Musée Historique** (p. 186), installed in an 8th-century mill.

Remain in Murten for lunch then set out for Bern, the capital of Switzerland. Check in to a hotel for 2 nights. With the time remaining in the afternoon, visit the famous **Bärengraben** (**Bear Pits;** p. 202), and the **Cathedral of St. Vincent** (p. 202), with its celebrated tympanum over the main portal.

On the morning of **Day 8,** spend at least 1½ hours in the **Kunstmuseum (Fine Arts Museum),** with its exceptional collection of world art dating from the 1300s. Before the morning ends, take our **2-hour walking tour of Altstadt** (p. 205). After lunch spend about an hour visiting the **Historisches Museum Bern** (**Bern Historic Museum;** p. 204), followed by a tour of the **Bundeshaus** (p. 203), a Renaissance palace housing the Swiss Parliament. To cap your visit, take the cable train to **Mount Gurten** at 844m (2,768 ft.) for one of the grandest panoramas in the area. Spend your final night in Bern by going to a famous old wine tavern, the **Klötzlikeller** (p. 211).

Day ➒: Solothurn ★ & Basel ★★★

Leave Bern in the morning and drive 43km (27 miles) north to Solothurn. At the foot of the Jura mountains, Solothurn offers a rewarding 3 hours of exploration,

as you visit its **Old Town** (p. 177) on the left bank of the Aare River, taking in its **Cathedral of St. Ursus** (p. 177). With 45 minutes remaining, call at the **Kunstmuseum Solothurn (Municipal Fine Arts Museum),** taking in such paintings as the *Madonna of Solothurn* by Holbein the Younger (p. 178).

After lunch continue to drive north into Basel, a distance of 69km (43 miles). Try to visit Basel's two main attractions, the **Zoologischer Garten Basel** (p. 166), one of the greatest zoos in the world, and **Fondation Beyeler** (p. 162), one of Switzerland's finest museums of modern art. Overnight in Basel.

Days ⑩ & ⑪: Lucerne: Lake Tours & Mountain Vistas ★★★

From Basel, drive 96km (60 miles) southeast to the city of Lucerne. After checking in to a hotel for 2 nights, set out to conquer this lakeside town by spending 2½ hours taking our **walking tour** (p. 360), which covers the scenic highlights. In the afternoon head to the **Swiss Transport Museum** (p. 365), one of the finest museums of its kind in the world. If time remains, visit **Neues Kunstmuseum (Modern Art Museum;** p. 364), with both a permanent collection and temporary exhibitions.

Spend all of **Day 11** taking two of Switzerland's most popular mountain excursions:

one to **Mount Pilatus** in the morning (p. 378), the other to **Rigi** in the afternoon (p. 379). These are described above under "Switzerland in 1 Week," Day 4.

Day ⑫: Appenzell: Strong on Folklore ★

From Lucerne, drive 129km (80 miles) to Appenzell, the most folkloric town of northeastern Switzerland. Take about 2 hours to explore the town, doing some shopping along its Hauptgasse for regional handicrafts. Have lunch at **Hof** (p. 148), before heading out in the afternoon to visit **Ebenalp** (p. 148), a distance of 6km (4 miles). This jagged promontory at 1,620m (5,314 ft.) offers one of the most stunning panoramas of the Appenzell district. For an even grander look, visit **Mount Säntis** (p. 148), the highest peak at 2,463m (8,079 ft.), for the single most spectacular view of eastern Switzerland. It's 14km (9 miles) west of Appenzell. Return to Appenzell for the night.

Days ⑬ & ⑭: Zurich ★★★

For your final look at Switzerland, head west from Appenzell for 99km (62 miles) to Zurich, the country's largest city. But there is reason to go here even if you don't dress in an Armani suit and carry a briefcase. For general orientation, follow our **two walking tours** (p. 118), which will take you into the **Altstadt** and along the historic quays by the Limmat River.

In the afternoon, pay a visit to one of the city's greatest attractions, the **Landesmuseum (Swiss National Museum;** p. 115). This is your best introduction to the history and culture of the Swiss people.

On **Day 14,** your final day in Switzerland, see the stained-glass windows of the **Fraumünster** (p. 114), admire the Romanesque and Gothic cathedral of **Grossmünster** (p. 114), and spend some time at the **Kunsthaus Zürich (Fine Arts Museum;** p. 115) viewing its treasure-trove of art.

After lunch take in the **Botanischer Garten** (p. 116), filled with works of the Impressionists. If enough time remains, take the mountain railway to **Uetliberg** (p. 139) for one of the great panoramic views of the area. Return to the city center for the night, perhaps spending it at **Bierhalle Kropf** (p. 103), the city's most famous beer hall, serving a hearty regional cuisine.

The next morning you'll find that Zurich has the best rail and air connections of any city in Switzerland, whether you're returning home or going somewhere else in Europe.

4 SWITZERLAND FOR FAMILIES

Many of Switzerland's pleasures and pastimes, such as alpine skiing and mountain trekking, are strictly adult-oriented. Nonetheless, it's one of the great outdoor countries in Europe, and all its major cities, such as Geneva and Zurich, offer activities that the entire family can enjoy.

If you're on a rushed weeklong schedule, our suggestion is to spend only 1 night in the two main cities, Geneva and Zurich, but 2 nights each in the more kid-friendly cities of Interlaken and Lucerne, because of all the thrilling mountain excursions possible from these two resorts.

Day ①: Zurich: Your Arrival Point ★★★

On **Day 1** arrive as early as you can to crowd in as much sightseeing as possible, since you have only a day. The best and quickest way to see the city is to walk about the famous **quays of Zurich** (p. 114), which are riverside promenades along the Limmat. Many of these quays open onto beautiful gardens where the

Day 1
1 Zurich

Days 2 & 3
2 Lucerne

Day 4
3 Bern

Days 5 & 6
4 Interlaken

Day 7
5 Geneva

entire family can rest their feet. The town's major attraction is the **Landesmuseum** (**Swiss National Museum;** p. 115), which has something for all ages, such as antique dollhouses built over various periods for the very young. Older boys will be fascinated by the display of weapons and armor, and there are always special exhibitions. After lunch families can head for the **Botanischer Garten** (p. 116), which features some 15,000 living specimens. If you've gotten through the day with time to spare, you can visit either the **Zürcher Spielzeugmuseum** (**Zurich Toy Museum;** p. 118) or one of the best zoos in Europe, **Zoologischer Garten** (p. 117). You can

also pick up a map listing 80 different playgrounds at the tourist office.

Days **2** & **3**: Lucerne: Mountains & Lakes ★★★

On **Day 2** leave Zurich and head 50km (31 miles) south to Lake Lucerne and its "queen," the city of Lucerne itself. Check in to a hotel for 2 nights, and take the whole family on our **walking tour** (p. 360), which will take you by the big attractions. The major sight of Lucerne is something the whole family can enjoy: the **Verkehrshaus der Schweiz** (**Swiss Transport Museum;** p. 365). There's everything from spaceships to an adventure ride called the Gotthard Tunnel Show here. There's even the Longies planetarium where space travel is simulated. In the afternoon take the kids to the **Bourbaki Panorama** (p. 363), a replica of the famous 19th-century battle, followed by an excursion on one of the flotilla of lake steamers plying across Lake Lucerne. Some **summer boat excursions** last 4 hours, and there is a cafeteria onboard. (Ships are operated by Lake Lucerne Navigation Co.; p. 366.)

On **Day 3,** while still based in Lucerne, take your family on two of the most famous mountain excursions in Switzerland, **Mount Pilatus** and **Rigi** (see Day 4 under "Switzerland in 1 Week," earlier in this chapter). Because of public transportation, such as a cog railway, getting there is part of the fun.

Day ❹: Bern: Capital of Switzerland ★★★

On **Day 4** leave Lucerne heading for the capital city of Bern, 111km (69 miles) to the west. Swiss politics will hold little interest for children, but the **Bärengraben** (**Bear Pits;** p. 202) is a surefire winner. These pampered bears are the best fed in Europe, carrots being their favorite food. Families may also enjoy the **Zytgloggeturm** (**Clock Tower;** p. 202), which, 4 minutes before the hour, stages the oldest and biggest horological puppet show, with mechanical bears and the like. Another popular attraction is the **Dählhölzli Tierpark** (p. 204), one of the best zoos in Switzerland, with everything from exotic reptiles to musk oxen. Later, an excursion to **Mount Gurten** at 844m (2,768 ft.) is in order. Not only do you get a panoramic view, but there's also a children's fairyland on-site. After a final stroll along **Marktgasse,** the main street of Old Town, you can call it a day.

Days ❺ & ❻: Interlaken: The Bernese Oberland ★★★

On **Day 5** drive 54km (34 miles) south-east of Bern to reach Interlaken, the tourist capital of the Bernese Oberland. This will

be your launchpad for exploring the mighty **Jungfraujoch** at 3,400m (11,152 ft.), reached by traveling to the highest railway station in Europe.

Arriving in the morning in Interlaken, check in to a hotel for 2 nights and spend the rest of the morning exploring parklike **Höheweg** (p. 215), covering 14 hectares (35 acres) in the center of town. All ages can admire the view of Jungfrau mountain and the famous flower clock. In the afternoon, take an excursion to the **Wilderswil/Schynige Platte** (p. 223) at 1,936m (6,350 ft.), where you'll find an alpine garden. If time remains, try to fit in an excursion to Giessbach Falls, accessible by funicular, allowing about 2 hours for the excursion. Return to Interlaken for the night.

On the morning of **Day 6,** set out by Jungfrau Railways (p. 222) for a day's excursion to the aforementioned **Jungfraujoch** (p. 222). Families can purchase a Family Card for the whole brood. Attractions at the top include the famous **Eispalast (Ice Palace),** and there are lofty alpine restaurants as well. Later you can take the family on a sleigh ride pulled by huskies. Departures from Interlaken are daily at 8am, with a return at 4pm. Overnight once again in Interlaken.

Day ❼: Geneva ★★★

On your final day in Switzerland, **Day 7,** leave Interlaken in the morning and drive 218km (135 miles) southwest across some of the most beautiful scenery in the country, both lake and mountain, until you come to Geneva. After checking in to a hotel, set out to discover one of Europe's most regal cities. Kids delight in seeing the famous fountain, **Jet d'Eau** (p. 336), and the **Flower Clock** (p. 336) in the Jardin Anglais. A walk through the **Old Town** or **Vieille Ville** (p. 336) can be a highlight of the trip. Wind down in the **Parc MonRepos** (p. 340), perhaps securing the makings of a picnic. Later you can visit the **Jardin Botanique (Botanical Garden;**

p. 340), with its alpine garden and little zoo. Older children are often interested in the adventure movie and exhibitions at the Musée International de la Croix-Rouge et du Croissant-Rouge, devoted to the Red Cross (p. 337). Overnight in Geneva.

5 THE GRISONS, THE ENGADINE & TICINO

Graubünden (the Swiss name for the Grisons) is crowned by St. Moritz but also shelters such fabled resorts as Klosters and Davos. The province covers more than one-sixth of Switzerland and many—certainly the local residents—consider it the most beautiful part of the entire country. Its geographic landscape has staggering statistics: 615 lakes, 150 valleys, and 937 mountain peaks.

Bordering it is the dramatically different Ticino, centering around Locarno and Lugano. This is Switzerland with an Italian accent, and the look of the resorts with their date palms and manicured gardens is Mediterranean. In its heart, the Ticino belongs to sunny Italy, but German-speaking Switzerland dominates the district politically. However, their culture and language are strictly Italian.

Day ❶: Klosters: Prince Charles & Movie People ★★

Begin your trip to the Grisons in the Prattigau Valley resort of Klosters, a favorite retreat for Prince Charles and his sons today, and, in the past, literary figures such as Robert Louis Stevenson, who wrote *Treasure Island* here. If you're driving here from Zurich, your gateway city can be Chur, which is 122km (76 miles) southeast of Zurich. Once at Chur, you still have a 29km (18-mile) drive east to arrive at Klosters. If you visit in winter, you've come to ski. But most visitors making these driving tours do so in the summer. In that case, you can spend the rest of the afternoon taking in the mountain beauty of the resort. Both the **Madrisa** (p. 403) and the **Gotschna-Parsenn** (p. 403) cable cars will take you to the most scenic points in the mountains, where you can hike through woods and alpine meadows along well-marked trails. Allow at least 4 hours for these treks. Overnight in Klosters.

Days ❷ & ❸: St. Moritz: The Ne Plus Ultra ★★★

On the morning of **Day 2,** leave early to get some sightseeing time in at Klosters's rival resort, Davos, 11km (7 miles) south of Klosters (many expat writers and artists have preferred Davos to Klosters). Take the cableway to **Weissflühgipfel** (p. 410) at a height of 2,778m (9,112 ft.) for the best panorama in this part of eastern Switzerland. Transit time is only half an hour.

After returning to your car, continue the drive 80km (50 miles) south of Davos to St. Moritz, where you can check in to a hotel for 2 nights. Although St. Moritz is at its ritzy best in winter, it also attracts summer visitors to the mountain beauty of the Engadine (you've left the Grisons at this point). After lunch in St. Moritz, you can visit the **Engadine Museum** (p. 423) to view artifacts of the history of the region. Part of the fun of a summer visit is selecting from an array of **summer sports** (p. 424) that include windsurfing on the lakes, golfing, tennis, hiking, and even fishing. Plan an activity that fits your interest or just spend the day walking around the streets of this posh resort window-shopping (or shopping-shopping, if your budget allows).

If you're into panoramas, you can go to **Piz Nair** (p. 424), the highest skiable mountain at 3,251m (10,663 ft.). The trip up takes 30 minutes by funicular to Corviglia.

SUGGESTED SWITZERLAND ITINERARIES

Day 1	
1	Klosters
Days 2 & 3	
2	St. Moritz
Day 4 & 5	
3	Bellinzona
4	Locarno
Days 6 & 7	
4	Lugano
6	Morcote

4

THE GRISONS, THE ENGADINE & TICINO

You go the rest of the way by cable car and on foot. Your reward from the terrace of the upper cable-car station is to look down on the Upper Engadine and its lakes, a vast panorama embracing the Bernina Alps.

On the morning of **Day 3,** while still based in St. Moritz, set out to explore some of the mountain scenery and the satellite towns of Engadine. One of the great drives in the area is to head southwest from St. Moritz, going through the resorts of Silvaplana and Sils-Maria until you reach **Maloja Pass** (p. 416) at 1,786m (5,858 ft.). Hikers come to Maloja to begin one of the great walks in the Engadine—or all of Switzerland, for that

matter—going for 14km (8.5 miles) to the resort of Silvaplana, taking about 3 to 3½ hours for this alpine trek. If you'd like something less strenuous, take the 2-hour drive to the **Bernina Pass** (p. 416), going 55km (34 miles) between St. Moritz and Tirano in Italy. This is one of the great drives in Europe, possible from June to September. Return to St. Moritz for a final night.

Days ❹ & ❺: Bellinzona & Locarno ★★

Leave St. Moritz on the morning of **Day 4** via the Julierpass, cutting across a broad stretch of southeastern Switzerland's great mountain scenery on your way. Follow the signs to the **Passo del S. Bernardino,** which you can take south into the Ticino, that Italian-speaking part of southern Switzerland. Your first stop can be in the town of **Bellinzona,** 152km (94 miles) southwest of St. Moritz. The town has three medieval fortifications. The best views are possible from **Schwyz Castle** (p. 441).

After a lunch stopover, press on to the southwest, a distance of 22km (14 miles) from Bellinzona. Plan to stay 2 nights in Locarno, a vacation resort opening onto Lake Maggiore. You'll probably arrive too late in the day for much sightseeing, but you can at least explore the main square, **piazza Grande** (p. 445), and take a lakeside promenade.

On the morning of **Day 5,** visit the **Santuario della Madonna del Sasso** (p. 445), lying on a wooden crag above the resort in Orselina, where you'll be rewarded with a panoramic view. For a dramatic drive, explore the **Gambarogno Riviera** (p. 446), with its evocative Ticinese villages spread across a distance of 11km (6½ miles) stretching to the Italian border. While still based in Locarno, and as part of the same day's activities, drive southwest to the resort of **Ascona,** a distance of only 4km (2½ miles). You can spend at least 2 hours visiting its Old Town and wandering its narrow streets, checking out the botanical garden on the **Isole di Brissago** (p. 451). If time remains, head for the little village of **Ronco** (p. 451), lying along the corniche, a distance of 18km (11 miles). A Mediterranean-style village, it's one of the most evocative in the Ticino. Return to Locarno for the night.

Days ❻ & ❼: Lugano ★★★ & Morcote ★★

On the morning of **Day 6,** drive 39km (24 miles) southeast of Locarno to the even larger and more famous waterfront resort of Lugano, which tops even Locarno for natural beauty and architecture. Check in to a hotel for 2 nights. Before lunch, walk around the city park, **Parco Civico** (p. 457), which opens onto Lake Lugano. There may even be time to duck into **Chiesa di Santa Maria degli Angeli** (p. 457) to see its famous frescoes by Bernardino Luini.

In the afternoon we suggest renting a bike (perhaps from your hotel) and getting a map from the tourist office. Set out to explore the nature reserve of **Origlio Lake** (p. 457) and the villages of **Tesserete** and **Colla** (p. 457). In all, the 4-hour trips goes for 37km (23 miles) and will give you some real atmosphere of the Ticino landscape. Then return to Locarno.

On the morning of **Day 7,** drive to the town of **Morcote,** 11km (7 miles) south of Lugano. We consider this the most idyllic in the Ticino. You can also reach it by a summer boat. Spend at least 2 hours exploring this village and plan on an early lunch at one of its fine restaurants. In the afternoon, head back to Lugano where you can go shopping for Ticino crafts or participate in one of a dozen or so summer activities— golf, tennis, boating, sailing, swimming, water-skiing, or windsurfing. See **"The Active Vacation Planner"** (p. 458) for suggestions. From Lugano you can make connections the following morning for a long trip back home or else another destination in Switzerland or Europe.

Zurich

Switzerland's largest city is surely among the most beautiful in all of Europe, and even today, Zurich retains much of its 19th-century charm. Situated on the northern shore of Lake Zurich in the heart of the country, the city is both large enough to offer all amenities to its visitors and small enough for you to discover on your own.

Zurich is the capital of a canton of the same name that joined the Swiss Confederation in 1351. Most of the more than 375,000 residents speak a form of German called Schwyzerdütsch (Schweizerdeutsch, in standard German). A former seat of the Reformation, Zurich is a staunchly Protestant—some say Puritan—city.

Zurich is less industrialized today than in recent decades, its economy having shifted away from heavy industry and toward the service industries, high-tech computer development, banking, insurance, and diplomacy. The factories that remain within the city limits run on electricity, and as a result, the city's skies remain relatively unpolluted. Zurich is also a major center of international finance; the headquarters of at least five major banks are on Bahnhofstrasse, in the heart of the city. The bankers are sometimes referred to as gnomes because many of the banks store mountains of gold in underground vaults.

Zurich produces one-fifth of the nation's income, but it's far from being a dreary city of commerce. It's long been a great center of liberal thought, attracting such scholars as Lenin, Jung, Joyce, and Mann. The Dadaist school (an early-20th-c. precursor of surrealism) was founded here in 1916. And the increase of visitors in the last 2 decades has spurred the development of a livelier nightlife and entertainment scene.

Built between the wooded slopes of the Uetliberg and the Zürichberg, Zurich is split by the Limmat River. There is no finer pleasure to be had in Zurich than walking along its quays, which line the banks of the Limmat and Lake Zurich. Sailboats and motorboats take visitors across Lake Zurich. Zurich's Altstadt (Old Town) is one of the most prosperous and intriguing in Switzerland, with two giant cathedrals and dozens of streets ideal for exploring at leisure. It's also a city of parks and gardens, with a particularly outstanding botanical garden.

While based in Zurich you can also take easy side trips to some of the most panoramic views of Switzerland, including to the Uetliberg, the king of picnic spots and known as the "top of Zurich."

1 ORIENTATION

ARRIVING

BY PLANE   **Kloten Airport** (✆ **044/816-22-11;** www.zurich-airport.com), the international airport of Zurich, is the biggest airport in Switzerland and the most popular gateway to the country; in fact, it's among the 10 busiest airports in Europe. The airport is approximately 11km (7 miles) north of the city center, and the trip by taxi costs between 55F and 60F. A far better and cheaper option is to take the Swiss Federal Railways train service; for 6F—press the solid red button on the automated ticket machine—you'll arrive in less than 15 minutes at the **Zurich Hauptbahnhof,** the main railway station in the center of town. Zurich is a fairly compact town—from the train station, you can walk or hop on a tram or bus to most Zurich hotels in less than 30 minutes. (The train ticket you purchase at the airport is valid for 1 hr. and includes connecting travel on the trams and buses within central Zurich. Alternatively, you can purchase a 24-hr. version of the same ticket for 15F—press the solid red button followed by the silver button with arrows). The train runs every 15 to 20 minutes between 5:36am and 12:20am. You can also take bus no. 768 (Zurich Airport–Seebach), but you'll have to change to tram no. 14 to get to the center of town.

BY TRAIN   Several trains bound for Switzerland leave from the Gare de l'Est in **Paris.** Two nonstop trains leave from Paris to Zurich daily, taking 6 hours. There are also good links between Austria and Switzerland, with trains arriving from **Salzburg** in 6 hours or **Vienna** in 9 hours. The best connection from Italy is via **Milan** (4½ hr.). Trains to Zurich run every hour from **Geneva** (a 3-hr. journey) and from **Basel** (1¼ hr.). From **Munich,** high-speed express trains depart for Zurich frequently. All trains arrive at the **Zurich Hauptbahnhof** (✆ 0900/300-300).

BY BUS   Zurich's bus routes function only as feeder lines from outlying suburbs, which lie off the train lines, into the vicinity of the town's railroad station.

BY CAR   From Basel, take N3 east, and from Geneva, take N1 northeast, going via Bern, where you'll connect with E4 and E17 heading east into Zurich.

BY BOAT   The **Zurichsee-Schifffahrtsgesellschaft,** Mythenquai 333 (✆ 044/487-13-33; www.zsg.ch), offers regularly scheduled service on modern passenger ships as well as old steamers plying both sides of Lake Zurich. The service is operated from Easter to October, going from Zurich as far as Rapperswil.

VISITOR INFORMATION
The **Zurich Tourist Office,** Bahnhofplatz 15 (✆ 044/215-40-00; www.zuerich.com), is in the main railway station. It's open November to April, Monday to Saturday from 8:30am to 7pm and Sunday 9am to 6:30pm; May to October, hours are Monday to Saturday 8am to 8:30pm and Sunday 8:30am to 6:30pm.

CITY LAYOUT
Zurich lies situated on both shores of the Limmat River, which flows from the northern end of Lake Zurich. The Sihl River, a tributary of the Limmat, also flows through the city, and quays line the riverbanks and the lake. The city spreads across a ravine in the eastern hills between the wooded slopes of the Zürichberg and Kääferberg hills into the Glatt River Valley.

The hamlet that became Zurich began at the **Lindenhof,** which is where you, too, may begin your orientation to the city. This square is the architectural center of historic Zurich. From here, you can survey the city as it rises on both banks of the Limmat from Bahnhofbrücke (*brücke* means bridge) to Quaibrücke. Between these two bridges are four other spans over the river: Muhle-Steg, Rudolf Brun-Brücke, Rathausbrücke, and Münsterbrücke.

Below this square runs **Bahnhofstrasse,** one of the most elegant and expensive shopping streets in the world. It begins in the north, at the Hauptbahnhof (the railway station), opening onto Bahnhofplatz, and runs south to the lake. It crosses **Paradeplatz,** a converging point for trams and the modern center of the city. From Paradeplatz continue east, passing Fraumünster church and crossing Münsterbrücke to reach the right bank of the river. Here, the narrow streets of the **Limmatquai** are the second-best place in the city to shop. Running parallel to Limmatquai is **Niederdorfstrasse,** in the so-called red-light district of Zurich.

Old Town, or **Altstadt,** was developed during the early medieval period and is focused on Lindenhof, Fraumünster, Grossmünster, and St. Peter's. It expanded to **Weinplatz,** the oldest market square, and **Strehlgasse.** By the 11th century, the city developed on the right bank with such centers as **Kirchgasse** and **Neumarkt.**

FINDING AN ADDRESS In a system that developed during the Middle Ages, all Swiss cities, including Zurich, begin their street-numbering system with the lowest numbers closest to the center of town. In Zurich the center is the **Hauptbahnhof.** All even numbers lie on one side of the street, and all odd numbers are on the other.

MAPS The best map, published by Falk, is a pocket-size Stadtplan (city plan) with an index. Copies are available at various newsstands and bookstores. Try the **Travel Book Shop,** Rindermarkt 20 (✆ **044/252-38-83;** www.travelbookshop.ch). Hours are Monday 1 to 6:30pm, Tuesday through Friday from 9am to 6:30pm, and Saturday 9am to 4pm.

NEIGHBORHOODS IN BRIEF

Zurich is divided by the Limmat River into the following two general areas:

WEST OR LEFT BANK

This district is dominated by Bahnhof-platz, center of rail connections, and Bahnhofstrasse, which is the main commercial and banking thorough-fare. This is the Zurich world of high finance and elegant shops. The vener-able Fraumünster church, on Frau-münsterstrasse, dominates the west bank. Included within the west bank, but somewhat removed from its sense of high-flying prosperity, is the increas-ingly visible, increasingly gentrified, warehouse-cum-*artmeisters* district of Zurich West.

EAST OR RIGHT BANK

Opposite Fraumünster, on the other side of the river, rises Grossmünster church, on Grossmünsterplatz; its two Gothic towers are an east-bank landmark. The historic guildhalls of Zurich, such as the Zunfthaus zur Saffran, rise on the east bank of the river. So, too, does the Rathaus, the city's town hall, completed in 1698. On the east bank you can explore the eastern part of Altstadt, strolling along Neumarkt, one of the best preserved of the old streets. The area beyond is Niederdorf, the center of the town's hot spots.

2 GETTING AROUND

Zurich is an easy city to navigate, and the trams (streetcars) and buses are reliable.

BY PUBLIC TRANSPORTATION

The public transport system of Zurich is operated by ZVV, or **Zurich Public Transport** (✆ **0848/801-880;** www.vbz.ch). The modern and extensive network of trams and buses (there is no subway) runs daily from 5:30am to 12:30am. You should have to wait no

longer than 6 minutes during rush hours. Most trams and buses connect at the Zurich
Hauptbahnhof, in the heart of the city.

You can buy tickets from automatic vending machines located at every stop. You must have a ticket before you get on a vehicle; if you're caught without one, you'll pay a fine of 50F. The fare is 4F for a trip of 1 hour. Visitors can get the most for their money by ordering a *Tageskarte* (1-day ticket), which costs 8F and allows you to travel on all city buses and trams for 24 hours.

BY TAXI

Taxis are very expensive. The budget-conscious will only want to use them as a last resort. Your hotel will usually be glad to call a taxi for you, but if you're making the call yourself, call **Taxi 444** (✆ **044/444-44-44;** www.taxi444.ch). The basic charge before you even get into the vehicle is 6F, plus 3.80F for each kilometer you travel.

BY CAR

We don't recommend attempting to see Zurich by car—the city is way too congested, and parking is too scarce and too expensive. Save the car for exploring the environs.

RENTAL CARS All the major car-rental firms are represented in Zurich, with offices at both Kloten Airport and downtown. Representative firms include **Avis,** with offices at Gartenhofstrasse 17 (✆ **044/296-87-87;** www.avis.com) or at the airport (✆ **044/800-77-33;** www.avis.com); **Budget,** with an office at the airport (✆ **044/813-31-31;** www.budget.com); and **Hertz,** with a base at Morgartenstrasse 5 (✆ **044/298-84-84;** www.hertz.com).

PARKING You should get a street plan (see "Maps" under "City Layout," above), which indicates parking garages with a P sign; a similar leaflet is available from the Zurich police. Some hotels have their own parking garages, for which there is an extra charge; others, especially those in congested Old Town, do not. You'll have to inquire at your hotel for the location of the nearest public garage. Parking costs range from 6F to 10F per hour in most of the city's public garages.

BY BIKE

Biking is a good way to get around Zurich, especially in the outlying areas. Bicycles can be rented at the baggage counter of the railway station, the **Hauptbahnhof** (✆ **051/222-29-04**), for 27F per day or 21F for a half-day for a city bike. Hours are daily from 7am to 7:30pm.

ON FOOT

Zurich and its quays are ideal for walking, and many of the places of interest, such as the sights of Altstadt on both sides of the Limmat, are conveniently grouped together.

ZURICH

5

FAST FACTS: ZURICH

(Fast Facts Zurich

Babysitters If enough advance notification is given (at least a day in advance), virtually any hotel in Zurich can arrange for a babysitter. Another option is the child-care facilities at one of Zurich's largest department stores, **Jelmoli,** Seiden-gasse 1 (✆ **044/220-44-11;** www.jelmoli.ch).

Banks Banks are generally open Monday to Wednesday and on Friday from 8:15am to 4:30pm, and on Thursday from 8:15am to 6pm. A convenient bank is **Crédit Suisse** at Paradeplatz 8 (© 044/333-99-11), open Monday to Friday 8am to 7pm.

Climate Summers in Zurich are not as warm as on the French Riviera, but the lake is usually warm enough to swim in during July and August. Many days are chilly, and spring and fall can be quite cold. In winter the temperature rarely goes below zero. The average temperature in January is 30°F (–1°C); in July the average is only 61°F (16°C). On cloudy days the view of the Alps is obscured.

Consulates If you lose your passport or have another emergency, go to the **U.S. Consulate,** Dufourstrasse 101 (© 043/499-29-60) or the **Consulate of the United Kingdom,** Hegibachstrasse 47 (© 044/383-65-60). Canadians and Australians should contact their respective embassies in Bern.

Currency Exchange Most banks and travel agencies will exchange money for you. There's also an exchange office of **Credit Suisse** at the Zurich Hauptbahnhof, the main railway station, open daily from 6:30am to 11:30pm at Minervastrasse 117. Incidentally, there are ATMs all over the city.

Dentists For emergency dental problems, call © **044/269-69-69.** An appointment with an English-speaking dentist can be arranged for you.

Doctors Contact the **Zurich Universitätsspital (University Hospital),** Rämistrasse 100 (© **044/255-11-11**).

Drugstores For 24-hour service, **Bellevue Apotheke,** at Theaterstrasse 14 (© **044/266-62-22;** www.bellevue-apotheke.com), lies off Bellevueplatz.

Emergencies Call the **police** at © **117.** For **first aid,** phone © **114;** for the **City Ambulance Service,** dial © **144.** There's an accident center at the **University Hospital,** Rämistrasse 100 (© **044/255-11-11**). For a fire, dial © **118.** Zurich's Bahnhof (main railway station) contains a limited roster of medical and dental facilities which, if they can't treat an ailment effectively themselves, will at least direct you to larger medical facilities that can.

Hairdressers & Barbers Women do not need a reservation at **Gidor,** Theaterstrasse 8 (© **044/251-90-18**). Men can get their hair cut at the Hauptbahnhof (rail station).

Hospitals See "Doctors" or "Emergencies," above.

Information See "Visitor Information," above.

Internet Access Head for an Internet cafe such as **Telefon-Corner,** Kanzleistrasse 57 (© **044/297-20-80;** www.telefoncorner.ch), open Monday to Thursday 9am to midnight, Friday and Saturday 9am to 2am, and Sunday 10am to 11pm.

Laundry & Dry Cleaning One of the best and most centrally located of Zurich's self-service laundries is Wäscherei TBTV, Dienerstrasse 70 (© **043/243-80-73**). A dry-cleaning service is also on-site.

Libraries The main branch of the **Pestalozzi Bibliothek (Pestalozzi Library),** the largest in Zurich, is at Zähringerstrasse 17 (© **044/204-96-96;** www.pbz.ch). You must maintain a permanent address in Switzerland to be able to borrow books, but even if you don't, you're welcome to browse the stacks and read anything you want on-site. It's open Monday to Friday 10am to 7pm and Saturday 10am to 2pm (till 4pm Sept–May).

Lost Property There is a lost-property office at Werdmühlestrasse 10 (📞 **044/216-25-50**), open Monday to Friday 7:30am to 5:30pm.

Luggage Storage & Lockers These are available at several locations throughout the vast Hauptbahnhof.

Newspapers & Magazines The major newspaper of Zurich is the German-language **Neue Zürcher Zeitung.** The **International Herald Tribune** is printed in Zurich. Several German-language magazines are published in Switzerland, and the latest copies of **Newsweek** and **Time** (European editions) are available at most newsstands and in big-hotel lobbies.

Police See "Emergencies," above.

Post Office The main post office is the **Sihlpost,** Kasernenstrasse 95–97 (📞 **044/296-21-11**), across the Sihl River from Löwenstrasse; an emergency-service window is open from 6:30am to 10pm daily. Most post offices—listed under "Post" in the phone directory—are open Monday to Friday 7:30am to 6:30pm and on Saturday from 6:30 to 11am.

Safety Zurich is one of the safest cities in Europe, both during the day and at night. The most potentially dangerous place is Niederdorf, the red-light district in Altstadt.

Taxes A 7.6% VAT (value-added tax) is added to hotel and restaurant bills. There are no other special taxes.

Taxis See "Getting Around," above.

Telephone, Telex & Fax A telephone, telex, and fax office is open at the **Zurich Hauptbahnhof,** the main railway station, Monday to Friday from 7am to 10:30pm and on Saturday and Sunday from 9am to 9pm.

Toilets Public toilets are located at all central points, including the Hauptbahnhof and such locations as Bellevueplatz, Paradeplatz, and Heimplatz. They are open daily, generally from 5am to midnight.

Transit Information For bus and tram information, call 📞 **0848/801-880.**

Weather See "Climate," above.

3 WHERE TO STAY

Zurich is an ideal place to get acquainted with Swiss hospitality. More than 120 hotels offer accommodations ranging from the most sumptuous suites in Europe to simple, clean pensions (boardinghouses). Finding a room can be a problem, however. The top hotels are usually filled with business travelers, and the city frequently hosts conventions and fairs. So, if possible, make a reservation in advance.

For top-rate comfort in Zurich, you'll have to pay. Inexpensive hotels are often spartan and definitely have no frills, and many of the budget hostelries are in dire need of renovation. Don't believe the myth that you can't find a bad hotel in Switzerland: It's not true and probably never was.

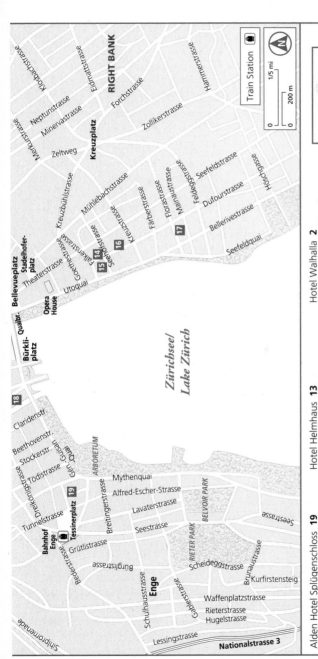

Train Station

RIGHT BANK

Zürichsee/
Lake Zürich

SWITZERLAND
Basel
Zurich
Bern
Geneva

Alden Hotel Splügenschloss 19
Bar Hotel Seehof 16
Baur au Lac 18
Hotel Ambassabor 15
Hotel Bristol 3
Hotel du Theatre 7
Hotel Goldenes Schwert 11

Hotel Helmhaus 13
Hotel Kindli 9
Hotel Limmatblick 6
Hotel Opéra 14
Hotel Romantic Florhof 10
Hotel Schweizerhof 4
Hotel St. Gotthard 5

Hotel Walhalla 2
Hotel Zum Storchen 12
Lady's First 17
Widder Hotel 8
X-tra Hotel Limmat 1

ZURICH

5

WHERE TO STAY

The division between the left bank and the right bank of Zurich isn't as sharply divided as it is in Paris, for example. You stay on the left bank for greater convenience, as it is the site of the rail terminus, all the major banks, and some of the grandest shops and restaurants. However, the right bank is the site of the Altstadt (Old Town), and for many visitors this section of Zurich has far greater atmosphere. It's also the site of many of the historic guildhalls of Zurich (some of which are now restaurants). A stay here is for those who seek ambience and an old-style atmosphere when lodging in a European capital.

Note: Rooms in all our recommended hotels have private bathrooms with tub and shower unless otherwise indicated.

ON THE LEFT BANK
Very Expensive
Alden Hotel Splügenschloss ★★ (Finds) A little *city-palais* and a little Relais & Châteaux, this is a gem of a hotel, each room a suite. At the turn of the 20th century, it was a luxury apartment house, home to rich merchants, but its historic decor has been successfully adapted into the midsize charmer that you see today. Bedrooms are spacious and tastefully furnished, including such extras as a sitting area and a luxury bathroom with Jacuzzi and separate shower. Many of the accommodations contain antique wardrobes and are decked out in soothing pastels. One, for example, has been paneled in Graubünden pine from eastern Switzerland. The location is just a 6-minute walk from the Bahnhofstrasse and a 3-minute walk from the Enge rail depot. The restaurant is a virtual art gallery and serves a refined international cuisine.

Splügenstrasse 2, CH-8002 Zurich. ℭ **044/289-99-99.** Fax 044/289-99-98. www.alden.ch. 22 units. 700F–1,100F junior suite; 960F–1,500F suite. Rates include buffet breakfast. AE, DC, MC, V. Tram: 5, 6, 7, or 13. **Amenities:** 2 restaurants; bar; airport transfers (150F); concierge; room service. *In room:* A/C (on request), TV, hair dryer, minibar, Wi-Fi (free).

Baur au Lac ★★★ One of the world's great hotels, owned by the same family since it opened in 1844, Baur au Lac is ideally located at the end of Bahnhofstrasse, right next to the Schanzengraben Canal. The three-story stone building is surrounded by a private park that's filled with red geraniums in summer. In grandeur, style, service, and amenities, it's superior to its nearest competitor, the Widder. The dining facilities are among the finest in Zurich.

In rooms where Richard Wagner and Franz Liszt once entertained at the piano, guests today are treated to Jugendstil glass, tapestries, antiques, marble floors, and Oriental carpets. All bedrooms and suites are luxuriously and uniquely furnished. Suites have the best antiques, but regular rooms may have an Empire piece, a style from one of the Louis periods, or modern furnishings. Try for a room with a lake view.

Talstrasse 1, CH-8022 Zurich. ℭ **044/220-50-20.** Fax 044/220-50-44. www.bauraulac.ch. 130 units. 820F double; from 1,800F suite. AE, DC, MC, V. Parking 35F. Tram: 4. **Amenities:** 3 restaurants; bar; airport transfers (150F); concierge; exercise room; room service. *In room:* A/C, TV, hair dryer (in some), minibar, Wi-Fi (free).

Hotel Kindli ★ Set at the end of a steep street (Rennweg) in Old Town, in a pedestrian zone, this 16th-century building is one of Zurich's most well-recommended middle-bracket hotels. It's been completely renovated, with a different color scheme designed for each of the bedrooms. Although each is relatively small, they contain flowery overlays of Laura Ashley fabrics throughout. Each room contains an eclectic blend of old and new furniture and an efficient bathroom.

Pfalzgasse 1, CH-8001 Zurich. ✆ **043/888-76-76.** Fax 043/888-76-77. www.kindli.ch. 20 units. 420F–460F
double. Rates include buffet breakfast. AE, DC, MC, V. Parking 40F. Tram: 7, 11, or 13. **Amenities:** Restaurant. *In room:* A/C, TV, minibar, Wi-Fi (free).

Hotel St. Gotthard ★

A longtime favorite of the Swiss, Hotel St. Gotthard is located on the main shopping street, only a block from the railroad station. For more than a century, it has been convenient for shops, transportation, business centers, bus terminals, and restaurants. Rooms and suites, including a collection of business-class units, are generously furnished in various styles and come in a range of sizes. Amenities include voice mail and videos, along with deluxe toiletries in the bathrooms. Suites and business-class rooms have fax machines. The welcome here is warmer and more personal than it is at the giants recommended elsewhere in this section.

Bahnhofstrasse 87, CH-8023 Zurich. ✆ **800/457-4000** in the U.S. or 044/227-77-00. Fax 044/227-77-50. www.hotelstgotthard.ch. 150 units. 500F–625F double; from 900F suite. AE, DC, MC, V. Parking 35F. Tram: 6, 7, 11, or 13. **Amenities:** Restaurant; 3 bars; babysitting; room service; sauna. *In room:* A/C, TV, CD player, hair dryer (in some), minibar, Wi-Fi (free).

Hotel Schweizerhof ★★

Located in one of the city's busiest areas, the landmark Schweizerhof is accessible from anywhere in town by tram. This is a grand old station hotel in turn-of-the-20th-century tradition, although major renovations have kept it in step with the times. When stacked up against the Baur au Lac, Widder, and Savoy, it would definitely be number four, although the Schweizerhof is far superior to the average station hotel in a European capital. The stone building has gables, turrets, and columns and is decorated with flags. Inside, the public rooms are pleasant and unpretentious. The ideal rooms are the semicircular corner units. In spite of its central location, rooms are generally quiet because of the triple glazing on the windows. Most units are roomy and filled with many thoughtful extras, including spongy carpeting, alarm clocks, fruit baskets, and deluxe toiletries.

Bahnhofplatz 7, CH-8023 Zurich. ✆ **044/218-88-88.** Fax 044/218-81-81. www.hotelschweizerhof.com. 115 units. 550F–770F double; 790F junior suite; 1,240F suite. Rates include buffet breakfast. AE, DC, MC, V. Parking 30F. Tram: 3 or 4. **Amenities:** 2 restaurants; bar; babysitting; concierge; room service. *In room:* A/C, TV, hair dryer, minibar, Wi-Fi (free).

Hotel zum Storchen ★★

This hotel claims to be the oldest in Europe, with origins going back to 1357. A traditional government-rated four-star hotel, it's an unusual choice for Zurich. Although Zurich's deluxe hotels are far better known, this is the only one directly on the Limmat River and seems more overrun with tourists than the prestigious Baur au Lac, which also lures discerning clients seeking an old-world ambience. Supposedly named for the storks that nested on the roof, and the former guildhall during the Middle Ages of the fishermen and boat-transport workers, the Storchen is undeniably romantic. A favorite feature is the cafe terrace, which provides a sweeping panorama of Old Town. The midsize rooms are warmly and invitingly decorated and maintained in state-of-the-art condition. The most desirable units have French windows opening onto the water, with views across to the floodlit Rathaus.

Am Weinplatz 2, CH-8001 Zurich. ✆ **800/457-4000** in the U.S., or 044/227-27-27. Fax 044/227-27-00. www.storchen.ch. 73 units. 600F–850F double; 790F–1,050F suite. Rates include buffet breakfast. AE, DC, MC, V. Parking 30F. Tram: 4 or 15. **Amenities:** 2 restaurants; bar; babysitting; concierge; room service. *In room:* A/C, TV, hair dryer, minibar, Wi-Fi (free).

Widder Hotel ★★★

This is Zurich's most up-to-date deluxe hotel, rivaled in the neighborhood only by the superior Baur au Lac, but ahead of the Savoy in overall tranquillity and comfort. In the early 1990s the Union Bank of Switzerland managed to acquire 10 individual, interconnected buildings—some associated with the city's medieval butchers' guild—clustered around a central courtyard in the capital's historic core. The buildings were then combined into this sophisticated international hotel. During the renovations, great care was used to retain the original stone walls, murals, frescoes, and ceilings. The result is a unique hotel where every room is different—sometimes radically so—from its neighbors, and where the color scheme (pastel beige, pink, blue, or yellow) reflects the color of the exterior of whichever of the 10 buildings you happen to be in. Interior furnishings range from the metallic, minimalist, and very modern to the traditional.

Rennweg 7, CH-8001 Zurich. ℂ **044/224-25-26.** Fax 044/224-24-24. www.widderhotel.ch. 49 units. 740F–920F double; 1,400F–1,950F suite. Rates include buffet breakfast. AE, DC, MC, V. Parking 35F. Tram: 6, 7, or 11. **Amenities:** Restaurant; bar; airport transfers (150F); babysitting; concierge; exercise room; room service. *In room:* TV, fax, hair dryer (in some), minibar, Wi-Fi (10F per day).

Moderate

Hotel du Theatre ★ (Finds)   This bed-and-breakfast hotel is aptly named, as it harbored a German-speaking Broadway-style stage in the 1950s before its conversion to a top-notch urban hotel. The tall, thin architecture of the building itself, along with a glass facade, sets the stage for the drama going on inside. The tranquil, comfortably furnished rooms are more traditional than theatrical. However, they possess character and are equipped with a cornucopia of audio books, plays, music, drama, crime stories, philosophy tomes, and even erotica. When this library of goodies has tired you, you're prepared for a rest before breakfast the following morning in a beautiful room. The city center, only a short walk away, can be seen from the dining room, and the location is a 5-minute walk from the Bahnhof.

Seilergraben 69, CH-8001 Zurich. ℂ **044/267-26-70.** Fax 044/267-26-71. www.hotel-du-theatre.ch. 50 units. 195F–305F double; 280F–335F junior suite. AE, DC, MC, V. Tram: 4 or 10. *In room:* TV, minibar, Wi-Fi (25F per day).

Inexpensive

Hotel Bristol ★ (Value)   This conservative, small-scale hotel stands on a hill near the main train station, behind the major road to the airport. For many years, Hotel Bristol has been one of Zurich's best-known and most successful small hotels despite its conventional format and lack of amenities. The bedrooms are well maintained, frequently renovated, and furnished to a high standard of comfort. The helpful staff makes you feel right at home in the center of Zurich. No alcoholic beverages are sold, and only breakfast is served.

Stampfenbachstrasse 34, CH-8035 Zurich. ℂ **044/258-44-44.** Fax 044/258-44-00. www.hotelbristol.ch. 53 units. 170F–270F double; 220F–310F triple; 240F–350F quad. Rates include continental breakfast. AE, DC, MC, V. Tram: 11 or 14. **Amenities:** Room service. *In room:* TV, hair dryer.

Hotel Walhalla (Value)   Set close to the railway station, this hotel is one of the relatively cheap bargains in central Zurich. It occupies two five-story buildings, one with more up-to-date bedrooms. The other is older and a bit dowdier, with high-ceilinged bedrooms and very little architectural flair. All rooms and bathrooms, however, are comfortable and well maintained. The dining room serves breakfast only. Don't expect glamour or even much originality—what you get is price conscious, and without too many surprises.

Limmatstrasse 5, CH-8005 Zurich. ✆ **044/446-54-00.** Fax 044/446-54-54. www.walhalla-hotel.ch.
48 units. 235F–275F double; 300F–350F triple. Rates include buffet breakfast. AE, DC, MC, V. Tram: 3 or 14.
Amenities: Restaurant. *In room:* TV, hair dryer, Wi-Fi (free).

X-Tra Hotel Limmat ★ (Finds)   The Limmat is one of the most durable of the cost-conscious hotels of downtown Zurich. The hotel occupies part of a four-story building erected in 1935 in the Bauhaus style as a convention center, and whose boxy-looking facade is today protected as a historic monument. You can expect more here than just a place to stay: Its management, in place since 1997, is one of the largest organizers of rock-'n'-roll concerts in Switzerland, often staging their acts in the cavernous restaurant and nightclub that occupies the ground floor. Consequently, members of the bands that play here are often in residence, a policy that adds to the cachet of the place for counter-culture rock-'n'-roll enthusiasts across Switzerland. (Hotel guests receive a 15F discount off their admission to the nightclub.) Accommodations are streamlined, partially paneled, and outfitted in a style reminiscent of Danish modern.

In the Limmathaus, Limmatstrasse 118, CH-8005 Zurich. ✆ **044/448-15-00.** Fax 044/448-15-01. www.x-tra.ch. 43 units. 166F–205F double; 204F–230F triple. Rates include buffet breakfast. Parking 15F per night. AE, DC, MC, V. Tram: 4 or 13 to Limmatplatz. **Amenities:** Restaurant; bar; discounted admission at a nearby health club. *In room:* TV, minibar, Wi-Fi (30F per day).

ON THE RIGHT BANK
Expensive
Hotel Ambassador ★★   One of our favorite hotels in Zurich is a small-scale gem with a lot of charm and pizazz. It was originally built late in the 19th century as the "Falkenschloss," a then-private villa whose distinguished Beaux Arts facade complements the opera house immediately across the street, near the important tramway junction at Bellevue Platz. After the turn of the millennium, its interior was radically upgraded into the modernized baroque decor you see today. Bedrooms are high ceilinged, with supremely comfortable beds (each adjusts, hospital style, to whatever angle and configuration you want), and generally spacious. A well-trained staff attends to your comfort, providing the services that a traveling business representative may need. The on-site restaurant, À l'Opéra (p. 105), is one of the best restaurants in Zurich, but more reasonably priced than you might expect.

Falkenstrasse 6, CH-8008 Zurich. ✆ **044/258-98-98.** Fax 044/258-98-00. www.ambassadorhotel.ch. 45 units. 350F–490F double; 420F–640F suite. Breakfast 25F extra. AE, DC, MC, V. Parking 31F. Tram: 4. **Amenities:** Restaurant; bar; concierge; room service. *In room:* A/C, TV, hair dryer, minibar, Wi-Fi (free).

Hotel Romantik Florhof ★ (Value)   This is the most charming and tranquil of the little boutique hotels of Zurich, located on the eastern edge of the Old Town. Originally built in the 15th century as a merchant's home, these premises became a hotel during the 1920s. The Florhof represents top value in Zurich, and is known as a gracious and well-managed hotel with a loyal clientele. Although the public rooms retain much of their antique glamour (including a noteworthy blue-and-white Kachelofen often used long ago for heating), many of the bedrooms are modern and functional. The single units are a bit small, but most doubles are of decent size and are nicely outfitted with plasterwork on the ceilings, exceedingly comfortable beds, stone-topped nightstands, and generous bathrooms.

Florhofgasse 4, CH-8001 Zurich. ✆ **044/250-26-26.** Fax 044/250-26-27. www.florhof.ch. 35 units. 360F–410F double; 630F–670F junior suite. Rates include continental breakfast. AE, DC, MC, V. Parking 17F. Tram: 3. **Amenities:** Restaurant; room service. *In room:* TV, hair dryer, minibar, Wi-Fi (free).

Bar Hotel Seehof Set close to the opera house and the promenade that parallels the lake, this small-scale, postmodern hotel was opened in 1999 after a radical renovation and modernization of the original 1930s-era private house. The hotel retains the original russet-colored exterior, but the interior decor is angular and efficient, with stark white walls and the kind of black furniture that you'd expect in a trendy art gallery. Fortunately, the angularity is softened, in both the public areas and the bedrooms, with varnished and beautifully crafted oaken floors and a revolving series of artworks (usually photographs by Swiss artists). Many of the rooms are reserved by opera singers performing at the nearby opera house.

Seehofstrasse 11, CH-8008 Zurich. ✆ **044/254-57-57.** Fax 044/254-57-58. www.hotelseehof.ch. 19 units. 290F–380F double; 390F–420F junior suite. Rates include buffet breakfast. AE, DC, MC, V. Parking 15F. Tram: 4. **Amenities:** Restaurant; bar; room service. *In room:* TV, hair dryer, minibar (in some), Wi-Fi (free).

Hotel Helmhaus ★ In the center of Zurich, Helmhaus is 5 minutes from Parade-platz/Bahnhofstrasse, the opera house, major museums, and the lake. Set on a boat-landing square, it stands a block from the river at the corner of Limmatquai. The hotel is one of the best in its price range, with a pleasantly personal atmosphere. The bedrooms are attractively furnished, often in bright florals, and the bathrooms are of medium size.

Schifflände 30, CH-8001 Zurich. ✆ **044/266-95-95.** Fax 044/266-95-66. www.helmhaus.ch. 24 units. 270F–430F double. Rates include buffet breakfast. AE, DC, MC, V. Parking 30F. Tram: 4 from the Hauptbahnhof, or shuttle-bus service btw. the hotel and the airport. *In room:* A/C, hair dryer, minibar, Wi-Fi (free).

Hotel Opera ★ (Finds) Cozy, comfortable, and unpretentious, this hotel was built in 1970 as a cousin to the also-recommended and more elegant Hotel Ambassador, which shares the same owner and management, and is located a few steps away. Set about 25 paces from the opera house, it's deliberately short on facilities, but it's a favorite among many business travelers seeking a central location. Try for one of the corner rooms or one on the fourth or fifth floor. The Opera boasts a large, carpeted lobby, with an assortment of armchairs, where you can purchase beer and soft drinks. Other than breakfast, no meals are served on-site, but clients have easy access to the Hotel Ambassador's superb restaurant, **À l'Opéra** (p. 105).

Dufourstrasse 5, CH-8008 Zurich. ✆ **044/258-99-99.** Fax 044/258-99-00. www.operahotel.ch. 62 units. 320F–450F double. Breakfast 25F extra. AE, DC, MC, V. Parking 31F nearby. Tram: 4. **Amenities:** Restaurant; bar; room service. *In room:* A/C, TV, hair dryer, minibar, Wi-Fi (free).

Lady's First ★ (Finds) The first hotel of its type in Switzerland, this is a boutique hotel with its top floor, rooftop terrace, and its spa facilities available only to women. It's installed in an elegant town house from the 1880s, which lies close to the core of town and Lake Zurich. Bedrooms come in various shapes and sizes, and each is furnished in a sleekly modern and tasteful way, with well-maintained bathrooms with tub or shower. The best rooms open onto a small balcony with a view of the lake. Along with chic furnishings, rooms have parquet floors and high ceilings. Grace notes include a fireplace in the lounge and a summer rose garden.

Mainaustrasse 24, CH-8008 Zurich. ✆ **044/380-80-10.** Fax 044/380-80-20. www.ladysfirst.ch. 28 units. 275F–340F double. Rates include buffet breakfast. AE, DC, MC, V. Tram: 2 or 4. **Amenities:** Spa. *In room:* TV, hair dryer, minibar, Wi-Fi (free).

Inexpensive

Hotel Goldenes Schwert   The "Golden Sword" caters to a clientele that's almost exclusively out, proud, and eager to patronize some of the many nightlife options that ring it within this bustling neighborhood of Zurich's historic Altstadt. Set behind a simple white stucco facade within a century-old building, it maintains a pair of gay nightclubs (see "Zurich After Dark," later in this chapter) on its lower floors, and comfortable bedrooms on floors four, five, and six, each accessible by elevator from the street level. Each of the rooms is individually decorated and outfitted in styles that range from the artfully minimalist to several that are a bit more cluttered, in a cozy way, with wooden furniture and original paintings.

Marktgasse 14, CH-8001 Zurich. ✆ **044/250-70-80.** Fax 044/250-70-89. www.gayhotel.ch. 22 units. 170F–250F double; 250F–380F suite. AE, DC, MC, V. Parking 28F. Tram: 4 or 15. **Amenities:** Bar; room service. *In room:* A/C, TV, minibar.

Hotel Limmatblick   This hotel is permeated with a theme that's a particular source of fascination to its owner, Claude Dreifuss, and members of his family: Dadaism. Throughout, this hotel, beginning with the small cafe-cum-reception area, you'll find a Dada theme, as evidenced by rooms which each contain artworks associated with the Dada movement. What, you might ask, is Dadaism, or Dada? An early precursor to surrealism, Dada flourished in Zurich, its birthplace, just prior to the First World War, permeating the city's art and contemporary theater with a sense of often politicized absurdity. The hotel is located near the crowded edge of the Limmat, a 10-minute walk from the main railroad station. Rooms are unfrilly and small scale—in some cases, somewhat claustrophobic. Each contains twin beds, a rather cramped bathroom with shower, and a sense of the Dadaist movement that, around 1912, generated screaming controversies within most of the bourgeois circles of Europe.

Limmatquai 136, CH-8001 Zurich. ✆ **044/254-60-00.** Fax 044/254-60-10. www.limmatblick.ch. 16 units. 210F–240F double. Rates include continental breakfast. AE, DC, MC, V. Closed mid-Dec–early Jan. Tram: 4 or 15. **Amenities:** Bar; room service; Internet (free, in lobby). *In room:* TV, hair dryer, minibar.

4 WHERE TO DINE

Zurich restaurants feature a selection of both international and Swiss specialties. The local favorite is *rösti* (potatoes grated and fried). You should also try *Züri-Gschnätzlets* (shredded veal cooked with mushrooms in a cream sauce laced with white wine) and *Kutteln nach Zürcherart* (tripe with mushrooms, white wine, and caraway seed). Another classic dish is *Leberspiesschen* (liver cubes skewered with bacon and sage and served with potatoes and beans).

Among local wines, the white Riesling Sylvaner is outstanding and great with fish. The light Clevner wines, always chilled, are made from blue Burgundy grapes that grow around the lake. You should be able to order wine by the glass, even in first-class restaurants.

ON THE LEFT BANK

Expensive

Accademia ★★ ITALIAN   The finest and most elegant Italian restaurant in Zurich, Accademia is much appreciated at lunchtime by bankers and businesspeople, who use it

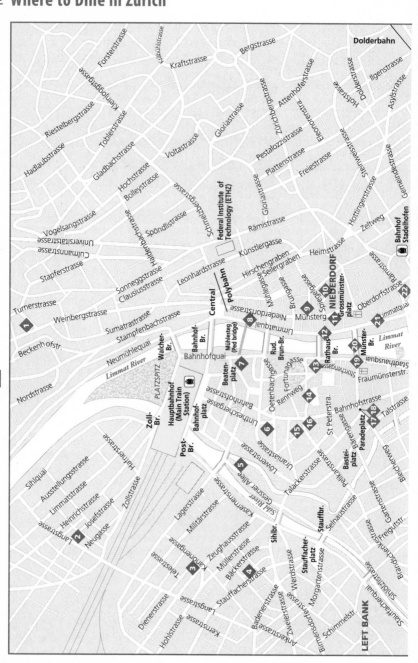

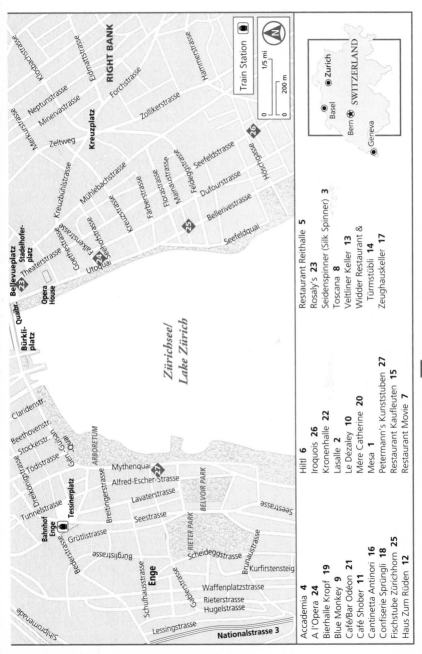

Accademia 4
A l'Opera 24
Bierhalle Kropf 19
Blue Monkey 9
Café/Bar Odéon 21
Café Shober 11
Cantinetta Antinori 16
Confiserie Sprüngli 18
Fischstube Zürichhorn 25
Haus Zum Rüden 12

Hiltl 6
Iroquois 26
Kronenhalle 22
Lasalle 2
Le Dézaley 10
Mère Catherine 20
Mesa 1
Petermann's Kunststuben 27
Restaurant Kaufleuten 15
Restaurant Movie 7

Restaurant Reithalle 5
Rosaly's 23
Seidenspinner (Silk Spinner) 3
Toscana 8
Veltliner Keller 13
Widder Restaurant &
Türmstübli 14
Zeughauskeller 17

to entertain their clients. In an Art Deco setting scattered with a collection of oil paintings, a uniformed staff politely serves Italian regional dishes, ranging from Venetian to Neapolitan. Specialties include ravioli filled with black truffles, or baked veal chop with mozzarella and tomato petals seasoned with fresh oregano. Daily specialties, when in season, may include various game dishes, including pheasant, venison, wild boar, and partridge. Offerings here rarely disappoint.

Rotwandstrasse 48. ℂ **044/241-42-02.** www.accademiadelgusto.ch. Reservations recommended, especially in summer. Main courses 28F–58F. AE, DC, MC, V. Mon–Fri noon–2pm and 6:15–10pm; Mar–Oct also Sat 6:15–10pm. Tram: 2, 3, 9, 10, or 14.

Cantinetta Antinori ★ ITALIAN   The Antinori marchesi launched the vineyards that became a wine empire some 26 generations ago. Their first wine bar (still going) was installed in a 15th-century *palazzo* in Florence. Today, this Zurich branch brings their high-quality ingredients—often from Antinori farms—and aromatic wines to the city on the Limmat. The waiters speak all known languages (well, almost) and are most helpful in guiding you through the delectable menu. Over the bar a sign reads TARTUFFO, ANCORA TARTUFF, SOLO TARTUFFO, meaning "Truffles, more truffles, and only truffles." This seems to be a mantra that the chefs live by, as evoked by their superb filets of veal with a generous portion of white truffles. Some of the specialties seemed to have arrived intact from their Florentine branch, including sausages with white haricot beans and thick oven-roasted Chiana beef. Top off your meal with an espresso macchiato, accompanied by a small dish of *cantuccini* (biscuits with almonds).

Augustinergasse 25. ℂ **044/211-72-10.** www.antinori.it. Reservations recommended. Main courses 40F–65F. AE, DC, MC, V. Daily 11am–11pm. Tram: 6, 7, or 11.

Veltliner Keller ★ SWISS/ITALIAN/FRENCH   If endurance and longevity are hallmarks of a good restaurant, this dining room would emerge near the top. Veltliner Keller has been a restaurant since 1551; before that it was a wine cellar. Located next to St. Peter's Church in Old Town, it has an ancient interior of carved mountain pine wood called *arve* (grown only in Switzerland). The chef prepares familiar Swiss specialties, and does so exceedingly well, including *züri-gschnätzlets,* the classic chopped-veal dish of Zurich. Several Italian dishes are also featured, including veal piccata and *osso buco.* A lot of the seafood is grilled or poached, including salmon. Ingredients change with the season, but you can always count on the house's signature dish, a Veltliner pot—baked macaroni with meat and beef liver cooked in a casserole.

Schlüsselgasse 8. ℂ **044/225-40-40.** www.veltlinerkeller.ch. Reservations recommended. Main courses 42F–50F. AE, DC, MC, V. Mon–Fri 11:30am–2pm and 6:30–9:30pm. Closed mid-July to mid-Aug. Tram: 2, 9, 11, or 13.

Widder Restaurant & Türmstübli ★ INTERNATIONAL   When this restaurant opened in the mid-1990s, many of its clients came as an excuse to view the iconoclastic architecture of the hotel that contained it (p. 95). But since then, these twin dining rooms have taken on a life of their own, and are now sought out as independent eateries in their own right. Although the Widder Restaurant is outfitted in a rustic, folksy style, and the Türmstübli is angular, minimalist, and devoid of most alpine reminders, the same menu is served in both. Look for a clientele from Zurich's financial community, along with a scattering of wealthy bohemians. Menu items include well-prepared versions of roast goose liver with a rhubarb compote served in crepe-style pastry with applesauce; a sumptuous breast of Barbary duckling in an orange-flavored crust served with a

pumpkin-and-lettuce-based piccata sauce and galettes of sweet corn; a delectable scampi
with morel-stuffed ravioli in a pepper-flavored butter sauce; and a particularly delicious
gratin of salmon-trout with cucumber sauce, dill weed, and new potatoes.

In the Widder Hotel, Rennweg 7. ✆ **044/224-25-26.** www.widderhotel.ch. Reservations recommended.
Main courses 29F–55F; fixed-price 4-course dinner menu 125F, 5-courses 140F. AE, DC, MC, V. Daily
11:30am–2pm and 6:30–11pm. Tram: 6, 7, 11, or 13.

Inexpensive

Bierhalle Kropf ★ (Kids) SWISS/BAVARIAN/AUSTRIAN   Everyone in Zurich goes
to "Der Kropf" for its old-fashioned ambience and generous portions at reasonable
prices. The restaurant is in one of the oldest burgher houses in town, a few steps from
Paradeplatz. Its dining room has stained-glass windows, polished paneling, chandeliers,
and plaster columns. On the walls hang stag horns and painted hunting scenes. You get
authentic and well-prepared dishes here. Almost no one, including visiting personalities,
local political figures, and finicky children, leaves disappointed. Bring along a healthy
appetite. Specialties include chopped veal with *rösti*, stewed meats, pork shank, and *pot-
au-feu* Zurich style. For dessert, we recommend *Palatschinken* (a chocolate crepe) or
Apfelstrudel (apple strudel).

In Gassen 16. ✆ **044/221-18-05.** www.zumkropf.ch. Reservations recommended. Main courses 18F–
55F. AE, MC, V. Mon–Sat 11:30am–11:30pm. Closed Easter, Dec 25, and Aug 1. Tram: 2, 8, 9, or 11.

Hiltl VEGETARIAN/INDIAN   Founded in 1898, this bright, inviting place is Zurich's leading vegetarian restaurant. Its main attraction is a large salad bar, containing more
than 40 different types of freshly prepared vegetables. House creations include vegetable
paella, mushrooms stroganoff, and curry colonial. There's a vast choice of fruit juices,
teas, draft beer, and wines priced by the glass. The restaurant is also known for its vegetarian Indian specialties.

Sihlstrasse 28. ✆ **044/227-70-00.** www.hiltl.ch. Reservations recommended. Main courses 19F–36F. AE,
MC, V. Mon–Sat 7am–11pm; Sun 11am–11pm. Tram: 6, 7, 11, or 13.

Restaurant Kaufleuten (Finds) INTERNATIONAL   Despite its location in the heart
of one of Europe's most gilt-edged neighborhoods, a few steps from the Bahnhofstrasse,
there's something artfully disheveled and happy-go-lucky about this restaurant. You'll
find a deliberately mismatched collection of tables and chairs. The menu is just as eclectic, with offerings derived from virtually everywhere. These include favorites from Thailand (including *tom kha kai,* made of chicken, coconut, and fiery spices), Japan (sushi,
sashimi, and miso soup), and Austria (Wiener schnitzel). Also available are tender steaks
and several kinds of saltwater and freshwater fish, including salmon, sole, and sea bass.
The setting is pleasant, and the place is a fine cost-conscious alternative to more formal
spots nearby. The site contains a worn, heavily trafficked bar area that's open daily from
9am till whenever the restaurant closes, and a nightclub that's separately recommended
(p. 130).

Pelikanstrasse 18. ✆ **044/225-33-33.** www.kaufleuten.com. Reservations recommended. Main courses
26F–58F. AE, DC, MC, V. Mon–Fri 11:30am–2pm; daily 7pm–1am (till 2am Fri–Sat). Tram: 6, 7, 11, or 13.

Restaurant Reithalle INTERNATIONAL   One of Zurich's most genuinely unpretentious restaurants occupies the battered premises of what was originally built as a stable
and horseback-riding rink. Cost-conscious locals frequent the Reithalle, which is set on
a small island in downtown Zurich, bordered by the Schanzengraben Creek and the Seil

Canal. It's at its most fun in midsummer when picnic tables are set up on the quiet, cobblestone inner courtyard, which is mobbed every day at lunch and dinner. The rest of the year, tables are moved into the severe-looking, heavily timbered interior that once sheltered horses and riding equipment from the city and weather outside. Menu items are hearty and generous and include beef curry, peppered paillard of veal, Iranian-style lamb stew, grilled squid with lemon sauce, and several kinds of pastas and salads. Saturday nights from 11pm till around 3am, the interior of this place becomes a disco, charging an entrance price of 15F per person (patrons of the restaurant enter free).

In the Theaterhaus Gessnerallee, Gessnerallee 8. (©) **044/212-07-66.** www.restaurant-reithalle.ch. Reservations not necessary. Main courses 20F–25F lunch, 23F–35F dinner. AE, DC, MC, V. Mon–Fri 11am–midnight; Sat–Sun 6pm–midnight. Tram: 2, 3, or 14.

Zeughauskeller ★ SWISS   This mammoth restaurant, dating from 1487, was once an arsenal; its vast dining room now seats 200. Large wooden chandeliers hang from cast-iron chains, and the walls are decorated with medieval halberds and illustrations of ancient Zurich noblemen. Generous portions of traditional and tasty Swiss dishes are served with steins of local beer. Owners Kurt Andreae and Willy Hammer say that patrons consume some 30 tons of potato salad a year. Hurlimann draft beer is poured from 1,000-liter barrels. Specialties, and excellent ones at that, include calves' liver, Wiener schnitzel, and regional sausages, such as *saucisson* of Neuchâtel. For 84F, you can order a meter-long sausage—enough to feed four hungry people. Service is quick and efficient.

Bahnhofstrasse 28a (near Paradeplatz). (©) **044/211-26-90.** www.zeughauskeller.ch. Reservations recommended. Main courses 13F–33F. AE, MC, V. Daily 11:30am–11pm. Tram: 2, 6, 7, 8, 9, 11, or 13.

ON THE RIGHT BANK
Very Expensive

Haus Zum Rüden ★★ SWISS/FRENCH   The Gothic room in this historic guild house dating from 1295 contains one of the best restaurants in the city. It's especially popular with foreign visitors, even though they often get a somewhat stuffy greeting from the staff. The spacious yet intimate dining room has a hardwood ceiling and stone walls decorated with medieval halberds and stag horns. The chef specializes in *cuisine du marché* (market-fresh cuisine). Foie gras sautéed with a salad makes a stunning opening, followed by salmon prepared in the style of Carcassonne or aromatic roast Scottish lamb delectably flavored with mustard grains. Other special dishes include grilled veal medallions with lemon olive oil or grilled filet of turbot with a grape-mustard sauce.

Limmatquai 42. (©) **044/261-95-66.** www.hauszumrueden.ch. Reservations required. Main courses 48F–76F; fixed-price menu 138F. AE, DC, MC, V. Mon–Fri noon–2pm and 6:30–9:30pm. Tram: 4 or 15.

Mesa ★★★ INTERNATIONAL   This is one of the grandest restaurants of Zurich, and one of the few in the country to receive a coveted Michelin star. Marcus G. Lindner, one of the most talented chefs of Switzerland, knows about balanced sauces and split-second timing, and we urge you to sample some of his intensely flavored dishes. His vibrant cuisine is as modern as tomorrow and highly innovative, and the menu changes every day—when you show up, expect to be surprised. We take delight in such dishes as mussels in a white-wine sauce, or else the marinated lamb cutlets with a saffron, mint, and herb sauce. Desserts are memorable, including a yogurt mousse with strawberry-and-basil ice cream. The chef aims to please and, indeed, he rarely disappoints.

Weinbergstrasse 75. ⓒ **043/321-75-75**. www.mesa-restaurant.ch. Reservations required. Main courses 52F–79F; fixed-price lunch 65F, dinner 142F. AE, DC, MC, V. Tues–Fri 11:45am–3pm; Tues–Sat 6:45pm–midnight. Tram: 7 or 15.

Expensive

À l'Opéra ★★ (Finds) CONTINENTAL   In 2007 a rising young artist, Tatiana Tiziana, slap-dashed, in fewer than 10 hysterical days, a sprawling series of neo-baroque *trompe l'oeil* murals onto this restaurant's ceiling. Since then, diners invariably look upward, between courses, at the world's most amusing take on Michelangelo's Sistine Chapel. Fish is particularly well prepared here within a culinary palette that changes monthly. Menus might focus heavily on, among others, fresh asparagus, fresh peaches, exotic mushrooms, and even ripe olives from Spain, Italy, or North Africa. Service is impeccable and laced with genuine sensitivity on the part of the staff. The best specialties include goat cheese pickled in olive oil on beet root–yogurt salad with slices of Serrano ham; a superb version of icy-cold tomato-olive soup; fried veal steak in an olive crust with lime sauce and slices of grilled zucchini; and filet of arctic char coated in pulverized olives with a sour cream and strawberry sauce.

In the Hotel Ambassador, Falkenstrasse 6. ⓒ **044/258-98-98**. Reservations recommended. Main courses 36F–57F; fixed-price menus 68F for 3 courses, 96F for 5 courses, 115F for 7 courses. AE, DC, MC, V. Daily 11:30am–2pm and 5:30–11:30pm. Tram: 4.

Blue Monkey THAI   It may seem incongruous to find a Thai restaurant, replete with Thai paintings and sculptures, and a staff that seems to have been trained in Bangkok, within this medieval-looking guildhall in the center of historic Zurich. But once you get here, you may appreciate its cultural ironies, and even be grateful for a break from too constant a diet of Teutonic food. The street-level venue, known as the Bistro, has tables that are a bit more crowded together, and prices that are a bit lower, than the setting upstairs (the restaurant), where there's a bit more privacy (theoretically at least), better service, and greater attention to detail. Menu items on either level include four different kinds of curry (red, brown, green, and yellow) to accompany, among others, pork, chicken, tofu, or fish. Delectable specialties include roasted duck breast in red curry and coconut milk, or grilled marinated beef with lemon grass and a chili and coriander sauce.

Stüssihofstatt 3. ⓒ **044/261-76-18**. www.kramergastronomie.ch. Reservations recommended. Main courses bistro 27F–39F, restaurant 32F–49F. AE, DC, MC, V. Mon–Fri 11am–2pm; daily 6–11:30pm. Tram: 4 or 15.

Kronenhalle ★ SWISS/FRENCH   This is one of Zurich's most famous restaurants, and it also serves some of the best cuisine. The restaurant is in a five-story, gray Biedermeier building with gold crowns above the six windows on the first floor. The decor includes original paintings by Klee, Chagall, Matisse, Miró, Kandinsky, Braque, Bonnard, and Picasso. Each was acquired, inexpensively, by the restaurant's early-20th-century founder and reigning matriarch. Regional specialties are served on a trolley and include smoked pork with lentils and *bollito misto* (boiled beef, chicken, sausage, and tongue). For a main dish, try shredded calves' liver with *rösti* or filet of sole baked with olives and tomatoes. You may also enjoy *bündnerfleisch*—thinly sliced, smoked, dried beef. This is one of the most outstanding and consistently reliable restaurants in Zurich. In the Kronenhalle Bar the specialty is the Ladykiller.

Rämistrasse 4. ⓒ **044/262-99-00**. www.kronenhalle.com. Reservations required. Main courses 34F–55F. AE, DC, MC, V. Daily noon–midnight. Closed Dec 24. Tram: 2, 4, 5, 9, 11, or 15.

Rosaly's ★ SWISS/INTERNATIONAL   Set about a block from the Bellevueplatz and the clamor of its tram junctions, this restaurant occupies what looks like a mountain chalet that's incongruously perched on a narrow alleyway amid the midtown urban sprawl. There's a bar (p. 131) on the premises—a half-moon-shaped affair whose clients spill out into the dining room as the evening gets late—but the real appeal here is the reasonably priced, well-prepared food. Part of its allure lies in the hints of California you may detect in the cuisine and the relaxed charm of the staff. (The owner named the restaurant after one he once visited in San Francisco.) The chef here is particularly proud of his butter-braised calves' liver, braised strips of veal prepared "Zurich style" in cream sauce, and a wide range of salad, vegetarian, and fish dishes. A particularly well-received side dish is Rosaly's Rice, prepared with herbs and cheese. Consider dining at one of the geranium-flanked tables lined up along the alleyway outside, weather permitting.

Freieckgasse 7. ℂ **044/261-44-30.** www.rosalys.ch. Reservations recommended. Main courses 26F–35F. AE, MC, V. Mon–Thurs 11:30am–midnight; Fri 11:30am–1am; Sat 4pm–1am; Sun 10am–midnight. Tram: 2, 4, 7, 9, 11, or 13.

Moderate

Fischstube Zürichhorn (Kids) SWISS   Ideal on a summer evening, this seafood restaurant with outdoor tables is built on pilings over the lake. The scenery, service, and cuisine make it a worthy choice if the weather is balmy. We recommend the lake trout, filet of Dover sole Champs-Elysées, grilled lobster with curry butter, and lake fish sautéed in butter and served with market-fresh vegetables. The cuisine here has a sprightly, original taste, flavored with a dash of this or a dab of that. The chefs rely on the sound principles of simplicity and accurate timing in all their dishes, and the servings are generous. Kids delight at sitting outside overlooking the lake and even like the vegetables cooked here since they're so fresh and delectably prepared.

Bellerivestrasse 160. ℂ **044/422-25-20.** www.fischstube.ch. Reservations required. Main courses 18F–45F; fixed-price lunch 39F. AE, MC, V. Daily 11am–11pm. Closed late Sept to Easter. Tram: 2 or 4.

Iroquois INTERNATIONAL   The Swiss have never really gone gaga over American-style bars and grills, but of the several that exist within Zurich, this is the busiest and most popular. Always crowded (and sometimes mobbed), it's a neighborhood tavern whose rough edges and spilled beer add to its image as a rough-and-ready burger-and-fajitas joint that just happens to have a distinctive Swiss accent. Come here for sports TV and the possibility of striking up a neighborhood friendship. The house cocktail is an Iroquois, made with vodka, Galliano, *maracuja* (star fruit), and orange juice. If you come with a group that tends to get the munchies, consider a Surfer's Platter prepared for multiple diners, with chicken wings, tortilla chips, quesadillas, and guacamole. Other food choices include ostrich-meat fajitas, burritos, chicken chili burgers, and turkey tacos. Don't expect grandeur, as virtually everything and everyone here is aggressively unpretentious.

Seefeldstrasse 120. ℂ **044/383-70-77.** www.iroquois.ch. Reservations not necessary. Main courses 16F–32F. AE, DC, MC, V. Daily 11am–2pm and 6–10pm. Bar daily 5pm–midnight. Tram: 2 or 4.

Le Dézaley ★ (Finds) SWISS/FRENCH   Named after a remote corner of the Vaud region of French-speaking Switzerland, this restaurant celebrates the food and traditions of the countryside north of Lake Geneva. Many of the regular clients speak French as they dine on an array of fondues (cheese, chinoise, and bourguignon) or other dishes such as minced liver, veal kidneys with *rösti,* pork sausages flavored with leeks, and shredded veal Zurich style. The chefs are more obsessed with flavor than novelty, and they certainly succeed. Many wines from the Dézaley region, some rather rare, are offered. The large, wood-paneled dining room is set in a pair of interconnected houses originally built during the late 13th century. In summer you can dine in a little garden out back. The restaurant is located close to the Grossmünster church.

Römergasse 7–9. ✆ **044/251-61-29.** www.le-dezaley.ch. Reservations recommended. Main courses 22F–40F; fondues 25F–43F. AE, DC, MC, V. Mon–Sat 11:30am–2pm and 6pm–midnight. Tram: 4 or 15.

Mère Catherine PROVENÇAL/FRENCH This small courtyard restaurant nestled among the back streets of Old Town offers quiet cafe tables, ivy, and, at times, a lot of sun. Anybody who knows backstreet Paris or a small town in France will feel at home here. Unpretentious French food, especially Provençal bistro fare, is served here. Fresh sea fish is a feature, but the specials change every day. You can always find various meatless platters on the menu. *Salade paysanne* with a Roquefort sauce is the most popular appetizer, and you can usually order snails *en brioche* or, for something more exotic, terrine of quail. The dishes are painstakingly prepared and usually get diners salivating in no time flat. You may want to arrive before your reservations to have an aperitif at the Bar Philosophe, the cozy marble bar next to the restaurant.

Nägelihof 3. ✆ **044/250-59-40.** www.commercio.ch. Reservations required. Main courses 24F–45F. MC, V. Daily 11:30am–2:30pm and 6–11:30pm. Tram: 4 or 15.

Restaurant Movie AMERICAN/INTERNATIONAL This is one of the most consistently popular theme restaurants in Zurich. Hip, artful, and fun, and positioned adjacent to one of the city's biggest movie theater complexes, it boasts a campy faux-Hollywood decor that includes a gilded version of the Statue of Liberty, industrial-style ventilation tubes, and the kind of lighting fixtures you'd expect on the original soundstage of *Gone With the Wind.* Even the place mats are emblazoned with publicity stills from about-to-be-screened American movies, with menus printed on round aluminum canisters that traditionally hold a reel of celluloid. Many of the dishes are named after movies and actors. All of this would be hopelessly corny if the food weren't genuinely well prepared and the place packed, especially during the dinner and after-dinner bar hour. Menus include pastas, sandwiches, salads, quesadillas, fajitas, and grills. Don't overlook the bar area at this place as a California-inspired (and very popular) nightlife option. Outfitted with a black-and-gold ancient Egyptian theme, it has tables spilling out onto the Beattenplatz and dance music that actually encourages you to rock 'n' roll.

Bahnhofquai 7, at Beattenplatz. ✆ **044/211-66-77.** www.dinner.ch. Reservations not necessary. Main courses 27F–40F. AE, MC, V. Daily 11:30am–midnight. Tram: 6 or 10.

Seidenspinner (Silk Spinner) ★ Finds ORGANIC CONTINENTAL One of the city's most stylish and offbeat restaurants occupies a small but high-ceilinged dining room near Helvetiaplatz. You'll find a roster of glass mosaics, enormous bouquets of artfully arranged flowers, and elaborate table settings. The list of food options here is limited but choice, often with no more than four appetizers, four main courses, and four desserts offered for consumption on any given evening. All ingredients are organic and seasonal, listed on an oft-changing handwritten menu, and "spun" into a frequently changing array of dishes likely to include elaborate salads; a "trio" of soups served within three espresso cups (they are likely to include potato leek soup, creamy red-beet soup, and a carrot-with-orange soup); homemade ravioli stuffed with ricotta and strips of organic salmon; succulent pastas; roasted filet of lamb served with olives and roasted potatoes; and stroganoff of beef.

Ankerstrasse 120. © **044/241-07-00.** www.seidenspinner.ch. Reservations recommended. Main courses 45F–55F. AE, DC, MC, V. Lunch Wed 11:30am–2pm; dinner Tues–Sat 6–10:30pm. Bus: 31.

Toscano ITALIAN   Cozy and well respected for fair prices and well-prepared Italian food, this is the kind of restaurant where local office workers go for a celebratory meal, whenever they're in the neighborhood late after work with a hankering for Mediterranean flavors and memories. It offers a pair of dining rooms, one at street level, the other immediately upstairs, each sheathed in medium-brown wood paneling, with tables draped in starched white linens. Established in 2000, it offers menu items that include three kinds of carpaccio (beef, tuna, and freshwater lake fish); skewers of grilled octopus; mussels steamed with tomatoes, garlic, and white wine; grilled seawolf or dorado with fresh vegetables; and many different kinds of pasta.

Schmidgasse 3. © **044/261-54-50.** www.ristorante-toscano.ch. Reservations recommended Fri–Sat nights. Main courses 17F–43F. AE, DC, MC, V. Mon–Fri noon–3pm and 6–10pm; Sat 6pm–midnight. Tram: 4 or 13.

SOUTH OF THE CENTER

Petermann's Kunststuben ★★★ CONTINENTAL   Arguably this is the best restaurant in Switzerland. Relentlessly elegant, but with a staff that's more hip and alert than you may expect, it lies 10km (6 miles) south of Zurich in the hamlet of Küsnacht, near Rapperswil, within a house whose date of construction (1873) is marked above a wood-burning stove in the dining room.

Most of the year, the restaurant accommodates only 45 diners, but in summer an outdoor terrace ringed with shrubs and flowers adds another 40 seats. You can enjoy such inventive dishes as a "cigar" of foie gras with black truffles and sauterne aspic, roasted duck with honey-lemon sauce, lobster with a purée of celery, lobster-studded potato salad with a leek-based cream sauce, stuffed squid with a confit of fennel, and young hen stuffed with shrimp. Dessert may include a gratin of wild strawberries with cannelloni stuffed with almond paste. You'll find almost anything you order irresistible within a setting that some of the most seasoned and jaded diners in the world have found utterly charming.

Seestrasse 160, Küsnacht. © **044/910-07-15.** www.kunststuben.com. Reservations required. Main courses 58F–85F; fixed-price menus 78F–135F. AE, DC, MC, V. Tues–Sat noon–2pm and 7pm–midnight. Closed 2 weeks in Feb and 2 weeks in Aug. Take a taxi or the train from Zurich's Hauptbahnhof to Küsnacht, then walk for 5 min.

NORTH OF CENTER

Restaurant Spice/Brasserie Quadrino ★★★ PACIFIC RIM/INTERNATIONAL   This pair of likable restaurants lies about 4km (2½ miles) north of Zurich's main railway station, within an apartment complex whose units are often rented out to European families with children or to business travelers for short-term stays. The gastronomic centerpiece is the Restaurant Spice, whose minimalist decor focuses on a large boulder artfully positioned in an otherwise simple setting with a maximum emphasis on the feng shui aspects of its position. Expect a cultivated, fussed-over menu that includes duck liver with honey sauce; fried halibut with salad and passion-fruit vinaigrette; and platters piled high with a combination of filet steak and ragout of beef in a spice marinade. The chef is especially proud of his rack of venison stuffed with apricots that is served with Brazilian tonga beans, onions, and a sauce concocted from port wine with hints of coffee and chocolate.

Prices are less expensive and service rituals a lot less elaborate in the Brasserie, where pastas, salads, grilled meats, and seafood platters are the norm. Seating in the Brasserie includes small, slightly claustrophobic tables for two, as well as sprawling communal tables where strangers sometimes get acquainted with strangers.

In the Rigiblick Apartment Hotel, Germaniastrasse 99. © 043/255-1570. www.restaurantrigiblick.ch. Restaurant set menus 62F–158F, main courses 55F–65F; brasserie set menus 24F–26F, main courses 18F–20F. AE, DC, MC, V. Restaurant Tues–Sat 11:30am–2pm and 6–10pm. Brasserie Tues–Sat 9am–midnight. Tram: 9 or 10.

WEST OF THE CENTER

Caduff's Wine Loft ★ (Finds CONTINENTAL   Set within a hilly residential neighborhood 3km (2 miles) west of Zurich's center, this hip and stylish restaurant occupies what was originally, from around 1900, an industrial warehouse. Today, it's a minimalist-chic bastion of Pan-European charm, with sleek furniture, sophisticated lighting, and one of the most appealing wine cellars in Zurich. Don't expect much of a view, since the windows look out on the somewhat drab neighborhood that surrounds the place. A seasonally changing menu reflects very fresh ingredients. The best examples include platters of shrimp and scallops drizzled with saffron sauce and served with fresh asparagus; a mixed grill that includes portions of calves' liver, veal, beef, and chicken; house-made ravioli stuffed with a mixture of tomatoes and basil; medallions of veal served with saffron-flavored risotto and rosemary; turbot in champagne sauce; and filets of venison with port-wine sauce and ricotta-flavored gnocchi.

Kanzleistrasse 126, Unit 4. © 044/240-22-55. www.wineloft.ch. Reservations recommended. Main courses 28F–60F; fixed-price menus 82F–130F. AE, DC, MC, V. Mon–Fri 11:30am–2:30pm and 6pm–midnight; Sat 5pm–midnight. Bus: 32. Tram: 3 or 9.

LaSalle ★ INTERNATIONAL   One of the most hip and sought-after restaurants in Zurich today is housed within a severe-looking factory built during the 19th century to manufacture boats and lake cruisers. Today it's the centerpiece of an urban renewal known as Zurich-West. The restaurant is enclosed within an enormous but delicate-looking high-tech box of steel beams and Plexiglas, all of it suspended from the building's ceiling and redbrick walls. Centered within the area's core is a massive blown-glass (Murano) chandelier. Menu items seem deceptively simple when listed on the stark-white menu, and except for an occasional gaffe, are incredibly flavor-filled and artful upon delivery. Examples include vitello tonnato (filets of veal with Italian-style tuna sauce); homemade terrine; thinly sliced veal liver Provençal; filets of pikeperch with spinach and coconut milk; cannelloni with ricotta, spinach, and a truffle-flavored cream sauce; and a vegetarian version of tortilla with guacamole and sour cream. There are also daily variations of fish, vegetarian dishes, and raviolis of the day.

Schiffbaustrasse 4. © 044/258-70-71. www.lasalle-restaurant.ch. Reservations necessary. Main courses 28F–55F. AE, DC, MC, V. Mon–Fri 11:30am–2pm and 5–11pm; Sat–Sun 5:30–10:45pm. Closed Sun July–Aug. Tram: 4 or 13.

CAFES

Café/Bar Odéon   This legendary and somewhat schmaltzy 1912 bohemian landmark is a popular singles and gay hangout in the evening. Lenin came here during World War I to make such pronouncements as, "The neutrality of Switzerland is a bourgeois fraud and means submission to the imperialist war." Thornton Wilder also sloshed down a few here, as did Mussolini and Mata Hari. The intimate, Art Nouveau cafe has banquettes and cubbyholes. It also sports a curved bar and many sidewalk tables.

Limmatquai 2. ℂ **044/251-16-50.** www.odeon.ch. Light meals 8.50F–26F; coffee 4F–6F. No credit cards. Mon–Thurs 6:30am–2:30am; Fri–Sat 7am–4:30am; Sun 9am–2:30am.

Café Schober   One of the most select cafes in Zurich is located in Zum grossen Erker (the Great Alcove), a building dating from 1314 that was turned into a confectionery and coffee shop by Theodor Schober after 1875. When the last Schober retired, the well-known meeting place was bought and renovated by Teuscher, the epicurean name brand in chocolates. The old-fashioned cafe, tastefully renovated in 2007, with its beautiful lighting fixtures and molded ceilings, is known for its hot chocolate. It also offers an array of homemade pastries, cakes, and ice cream.

Napfgasse 4. ℂ **044/251-80-60.** www.cafe-conditorei-schober.ch. Hot chocolate 10F. No credit cards. Mon–Fri 8am–6:30pm; Sat 8am–5:30pm; Sun 10am–5:30pm.

A PASTRY SHOP

Confiserie Sprüngli   This old-fashioned pastry shop on Bahnhofstrasse, founded in 1836, is comparable to the legendary Demel in Vienna. Many Zurichers remember this place fondly from their childhood. A variety of pastries and chocolates are sold on the ground floor. The famous Lindt chocolates and the house specialties are about the best you'll ever find. Fixed-price lunches, tea, and coffee are also available. Many old-time Zurichers journey across town for a cup of hot chocolate here.

Am Paradeplatz. ℂ **044/224-46-15.** www.confiserie-spruengli.ch. Fixed-price lunch 22F–29F; tea or coffee from 4F. AE, DC, MC, V. Mon–Fri 7am–6:30pm; Sat 8am–6pm.

5 ATTRACTIONS

Zurich has a rich history and many reminders of its past. There are 20 museums, nearly 100 galleries, and 24 archives (including one devoted to Thomas Mann). The historic buildings, religious monuments, and quays are worth discovering, as are the well-preserved homes of rich burghers, lovely parks, and gardens. Even if you don't have time to visit all those museums and galleries, a walk along the quays of Zurich shouldn't be missed.

You can also visit Uetliberg, southwest of Zurich, the northernmost peak in the Albis ridge (see "Side Trips from Zurich," later in this chapter).

(Finds)   An Open Sesame & Bargain Pass

Inaugurated in 2003, the ZurichCARD offers 50% reduction on public transportation, free visits to 43 museums, reduced prices at the zoo, and a welcome drink at more than two dozen restaurants. The pass is widely available, sold at such outlets as the Zurich Main Rail Station, the airport, and at certain hotels. It costs 19F for 24 hours or 38F for 72 hours.

Zurich Street Parade

You'll either flock to or flee from this bash, depending on your personality and music preferences. The Zurich Street Parade is one massive rave/techno dance party, filling the city streets for 1 day and night each August in an outdoor, over-the-top party. The event, meant to symbolize love, peace, freedom, generosity, and tolerance, started in 1992 with 2,000 partyers and has mushroomed to attract more than half a million international visitors. Modeled after Berlin's Loveparade, the Zurich Street Parade kicks off on a Saturday in early August with a parade of floats (lovemobiles) blaring their way along city streets, each with its own dance and music theme. In three words—exuberant, energetic, and fun. And just as the party starts winding down (around 3am, when other, more bacchanalian parties move into private homes and hotel rooms), special cleaning vans sweep and clean the streets, leaving the town spotless and perfect by the next day—only in Switzerland. If this is your thing, book early, or plan to stay in a nearby city such as Basel or Lucerne (both 1 hr. away by train). If this sounds like your biggest nightmare, stay away, and if it sounds like your thing, come in and play. For dates and details, visit the Street Parade's official website (www.streetparade.ch).

Less raucous and a bit more historical and dignified is Zurich's Sechsenlauten party, conducted on the third Monday of April. With origins going back to the mid-19th century, and centering around the Sechsenlauterplatz, near Zurich's opera house, the party celebrates the end of winter with as many pagan allegories as reasonably possible. It's sponsored by an association of Zurich's remaining guilds, and culminates in a parade and the "burning of the snowman," which symbolizes, perhaps somewhat unsubtly, the melting of the ice that can grip the human heart, the rebirth of life after a barren period of cold, and the beginning of spring.

—Caroline Sieg

ZURICH

5

SUGGESTED ZURICH ITINERARIES

SUGGESTED ZURICH ITINERARIES

IF YOU HAVE 1 DAY

Take **"Walking Tour 1: Zurich's Bahnhofstrasse"** (p. 118) to Lake Zurich, where you can board a steamer for a 1½-hour ride on the lake. Return to shore and visit either the **Kunsthaus Museum** or the **Landesmuseum.** In late afternoon take **"Walking Tour 2: Zurich's Altstadt"** (p. 120), along the famous quays of Zurich and through Old Town, where you might have a raclette dinner in an old tavern.

IF YOU HAVE 2 DAYS

Spend the first day as suggested above. On the morning of the second day, visit **Fraumünster** or **Grossmünster,** the two most famous churches of Zurich. Enjoy lunch in a typical Zurich cafe. In the afternoon leave Zurich for **Uetliberg** for a panoramic view of the Alps and the city. Have a beer and listen to the oompah band at the **Bierhalle Wolf** in the evening.

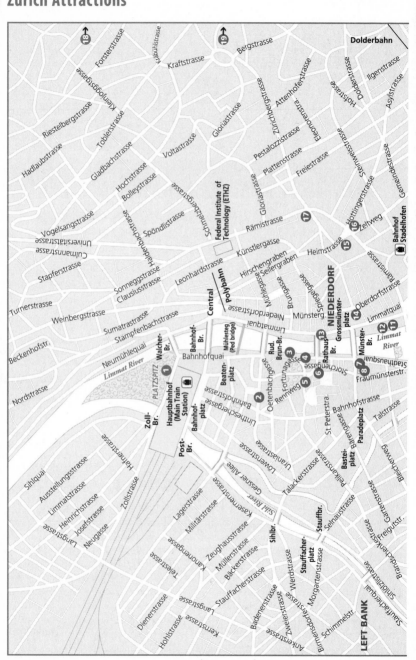

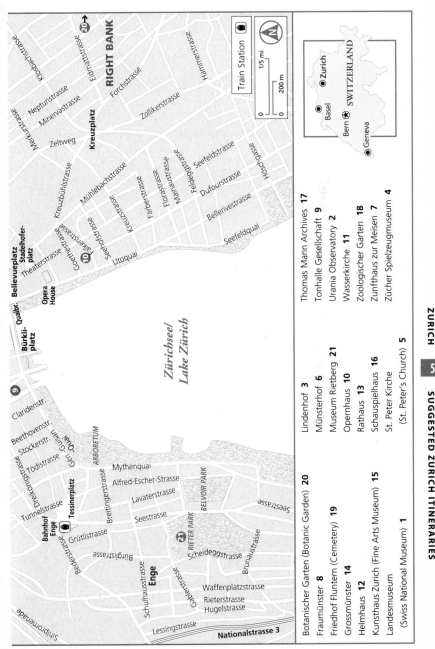

ZURICH

5 SUGGESTED ZURICH ITINERARIES

Botanischer Garten (Botanic Garden) **20**
Fraumünster **8**
Friedhof Fluntern (Cemetery) **19**
Grossmünster **14**
Helmhaus **12**
Kunsthaus Zurich (Fine Arts Museum) **15**
Landesmuseum
(Swiss National Museum) **1**

Lindenhof **3**
Münsterhof **6**
Museum Rietberg **21**
Opernhaus **10**
Rathaus **13**
Schauspielhaus **16**
St. Peter Kirche
(St. Peter's Church) **5**

Thomas Mann Archives **17**
Tonhalle Gesellschaft **9**
Urania Observatory **2**
Wasserkirche **11**
Zoologischer Garten **18**
Zunfthaus zur Meisen **7**
Zücher Spielzeugmuseum **4**

Spend the first 2 days as outlined above. On the third day, see all the attractions you've missed before, including two museums: the **Rietberg,** with its great non-European art collection, and the **Bührle,** with its collection of modern art. Visit the **Botanischer Garten (Botanic Garden)** and the **zoo** in the afternoon, if time remains.

Spend the first 3 days as outlined above. On the morning of the fourth day, go to **Winterthur,** only a 25-minute ride from Zurich, to see its many attractions, including the Museum Oskar Reinhart, the Kunstmuseum, and the Schloss Kyburg.

THE TOP ATTRACTIONS

The **quays of Zurich** ★★, with their promenades, are among the city's most popular attractions. They're made for walking. The most famous is **Limmatquai,** in the center of Zurich. It begins at the Bahnhof Bridge and extends east to the Rathaus (town hall) and beyond. Many of the quays have lovely gardens. **Uto Quai** is the major promenade along Zurichsee (Lake Zurich), running from Badeanstalt Uto Quai (a swimming pool) to Bellevueplatz and Quaibrücke. The pool is open daily from 8am to 7pm. If you stroll as far as **Mythenquai,** you'll be following the lake along its western shore and out into the countryside.

Fraumünster   This church, with its slender, blue spire, is on the left bank overlooking the former pig market, Münsterhof. Münsterhof is one of the historic old squares of Zurich and is well worth a visit. A Benedictine abbey was founded at the site in 853 by Emperor Ludwig (Louis the German), the grandson of Charlemagne. His daughter became the first abbess. The present church dates from the 13th and 14th centuries, but the crypt of the old abbey church is preserved in the undercroft.

The chief attractions of Fraumünster are five **stained-glass windows** ★—each with its own color theme—designed by Marc Chagall in 1970. They are best seen in bright morning light. The Fraumünster is also celebrated for its elaborate organ. The basilica has three aisles; the nave is in the Gothic style.

From Fraumünster you can cross the Münsterbrücke, an 1838 bridge that leads to Grossmünster. On the bridge is a statue of Burgomaster Waldmann, who was beheaded in 1489 when his political enemies seized power. During his rule the city gained influence over much of the surrounding lands.

Fraumünsterstrasse. ✆ **044/211-41-00.** www.fraumuenster.ch. Free admission. May–Sept Mon–Sat 9am–noon, daily 2–6pm; Oct and Mar–Apr Mon–Sat 10am–noon, daily 2–5pm; Nov–Feb Mon–Sat 10am–noon, daily 2–4pm. Tram: 4 to City Hall.

Grossmünster   This Romanesque and Gothic cathedral was, according to legend, founded by Charlemagne, whose horse bowed down on the spot marking the graves of three early Christian martyrs. The cathedral has two three-story towers and is situated on a terrace above Limmatquai, on the right bank. Despite the legend, construction actually began in 1090 and additions were made until the early 14th century. The choir contains stained-glass windows completed in 1932 by Augusto Giacometti. (Augusto is not to be confused with his more celebrated uncle, Alberto Giacometti, the famous Swiss abstract artist.) In the crypt is a weather-beaten, 15th-century statue of Charlemagne, a copy of which crowns the south tower.

The cathedral is dedicated to the patron saints of Zurich: Felix, Regula, and Exuperantius. In the 3rd century the three martyrs attempted to convert the citizens of Turicum (the original name for Zurich) to Christianity. The governor, according to legend, had them plunged into boiling oil and forced to drink molten lead. The trio refused to renounce their faith and were beheaded. Miraculously, they still had enough energy to pick up their heads and climb to the top of a hill (the present site of the cathedral), where they dug their own graves and then interred themselves. The seal of Zurich honors these saints, depicting them carrying their heads under their arms. The remains of the saints are said to rest in one of the chapels of the *Münster* (cathedral).

The cathedral was once the parish church of Huldrych Zwingli, one of the great leaders of the Reformation. He urged priests to take wives (he himself had married) and attacked the "worship of images" and the Roman Catholic sacrament of mass. In 1531 Zwingli was killed in a religious war at Kappel. The hangman quartered his body and soldiers burned the pieces with dung. The site of his execution is marked with an inscription: "They may kill the body but not the soul." In accordance with Zwingli's beliefs, Zurich's Grossmünster is austere, stripped of the heavy ornamentation you'll find in the cathedrals of Italy. The view from the towers is impressive.

Grossmünsterplatz. ℭ **044/252-59-49.** www.grossmuenster.ch. Free admission to cathedral; towers 2F. Cathedral Mar 15–Oct daily 9am–6pm; Nov–Mar 14 daily 10am–4pm. Towers (weather permitting) Mar–Oct daily 9am–6pm; Nov–Feb Sat–Sun 10am–4pm. Tram: 4.

Kunsthaus Zürich (Fine Arts Museum) ★★ One of the most important art museums in Europe, the Kunsthaus Zürich is devoted mainly to the 19th and 20th centuries, although the range of paintings and sculpture reaches back to antiquity. The museum was founded in Victorian times and was overhauled in 1976. Today it's one of the most modern and sophisticated museums in the world, both in its lighting and its display of art.

Our favorite exhibits include Rodin's *Gate of Hell,* near the entrance, and the Giacometti wing, showing the development of this Swiss-born artist. The collection of modern art includes works by all the greats—Bonnard, Braque, Chagall, Lipschitz, Marini, Mondrian, Picasso, and Rouault. The gallery owns the largest collection of works by the Norwegian artist Edvard Munch outside of Oslo. Two old masters, Rubens and Rembrandt, are also represented. To brighten a rainy day, come see the pictures by Cézanne, Degas, Monet, Toulouse-Lautrec, and Utrillo.

Heimplatz 1. ℭ **044/253-84-84.** www.kunsthaus.ch. Admission 18F adults, 12F seniors and students, free for children 16 and under; special exhibitions 16F adults, 10F children. Tues 10am–6pm; Wed–Fri 10am–8pm; Sat–Sun 10am–6pm. Tram: 3 (marked KLUSPLATZ).

Landesmuseum (Swiss National Museum) ★★★ This museum offers an epic survey of the culture and history of the Swiss people. Its collection, housed in a feudal-looking, 19th-century building behind the Zurich Hauptbahnhof, contains works of religious art, including 16th-century stained glass from the Tanikon Convent and frescoes from the church of Mustair. Some of the Carolingian art dates from the 9th century. The altarpieces are carved, painted, and gilded.

The prehistoric section is also exceptional. Some of the artifacts are from the 4th millennium B.C. There's a large display of Roman clothing, medieval silverware, 14th-century drinking bowls, and 17th-century china, as well as painted furniture, costumes, and dollhouses of various periods. A display of weapons and armor shows the methods of Swiss warfare from 800 to 1800. There's also an exhibit tracing Swiss clock making from the 16th to the 18th centuries.

Special exhibitions are presented twice annually, lasting between 3 and 6 months. Themes are always different; a recent one was devoted to Swiss fashion design.

Museumstrasse 2. ℂ **044/218-65-11.** www.musee-suisse.com. Admission 10F, 8F students and seniors. Tues–Sun 10am–5pm (until 7pm Thurs). Tram: 3, 4, 5, 11, 13, or 14.

Museum Rietberg ★ Finds A real discovery, the neoclassical Villa Wesendonck, set in the lush Rieter-Park overlooking Zurich, was once occupied by Richard Wagner, who wrote his *Wesendonck Songs* to the lady of the manor. Today that mansion and an adjoining one, Park-Villa Rieter, have been converted into an exquisite museum that showcases Asian, African, and other non-European art. The collection grew from an initial trove collected by Baron von der Heyt. The collection is rich in highly acclaimed exhibits of Japanese, Chinese, and Indian drawings and paintings, including Bodhisattvas from India, China, Tibet, and Nepal. Here you can enjoy viewing everything from Tibetan bronzes to jade Chinese funeral art, even the bizarre Japanese Noh masks. The location of the museum is along Seestrasse, 1.8km (1 mile) south of the center.

Gablerstrasse 15, Kreis 2. ℂ **044/206-31-31.** www.rietberg.ch. Admission 12F adults, 10F students and children; special exhibitions 12F–16F. Fri–Tues 10am–5pm; Wed–Thurs 10am–8pm. Tram: 7.

MORE ATTRACTIONS

Botanischer Garten (Botanic Garden) ★ The gardens contain 15,000 living species, including some rare specimens from New Caledonia and southwest Africa. The herbarium contains three million plants. The gardens, owned by the University of Zurich, were laid out on the site of a former private villa.

Universität Zurich, Zollikerstrasse 107. ℂ **044/634-84-61.** www.bguz.uzh.ch. Free admission. Park Mar–Sept Mon–Fri 7am–7pm, Sat–Sun 8am–6pm; Oct–Feb Mon–Fri 8am–6pm, Sat–Sun 8am–5pm. Greenhouses daily 9:30–11:30am and 1–4pm. Tram: 11 to Hegibachplatz, or 2 or 4 to Höschgasse. Bus: 33 to Botanischer Garten.

Friedhof Fluntern (Fluntern Cemetery) James Joyce, the author of *Ulysses,* lived in Zurich from 1915 to 1919, at Universitätsstrasse 38. In 1941 he returned to Zurich from Paris, only a month before his death. Near his tomb is a statue depicting the great Irish writer sitting cross-legged with a book in his hand. Elias Canetti, winner of the Nobel Prize for literature in 1981, died in August 1994; his grave lies to the left of Joyce's. The grave of Johanna Spiri (1827–1901), who wrote the famous story *Heidi,* is in the Central Cemetery.

Zürichberg district. Free admission. May–Aug daily 7am–8pm; Mar–Apr and Sept–Oct daily 7am–7pm; Nov–Feb daily 8am–5pm. Tram: 6 to zoo.

St. Peter Kirche (St. Peter's Church) Built in the 13th century, St. Peter's—on the left bank south of Lindenhof—is the oldest church in Zurich. It has the largest clock face in Europe: 9m (30 ft.) in diameter; the minute hand alone is almost 4m (13 ft.) long. Inside, the choir is Romanesque, but the three-aisle nave is baroque.

St. Peterhofstatt 1. ℂ **044/211-25-88.** www.st-peter-zh.ch. Free admission. Mon–Fri 8am–6pm; Sat 9am–4pm; Sun noon–5pm.

Thomas Mann Archives Thomas Mann, the German writer who won the Nobel Prize for literature in 1929 for such works as *Death in Venice* and *The Magic Mountain,* died in Kilchberg, near Zurich, in 1955. An opponent of the Nazi regime, he had lived outside Germany after 1933—in the United States and Switzerland during most of the period. The archives, located next to the university, contain manuscripts and mementos.

Urania Observatory   The observatory is halfway between Bahnhofstrasse and the Limmat River on Uraniastrasse. On clear days you can look through the telescope, while on bad days the observatory doesn't open. Call in advance to find out. The observatory has been at this site since 1907. Because of its central location, you have a panoramic view not only of Zurich but also of the lake and the distant Alps. You can see the stars, planets, and galaxy through a big Zeiss telescope that weighs 20 tons. This observatory is the site of an unusual and highly popular bar, the Jules Verne Bar (p. 131).

Uraniastrasse 9. ℂ **044/211-65-23.** www.urania-sternwarte.ch. Admission 15F adults, 10F children. Apr–Sept Tues–Sat noon–4pm and 7–11pm; Oct–Mar Tues–Sat noon–4pm and 6–9pm. Tram: 7, 11, or 13.

Zunfthaus zur Meisen   Across the bridge from the Wasserkirche is one of the city's famous old guildhalls. It has a wrought-iron gatehouse that opens onto Münsterhof. Dating from 1752, it's a branch museum of the overstuffed Swiss National Museum. It's devoted mainly to 18th-century Swiss ceramics, the porcelain of Zurich, and several antiques. The beauty of the stuccoed rooms competes with the exhibits.

Münsterhof 20. ℂ **044/211-21-44.** www.zunfthaus-zur-meisen.ch. Admission 3F adults, free for children 15 and under. Tues–Sun 10:30am–5pm. Closed holidays. Tram: 3.

ESPECIALLY FOR KIDS

There are 80 playgrounds in Zurich. For the one nearest your hotel, ask either at your hotel or at the local tourist office (see "Visitor Information," p. 87). Most boat trips (see "Organized Tours," p. 123) leave from the end of Bahnhofstrasse on the right. You may also combine a train ride with a trip to an attraction outside Zurich.

Select theaters also present changing programs for children. Ask at the tourist office or get a copy of *Zurich Weekly Official,* available at most newsstands.

Several stores may be fun spots to visit with your kids. Artfully old-fashioned is **Pastorini,** Weinplatz 3 (ℂ **044/228-70-70;** www.pastorini.ch), which specializes in wooden toys—the kind your parents might have played with—and is one of the biggest toy stores in Zurich, spread over five floors.

The best-stocked children's bookstore in Switzerland is **Kinderbuchladen Zurich,** Oberdorfstrasse 32 (ℂ **044/265-30-00;** www.kinderbuchladen.ch), which carries many English-language books.

In addition, the following two attractions may be of special interest to children:

Zoologischer Garten (Zoological Garden) ★   One of the best-known zoos in Europe, Zurich's Zoological Garden contains some 2,200 animals of about 260 species. It also has an aquarium and an open-air aviary. You can visit the Africa house, the ape house, and the terrariums, along with the elephant house and the giant-tortoise house. There are special enclosures for red pandas, otters, and snow leopards, and a house for clouded leopards, tigers, Amur leopards, and Indian lions. The zoo contains a replica of a tropical rainforest, lodged within a state-of-the-art building which successfully replicates the temperatures, light levels, and humidity of Madagascar. This added attraction has become one of the most frequently visited attractions in Zurich, and one of the prides of the zoo itself.

Zürichbergstrasse 221. ℂ **044/254-25-00.** www.zoo.ch. Admission 22F adults, 11F children 6–12, free for children 5 and under. Mar–Oct daily 9am–6pm; Nov–Feb daily 9am–5pm. Tram: 6 from the Hauptbahnhof; the zoo is in the eastern sector of the city, called Zürichberg, on a wooded hill.

ZURICH

5

ATTRACTIONS

Frommer's Favorite Zurich Experiences

Shopping along Bahnhofstrasse It has been called the most beautiful shopping street in the world, and perhaps it is. Built a century ago on the site of the ancient moat, it's a stroller's paradise. In stores on both sides of the street is some of the world's greatest merchandise.

Taking a Boat Trip on Lake Zurich or along the Limmat River On a sunny day, this is the best way to spend time in Zurich. Cruises on one of Europe's most beautiful lakes last 1½ to 4 hours. Boats depart from Bürkliplatz, the lake end of Bahnhofstrasse.

Visiting Uetliberg If the day is sunny, you can take an electric train to this parklike, 840m (2,755-ft.) hill. Once here, you can wander about, enjoying the natural surroundings and scenic vistas at every turn. It's best to take a picnic.

Biking & Swimming on the Lake In July and August, one of the most peaceful experiences is to bike from Seebach station through the forest to Katzenruti, where you'll find several places ideal for a picnic. After lunch you can cycle to the Katzensee with its sandy beach, returning later via Affoltern. The tourist office in Zurich will help you plot this course, which takes about 1½ hours to go the full 13km (8 miles).

Zürcher Spielzeugmuseum (Zurich Toy Museum) This museum, in one of the oldest parts of the city, contains more than 1,200 antique toys from all over Europe. Everything that seemingly belongs to the world of toys can be found here: miniature railroads and steam engines, dolls (some of which date from the 18th century), doll houses, miniatures, century-old games for kids, dozens of wooden toys, books, and even cooking stoves for kids. The collection is displayed on the fifth floor of a house and is accessible by elevator. Allow at least an hour to view this collection, although your kid may want to stay longer.

Fortunagasse 15. ℂ **044/211-93-05.** www.zürcher-spielzeugmuseum.ch. Free admission. Mon–Fri 2–5pm; Sat 1–4pm. Tram: 6, 7, 11, or 13.

WALKING TOUR 1	ZURICH'S BAHNHOFSTRASSE

START:	Bahnhofplatz.
FINISH:	Bellevueplatz.
TIME:	1 hour.
BEST TIMES:	Monday through Friday from 9am to 5pm or on Saturday from 9am to 1am (when most stores are open).
WORST TIMES:	Rush hours, Monday through Friday from 8 to 9am and 5 to 6pm.

If you do nothing else in Zurich, walk along world-famous Bahnhofstrasse. One of the most beautiful shopping streets on earth was built on the site of a frogs' moat. The street is free from all traffic except trams.

Post-Br.

Hauptbahnhof (Main Train Station)

start here

Bahnhof-platz

1

Bahnhof-Br.

Central

Polybahn

Sihl River

Schuttengasse

Beaten-platz

2

Beatengasse

3

Mühlesteg (Ped bridge)

Linthescher gasse

Bahnhofstrasse

Löwenstrasse

Usteristrasse

Bahnhofquai

Neumühlequai

Stampfenbachstr.

Weinbergstrasse

Leonhardstrasse

Hirschengraben

Seilergraben

Uraniastrasse

Rud. Brun-Br.

Limmatquai

Niederdorfstrasse

Zähringerstrasse

Oetenbachgasse

Zähringer-platz

Spitelgasse

Mühlegasse

Fortunagasse

Rennweg

Lindenhof

Brungasse

Pelikanstrasse

St Peterstrasse

Rathaus-Br.

Wein-platz

NIEDERDORF

Münstergasse

Spiegelgasse

Obmannamtsgass

Talackerstrasse

Bärengasse

Storchengasse

Grossmünster-platz

Kirchgasse

Paradeplatz

4

Poststrasse

Fraumünster

Münster-Br.

Grossmünster

Bleicherweg

Talstrasse

Bahnhofstrasse

Kappelerstrasse

Fraumünsterstr.

Stadthausquai

Limmat River

Limmatquai

Oberdorfstrasse

Rämistrasse

Dreikönigstr.

Claridenstrasse

finish here

6

Beethovenstr.

Bürkli-platz

5

Quaibr.

Bellevueplatz

Stadelhofer-platz

Gen.-Guisan-Quai

Utoquai

Theaterstrasse

Opera House

Train Station

1 Bahnhofplatz
2 Bahnhofstrasse
3 Pestalozzi Park
4 Paradeplatz
   Confiserie Sprüngli
5 Bürkliplatz
6 Bellevueplatz

Basel

Zurich

Bern

SWITZERLAND

Geneva

0   200 yds
0   100 m

ZURICH

5

WALKING TOUR 1: ZURICH'S BAHNHOFSTRASSE

Begin the tour at:

❶ Bahnhofplatz

The site of the Hauptbahnhof, the central railroad station, this is the beginning of Bahnhofstrasse. The square itself is rather drab, but the scenery improves as you go along (the street extends almost a mile to the lake). The Hauptbahnhof was built in 1871.

Escalators take you from Bahnhofplatz past an underground shopping mall called ShopVille to:

❷ Bahnhofstrasse

With your back to the railway terminus, you can head up Bahnhofstrasse, which is lined with linden trees as well as some of the world's most prosperous banks and expensive shops, selling such luxury merchandise as Swiss watches and jewelry.

Continue up the street to:

❸ Pestalozzi Park

The park appears on your right, 2 blocks from Bahnhofplatz, between Schweizergasse and Usteristrasse. You can stop here and rest on one of the park benches by a statue of Johann Heinrich Pestalozzi (1746–1827), an educational reformer who influenced school standards in the United States.

Farther along, near Augustinergasse and Pelikanstrasse, you'll see a small pedestrian walkway where you can stop to admire the sculptures in the area. After you pass St. Peter Strasse and Bärengasse, you'll reach:

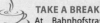

TAKE A BREAK
At Bahnhofstrasse 21 (Am Paradeplatz) is the **Confiserie Sprüngli** (ℂ **044/224-47-11;** www.confiserie-spruengli.ch), the most elegant and fashionable place on this chic shopping street to meet for tea and pastries (which are the best in the city). Try one of the daily lunch specials.

❹ Paradeplatz

This is the hub of Zurich and the central tram interchange. In the 18th century, it was a cattle market. The square is dominated by the 1876 mansion of Crédit Suisse. East of the plaza is the Savoy Baur en Ville hotel.

Continue along Bahnhofstrasse until you reach:

❺ Bürkliplatz

On the shore of Lake Zurich, this is the point where the Limmat River empties into the lake. This square overlooks Quaibrücke, a bridge across the Limmat that connects the left bank with the right bank. After stopping to admire the lake, you may also consider a boat excursion if it's summer.

If you cross Quaibrücke, you'll arrive on the right bank at:

❻ Bellevueplatz

Here you can enjoy the view of the lake and river as you rest on a park bench and watch all of Zurich pass by.

WALKING TOUR 2   **ZURICH'S ALTSTADT**

START:	Münsterhof.
FINISH:	Helmhaus.
TIME:	1½ hours.
BEST TIMES:	Any sunny day between 10am and 4pm (when there's less traffic).
WORST TIMES:	Rush hours, Monday through Friday from 8 to 9am and 5 to 6pm.

Situated on both sides of the Limmat River, Altstadt (Old Town) is known for its squares, narrow cobblestone streets, and winding alleys. There are fountains, medieval houses, art galleries, boutiques, quaint restaurants, hotels (many moderately priced), and antiques shops. To walk its old streets is to follow in the footsteps of such famous figures as Charlemagne, Goethe, Einstein, and Lenin. The oldest houses date from the 1100s.

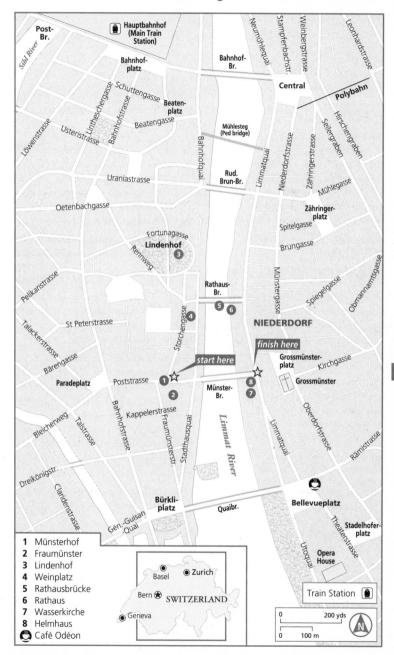

1 Münsterhof
2 Fraumünster
3 Lindenhof
4 Weinplatz
5 Rathausbrücke
6 Rathaus
7 Wasserkirche
8 Helmhaus
🔵 Café Odéon

Train Station 🏛

0   200 yds
0   100 m

A good place to begin your exploration of Altstadt is the former swine market:

❶ Münsterhof

This square, on the left bank, is near such landmarks as Fraumünster and the Rathaus. You can reach it by walking along Schlüsselgasse. At Münsterhof 8 is the guildhall Zunfthaus zur Waag, erected in 1637, with late Gothic windows and a gabled facade.

Across the square is:

❷ Fraumünster

The entrance is on Fraumünsterstrasse. A church has stood on this site since 853, when it was a convent for noblewomen. It contains artwork by Chagall and Giacometti, among others.

After the church, your next target can be:

❸ Lindenhof

To get here, you must climb narrow medieval alleyways from Fraumünster. Continue north along Schlüsselgasse, heading in the direction of the railroad station. Shaded by trees, the belvedere square of Lindenhof is one of the most scenic spots in Zurich, especially romantic at twilight. Once the site of a Celtic and later a Roman fort, Lindenhof is a good place from which to view the Limmat River; the lookout point has a fountain. There's also a good view of the medieval old quarter, which rises in layers on the right bank.

From Lindenhof, head down Pfalzgasse, forking left onto Strehlgasse to Waggengasse and Rathausbrücke, the city hall bridge spanning the Limmat. You have arrived at the landmark square:

❹ Weinplatz

The site of the Corn Exchange until 1620, this is presumably the oldest market square in Zurich. It's named for its 1909 Weinbauer fountain, which depicts a Swiss winegrower with a basket of grapes in hand. Most visitors pause to photograph the Flemish-roofed burghers' houses on the opposite bank.

Here you can also look at the:

❺ Rathausbrücke

The present City Hall Bridge spanning the Limmat was built in 1878, at the site of the first span in Zurich.

Cross the bridge to visit the:

❻ Rathaus

Here you'll find the late Renaissance town hall of Zurich, which opens onto Limmatquai. Built in the late 17th century, it has darkly paneled rooms and antique porcelain stoves. Canton councils still meet here in a setting of rich sculptural adornment. The town hall is open on Tuesday, Thursday, and Friday from 10 to 11:30am. Admission is free, but you should tip your guide a couple francs.

Walk south along Limmatquai until you reach Münsterbrücke, a bridge across the Limmat, and the site of:

❼ Wasserkirche

Also called Water Church, this church got its unusual name because it was surrounded by water when it was built in 1479. There's a statue of Zwingli, the famous Swiss reformer, here.

Directly north of the church at Limmatquai 31 is the:

❽ Helmhaus

Built in 1794, the Helmhaus has a fountain hall and a gallery on the second and third floors, where the city shows changing exhibitions of Swiss art. The gallery is open Tuesday through Sunday from 10am to 6pm and also on Thursday from 8 to 10pm.

At the end of your walking tour, you can continue over to Zurich's most famous cafe:

❾ Café Odéon

This Belle Epoque cafe, at Limmatquai 2 (✆ 044/251-16-50), is the place where Lenin sat out most of World War I, plotting the Russian Revolution. It was also popular with the iconoclastic Dada artists of the same era. Stop for a cup of coffee in this historic setting.

TRAM TOURS   The quickest and most convenient way to get acquainted with Zurich is with a 2-hour trolley tour, which rolls through various neighborhoods of interest. There's no live spokesperson pointing out the sights, but you'll be given a headset, which delivers a running commentary in seven languages. Between May and October, for a fee of 32F per person, tours depart daily at 9:45am, noon, and 2pm. The tour takes in the commercial and shopping center and Old Town, and goes along the lakefront for a visit to Fraumünster or one of the historic guildhalls beside the Limmatquai.

BOAT TOURS   At some point during your stay in Switzerland's largest city, you'll want to take a lake steamer for a tour around Lake Zurich. Walk to Bahnhofstrasse's lower end and buy a ticket at the pier for any of the dozen or so boats that ply the waters from late May to late September. The boats are more or less the same, so it doesn't matter which one you take. Most of the steamers contain simple restaurant facilities, and all have two or three levels of decks and lots of windows for wide-angle views of the Swiss mountains and shoreline. During peak season, boats depart at approximately 30-minute intervals. The most distant itinerary from Zurich is to Rapperswil, a historic town near the lake's southeastern end. A full-length, round-trip tour of the lake from Zurich to Rapperswil will require 2 hours each way, plus whatever time you opt to explore towns en route. This trip is the highlight of the boat tours offered, and if you can spare the time, you'll find it a rewarding way to see the area in and around Zurich. Many visitors opt for shorter boat rides encompassing only the northern third of the lake; those trips take about 90 minutes total.

The full-length tour of the lake costs 27F in second class and 42F in first class. The shorter boat ride on the northern third of the lake costs 11F.

You may also want to take a 1½-hour boat trip along the Limmat River for a closer view of Zurich's historic bridges and riverfront buildings. Boats depart daily at 30-minute intervals in the summer months, costing 40F per person, from a pier in front of the Landesmuseum, near Zurich's main railway station. The boats travel downriver to the lake as far as the Zurichhorn or the Wollishofen railway station before retracing their paths back upriver to the pier.

For more information on all the boats mentioned above, contact the **Zürichsee Schifffahrtsgesellschaft** by calling ℂ **044/487-13-33**, or go online at www.zsg.ch.

WALKING TOURS   One of the most appealing walking tours in Zurich is a 2-hour guided stroll through the Old Town. If you're interested in participating, meet in the main hall of Zurich's railway station, at the Tourist Service office (ℂ **044/215-40-00**). The cost of the tour is 20F for adults, 10F for children 6 to 16, and free for children 5 and under. From April through October, tours in German and English are operated Monday to Friday at 3pm, and on Saturday and Sunday at 11am.

ACTIVE PURSUITS

Zurichers are not big on spectator sports—they like to get out and participate.

Many of the larger hotels have added swimming pools and tennis courts or handball and racquetball facilities. Some also have fitness centers.

GOLF   The premier golf club in Switzerland, **Golf & Country Club Zurich,** Wied 9, Aiderstrasse, in the suburb of Zumikon (ℂ **043/288-10-88**), 12km (7½ miles) southeast of the center, was laid out in 1931 and has the most prestigious reputation in the country. An 18-hole, par-72 course, it welcomes nonmembers who phone in advance, but only if they have a handicap of 30 or less, and only if they present a membership at a golf club in another part of the world. Greens fees are 200F per person, and clubs can be rented for 30F per set. To get there from downtown Zurich, take the Forchbahn tram from the Stadelhofen Bahnhof, near the Zurich opera house, then ride for 20 minutes to the tram station in the suburb of Zumikon. From there, it's a 6-minute walk to the golf course.

HIKING   Zurich has seven Vita-Parcours, or keep-fit trails. Someone at the Zurich Tourist Office, Bahnhofplatz 15 (© **044/215-40-00**), will map these trails for you.

JOGGING   The nearest woodland jogging route is on the **Allmend Fluntern,** which is a wide-open public park, crisscrossed with jogging paths, on the northeastern outskirts of Zurich, near the zoo. To get here from the center, take tram no. 6. Joggers are also seen frequently along the quays and elsewhere in the city.

SWIMMING   You can go swimming in Lake Zurich, which has an average summer temperature of 68°F (20°C). The finest beach is the **Tiefenbrunnen.** To get to Tiefenbrunnen (which is also popular with the gay crowd), take tram no. 4 from central Zurich (Bahnhofplatz) to Tiefenbrunnen Bahnhof, a ride of about 15 minutes. The **public pool** at Sihlstrasse 71 also has a sauna with its indoor swimming facilities.

6 SHOPPING

In the heart of Zurich is a square kilometer (about ⅓ sq. mile) of shopping, including the exclusive stores along **Bahnhofstrasse.** Your shopping adventure might begin more modestly at the top of the street, at Bahnhofplatz. Below this vast transportation hub is a complex of shops known as **ShopVille.**

ShopVille is open from 8am to 8pm every day except Christmas. Most shops are open Monday to Friday from 8am to 6:30pm and on Saturday from 8am to 4pm. Some of the larger stores stay open until 9pm on Thursday, and other shops are closed on Monday morning.

ART

Löwenbräu   We (along with most of our readers) realize that Löwenbräu is the name of a widely sought-after brand of beer, but when it comes to art and art galleries within the rapidly emerging neighborhood of Zurich West, it takes on another meaning completely. Massively built of red brick around 1900 as a brewery by the you-know-who company, its fortresslike interior was radically transformed a few years ago into one of the biggest art exhibition spaces in town—an ugly, industrial-looking mixed-use showplace for both publicly funded museums and privately owned art galleries where artworks are for sale. Of the six or seven private art galleries inside, one of the most impressive is **Daros Exhibitions** (© **044/447-70-00;** www.daros.ch), whose works are about as cutting edge as they come. Also on-site, and funded by a chain of local grocery stores, is the **Migros Museum for Contemporary Art** (© **044/277-20-50;** www.migrosmuseum.ch). The best way to decipher the various venues within this place involves tramping through its maze of labyrinthine corridors and stairwells. *Tip:* Avoid the place on Monday, when virtually everything inside this sprawling place is closed. Limmatstrasse 268, in Zurich-West.

BAGS & KNAPSACKS

Freitag Shop Zurich   Set within a drab and shadowy neighborhood of Zurich West, and flanked with roaring traffic ramps and overpasses, this shop achieved fame and notoriety throughout Switzerland, thanks to a physical plant that's composed of 17 seagoing containers piled to a height of 85 feet. In Zurich, it ranks as a tall building. Inside, you'll find the entire line of backpacks, wallets, bike saddlebags, dopp kits, wallets, and duffel bags for which Freitag, within counterculture fashion accessories for the young and the restless, is famous. Many of the goods sold here are crafted from colorful scraps of canvas, and some have been singled out by Manhattan's Museum of Modern Art for the integrity and originality of their designs. Geroldstrasse 17, in Zurich West. (℃ 043/366-95-20. www.freitag.ch.

BOOKS

Orell Füssli   Zurich's premier book department store stocks a large inventory of German- and English-language books. In addition to books on Switzerland, you'll find everything from the latest novels to your favorite classics, as well as many contemporary nonfiction titles on every subject. Füsslistrasse at Bahnhofstrasse. (℃ 044/455-56-17.

The Travel Book Shop   This shop has a complete selection of travel books, as well as one of Europe's best map collections. While many of the books are in German, about half the stock is in English. Maps for trekking and mountaineering from all over the world are also sold. Rindermarkt 20. (℃ 044/252-38-83. www.travelbookshop.ch.

CHOCOLATES

Sprüngli ★★★   In a country famous for its chocolates, Sprüngli is the most famous chocolatier, although we still consider it second best to Teuscher (see below). The inventory of virtually everything dark and "meltable in your mouth" is featured at this temple to chocolate. Adjacent to the store, you'll find a coffee shop, a small restaurant with a limited menu, and a room exclusively for mailing your next high-caloric gifts to friends and family abroad. Additional outlets of Sprüngli are located at Bahnhofstrasse 67, Löwenplatz, Stadelhoferplatz, and, to tempt last-minute buyers, the Zurich International Airport. Paradeplatz. (℃ 044/224-47-11. www.spruengli.ch.

Teuscher   Located on a narrow cobblestone street in Old Town, this small store is the original epicurean chocolate shop. You can tell you're in the area by the smell of chocolate truffles, which come in such flavors as champagne, orange, and cocoa. Storchengasse 9. (℃ 044/211-51-53. www.teuscher.com.

CRAFTS

Schweizer Heimatwerk ★ Finds   In 1930, in an effort to help economically distressed areas, a nonprofit society, Schweizer Heimatwerk, was created to keep traditional crafts alive. Today, Heimatwerk shops sell only items designed and made in Switzerland, most of them handcrafted. Items include copperware, ceramics, woodcarvings, ironwork, jewelry, toys, nave paintings, crystal, tinware, baskets, music boxes, and paper-cutout pictures. Puzzles, games, and puppets—even a Noah's ark with its carved wooden animals—are sold here as well. The headquarters shop and four other outlets of Schweizer Heimatwerk are in Zurich. The prices range from reasonable to expensive. Other branches are at Bahnhofstrasse 2, at Rennweg 14, at the Hauptbahnhof, and at the Zurich airport in Transit Halls A and B. Rudolf Brun-Brücke. (℃ 044/217-83-17. www.heimatwerk.ch.

Teddy's Souvenir Shop   Swiss-made handicrafts here evoke a nostalgia for old-fashioned Switzerland with the type of gifts a Teutonic Santa Claus might stuff into his bag of Christmas gifts. Items for sale include cuckoo clocks, T-shirts with an assortment of Swiss-inspired sayings, an impressive array of music boxes and beer steins, Swiss Army knives, and woodcarvings. Anything you buy can be shipped abroad. Limmatquai 34. © **044/261-22-89.** www.teddyssouvenirshop.ch.

DEPARTMENT STORES

Grieder les Boutiques ★★ This is one of the best department stores in Switzerland, offering both ready-to-wear and couture by such designers as Valentino, Dior, Escada, and Montana. The store fills two floors of a stone building on Zurich's most fashionable commercial street, where the salespeople tend to be bilingual and formidably well dressed. The accessories, including purses, scarves, and leather goods, are well selected. There's a wide choice of shoes—many Swiss-made—for both men and women, plus a good men's department. Bahnhofstrasse 30. © **044/224-36-36.** www.bongenie-grieder.ch.

Jelmoli Department Store ★ This Zurich institution has everything a large department store should have, from cookware to clothing. Founded more than 150 years ago by the Ticino-born entrepreneur Johann Peter Jelmoli, the store is a legend in the Zurich business community. Seidengasse 1. © **044/220-44-11.** www.jelmoli.ch.

FASHIONS

Le Mouton a Cinq Pattes This is the Zurich branch of a well-known Paris-based discount outlet for high-end fashion for men and women. It maintains direct pipelines to upscale manufacturers including Moschino, Issey Miyake, Thierry Mügler, Cerrutti 1881, Armani, Versace, Gucci, Cavalli, and—for the very youthful-looking—Exte. Unless you're a very tall, very muscular, or very bulky man, the store will probably have something to fit you. Ask the multilingual staff for help. They're genuinely charming and willing to help. Usteristrasse 23. © **044/212-00-68.** www.moutona5pattes.com.

Modeshaus Feldpausch Spread across four floors, this outlet is devoted mainly to women's wear. With some of the deepest discounts available in the basement, inventories include designs from fashion moguls Mark Kane, Hugo Boss, Orvell, and Akris. On the street level they sell casual wear along with a selection of clothing for young women. On the next level is the house's selection of designer clothing, with cocktail dresses and ensembles on the floor above. Check for sales in late summer and late winter. Bahnhofstrasse 88. © **044/225-11-11.** www.pkz.ch.

Thelma Selection Around 1912, when this premises in the Old Town first opened as a butcher shop, the Russian political theorist Vladimir Lenin lived next door, surviving on starvation rations of bread, milk, and coffee, and complaining bitterly about the smells that emanated from the shop whenever it prepared sausages. Today, the site functions as a purveyor of stylish women's clothing, much of it designed in-house by a local personality known as Thelma. If you enter for a look at the evening wear and sportswear, you'll invariably notice an elaborate Jugendstil ceiling fresco that has been in place since its beginning. The clothes are breezy, comfortable, and hip, conveying a wide spectrum of various degrees of formality. Spiegelgasse 16. © **044/261-78-42.**

GIFTS

Meister Silber ★ This elite shop, on prestigious Paradeplatz in the center of Zurich, has one of the widest selections of gift items in Switzerland. The prices are high but reasonable, considering that every article is either exquisitely handcrafted or comes from producers internationally known for quality and fine design. Bahnhofstrasse 28A. © **044/ 221-27-30.** www.meister-zurich.ch.

Les Ambassadeurs Benefiting from a stylish location on the city's most prestigious shopping street, this well-known jeweler sells gemstones and such watches as Breitling, Cartier, Longines, Omega, and Constantin. Also featured are the baubles of Italian jeweler Mandredi and the Cleopatra line. Bahnhofstrasse 64. *©* **044/227-17-17.** www.les ambassadeurs.ch.

Tiffany & Co. ★★★ The Swiss branch of America's most famous jeweler, this well-upholstered boutique sells the full line of products originally made famous in New York, including those by artists such as Paloma Picasso. No crystal or china is offered, but small gift items are sold, as well as a choice of the famous gold and silver chains. Bahnhofstrasse 14. *©* **044/211-19-45.** www.tiffany.com.

Türler ★★ On the ground level of the Savoy Hotel, this outlet has a goldsmith and a watchmaker on staff and is known throughout Zurich for its custom-made watches and jewelry. If you have a special design, they'll make it for you. They also carry a wide variety of watches from other designers—some 30 different brands in all—and they sell both these and a selection of jewelry in a wide range of prices. Bahnhofstrasse 28. *©* **044/221-06-08.** www.tuerler.ch.

LEATHER GOODS

Leder-Locher ★★ Established 150 years ago, this venerable leather store has maintained high standards despite the changing tides of fashion throughout the years. Its inventory includes handbags, purses, wallets, suitcases, garment bags, and an unusual collection of small but charming gift items and accessories. The store maintains another branch at Bahnhofstrasse 91. Münsterhof 18–19. *©* **044/211-18-64.** www.leder-locher.ch.

LINENS & COTTONS

Spitzenhaus An air of old-fashioned charm permeates this store specializing in carefully crafted linens, cottons, and silks for the dining table. Most of the linen comes from Bern and Zurich (both specialists in linen), while most of the lace is handmade in either St. Gallen or Appenzell. The place also sells embroidered blouses and table scarves. Börsenstrasse 14. *©* **044/211-55-76.**

MUSIC

Musik Hug This is the largest branch of the best music chain in Switzerland. Conveniently located in the center of Zurich, it stocks thousands of CDs, and even some tapes, from around the world and has a helpful staff. Its selection of Swiss folkloric music, classical recordings, and modern jazz is especially rich and varied. Limmatquai 28–30. *©* **044/269-41-41.**

PERFUMES

Parfumerie Schindler This store on the Paradeplatz is devoted exclusively to one of the city's most comprehensive selections of perfumes and fragrances. If you can name it, this store will probably have it. Bahnhofstrasse 26. *©* **044/221-18-55.**

PORCELAIN

Ursula Riedi ★ Whatever you do, don't make any sudden moves in this shop. It's loaded from floor to ceiling with some of the most exquisite and valuable antique Meissen porcelain in Zurich. Everything is breathtakingly fragile—and breathtakingly valuable. It's a safe haven for aficionados of Europe's most ephemeral art form: antique porcelain. Leave the kids at home, and keep in mind that hours here tend to be a bit irregular and whimsical. If you're absolutely intent of visiting this place, it's best to phone before you go. Torgasse 5. ℂ **044/262-35-10.** www.ursulariedi.com.

SCHNAPPS

Distillerie zur Schnapsboutique   The light within this small and aromatic shop seems to shimmer in tones of honey and amber, thanks to the oversized, balloon-shaped glass decanters which nestle side by side within specially designed wooden racks. Each is filled to the brim with various vintages of schnapps from local distillers, sherry from selected bodegas throughout Spain, and rare plum wines from Japan. A staff member will advise you of what you're seeing (and smelling) here, but if you think you can plunk down some money and walk out with a bottle, think again, since it gets more compli-cated than that. Before your liqueur of choice is decanted, you'll have to select, and pay for, a container. These range from the utilitarian and relatively ordinary—a glorified milk bottle with a cap, for example, for 2.90F—to high-tech, labor-intensive crystal decanters priced at around 180F each. The contents of your decanter, depending on the vintage and its age, begin at around 30F and can go up to 10 times that amount. This is liquor as it was sold several generations ago, within a venue that we were told is now unique within Switzerland. Napfgasse 3. ℂ **044/262-32-27.**

SHOES

Andy Jllien   This is the quintessential boutique, with a carefully chosen but limited inventory of shoes that appeal to fashion-conscious women. Torgasse 5–6. ℂ **044/252-19-11.**

Graziella   Graziella's inventory of shoes comes from throughout Europe. There's everything from sensible oxfords to the kind of flimsy but oh-so-attractive footwear a woman might wear to a Hollywood premier or a glamorous casino. Löwenstrasse 30. ℂ **044/221-11-93.**

Stefi Talman   Some of the most whimsical and festive shoes in Zurich are designed by this store's namesake, many of them in electric tones of blood red, purple, pink, and apple green. The darling of the Swiss fashion media, Ms. Talman and her works are widely publicized. Only shoes for women, and sometimes the purses and bags that accompany them, are available. Oberdorfstrasse 13. ℂ **044/252-81-10.** www.stefitalman.ch.

WATCHES

Beyer ★   If you have your heart set on buying a timepiece in Zurich, try this well-established store midway between the train station and the lake. Besides carrying just about every famous brand of watch made in Switzerland—Rolex, Corum, Cartier, and Patke Philippe—it also has a museum in the basement, containing timepieces from as early as 1400 B.C. Exhibitions include all kinds of water clocks, sundials, and hourglasses. Bahnhofstrasse 31. ℂ **044/344-63-63.** www.beyer-ch.com.

Bucherer   A longtime name in the Swiss watch industry, this store also carries an impressive collection of jewelry. Some of the most famous names in watchmaking are represented in their latest offerings, including Chopard, Rado, and Rolex. Bahnhofstrasse 50. ℂ **044/211-26-35.** www.bucherer.com.

7 ZURICH AFTER DARK

The city's nightlife is becoming less conservative, but don't expect it to be too wild. Most of the nightspots in Zurich close down early, so you should begin early. Concerts, theater, opera, and ballet all flourish here.

To learn what's on during your visit, pick up a copy of *Zurich News,* available free at the tourist office and distributed at the front desks of most hotels.

THE PERFORMING ARTS

No special discount tickets are granted, but for regular tickets to operas, theaters, and concerts, go to **Billettzentrale** (BiZZ for short), Stadthausquai 17 (⒞ **044/221-22-83**), open Monday to Friday from 10am to 6:30pm and on Saturday from 10am to 2pm.

The **Zurich Opera** is the most outstanding local company, performing at the Opernhaus. The **Zurich Tonhalle Orchestra,** performing at Tonhalle, also enjoys an international reputation.

Opernhaus ★ The Zurich opera house, near Bellevueplatz in the center of the city, was founded in 1891. The history of the opera house forms part of the cultural history of Europe; the house was the venue of several world premières, including performances of *Lulu* by Alban Berg and *Mathis der Maler* by Hindemith. The opera house is also a repertory theater, hosting ballets, concerts, and recitals. The hall is dark in July and August. The box office is open daily from 10am to 6:30pm. Falkenstrasse 1. ⒞ **044/268-66-66.** www.opernhaus.ch. Tickets 16F–380F.

Schauspielhaus This is one of the most famous theaters in Switzerland, generally performing plays in German that range from classic to modern. It's a repertoire theater that performs different works nearly every evening, not long-running shows. The box office is open daily from 10am to 7pm (closed mid-June to Sept). Rämistrasse 34, at Heimplatz. ⒞ **044/268-66-66.** www.schauspielhaus.ch. Tickets 23F–97F.

Tonhalle Gesellschaft ★ This concert hall facing Bürkliplatz is the biggest and most famous concert hall in Zurich, with 1,500 seats in the big hall and 700 seats in the small hall. Brahms opened Tonhalle Gesellschaft in 1895 with a presentation of "Song of Triumph." It's home to the Zurich Tonhalle Orchestra and the venue for appearances by many internationally known soloists. Recitals and chamber music presentations are also staged here. Try to purchase your tickets as early as possible because many seats are sold by subscription. Reservations can be made 2 weeks prior to any concert. The box office is open daily from 10am to 6pm, except concert days when it closes at performance time. Claridenstrasse 5. ⒞ **044/206-34-34.** www.tonhalle.ch. Tickets 20F–141F.

THE CLUB & MUSIC SCENE

Adagio In a city building frequently used for public meetings (the Kongresshaus), this nightclub sets strict standards of respectability for its relatively conservative clientele, generally attracting an over-35 crowd. Adagio is a dance club—mainly ballroom stuff in a big hall decorated like a church, replete with baroque-style ceiling frescoes with a chorus of chubby cherubs gazing down from above. The staff wears medieval costumes, and fresh flowers and burning candles abound. The club is extremely crowded on weekends. Open year-round Sunday to Thursday 5pm to 2am, Friday and Saturday 5pm to 4am. In the Kongresshaus, Gothardstrasse 5. ⒞ **044/206-36-66.** http://zh.adagio.ch. No cover.

Bierhalle Wolf   With 160 seats, this is the best-known beer hall in Zurich, drawing people of all ages and all walks of life. It features "evergreen music" in a sometimes rowdy but safe environment. Folk music is played by an oompah band in regional garb whose instruments include a tuba, accordion, saxophone, clarinet, and bass. The large beer hall is decorated with pennants and flags of different cantons. Beer is available in tankards costing 7F and up. Live music is presented every day from 4 to 6:30pm and from 8:30pm to midnight, and every Sunday morning from 10am to noon. During the breaks, slides of alpine scenery are shown. You can also dine on hearty robust fare, with main courses starting at 14F. Open daily from 11am to 2am. Limmatquai 132. ℂ **044/251-01-30.** www. bierhalle-wolf.ch. Cover 4F–5F.

Casa-Bar   When Zurichers want to hear New Orleans–style Dixieland jazz, they head here. Some rhythm and blues from the '50s and '60s is regularly featured as well. The dark-paneled decor is inspired by the forests of Switzerland. On a busy night, at least 60 patrons of varying ages can crowd in here. A beer costs 10F and up, or you can order hard liquor beginning at 16F. Wine by the glass starts at 16F. Open Tuesday to Saturday from 5pm to 2am. Münstergasse 30. ℂ **044/261-20-02.** www.casabar.ch. No cover.

Kaufleuten   This club attracts a wide cross section of Zurich society, partly because of the central location and partly because of the comfortably battered, old-fashioned interior whose mismatched tables and chairs imply a certain unstructured comfort. Inside are four different bar areas with mostly house and garage music playing. The Restaurant Kaufleuten is separately recommended (p. 103). Open daily 11pm to 2am (till 4am Fri–Sat). Pelikanstrasse 18. ℂ **044/225-33-22.** www.kaufleuten.com. Cover 15F–25F, depending on the night of the week.

Palais X-tra   This is the largest nightclub in Zurich. It's a cavernous, high-ceilinged affair, partially painted in strident colors of red and black, with a long, long bar, an outdoor terrace, and restaurant facilities that seem to be less popular than the bar and rock-'n'-roll club that fill the same place. Between bouts of recorded music, a changing ensemble of live acts will appear, drawing counterculture and youthful fans from throughout Switzerland. This is a trendy and creative address, beloved by persons in their 20s, and respected by parents throughout the city as a spot where their children are likely, at least once, to have spent some time meeting and mingling. Open Monday, Wednesday, and Saturday 8pm to 2am. In the Limmathaus, Limmatsrasse 118. ℂ **044/448-15-00.** www. x-tra.ch. Cover 30F–45F, depending on the performers.

THE BAR SCENE

Blaue Ente   Although Blaue Ente is best known as a restaurant, many locals, especially young professionals, come here for its bar. In a high-tech setting, you can enjoy beer beginning at 7F, or whiskey at 16F. The restaurant is open Monday to Friday 11:30am to 12:30am, Saturday 11:30am to 11pm; the bar is open Monday to Friday noon to 2pm and 5pm to midnight, Saturday 4pm to 12:30am. Both the bar and its restaurant are closed from late-July to mid-August. Seefeldstrasse 223 at Mühle Tiefenbrunnen. ℂ **044/388-68-40.** www.blaue-ente.ch.

James Joyce Pub   The furnishings and paneling of this pub were acquired in the early 1970s by the Union Bank of Switzerland, when Jury's, an 18th-century hotel in Dublin, was demolished. The Union Bank reassembled the bar (with slightly more comfortable banquettes) near Bahnhofstrasse to entertain business clients and named it after famous Dubliner James Joyce, who had described its decor in certain passages of *Ulysses*.

The blackboard menu lists the daily specials *(Plattes)*. In December, Irish stew is tradi- tionally served. Other fare includes fish and chips, hamburgers, and fried chicken legs. Open Monday to Friday 11am to 12:30am and on Saturday from 11:30am to 6pm. Pelikanstrasse 8. (C) **044/221-18-28**. www.jamesjoyce.ch.

Jules Verne Bar   To reach the bar, you'll have to ride an elevator to the 11th floor of the Urania Observatory (p. 117), after passing through the street-level restaurant (Brasserie Lipp) with which it's associated. Views from the windows encompass the center of Zurich and some of the surrounding scenery, and the decor includes nostalgic references to what the bar's namesake envisioned as the technology of the future. The place can get crowded with talkers and drinkers in their 30s and 40s as music plays in the background. You can expect conviviality but not necessarily intimacy here. It's a great happy-hour spot. Open Monday to Thursday 11am to midnight, Friday and Saturday 11am to 1am, Sunday 3 to 11pm. Uraniastrasse 9. (C) **044/888-66-66**. www.jules-verne.ch.

Rosaly's   The structure looks a lot like a geranium-studded alpine chalet that's oddly positioned on a narrow alleyway near the most congested part of the Bellevueplatz, a busy downtown tram junction. During the dinner hour, patrons huddle around a half-moon-shaped bar area, leaving most of the tables to diners (p. 106). Later in the evening, however, more and more of the tables—both indoor and outdoor—become devoted to the bar. There's a sense of hipness and whimsy to this place, and an occasional subtle reference to big-city life in faraway California. The list of cocktails include kamikazes, Rob Roys, Side Cars, and margaritas. Open daily 4pm to midnight or 1am, depending on business. Freieckgasse 7. (C) **044/261-44-30**.

2 Akt   By daylight, this place resembles a simple bistro, with varnished pine paneling, high ceilings, and accessories that hint at its beer-hall-style origins around the turn of the 20th century. A simple menu of Wiener schnitzels and roasted chicken accompanies mugs of beer and glasses of wine. By nightfall, however, the place is filled with the young and the restless, and on nights when a DJ spins state-of-the-art dance music, the place is mobbed. It isn't a disco per se, but rather a bar and restaurant that just happens to play dance music, and which just happens to attract a crowd of TV announcers, journalists, and artists in modern-day Zurich. As such, you'll probably be tapping your feet to the music but not actually dancing, unless a group of rowdies breaks loose from their drinking and spontaneously begins to gyrate. The weekly schedule of which spinmeister will be on duty is clearly marked on a blackboard several days in advance, adding an element of star quality to the artist who's actually selecting the music. Food is served Monday to Saturday from 9am to 10pm, and Sunday from 5 to 10pm. A DJ plays Thursday to Saturday from 9pm to 4am. Open Monday to Saturday from 9am to 2 or 4am, Sunday from 5pm to 2am. Selnaustrasse 2. (C) **044/201-65-64**.

Wings ★   This is the most unusual bar in Zurich, with memorabilia gathered in the wake of the bankruptcy of Swissair in 2001 (a cataclysm that shocked and deeply wounded, it's been said, the national psyche of Switzerland). A small group of pilots and flight attendants saved what they defined as the "essence" of the Swissair spirit, airline seats removed from the first-class cabins of Boeing 747s and MD-11s formerly associated with the airline, and some of the battered aluminum carts that a generation of stewards rolled up and down the aisles.

And if you have an ongoing obsession about meeting the flight attendant of your dreams, there's likely to be a bigger concentration of them on a hard-drinking Friday or Saturday night than at any equivalent bar in Zurich. Drinks cost 16F each, and include cocktails with names like Sex on the Wings, Jet Lag, Turbulence, and Grounding. Don't overlook the viability of this place as a lunch or dinner stopover, since rib-sticking platters, priced at 14F to 24F, are served Monday to Friday noon to 2pm and 5 to 10pm. Bar hours are Monday to Thursday noon to midnight, Friday and Saturday noon to 2am, and Sunday 2 to 10pm. Limmatquai 54. ℭ **043/268-40-55.** www.wings-lounge.ch.

THE GAY SCENE

Barfüsser Long gone are the raucous and raunchy old days when a sprinkling of sawdust soaked up any beer that was spilled onto the floor of this place, and when most of the mostly male and mostly gay clientele looked like amiably scruffy refugees from a logging camp. A few years ago, in the rush to "gentrify" the place, this Zurich institution was scrubbed squeaky-clean, a sushi bar was installed, a yuppy-style cocktail menu was made available, and everyone began looking like metrosexual wannabes. Despite the controversial cleanup, which hasn't been universally well received, Barfüsser proudly lays claim to being the oldest continuously operated gay bar in Europe, with occasional (but increasingly rare) sightings of a clientele that has patronized the place since its establishment in 1956. Most show up after 8pm, and it's especially popular on weekends. The sushi bar serves continuously throughout the day until 11pm. It's open Monday to Wednesday from 11am to 1am, Thursday 11am to 2am, Friday and Saturday 11am to 3am, and Sunday 3pm to 1am. Spitalgasse 14. ℭ **044/251-40-64.** www.barfuesser.ch.

Club Aaah! Set on the third floor of the same building as the all-gay hotel recommended previously, but with which it is not associated (the Hotel Goldenes Schwert, p. 99), this is a techno-rock dance club with a bar; a minimalist, vaguely industrial-looking decor; and an animated, rather sweaty dark room in back. It isn't for everybody, although if you're absolutely intent on exploring as many gay dives as possible during one of your counterculture explorations of a town whose gay life has considerably expanded recently, it's worth a brief hello. There's a cover charge of 25F per person that's imposed only on Friday and Saturday nights. Otherwise, entrance is free, and beers cost around 9F each. Open daily 9:30pm to 2am. For more gay action, refer to the Pigalle Bar (see below) at the same address. In the Hotel Goldenes Schwert, Marktgasse 14. ℭ **044/253-20-60.**

Cranberry's Of the many gay bars that compete with the deeply entrenched Barfüsser, this one is the most successful. It's definitely not a disco (no one comes here to dance), but for an ambience that's like that of a classy and minimalist-looking American-style cocktail bar, and where virtually everyone is gay or gay-friendly, it's a solid and reliable bet. Scattered over two floors of a building on a sloping street within Zurich's historic Altstadt, cocktails cost from 10F to 17F. It's open Monday to Wednesday 5pm to 1am, Thursday 5pm to 2am, Friday and Saturday 5pm to 3am, and Sunday 5pm to 12:30am. Metzgergasse 3. ℭ **044/261-27-72.** www.cranberry.ch.

Labor Bar Most of the week, this place operates like a well-oiled, mostly heterosexual club where teeny-boppers release pent-up energy, and where recent divorcés mingle and flirt and sometimes get lucky. Upcoming musical venues are scheduled online (www. laborbar.ch) several months in advance, and if you happen to be caught in the flashbulbs of the resident paparazzi, it's likely that it will be posted on the Internet within a day or two. But every Sunday night, beginning around 7pm, the place goes gay, and if a recently divorced (presumably heterosexual) single happens to wander in, he or she usually tends to have a marvelous time. And in some instances, a radio commentator might be broadcasting an overview of recent cultural and nightlife events from the floor of this place, for all of trend-conscious Zurich to hear. Entrance is usually free for these "Trash Sundays," and beers cost around 7F each. Open Friday and Saturday from 10pm to 3am, Sunday 9pm to 2am. Schiffbaustrasse 3. © 044/272-44-02. www.laborbar.ch.

The Labyrinth This place switch-hits between its straight and gay identities depending on the night of the week. But at press time the prevalent wisdom assigned Wednesday, Friday, and Saturday (from around 9:30pm till between 1 and 3am, depending on business) to a mostly gay—and youthful—clientele. There's a bar or two on the premises, but most of the crowd comes here just to dance, dance, dance, and perhaps to explore the shadowy premises this place maintains in its nether areas. Entrance costs 25F per person, a price that includes the first drink. Open Friday and Saturday from 11:30pm till late. Hohlstrasse 452. No phone. www.laby.ch.

Pigalle Bar Another hot spot is a vaulted cubbyhole whose walls were adorned in 1951 with mosaics that showcase a version of Paris that Jacques Brel might have appreciated. (Though they were installed during the administration of other owners, they seem completely appropriate to the context of this sometimes giddy, ooh-la-lah bar where many of the clients seem to know one another.) Remo, the multilingual owner, charges 3.50F for a beer. Marktgasse 14. © 079/707-25-20. www.pigalle-bar.ch.

Predigerhof This is a warm, friendly, and sometimes very busy men's pub that makes every effort to welcome the widest possible cross section of the local gay community. Despite its attempts to draw a broad clientele, the bar tends to attract the kind of machos you might have expected in a high-altitude hut in the Swiss Alps. Sandwiches, salads, and soups are served, each item priced from 6F to 12F. Beers cost 6F. Open Sunday to Thursday 2pm to 2am, Friday and Saturday 11am to 4am. Mühlegasse 15. © 044/251-29-85. www.predigerhof.ch.

8 SIDE TRIPS FROM ZURICH

Zurich is surrounded by some of the most interesting sightseeing areas in Switzerland. The following are a few of exceptional interest. All these attractions can easily be reached on a short trip from your hotel in Zurich, either by train or by lake steamer.

WINTERTHUR

This industrial town in the Toss Valley, 20km (12 miles) northeast of Zurich, is also a music and cultural center, with an art collection that makes the short train trip from Zurich worthwhile. Winterthur was once a Roman settlement and became the seat of the counts of Kyburg. It later was a stronghold of the Habsburgs, until it was sold to Zurich. In the United States the name Winterthur conjures up the du Pont mansion in Delaware with its museum of Americana, or a reference to the financial giant, Winterthur Insurance. Both of these take their name from this Swiss city.

Winterthur is best explored on foot. City officials have signposted an itinerary that takes in the history, architecture, and culture of the town.

A **tourist office** is at Im Hauptbahnhof (© 052/267-67-00), open Tuesday to Friday 8:30am to 6:30pm, and on Saturday from 8:30am to 4pm.

From Zurich's Hauptbahnhof, **trains** depart about every 20 minutes throughout the day (trip time: 20–26 min.).

The skyline of Winterthur is dominated by the twin towers of its parish church, the Stadtkirche, built from 1264 to 1515 (the towers were added later).

Kunstmuseum ★ Located a 10-minute walk north of the Stadthaus on Stadthausstrasse and Lindstrasse, this fine-arts museum contains an impressive collection of European and American art and sculpture from the late 19th century to the present. Giacometti and such French artists as Bonnard and Vuillard are well represented. Highlights are works by van Gogh, Miró, Magritte, Mondrian, Kokoschka, Calder, and Klee. There are sculptures by Rodin, as well as works by Medardo Rosso and Maillol. The permanent collection is on display from June to August; temporary exhibits are presented the rest of the year.

Museumstrasse 52. ✆ **052/267-51-62.** www.kunsthaus.ch. Admission 18F adults, 12F seniors and students 16-18, free children 16 and under with adult. Sat–Sun and Tues 10am–6pm; Wed-Fri 10am–8pm. Bus: 1, 3, or 6 to Stadthaus.

Museum Oskar Reinhart am Stadtgarten ★★ Oskar Reinhart, a famous art collector who died in 1965, willed many of his treasures to the city. Displayed in this gallery are works of Austrian, German, and Swiss artists, with a fine representation of the Romantic painters, including Blechen, Friedrich, Kersting, and Runge. Many canvases are by Hodler. There are some 600 works in all, from the 18th to the 20th centuries.

Stadthausstrasse 6. ✆ **052/267-51-72.** www.museumoskarreinhart.ch. Admission 15F adults, 12F children 8 and under. Wed–Sun 10am–5pm, Tues 10am–8pm. Bus: 1, 3, or 6.

Schloss Kyburg Six kilometers (4 miles) from Winterthur, Schloss Kyburg is the largest castle in eastern Switzerland, dating from the Middle Ages. The stronghold was the ancestral home of the counts of Kyburg until 1264, when the Habsburgs took over. These counts were local rulers and of little interest to visitors today, as their history has long been overshadowed by the more powerful and more famous Habsburg dynasty. It was ceded to Zurich in the 15th century and is now a museum of antiques and armor. There's a good view from the keep. You may also visit the residence hall of the knights, parapet, and chapel.

Kyburg 8314. ✆ **052/232-46-64.** www.schlosskyburg.ch. Admission 8F adults, 6F students and seniors, 3F children 6–16, free children 5 and under. Mar 21–Oct Tues–Sun 10:30am–5:30pm; off-season Sat–Sun 10:30am–4:30pm. From Zurich, take the Winterthur rail line, get off at the Fretekon stop, and transfer to a bus for the 10-min. ride to the castle; buses depart every hour throughout the day. The castle is not on a street (or road) map.

Swiss Technorama (Kids) Technorama is the Swiss National Center for Science and Technology. Its permanent exhibition is divided into eight areas, with many interactive experiments and phenomena: Physics, Energy, Water/Nature/Chaos, Mechanical Music, Math/Magic, Materials, Textiles, and Automation. Technorama also has the world's greatest tin-plate train collection. In the hands-on Youth Laboratory, children can learn from some 100 experiments about science, mathematics, and biology. A self-service restaurant is at the site, and a big park features a steam train and muscle-powered flying machines.

Technoramastrasse 1. ✆ **052/244-0844.** www.technorama.ch. Admission 24F adults, 22F students and seniors, 13F ages 6–15, free children 5 and under. Tues–Sun 10am–5pm. Closed Dec 25. Take motorway N1, exit at Oberwinterthur, and drive a mile toward Winterthur. Or take a train to the Winterthur main station and switch to bus no. 5, marked TECHNORAMA.

Banana City ★   Lacking the elegance of the Park, this hotel under private ownership is nonetheless a comfortable, serviceable, and well-run complex close to the central rail station. The complex is some 200 meters long, and locals have dubbed it "the banana." In its former life, the building was an industrial site until its successful conversion into one of Winterthur's most beautiful landmark buildings thanks to its modern glass façade. A frequent venue for conferences, the hotel has attractively furnished bedrooms.

Schaffhauserstrasse 8, CH-8400, Winterthur. (© 052/268-16-16. Fax 052/268-16-00. www.bananacity.ch. 101 units. 250F–270F double, 330F junior suite, 430F–480F suite. AE, DC, MC, V. **Amenities:** Restaurant; bar; exercise room; room service. *In room:* TV, hair dryer, minibar, Wi-Fi (free).

Park Hotel ★★   This is the town's best address, offering the finest accommodations in the city plus a gourmet restaurant. Its "green belt" location is in the heart of the city, in an idyllic park a few steps from the Altstadt or Old Town. All the rooms, spacious for the most part, are tastefully decorated and equipped with modern conveniences. The top floor rooms have private terraces with panoramic views over the city.

Stadthausstrasse 4, CH-8402 Winterthur. (© 052/265-02-65. Fax 052/265-02-75. www.phwin.ch. 73 units. 298F–335F double. AE, DC, MC, V. Parking: 18F. **Amenities:** Restaurant; bar; exercise room; room service. *In room:* TV, minibar, hair dryer, Wi-Fi (free).

Where to Dine

Restaurant Taggenberg ★★★ CONTINENTAL   The best and most fussed over cuisine in the region is crafted within the kitchens of this circa 1901 villa, 20km (12 miles) northwest of Winterthur on a mountainside in the hamlet of Winterthur-Wülflingen. From the windows of the dining room, whose décor changes with the seasons and whatever temporary theme the owners opt to give it, views sweep down onto the surrounding fields and forests. In summer you can dine outside on the terrace. Menu items, as conceived by the owners, Margriet and Peter Schnaibel, include a sophisticated blend of such dishes as a terrine of goose liver and tafelspits (boiled beef) served with "pralines" of goose liver mousse; pink-cooked rack of local lamb with a Burgundy-flavored mustard sauce, braised vegetables, and truffled potatoes; and a warm (dessert) salad of passion fruit, mandarin orange segments, and fresh figs with Bolivian chocolate and coffee-flavored ice cream.

Taggenbergstrasse 79. (© 052/222-05-22. Reservations required. Four-course fixed-price menus 94F–119F; 6-course fixed-price menus 128F–148F. AE, DC, MC, V. Tues–Sat noon–2:30pm and 6:30–10:30pm.

Restaurant Trübli ★ INTERNATIONAL   Solidly reliable and set within a severely dignified antique building that's only a block or two from the railway station, this is a well-respected restaurant whose stately looking dining rooms contrast with the hubbub and conviviality of its popular, woodsy bar—the Boss-Bar. In the restaurant, crisp napery adorns tables, which have enough space between them to allow discreet conversations, all of it amid a prosperous and dignified Teutonic decor of framed prints and hunting trophies. The best menu items include a salad of forest mushrooms with strips of foie gras, tagliata pasta served with strips of beef, leaf-green salads with hazelnut dressing and grated parmesan, braised sea wolf with champagne sauce, and cordon bleu of veal with roasted potatoes and butter sauce.

Bosshardengässchen 2. (© 052/212-55-36. Reservations recommended. Main courses 38F–52F. AE, MC, V. Restaurant Tues–Sat noon–2pm and 7:30–10pm; Boss-Bar Tues–Sat 10am–12:30am.

Lake steamers from Zurich in summer take you to Rapperswil, "the town of roses" lying on the northern shore of Lake Zurich, a distance of 39km (25 miles) from the Swiss capital. If you're in Zurich for just a short time and have no other chance to visit the rest of the country, then spend a day (and/or night) at Rapperswil to see a typical Swiss town.

In recorded history, its vineyards were first mentioned in 981. It was once a town of prestige, with a fortified castle dating from 1229. The Counts of Rapperswil controlled parts of Eastern and Central Switzerland. But in 1283 the House of Rapperswil became extinct upon the death of the 18-year-old Count Rudolf V. After that time, the Emperor Rudolf I acquired the fiefs. Eventually, the possession of the former nobles became part of the Habsburg kingdom.

In January of 2007, the towns of Rapperswil and Jona merged to form a new municipality, Rapperswil-Jona, with a population of about 26,000, making it the second largest town in its canton, with St. Gallen as its capital.

The town's main sights are centered around the Old Town or **Altstadt** of Rapperswil. You can spend about 1½ hours strolling through its medieval alleys.

Rapperswil is called the *Rosenstadt* or the "town of roses" because of its displays of the flower in its trio of parks in the center. Some 600 different kinds of roses can be seen between June and October.

Seeing the Sights

The chief attraction is **Schloss Rapperswil.** Lying on the Rapperswil Peninsula on Lake Zurich, this early 13th-century castle is perched atop a hill, dominating the town. Deer roam the grounds around the castle. Since 1870, the castle has been home to the **Polish National Museum** created by Polish émigrés. You can see mementos of everybody from Copernicus to Chopin, even from Kosciuszko.

Herrenberg. © **055/210-18-28.** Admission 10F adults, 5F children 4–16. Mon–Sat 9am–6pm, Sun 9am–7pm.

Knie's Kinderzoo (Children's Zoo) (Kids) On the north side of Castle Hill (Herrenberg) lies this children's zoo run by the Knie National Circus. It fronts a road that borders the lake to the south of the rail station; nearby is the **Hirschgarten** or deer park in the Linderhof. Kids can pet and feed the elephants, rhinos, and zebras among other animals and also take camel or pony rides. Attractions range from a pirate ship to an original steam engine locomotive as well as an adventure playground.

Oberseestrasse. © **055/220-67-60.** Admission 10F adults, 5F children 4–16, free children 3 and under. Mon–Sat 9am–6pm, Sun 9am–7pm.

Heimatmuseum This is a Gothic hall with flower garlands and beamed ceilings housing historical relics of the region, ranging from an oven dating back to the Roman Empire to medieval works of art from a goldsmith, plus engravings 2 centuries old. The museum also exhibits other Roman artifacts, a weapon collection, paintings, and antiques.

Admission 6F adults, free children 16 and under. Wed–Sat 1–4pm, Sun 11am–4pm. Closed Dec–Mar.

Where to Stay

Schwanen ★★ Lying on the lakeshore promenade, this is the most prestigious hotel in the area with the finest accommodations, cuisine, and comfort. The hotel has been carefully restored and modernized, and is the most tranquil in the area, often a venue for

wedding receptions and family reunions. Bedrooms are beautifully maintained and elegantly furnished. Le Jardin, a gourmet restaurant, and the chic Schwanen Bar, draw both
visitors and locals to its precincts.

Seequai 1, CH-8640 Rapperswil. ℂ **055/220-85-00.** Fax 055/210-77-77. 25 units. 215F–320F double,
490F suite. AE, DC, MC, V. Parking: 18F. **Amenities:** Restaurant; bar; exercise room; room service. *In room:*
TV, minibar, hair dryer, Wi-Fi (free).

Where to Dine

Schloss Restaurant FRENCH/ITALIAN   Permeated with a sense of medieval solidity, this restaurant occupies the street level of Rapperswil's 12th-century castle, a brood-
ing stone monument rising from a hilltop in the center of town. The upper floors of this
monument contain a Polish Museum and a concert hall. Don't expect views of the surrounding township and forests, since windows inside correspond to the narrow, high
openings of the castle's medieval, once-fortified design. You'll find yourself within a
stone-sided, stone-floored dining room with a wooden ceiling and a circa 1989 decor of
warm creams and beiges, all within a space that's big enough for 40 diners at a time.
Menu items tend to be configured without heavy sauces and include, among others, filet
of beef that's stuffed, Rossini style, with foie gras; braised rump roast with mashed potatoes and red cabbage; and a medley of fish and vegetarian dishes that might remind you
of the Mediterranean.

Llindenhugel. ℂ **055/210-18-28.** Reservations recommended. Main courses 42F–48F; fixed-price
lunches 50F; fixed-price dinners 58F–98F. AE, DC, MC, V. Wed–Sun 11:30am–1:45pm, Wed–Sat 6:30–
9:45pm. Closed lunch Oct–May.

Villa Aurum ★ INTERNATIONAL   Permeated with a sense of solid comfort and
stability, this modern, yellow-and-white restaurant occupies the street level of a neoclassical, 18th-century villa in the heart of town, within a 5-minute walk of the railway station. It's the kind of place where leisurely lunches and even longer dinners attract a wide
assortment of the resort's business communities. In the most tranquil dining room in
town, the cuisine is based on seasonal, scrupulously selected ingredients. The cookery is
inventive, a lightened version from a classic repertoire. Starters include a salad of marinated scallops on a bed of seasonal greens; and braised filet of beef with mashed potatoes,
fresh vegetables, and a creamy mustard sauce.

Alte Jonastrasse 23. ℂ **055/220-72-82.** Reservations recommended. Main courses 45F–50F; fixed-price
lunches 65F; fixed-price dinners 98F. AE, DC, MC, V. Tues–Sat 11:30am–2:30pm and 6pm–midnight.
Closed 2 weeks in late Jan.

GREAT RIDES THROUGH THE ENVIRONS

A few fun, quick tours you can take on your own make use of funiculars and trains. If
you have time for only one of these trips, make it the Uetliberg (see below).

ALPAMARE   We recommend a visit to Alpamare (ℂ **055/415-15-87;** www.alpamare.
ch), Europe's largest water park (as certified in the *Guinness Book of World Records*). It lies
at Churstrasse 111, in the village of Pfäffikon on Lake Zurich, offering year-round fun
in and around the water on four body flumes and both indoor and outdoor tube slides.
There's also an indoor swimming pool with breakers, a bubbling hot spring, and an
open-air pool with underwater music and massage jets, as well as 90m (295 ft.) of lazy
river. An outdoor thermal pool contains iodine. The attraction is open daily from 10am
to 10pm. Weekdays adults pay 38F for a visit of up to 4 hours, or 48F for a daylong visit.
Children 15 and under are charged 32F for a visit of up to 4 hours or 39F for a daylong

visit. Weekends adults pay 41F and 51F, respectively, and children 34F and 41F. Children 2 and under are not allowed in the water.

THE DOLDERBAHN ★ Take the Dolderbahn for a short aerial cable ride to the **Dolder Recreational Area,** 596m (1,955 ft.) above the city. Trains leave every 10 minutes from Römerhofplatz, which you can reach by taking tram no. 3, 8, or 15. The recreational area is open year-round and has restaurants, nature trails, old rustic taverns, a path to the zoo, a miniature golf course, and, from October to March, a huge ice-skating rink. There's a place to swim, the **Dolder Schwimmbad** (✆ **044/267-70-80**), which is carved into a hillside with a view of Zurich. The swimming area is a 5-minute walk along a forest trail from the end of the cable-car line; follow the signs to Dolder Wellenbad. Admission to the pool with its artificial waves is 8F, 5F for children 5 and under. The Dolderbahn funicular ride costs 5F; buy your tickets from the machine.

FELSENEGG ★ An excursion to the alpine aerie at Felsenegg isn't as vertiginous as other mountain stations in higher-altitude regions of Switzerland, but its proximity to Zurich makes it one of the most consistently popular. To reach it, take one of the frequent (every 25 min.) trains from Zurich's Hauptbahnhof for the 14-minute ride to the residential suburb of Adliswil, 10km (6 miles) south, for a cost of 9F each way. Get off in Adliswil, then embark on a brisk, 10-minute uphill climb to an aerial cable car, the Luftseilbahn Adliswil-Felsenegg (LAF; ✆ **044/710-73-30**; www.laf.ch), for a 6-minute uphill ride to the top of Felsenegg, at 795m (2,608 ft.) above sea level. Expect to pay 8F round-trip. From here, it's a 10-minute hike to the **Restaurant Felsenegg** (✆ **044/710-77-55**; www.felsenegg.com), which serves typical alpine food on a panoramic outdoor terrace or indoors. Main courses range in price from 9.50F to 34F. The restaurant is open May to September Monday to Friday 11am to 10pm, Saturday 11am to 11pm, and Sunday 10am to 6pm; October to April, hours are Monday to Friday 11am to 8pm, Saturday 11am to 11pm, and Sunday 10am to 6pm.

THE FORCHBAHN For a close-up view of some of the most desirable residential real estate in Zurich, consider a ride on the Forchbahn, a short-haul railway line originating in downtown Zurich at the Stadelhofen Bahnhof, which lies at the junction of the Bellevueplatz and the Limmatquai, adjacent to the Quaibrücke (✆ **044/434-41-11** for more information). The Forchbahn travels through the capital's staid and endlessly respectable suburbs (local wits refer to it as "the Gold Coast") to endpoints at Esslingen and Forch, both of which lie within 30-minute rides south of the city center. The area is noted for its sunlight, and gardening seems to be a passionate pastime for local residents. You can get off the train at any of the stops, and pick any of the signposted trails that meander to nearby points of scenic interest. (The tourist office in Zurich is a good source of information. Otherwise, just ask a local or set out on a brief excursion on your own.) The shores of both the Greifensee and the Zurichsee are good bets for a walk, with paths that meander down from many points en route. Trains on the Forchbahn run without conductors, so you must buy your tickets from a machine at whatever point you happen to get on.

A round-trip ticket from Stadelhofen Bahnhof to Forch costs 18F; a round-trip ticket from Stadelhofen Bahnhof to Esslingen costs 22F. Trains depart from downtown Zurich (Bellevueplatz) at 30-minute intervals throughout the day and evening.

KILCHBERG If you're an admirer of Thomas Mann, we recommend a visit to Kilchberg, 6km (4 miles) from Zurich along the southwestern shore of the lake. Mann spent the last years of his life here and was buried on the south side of the small church in the village in 1955. His wife died here in 1980. Fans of the author still flock here to see the grave site, but Kilchberg is more famously associated with the 19th-century Swiss author Conrad Ferdinand Meyer. Train S8 departs from the Zurich Hauptbahnhof every half-hour for an 11-minute ride to the village. If traveling by car, proceed along the southwestern shore route of Lake Zurich following the signposts to Kilchberg.

UETLIBERG   Southwest of Zurich, Uetliberg, the northernmost peak in the Albis ridge, is one of the most popular excursions from the city, reached in only 15 minutes. Take the mountain railway Uetlibergbahn from the Selnau station in Zurich. A round-trip costs 17F and takes half an hour. You arrive near the Sihl River, at an elevation of 840m (2,755 ft.).

From the station, you can hike 10 minutes to the summit, where there's a cafe and restaurant. The tower is a climb of about 170 steps; from the lookout, on a clear day, you can see as far away as the Black Forest. For more information about the train, call ⓒ **044/ 206-45-11.**

Northeastern Switzerland

The northeastern region of Switzerland—one of the country's most unspoiled areas—contains the cantons of Appenzell, Glarus, St. Gallen, Schaffhausen, and Thurgau, and such wondrous natural sights as St. Gallen's Rhine Valley and the Rhine Falls. St. Gallen is the region's bustling cultural and economic center, and some of the most abundant orchards in the country dot the shores of Lake Constance.

For the athletic, there are plenty of sports and adventure to be found. Skiing, snowboarding, tobogganing, and hiking are easily accessible in the mountain areas. Sailing schools abound in the lakeside communities of Rorschach and Kreuzlingen, and the flat countryside along the lake is perfect for biking.

The northeastern region is also a sensible destination economically, as food and lodging prices are among the lowest in the country.

For an overnight stopover in the area, our money is on Stein-am-Rhein, one of the most perfectly preserved medieval villages in Europe and also one of the most charming of all Swiss towns. It lies at the point where the Rhein leaves Lake Constance. It also has the most charming old-world hotels.

However, that doesn't mean that other towns in northeastern Switzerland are without their allure. If you like your cities historic, make it St. Gallen, the largest city in eastern Switzerland. However, if you've come to the area for its folkish charm, head for Appenzell, the country's most traditional town (some Swiss speak of locals here as virtual hillbillies).

If boating and views of Lake Constance are your passion, take a promenade along the seafront, then settle into one of the resorts along Lake Constance—Rorschach has the widest choice of hotels and restaurants.

1 ST. GALLEN ★★

85km (53 miles) E of Zurich; 156km (97 miles) E of Basel; 15km (9 miles) SW of Rorschach

At 660m (2,165 ft.) above sea level, this valley is one of the primary stops in northeastern Switzerland. St. Gallen, which is the highest city of its size in Europe, is a good base for exploring Lake Constance (a 15-min. drive away), Mount Säntis, and the Appenzell countryside. This ancient town in the foothills of the Alps was founded by Gallus, an Irish monk who built a hermitage here in 612. By the 13th century his humble cell had developed into an important cultural outpost. St. Gallen became a free imperial city in 1212, and in 1454 it joined the Swiss Confederation. With a population of approximately 75,000, St. Gallen is the capital of a canton of the same name.

St. Gallen is the embroidery and lace capital of Europe; here, three dozen seamstresses worked for a year and a half to make a lace gown for Empress Eugénie, the wife of Napoleon III. Today most of the embroidery is done by computer-driven machines. However, you can still purchase handmade items (see "Shopping," below).

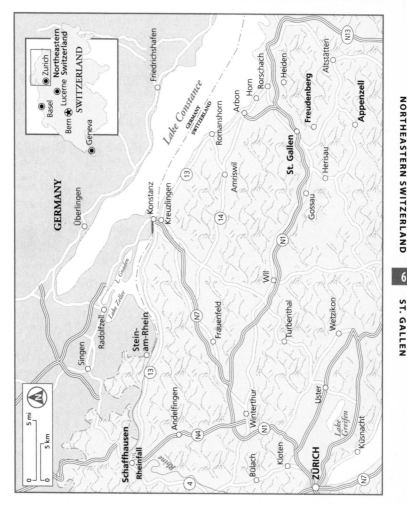

Freudenberg, 3km (2 miles) south of St. Gallen, at an altitude of 900m (2,952 ft.), offers a panoramic view of Mount Säntis, St. Gallen, and Lake Constance (known in this part of the country as Bodensee).

ESSENTIALS

GETTING THERE   St. Gallen is on the main **train** lines connecting Zurich with Munich. At least a dozen trains per day arrive from both directions. Trip time from Zurich is about 75 minutes. St. Gallen is the railway linchpin for at least four local lines. Call ② **0900/300-300** for more information.

As in most other Swiss cities, **bus** connections in St. Gallen are meant to supplement railroad service. Buses connect St. Gallen mainly with such outlying villages as Rorschach and Appenzell, with many stops at local villages along the way. Call the tourist office (see below) for more information.

By **car** from Zurich, head east on N1 (also called E17).

VISITOR INFORMATION The **St. Gallen Tourist Office** is located at Bahnhofplatz 1A (✆ **071/227-37-37;** www.st.gallen-bodensee.ch). It's open Monday to Friday from 9am to noon and 1 to 6pm, and Saturday 9am to 3pm. From November to April Saturday hours are 9am to 1pm.

EXPLORING THE TOWN

The **Old City** ★ is a must-see here, with its restored, half-timbered houses and their turrets and oriels. Wander the lanes and alleys laid out during the Middle Ages; some of them are closed to traffic.

The Protestant Reformation was victorious in St. Gallen, but the **Benedictine monastery at Klosterhof** remained virtually unaffected. The monastery contains the Catholic bishop's residence, the abbey library, and the canton's government offices. This area is also the site of the Domkirche (see below). The buildings that remain of the abbey date from the 17th and 18th centuries. Its walls were razed, and the best view is from the abbey yard, called the Klosterhof. To reach the abbey from Marktplatz in the center of town, take Marktgasse south, past St. Lawrence's Church, to the large Klosterhof.

St. Gallen offers many sports facilities, including tennis courts and three outdoor swimming pools. The region's best golf course lies 4km (2½ miles) from St. Gallen at the **Waldkirch Golf Park,** Golfpark Waldkirch, St. Gallen (✆ **071/434-67-67;** www.golf waldkirch.ch). To get here, follow the road signs to Gosau. An 18-hole round of golf costs from 80F to 100F per person. Because much of the area is relatively flat, consider renting a bicycle (available at the federal rail station). The tourist office (see "Essentials," above) is helpful in outlining bike routes that aren't too strenuous.

Serious climbers tend to dismiss the region around St. Gallen as being too flat, and they will consequently direct you to loftier altitudes near Appenzell. But if you don't mind a softly undulating landscape that's forested with deciduous trees, and accessible even to those not in the best shape, consider an 8km (5-mile) trip that incorporates the best and most panoramic of the local low-lying hills. From the center of St. Gallen, take bus no. 5 to the satellite hamlet of Reithüsli. From there, you'll climb a low hill, **Bernegg,** whose views sweep out over the Bodensee. There's a cozy wood-sheathed restaurant near its summit (the **Falkenburg Restaurant;** ✆ **071/222-55-81**), where air-dried beef, hearty stews, and steaks are the norm every day at lunch and dinner. Walk about a mile to **Drei Weiher,** a trio of small, clear lakes, where you can swim. Afterwards you can walk back to St. Gallen directly, or retrace your steps to the hamlet of Reithüsli. The complete excursion can last between 4 and 6 hours, depending on how much you dawdle en route. For more information on this and other treks near St. Gallen or Appenzell, contact the local tourist office.

Domkirche (Cathedral) The twin-towered Domkirche at Klosterhof is Switzerland's best example of baroque architecture. It was erected in 1756 on the site of the celebrated 14th-century Gothic abbey. Be sure to check out the cathedral chancel, one of its more interesting architectural features.

Klosterhof. ✆ **071/227-34-88.** Free admission. Daily 9am–7pm.

Stiftsbibliothek (Abbey Library) ★★★ This world-famous library contains some 130,000 volumes, including manuscripts dating back to the 8th through the 15th centuries (several of the Renaissance manuscripts have well-preserved illustrations). The library hall is built in a rococo style, with stucco art and ceiling paintings. A plan of the St. Gallen Abbey in the year 830 is displayed, preserved under glass.

Klosterhof 6. ✆ **071/227-34-16.** www.stiftsbibliothek.ch. Admission 10F adults, 7F students and seniors, free for children 15 and under. Apr–Nov Mon–Fri 10am–5pm; Dec–Mar Mon–Fri 10am–noon and 1:30–4pm.

SHOPPING

Many shoppers come to St. Gallen seeking embroideries. You can find real bargains when the local textile factories have clearance sales, usually in January and July. The tourist office can provide specifics.

To see how the embroideries—both hand- and machine-made—of St. Gallen are produced, call **Försterhoner Embroiderie,** Flurhofstrasse 150 (✆ **071/243-15-15**), which is 10 minutes by car from the center of town in the direction of Bodensee. You need an appointment, but they'll show you the factory and explain the process to you.

Finally, **Graphica Antiqua,** Marktgasse 26 (✆ **071/223-50-16**), is a real shopping find, selling an array of antique prints of Swiss landscapes, including the Alps and "Heidi meadows." Prints are available from all parts of Switzerland, and each region is clearly identified in the shop.

WHERE TO STAY
Expensive

Einstein Hotel ★★ The most desirable hotel in town, the Einstein is near the center of the historic district. Built some 150 years ago, originally as a Swiss embroidery factory, it was converted in 1983 into a stylish provincial hotel. It has a gray-and-white neoclassical facade and a marble lobby, and you're likely to hear live piano music playing in the pub/cocktail bar. The midsize guest rooms are conservatively furnished and well maintained, each fitted with neatly kept bathrooms.

Berneggstrasse 2, CH-9001 St. Gallen. ✆ **071/227-55-55.** Fax 071/227-55-77. www.einstein.ch. 113 units. 400F–500F double; 550F–600F suite. Rates include buffet breakfast. AE, DC, MC, V. Parking 30F in the garage, free outside. Bus: 1, 3, or 11. **Amenities:** Restaurant; bar; concierge; room service. *In room:* TV, hair dryer, minibar, Wi-Fi (35F per day).

Moderate

Hotel Ekkehard Located in the center of town, this government-rated three-star Swiss hotel was closed for renovations in 2009 and is scheduled to open sometime in 2010. Check in advance before booking in here and expect some adjustment in the prices listed below. All are equipped with tidily kept bathrooms. The hotel offers a wood-trimmed restaurant with modern decor serving Austrian food at reasonable prices, as well as a more upscale option.

Rorschacher Strasse 50, CH-9000 St. Gallen. ✆ **071/222-04-44.** Fax 071/222-04-74. www.ekkehard.ch. 29 units. 250F–280F double. Rates include buffet breakfast. AE, DC, MC, V. Bus: 1 or 7. **Amenities:** 2 restaurants; room service. *In room:* TV, hair dryer, minibar, Wi-Fi (free).

Hotel Gallo This hotel—a former apartment house—lies along a busy traffic artery, about a 10-minute walk from the town center. Windows are double glazed to shut out the noise. Some of the details of its Art Nouveau facade are still visible. The renovated rooms have tall windows and contain big, tiled bathrooms. Our favorites are two cozy attic rooms under beamed ceilings with dormer windows.

St. Jacobstrasse 62, CH-9000 St. Gallen. ☎ **071/242-71-71.** Fax 071/242-71-61. www.hotelgallo.ch. 24 units. 220F–240F double; 270F triple; 420F–460F junior suite. Rates include buffet breakfast. AE, DC, MC, V. Parking 20F. Bus: 3. *In room:* A/C, TV, hair dryer, minibar.

Hotel Walhalla ★ This modernized Best Western is a first-class hotel in the shopping district. It faces the main railroad station and parking garage and is about a 3-minute walk from the Old Town. Many visitors use the Walhalla as a base for excursions to Appenzellerland and the Lake Constance area. The rooms are nicely furnished and include well-scrubbed bathrooms. The hotel has a Mediterranean-style restaurant, which also serves typical Swiss cuisine.

Bahnhofplatz, CH-9001 St. Gallen. ☎ **800/528-1234** in the U.S. or 071/228-28-00. Fax 071/228-28-90. www.hotelwalhalla.ch. 57 units. 200F–280F double; 250F–350F suite for 2. Children 11 and under stay free in parent's room. Rates include buffet breakfast. AE, DC, MC, V. Parking 30F in garage (only 2 spaces), 20F outside. Bus: 1. **Amenities:** 2 restaurants; bar; room service. *In room:* TV, hair dryer, minibar, Wi-Fi (free).

Radisson SAS Hotel ★★ At last a hotel has come along to challenge the long-established Einstein. This is the largest, newest, and most modern hotel in town, rated four stars by the government. A good choice for commercial travelers, it's also ideal for a vacationer who prefers contemporary styling to the more traditional choices in town. Opposite the trade fair grounds, it lies within an easy walk of the Altstadt (Old Town). Even the standard rooms are well furnished, though not overly spacious, and a sleek contemporary styling prevails throughout. Business-class rooms come with an individual espresso machine, daily newspaper, and an excellent breakfast buffet. The on-site Restaurant Olive is one of the city's best hotel dining rooms, with mix of both modern Swiss and Asian-inspired dishes.

St. Jakob-Strasse 55, CH-9000 St. Gallen. ☎ **071/242-12-12.** Fax 071/242-12-00. www.stgallen.radisson sas.com. 123 units. 210F–295F double; 750F–850F suite. AE, DC, MC, V. **Amenities:** Restaurant; bar; babysitting; exercise room; room service; sauna. *In room:* A/C, TV, fax, minibar, Wi-Fi (free).

Inexpensive

Hotel Dom This simple but adequate hotel is one floor above street level, near the cathedral in the center of town. Originally built in 1966, it has been renovated slowly and gradually many times since. The hotel offers small, basic units with comfortable furniture, some with private bathrooms.

Webergasse 22, CH-9000 St. Gallen. ☎ **071/227-71-71.** Fax 071/227-71-72. www.hoteldom.ch. 40 units (32 with bathroom). 120F double without bathroom, 205F with bathroom. Children 11 and under stay free in parent's room. Rates include continental breakfast. AE, DC, MC, V. Parking 10F. Bus: 1. **Amenities:** Restaurant; room service. *In room:* TV, hair dryer, Wi-Fi (free).

WHERE TO DINE

In the restaurants recommended below, as well as in the area's tearooms and inns, make an effort to try the famous local sausage—bratwurst—and to sample St. Gallen's rich regional pastries.

Am Gallusplatz ★★ FRENCH/SWISS Am Gallusplatz is the most famous restaurant in the Old Town and has a dining room that dates from 1606. Finding it is part of the pleasure of dining here. It's opposite the cathedral, behind a low wall and a pink facade. The five- or seven-course "menu surprise" dinner includes wine and champagne, and the regular menu changes frequently and is always based on fresh ingredients. If available, we recommend bouillabaisse "chef," *pot-au-feu* of fish, garnished goose liver with fresh herbs, grilled sole and salmon Florentine style, and lamb medallions Provençal.

The savory dishes are prepared with flair, with perfectly balanced flavors and textures. **145**
The wine list, one of the most extensive in Switzerland, includes 450 choices, the oldest
dating from 1893. The restaurant also offers a nice selection of Armagnacs and brandies.

Gallusstrasse 24. ✆ **071/223-33-30.** www.gallusplatz.ch. Reservations recommended. Main courses
33F–52F; 4-course menu surprise 125F, 6 courses 165F. AE, DC, MC, V. Tues–Fri and Sun 11:30am–2:30pm;
Tues–Sun 6pm–midnight. Closed last week of July through the 1st 2 weeks of Aug. Bus: 1.

David 38 ★★ MEDITERRANEAN/ASIAN   This is the chic, hip, and trendy dining
address in the city. It lies right outside the center of the Altstadt (Old Town), and is
decorated in a fashionable brasserie style, almost evoking Paris. There's garden seating in
fair weather. The chefs are well trained, and base their dishes on regional produce whenever possible. The cooking is deft, delicious, and sometimes classic, but not always: They
rely on many Asian influences. The house specialty, for example, is lobster in a fiery hot
pepper sauce with a lemon grass–laced risotto. Many dishes, especially their succulent
pastas, are inspired by Italy to the south. Try the roasted goose liver with a sweet-and-sour
rhubarb glaze or the daily fish of the day, perhaps a roasted *loup de mer* (sea bass). A tasty
beginning might be the carrot foam soup flavored with red Thai curry. Desserts are
sumptuous and made fresh daily.

Davidstrasse 38. ✆ **071/230-28-38.** www.david38.ch. Reservations required. Main courses 18F–60F.
Fixed-price menus 72F for 3 courses, 82F for 4 courses, 98F for 5 courses. AE, MC, V. Mon–Wed 9am–
midnight; Thurs–Sat 9am–2am.

Einstein Hotel Restaurant ★ FRENCH/SWISS   One of the finest restaurants in
the city is located on the fifth floor of the Hotel Einstein, with the best panoramic view
in town. The decor blends rustic timber with marble trim. Specialties include pan-fried
pikeperch with apple risotto and baked fennel or a rare loin of tuna on ginger-flavored
noodles. You might begin with a cream of potato soup with wasabi and smoked eel. The
food is rather hearty but often prepared with a sense of delicacy, too.

Berneggstrasse 2. ✆ **071/227-55-55.** Reservations recommended. Main courses 20F–46F. AE, DC, MC, V.
Daily noon–2pm and 6:30–10pm. Bus: 1, 3, or 11.

Restaurant Neubad ★★★ SWISS/FRENCH/ITALIAN   Set in a 300-year-old
house in the historic center of St. Gallen, this restaurant contains a street-level bistro and
a more formal (and expensive) restaurant upstairs, which is one of the finest in northeastern Switzerland. The setting's antique charm is most visible in the two dining rooms
upstairs. Here, a *cuisine du marché,* featuring menu items that change with the seasons,
may include roast haunch of venison with fresh spaetzle, several preparations of fresh fish,
filet of veal with alpine herbs and vegetable risotto, and roast lamb with rosemary sauce
and garlic. Wild-game dishes are featured in autumn, and the salads are usually very, very
fresh. The dishes prepared here seem more engaging year after year, and you can always
count on first-rate cuisine.

Bankgasse 6. ✆ **071/222-86-83.** www.restaurant-neubad.ch. Reservations recommended for the restaurant, not required for the bistro. Restaurant main courses 32F–62F. Bistro main courses 17F–42F. AE,
DC, MC, V. Mon–Fri 10am–2pm and 6–10:30pm. Closed 2 weeks in July. Bus: 1.

ST. GALLEN AFTER DARK
Many locals head for the town's main hotel, **Einstein Hotel** (see "Where to Stay," above),
which has the best pub/cocktail bar in town. If you're lucky, you'll catch a set of live piano
music in this dark, leathery enclave.

Another good spot on the after-dark circuit, for those who like a bustling, noisy Teutonic atmosphere, is the **Weinstube zum Bäumli,** Schmiedgasse 18 (© **071/222-11-74;** www.weinstube-baeumli.ch), convenient to the Old Town, which has been in business for 5 centuries. It has the town's best wine collection, and you can order inexpensive food here, mainly regional fare such as bratwurst. It's closed Sunday and Monday.

You can also check the program at the local tourist office to find out what's scheduled at the **Stadttheater,** Museumstrasse 24 (© **071/242-05-05;** www.theatersg.ch), which presents at least 200 concerts and dramatic performances during its annual season from September to June. Ticket prices depend on the presentation.

Local bands often appear at the **Trischli,** Brühlgasse 18 (© **071/226-09-00**), which also sponsors the occasional karaoke or theme night. The club is open in July and August daily from 10pm to 5:30am, and from September to June daily from 9pm (closing hours vary). There's a cover charge of 10F on Friday and Saturday.

2 APPENZELL ★

18km (11 miles) S of St. Gallen; 20km (12 miles) SW of Altstätten

In the rolling, verdant foothills of the Alpstein, south of Lake Constance, the Appenzell district retains some of Switzerland's strongest folklore. However, in recent years, in an attempt to attract the tourist purse, the area has become somewhat self-conscious and commercial about its traditions. Its hamlets contain intricately painted houses whose colorful decorations are distinctive to the region. The inhabitants, proud of their cultural distinctions, sometimes wear folk costumes, which include an elaborate coif with large wings made of a fabric called tulle. Local men are known for their rakish earrings and their habit of going barefoot in the summer.

Appenzell is famous for three reasons: for its baked goods such as pear bread and chocolates, for the artists who adhere to a certain school of naive art (which some observers compare to paintings by the late American primitivist Grandma Moses), and for its status as the yodeling headquarters of Switzerland. For centuries the district was relatively isolated from the rest of Switzerland, but modern roads and trusty cable cars now ferry sightseers across the otherwise inaccessible terrain.

Appenzell's main square, **Landsgemeindeplatz,** and its main street, **Hauptgasse,** are lined with traditional painted houses. Here, shops sometimes sell the famous embroidery of the area—but examine items carefully before you buy, as some embroideries are made in China or Portugal. Appenzell is an excellent base for exploring two nearby peaks, the **Ebenalp** and **Mount Säntis.**

ESSENTIALS

GETTING THERE From Zurich, you can take a slow local train without transferring; you'll reach Appenzell in about 2 hours. A faster way is to take an express train from Zurich to Gossau, a satellite village of St. Gallen, and transfer to the local train. Trip time from St. Gallen or Gossau to Appenzell on one of the 30 or so daily locals is about 45 minutes. Call © **0900/300-300** for information.

The town's only bus line goes between Appenzell and St. Gallen via a meandering path through local villages not serviced by rail. From St. Gallen, you'll have to transfer buses in a village called Teufen. For more information, call © **071/227-37-37.**

By car from St. Gallen, drive south from the city toward Teufen, where the road is **147** signposted south to Appenzell.

VISITOR INFORMATION The **Appenzell Tourist Office,** Hauptgasse 4 (𝄐 **071/788-96-41;** www.appenzell.ch), is open Monday to Friday from 9am to noon and 2 to 6pm, Saturday and Sunday 10am to noon and 2 to 5pm.

SHOPPING

The main street is filled with shops hawking souvenirs and gifts, some of dubious origin. However, for the best and most authentic handicrafts, head for **Trachtenstube,** Hauptgasse 23 (𝄐 **071/787-16-06**). On the second floor of this outlet you'll find a wide array of traditional Appenzeller clothing, along with farmers' floral work shirts and hand-embroidered handkerchiefs. A wide selection of lace, embroidery, and crafts are sold here as well. Even the locals come here to shop for costumes during festivals.

Another outlet on the main street, **Margreiter,** Hauptgasse 29 (𝄐 **071/787-33-13**), offers machine-made work produced in neighboring factories that's often quite stunning. Embroideries decorated with edelweiss or other alpine flora seem to be the fastest-moving items.

WHERE TO STAY

Hotel Appenzell ★ (Finds) Located on the town's main square, this cozy retreat, built in 1983, is painted with whimsical folk colors on its gabled facade with shuttered windows. The comfortable rooms include conservative, modern walnut furniture, and the bathrooms are lined with marble. It's rather luxurious for the prices charged.

The hotel's street-level cafe, with an outdoor terrace, is a comfortable stop for daily meals, which are really well prepared and based on fresh ingredients. Through the cafe is an elaborately paneled dining room, which is best for a more intimate experience.

Landsgemeindeplatz, CH-9050 Appenzell. 𝄐 071/788-15-15. Fax 071/788-15-51. www.hotel-appenzell. ch. 16 units. 200F–220F double. Rates include buffet breakfast. AE, DC, MC, V. Free parking. Closed 3 weeks in Nov. **Amenities:** 2 restaurants; bar; babysitting; room service. *In room:* TV, hair dryer, minibar.

Hotel Hecht This 18th-century hotel, in the center of town opposite the Catholic church, is the biggest alpine inn in Appenzell. The Knechtle family has owned the place for more than 50 years, keeping it clean, attractive, and conservative. The overall effect is cheerful and comfortable. Bedrooms are small but tastefully furnished with private bathrooms.

Hauptgasse 9, CH-9050 Appenzell. 𝄐 071/788-22-22. Fax 071/788-22-88. www.hecht-appenzell.ch. 42 units. 180F–260F double. Rates include buffet breakfast. AE, DC, MC, V. *In room:* TV, hair dryer, minibar, Wi-Fi (30F per day).

Romantik Hotel Säntis ★★ Appenzell's best hotel in the town center is decorated with dozens of stenciled, symmetrical designs. Its traditional rooms are cozy, and many are filled with regional antiques. Try for a room in the old wing, dating from 1835, if you like painted beams and provincial wooden furnishings. Some accommodations have four-poster or canopy beds. There's a small Appenzell-style dining room with a wood ceiling and colorful tablecloths (see "Where to Dine," below). The Heeb family offers a cordial welcome.

Landsgemeindeplatz 3, CH-9050 Appenzell. 𝄐 071/788-11-11. Fax 071/788-11-10. www.saentis-appenzell.ch. 37 units. 230F–320F double; 340F suite. Rates include buffet breakfast. Parking 6F. AE, DC, MC, V. **Amenities:** Restaurant; room service. *In room:* TV, hair dryer, Wi-Fi (30F per day).

Hof ★ SWISS   One of Appenzell's most consistently crowded and popular restaurants occupies a prominent location in the town center, within a relatively modern-looking decor that's accented with many yards of varnished pinewood planking. Inside, you'll find a collection of local sports trophies and memorabilia, rustic artifacts straight from an alpine farm, wooden tables and chairs, and a fireplace that burns brightly throughout the winter. Menu items include all manner of grilled steaks and meats, fondues, spaetzle with cheese, and a house potato-based specialty loaded with ham, cheese, onions, and spices known as Rösti Hof.

Upstairs are 20 cozy but compact bedrooms, each with private bathroom (tub/shower combination) and TV. None has air-conditioning, but given the relatively cheap price (130F double with breakfast), they tend to be popular.

Engelgasse 4. ℂ **071/787-40-30.** Fax 071/787-58-83. www.gasthaus-hof.ch. Reservations not necessary. Main courses 14F–29F. AE, DC, MC, V. Daily noon–10pm.

Restaurant Säntis ★★ SWISS   This restaurant on the first floor of the popular Romantik Hotel Säntis offers a view over the elaborately detailed houses of the main square. The menu changes frequently. Typical appetizers include a nourishing bouillon or alpine dried beef garnished with pickles and onions. Main courses may include loin of lamb Provençal or roast filet of pork. Some of the meat and fish dishes are accompanied by homemade noodles, served with al dente carrots and spinach.

In the Romantik Hotel Säntis, Landsgemeindeplatz 3. ℂ **071/788-11-11.** Reservations recommended. Main courses 44F–55F; fixed-price menus 88F–115F. AE, DC, MC, V. Daily 11am–2pm and 6:30–11pm. Closed Jan 15–Feb.

EASY EXCURSIONS

Either of the following excursions would be ideal for a picnic, with some of the most dramatic mountains in eastern Switzerland as your backdrop. Before heading here, pick up supplies in Appenzell and the day is yours. We hope it's a sunny one.

EBENALP ★★   Visit Ebenalp, 6km (4 miles) away, for a spectacular view of the hills and pastures of the Appenzell district. The jagged promontory is at an elevation of 1,620m (5,314 ft.). Wear sturdy walking shoes so that you can walk down to **Wildkirchli**—a chapel in a grotto that was inhabited by hermits from the mid–17th to the mid–19th centuries. Paleolithic artifacts discovered here at the turn of the 20th century indicate that it is the oldest prehistoric settlement found in Switzerland so far.

To get here, drive to the end of the Weissbad-Wasserauen road, then take a cable car for an 11-minute ride to the summit. The cable car leaves every 45 minutes in season; a round-trip costs 27F for adults, 10F for children. For information, call ℂ **071/799-12-12** or visit www.ebenalp.ch.

MOUNT SÄNTIS ★★★   The major attraction in the area is Mount Säntis, the highest peak (2,463m/8,079 ft.) in the Alpstein massif. It offers a panoramic view of eastern

---

> (**Tips**)   **A Must-Have Picnic Item**
>
> If you're planning a picnic in the mountains, stock up on some of the local Appenzeller cheese at **Chäs Sutter,** Marktgasse 8 (ℂ **071/787-13-33;** www. chaes-sutter.ch). This cheese tastes like nothing else found in Europe.

Switzerland, including the Grisons, the Bernese Alps, the Vorarlberg mountains, Lake Constance, and even Lake Zurich. On a clear day you can see as far as Swabia in southern Germany.

To reach the departure point for the cable car (whose German name is Säntis Schwebebahn), drive 14km (9 miles) west of Appenzell, following the signs pointing to Urnäsch and Schwägalp. The cable car departs at 30-minute intervals year-round; round-trip passage costs 41F. For more information, call ℰ **071/365-65-65** or visit www. saentisbahn.ch.

Instead of driving, you can take one of the most dramatic walks in the area from the village of Wasserrauen to the village of Schwägalp, at which point you can take a cable car to the belvedere overlooking Säntis. Hourly trains from Appenzell will take you to Wasserrauen. The walk between Wasserrauen and Schwägalp is 8km (5½ miles), taking anywhere from 4½ to 5½ hours, depending on your stamina. As you hike along, you'll see some of the most scenic panoramas in this part of Switzerland.

3 LAKE CONSTANCE ★★★

The 261km (162-mile) shoreline of Lake Constance is shared by three countries—Switzerland, Germany, and Austria. The surrounding hills are covered with vineyards and orchards and are dotted with many farming villages. Vacationers are drawn here by the sunny, mild climate and nice beaches.

Lake Constance is divided into three parts, although the name is frequently applied to Bodensee, the largest part. At the western end of Bodensee, the lake splits into two branches: a long fjord called Überlingersee and an irregular marshland known as Untersee. Untersee is connected to the rest of the lake by a narrow channel of water, which is actually the young Rhine River. The blue felchen, a pikelike fish found only in Lake Constance, furnishes the district with a tasty and renowned specialty.

The Swiss gateway to Lake Constance is **Rorschach,** 11km (7 miles) northeast of St. Gallen. You can get here by **train** from Zurich in 1½ hours (the train departs every hour) or from St. Gallen in 20 minutes. From Rorschach, you can continue on—by frequent local trains or buses along the lake—to the three major centers: **Arbon, Horn,** and **Romanshorn.** A well-organized network of modern passenger **ferries** links all these towns along the shore and connects Switzerland with Germany and Austria.

The **Rorschach Tourist Office,** Hauptstrasse 63 (ℰ **071/841-70-34;** www.rorschach. ch), provides an up-to-date timetable for all forms of transportation. They are open Monday to Friday 8:30am to noon and 1:30 to 6pm. From May 1 to September 15, the office is also open on Saturday 10am to 6pm. You can also contact one of the most popular boat lines, **Schiffahrtsbetrieb Rorschach** (ℰ **071/846-60-60;** www.schifffahrt-rorschach.ch), the best and most economical way to cruise from one town along the lake to another, thereby transforming a commuter trip into a cruise. This is easiest to do from May to September.

Your choice of towns along Lake Constance will depend almost entirely on your selection of a hotel. The towns and attractions are so similar that it is hard to tell where one town ends and another begins. All of them offer lakeside promenades and flower gardens overlooking the lake, and all of them can become centers for pleasure boating and trips on the lake. The towns are also so close together that even if you're in Romanshorn in the west, you can arrive at Rorschach in the east in minutes. Because it has a greater choice of hotels, we'd give the nod to Rorschach.

Once at Lake Constance, you'll find dozens of bike trails, each marked with a red sign, and each running around the southern tier (the Swiss side) of the lake.

RORSCHACH

This medieval harbor town at the foot of the Rorschacher Berg is at the southern tip of the lake. It has lakeside gardens, an extensive promenade, a good choice of hotels, and facilities for sailing, rowing, swimming, fishing, and windsurfing. Passenger ships pass through Rorschach en route to Germany, Austria, and Liechtenstein.

Rorschach's illustrious past is reflected in its buildings, which include the **Kornhaus,** a granary built in 1746; the former **Mariaberg cloister;** and **18th-century painted houses** with oriel windows along Hauptgasse. If you'd like to bike along the lake, you can go to the railway station and rent a bike for the day for about 30F.

Where to Stay & Dine

Hotel Mozart   Opened in 1986, this comfortable hotel with its own garage is situated between the main street of town and the lake. The polished-granite building has well-maintained, midsize rooms, eight overlooking the lake.

The old-world ambience of the hotel's Café Mozart complements its variety of famous pastries. Another specialty is tea—19 varieties, including essence of kiwi, linden blossom, and tea leaves grown on the foothills of Mount Everest. The cafe also offers simple meals.

Hafenzentrum, CH-9400 Rorschach. ⓒ **071/844-47-47.** Fax 071/844-47-48. www.mozart-rorschach.ch. 33 units. 155F–195F double; 235F–350F suite. Rates include buffet breakfast. AE, DC, MC, V. Parking 5F. **Amenities:** Restaurant. In room: TV, minibar.

Parkhotel Waldau ★★   This country manor was built after World War II as a private school for boys, then transformed into a government-rated five-star hotel (the best in town). The hotel sits on a hill overlooking the lake 6km (4 miles) southwest of the center. As a first-class hotel, Parkhotel Waldau has far larger and better-furnished rooms and more spacious and well-equipped bathrooms than its more modest and smaller competitor, the Mozart. In addition, it has all the amenities of a deluxe hotel (including a swimming pool, tennis courts, and a health club), with which no other hotel in town can compete. And if that wasn't enough, Parkhotel Waldau also has the finest and most varied cuisine in town.

Seebleichestrasse 42, CH-9400 Rorschach. ⓒ **071/858-70-70.** Fax 071/858-70-71. www.parkhotel-waldau.ch. 42 units. 215F–225F double; 270F–280F junior suite. Rates include buffet breakfast. AE, DC, MC, V. Free parking. **Amenities:** Restaurant; babysitting; indoor heated pool; exercise room; room service; sauna; outdoor tennis court (lit). In room: TV, hair dryer, minibar, Wi-Fi (30F per day).

HORN

This old fishing hamlet is a 5-minute drive east of Arbon. Set in the canton of Thurgau, it provides another base for exploring the shores of Lake Constance. Frankly, the main reason to visit is to stay or dine at the Hotel Bad Horn; otherwise, you'll find more facilities at Rorschach, only a 10-minute car or bus ride to the east.

Where to Stay & Dine

Hotel Bad Horn ★ ⓕⓘⓝⓓⓢ   This large blue-and-white hotel is located in the town center at the end of a small peninsula on the lakefront. Built in 1827, it is fully restored with big windows, gables, a tile roof, rooftop terraces, and an expanse of lawn extending

almost to the lake. The midsize bedrooms are well furnished and comfortably appointed,
each with a neatly kept bathroom.

At the Captain's Grill, with its nautical decor, specialties include aiguillettes of pink
duck, quenelles of local fish, scampi with Calvados, and filet of beef with Armagnac.

Seestrasse 36, CH-9326 Horn. ℂ **071/841-55-11.** Fax 071/841-60-89. www.badhorn.ch. 54 units.
190F–260F double; 310F suite. Rates include buffet breakfast. AE, DC, MC, V. Free parking. **Amenities:** 2
restaurants; room service. *In room:* TV, hair dryer, minibar, Wi-Fi (35F per day).

ARBON ★

One of the best spots along the lake is Arbon, the lakefront promenade that offers a view
of Constance, the German shore, and the Alps. It has far more facilities than Horn (see
above), although the views and ambience are pretty similar. If lakeside walks appeal to
you, this might be the place, as most of the town lies on a promontory jutting out into
Lake Constance. In summer you're surrounded by orchards and lake meadows, so strolling is what to do here. Facilities include a large boat harbor, swimming pools, and a
school for sailing and surfing. The town was built on the site of an ancient Celtic community and was called Arbor Felix by the Romans.

After leaving Rorschach, continue northwest along Route 13 for 15 minutes until you
reach Arbon. The town is also a major stopover for all the trains and buses running along
the southern tier of Lake Constance.

The town's most visible monument is its 13th- or 14th-century castle, **Schloss Arbon,**
Hauptstrasse (ℂ **071/446-10-58**), which broods over the town from its hilltop. Most of

its interior is devoted to a technical school for adults, but you can visit the small-scale
museum during its limited open hours. Exhibits include ancient Roman artifacts
unearthed in the region, and displays relating to the once-potent, now-defunct industries
that used to call Arbon home. Premier among these is the Saurer Truck Company, which
employed up to 3,000 local workers between its 1906 founding and its merger with
Mercedes-Benz in 1982. Frankly, unless you're terribly interested in the history of the local
region, you can skip this museum entirely. Between May and September, the museum is
open daily from 2 to 5pm; March, April, October, and November, it's open Sunday only,
from 2 to 5pm. Admission costs 4F for adults and 2F for children 14 and under.

For tourist information, go to **Infocenter Arbon,** Schmiedgasse 6 (ℂ **071/440-13-
80**), open Monday to Friday 9 to 11:30am and 2 to 6pm. From mid-June to August it
is also open on Saturday from 9 to 11:30am.

Where to Stay & Dine

Gasthof Bräuerei Frohsinn ★   Originally built in 1822, and located near the edge
of the Bodensee, within a 5-minute walk west of the town center, this four-story historic
hotel contains 13 simple and nostalgically decorated bedrooms, a brewery that chugs out
many gallons of both light and dark beer (the brand name is Frohsinn), a popular bowling alley, and a trio of restaurants. The most formal and gourmet conscious of the three
is the Fisch Restaurant. Focusing on upscale, gourmet-inspired Continental food, its
prices begin at 75F for a fixed-price menu.

Less lofty and less ambitious in their cuisine are Le Bistro and, in the cellar, the
Bräukeller. Both restaurants charge from 20F to 48F for rib-sticking main courses that
include grilled steaks; calves' liver with bacon; roulades of beef, chicken, or veal layered
with herbs and cheese; noodles studded with ham and a cream-flavored cheese sauce; and
as much beer from the local brewery as you can handle.

Romanshornerstrasse 15, CH-9320 Arbon. $\mathcal{C}$ **071/447-84-84.** Fax 071/446-41-42. www.frohsinn-arbon. ch. 13 units. 180F double; 220F suite. Rates include buffet breakfast. AE, DC, MC, V. **Amenities:** 3 restaurants. *In room:* TV.

Hotel Metropol ★   This hotel, across from the train station, is part of a lakeside complex that exemplifies creative urban planning. It's Arbon's best choice for overnighting. The complex includes a department store, a grocery store, and a busy cafeteria. The hotel lobby is Nordic modern, and the rooms are comfortable but plain, each with a loggia facing the lake and well-maintained bathrooms. The best place to dine is the second-floor restaurant, serving Swiss cuisine and specializing in fish caught in the lake.

Bahnhofstrasse 49, CH-9320 Arbon. $\mathcal{C}$ **071/447-82-82.** Fax 071/447-82-80. www.metropol-arbon.ch. 42 units. 200F–260F double; 170F–320F suite for 1–3. Rates include buffet breakfast. AE, DC, MC, V. Free parking. **Amenities:** 2 restaurants; bar; outdoor pool; room service; sauna. *In room:* TV, hair dryer, minibar.

Hotel Rotes Kreuz   This is a stucco house with a lake terrace built in 1760. The handful of rooms it contains are simple, small, and clean. All contain a private bathroom. You can dine in a glass-enclosed solarium or a cozy pine-paneled room. Specialties include a variety of lake fish.

Hafenstrasse 3, CH-9320 Arbon. $\mathcal{C}$ **071/446-19-18.** Fax 071/446-24-85. www.hotelroteskreuz.ch. 20 units. 150F double. Rates include continental breakfast. MC, V. Free parking. **Amenities:** Restaurant. *In room:* TV.

ROMANSHORN

This town is the largest port on the lake and the base for Swiss steamers. In spite of the industrial overlay, Romanshorn is also a successful summer lakeside resort. Popular with Swiss, German, and Austrian tourists, it's set against a backdrop of panoramic views of the Austrian and Swiss mountains nearby. The resort offers a swimming pool, a sailing school, a water-skiing school, and tennis courts. There's also a park and a zoo.

A year-round ferry service links Romanshorn with Friedrichshafen, Germany. Boats operated by the **Schweizerische Bodensee Schiffahrtsgesellschaft** ($\mathcal{C}$ **071/446-78-88;** www.sbsag.ch) make hourly transits to Friedrichshafen, beginning at 8:30am daily between May and October, and ending between 6:30 and 7:30pm, depending on the day of the week. One-way transit, which requires about an hour, costs 15F. The attractions on the German side of the lake are actually far more interesting than anything on the Swiss border, and there's no hassle or fees to cross, so we recommend you take the chance to visit **Friedrichshafen.** Here you can stroll its lakefront promenade, with a sweeping view of the Swiss Alps. Biking along the broad Seestrasse is also a delight. A kiosk within the Stadtbahnhof (local rail station) rents bikes for 28F to 33F per day. You can also visit the **Zeppelin Museum** in the Hafenbahnhof on Seestrasse 22, with its fascinating re-creation of the historic *Hindenburg,* which exploded in a fire in New Jersey in 1937.

In summer, boat trips are organized to Mainau, a German island about 6km (4 miles) north of Constance that was once the home of the grand duke of Baden. Boats operated by the **Schweizerische Bodensee Schiffahrtsgesellschaft** ($\mathcal{C}$ **071/466-78-88;** www. sbsag.ch) make two daily transits from May to October, from Romanshorn to Mainau. Trips take 90 minutes each way and cost 30F round-trip. You'll have to pay an entrance fee of 15F to gain access to the island. **Mainau Island** is well worth your time. Because of the mild climate, the island is almost tropical, filled with palms and orange trees, along with fragrant flowers in bloom year-round—even though the island lies practically in the shadow of the snow-covered Alps. In the center of the island is a botanical garden, set on the site of an ancient castle, once a residence of the Knights of the Teutonic order.

In Romanshorn, two other worthy options involve hopping aboard any boat operated by Schweizerische Bodensee Schiffahrtsgesellschaft (see above). If you go on the one bound for Rorschach (three departures per day), you'll pay about 15F one-way. Then you can explore the town of Rorschach before returning to Romanshorn by any of the many trains (a 20-min. ride).

A second option involves sailing from Romanshorn to **Kreuzlingen** or the German town of **Konstanz,** a 1-hour ride (btw. two and three departures per day), and taking the train back (a 20-min. ride). One-way boat transit to either Kreuzlingen or Konstanz costs 14F.

For tourist information in Romanshorn, contact **Verkehrsbüro,** Bahnhofplatz (✆ 071/ 463-32-32), open Monday to Friday from 8am to noon and 2 to 6pm, Saturday 9am to noon. If you'd like to bike along the lake, you can go to the railway station, where a kiosk rents bikes from 28F to 33F per day.

Where to Stay & Dine

Park-Hotel Inseli ★ This model hotel, the best in town, is secluded in a grove of trees a 10-minute walk from the center, directly on the lake. Its comfortable and spacious bedrooms offer views of the park or the lake; the public rooms are decorated with chrome and plush carpeting. Manager Anton Stager and his family keep up the hotel's informal ambience. There's a sunny, indoor-outdoor cafe and a more formal rotisserie where French cuisine is served daily. There's a pretense to grandeur, and those in the know order the local fish caught from Lake Constance. The cafe offers a panoramic view all the way to Austria.

Inselistrasse 6, CH-8590 Romanshorn. ✆ **071/466-88-88.** Fax 071/466-88-77. www.hotel-inseli.com. 39 units. 210F–280F double. Rates include buffet breakfast. AE, DC, MC, V. Free parking. **Amenities:** 2 restaurants; bar; exercise room; room service; sauna. *In room:* TV, hair dryer, minibar, Wi-Fi (30F per day).

4 STEIN-AM-RHEIN ★★

20km (12 miles) east of Schaffhausen; 27km (17 miles) N of Winterthur

Dating from 1094, Stein-am-Rhein is pure old town, one of the most authentic and best-preserved medieval towns in Switzerland. It's on the right bank of the Rhine, west of Untersee, an arm of Lake Constance. The town is blessed with the finest half-timbered houses in northeastern Switzerland, and the foundations of some of them dip into the river itself. Flower-decked fountains and oriel-windowed houses are grace notes. The facades, which are often fully painted, beckon the photographer in all of us. Nearby was the first Roman bridge ever built over the Rhine.

ESSENTIALS

GETTING THERE Stein-am-Rhein lies midway along the railway link connecting Schaffhausen with Kreuzlingen, on the edge of Lake Constance. From Zurich, passengers take an express train to Schaffhausen, then change for a less frequent local train to Stein-am-Rhein; trip time from Zurich is just under 2 hours. There are also good train connections to Stuttgart, Germany. For **rail schedules** or more information, call ✆ **0900/ 300-300.**

The only **bus** connection to Stein-am-Rhein crosses the border into a German village named Singen, from which there are rail connections to Stuttgart, Germany. Call ✆ **0900/300-300** for information.

By **car** the trip from Zurich takes less than an hour. Head north on N1 until a point near Winterthur, where you connect with E41 going north to Schaffhausen. This route becomes N4, connecting with Route 13, heading east toward Stein-am-Rhein.

VISITOR INFORMATION   The Stein-am-Rhein **Tourist Office,** at Oberstadt 3 (© **052/ 742-20-90;** www.stein-am-rhein.ch), maintains up-to-date bus and rail schedules. It's open year-round Monday to Thursday 9:30am to noon and 1:30 to 5pm, with additional operation April to December Friday 9:30am to noon and 1:30 to 5pm, and also Saturday in July and August 9:30am to noon and 1:30 to 4pm.

SEEING THE SIGHTS

A number of quaint houses line **Rathausplatz (Town Hall Square)** and **Hauptstrasse (Main Street).** Many have oriel windows, rich frescoes, timberwork, and fountains.

The **Historische Sammlung (Historical Museum)** is in one of the rooms of the town hall, on Rathausplatz (© 052/741-21-42). The collection includes weapons, banners, and stained glass. Admission is 3F. The exhibit keeps no set hours; you have to call and arrange for an appointment to view it.

A Benedictine abbey was built near Rathausplatz during the 11th century; it was abandoned during the Protestant Reformation in 1524. Today it's the **Kloster-museum St. Georgen (St. George's Abbey Museum;** © 052/741-21-42), devoted to local history and art. The rooms, because of their rich ceilings, paneling, and 16th-century murals by Thomas Schmid and Ambrosius Holbein, are often more interesting than the exhibits. Admission to the museum is 4F for adults, 2F for children. The museum is open April to October, Tuesday to Sunday 10am to 5pm. The restored Convent Church of St. George, a Romanesque basilica built by the Catholics and later transformed into a Protestant church, has sections dating from the 12th century.

Wohnmuseum Lindwurm, Understadt 18 (© **052/741-25-12;** www.museum-lindwurm.ch), lies in an old, 19th-century *bürgerhaus* (community center). With exhibits and artifacts, it re-creates life here in that century. You learn how the townspeople and their servants lived, and something about their farming methods. It's open March to October Wednesday to Monday from 10am to 5pm, charging 5F for adults and 3F for children.

If riding a **bike** appeals to you, consider renting one from the kiosk within the railway station, and then heading off for a 20km (13-mile) westbound excursion to Schaffhausen, or a 29km (18-mile) eastbound excursion to Kreuzlingen. The cost is about 32F per day. The edges of both the Rhine and the Bodensee are flanked with "velo-routes" (bicycle paths) that are clearly marked with red-and-white signs that display a bicycle.

Ecologically and panoramically, the area where the Rhine widens into a lake is particularly interesting for sightseeing and cruising. If you're in Stein-am-Rhein, you'll find yourself midway along the route of a series of cruises that depart from Schaffhausen, to the west, and meander their way into the Untersee, the lake just to the west of the Bodensee. The terminus of the cruise is in the Swiss town of Kreuzlingen, just across the water from the German city of Konstanz. If you opt for a full round-trip excursion from Schaffhausen to Kreuzlingen, a travel time of 4 hours each way, you'll spend a full day in some of the most appealing waterways of central Europe. The cost is 86F round-trip. There are between three and four departures per day from both Schaffhausen and Kreuzlingen, but only between April and early October. For reservations and more information, contact **Schiffahrtsgesellschaft Untersee und Rhein,** Freierplatz 7, 8200 Schaffhausen (© **052/634-08-88;** www.urh.ch).

SHOPPING

Most of the town's shopping options line either side of the **Understadt,** a thoroughfare that some old-time residents still refer to as Hauptstrasse. Set near the town's railway station and Rathaus, its most appealing shop is **Heimatwerk,** Understadt 28 (© **052/ 741-33-92**). Devoted to the merchandising of artifacts made exclusively in Switzerland, it inventories glass, ceramics, woodcarvings, textiles, Swiss Army knives and watches, and lots of small and usually inexpensive art objects guaranteed to collect dust after you display them in your home for a while.

WHERE TO STAY

Hotel Chlosterhof ★★★   The finest hotel in town, situated on the Rhine east of Rathausplatz, was created from an abandoned shoe factory and now has a brick facade with angled glass. Its interior includes an open fireplace and a lobby with a cruciform vault. The rooms, which come in various shapes and sizes, are stylized; 10 have four-poster beds and most of the suites open onto the Rhine. All units contain neatly kept bathrooms. The restaurant, Le Bâteau, offers fine dining amid a nautical decor, and Le Jardin is a little in-house bistro.

Oehningerstrasse 2, CH-8260 Stein-am-Rhein. © **052/742-42-42.** Fax 052/741-13-37. www.chlosterhof. ch. 69 units. 270F–310F double; 370F–600F suite. Rates include buffet breakfast. AE, DC, MC, V. Parking 15F. **Amenities:** 2 restaurants; bar; indoor heated pool; room service; spa. *In room:* TV, hair dryer, minibar, Wi-Fi (18F per hour).

Hotel-Restaurant Adler ★ (Finds)   This tasteful, comfortable hotel has one of the most flamboyant facades in the old city: It's painted with characters from Rhenish legends, depicting such medieval scenes as a tree of life, martyrs at the stake, and characters groveling before Asian potentates. The hotel has two sections: One dates from 1461, and the other, rather plain guesthouse annex was built in 1957. The rooms, streamlined with a Nordic design and equipped with firm beds, often attract traveling families.

Rathausplatz, CH-8260 Stein-am-Rhein. © **052/742-61-61.** Fax 052/741-44-40. www.adlersteinamrhein. ch. 25 units. 180F–200F main house double; 120F–150F annex double. Rates include buffet breakfast. AE, DC, MC, V. Free parking. **Amenities:** Restaurant. *In room:* TV, hair dryer, Wi-Fi (free).

Hotel Rheinfels ★   This is a large and commodious building built in 1448 near the entrance to Stein-am-Rhein beside the Rhine. It's well known for its pleasantly decorated bedrooms and for its popular restaurant with family-style tables. Bedrooms range from small to midsize, and each is traditionally furnished with comfortable beds. Upstairs from the restaurant is an antique room with wide, creaking floorboards, massive chandeliers, old portraits, and a collection of medieval armor.

Rhygasse 8, CH-8260 Stein-am-Rhein. © **052/741-21-44.** Fax 052/741-25-22. www.rheinfels.ch. 16 units. 190F–260F double. Rates include continental breakfast. AE, MC, V. Closed Jan–Feb. **Amenities:** Restaurant; room service. *In room:* TV, hair dryer, minibar.

WHERE TO DINE

Hotel Rheinfels Restaurant SWISS   This regional restaurant offers a view of the head of the Rhine, where it exits from Lake Constance. Typical dishes include filet of fera (a lake fish) with lemon and capers, fricassee of Rhenish fish with baby vegetables, hot *Bauern-schinken* (farmer's ham), and grilled veal steak. A potpourri of desserts is offered. The cuisine is based on very fresh and quality ingredients that are deftly handled by the kitchen staff.

Rathausplatz. © **052/741-21-44.** Reservations recommended. Main courses 35F–52F. AE, MC, V. July–Aug daily 11am–2pm and 6–9:30pm; Sept–Dec and Mar–June Thurs–Tues 11am–2pm and 6–9:30pm.

Restaurant Le Bateau ★★ INTERNATIONAL   In the Hotel Chlosterhof, this deluxe restaurant is a bastion of elegance and a refined cuisine. The chefs have honed their technique to an amazing sharpness, and they follow their inspiration wherever it leads. Their fixed-price menus are arguably the finest in town. You can also order a la carte, beginning with such starters as an avocado carpaccio with lime dressing and a smoked salmon tartar with a sautéed quail's egg. For a fish course we'd recommend the poached sole in a whiskey-lobster sauce, or else a poultry dish such as quail breast and corn-fed chicken breast with a mushroom risotto. The desserts are rich enough to be sinful, including, for example, homemade nougat dumplings with an apricot ragout and macadamia ice cream.

In the Hotel Chlosterhof, Oehningerstrasse 2. ✆ **052/742-4242.** Reservations required. Main courses 39F–45F. AE, MC, V. Daily 6–10pm.

Weinstube zum Rothen Ochsen INTERNATIONAL   The Inn of the Red Ox opens onto the main square of town, sharing space with the city hall. It is the most revered wine tavern in town, a bastion of good food at affordable prices. Its frescoed facade will draw you inside a cozy atmosphere with an old-fashioned *Kachelofen* (tiled stove). At night candles flicker on the wooden tables. Begin with a sausage salad, dried alpine ham, or a tempting antipasti. For the main course, try the savory goulash soup or beef Stroganoff. A selection of vegetarian dishes is also offered, along with some market-fresh fish, poultry, and beef dishes.

Rathausplatz 9. ✆ **052/741-2328.** Reservations recommended. Main courses 20F–25F. No credit cards. Mon and Thurs–Fri 11am–11pm; Sat 10am–11pm; Sun 10am–5pm.

STEIN-AM-RHEIN AFTER DARK

Most city residents head home after work in a city that's not noted for its raucous night-life. But the bar that attracts more business than any other, **Le Papillon,** is in the Hotel Chlosterhof (see above), Oehningerstrasse 2 (✆ **052/742-42-42**). It opens every night at 6pm and offers lots of varnished paneling, a woodsy kind of coziness, and views of the river. They will happily stay open until the last customer leaves.

5 SCHAFFHAUSEN ★ & THE RHEINFALL ★★

51km (32 miles) N of Zurich; 27km (17 miles) N of Winterthur

Once a major depot for river barges, Schaffhausen is built on terraces along the steeply inclined right bank of the Rhine. Although many sections of the city are modern and heavily industrialized, Schaffhausen retains its medieval spirit, exemplified by its roman-tic fountains and old, brown-roofed houses, dotted with oriel windows and decorated with statues in niches. It's a center for visiting the Rhine Falls (Rheinfall), one of the most popular sights in northeastern Switzerland.

Once ruled by the Habsburgs, Schaffhausen became an imperial free city and later the capital of a Swiss canton of the same name. Germany borders the canton on three sides, heavily influencing the Teutonic flavor of much of the city's architecture.

ESSENTIALS

GETTING THERE   Schaffhausen is on all major north-south **train** lines between Stutt-gart and Milan. There are at least 14 express trains from Zurich every day (trip time 40

min.). Call © **0900/300-300** for more information. If **driving** from Zurich, head north
on Route 4 all the way, which takes about 1 hour.

VISITOR INFORMATION   The Schaffhausen **Tourist Information Office,** at Herrenacker 15 (© **052/632-40-20;** www.schaffhauserland.ch), is open in summer Monday to Friday 9:30am to 6pm, Saturday 9:30am to 4pm, and Sunday 9:30am to 2pm; winter hours are Monday to Friday 9:30am to 5pm and Saturday 9:30am to 2pm.

SEEING THE SIGHTS

Spend a morning touring the **Old Town** ★ on foot. There's a good view of the town from the battlements of the **Munot,** which dates from 1564. The round fortress has a tower, platform, and parapet walks. It can be reached by stairs and has a covered footbridge across the moat. The Munot is the only fortress to be based on a book by Albrecht Dürer, published in Nürnberg in 1527. It's open May to September daily from 9am to 8pm, October to April daily from 10am to 5pm. Admission is free.

The crowning glory of the Old Town is the **Münster (All Saints' Church),** on Münsterplatz. Now Protestant, it was formerly a Benedictine monastery, consecrated in 1052. Its Romanesque architecture is stern and plain. In a nearby courtyard is the 15th-century bell that inspired Schiller's poem "Song of the Bell" and the opening of Longfellow's "Golden Legend."

The most characteristic street is **Vordergasse** ★, where visitors usually stop to photograph the frescoed Haus zum Ritter, dating from 1485. On Fronwegplatz you'll find two outstanding fountains from the 1520s.

Museum zu Allerheiligen (All Saints' Museum) ★, Baumgartenstrasse (© **052/633-07-77;** www.allerheiligen.ch), is one of the most important national museums in Switzerland. The exhibits range from prehistoric times to the present, including traditional garb of the province, old weapons, and period furnishings. Visit the Treasury in the former abbots' salon. The museum is open Tuesday to Sunday from 11am to 5pm. Admission is 9F for adults, free for children 15 and under.

A SPECTACULAR WATERFALL

The Rheinfall (or Rhine Falls) is the most celebrated waterfall in central Europe. It's also the most powerful—700 cubic meters of water per second rush over a width of 137m (449 ft.). The water falls 21m (69 ft.), a sight that inspired Goethe to liken it to the "source of the ocean." This natural wonder is most spectacular in early summer when it's fed by mountain snows.

From the bus station at Schaffhausen, take bus no. 1. There are frequent departures for the 10-minute ride. A train runs every 30 minutes during the day from the station at Schaffhausen to Rheinfall.

To get to the Rheinfall from Zurich, take a train from the Hauptbahnhof to Neuhausen and get off at the Rheinfall stop. The trip takes less than an hour. It's a 15-minute walk from the train depot at Neuhausen to the waterfall. To further enhance the experience, you can take an 10F boat trip to the rock in the center of the Rheinfall from April to October.

In addition, the falls can be viewed from the belvedere of **Laufen Castle** on the left bank. The castle has been converted into a restaurant with a staircase that leads to the view. Bring a raincoat.

You can also take a ferry across the river to Neuhausen and the little castle of **Schlöseli-Wörth** (© **052/672-24-21;** www.schloessliwoerth.ch), built in the 12th century as a Customs post. Today it's a restaurant, open daily from March through November.

Consistent with its role as a hardworking, industry-conscious border town, Schaffhausen doesn't place too much emphasis on folklore, so the handful of kitschy souvenirs you're likely to find will probably be sold from small shops around the railway station, or from nondescript outlets beside either of the town's main shopping streets, **Vordergasse** and **Fronwegplatz.** More appealing is a shop that specializes in equipment designed for climbing, skiing, and virtually every other sport you can think of: **Benz,** Schützengraben 9 (② **052/624-56-93;** www.schaffhausen.ch). In addition to everything from tennis racquets to snowshoes, the outlet sells clothing suitable for any weather Switzerland can dish out.

WHERE TO STAY

Hotel Park Villa ★ This chiseled gray hotel is located near the train station in a municipal park with massive trees. Originally built as an opulent private home around 1900, it was converted into a hotel in the 1960s. It's designed very much like a castle, with towers and steep roofs. The interior is as graceful as the exterior is rough, containing crystal chandeliers and several public rooms with fresh flowers, comfortable chairs, and oil paintings. A few bedrooms are decorated regally with antiques; others are in an uninspired modern style. All units are well maintained.

Parkstrasse 18, CH-8200 Schaffhausen. ② **052/635-60-60.** Fax 052/635-60-70. www.parkvilla.ch. 20 units. 215F–235F double; 250F–308F suite. Rates include buffet breakfast. AE, DC, MC, V. Free parking. **Amenities:** Restaurant; room service; outdoor tennis court (lit). *In room:* TV, hair dryer, minibar, Wi-Fi (free).

Rheinhotel Fischerzunft ★★★ Located on Freier Platz next to a promenade along the Rhine, this is an inviting inn that was formerly occupied by the fishermen's guild. The Jaeger family converted it to a hotel in 1898. The main public room has Chinese decor. Since there are so few bedrooms, and this place is so well known, reservations are especially important in summer. The château-style, contemporary bedrooms at first appear out of place in such a medieval city, but they're soothingly comfortable. The six with views of the Rhine carry higher price tags.

The excellent restaurant mixes classic European and Asian influences, featuring curried chicken consommé with Chinese ravioli, filet of venison with Chinese five-spice powder and sautéed mustard cabbage, ravioli of crayfish, and an assortment of dim sum. The dishes are rich in taste, texture, and presentation. The desserts include a medley of passion fruit and papaya.

Rheinquai 8, CH-8202 Schaffhausen. ② **052/632-05-05.** Fax 052/632-05-13. www.fischerzunft.ch. 10 units. 295F–360F double; 460F junior suite. Rates include buffet breakfast. AE, DC, MC, V. **Amenities:** Restaurant; room service. *In room:* TV, hair dryer, minibar.

WHERE TO DINE

Consider an elegant dinner at the Rheinhotel Fischerzunft (see above), which is one of the top three restaurants in Switzerland.

Restaurant Gerberstube ITALIAN The Guidi family runs the finest Italian restaurant in Schaffhausen. The dining room is in a 17th-century guildhall, which contains a changing exhibit of modern paintings. You may begin with *stracciatella,* the famous egg-and-consommé soup of Rome, and follow it with spaghetti, cannelloni, or a veal schnitzel pizzaiola. They also serve many classic dishes, including chateaubriand with béarnaise sauce and various preparations of veal and pasta. The cooking, although not exactly innovative or exciting, is always reliable and satisfying and is prepared with quality ingredients.

Bachstrasse 8. 𝄐 **052/625-21-55.** www.gerberstube.ch. Reservations required. Main courses 21F–69F. AE, DC, MC, V. Tues–Sat 11am–3pm and 6–10:30pm.

Wirschaft zum Frieden ★ SWISS   One of Schaffhausen's most folkloric and romantic-looking restaurants occupies five richly paneled dining rooms within the thick and solid walls of a building that dates from 1445. In summer expect masses of flowers on the building's balconies, and even more pleasingly, one of the city's finest gardens in back, where tables are set up beneath wisteria vines and venerable trees as a means of appreciating the seasonal warmth. Menu items include carpaccio of beef; fresh-made soups that include cream of broccoli and cream of tomato with basil; Zurich-style minced veal in an herb-flavored cream sauce; an excellent version of calves' liver with *rösti* potatoes; and a mixed grill that combines portions of veal, beef, calves' liver, and chicken. Dessert may include a satisfying dish of poached seasonal fruit (including plums, peaches, and/or apricots), sometimes garnished with ice cream.

Herrenacker 11. 𝄐 **052/625-47-15.** www.wirtschaft-frieden.ch. Reservations recommended only for dinner on weekends. Main courses 37F–48F. AE, DC, MC, V. Tues–Sat 11am–2:30pm and 6pm–midnight. Bus: 1, 2, 6, or 10.

SCHAFFHAUSEN AFTER DARK

Many night owls gravitate toward Schaffhausen's **Saffrangasse,** a narrow historic street with the most crowded and popular bars in town. Two of them stand out. The **Bar Orient,** Stadthausgasse 13 (𝄐 **052/633-02-02**), a loud, sometimes raucous hangout for folks under 35, offers high energy, foaming mugs of beer, and occasional bouts of live music. Its most visible competitor is the smaller, somewhat calmer **Cuba Club,** Saffrangasse 2 (𝄐 **052/625-34-98**), which is also favored by clients under 40. Catering to an older and somewhat more sedate crowd is the **Piano Bar Eckhaus,** Stadthausgasse 1 (𝄐 **052/ 624-55-55**), where stiff drinks, a cozy setting, and live piano music help keep the conversation rolling. Most spots are open 7 days a week.

Basel & the Jura

Northwestern Switzerland, with its valleys, waterfalls, and old-world villages, is one of the most beautiful regions in the country. Most of the region has a medieval feel, reflected mainly in the ancient architecture.

The area lies at the juncture of Germany and France and encompasses the Jura mountain range, Basel, and the surrounding towns. During this part of your journey, you'll zigzag between two cultures, and the names of the towns—for example, Morat in French and Murten in German—will often confuse you. Most citizens of Basel, for instance, speak German, although many, living so close to France, also speak French and often English. To confuse the cultural brew, every weekday some 30,000 commuters from both France and Germany cross into Basel to work, returning to their homes in the evening.

Some of the towns may sound familiar to you: Gruyères is well known for its cheese. Other places, such as the walled university town of Fribourg and historic Neuchâtel, are also well worth a visit. You'll probably be based in Basel (or Basle), which straddles the Rhine, between Alsace in France and the Jura in Switzerland.

The canton of Jura was established in 1979 as the 23rd member of the Swiss Confederation. A total of 82 communes make up the canton, with Delemont as its capital. Nearly 88% of the population is Roman Catholic, and French is the predominant language.

Situated between the Rhine and the Rhône, the geological folds and faults of the Jura mountain range form the border between Switzerland and France and extend from Geneva, in the southwest, to Schaffhausen, along the northern border. Vastly different in height and character from the Alps, few peaks in the Jura exceed 1,650m (5,412 ft.).

The center of the Swiss watchmaking industry is here. Winter-sports resorts also thrive throughout the region, although most of them draw a local rather than an international clientele.

1 BASEL ★★★

85km (53 miles) NW of Zurich; 98km (61 miles) N of Bern

The third-largest city in Switzerland, Basel stands on the Rhine at the point where the French, German, and Swiss borders meet. At the entrance to the Swiss Rhineland, Basel is the capital of the half-canton of Basel-Stadt. On its borders are the French Vosges, the German Black Forest, and the Swiss Jura Mountains. Grossbasel (Greater Basel) lies on the steep left bank, and Kleinbasel (Lesser Basel) is on the right bank. The old imperial city stood at Grossbasel. The two parts of the city are linked by half a dozen bridges, plus four ferries powered by river currents. The first bridge, erected in 1225, was for centuries the only one spanning the Rhine; it has since been replaced by the Mittlere Rheinbrücke (Middle Rhine Bridge).

The town was a Roman fort in A.D. 374, named Basilia, and was later ruled by prince-bishops for about 1,000 years. The Great Council met in Basel between 1431 and 1448, during which time a pope was crowned here. After Basel joined the Swiss Confederation in 1501, it became a Protestant region. During the onset of the Reformation in 1529, it served as a refuge for victims of religious persecution. They flooded in from Holland, Italy, and France, bringing renewed vitality to Basel and laying the foundation for the city's great golden age in the 18th century.

As one of Switzerland's most important cultural centers, Basel saw the development of the printing press and the book trade. In 1516 Erasmus, the great Dutch humanist and writer, published here the first edition of the New Testament in the original Greek. He is buried in the cathedral. Other notable Basel residents were the painter Holbein the Younger, who made portraits of Erasmus; the German philosopher Friedrich Nietzsche, who taught at the University of Basel; Theodor Herzl, who addressed the first Zionist World Congress here in 1897; and Jacob Burckhardt, a native, who achieved fame with his history of the Italian Renaissance.

Today the cultural traditions of Basel live on in its many museums (27 in all), art galleries, and schools. The city has become known as an international marketplace for art and antiquities. In 1967 its citizens voted by referendum to purchase two well-known works by Picasso, *The Seated Harlequin* and *The Two Brothers.* Picasso was so moved that he donated four other paintings to Basel.

Basel, which is also a banking and industrial center, is headquarters of the Bank for International Settlement. In addition, Basel's chemical and pharmaceutical industry is one of the most important in the world.

Except at Carnival, the citizens of Basel are self-restrained and industrious. The German dramatist Rolf Hochhuth has observed: "English understatement looks like megalomania when compared to the people of Basel."

ESSENTIALS

GETTING THERE **EuroAirport** (© 061/325-25-11; www.euroairport.com) lies across the border in France and is shared by Basel, Mulhouse (France), and Freiburg (Germany). The location is 9km (5½ miles) northwest of Basel. Many major European cities have direct flights into EuroAirport, but the nearest intercontinental airport is at Zurich, 80km (50 miles) southeast of Basel.

Located on the major rail lines between Paris and Zurich, Basel is the most important railroad junction in the Juras. Trip time from Paris is between 4½ and 5 hours, depending on the train; from Zurich, an express train can take as little as an hour. Call © **0900/ 300-300** for **rail information.**

Basel is a junction point for highways from all over Europe. From Bern, head north on N1, continuing north on N2 at the junction. From Zurich, drive west on the same N1, turning north onto N2 at the junction.

ARRIVING If you're flying to Basel, your plane will land at the **EuroAirport Basel-Mulhouse-Freiburg** (see above). A road links the Swiss sector of the airport with Switzerland. A city **bus** runs between the airport and Basel's main railway station, departing every 30 minutes daily between 5:10am and 11:30pm; the 15-minute trip costs 3.80F one-way. A **taxi** costs from 40F and takes from 15 to 30 minutes depending on traffic.

Basel has three **railroad** stations—Swiss, French, and German—making it one of the largest rail junctions in Europe. The SNCF station is on Centralbahnplatz, as is the SBB station. The DB station is across the Rhine and down Richenstrasse.

VISITOR INFORMATION The **Basel Tourist Office** is at im Bahnhof, the main rail station at Centralbahnplatz (© **061/268-68-68;** www.baseltourismus.ch), open Monday to Friday 8:30am to 6:30pm, Saturday 9am to 5pm, and Sunday 9am to 4pm.

Tips **An Open Sesame to Discounts in Basel**

While at the **tourist office** (see above), you can purchase a **Basel Card** for 20F, good for 24 hours and entitling you to a guided walking tour, discounts at some restaurants, and admission to all city museums. It's a worthy investment.

GETTING AROUND   Basel has a good, relatively cheap public transportation system. Bus or tram tickets must be purchased at a station in advance. Clear maps will help you find your way. For 14F you can buy a ticket allowing you unlimited travel in two geographical zones for a 24-hour period. A single, once-only tram ride costs 3F within one zone.

Basel is best covered on foot, as most of its attractions radiate from the historic heart of this ancient city on the Rhine. When you need to go farther afield, you can take public transportation such as a tram. Taxis tend to be expensive.

Another way of getting around is to rent a bike at the kiosk next to the information booth at the rail station in the center of town. The cost is 33F per day, and an ID deposit is required. Bikes are rented daily from 7am to midnight.

SPECIAL EVENTS   Dating from the Middle Ages, **Fasnacht** is the most exciting time to be in Basel. All the city seems caught up in the revelry beginning the Monday after Ash Wednesday (usually in late Feb or early Mar). Motorized and horse-drawn parades highlight the activities, along with music from dozens of bands—fifes, trumpets, trombones, and drums.

The **Basel Art Fair** in mid-June (✆ 061/686-20-20 for more information) grows larger every year, with 260 dealers displaying the work of some 1,000 artists. The fair also generally hosts more than two dozen solo shows. Basel's most traditional festival is **Vogel Gryff Volksfest,** when a griffin, a lion, and a "wild man of the woods" float down the Rhine on a raft. This event occurs either on January 13, 20, or 27 (it changes every year). The event is followed by street dancing. The Wilder Mann, the lion, and the griffin are traditional symbols for the three main neighborhoods of Basel.

SEEING THE SIGHTS

As a city, Basel is visited primarily for its urban attractions such as museums and shopping. However, if you'd like to escape the congestion and get out and see some countryside, you're at the right place. On the outskirts of the city are 1,198km (744 miles) of **Wanderweg,** which are marked trails crisscrossing the scenic highlights of the area. To get you going on your journey, catch bus no. 70 to Reigoldswil. Here you can board the Gondelbahn cable to take you to the mountain peak of Wasserfallen at 922m (3,024 ft.). Once here, you can set off on hikes in many directions. Call ✆ 061/601-15-35 for information about the best hikes in the Reigoldswil and Wasserfallen region.

THE TOP ATTRACTIONS

Fondation Beyeler ★★★   Some half a century ago, Ernest and Hildy Beyeler set out to acquire some modern paintings to decorate their home. By the turn of the millennium, they had collected one of the greatest private art collections of Switzerland, which they now share with the public in the suburb of Riehen, 15 minutes by tram from the center near the Swiss borders with France and Germany. Talk about name-dropping: Andy Warhol, Georges Seurat, Jackson Pollock, Mark Rothko, Joan Miró, Léger, Max

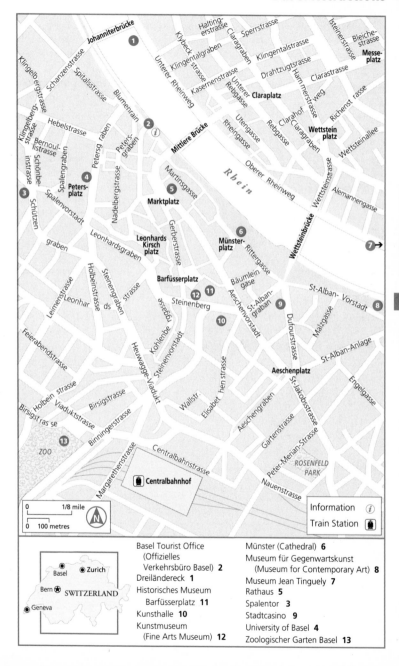

BASEL & THE JURA

7

BASEL

Basel Tourist Office
(Offizielles
  Verkehrsbüro Basel) **2**
Dreiländereck **1**
Historisches Museum
  Barfüsserplatz **11**
Kunsthalle **10**
Kunstmuseum
  (Fine Arts Museum) **12**

Münster (Cathedral) **6**
Museum für Gegenwartskunst
  (Museum for Contemporary Art) **8**
Museum Jean Tinguely **7**
Rathaus **5**
Spalentor **3**
Stadtcasino **9**
University of Basel **4**
Zoologischer Garten Basel **13**

Information ⓘ
Train Station 🏛

> **(Tips)** **The Mobility Ticket**
>
> Any tourist staying in Basel at paid accommodations is entitled to a **mobility ticket,** which allows free use of Basel's public transport for the duration of your stay. The reception desk at your hotel should provide you with your ticket upon check-in.

Ernst, van Gogh, Kandinsky, Edgar Degas, Cézanne, Alexander Calder, and Georges Braque, among others. These artists' works are stunningly displayed in Renzo Piano's avant-garde building, which is evocative of a ship lying at anchor. One of our favorite arrangements is a Monet water-lily triptych that seemingly spills from the canvas into a reflecting pool outdoors.

Seek out, in particular, Picasso's 1944 *Woman in Green,* believed to be his final portrait of Dora Maar, his longtime mistress and muse. A Picasso oddity is his sculpture of the head of Marie-Thérèse Walter. The protuberances and hollows of her face evoke male and female genitalia. The Picasso is remarkable, although Matisse is more thinly represented except for some dazzling cutouts.

A series of eight Giacometti bronze figures are complemented by some of his magnificent portraits in oil. Francis Bacon's canvas, *Lying Figure,* from 1969 depicts a naked man writhing on a striped mattress. Paul Klee painted *MOMOM Sinks, Drunk, Into the Chair* in black paste on mounted paper 3 months before his death in 1940.

Baselstrasse 101, Riehen. (©) **061/645-97-00.** www.beyeler.com. Admission 23F adults, 12F students, 6F children 11–19, free for children 10 and under. Thurs–Tues 10am–6pm; Wed 10am–8pm. Tram: 6.

Historisches Museum Barfüsserplatz ★ This former 14th-century Franciscan church on Barefoot Square (named for the unshod friars) contains many relics of medieval Basel, including rare 15th-century tapestries and specimens of ecclesiastical art. One of the best-known sculptures is in the late Gothic style, depicting a babbling king. Its greatest exhibit is a reliquary bust of St. Ursula, in silver and gold, commissioned by the people of Basel to contain the saint's relics.

Barfüsserplatz. (©) **061/205-86-00.** www.hmb.ch. Admission 7F adults, 5F students, free for children 15 and under. Wed–Mon 10am–5pm. Tram: 3, 6, or 8.

Kunsthalle A 5-minute walk from the Kunstmuseum, this gallery offers experimental works by contemporary artists. Banners displayed throughout the town announce current exhibitions. Since 1872 its changing program of exhibitions has featured many of the leading artists of classical modern and abstract expressionism before they became household names. Since the early 1980s it has been among the leading spaces in Switzerland to exhibit the most recent trends in modern art.

Steinenberg 7. (©) **061/206-99-00.** www.kunsthallebasel.ch. Admission 10F adults, 6F seniors and children. Tues 11am–8:30pm; Wed–Fri 11am–6pm; Sat–Sun 11am–5pm. Tram: 3, 6, 8, 11, or 14. Go left from the Kunstmuseum on St. Alban–Graben, cross Bankenplatz, and follow Theaterstrasse.

Kunstmuseum (Fine Arts Museum) ★★★ This is the oldest museum in Switzerland, offering one of Europe's most remarkable collections—everything from the old masters to 20th-century paintings. You approach the massive building through a courtyard graced with sculptures by Rodin, Calder, and others. The collections represent the development of art of the Upper Rhine Valley from the 14th to the 17th centuries, as **165** well as works by outstanding modern artists.

In addition to paintings by Holbein the Younger (who lived in Basel 1515–38) and Konrad Witz, the Kunstmuseum has a collection of Impressionist and modern art, including works by van Gogh, Picasso, Gauguin, Klee, Chagall, and Giacometti.

St. Alban–Graben 16. © **061/206-62-62.** www.kunstmuseumbasel.ch. Admission 12F adults, 10F seniors and children 6–16. Tues–Sun 10am–5pm. Tram: 2 or 15.

Münster (Cathedral) This red sandstone building towering over the Old Town was consecrated way back in 1019. Destroyed by an earthquake in 1356, it was rebuilt along Romanesque and Gothic lines with a green-and-yellow-tile roof. The cathedral has functioned as an Evangelical Reformed church since 1529.

The facade is richly decorated, depicting everything from prophets to virgins. The pulpit, which dates from 1486, was carved from a single block of stone. One of its many treasures, at the end of the south aisle, is an 11th-century bas-relief. There's a monumental slab on one of the pillars honoring Erasmus of Rotterdam, who died in Basel in 1536. The church also contains the tomb of Anna von Hohenberg, wife of Rudolf of Habsburg. The double cloister can be entered from Rittergasse; it was erected in the 15th century on the foundations of a much earlier Roman structure. Visitors will find an excellent view from the twin Gothic towers of the cathedral. There are also two famous views of the cathedral—from the right bank of the Rhine and from the back of the Pfalz (palace). This 20m (65-ft.) terrace also provides a splendid panorama of the Rhine and Germany's Black Forest.

Münsterplatz. © **061/271-21-82.** www.muensterbasel.ch. Free admission to cathedral; towers 3F. Easter to Oct 15 Mon–Fri 10am–5pm, Sat 10am–4pm, Sun 1–5pm; Oct 16 to Easter Mon–Sat 11am–4pm, Sun 2–4pm. Tram: 1, 6, 8, or H.

Museum für Gegenwartskunst (Museum for Contemporary Art) ★ This is one of Europe's leading museums, highlighting artists from the 1960s to the present, with works by Bruce Nauman, Richard Long, Jonathan Borofsky, Joseph Beuys, Frank Stella, and Donald Judd. Opened in 1980, this was the first museum in Europe dedicated exclusively to contemporary art. A 19th-century paper factory was converted to showcase the collection. Of course, the museum can display only a small part of its collection, and individual paintings and sculpture are forever changing. Guided tours can be arranged. As a living museum in an ever-changing art world, the museum stays abreast of modern trends, adding to its vast collection whenever possible.

Alban-Rheinweg 60. © **061/272-81-83.** www.kunstmuseumbasel.ch. Admission 12F adults, 5F students and seniors, free for children 15 and under. Tues–Sun 11am–5pm (until 7pm Wed). Tram: 2.

Museum Jean Tinguely ★ (Finds) The museum is dedicated to the work of Jean Tinguely, one of Switzerland's greatest sculptors, who died in 1991. The 70 mechanical sculptures in the collection span 4 decades of artistic evolution, beginning with reliefs and printing machines from the 1950s and progressing to later pieces like the Mengele-Totentanz cycle and huge, clanking metaharmonies. Further insight into the artist's life and times can be found in the many drawings and writings that document his projects around Europe and the United States.

The museum is a delight. All four levels are alive with ponderous movement, musical with the clean notes of working machinery. "Works of art usually make their statements silently," said Mario Botta, the Swiss architect who designed the museum specifically to house the collection. "These works are the exception, for they communicate through sound engendered by their movements." Many of the exhibits in the museum were donated by Tinguely's wife and fellow artist, Niki de Saint Phalle.

Botta's dramatic architectural vision has made the museum building an attraction in its own right, a modern landmark in Solitude Park on the right bank of the River Rhine. The red sandstone building is topped by the "barca," a bold steel construction.

Paul Sacher–Anlage 1. (C) 061/681-93-20. www.tinguely.ch. Admission 15F adults, 10F seniors and students, free for children 16 and under. Tues–Sun 11am–7pm. Bus: 31 or 36.

Zoologischer Garten Basel ★★★   Established in 1874, the Zoologischer Garten is one of the greatest zoos in the world, famous for breeding endangered species in captivity. Covering 11 hectares (26 acres) in an urban setting within a 7-minute walk of the railway station, it has some 4,500 animals of 600 different species. Trained elephants and sea lions perform tricks. The Vivarium is filled with everything from penguins to reptiles. Baselers call this attraction *Zolli* and often go here several times a year to see the "armored" rhinoceroses along with Japanese monkeys and gorillas. Ever seen a pygmy hippopotamus? This is one of the most kid-friendly zoos in Europe; the restaurant pavilion in the center even serves special meals for children.

Binningerstrasse 40. (C) 061/295-35-35. www.zoobasel.ch. Admission 18F adults, 7F children, 39F family ticket. May–Aug daily 8am–6:30pm; Mar–Apr and Sept–Oct daily 8am–6pm; Nov–Feb daily 8am–5:30pm. Tram: 1, 2, 6, 8, 10, or 17.

MORE ATTRACTIONS

The **Rathaus (town hall)** on Marktplatz dominates the market square of Basel. It was built in 1504 in the late Burgundian style, but additions have been made since. The sandstone building is decorated with shields of the ancient city guildhall and adorned with frescoes.

You may also want to visit the **University of Basel,** on the south side of Petersplatz. Founded in 1460, it's one of the oldest academic institutions in Switzerland (the school's charter was signed by Pope Pius II). Its library contains a collection of rare manuscripts, as well as works by Martin Luther, Erasmus, and Zwingli.

Spalentor (Spalen Gate), west of the university, marks the end of the medieval sector. It's one of the most beautiful gates in the country. Built in the 1400s, it was heavily restored in the 19th century, and has a pointed roof and two towers with battlements.

Finally, **Dreiländereck (Three Countries' Corner),** which juts out into the Rhine, is one of Basel's more unusual sites. If you walk around a pylon marking the spot, in just a few steps you can cross from Switzerland into Germany and then into France—and you don't even need a passport.

ORGANIZED TOURS

Basel is a popular embarkation point for cruises on the Rhine. From May to mid-October, **Basler Personenschiffahrt,** Blumenrain 2 ((C) 061/639-95-00; www.basler personenschifffahrt.ch), conducts cruises to Rheinfelden. Ships leave Monday to Saturday at 1:45pm and on Sunday at 9:15am. A one-way ticket costs 26F, or 49F round-trip; children travel for half price. Evening cruises are often conducted, costing 50F to 75F, depending on the cruise. The theme of the night cruise changes daily—a fondue cruise, a captain's dinner, a Gypsy evening. Check with the tourist office or with Basler Personenschiffahrt for last-minute changes in these schedules.

Cosmopolitan, sophisticated, and prosperous, Basel shelters a medley of shops whose merchandise rivals that found in much larger cities. The finest antiques shop in the region is **Antiquités M. & G. Ségal,** Aeschengraben 14 (✆ **061/272-39-08**). Founded in 1862, it's run by the articulate and knowledgeable fourth-generation owner, Georges Ségal, and his North Carolina–born wife, Margaret. Their specialties include 18th-century Continental paintings, silver, furniture, ceramics (including antique Meissen porcelain), and art objects, all of which are displayed over four floors of a building bulging with treasures. You'll also find two impressive art galleries in town. The immensely prestigious **Ernest Beyeler Gallery,** Baunleingasse 9 (✆ **061/206-97-00**), is a cultural focal point that's famous throughout Europe for its roster of Impressionist, modern, and contemporary paintings. Also, a more avant-garde gallery with more emphasis on minimalist, hypercontemporary art, is the well-respected **Galerie Gisele Linder,** Elisabethenstrasse 54 (✆ **061/272-83-77**).

Seeking a suitcase to pack the loot you've already acquired in Basel? Head for **Droeser,** Martinskirchplatz 15 (✆ **061/261-42-53**), where wallets, valises, purses, handbags, shaving kits, even gym bags, offer leather making at its best. If you have a yen for fine tobaccos, check out **Oettinger Cigares,** Aeschenvorstadt 4 (✆ **061/272-47-70**), where brierwood and meerschaum pipes, along with cigarettes and cigars from around the world (including Cuba), are sold along with their appropriate accessories. And finally, dozens of emporiums in Basel are ready, willing, and able to sell you a wristwatch. One of the city's most upscale shops is **Gübelin,** Freie Strasse 27 (✆ **061/261-40-33**).

The premier chocolatier in town is **Confiserie Schiesser,** 19 Marktplatz (✆ **061/261-60-77**), which sells expensive but delectable confections in its downstairs shop. Upstairs is a Viennese tearoom founded in 1870, where you can order delicate pastries and tasty little sandwiches while enjoying views of the bustling market square and the Gothic City Hall.

The best place to shop for handicrafts and gifts is **Heimatwerk,** Schneidergasse 2 (✆ **061/261-91-78**), which carries an array of tasteful merchandise from all parts of the country. You'll find everything from ceramics to wooden toys here.

If you're just seeking general merchandise, head for the leading department store in Basel, **Globus,** Marktplatz 2 (✆ **061/268-45-45**).

WHERE TO STAY

Keep in mind that it's almost impossible to get hotel reservations during the Swiss Industries Fair, which attracts about a million visitors every spring. Rooms are also impossible to find at Carnival time, when hotels often raise their prices by as much as 40%. Check with the Basel tourist office for exact dates. Even when hotels aren't raising their prices in Basel, the prices strike many visitors as being extremely high, even when they shouldn't be for what they offer. That's because Basel usually fills up its rooms with business clients and doesn't have to rely primarily on tourists.

BASEL & THE JURA

7

BASEL

Impressions

Once people have been to Basel, they keep coming back. The only difficulty we have is in getting them to come for the first time.

—Urs Hitz, 1992

Hotel Drei Könige (Hôtel des Trois Rois) ★★★ Established in 1026, this is the oldest government-rated five-star hotel in Europe, although most of the building you see today was constructed in the 18th century. Originally named Zur Blume (At the Flower), the white building, situated on the Rhine, houses a guest book, now a museum piece, containing the names of Voltaire, Napoleon, Princess (later Queen) Victoria, and Kaiser Wilhelm II. History records that soon after the establishment of the inn, three kings (Conrad II, emperor of the Holy Roman Empire; his son, Henry III; and Rudolf III, the last king of Burgundy) drew up a treaty here that divided western Switzerland and southern France.

A tapestry resembling a Gobelin tapestry hangs in the wood-paneled lobby; the bar area is accented with pin lights and brass detail. Some of the traditional guest rooms have their original ornamentation on the ceilings. Even the stables and old servants' quarters have been converted into comfortable rooms. Most units are spacious, and all are up-to-date with soft robes and well-kept bathrooms. Try for a room opening onto the river.

Blumenrain 8, CH-4001 Basel. ⟨ℭ⟩ **061/260-50-50.** Fax 061/260-50-60. www.drei-koenige-basel.ch. 101 units. 385F–750F double; from 1,325F suite. AE, DC, MC, V. Parking 35F. Tram: 1, 6, 8, 14, or 15. **Amenities:** 2 restaurants; bar; babysitting; concierge; exercise room; room service; sauna. *In room:* A/C, TV/DVD, CD player, hair dryer, minibar, Wi-Fi (free).

Hotel Euler und Central ★ This hotel offers everything you'd expect from a grand hotel in Basel. Built in 1865 near the railroad station, it's elegantly detailed in white, with gray-stone half columns. The bedrooms are luxuriously paneled and impeccable. Rooms have traditional styling with original paintings, some period furnishings, and spacious closets. All the bathrooms are maintained in excellent condition with heated towel racks. The chandeliered dining room, Le Jardin, serves first-class cuisine, mainly French with a lot of fish and a changing menu that takes advantage of the best of seasonal produce. The famous bar is richly ornamented with leather, wood, and red velvet, and is a favorite of visiting businesspeople and local bankers.

Centralbahnplatz 14, CH-4002 Basel. ⟨ℭ⟩ **061/275-80-00.** Fax 061/275-80-50. www.hoteleuler.ch. 65 units. 480F double; 600F suite. AE, DC, MC, V. Tram: 6, 10, 16, or 17. **Amenities:** 2 restaurants; bar; babysitting; room service. *In room:* TV, hair dryer, minibar, Wi-Fi (free).

Swisshotel Le Plaza ★★★ This elegant government-rated five-star hotel is the best in Basel, a favorite of both commercial travelers and well-heeled vacationers. In the heart of the city, the hotel is linked to the Basel Congress Centre. Le Plaza is a formidable challenger to the long-established Hilton, and is superior to it in amenities, taste, and general ambience. Bedrooms, ranging from midsize to spacious, are both tastefully and comfortably furnished, and the deluxe suites are the best in town, containing such extras as a personal espresso machine and a private fax. There's even a presidential suite, should any king or visiting head of state arrive in Basel. The roomy, well-equipped bathrooms are the best in town. The health facilities contain all the latest equipment, and the hotel restaurant, Le Provence, specializes in both Asian dishes and traditional Swiss cuisine. Its adjoining Plaza bar is a chic rendezvous with an Iberian flavor.

Messeplatz 25, CH-4005 Basel. ⟨ℭ⟩ **061/555-33-33.** Fax 061/555-39-70. www.swissotel.com. 238 units. 610F–650F double; 830F junior suite; 1,640F suite. AE, DC, MC, V. **Amenities:** Restaurant; bar; concierge; exercise room; indoor heated pool; room service. *In room:* A/C, TV, minibar, Wi-Fi (free).

Expensive

Hilton Basel ★★ Visitors can expect the customary Hilton service in this black steel-and-glass hotel built in 1975. In the center of town, it's connected via an underground

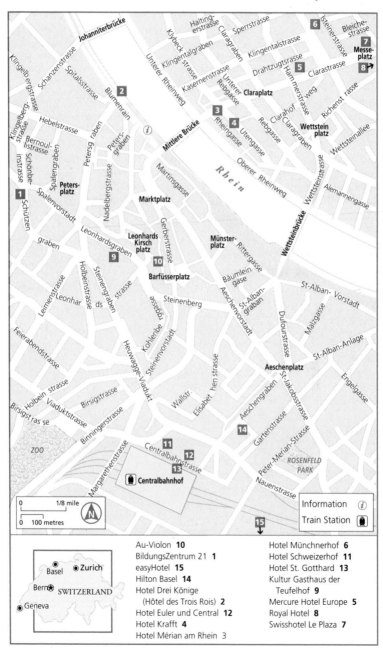

Au-Violon **10**
BildungsZentrum 21 **1**
easyHotel **15**
Hilton Basel **14**
Hotel Drei Könige
(Hôtel des Trois Rois) **2**
Hotel Euler und Central **12**
Hotel Krafft **4**
Hotel Mérian am Rhein **3**

Hotel Münchnerhof **6**
Hotel Schweizerhof **11**
Hotel St. Gotthard **13**
Kultur Gasthaus der
Teufelhof **9**
Mercure Hotel Europe **5**
Royal Hotel **8**
Swisshotel Le Plaza **7**

shopping arcade to the main railway station. Bedrooms are generally roomy and comfortable, with built-in furnishings, blackout draperies, abstract paintings, easy chairs, and plenty of work space. Bathrooms are large and well equipped. There are even some rooms for tall people.

Aeschengraben 31, CH-4002 Basel. ☎ **061/275-66-00.** Fax 061/275-66-50. www.basel.hilton.com. 214 units. 445F–615F double; from 778F suite. AE, DC, MC, V. Parking 24F. Tram: 1, 2, or 8. **Amenities:** Restaurant; bar; airport transfers (150F); babysitting; concierge; exercise room; indoor heated pool; room service; sauna. *In room:* A/C, TV, hair dryer, minibar, Wi-Fi (25F per 24 hr.).

Hotel Krafft ★★ ⬭Finds⬭ Located across the river from the Old Town's Rathaus and Münster, this elegant little mansion is a real discovery. Its terrace cafe and its bedrooms open directly on the waterfront of Basel's right bank. The public rooms are decorated with 19th-century antiques, oversize gilt mirrors, and Oriental rugs. The comfortable, modernized rooms often have good views, and contain Oriental carpets and artwork. All units offer showers, and some contain tub/showers. The Waldmeyer-Schneiter family also manages the well-known restaurant Zem Schnooggeloch (Mosquito's Den) and the Restaurant Petit Bâle, both serving a mix of French and Swiss cuisine.

Rheingasse 12, CH-4058 Basel. ☎ **061/690-91-30.** Fax 061/690-91-31. www.hotelkrafft.ch. 52 units. 270F–295F double; 300F junior suite. Children 12 and under stay free in parent's room. Rates include continental breakfast. AE, DC, MC, V. Parking 25F. Tram: 8. **Amenities:** 2 restaurants. *In room:* TV, hair dryer, Wi-Fi (30F per 24 hr.).

Hotel Mérian am Rhein ★ This 1972 hotel lies just off the quay where a 13th-century bishop commissioned the construction of the only bridge across the Rhine between Lake Constance and the sea. Located in the oldest part of the city, the Mérian has updated conveniences, including very comfortable beds. Rooms with balconies overlooking the Rhine are more expensive. Ranging from midsize to spacious, units are well equipped with modern furnishings, glass-topped cocktail tables, well-lit desk space, and tiled bathrooms.

With its black lacquer and beech furnishings, the Café and Restaurant Spitz on the ground floor of the hotel is famous locally, especially because of its terrace by the Mittlerebrücke and the Rhine.

Rheingasse (at Greifengasse 2), CH-4058 Basel. ☎ **061/685-11-11.** Fax 061/685-11-12. www.best western.ch. 65 units. 260F–350F double. Rates include continental breakfast. AE, DC, MC, V. Parking 18F. Tram: 6, 8, or 14. **Amenities:** 2 restaurants; bar; room service. *In room:* TV, hair dryer, minibar, Wi-Fi (30F per 24 hr.).

Hotel St. Gotthard Opposite the train station, this building is graced with arched canopies stretching above the two doors and three picture windows. The hotel, run by the third generation of the Geyer-Arel family, offers comfortable, well-maintained, and individually decorated bedrooms. The staff is friendly and helpful.

Centralbahnstrasse 13, CH-4002 Basel. ☎ **800/780-7234** in the U.S. or 061/225-13-13. Fax 061/225-13-14. www.st-gotthard.ch. 104 units. 180F–680F double. Rates include buffet breakfast. AE, DC, MC, V. Parking 25F. Tram: 1, 2, or 8. **Amenities:** Bar. *In room:* A/C, TV, hair dryer, minibar, Wi-Fi (free).

Kultur Gasthaus der Teufelhof ★★★ ⬭Finds⬭ This is one of the most unusual hotels in Switzerland, if not all of Europe. Set in what was originally a 19th-century private home in the Spalen district, near the Academy of Music, it contains two restaurants, a charming bar, and handsomely decorated bedrooms featuring decor that's been written up in newspapers across the city. Each room was entrusted to the artistic inspiration of a different Swiss, Italian, or German "environmental artist." Each artist was given carte blanche to create whatever he or she decided. The result gives you the impression of living inside a work of art that happens to be exceedingly comfortable, with cozy chairs and modern plumbing. ***Heads-up:*** There is no air-conditioning and no room TV.

Leonhardsgraben 49, CH-4051 Basel. ℂ **061/261-10-10.** Fax 061/261-10-04. www.teufelhof.com. 33 units. 265F–375F double; 295F–550F suite. Rates include breakfast. AE, MC, V. Parking 27F. Tram: 3. **Amenities:** 2 restaurants; bar; room service. *In room:* Hair dryer, Wi-Fi (15F per 24 hr.).

Mercure Hotel Europe ★   Centrally located next to the Swiss Industries Fair and within easy access of the Swiss and German railway stations, this renovated hotel offers modern comforts and contemporary style. Most of its bedrooms overlook a quiet roof garden, and all units contain neatly kept bathrooms, which include two 1.5m-wide (5-ft.) mirrors. Le Quatre Saisons, the hotel's luxury restaurant, is among the top three in Basel, although some find it overrated and overpriced. An international market-fresh cuisine is served.

Clarastrasse 43, CH-4005 Basel. ℂ **800/223-5652** in the U.S. and Canada or 061/690-80-80. Fax 061/690-88-80. www.balehotels.ch. 158 units. 260F–420F double; 290F–520F suite. Children 12 and under stay free in parent's room. Rates include buffet breakfast. AE, DC, MC, V. Parking 15F; 30F for fairs and congresses. Tram: 2, 6, or 8. **Amenities:** 2 restaurants; bar; babysitting; room service. *In room:* TV, hair dryer, minibar, Wi-Fi (free).

Royal Hotel ★ (**Finds**)   This boutique hotel in a former office building is a bit of an oddity but one with charm for some clients, especially young travelers. Its bedrooms are aligned according to proper feng shui, and individually designed with your comfort in mind. The size—called "spatial environment" here—is generous with a certain elegant functionalism. The belief here is that "less is more." Opt for a meal in the 70-seat Royal Restaurant, where you can enjoy light, imaginative cuisine in its bright, airy rooms. Or you can choose a table in the garden.

Schwarzwaldallee 179, CH-4058 Basel. ℂ **061/686-55-55.** Fax 061/686-55-99. www.royal-hotel.ch. 15 units. 260F–310F double. Rates include buffet breakfast. AE, DC, MC, V. Tram: 2 or 6. **Amenities:** Restaurant; bar; room service. *In room:* A/C, TV, fax, hair dryer, minibar, Wi-Fi (free).

Moderate

BildungsZentrum 21 (**Value**)   More than a hotel, this building is also the headquarters of the Evangelische Missionswerk (Protestant Mission) of Basel and all profits go to their work. However, this isn't just a good place to stay for the religious. The hotel's central location, beautiful garden, and comfortable rooms make it a good value choice for any traveler. Most of the rooms are inexpensive, priced at the lower end of the scale. Zum Rosengarten, the on-site restaurant, is fine, but guests go here more for the convenience than for the food. The extensive library is a grace note.

Missionsstrasse 21, Postfach CH-4003 Basel. ℂ **061/260-21-21.** Fax 061/260-21-22. www.bildungszentrum-21.ch. 69 units. 200F–320F double; 290F–400F junior suite. Rates include buffet breakfast. AE, DC, MC, V. Free parking. Tram: 1. **Amenities:** Restaurant. *In room:* TV.

Hotel Münchnerhof   In front of the Basel Fair and Conference Center and close to the railroad station, Hotel Münchnerhof is housed in a brownish-ocher building with white trim and small balconies. Bedrooms are small to midsize, each well maintained and comfortable. Furnishings are a combination of modern and traditional. In addition to the hotel, the Früh family also operates a restaurant, known for its French, Swiss, and Italian cuisine.

Riehenring 75, CH-4058 Basel. ☎ **061/689-44-44.** Fax 061/689-44-45. www.muenchnerhof.ch. 32 units. 175F–290F double. Rates include buffet breakfast. AE, DC, MC, V. Parking 25F. Tram: 1, 2, 6, or 14. **Amenities:** Restaurant; bar; room service. *In room:* TV.

Hotel Schweizerhof ★   Located near the main train station across from a landscaped park, this ornate hotel is six stories high, with a terrace and wrought-iron balconies. It has been in the Goetzinger family for three generations. Built in 1864, it was once the most luxurious hotel in Basel, entertaining such greats as Casals, Menuhin, and Toscanini. Today it remains the traditional favorite of town, but is likely to attract more business travelers than its former clientele of the wealthy chic. The salons are decorated with Oriental rugs and some 19th-century antiques, while the bedrooms are both modern and traditional, sometimes blending Biedermeier with pine and beech. Half the accommodations are air-conditioned.

Centralbahnplatz 1, CH-4002 Basel. ☎ **061/560-85-85.** Fax 061/560-85-86. www.schweizerhof-basel.ch. 83 units. 189F–350F double. Rates include buffet breakfast. AE, DC, MC, V. Free parking. Tram: 6, 10, 16, or 17. **Amenities:** Restaurant; bar. *In room:* A/C (in some), TV, hair dryer, minibar, Wi-Fi (35F per 24 hr.).

Inexpensive

Au-Violon ★★ (Finds)   One generally tries to avoid overnighting in a prison, but not in this case. This historic site, once a 12th-century cloister for priests and from 1835 to 1995 a famous prison, is now an offbeat hotel of comfort and grace. If you want that jailhouse feeling, ask for one of the bedrooms fronting the courtyard. These units still adhere to their cellblock plan, and space is tight. Accommodations whose windows open onto the Altstadt are larger and more comfortable. All units come with well-maintained but rather small private bathrooms with shower stalls. Some of the doors leading to the bedrooms are 1.5m (5 ft.) tall, so be duly warned. Even if you don't stay here, consider a visit to its charming old-world brasserie with its classic French cuisine. Tables are placed outside on a terraced garden in fair weather.

Im Lohnhof, CH-4051 Basel. ☎ **061/269-87-11.** Fax 061/269-87-12. www.au-violon.com. 20 units. 160F–202F double. MC, V. Tram: 3. **Amenities:** Restaurant. *In room:* TV, hair dryer.

easyHotel (Value)   A friend of the frugal traveler, this minimalist hotel is the second easyHotel to open in the world, the first having made its debut in London. You have to sacrifice space for an affordable price and value, but the very small bedrooms are a safe, clean haven for the night. Don't expect luxuries. The main appeal of the place is for people who want to spend most of their day sightseeing, using the hotel mainly for a good night's sleep and little more. All units have one double bed and a private bathroom with shower. Twenty-one of the units have a window; those without a window offer air-conditioning. There are vending machines in the lobby for emergencies, although a full-service restaurant is next door. If you want maid service during your stay, you'll have to pay extra. To activate your TV, you must purchase a remote control from the reception desk.

Rheing 8, Kleinbasel, CH-4058 Basel. ☎ **0900/327-927.** www.easyhotel.com. 24 units. 45F–91F double. AE, MC, V. Bus: 50. **Amenities:** Internet (5F per hour, in lobby). *In room:* A/C (in some), pay TV, no phone, Wi-Fi (5F per hour).

WHERE TO DINE

Five centuries ago the humanist Enea Silvio de' Piccolomini (who later became Pope Pius II) said about Baslers: "Most of them are devotees of good living. They live at home in style and spend most of their time at the table." Not much has changed.

Cheval Blanc ★★ FRENCH   This elegant restaurant is famous for its riverside terrace, where in midsummer tables are set close to the waters of the Rhine. The restaurant offers a *cuisine du marché*—that is, a cuisine based on the best of market-fresh ingredients. Original seasonings and a sound classic technique characterize this refined cuisine, which is exceptionally flavorful—no wonder the locals flock here. Specialties change with the seasons. Begin with a warm carpaccio of lobster with a lemon-grass vinaigrette, or else gâteau of duck foie gras with green peppercorns and fresh rhubarb. Among the best of the main courses are monkfish medallions with a fennel purée and star-anise sauce, or filet of John Dory glazed with mustard and herbs. Another specialty is rack of lamb baked with a crisp bread crust and flavored with Mediterranean spices. You might also try the smoked breast of Bresse pigeon with a pepper *jus* and a celery mousseline. Desserts we find tempting include wild strawberries in their own juice with a white cheese sorbet or an iced parfait with a lime zest and raspberry *jus*.

In the Hotel Drei Könige, Blumenrain 8. ℭ **061/260-50-50.** Reservations recommended. Main courses 62F–72F; 6-course gourmet menu 180F. AE, DC, MC, V. Tues–Sat noon–2pm and 7–10pm. Closed July. Tram: 1, 6, 8, 14, or 15.

Restaurant Stucki Bruderholz ★★★ FRENCH   Located a short distance south of the city limits, Hans and Susi Stucki's gourmet restaurant—an elegant shrine of haute cuisine—is renowned throughout Switzerland. Customers may dine inside or on the backyard terrace by the garden. The former private residence is decorated with antiques and oil paintings. Our favorite room is the Salon Vert, with its green napery, Empire chairs, and light-patterned Oriental rug.

The chef produces a refined yet lively cuisine known for its intense flavor and use of top-quality ingredients. Specialties may include a filet of saltwater red mullet with coriander, a terrine of foie gras, sliced veal kidneys in a tarragon vinaigrette sauce, or a lobster ragout with truffles and baby leeks. The *selle d'agneau* (lamb) is cooked with a gratin of green beans, and the sweetbreads are masterful. For dessert, we'd suggest a compote of pears or a soufflé made with the fresh fruit of the season.

Bruderholzallee 42. ℭ **061/361-82-22.** www.stucki-bruderholz.ch. Reservations required. Main courses 59F–65F; fixed-price menus 59F for 3 courses, 75F for 4 courses, 150F for 6 courses. AE, DC, MC, V. Tues–Sat 11:30am–1am. Bus: 15.

Expensive

Chez Donati ★★ ITALIAN   This is Basel's best Italian restaurant, the creation of Romano Villa and Peter Wyss, whose viands are just as fine as those south in Italy itself. This has long been a favorite of artists visiting Basel; it was a former haunt of Andy Warhol and Jean Tinguely. Ancient statuary is placed against periwinkle blue walls, and chandeliers light the dark woodwork. All that is a mere backdrop for the first-class cuisine, though, which some critics have hailed as the finest Italian dining in the entire country. The chefs are justifiably celebrated for the best antipasti table in this part of the world. One of their premier dishes is *osso buco* (braised veal knuckles). The meat is incredibly tender, and this Lombard specialty would hold up against any competition in Milan. Braised beef and fresh fish are other specialties, and all of this fare is enjoyed on a white-covered table with a view of the fast-flowing Rhine.

St. Johanns-Vorstadt 48, Grossbasel. ℭ **061/322-09-19.** Reservations required. Main courses 42F–65F. AE, DC, MC, V. Tues–Sat 11:30am–2pm and 6:30–10pm. Closed mid-July to mid-Aug. Tram: 11. Bus: 3.

St. Alban-Eck ★ (Finds) SWISS/FRENCH   Set in the antiques district and filled with architectural charm, this small and intimate restaurant is a 5-minute walk from the Museum of Fine Arts. The historic 750-year-old building has retained its beautiful original stone and oak door. The kitchen is known for its high-quality French and Swiss specialties. You might try the homemade ravioli stuffed with salmon in a creamy truffle sauce, grilled turbot with potatoes and vegetables, or suprême of duckling with honey sauce or coriander. The chef also prepares grilled U.S. beef with arugula and rack of veal with potatoes and chanterelles. We are exceedingly fond of this place, and after sampling the meticulously prepared cuisine, we think you will be too.

Malzgasse–St. Alban-Vorstadt 60. ℂ 061/271-03-20. www.st-alban-eck.ch. Reservations recommended. Main courses 42F–59F; fixed-price 5-course menu 92F. AE, DC, MC, V. Mon–Fri 11:30am–2:30pm and 6:30–11:30pm; Sat 6:30–11:30pm. Closed mid-July to mid-Aug. Tram: 2 or 14.

Schloss Binningen ★★ FRENCH   This 16th-century château and its grounds are owned by the township but managed by independent entrepreneurs. The entrance hall is appropriately baronial, and the grand dining rooms contain an antique loggia (presumably used long ago by chamber orchestras). The wine cellar is among the best in the region, with at least 50 vintages not listed on the menu (the wine steward will make appropriate suggestions). The menu changes at least three times a year but is likely to include a *timbale de langoustines* (crawfish served in a pie crust) with caviar, a *selle de chevreuil rösti* (saddle of roast roebuck), or fresh lobster, followed by a cold soufflé. This restaurant is tranquil and charming. Dishes are carefully prepared, and lighter versions of classic dishes appear frequently.

Schlossgasse 5, Binningen. ℂ 061/425-60-00. www.schluessel-binningen.ch. Reservations required. Main courses 32F–66F; fixed-price menus 39F–90F. AE, DC, MC, V. Tues–Sat noon–2pm and 7–9:30pm. Closed 2 weeks in Feb. Tram: 2, 10, or 17.

Moderate

Löwenzorn (The Angry Lion) ALPINE SWISS   This is one of the most famous and best-managed regional restaurants in Basel, with foundations that go back to the 13th century, and a warren of cozy dining rooms (five in all, plus some private dining rooms) with, in some cases, paneling and accessories from the 16th and 17th centuries. During clement weather, a garden seats an additional 200 diners. Come here for oompah Switzerland and the kind of *gutburgerlich* (home-cooking) cuisine that many locals remember, in less copious portions, from their childhoods. Examples include sliced veal with dark beer sauce and *rösti* potatoes; *cordon bleu*–style veal layered with ham and cheese; barbecued steaks and grilled kabobs; and, in winter, at least three different kinds of fondue.

Gemsberg 2–4. ℂ 061/261-42-13. Reservations recommended. Fixed-price menus 15F–51F; main courses 25F–40F. AE, DC, MC, V. Daily 11am–midnight. Tram: 6, 8, 10, or 11.

Safran-Zunft (Value) SWISS/SOUTH AFRICAN   Upon entering this medieval stone building, you'll notice the wrought-iron depiction of the restaurant's logo, a gluttonous monk inhaling the aroma from a goblet of wine. That sets the tone for this time-tested favorite, which attracts faithful devotees (primarily those drawn by its bargain lunches). Inside, the restaurant is set up tavern style, with red-checked tablecloths, wood paneling, and oversize Gothic windows.

The kitchen is equally adept at preparing either Swiss or South African specialties. Among the Swiss favorites are sliced veal in either a butter or Madeira sauce served with *rösti*, pork filets with a peach and port-wine sauce, and, finally, chicken breasts roasted

with lemon zest and fresh rosemary. The best African dishes include a lamb filet with a
zesty tomato sauce or king prawns flavored with exotic spices and served with sweet
potatoes. The stroganoff (ostrich in a peanut and ginger sauce) is better than your own
mother used to make for you.

Gerbergasse 11. ✆ **061/269-94-94.** www.safran-zunft.ch. Reservations recommended. Main courses 35F–47F. AE, DC, MC, V. Sept–June Mon–Sat 11:30am–11pm; July–Aug Mon–Fri 10am–2pm and 5pm–midnight. Tram: 1, 6, 8, 11, or 14.

Schlüsselzunft ★★ FRENCH   This is one of the oldest guildhalls in Basel, built in
the 12th century by cloth merchants. The restaurant has a menu offering seasonal specialties, including various types of fish and, in the autumn, venison. The cooking is
careful, and the talented kitchen delivers solid flavors using quality ingredients. Regular
specialties include veal curry, tenderloin steak with goose liver and morels, shredded
calves' kidney in a Madeira sauce, and shredded veal and kidney in a cream sauce with
spaetzle. It also serves well-prepared traditional soups and a fine selection of pasta,
including cannelloni au gratin.

Freie Strasse 25. ✆ **061/261-20-46.** www.schluesselzunft.ch. Reservations recommended. Main courses 36F–60F; fixed-price lunch 55F, dinner 78F. AE, MC, V. Mon–Sat 11:30am–3pm and 6pm–midnight. Tram: 6 or 14.

Zum Goldenen Sternen CONTINENTAL   Set near the edge of the Rhine and
established in 1421, this is one of the oldest restaurants in Switzerland. Decorated in a
conservative mixed style of old and modern architectural elements, it's known to many
different generations of Baslers. The well-prepared dishes are traditional, influenced by
neighboring France. Impeccable ingredients and harmonious sauces go into such dishes
as filet of red mullet and scallops with spicy chorizo sausages and spring onions, or St.
Peter's whitefish steamed with fresh tomatoes, olives, capers, and herbs. One specialty we
especially like is the tenderloin of beef poached in an essence of fresh tomatoes and served
with whipped horseradish cream. The chefs take special care with their vegetables, never
boiling them until they're soggy.

St. Albanrheinweg 70. ✆ **061/272-16-66.** www.sternen-basel.ch. Reservations recommended. Main courses 45F–56F. AE, DC, MC, V. Daily noon–2pm and 6–10pm. Tram: 6 or 12.

Inexpensive

Brauerei Fischerstube BREWERY   No one comes to this restaurant expecting a
mind-boggling culinary experience. People visit because they want to drink one of the
fresh-brewed local lagers and ales. Order the house ale, named Ueli Bier after a Fasnacht
clown, and you'll be expected to drink every drop of the mammoth 5-liter serving you're
given. If you'd rather drink at a slower pace in the comfort of your own hotel room, the
brewers also sell 15-liter kegs. The food here isn't anything special. Expect such hearty
fare—good with beer—as regional sausages and a big serving of rump steak. This is one
of the most fun spots in Basel for devotees of the brew.

Rheingasse 45. ✆ **061/692-94-95.** www.restaurant-fischerstube.ch. Reservations not required. Main courses 22F–43F. MC, V. Mon–Thurs 10am–midnight; Fri–Sat 10am–1:30am; Sun 5pm–midnight. Tram: 6, 8, or 14.

Da Roberto ⟨Value⟩ ITALIAN   Located on a narrow side street 1 block from the central
train station, this restaurant attracts younger Baslers, many of whom appreciate its nonsmoking area. You can dine here rather inexpensively (depending on what you order),

enjoying good food, a lively atmosphere, and polite but informal service. There are three separate seating areas, decorated with checkered tablecloths and paneled walls. At night a young crowd often drops in for the tasty pizzas. The soups are a good value, as are the 15 different spaghetti dishes.

Kuchengasse 3. (C) **061/205-85-50.** www.da-roberto.ch. Main courses 30F–48F; pizzas and salads 8.50F–25F. AE, DC, MC, V. Sun–Fri 11:45am–2pm; daily 5:30–11pm. Tram: 1, 2, 8, 10, or 11.

BASEL AFTER DARK

Regardless of which language you speak, you'll find lots of options for nightlife, whether you're looking for a sophisticated cocktail lounge or a funky alternative club. A worthwhile cluster of them are in the **Stadtcasino,** Barfüssenplatz ((C) **061/225-93-93;** www. casinobasel.ch), a venue that contains a stage (Musik Halle) for live musical acts, plus at least three other bars and restaurants. On Steinenberg 14, look for the American-inspired **Papa Joe's** ((C) **061/225-93-94;** www.papajoes.ch), a restaurant containing vague references to Hemingway and a commodious bar area. A few steps away, at Steinenberg 7, directly opposite the whimsical fountain designed by mega-artist Jean Tinguely, is the **Campari Bar** ((C) **061/272-83-83**), a youthful site for drinking, gossiping, or whatever.

The appealing and discreetly prosperous **City Bar** is in the previously recommended Hilton Basel, Aeschengraben 31 ((C) **061/275-66-00;** p. 168). Its decor evokes a prestigious men's club in London; you'll get the distinct feeling that everything from billion-dollar bank transfers to romantic assignations has been discreetly and stylishly conducted here. Several notches upscale, with older and more prestigious antecedents, is the **Euler Bar,** in the Hotel Euler, Centralbahnplatz 14 ((C) **061/275-80-00**). Popular with the international business community, it contains a lavishly coffered ceiling, a live pianist, lots of leather upholstery, a noise level that rarely rises above a murmur, and stiff drinks. More raucous and earthy is the popular bar in the oldest hotel in Europe, the **Drei Könige,** Blumenrain 8 ((C) **061/260-50-50**), which is smaller and more bohemian than the previously recommended bars.

The city's most entrenched bastion of electronic music, avant-garde jazz, and rock 'n' roll is the **Café Atlantis,** Klosterberg 13 ((C) **061/228-96-96;** www.atlan-tis.ch). Favored by rock-star hopefuls and college students, it contains a labyrinth of bars and balconies, and views of the medieval cathedral from the second-floor windows. On Friday and Saturday nights, it becomes a disco. During the week it has occasional live music. Admission is free. The quintessential smoke-filled cafe is **Zum Roten Engel,** Andreasplatz 15 ((C) **061/261-20-08**), filled mainly with students and other young people.

Young Basel residents, enjoying their position at the "crossroads" of Europe, are constantly discovering and patronizing new bars and nightspots that keep them on the cutting edge, making Bern look absolutely provincial. Follow the sound of soul and funk echo to **NT/Areal,** Erlenstrasse 21–23 ((C) **061/683-35-45;** www.areal.org), a music spot that grows hotter as the night goes on.

You're always likely to strike up an interesting conversation when you drop in at any of Basel's gay bars, which tend to get going relatively late at night, around 11pm. Try **Elle et Lui,** Rebgasse 39 ((C) **061/692-54-79**).

On a more cultural note, the **Basel Stadttheater,** Theaterstrasse 7 ((C) **061/295-11-33;** www.theater-basel.ch), presents an array of opera, operetta, dance concerts, and plays in German. The box office is open Monday to Saturday from 10am to 1pm and 3:30 to 5:30pm, and 1 hour before any performance. It is closed in July and August.

2 SOLOTHURN ★

The capital of a canton by the same name, Solothurn, according to a 16th-century rhyme, is "the oldest place in Celtis save Trier." Located on the banks of the Aare at the foot of the Jura Mountains, it has been fortified many times. Roman inscriptions calling it Salodurum have been found, as have the remains of a Roman castrum. But today the town is celebrated for its baroque architecture—reason enough for a visit.

Many guidebooks ignore the town completely, and many visitors relegate it to a day trip from Bern, but there are rewards to be found here.

ESSENTIALS

GETTING THERE Solothurn has frequent train connections to the major cities of Switzerland, including Zurich (65 min.), Geneva (2 hr.), and Biel (1 hr.). Call ✆ **0900/ 300-300** for **rail information.** If **driving,** head north from Bern on the N1, veering west at the turnoff to Solothurn.

VISITOR INFORMATION The Solothurn tourist office, the **Verkehrsbüro,** Hauptgasse 69, am Kronenplatz (✆ **032/626-46-46**), will provide you with a map and pinpoint some of the best hiking in the area. It's open Monday to Friday from 8:30am to 12:30pm and 1:30 to 6pm, Saturday 9am to noon.

SEEING THE SIGHTS

Solothurn is Switzerland's finest baroque town. It was at its peak from the 16th to the 18th centuries, when it was the residence of the French ambassadors to the Swiss Confederation. Solothurn became part of the Confederation in 1481.

Exploring Solothurn on foot is the typical way to see the town's attractions, although you may opt for a **rental bike** instead. At the Solothurn rail station on Hauptbahnhofstrasse (✆ **0512/26-98-15**), you can rent a bike for 33F daily from 8am to 7pm.

Solothurn's **Old Town** ★ is on the left bank of the river, partially enclosed by 17th-century walls. Inside those walls you'll find many Renaissance and baroque buildings. The Old Town is entered through the **Biel Gate,** or the Basel Gate. The heart of the old sector is **Marktplatz,** with its clock tower and a produce market on Wednesday and Saturday mornings from 9am to noon. The 15th-century **Rathaus (town hall)** has a notable Renaissance doorway. The two most colorful streets are **Hauptgasse** and **Schaalgasse,** where you'll find many wrought-iron signs and brightly painted shutters.

The baroque **Cathedral of St. Ursus** ★—said to stand on the spot where its namesake was martyred—dates from the 18th century and has been the seat of the bishop of Basel since 1828. The cathedral, just inside Basel Gate, was constructed by builders from Ticino, which explains its Italian artistry. Try to visit the gardens on the east side.

The **Jesuitenkirche (Jesuits' Church),** on Hauptgasse between the cathedral and the marketplace, dates from 1680 and contains a frescoed **three-bay nave** ★.

After you've absorbed the town's beauty, you might want to see some of the **Juras,** which tower in the background. There are many marked trails in the area for biking or hiking. The most scenic trail leads from the center of Solothurn to the Weissenstein Alpine Center, which will take about 2 hours by foot. Start out at the corner of Wengisteinstrasse and Verenawegstrasse in Solothurn and follow signs leading to Weissenstein.

Once there you can board a chairlift that takes you down from Weissenstein to a station in Oberdorf, where you can return to Solothurn by rail.

In summer, consider a **boat tour** leaving from the quays at Solothurn to the towns of Biel, Murten, or Neuchâtel. A round-trip fare costs 50F, and the tourist office (see above) keeps a list of departure times, which vary depending on the weather.

Kunstmuseum Solothurn (Municipal Fine Arts Museum) ★ Visit this museum if only to see the *Madonna of Solothurn,* by Holbein the Younger. Also outstanding is a 15th-century painting on wood from the Rhenish school, the *Virgin with Strawberries.* The museum emphasizes Swiss art from the mid–19th century to the present. A collection of excellent works represent Frölicher, Hodler, Vallotton, Trachsel, Amiet, Berger, Gubler, and others.

Werkhofstrasse 30. ✆ **032/622-23-07.** www.kunstmuseum-so.ch. Free admission; contribution requested. Tues–Fri 10am–noon and 2–5pm; Sat–Sun 10am–5pm.

Museum Altes Zeughaus (Old Arsenal) Slightly to the northwest of the cathedral stands this museum, which houses one of the largest collections of weapons in Europe. There are fascinating exhibits of medieval weaponry, flags, and Swiss military uniforms.

Zeughausplatz 1. ✆ **032/623-35-28.** www.altes-zeughaus.ch. Admission 6F adults, 4F children and seniors, 10F family ticket, free for children 7 and under. June–Oct Tues–Sun 10am–noon and 2–5pm; Nov–May Tues–Sun 2–5pm, Sat–Sun 10am–noon.

WHERE TO STAY

Hotel Krone ★ This hotel is clearly the front-runner in town. Hotel Krone, near the clock tower, basks in its reputation as the hotel where Napoleon's wife, Josephine, stayed for several days in 1811. Run by the Küng family, the inn still attracts history buffs. The gilt lettering on the pink facade spells out the name in French—Hôtel de la Couronne. The bedrooms are old-fashioned but exceedingly comfortable and well maintained. Most of the units are quite spacious, and all contain neatly kept bathrooms.

Hauptgasse 64, CH-4500 Solothurn. ✆ **032/626-44-44.** Fax 032/626-44-45. www.hotelkrone-solothurn. ch. 42 units. 220F–260F double; 300F junior suite. Children 11 and under stay free in parent's room. Rates include buffet breakfast. AE, DC, MC, V. Parking 12F. **Amenities:** 2 restaurants; bar; room service. *In room:* TV, hair dryer, minibar, Wi-Fi (15F per 4 hr.).

Roter Turm Parts of this hotel date from the 1100s; others were added throughout the centuries to create the inner labyrinth of rooms and corridors that make the architecture of this place the most complicated and intriguing in town. An inn has been on-site since the 1840s, and the current Swiss-family owners provide modern, comfortable bedrooms; the largest overlook the front square. Accommodations come in a range of sizes and shapes, and most furnishings are traditional. All units are equipped with well-maintained bathrooms. The staff keeps the place in tiptop shape.

Hauptgasse 42, CH-4500 Solothurn. ✆ **032/622-96-21.** Fax 032/622-98-65. www.roterturm.ch. 36 units. 200F–260F double. Rates include buffet breakfast. AE, DC, MC, V. **Amenities:** 2 restaurants. *In room:* TV, hair dryer, minibar, Wi-Fi (15F per 4 hr.).

WHERE TO DINE

Zum Alten Stephan ★★★ SWISS This restaurant is the finest in this region of Switzerland. Parts of the structure that contain this place were built 1,000 years ago as housing for the staff of a nearby chapel, St. Stephan's Kappelle. Later it functioned as the

6, Grand Rue. (✆) **026/321-23-67.** Reservations recommended. Fixed-price lunch menu 26F, dinner 68F; **183**
main courses 29F–49F. AE, DC, MC, V. Wed–Sat noon–1:30pm; Tues–Sat 6:30–11:30pm. Closed mid-July
to mid-Aug.

FRIBOURG AFTER DARK

You'll find more cafes and hole-in-the-wall bars around Fribourg's railway station than anywhere else in town, especially along either side of boulevard de Pérolles, rue de Romont, and rue de l'Hôpital. A particularly cozy bar is **La Cave de la Rose,** in the cellar of the Hôtel de la Rose, 1, rue de Morat ((✆) **026/351-01-01**). Rather mellow is the disco in the cellar of the **Restaurant l'Escale,** 3, rte. de Belfaux, in the suburb of Givisiez ((✆) **026/466-27-67;** www.escale-hotel.ch), about 1km (half a mile) west of Fribourg's commercial core.

One hot spot is **Planet Edelweiss,** Mariahilf, Düdingen ((✆) **026/492-05-05;** www. planet-edelweiss.ch), an 18th-century inn converted into a bustling restaurant and dance club. It draws a young crowd to its location a 5-minute ride northeast of the center. The club keeps the latest hours in the area: until 2am Sunday to Tuesday, 3am Wednesday and Thursday, and 4am Friday and Saturday.

4 GRUYÈRES ★★

6km (4 miles) S of Bulle; 64km (40 miles) SW of Bern; 43km (27 miles) E of Palézieux

This small town, which once belonged to the counts of Gruyères, is known for its castle and its cheese. It's a highlight for anyone taking the "cheese route" through Switzerland. It's also a good base for exploring the district of Gruyère (the region is spelled without an "s").

In the canton of Fribourg, the little town of Gruyères seems to slumber somewhere back in the Middle Ages. Enclosed by 12th-century ramparts, it's dominated by a castle, where the counts lived from the 12th to the 16th centuries. Their crest, which bears a crane, is still used in Gruyères.

Cars are forbidden to enter between Easter and the first of November (and on Sun year-round). Therefore you must park your car outside the gates and walk into town. Everything can be explored on foot.

ESSENTIALS

GETTING THERE   From either Lausanne or Zurich, most Gruyères-bound passengers transfer at the busy railway junction of Palézieux. From here, a secondary railway spur leads to Gruyères, stopping at about 20 other hamlets along the way. Trip time from Zurich to Gruyères is about 4½ hours; from Palézieux to Gruyères, about 1 hour. For **train information,** call (✆) **0900/300-300.**

About seven buses a day connect Gruyères with the rail and bus junction of Bulle, a 10-minute drive northwest of Gruyères. From Bulle, you can make bus connections to Fribourg and rail connections to the rest of Switzerland. For **bus schedules** and information, call (✆) **026/913-05-21.**

If you're **driving** from Bern, head southwest along N12 and take the southeast turnoff to Bulle; Gruyères is signposted from there.

VISITOR INFORMATION   The **Office du Tourisme** ((✆) **026/921-10-30;** www.la-gruyere.ch) is in the village center, open Monday to Friday 9am to noon and 1:30 to 5pm, Saturday and Sunday 10am to 4pm. Street names aren't used—the village is very small.

Moments **Fantasy Porn, Gynecological Obsessions & More**

There's nothing quite like the **H. R. Giger Museum,** Château St-Germain (© **026/ 921-22-00;** www.hrgigermuseum.com), in all of Switzerland. The Swiss-born graphic artist H. R. Giger won an Oscar for the special effects he created for the film *Alien.* He brought his obsessions of sexualized surrealist visions to the quaint town of Gruyères, where he opened this museum. Many of his key works are on display here, including grotesque paintings and sculpture, bizarre furniture, and film designs, many from the early 1960s. On the top floor is a permanent display of Giger's own private collection. Wait until you see the glowing red room with "erotic aliens" in compromising positions—it's something to write home about. Admission is 13F for adults and 8.50F for students. April to October, hours are daily 10am to 6pm. In winter, hours are Tuesday to Friday 11am to 5pm, Saturday and Sunday 10am to 6pm.

SEEING THE SIGHTS

If you're here when the tour buses aren't, you'll discover one of the most charming villages on the Continent.

At the entrance to town, at the foot of a hill near the railway station, the Swiss Cheese Union operates a model dairy, **Fromagerie de Démonstration,** près de la Gare, at Pringy (© **026/921-84-00**), for demonstration purposes. Here you can see workers produce the famed Gruyère cheese (a single wheel weighs 75 lb.), which is a more piquant version of the equally famous Emmenthaler. An audiovisual show reveals how the cheese is made. The dairy is open daily from 9am to noon and 1:30 to 7pm, but it's best to go between 10 and 11am or 2 and 3pm, when the cheese is actually being made. In July and August, daily hours are 7am to 7pm. For more information, contact the tourism office (see above).

The traditional lunch in all the restaurants here is **raclette.** A machine is usually placed on your table, so you can melt and scrape the cheese at your own speed. You can eat right down to the rind, which is crunchy and considered by many to be the best part of the raclette. In the right season, you can finish with a large bowl of fresh raspberries in thick cream.

You can walk the cobblestone road to the **Château Gruyères** ★ (© **026/921-21-02;** www.chateau-gruyeres.ch), passing the house of the famed court jester Chalamala. Dating mostly from the 15th century, the castle, or château, is owned today by the canton of Fribourg. In 1848 the Bovy family of Geneva acquired it and ordered many of its embellishments. Several famous artists, including Corot, have lived here. The château is filled with objets d'art, the most outstanding of which are three mourning copes from the Order of the Golden Fleece—part of the bounty grabbed up in the Burgundian wars. It's open April to October daily 9am to 6pm, November to March daily 10am to 4:30pm. Admission is 9.50F.

WHERE TO STAY

Hostellerie de St-Georges ★★★ This peaceful hideaway is the best place to stay in the region. The building, which dates from the 1500s, offers well-furnished bedrooms, all with new beds and bathrooms. There's a cozy cafe suitable for drinks, snacks, and light lunches. But many guests prefer the old-world charm of the formal dining room in back, where specialties include filet of beef served on a slate platter, breast of duckling with green peppercorns, and a quiche made with—of course—Gruyère cheese.

CH-1663 Gruyères. (✆ **026/921-83-00.** Fax 026/921-83-39. 14 units. 180F–280F double. Rates include continental breakfast. AE, DC, MC, V. Closed Nov and last 2 weeks of Jan. **Amenities:** 2 restaurants; Wi-Fi (free, in lobby). *In room:* TV, hair dryer, minibar.

Hostellerie des Chevaliers ★★ This atmospheric hotel is set at the end of a private driveway near the main town square and thus avoids the bus hordes that descend upon Gruyères. The restaurant section is in a 1950s private villa. The comfortable, conservative, midsize bedrooms are situated a few steps away in a more recent addition, and the best rooms offer sweeping views of the valley. All units are well maintained and contain neatly kept bathrooms.

Both guests and nonguests are welcome to visit the three elegant dining rooms. The one with the best view is covered from floor to ceiling with garden lattices. The others have a scattering of antiques, Delft tiles, and paneling.

CH-1663 Gruyères. (✆ **026/921-19-33.** Fax 026/921-25-52. www.gruyeres-hotels.ch. 34 units. 190F–260F double. Rates include breakfast. AE, DC, MC, V. Free parking. Closed Jan. **Amenities:** Restaurant; room service. *In room:* TV, minibar.

Hôtel de Ville (Value) In a historic building in the center of the Old Town, Jean-Luc Dumas's hotel offers comfortable, pleasantly furnished rooms, all of which contain tidy bathrooms. There is a terrace cafe in front. The restaurant, one of the best bargains in town, serves such specialties as ham and trout.

CH-1663 Gruyères. (✆ **026/921-24-24.** Fax 026/921-36-28. www.hoteldeville.ch. 8 units. 190F–230F double; 290F–320F junior suite. Rates include continental breakfast. AE, DC, MC, V. **Amenities:** Restaurant; Wi-Fi (free, in lobby). *In room:* TV.

WHERE TO DINE

Restaurant le Chalet de Gruyères ★ (Finds) SWISS One of the most popular and evocative restaurants in town specializes in any dish that can be made with the region's most famous product—cheese. Built in the 1700s a few paces from the château, and functioning as a traditional restaurant since the early 20th century, it counts former U.S. president Jimmy Carter as one of its patrons. Amid aged timbers, honey-colored planks, and polished farm tools, you can order *assiettes gruyèriennes* (Gruyères plates) piled high with ham, cheese, sausages, and air-dried beef; Gruyère salads; *croûtes aux Gruyère* garnished with salad and ham; several kinds of fondues with bread and potatoes; and raclettes. For anyone not interested in cheese, there's a savory mixed grill of meats and sausages.

Rue Principale. (✆ **026/921-21-54.** Reservations recommended. Main courses 16F–50F. AE, DC, MC, V. Daily 11am–10:30pm.

5 MURTEN ★★

18km (11 miles) N of Fribourg; 30km (19 miles) W of Bern

Of the many ancient towns in Switzerland, we find Murten to be one of the most idyllic and beautifully preserved. The town sits on what is called the "language demarcation line," and its residents speak either French or German, and quite often both. Lying on the southern side of the lake Murtensee, known in French as Lac de Morat, Murten forms a gateway into French-speaking Switzerland.

GETTING THERE Murten is connected by direct rail line to Fribourg, a 30-minute ride away. About 20 trains a day make the run, stopping off at about six hamlets along the way. Murten also has good connections to the nearby town of Ins, which lies directly on most of the train routes between Zurich and Paris. For **train information,** call ℂ **0900/300-300.** If you'd like to rent a bike, stop in at the station; a kiosk rents bikes for 33F a day.

A **boat ride** over the lakes that lie to the north and west is quite a restful way to reach Murten. Ferries cross between Neuchâtel and Murten about five times daily between late May and late September. It takes about 1¼ hours to cross the two lakes (Lac de Neuchâtel and Murtensee) and the canal (La Broye) that connects them; the one-way boat fare is 23F. Call ℂ **026/670-26-03** for more information.

In midsummer another way to reach Murten is from Biel (Bienne). Between late May and late September, a ferry departs Tuesday to Sunday from the central piers in Biel at 11:20am, arriving in Murten at 3:30pm. One-way transit costs 51F and will take you through three lakes (Bielersee, Lac de Neuchâtel, and Murtensee) and across the canals connecting them.

If you're driving, head west from Bern on Route 10 and turn south to Murten at the junction with Route 22.

VISITOR INFORMATION The **Murten Tourist Information Office** is at Französische Kirschgasse 6 (ℂ **026/670-51-12;** www.murtentourismus.ch). It's open Monday to Friday 9am to noon and 2 to 6pm, Saturday 10am to 2pm.

EXPLORING THE AREA

Many houses date from the 15th to the 18th centuries, and the town itself is surrounded by **medieval ramparts** ★★ with a wall walk. Today you can stroll along the wall, taking in the view over Altstadt (Old Town) with the castle, lake, and Jura Mountains as a backdrop.

Duke Peter of Savoy built the town's **castle** in the 13th century. It's bleak and foreboding, but impressive nevertheless, and from its inner courtyard (which you can enter for free), there's a vista of the lake and the Jura foothills.

The main street, **Hauptgasse** ★, is the major attraction of Murten, running through the center of the old quarter. It leads to the baroque **Bernegate,** which contains one of the oldest clock towers in the country, dating from 1712.

Musée Historique, adjacent to the castle (ℂ **026/670-31-00;** www.museummurten. ch), contains everything from archaeological excavations revealing the city's earliest history to a diorama of the 15th-century Battle of Morat. It's housed in an 8-century-old mill a few steps from the walls of the castle. The museum shows a film featuring the Battle of Murten, one of the defining moments in the history of the Swiss cantons. It's open April to November, Tuesday to Saturday from 2 to 5pm, Sunday 10am to 5pm. Admission is 6F for adults, 5F for seniors, 2F for students and children 6 to 16, and free for children 5 and under.

Nearby, **Murtensee** ★, or Lac de Morat, spread over nearly 26 sq. km (10 sq. miles), has a maximum depth of 45m (148 ft.). Between late May and September, you can take boat trips and circular tours on the three lakes from Murten to Neuchâtel to Biel (Bienne), with trips through the canals in the Great Marshes. Check with the tourist office for information on these excursions.

One of the most enchanting **bike rides** in this part of Switzerland is around Lake Murten. The tourist office (see above) will provide maps, and you can set out on your own. You can rent a bike at the rail station (33F) and visit such lakeside villages as Faoug, Salavaux, Bellerive, and Vully. Allow about 4 hours for this 40km (25-mile) jaunt.

WHERE TO STAY & DINE

Hotel Krone (Hôtel de la Couronne) (Value) This is a heavily gabled building in the center of town that was originally a 15th-century inn. It offers well-maintained, orderly accommodations at reasonable prices. All units contain neatly kept bathrooms. Some rooms are small; those opening onto the lake are the most sought after. The owners, Werner and Christine Nyffeler, oversee service at the hotel's five eating areas. You can opt for the street-level pizzeria, which also serves fondue, or the adjacent Café-Brasserie. A large, sunny restaurant and open-air terrace can be found one floor above the lobby, offering a salad bar with as many as two dozen varieties of vegetables.

Rathausgasse 5, CH-3280 Murten. ℂ **026/672-90-30.** Fax 026/672-90-39. www.krone-murten.ch. 33 units. 160F–280F double; 300F–430F junior suite. Rates include continental breakfast. AE, DC, MC, V. Parking 18F. Closed mid-Nov to mid-Dec. **Amenities:** 3 restaurants; bar. *In room:* TV, minibar.

Hotel Schiff Lying at the edge of the lake near the harbor, this hotel is surrounded by parks and operates a lakeside cafe. The building, with 19th-century gables and porches, has a modern extension containing well-decorated public rooms with Persian rugs, antiques, and lots of gilt. All units are comfortable and well maintained.

The hotel's restaurant, Lord Nelson, has large windows offering a view of lawns and chestnut trees down to the lake. The French menu is changed every 2 months; in September, during the hunting season, it features game selections. The hotel's dance club is yet another option for evening activity. Indoor and outdoor swimming pools are a short walk away.

Ryf 53, CH-3280 Murten. ℂ **026/672-36-66.** Fax 026/672-36-65. www.hotel-schiff.ch. 15 units. 170F–280F double. Rates include continental breakfast. AE, DC, MC, V. **Amenities:** 2 restaurants; bar; room service. *In room:* TV, hair dryer, minibar, Wi-Fi (free).

Le Vieux Manoir au Lac ★★★ (Finds) Located 2.4km (1½ miles) west of the town center (a 5-min. taxi ride from the train station), this is a gabled, stucco building in an idyllic setting. With a sun deck and balconies overlooking Lake Morat, this is the finest place to stay in the entire area. In the Belle Epoque era, a French military officer—homesick for his native Normandy—constructed this manor with the turrets and half-timbers of his homeland. Inside, the decor blends many periods and styles, with objects, such as Persian rugs, collected from all over the world. The nice-size bedrooms are comfortable and furnished with individual style and decor. Country prints abound, making for a cozy atmosphere, and the bedrooms open onto either a landscaped park or the lake.

The restaurant, which has a collection of antiques from around the region, serves excellent French cuisine.

Rte. de Lausanne, CH-3280 Murten-Meyriez. ℂ **026/678-61-61.** Fax 026/678-61-62. www.vieuxmanoir. ch. 33 units. 430F–590F double; 560F–745F suite. Rates include continental breakfast. AE, DC, MC, V. Free parking. Closed Jan to mid-Feb. **Amenities:** Restaurant; babysitting; bikes; outdoor pool; room service. *In room:* TV/DVD, CD player, hair dryer, minibar, Wi-Fi (free).

Bern

As the Swiss capital, Bern, with a relatively small population of only 130,000, is an important city of diplomats and the site of many international organizations and meetings. It's one of the oldest and loveliest cities in Europe, with origins going back to the 12th century. Since much of its medieval architecture remains today, Bern evokes the feeling of a large provincial town rather than a city. In 1983 the United Nations declared it a World Heritage Site.

Over the years the city landscape has been praised by many famous visitors, including Horace Walpole, who called it "the most Faire city." Dorothy, sister of William Wordsworth, gushed, "There is a beautiful order, a solidity, a gravity in this city, which strikes one at first sight and then never loses its effect."

The modern mingles harmoniously with the old in this charming city, and in recent years residents have discreetly added contemporary-style homes and structures to the historic environment. Such coexistence between the old and new is also evident in Bern's university, known equally for traditional studies and pioneering scientific research.

Bern joined the Swiss Confederation in 1353. In 1848, it became the seat of the federal government. The city stands on a thumb of land that's bordered on three sides by the Aare River, hence the several bridges connecting various sections of the city.

Market days in Bern are Thursday and Saturday. People from the outlying areas come to town to sell their produce and wares. The fourth Monday of November features the centuries-old **Zwiebelmarkt** (**Zibelemärit,** in the local dialect), or Onion Market. This is the city's last big event before winter, and residents traditionally stock up on onions in anticipation of the first snows. In Bern's historic core, vendors arrive before dawn to set up stalls featuring plaited strings of onions. It is customary to sell some 100 tons of onions in 1 day during the festival. It's not all salesmanship either—buffoons disguised as onions run about, barrels of confetti are thrown, and a good time is had by all. Naturally, local restaurants feature all their special dishes made with onions at the time.

Bern is also a popular starting point for many excursions, especially to the lakes and peaks of the Bernese Oberland (see chapter 9), a vast recreational area only minutes from the capital.

1   ORIENTATION

ESSENTIALS
Getting There
BY PLANE   The **Bern-Belp Airport** (© **031/960-21-11;** www.alpar.ch) is 9.6km (6 miles) south of the city in the area of Belpmoos. International flights arrive from Munich, Rome, and London, but transatlantic jets are not able to land here. Fortunately, it's a short hop to Bern from the international airports in Zurich and Geneva.

A taxi from the airport to the city center costs about 35F to 50F, so it's better to take the shuttle bus that runs between the airport and the Bahnhof (train station)—it costs 16F one-way.

BY TRAIN Bern has direct connections to the Continental rail network that includes France, Italy, Germany, the Benelux countries, and even Scandinavia and Spain. The TGV high-speed train connects Paris with Bern in just 4½ hours. Bern also lies on major Swiss rail links, particularly those connecting Geneva (90 min.) and Zurich (58 min.). For **rail information** and schedules, call ℂ **0900/300-300.**

The **Bahnhof** rail station, on Bahnhofplatz, is right in the center of town near all the major hotels. If your luggage is light, you can walk to your hotel; otherwise, take one of the taxis waiting outside the station.

BY CAR Bern lies at a major expressway junction, with A1 coming in east from Zurich, A2 heading south from Basel, and A12 running north from Lake Geneva.

Visitor Information

Bern Tourist Center, in the Bern Bahnhof, on Bahnhofplatz (ℂ **031/328-12-12;** www.berninfo.com), is open June to September daily 9am to 8:30pm, and October to May Monday to Saturday 9am to 6:30pm and Sunday from 10am to 5pm. If you need help finding a hotel room, the tourist center can make a reservation for you in the price range you select.

City Layout

MAIN ARTERIES & STREETS The geography of the city is neatly pressed into a relatively small area, so getting about is quite easy. You can walk to most of the major sights. **Altstadt,** or Old Town, lies on a high rocky plateau that juts out into a "loop" of the Aare River. A majority of the major hotels and attractions lie in this loop.

Most arrivals are at the Bahnhof on Bahnhofplatz, in the center of town. From here you can walk along the major arteries of Bern: **Spitalgasse, Marktgasse, Kramgasse,** and **Gerechtigkeitsgasse.** The town's major squares include **Theaterplatz,** with its famed Zytgloggeturm (Clock Tower), **Kornhausplatz** and its much-photographed Ogre Fountain, and **Rathausplatz,** on which stands the old Rathaus (town hall), seat of the cantonal government.

The three major bridges crossing the Aare into this historic loop are **Kirchenfeldbrücke, Kornhausbrücke,** and **Lorrainebrücke.**

FINDING AN ADDRESS In a system developed during the Middle Ages, street numbers in the city begin in the center of Altstadt, and the numbers increase as they fan out. Even numbers lie on one side of the street, odd numbers on the other.

MAPS Good local maps are available at the Bern Tourist Center (see above).

NEIGHBORHOODS IN BRIEF

Only two of Bern's many neighborhoods are of particular interest to tourists:

ALTSTADT

This is the heart of Bern, lying inside a bend of the Aare River. Filled with flower-decked fountains, it encompasses some 6km (3½ miles) of arcades and medieval streets, many reserved for pedestrians only. Its main street is Kramgasse, filled with luxury shops and 17th- and 18th-century houses.

You can reach this sprawling district by crossing the Kirchenfeldbrücke. The neighborhood has four major museums: Swiss Alpine Museum, Bern Historical Museum, Natural History Museum, and Museum of Communication.

2 GETTING AROUND

ON FOOT   This is the only practical means of exploring Altstadt and its many attractions. You can see what there is to see here in about 2½ hours.

Don't overlook the possibility of walks in Greater Bern, including Bern's own mountain, **Gurten,** a popular day-trip destination reached in 25 minutes by tram no. 9 and rack railway. Once here, you'll find walks in many directions and can enjoy a panorama over the Alps. There's also a children's playground.

Walks in and around Bern include 250km (155 miles) of **marked rambling paths.** One of the most scenic walks is along the banks of the Aare through the English gardens, the Dählhölzli Zoological Gardens, Elfenau Park, and the Bremgarten woods.

For **jogging and running,** the best spots are the Aare River Run (Dalmaziquai), stretching 4km (2¼ miles), or the Aare River Run—Bear Pits, which is 5km (3 miles) long.

BY BUS & TRAM   The public transportation system, the **Bernmobil,** is a reliable, 77km (48-mile) network of buses and trams. Before you board, purchase a ticket from one of the automatic machines (you'll find one at each stop) because conductors don't sell tickets. If you're caught traveling without one, you'll be fined 80F in addition to the fare for the ride. A short-range ride (within six stations) costs 2F; a normal ticket, valid for 60 minutes one-way, goes for 3.80F.

To save time and money, you might purchase a Bern Card (see the description in "Fast Facts: Bern," below) which, among other benefits, entitles you to unlimited travel on the city's bus and tram lines. Just get the ticket stamped at the automatic machine before beginning your first trip. Tickets are available at Rail City, Tourist Center, the Bear Pits Center, and in some hotels and museums.

BY TAXI   You can catch a taxi at the public cab ranks, or call a dispatcher. **Nova Taxi** is at ℂ **031/331-33-13, Bären Taxi** at ℂ **031/371-11-11.** The basic rate is 6.80F, plus 3.80F per kilometer.

BY CAR   Seeing Bern by car is very impractical due to traffic congestion in Old Town, its confusing layout of one-way streets, and a lack of on-street parking. If you have a car, it's best to park in a public garage and explore the city on foot; its miles of arcades were designed to protect pedestrians from rain, snow, and traffic.

If you want to rent a car to explore the environs, arrangements can be made at **Europcar,** Laupenstrasse 22 (ℂ **031/381-75-55;** www.europcar.com); **Hertz,** Kasinoplatz at Kochergasse 1 (ℂ **031/318-21-60;** www.hertz.com); or **Avis,** Wabernstrasse 41 (ℂ **031/ 378-15-15;** www.avis.com).

BY BICYCLE   Altstadt is compressed into such a small area that it's better to cover the historic district on foot rather than on a bike (bicycles aren't allowed on many pedestrian-only streets, anyway). However, in Greater Bern and its environs, there are 400km (248 miles) of cycling paths, which are marked on a special cycling map available at the tourist center (see above). The narrow yellow lanes throughout the road network are reserved

for bikers. The point of departure for most official routes is Bundesplatz in Parliament
Square. Special red signs will guide you through a wide variety of landscapes. Bikes can
be checked out free at the **Zeughausgasse** (© 079/277-28-57).

ⓕ *Fast Facts* **Bern**

The following is a quick-reference guide to Bern. For more information, see "Fast
Facts: Switzerland," p. 480.

Babysitters Babysitting can be arranged through most hotels. Try to make
arrangements as far in advance as possible.

Bern Card This is one of those touristic grace notes which, while not essential,
can certainly enrich a stopover in Bern and render it more economical. Sold at
any branch of the Bern Tourist Office, the card entitles its holder to free admission
to the permanent exhibitions within the city's museums; unlimited free use of
the city's bus and tram lines; and a 25% discount on guided walking tours of the
old town, the Clock Tower tour, and rental of any audio guide. Cards come in
validation periods of between 24 and 72 hours and are priced as follows: cards
valid for 24 hours cost 20F for adults and 16F for children 6 to 16 years old; cards
valid for 48 hours cost 31F for adults and 26F for children; cards valid 72 hours
cost 38F for adults and 31F for children. For information and sales, contact any
branch of the Bern Tourist Office or call © **031/328-12-12.**

Bookstores The best for English-language books is **Buchanlung Stauffacher,**
Neuengasse 25–37 (© **031/313-63-63).**

Business Hours Banks are open Monday to Friday 8am to 4:30pm (on Thurs until
6pm). Most offices are open Monday to Friday 9am to 5pm, and on Saturday 9am
to noon.

Car Rentals See "Getting Around," above.

Currency Exchange This is available on the lower level of the Bahnhof, on Bahnhofplatz, open Monday to Friday 7am to 8pm, Saturday 7am to 7pm, and Sunday
9am to 7pm.

Doctors & Dentists Call © **0900/576-747** for a referral to an English-speaking
doctor.

Drugstores Try **Central-Apotheke Volz & Co.,** Zytgloggelaube 2 (© **031/311-
10-94;** www.central-apotheke-volz.ch). It's near the Clock Tower in Old Town. The
staff speaks English and can suggest over-the-counter substitutes for foreign
drugs that can't be found in Europe. It's open on Monday 9am to 6:30pm, Tuesday to Friday 7:45am to 6:30pm, and on Saturday 7:45am to 4pm. **Bahnhof
Apotheke,** at the Bahnhofplatz (© **031/329-25-25),** is open daily 6am to 10pm.

Embassies & Consulates The **U.S. Embassy** is at Jubiläumsstrasse 93 (© **031/357-
70-11).** Other embassy addresses are **Canada,** Kirchenfeldstrasse 88 (© **031/357-
32-00),** and **United Kingdom,** Thunstrasse 50 (© **031/359-77-00).** New Zealand
citizens should call their consulate-general in Geneva (© **022/929-03-50).**

Emergencies Call © **117** for the police, © **144** for an ambulance, © **118** to
report a fire, or © **140** for the road patrol, but only for an emergency.

Eyeglasses **Augenwerk,** Marktgasse 52 (✆ **031/311-02-02**), can replace both eyeglasses and contact lenses.

Hairdressers & Barbers One of the city's best-known hairdressers is **Erminio,** Marktgasse 50 (✆ **031/312-22-33**). There are separate sections for men and women. Hours are Monday to Friday 9am to 6:30pm and Saturday 8am to 1pm.

Hospital The city's largest is **Insel Hospital,** Freiburgstrasse (✆ **031/632-21-11**), the clinic affiliated with the University of Bern.

Information See "Visitor Information," above.

Internet Access Internet access is available at **Internetcafé,** Aarbergergasse 46 (✆ **031/311-98-50;** www.internetcafe-bern.com).

Laundry & Dry Cleaning **Jet Wash** is a coin-operated, conveniently located laundry at Dammweg 43 (✆ **031/330-26-38**). For dry cleaning, try **Textilreinigung** (✆ **031/312-00-77**), which is located in the main railway station.

Lost Property The lost-property office at Predigergasse 5 (✆ **031/321-50-50**) is open Monday to Friday from 10am to 4pm (till 6pm Thurs).

Luggage Storage & Lockers Storage facilities are available on the lower level of the Bahnhof, on Bahnhofplatz.

Police The police station is at Waisenhausplatz 32 (✆ **031/321-21-21**).

Post Office The main post office (Schanzenpost), at Schanzenstrasse 4 (✆ **031/386-61-11**), is open Monday to Friday from 7:30am to 9pm, on Saturday from 8am to 4pm, and Sunday 4 to 9pm.

Safety Bern is Europe's safest capital. Nevertheless, you should take the usual precautions; protect your valuables. It's generally safe to walk the streets at night, and crimes against women are rare.

Taxes A 7.6% value-added tax (VAT) is included in the price of all goods and services rendered, including hotel and restaurant bills. There are no other special taxes.

Taxis See "Getting Around," above.

Telegrams, Telex & Fax Most hotels will arrange the expedition of faxes and telegrams. If not, head for the main post office (see above).

Toilets You'll find public facilities in the Bahnhof and in some squares in Old Town.

Transit Information Call ✆ **0900/300-300** for **rail information** or ✆ **031/370-88-88** for **postal-bus information.**

3 WHERE TO STAY

There are accommodations for most budgets in Bern, but as the federal capital, Bern hosts many conventions and international meetings, so the hotels are frequently fully booked; make a reservation. You can reserve a hotel room in advance either by phone (✆ **031/328-12-12**) or by Internet (www.berninfo.com). The service is free.

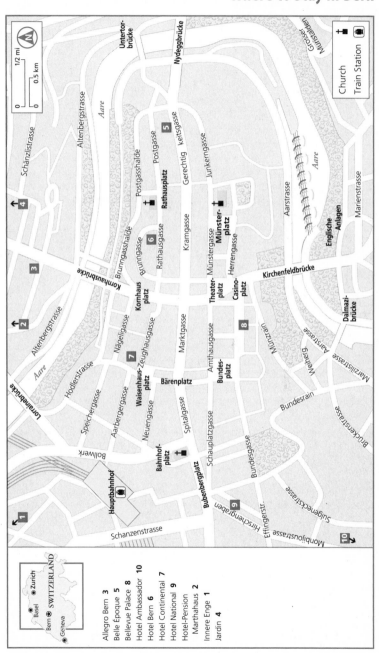

Allegro Bern **3**
Belle Époque **5**
Bellevue Palace **8**
Hotel Ambassador **10**
Hotel Bern **6**
Hotel Continental **7**
Hotel National **9**
Hotel-Pension
Marthahaus **2**
Innere Enge **1**
Jardin **4**

Altstadt is built on a peninsula so compact that everything is literally "around the corner," including nearly all hotels, more than 150 restaurants, the major sights, 6km (3½ miles) of arcades for shopping—even the weekly farmers market and the Houses of Parliament.

VERY EXPENSIVE

Bellevue Palace ★★★   Built in 1913 and located next to the Bundeshaus (the seat of the Swiss government), this grand old dame of Bern reopened in 2003 after massive renovations and improvements. It's the most lavish and opulent choice in town, with carved Corinthian columns and ornate details, and one of its grand salons is covered with a stained-glass ceiling. The setting is definitely old world, and the service is impeccable. The spacious and beautifully furnished bedrooms open onto views of the Jungfrau and the Bernese Alps. The trappings of the Belle Epoque era have been combined with a state-of-the-art infrastructure that still pays homage to its architectural heritage. The market-fresh cuisine is some of the most sophisticated in town—a parade of gourmet delicacies. Dining on the renowned Bellevue Terrace is one of the reasons to come to Bern.

Kochergasse 3–5, 3001 Bern. ℰ **031/320-45-45.** Fax 031/320-46-46. www.bellevue-palace.ch. 130 units. 495F–590F double; from 715F suite. Rates include buffet breakfast. AE, DC, MC, V. Parking 28F. Tram: 3, 9, or 12. **Amenities:** 2 restaurants; bar; babysitting; concierge; room service. *In room:* A/C, TV, hair dryer, minibar, Wi-Fi (25F per 24 hr.).

EXPENSIVE

Allegro Bern ★★★   This is the hippest, most savvy, and most sophisticated hotel in town, with a charming, well-trained, and hardworking staff and a flair for elegance. Guests appreciate the panoramic view of the medieval town center of Bern and the Swiss Alps. That's reason enough to check in—that and the fact that this is the best-rated hotel in town for comfort and a sense of grace. Set just across the river from the town's historic core, the hotel runs as efficiently as a Swiss clock. There is grand comfort everywhere, especially in the midsize to spacious bedrooms, which are well furnished, immaculately kept, and equipped with well-accessorized bathrooms. The best accommodations are in the Panorama Club at the front of the hotel. These are especially sought out for their view of the Bernese Alps.

Kornhausstrasse 3, CH-3000 Bern. ℰ **031/339-55-00.** Fax 031/339-55-10. www.allegro-hotel.ch. 171 units. 219F–410F double; 499F–900F suite. AE, DC, MC, V. Parking 24F. **Amenities:** 3 restaurants; 2 bars; babysitting; concierge; Jacuzzi; exercise room; room service; sauna. *In room:* A/C, TV, hair dryer, minibar, Wi-Fi (30F per 24 hr.).

Belle Epoque ★★ Finds   In 1989 an interconnected pair of historic Bern medieval houses were gutted, renovated, and turned into this small-scale boutique-style gem of a hotel. Throughout, its decor celebrates and promotes the Teutonic interpretation of Art Nouveau *(Jugendstil)*. Each of the bedrooms is outfitted with jewel-toned colors, big windows, turn-of-the-20th-century furniture and lighting fixtures, and unusual antique paintings and engravings. Minibars and closets are artfully concealed within *trompe l'oeil* replicas of steamer trunks, in a style that's in pleasing contrast to bathrooms that are immaculately tiled (some have Jacuzzis) and very modern, with free condoms on offer. Public rooms are somewhat cramped but beautifully decorated and convivial. They include a cozy bar whose cafe tables extend out under the 17th-century arcades in front.

Gerechtigkeitsgasse 18, CH-3011 Bern. ℰ **031/311-43-36.** Fax 031/311-39-36. www.belle-epoque.ch. 17 units. 290F–350F double; 250F–590F suite. AE, DC, MC, V. Bus: 12. **Amenities:** Restaurant; bar; babysitting; room service. *In room:* TV, hair dryer, minibar, Wi-Fi (10F per 24 hr.).

Hotel Bern ★ This six-story hotel, a frequent host to diplomats and business travel- **195** ers, sits behind one of Bern's most striking Art Deco facades ornamented with arches, columns, and a series of iconoclastic sculptures. The midsize guest rooms are comfortable and well furnished, with breakfast areas and firm beds, plus tidy bathrooms. The best rooms look out onto a garden courtyard. The hotel has nine dining rooms, but most of these are reserved for groups and banquets. The Grill Room is more formal, serving French cuisine.

Zeughausgasse 9, CH-3011 Bern. ✆ **031/329-22-22.** Fax 031/329-22-99. www.hotelbern.ch. 95 units. 250F–370F double; 300F–405F triple. Rates include buffet breakfast. AE, DC, MC, V. Tram: 9. **Amenities:** 2 restaurants; bar; room service. *In room:* TV, hair dryer, minibar, Wi-Fi (free).

Innere Enge ★★★ (Finds) When you tire of Bern's impersonal bandbox hotels, head for this inn that occupies a building from the 1700s. This small but choice hotel, a 20-minute walk from the center of town, has windows that open onto views of the Ber- nese Oberland; a tranquil setting within a verdant park; and a pervasive, and sometimes just a bit cloying, jazz theme—both its melodies and its history. The well-kept and indi- vidually designed bedrooms are often spacious and filled with sunshine. Furnishings are traditional, and maintenance meets the high standards set by the manager. The most romantic units are on the top floor, resting under the eaves with sloped ceilings. The Louis Armstrong Bar, also called Marians Jazzroom (p. 211), is linked to the hotel, offer- ing drinks, food, and traditional jazz performances February to June and September to December.

Engestrasse 54, CH-3012 Bern. ✆ **031/309-61-11.** Fax 301/309-61-12. www.zghotels.ch. 26 units. 330F–370F double; from 370F suite. AE, DC, MC, V. Free parking. Bus: 21. **Amenities:** Restaurant; bar; babysitting; room service. *In room:* A/C (in some), TV, hair dryer, minibar, Wi-Fi (36F per 24 hr.).

MODERATE

Hotel Ambassador ★ This restored nine-story hotel is the tallest building in a neighborhood of old houses with red-tile roofs, approximately 3km (2 miles) west of the center of Bern's Old Town. The guest rooms come with refrigerators, and many have a view of the federal palace, the Bundeshaus. They tend to be smallish and furnished in a minimalist style, but they are well maintained, with firm beds and neat bathrooms. Since the hotel caters to business travelers, its rooms offer fax and computer hookups. It's located about a mile from the train station and easily reached by tram. Dining choices include the Japanese Teppan Restaurant, surrounded by a Japanese garden. It's also the only hotel in Bern with an on-site spa.

Seftigenstrasse 99, CH-3007 Bern. ✆ **031/370-99-99.** Fax 031/371-41-17. www.fhotels.ch. 99 units. 235F–360F double. AE, DC, MC, V. Free parking. Tram: 9. **Amenities:** 2 restaurants; babysitting; indoor heated pool; room service; spa. *In room:* A/C, TV, hair dryer, minibar, Wi-Fi (free).

Hotel Continental Another of those fairly anonymous, relatively banal hotels clus- tered around the Bern rail station, this government-rated three-star choice is notable for its flower boxes blooming in spring at its bedroom windows. Filled with shops at ground level, the building lures mainly business travelers during the week, although weekends are more devoted to leisure travelers, often the Swiss themselves. The smallest bedrooms are a bit lackluster, but still well maintained and furnished with both traditional and modern pieces. In fair weather, breakfast is served under a canopied terrace upstairs.

Zeughausgasse 27, CH-3011 Bern. ✆ **031/329-21-21.** Fax 031/329-21-99. www.hotel-continental.ch. 43 units. 140F–205F double. Rates include buffet breakfast. AE, DC, MC, V. Tram: 3 or 9. **Amenities:** Babysit- ting. *In room:* TV, Wi-Fi (30F per 24 hr.).

Hotel National (Value) Originally built in 1908 as a brewery and later transformed into a textile factory, this simple but dignified government-rated two-star hotel enjoys a consistently high occupancy and many compliments based on its good value and well-scrubbed interior. It's run by two sisters, members of the Grünewald family, who maintain its very high ceilings and its confusing layout with verve and a kind of charm. The reception area lies one floor above street level, and to reach it, you'll either take the stairs or a "historically significant" elevator that might remind you of a rather quaint birdcage. Accommodations are sober but reliable, utterly devoid of any contemporary fashion statements or accessories, and occupied by a value-conscious clientele from throughout Europe and the world. Of particular note are the bedrooms on the uppermost floor, where a recent renovation exposed some of the massive timber trusses that form the exterior's mansard roof. The hotel's restaurant is recommended separately (p. 201).

Hirschengraben 24, CH-3011 Bern. ℭ **031/381-19-88.** Fax 031/381-68-78. www.nationalbern.ch. 46 units, 32 with private bathroom. Double with shared bathroom 130F, with private bathroom 150F–170F. AE, MC, V. Tram: 3, 5, or 9. **Amenities:** Restaurant. *In room:* TV, no phone (in some), Wi-Fi (35F per 24 hr.).

INEXPENSIVE

Hotel-Pension Marthahaus (Value) Set within a verdant suburb about a 12-minute walk to the city center, this five-story hotel was originally built around 1900 and has comfortably battered, semiantique bedrooms, each with a different floor layout (it may remind some visitors of a slightly dowdy college dormitory). There's a tiny elevator to carry guests upstairs, and a simple but respectable and clean format that symbolizes good value in an otherwise expensive town. Present management—an organization that directs a pension and retirement fund for women—has been in place here since the 1970s. The better rooms contain small private bathrooms.

Wyttenbachstrasse 22A, CH-3013 Bern. ℭ **031/332-41-35.** Fax 031/333-33-86. www.marthahaus.ch. 40 units, 6 with bathroom. 99F–110F double without bathroom, 140F–160F with bathroom. Rates include buffet breakfast. MC, V. Parking 10F. Bus: 20. **Amenities:** Bikes; Wi-Fi (free, in lobby). *In room:* TV.

Jardin (Value) Set less than a kilometer (½ mile) north of Bern's center, Jardin lies within a leafy residential suburb with lots of parking. This establishment functioned as a restaurant and apartment building between the year it was built (ca. 1900) and 1985. Then its apartments were transformed into modern, warmly appealing hotel rooms that are larger than virtually anything else within their price category. All rooms are equipped with private bathrooms. Your hosts are identical twins Andreas and Daniel Balz. Joggers and nature enthusiasts will appreciate the large verdant spaces (part of a military academy) across the street from this russet-brown, four-story hotel.

Militärstrasse 38, CH-3014 Bern. ℭ **031/333-01-17.** Fax 031/333-09-43. www.hotel-jardin.ch. 18 units. 160F double; 220F triple. Rates include buffet breakfast. AE, DC, MC, V. Free parking. Tram: 9 to Breitenrainplatz. **Amenities:** Restaurant. *In room:* TV, hair dryer.

4 WHERE TO DINE

Bern is a city of international cuisine. There are dozens of specialty restaurants offering everything from paella to porterhouse, in addition to the famous Swiss potato dish, *rösti*. We recommend sampling one of the charming country inns on the outskirts.

La Tavola Pronta ★ ITALIAN   From the agriculturally rich province of Piedmont in northwestern Italy comes a restaurant serving specialties of that region. These specialties are showcased in four- or five-course set menus, which are frequently changed. A skilled team of chefs from "south of the border" are employed to turn out these tantalizing dishes. The antipasti is the best in town, and sometimes the rare white truffle of Piedmont is used. Other main dishes such as beef are cooked with Parolo wine. From the cellar emerges some of the finest vintages of the Piedmont.

Laupenstrasse 57. ℂ **031/382-6633.** Reservations required. Fixed-price 4-course menu 88F, 5-course menu 98F. AE, DC, V. Tues–Fri 11:30am–2:30pm; Tues–Sat 6–11:30pm. Closed July.

Meridiano ★★ INTERNATIONAL   Virtually everybody in Bern agrees that since this restaurant opened on the sixth floor of its best-rated hotel, it has surpassed all of its competitors. It occupies a conservatively modern cream-colored dining room, whose focal point is a sweeping wall of windows with panoramic views that reach across the Aare River toward Bern's historic core. Menu items are impeccably fresh and presented with verve. Chefs search the world for the products used in their cuisine: oven-roasted Scottish Highland lamb; scampi from South Africa; fried scallops from the North Pacific; sautéed filet of Lake Constance pikeperch with fresh morels. Bern's only casino (p. 211) lies on the hotel's fifth floor, immediately downstairs from the restaurant, encouraging many diners to test their luck either before or after a meal.

In the Hotel Allegro Bern, Kornhausstrasse 3. ℂ **031/339-52-45.** Reservations required. Main courses 64F–75F; set-price menu 135F. AE, DC, MC, V. Tues–Fri noon–2pm and 6–9:30pm; Sat 6–9:30pm. Closed July. Tram: 9.

Restaurant la Terrasse ★ INTERNATIONAL   For a unique gastronomic experience with the Alps as a backdrop, try the refined cuisine in this dining room high above the Aare River. The kitchen is resolutely contemporary, although it draws inspiration from the classic repertoire. All the ingredients are carefully selected and inventively paired. This is the quintessential choice for haute-cuisine dining in Bern. The chefs are known for their imaginative pairing of ingredients—filet of tuna with calves' sweetbread fritters served with candied tomatoes, focaccia with wild garlic and herbs, or a parsnip sabayon with morels stuffed with pistachios. In fair weather, grilled fish is often served on a summer salad. A pianist adds to the soothing atmosphere.

In the Bellevue Palace, Kochergasse 3. ℂ **031/320-45-45.** Reservations recommended. Main courses 44F–68F. AE, DC, MC, V. Daily noon–3pm and 6–11pm. Closed for dinner in winter. Tram: 3 or 5. Bus: 19.

Wein & Sein ★★★ INTERNATIONAL   In terms of underground, word-of-mouth chic, this is the most fashionable and hip restaurant in Bern today. Set within the cellar of a historic building in the city's medieval core, it's accessible via a steep staircase that leads you past an open kitchen where a view of the staff comprises part of the allure. Chef and owner Beat Blum, a celebrity whose fame derives from his former administration of a more expensive restaurant near Lucerne, is the impresario who directs the show here. Within a severely spartan-looking dining room, you can order a la carte, but many locals prefer the market-fresh fixed-price menu, which is written on a blackboard. The menu might consist of such heavenly concoctions as braised tuna and free-range chicken served with braised pepperoni in a sweet-and-sour sauce; terrine of melon; beef filet with a vegetable purée; and a quark (white cheese) mousse served with pineapple and home-made ice cream. You'll select your wine from racks at one end of the dining room, a system that affords lots of interplay with the staff over whatever it is that you propose drinking with your meal.

Münstergasse 50. (✆ **031/311-98-44.** www.weinundsein.ch. Reservations required. Main courses 37F–45F; fixed-price menu 95F. MC, V. Tues–Sat 6pm–midnight. Closed 3 weeks in July–Aug. Tram: 3, 5, or 9. Bus: 10 or 12.

EXPENSIVE

Della Casa ★ CONTINENTAL Entering this restaurant, immediately adjacent to the Hotel Bristol, you'll find yourself within what has been called Switzerland's "unofficial Parliament headquarters." The ground-floor dining room, which doubles as a cafe during the morning and afternoon, contains the day's newspapers. You'll find a quieter, more formal dining room upstairs. The menu features Continental and Italian dishes, such as *bollito misto* (a medley of mixed boiled meats) and rack of lamb. Two local favorites are the *ravioli maison* and the fried zucchini; a popular meat specialty is a filet mignon *a la bordelaise* with Creole rice. For the more adventurous, try the boiled veal head served with onions, tomatoes, and potatoes with an herbed vinaigrette. The cuisine is very authentic, very savory, and very satisfying.

Schauplatzgasse 16. (✆ **031/311-21-42.** www.della-casa.ch. Reservations recommended. Main courses 25F–45F. AE, DC, MC, V. Mon–Fri 9:30am–1:30pm; Sat 9:30am–3pm. Upstairs level closed July. Tram: 3, 5, or 9.

Frohsinn ★ (Finds) FRENCH/SWISS This restaurant, with only a dozen tables, stands in the shadow of the Zytgloggeturm (Clock Tower). It attracts businesspeople, journalists, and politicians as much for its traditional cuisine as for its cozy atmosphere. The menu may include filet of beef with whiskey sauce, goose liver mousse, liver with *rösti*, or filet of rabbit with watercress. Other dishes reflect a southern Italian influence, especially the homemade ravioli. Sabayon with strawberries is a seasonal specialty. You'll relish most of the dishes, as they are prepared with first-rate ingredients.

Münstergasse 54. (✆ **031/311-37-68.** www.froh-sinn.ch. Reservations required. Main courses 22F–52F. AE, DC, MC, V. Tues–Sat 8am–2pm and 6–10pm. Closed mid-July to mid-Aug. Tram: 3 or 5.

Gourmanderie Café Moléson ★ (Finds) INTERNATIONAL It looks like your basic cafe, but the food at this joint is rather uncafe-like. Market-fresh ingredients and a skilled preparation go into the pleasing dishes, attracting politicians from the Swiss Parliament and even artists (a combination that probably wouldn't be compatible elsewhere). The friendly staff speaks English and will guide you through their specials of the day. Try, for example, fresh sea devil roasted in olive oil, or breast of guinea fowl with fresh basil, oregano, and rose water. Another specialty is lamb from the Emmental roasted with coriander, black cumin, and salted lemon and ginger.

Aarbergergasse 24, 3011 Bern. (✆ **031/311-44-63.** www.moleson-bern.ch. Reservations not required. Main courses 35F–48F. AE, DC, MC, V. Mon–Fri 11:30am–2:30pm; Mon–Sat 6–11:30pm.

Jack's Brasserie (Stadt Restaurant) ★★ FRENCH/CONTINENTAL Although the once-imperial-looking white elephant of a hotel (the Schweizerhof) that contained this restaurant has closed, Jack's continues to flourish, and it's a congenial spot for a fine meal or even a celebratory dinner. Decorated in a style that might remind you of a Lyonnais bistro, replete with paneling, banquettes, and etched glass, it bustles in a way that's chic, friendly, and matter of fact, all at the same time. Menu items include fish soup; the kind of Wiener schnitzels that hang over the sides of the plate; succulent versions of sole meunière and sea bass; veal head vinaigrette for real regional flavor; and smaller platters piled high with salads, risottos, and pastas.

Bahnhofplatz 11. ℭ **031/326-80-80.** www.schweizerhof-bern.ch. Reservations recommended. Main courses 29F–60F; fixed-price menu 88F. AE, DC, MC, V. Daily 11:45am–10:45pm (limited menu 1:45–6:15pm). Tram: 3, 9, or 12.

Räblus FRENCH/SWISS REGIONAL   Centrally located near the Clock Tower, this spot offers dinner guests a chance to stop for an aperitif in the ground-floor bar before proceeding upstairs to the richly paneled and sculpture-filled dining room. The chef prepares French cuisine with a definite Swiss/German influence. Dishes include potpourri of seafood with Pernod, saffron-flavored sole, citrus-flavored veal, and those old reliables, tournedos Rossini and veal kidney flambé, that have appeared on French menus forever. The cuisine is satisfying, especially on a cold day, but not particularly imaginative. The kitchen is talented, and local produce is deftly handled.

Zeughausgasse 3. ℭ **031/311-59-08.** Reservations required. Main courses 26F–42F. AE, DC, MC, V. Mon–Wed 6pm–1:30am; Thurs 6pm–2:30am; Fri–Sat 6pm–3:30am. Tram: 9. Bus: 10.

Ratskeller (Kids) SWISS   Amid old masonry and modern paneling, a battalion of busy waitresses serve ample portions of good, rib-sticking food at this establishment. The dining room has long been the family favorite of locals; Swiss parents who take their children here were once taken here by their parents. Specialties include rack of lamb *a la diable* for two, an omelet soufflé aux fruits, veal kidneys Robert, and *côte de veau* (veal steak) in butter sauce. Your best bet is the tiny filet of perch (*egli* in German) with white sauce on a bed of spinach. Prized by gourmets, this tiny fish is native to the lakes around Bern.

Gerechtigkeitsgasse 81. ℭ **031/311-17-71.** Reservations recommended. Main courses 26F–42F. AE, DC, MC, V. Daily 11:30am–2pm and 6–11pm. Bus: 12.

Restaurant Harmonie SWISS/BERNESE   Located at the corner of Münstergasse, a few blocks from the Houses of Parliament, this Art Nouveau local favorite evokes 1890s Paris with its grimy overlay. It has been in the hands of the Gyger family since 1915. Service is efficient, and tables are spaced far enough apart to allow a feeling of privacy. There are two separate dining rooms and a handful of sidewalk tables set behind banks of potted geraniums. You get the same regional specialties that Grandmother Gyger might have served between the wars: pork sausage with *rösti,* tripe with tomatoes, and cheese fondues. If you're not ravenously hungry, go for the simple platter of cooked ham with pickles, pickled onions, and sliced bread.

Hotelgasse 3. ℭ **031/313-38-40.** www.harmonie.ch. Reservations recommended. Main courses 24F–55F. MC, V. Mon–Fri 8am–11:30pm. Closed mid-July to mid-Aug. Tram: 5.

Restaurant Zimmermania ★ (Value) FRENCH   This is a small and charming French bistro that's set on a quiet street in Bern's historic core. Inside, you'll find two dining rooms outfitted like something you might have expected in a small French town in the 1920s, a marble-topped service bar, and a menu that emphasizes many classic brasserie-style dishes from France. In addition to a short but well-chosen wine list, you can expect such wellprepared French classics as foie gras of duckling, carpaccio of beef, marinated herring with apple slices and sour cream, fresh oysters, veal kidneys in mustard sauce, rack of lamb with green beans, steak tartare, and guinea fowl roasted with rosemary.

Brunngasse 19. ℭ **031/311-15-42.** Reservations recommended. Main courses 32F–60F. AE, MC, V. Tues–Sat 11am–2:30pm and 5–11:30pm. Closed July. Tram: 12.

Verdi Ristorante, Bar & Enoteca ITALIAN   This is a charmingly decorated Italian hideaway that's more elegant and more sophisticated than its reasonable prices would imply. Set near the eastern terminus of one of the most important medieval streets of the Old Town, it includes at least three different dining areas, simultaneously evoking both a brick-lined trattoria and a grand gourmet restaurant. Accessories include a zinc-topped bar, a vast array of wine that's artfully arranged in a replica of an antique wine cellar, an antipasti buffet, and a fireplace that blazes merrily throughout the winter. Food items are good, classic Italian. The best examples include braised artichokes in herb-flavored olive oil, with Parma ham; medallions of angler-fish with white wine and saffron sauce; diced filets of rabbit with mushrooms, olives, and rosemary, served with risotto; and grilled filets of beef with arugula-basil sauce and risotto.

Gerechtigkeitsgasse 5. ☎ **031/312-63-68.** Reservations recommended. Pastas 20F–34F; main courses 34F–45F. AE, DC, MC, V. Mon–Sat 11am–12:30am; Sun 11am–11:30pm. Bus: 12.

Zum Zähringer ★ (Finds) CONTINENTAL   No restaurant in Bern projects such a high mountain atmosphere. It occupies a weathered chalet that sits across a quiet street from the surging waters of the Aare, at the bottom of the steep cliff whose top contains the cathedral and the rest of medieval Bern. Many aspects, particularly its riverfront terrace, evoke a country inn that's far removed from the politics of the Swiss capital, but with a menu that's much more modern than you might have expected. Menu items are creative and filled with flair. They include asparagus mousse served with a tartare of salmon; veal shank in wine sauce; house-made terrine with green peppercorn and chutney; braised chicken livers with arugula; pikeperch with chive-flavored cream sauce; an artfully composed "hamburger" of goose meat with Asian vegetables and basmati rice; and scallops with spring vegetables served with olive-studded mashed potatoes.

Badgasse 1 (corner of Aarbergergasse). ☎ **031/312-08-88.** www.restaurant-zaehringer.ch. Reservations recommended. Main courses lunch 16F–58F, dinner 28F–58F. MC, V. Tues–Fri 11am–2:30pm; Mon–Sat 6–11:30pm.

MODERATE

Altes Tramdepot Brauereï & Restaurant (Kids) INTERNATIONAL   One of the most visible and popular restaurants on Bern's tourist circuit lies immediately adjacent to the Bear Pits, within a former tramway depot. In 1999 the space beneath its soaring, heavily trussed ceiling was transformed into a brewery and brasserie. You'll have to descend into the cellar to see the complicated vats and pipes of the brewery, where any of three kinds of beer—blonde, dark, and white (wheat) beer—are likely to be percolating and fermenting. Many clients gravitate toward the sprawling terrace looking out over the city. Menu items focus on a hearty, wholesome cuisine that goes beautifully with beer. Examples include pork sausages with onion sauce and *rösti;* sliced veal Zurich style with mushroom sauce and *rösti;* Wiener schnitzels; chicken breast stuffed with mozzarella and sun-dried tomatoes; pork cutlet with mushroom sauce; and at least four different wok-prepared dishes inspired by the cuisine of Thailand. There's even a special menu, each dish of which is named after a species of bear, for children.

Am Bärengraben, Gr. Muristalden 6. ☎ **031/368-14-15.** www.altestramdepot.ch. Reservations necessary. Main courses 20F–43F; children's platters 8F–16F. AE, DC, MC, V. Daily 11am–12:30am. Bus: 12.

Flo's Kitchen ★ SWISS   Locals refer to this restaurant as "small and fine," and so it is, a cozy but uncluttered venue for no more than 30 diners. The atmosphere evokes the reading room of a public library, thanks to its bare wooden floors and tastefully conservative modern furniture. The culinary team of Florina, Tina, Gregor, and Tobias focuses on very fresh first-class ingredients prepared with creativity and in harmony with the season. All breads and pastries are prepared fresh and on-site. Start with a mixed green salad with watercress, bacon, and mushrooms, or else a cold tomato-and-pepperoni soup with fresh basil and sour cream. For a main, perhaps you'll opt for the house-made potato gnocchi with green asparagus and a beurre blanc sauce, or else veal schnitzel stuffed with ricotta and fresh herbs and served with a white tomato mousse. Another specialty is braised salmon with white asparagus, a passion-fruit sauce, and spicy couscous. The restaurant is mainly a weekend dinner-only happening and enjoys a long summer holiday.

Weissenbuhlweg 40. ✆ **031/372-0555.** Reservations required. Main courses 24F–36F. MC, V. Thurs–Sat 6–9pm. Closed mid-June to early Oct.

Kirchenfeld ★ INTERNATIONAL   A 10-minute walk southeast of Bern's railway station delivers you to this Swiss-style bistro, the domain of Charlotte and Maurice Rota. They've hired a hardworking team of chefs to tempt your palate with a number of delights. Their impressive repertoire of dishes includes such starters as a Thai-style lemon-grass soup flavored with red curry, tartare of veal flavored with olive oil and lemon zest, or medallions of sole with a lemon risotto. The same fine craftsmanship extends to their main dishes, especially the breast of chicken flavored with a port-wine sauce or the rack of New Zealand lamb with a parsley sauce, a tapenade of olives, and roast potatoes. Their desserts are made fresh daily, many of them rich and creamy. In summer, they open their garden for dining.

Thunstrasse 5. ✆ **031/351-0278.** Reservations recommended. Fixed-price lunch 20F–30F, dinner 68F; main courses 25F–43F. AE, DC, MC, V. Tues–Sat 8am–11:30pm.

Mille Sens ★ EUROPEAN FUSION   This old factory building converted into a restaurant by Urs Messerli is an intimate choice and one of the leading restaurants of Bern. The open kitchen and accessible wine cellar add to the warm ambience of this sophisticated eatery. Light menu items include a chicken club sandwich with curried mayonnaise, tomatoes, and pickles, and a vegetable-stuffed crepe with a sweet-and-sour sauce topping. If you want a more substantial meal, we recommend you start with the seasonal green salad with melon and summer herbs, or cured Parma ham slices in a roulade with walnut oil vinaigrette. For your main course, enticing dishes include sautéed breast of corn-fed chicken with strips of cured ham and saffron-flavored risotto, and filet of Angus beef in a red-wine sauce along with strips of Mediterranean polenta.

Markethalle, Bubenbergplatz 9. ✆ **031/329-29-29.** www.millesens.ch. Reservations recommended. Main courses 28F–45F; business lunch 68F. AE, DC, MC, V. Mon–Thurs 11am–11:30pm; Fri 11am–1:30am; Sat 4pm–12:30am.

Restaurant National CONTINENTAL   Few other restaurants in Bern convey as effectively a sense of difficult-to-influence, unhurried, old-fashioned Switzerland of the 1930s. It occupies a sprawling, high-ceilinged dining room on the street level of the also-recommended Hotel National, a stately looking building behind the railway station. The focus here is on "slow-cooked food," a low-key rebellion against anything edible that carries even a whiff of America-inspired modernity. Stews and ragouts here each tend to have been slow simmered for hours, and vegetables and salads are very fresh and prepared simply, with a maximum of the original nutrients still intact. Examples include a daily variation of vegetable soup; a ragout of beef with summer vegetables and polenta; stewed vegetables within a "ring" of couscous; braised filets of salmon with herbs and onions;

ricotta-stuffed tortellini with spinach and a tomato-enriched cream sauce; and calves' liver with Madeira sauce.

In the Hotel National, Hirschengraben 24. ☎ **031/381-19-88.** Reservations not needed. Main courses 21F–37F. AE, MC, V. Mon–Fri 11am–2pm; Mon–Sat 5:30–10pm. Tram: 3, 5, or 9.

---

5 ATTRACTIONS

Before you rush off to sample the sightseeing attractions of the capital of Switzerland, stop in at the **Brasserie zum Bärengraben,** Muristalden 1 (☎ **031/331-42-18**), immediately across the street from the Bear Pits, the town's major attraction (see below). At a table here you can enjoy a slice of local life better than anywhere else. Many habitués settle down to read the morning news, ordering their favorite coffee, a beer, or a glass of wine.

THE TOP ATTRACTIONS

Bärengraben (Bear Pits) ★ is a deep, half-moon-shaped den where the bears, Bern's mascots, have been kept since 1480. According to legend, when the duke of Zähringen established the town in 1191, he sent his hunters out into the surrounding woods, which were full of wild game. The duke promised to name the city after the first animal slain, which was a *Bär* (bear). Since then, the town has been known as Bärn (Bern). Today the bears are beloved, pampered, and fed by both residents and visitors (carrots are most appreciated). The Bear Pits lie on the opposite side of the **Nydegg Bridge (Nydegg-brücke)** from the rest of Old Town. The bridge was built over one of the gorges of the Aare River; its central stone arch has a span of 54m (177 ft.) and affords a sweeping view of the city. Below the Bear Pits, you can visit the **Rosengarten (Rose Gardens),** with its much-photographed view of the medieval sector of the city.

Zytgloggeturm (Clock Tower) ★ (*Zeitglocketurm* in standard German), on Kram-gasse, was built in the 12th century and restored in the 16th century. Four minutes before every hour, crowds gather for the world's oldest and biggest horological puppet show. Mechanical bears, jesters, and emperors put on an animated performance. Staged since 1530, it's one of the longest-running acts in show business.

Cathedral of St. Vincent ★★
The Münster is one of the "newer" Gothic churches in Switzerland, dating from 1421. The belfry, however, was completed in 1893. The most exceptional feature of this three-aisle, pillared basilica is the tympanum over the main portal, which depicts the Last Judgment and contains more than 200 figures. You'll see mammoth 15th-century stained-glass windows in the chancel, but the most remarkable window, the *Dance of Death,* can be found in the Matter Chapel. The cathedral's 90m (295-ft.) belfry dominates Bern and offers a panoramic sweep of the Bernese Alps; to reach the viewing platform, you must climb 270 steps. The vista also includes the old town, its bridges, and the Aare River. Outside the basilica on Münsterplatz is the Moses Fountain, built in 1545.

Münsterplatz. ☎ **031/312-04-62.** Free admission to cathedral; viewing platform 4F adults, 2F children. Easter to Oct Tues–Sat 10am–5pm, Sun 11:30am–5pm; Nov–Easter Tues–Fri 10am–noon and 2–4pm, Sat 10am–noon and 2–5pm, Sun 11:30am–2pm. Viewing platform closes 30 min. before cathedral. Bus: 12.

Kunstmuseum (Fine Arts Museum) ★
The focus of this museum is on a worthy collection of paintings, sculptures, and art objects crafted and created up until the end of the 19th century. There's a collection of Italian 14th-century primitives, including Fra Angelico's *Virgin and Child.* Swiss primitives include some from the "Masters of the

Carnation." Hodler, the romantic artist, is represented by allegorical paintings depicting day and night. Impressionists include Monet, Manet, Sisley, and Cézanne, along with Delacroix and Bonnard. Surrealistic painters represented here include Dalí, Seligman, Oppenheim, and Tschumi. You'll also see works by Kandinsky, Modigliani, Matisse, Kirchner, Soutine, and Picasso, as well as contemporary Swiss artists.

Hodlerstrasse 12. (✆ **031/328-09-44.** www.kunstmuseumbern.ch. Permanent collection 7F adults, 5F seniors; special exhibitions 14F–18F extra. Tues 10am–9pm; Wed–Sun 10am–5pm. Bus: 20.

The Paul Klee Collection (Zentrum Paul Klee) ★★★   Until around 2004, most of the artworks within this museum were contained within an overcrowded series of rooms within the also-recommended Kunstmuseum. That was before they were moved into a museum created expressly for them by Renzo Piano, one of the most celebrated architects of Italy. Today, in a location about 5km (3 miles) east of Bern's Altstadt, more than 4,000 works by the artist Paul Klee are proudly displayed as a kind of homage to Bern's "local son who made good." The painter was born in Switzerland in 1879. The local collection of his works includes 40 oils, 2,000 drawings, and many gouaches and watercolors. Klee had a style characterized by fantasy forms in line and light colors. There's a gift shop and a restaurant on the premises, serving platters of food Tuesday to Sunday 11:30am to 11:30pm.

Monument in Fruchtland 3. (✆ **031/359-01-01.** www.paulkleezentrum.ch. Admission 18F adults, 8F children 6–16, free for children 5 and under. Tues–Sun 10am–5pm (Thurs till 9pm). Tram: 5. Bus: 12.

MORE ATTRACTIONS
In Town
The town's old but dignified **Rathaus (town hall),** on Rathausplatz, is still a center of political life. Built in 1406 in the Burgundian Gothic style and restored during World War II, the town hall has a double staircase and a covered porch.

Botanischer Garten (Botanical Garden) ★   The University of Bern operates one of the nation's most extensive botanical gardens in an idyllic setting along the river at Lorrainebrücke. Gardens extend in vast descending terraces down to the banks of the Aare. What is amazing about these gardens is the number of exotic plants from around the world that survive alongside native alpine greenery. The collection includes both medicinal and fiber plants, woodland and water plants, and an impressive collection of botanical wonders from the cold steppes of Central Asia. Vegetation from various ecological zones from around the world grow both in greenhouses and outdoors. The giant lily pads in a tropical greenhouse are a wonder to behold.

Altenbergrain 21. (✆ **031/631-49-44.** http://unibe.ch. Free admission. Mar–Sept daily 8am–5:30pm; Oct–Feb daily 8am–5pm. Bus: 20.

Bundeshaus   This Renaissance building, the Federal Palace, contains the two chambers of Switzerland's Parliament. Inaugurated in 1902, the Parliament building has a glass dome that displays the coats of arms of all 23 Swiss cantons. Of interest are the stained-glass windows, which symbolize education, public works, defense, and justice. In the ground-floor rotunda a relief depicts the legend of the origin of Switzerland as dramatized in Schiller's saga of *Wilhelm Tell.* You can also visit the Chamber of the National Council, dominated by a large fresco by Gyron, and the Chamber of the Council of States, decorated with a mural painting by Albert Welti. Because of unexpected delays, the Federal Palace remained closed at the time of writing. Check its status upon your arrival in Bern.

Bundesplatz. ℰ **031/322-85-22.** Free admission. Call for details about scheduled tours, which are not conducted when Parliament is in session. Tram: 9.

Historisches Museum Bern und Einstein Museum (Bern Historical Museum and Einstein Museum) ★★ The bulk of this museum resembles a neo-Gothic castle inspired by the Swiss fortress style of the 16th century. It's a venerable and somewhat old-fashioned repository for historical relics, along with archaeological, ethnographic, and numismatic collections. One of its primary attractions is a series of seven 15th-century tapestries. A tapestry called *The Thousand Flowers,* plus four others telling the story of Julius Caesar, belonged to the dukes of Burgundy during the Middle Ages. A number of rural and urban rooms, filled with period furnishings and artifacts, are also open to the public. Within the larger context of the museum is a specialized submuseum, the **Einstein Museum,** where books, journal entries, and an ongoing roster of videotaped news bulletins illustrate the life of one of Switzerland's most famous émigrés, who lived in Bern for a while back in 1905. Animated films and a computer-simulated "virtual journey through the cosmos" help to illuminate Einstein's theories about the relationships between physical matter, energy, and time.

Helvetiaplatz 5. ℰ **031/350-77-11.** www.bhm.ch. Admission to Bern Historical Museum 13F adults, 8F students and seniors, free for children 16 and under. Admission to Einstein Museum 18F adults, 8F children 6–16, free for children 5 and under. Both museums Tues–Sun 10am–5pm. Tram: 3 or 5.

Nearby

The most panoramic attraction in the immediate vicinity of Bern is the belvedere atop **Mount Gurten** ★★ at 844m (2,768 ft.). At its summit, there's a children's playground, a network of hiking trails, and panoramas that sweep out over the surrounding mountains and valleys. The belvedere is accessible to Bern via the **Gurtenbahn,** a cable train that's one of the fastest in Europe. The train departs from a station beside the Seftigenstrasse, about a half-mile north from the center of Bern. To reach the departure platform, take tram no. 9, and get off at the Gurtenbahn station, for a cost of 3.60F each way. The trip takes 4 minutes each way. If driving, follow the road signs to Thun. A parking lot in the hamlet of Wabern is a short walk from the cable-train station.

Round-trip passage on the cable-train to the belvedere costs 9F. The train operates year-round daily from 7:30am to sunset (depending on the season). For information, contact **Gurtenbahn Bern,** Eigerplatz (ℰ **031/961-23-23**).

ESPECIALLY FOR KIDS

Dählhölzli Tierpark, Tierparkweg (ℰ **031/357-15-15;** www.tierpark-bern.ch), is one of the most interesting zoos in Europe. It offers a complete range of European creatures, from the tiny harvest mouse to the mighty musk oxen. You can admire more than 2,000 animals, including exotic birds, reptiles, and fish in the vivarium. Admission is 10F for adults, 6F for children 6 to 16, and free for children 5 and under. The zoo is open April through September daily from 8am to 6:30pm; off-season hours are daily 9am to 5pm. A family ticket sells for 24F. Take bus no. 19.

Kids will also enjoy the **Zytgloggeturm (Clock Tower)** and the **Bärengraben (Bear Pits).** The **Naturhistorisches Museum,** Bernastrasse 15 (ℰ **031/350-71-11;** www-nmbe. unibe.ch), with its fascinating reptile collection and gallery of stuffed African beasts, is best for a rainy day, and a picnic at **Mount Gurten** is a good way to cap any child's visit to Bern.

START:	Bahnhofplatz.
FINISH:	Swiss Parliament.
TIME:	2 hours.
BEST TIMES:	Any sunny day.
WORST TIMES:	Rush hours, Monday through Friday from 8 to 9am and 5 to 6pm.

Start at the city's commercial core, the

❶ Bahnhofplatz

Throughout 2007 and during part of 2008, this square, or plaza, in front of the city's main railway station witnessed a more thorough urban renewal (new underground parking, new pedestrian zones, new landscaping) than any other location within Bern. Expect a spanking-new urban layout around this square, one of the showcases of urban Switzerland.

Opening onto Bahnhofplatz is the:

❷ Church of the Holy Ghost

Also called the Heiliggeistkirche, this church dates from 1729 and seems out of place in such a traffic-congested area.

From the church, head east up Spittalgasse, coming first to:

❸ Bagpiper Fountain

The Pfeiferbrunnen, which depicts a bagpiper atop a column and capital, was erected around 1545, presumably by Hans Gieng. In 2007, the widely publicized cost of removing (temporarily) this statue from its pedestal, and its subsequent restoration, was 500,000F.

Directly east of the fountain, at Bärenplatz, is the:

❹ Prison Gate

Called the Käfigturm, this gate dates from the 1200s. It now shelters a tiny museum devoted to the cultural and business life of the city.

Continue east along:

❺ Marktgasse

This is the main street of Old Town, filled with fashionable shops and florists. Many of its buildings date from the 17th century.

The street leads into one of the principal squares of Altstadt:

❻ Kornhausplatz

This square is the site of the Ogre Fountain, which is a representation of a carnival figure, with a pillar and capital erected about 1544. The Kornhaus, an old granary from the 1700s, also stands on the square; today it's a restaurant and wine cellar.

> **TAKE A BREAK**
> The "nerve center" of Bern, **Café des Pyrénées,** Kornhausplatz (☎ **031/311-30-63**), is frequented by international journalists and visitors drawn to its sidewalk terrace. This bistro cafe also attracts many expatriates. Stop in for a drink—half a dozen types of Spanish brandy, for example—or any of the sandwiches and pasta dishes. It's open Monday to Friday 9am to 12:30am and Saturday 8am to 5pm.

Also opening onto this square is the celebrated:

❼ Clock Tower

Also called the Zytgloggeturm, the Clock Tower was the town's west gate from 1191 to 1250. Its chimes start pealing at 4 minutes before every hour. A picture postcard of this scene is the most popular souvenir of Bern.

Leaving Kornhausplatz, continue east along:

❽ Kramgasse

A continuation of Marktgasse, this street contains many old houses with corner turrets and oriel windows.

BERN

8

WALKING TOUR: BERN'S ALTSTADT

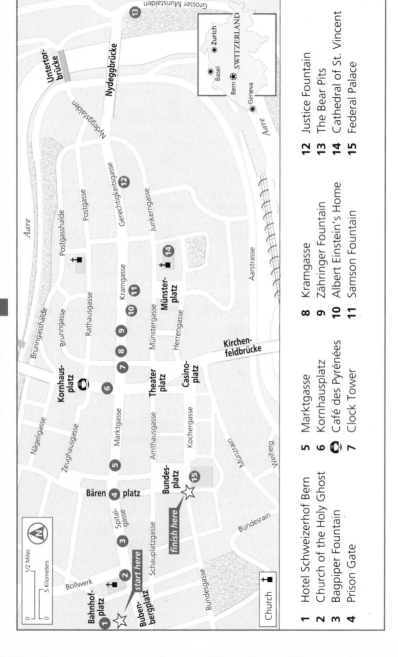

1 Hotel Schweizerhof Bern
2 Church of the Holy Ghost
3 Bagpiper Fountain
4 Prison Gate
5 Marktgasse
6 Kornhausplatz
7 Clock Tower
8 Kramgasse
9 Zähringer Fountain
10 Albert Einstein's Home
11 Samson Fountain
12 Justice Fountain
13 The Bear Pits
14 Cathedral of St. Vincent
15 Federal Palace

Another major fountain standing on this street is the:

⑨ Zähringer Fountain

This fountain was a monument to the city founder, Berchtold von Zähringen. Here you can see the Bern bear, mascot of the city, along with the Zähringer coat of arms. The pillar, capital, and figure were erected in 1535 by Hans Hiltprand.

Continuing, at Kramgasse 49 you come to:

⑩ Albert Einstein's Home

In 1905 the famous physicist wrote his "theory of relativity" here.

The next fountain encountered on this same street is the:

⑪ Samson Fountain

This notable fountain is an allegory of strength, with a pillar and capital from 1527 and the figure from 1544.

Continue east along the street, which now changes its name to Gerechtigkeitsgasse. In the center of the street stands yet another famous fountain, the:

⑫ Justice Fountain

This fountain is an allegory of Justice, with worshiping subjects, including the pope, at her feet. The statue was erected in 1543.

Walk to the end of the street and continue across the river, crossing the Nydeggbrücke, until you reach Bern's most visited sight:

⑬ The Bear Pits

The Bärengraben is immediately on your right. The city of Bern is named after the bear (now its official mascot), and bears have resided in these pits since 1480.

Cross back over the bridge, and this time take the street to the left, heading west along Junkerngasse until you reach the:

⑭ Cathedral of St. Vincent

In Münsterplatz, the cathedral's first stone was laid in 1421, but building went on until 1573. From the tower you'll get a panoramic view of Bern.

After leaving the cathedral, continue west along Münstergasse until you reach Theaterplatz, one of Altstadt's major squares. Continue west, following the same street, which has now changed its name to Amthausgasse. You'll then approach Bundesplatz, site of the:

⑮ Federal Palace

Also called the Bundeshaus (Swiss Parliament) and capped with a massive dome, it was inspired by the Italian Renaissance Cathedral in Florence. This is the seat of Swiss democracy and one of the nation's treasured symbols.

BERN

8

ATTRACTIONS

ORGANIZED TOURS

The tourist office conducts **walking tours** of Bern May to October. The daily meeting point is either at the tourist office at 11am or at Zytgloggeturm at 11am. The cost is 12F for adults, 6F for children 6 to 16, and free for children 5 and under. Depending on demand, this guided walking tour may or may not be offered by the time of your visit, since the focus of the tourist office's walking tours is to an increasing degree trained upon iPod-style audio guides that play a prerecorded 2-hour walking tour of Bern which can be started and stopped at any point, depending on the pace you want to maintain. Interspersed with descriptions of the Bernese monuments en route are anecdotes, folk songs, cheerful music, and far more than you might have initially thought of. These audio guides rent for 18F per day (14F per day for anyone who opts to buy a Bern Card), with a 50F deposit. For more information about how and where to acquire these audio guides, contact the Bern city tourist office (see "Essentials," earlier in this chapter).

Bern is accepted by many Swiss as the point of origin for several rail itineraries that are among the most spectacular in Europe. You'll probably need help from someone at the tourist office to organize one of these itineraries, but the staff at the Bern Tourist office is now capable of crafting and selling tickets for either one-way or circular itineraries which will take you through some of the most vertiginous landscapes in Europe. One of our favorites involves traveling from Bern through its Oberland region, with rail junctions in towns that include Interlaken, Lauterbrunnen, Wengen, and Kleine Scheidegg, then over the Jungfraujoch via Grindelwald and Interlaken, and back to Bern. Jungfraujoch, at 3,400m (11,152 ft.), has the highest railway station in Europe and offers panoramic views over glaciers and the Alps, including the so-called Ice Palace. The cost for this particular itinerary, which is self-conducted, self-guided, and self-scheduled, assuming that participants begin and end their journeys in Bern, is 148F in second class and 227F in first class. For anyone holding a valid Swiss Pass, prices of this itinerary are reduced to 52F for second-class travel, and 81F for first-class travel.

6 OUTDOOR PURSUITS

The people of Bern are not particularly addicted to spectator sports, but they're very fond of recreational sports. The vast playground of Europe, the Bernese Oberland (see chapter 9), is at their doorstep, and they tend to take full advantage of it.

BIKING   There are approximately 3,000km (1,860 miles) of roadway in the Bernese Oberland around Bern. Pick up a bicycle map that outlines the routes at the tourist office, then rent a bike at the Bahnhof and set off on your adventure. See "By Bicycle" in "Getting Around," earlier in this chapter, for more information.

FITNESS, SAUNA & SOLARIUM   Go to the **STB Training Center,** Seilerstrasse 21 (© **031/381-02-03**), where full facilities are available to keep you in shape.

GOLF   If you're a member of a golf club back home and have your membership card, you can patronize the **Golf and Country Club** in Blumisberg (© **026/496-34-38**), 18km (11 miles) west of Bern near Flamatt (on the road to Fribourg).

HIKING   There are an estimated 250km (155 miles) of marked walking trails in the area surrounding Bern. You can pick up a rambling map at the tourist office. See "On Foot" in "Getting Around," earlier in this chapter, for more information.

SWIMMING   The city's best indoor pool, along with a Turkish bath and sauna, is the **Hirschengraben Indoor Pool,** Maulbeerstrasse 14 (© **031/381-36-56**). The pool is open Tuesday, Thursday, and Friday 8am to 8:45pm. Admission is 7F to the pool and 17F to the sauna. The pool is closed July and August.

TENNIS   Courts are available at **Thalmatt,** Mettlenwaldweg 19, Herren-schwanden (© **031/307-33-33;** www.thalmattsport.ch).

7 SHOPPING

With a few exceptions, stores in the city center are open on Monday 9am to 7pm; on Tuesday, Wednesday, and Friday 8:15am to 6:30pm; on Thursday 8:15am to 9pm; and on Saturday 9am to 5pm.

With 6km (4 miles) of arcades, stores of all types are sheltered in Bern. The main shopping streets are **Spitalgasse, Kramgasse, Postgasse, Marktgasse,** and **Gerechtigkeitsgasse.**

You can begin your shopping excursion at **Globus,** Spitalgasse 17 (© **031/313-40-40**), a major department store comparable to Bloomingdale's, with departments for just about everything. Many people from the Bernese Oberland come into Bern just to shop at Globus. Also in the center of town, **Loeb ag Bern,** Spitalgasse 47 (© **031/320-71-11**), has a little bit of everything but is known chiefly for its high-quality fashions.

The best handicrafts, souvenirs, and gifts are found at **Heimatwerk,** Kramgasse 61 (© **031/311-30-00**), located on a historic street near the Clock Tower. This outlet sells handicrafts from all over Switzerland, including textiles, woodcarvings, music boxes, and jewelry.

A collection of Art Nouveau pewter pieces is found at **Galerie Trag-art,** Gerechtigkeitsgasse 9 (© **031/311-64-49**).

For antiques, dolls, and toys, the best outlet is **Puppenklinik,** Gerechtigkeitsgasse 36 (© **031/312-07-71**).

The coin and stamp collector should head for Bern's most famous dealer, **Zumstein,** Zeughausgasse 24 (© **031/312-00-55**).

A good outlet for leather footwear is **Bally,** Kramgasse 55 (© **031/311-54-81**), a branch of the famous Swiss shoe manufacturer that carries the complete line. Spitalgasse lies right off Bahnhofplatz. On the same street, **Gygax Mode,** Spitalgasse 4 (© **031/311-25-61**), is a leading name in leather goods. It sells locally produced items as well as some of the best from neighboring countries such as Italy.

For fashion, women gravitate to **Ciolina Modehaus,** Marktgasse 51 (© **031/328-64-64;** www.ciolina.ch), where clothes have fine styles and high prices. A leading men's store is **Zwald,** Neuengasse 23 (© **031/311-22-33**). Fashions here reflect a Continental flair.

Swiss chocolates (not always made in Switzerland these days) are sold at **Beeler,** Spitalgasse 29 (© **031/311-28-08;** www.confiserie-beeler.ch), one of the city's leading chocolatiers, and **Abegglen,** Spitalgasse 36 (© **031/311-21-11**).

Hats and handbags are the specialties at **KB Accessories,** Münstergasse 12 (© **031/312-01-15**), as designed by funky fashion iconoclasts Brigitte Keller and Stephan Billeter. Look for the kind of unusual and hip millinery that, if you're brave enough to wear it proudly and with good posture, will evoke comparisons to Marlene Dietrich.

Many of the art objects at **Galerie Granero/Erg du Ténéré,** Nydeggasse 15 (© **031/311-71-41**), derive from Africa's dusty sub-Sahara region, especially the arid and folklore-rich countries of Chad and Mali. The Swiss-born owners scour that region for silver jewelry crafted by members of the Tuareg tribes, some of which come adorned with mystical symbols that are believed to ward off evil and empower the wearer.

Chalk **Llhasa,** Münstergasse 51 (© **031/311-61-06**), up to offbeat shopping. Switzerland's status as a neutral nation has encouraged the emigration to Bern of some of Tibet's spiritual leaders, with this shop acting as a focal point for them. You'll find meditative aids, exotic jewelry, carpets and weavings, clothing, incense, and books describing various aspects of Tibet's unique points of view about politics, philosophy, and religion.

Here's a random sampling of funky shops in funky Bern. **Irmak und Wirz,** GmbH, Kramgasse 10 (© **031/312-06-04**), specializes in tribal rugs from Iran, many of them woven high in the Iranian mountains according to age-old geometric designs of the Quashquai tribes. **Trouvaillen am Münster,** Münstergasse 16 (© **031/312-79-82**), is dusty and overcrowded, containing an intriguing, sometimes bizarre collection of African and Swiss hunting trophies, antique lighting fixtures, bric-a-brac, and oddities that include an elephant embryo from the 1950s and a barely used motorcycle from the 1930s. This is counterculture Bern at its most genuinely eccentric. Visit **Marcopolo,** Münstergasse 47 (© **031/311-88-44**), for artifacts from the developing world, all arranged in glittering arrays of jewelry and weavings from Africa, India, Uzbekistan, and Afghanistan. Everything here seems exotic and ironically positioned a bit like a cleaned-up version of a Middle Eastern bazaar.

BERN

8

SHOPPING

8 BERN AFTER DARK

Most Bern residents get up early on weekday mornings, so they usually limit their evening entertainment to a drink or two at a historic cellar such as the Kornhauskeller or the Klötzlikeller. Nevertheless, the city offers several late-night clubs, with dancing and cabaret, for the nocturnally active international crowd. *Bern Guide,* distributed free by the tourist office, keeps a current list of cultural events.

THE PERFORMING ARTS

The **Bern Symphony Orchestra** is one of the finest orchestras in Switzerland. Concerts by the orchestra are usually performed at the concert facilities in the **Bern Kursaal,** Herrengasse 25 (✆ **031/328-02-28;** www.kursaal-bern.ch). Except for a summer vacation, usually lasting from July until mid-August, the box office is open Monday to Friday noon to 6:30pm, Saturday 10am to 2pm. Tickets range from 20F to 55F.

Concerts with fewer musicians, especially chamber music, are often performed in any of four or five churches; in the auditorium at the **Konservatorium für Musik,** Kramgasse 36 (✆ **031/326-53-53;** www.konsibern.ch); or in the concert and recording facilities of **Radio Studio Bern,** Schwarztorstrasse 21 (✆ **031/388-91-11**).

Major opera and ballet performances are usually staged in what is generally acknowledged as Bern's most beautiful theater, the century-old **Stadttheater,** Kornhausplatz 20 (✆ **031/329-51-11;** www.stadttheaterbern.ch). Performances are often in German, and to a lesser degree in French, but even if you don't understand those languages, you might want to attend a performance. Other plays and dance programs, including ballet and cabaret, are presented in the **Theater am Käfigturm,** Spitalgasse 4 (✆ **031/311-61-00;** www.theater-am-kaefigturm.ch).

THE CLUB & BAR SCENE

Bar aux Petits Fours   The best gay bar in Bern attracts a multilingual, attractive, and international group of gay people, mostly men. There's no dance floor and no restaurant on the premises, but what you get is a low-key bar, filled with regular clients, where a newcomer can usually break the glacial freeze of Swiss reserve with a bit of effort. It's open daily from 6:30pm to 12:30am. Kramgasse 67. ✆ **031/312-73-74.**

Cesary Bar   Some people in Bern consider this the most stylish and intriguing bar in the Swiss capital, with an ongoing stream of some of its most beautiful people. Set on one of the showcase squares of the Old Town (behind a terrace that opens during clement weather for an additional 30 seats), it evokes the kind of stylish Milanese modernity you might have expected far to the south, beyond the mountains. There's a sampling of simple platters, especially sandwiches, priced at 10F to 15F each, many different kinds of cocktails for the drink-a-holic set, and whiskeys with soda priced at around 14F each. It's open Monday to Saturday from 7:30pm to 12:30am. Kornhausplatz 11. ✆ **031/318-93-83.**

Come Back Bar   This isn't a gay bar in the strictest sense of the word, but a tavern that's cosmopolitan and tolerant, and likely to attract lots of genuinely cool artists and hipsters. It occupies the cellar vaults below the medieval buildings of the Rathausgasse. Inside, blinking lights frame a discreet dance floor and a long bar functions as a local hangout for many of the gay and gay-friendly residents of the Old Town. It's especially crowded on weekends, with a calmer, more low-key approach to things during weeknights. It's open daily from 6pm to 12:30am (until 3:30am Fri–Sat). Rathausgasse 42. ✆ **031/311-77-13.**

Klötzlikeller   The oldest wine tavern in Bern is near the Gerechtigkeitsbrunnen
(Fountain of Justice), the first fountain you see on your walk from the Bärengraben (Bear
Pits) to the Zytgloggeturm (Clock Tower). Watch for the lantern outside an angled cellar
door. The well-known tavern dates from 1635 and is leased by the city to an independent
operator. Some 20 different wines are sold by the glass, with prices starting at 8.50F. The
menu is changed every 6 weeks. The appetizing snacks are always traditional, including
sliced cheese, with prices ranging from 14F to 28F. The traditional Bernese kitchen
produces various dinner plates, reflecting regional specialties and costing 24F to 48F. In
summer, hours are Tuesday to Friday 4 to 11:30pm; off season, it's open Monday to
Saturday 4 to 11:30pm. Gerechtigkeitsgasse 62. (C) **031/311-74-56.** www.kloetzlikeller.ch.

Marians Jazzroom   The Louis Armstrong Bar, site of this jazz venue, has its own
separate entrance from the Innere Enge Hotel. Unique in Bern, it serves up not only food
and drink, but the finest traditional jazz performed live by top artists from around the
world. Hours are Tuesday to Thursday 7:30pm to midnight, Friday 7:30pm to 1am, and
Saturday 7:30pm to 2am. On Saturday there is a *concert apéro* from 4 to 6:30pm, and on
some Sundays there is a jazz brunch from 10am to 1:30pm. It's closed June through
August. In the Innere Enge Hotel, Engerstrasse 54. (C) **031/309-61-11.** www.mariansjazzroom.ch.
Cover 15F–50F, depending on the act.

GAMBLING

Grand Casino Kursaal Bern, on the fifth floor of the Allegro Hotel Bern, Kornhausstrasse
3 ((C) **031/339-55-55;** www.kursaal-bern.ch), is the only place in town to gamble. Indeed,
it's a great spot for novices to learn because the size of bets is limited, and consequently,
serious money rarely changes hands here. It's open daily noon to 2am, and admission is 10F.
Drinks cost 10F to 15F. Within the immediate vicinity, and managed by the Allegro Hotel
Bern, are three restaurants and two bars, plus a dance hall that charges a 10F cover. It's open
Friday and Saturday 9pm to 3:30am, and Sunday 3 to 10pm.

The Bernese Oberland

The Bernese Oberland is one of the greatest tourist attractions in the world, mainly because it's one of the best areas for winter sports. The region sprawls between the Reuss River and Lake Geneva, with the Rhône forming its southern border. The area contains two lakes, the Thun and the Brienz, and takes in a portion of the Alps (culminating in the Finsteraarhorn at 4,207m/13,799 ft.). The canton of Bern, which encompasses most of the area, is the second largest in Switzerland and contains about 160 sq. km (62 sq. miles) of glaciers.

The best center for exploring the Bernese Oberland is Interlaken, most popular as a summer resort. Other cities in the region, such as Gstaad, Grindelwald, Kandersteg, and Mürren, are both summer and winter playgrounds. You can ski the mountains during winter and swim, sail, and water-ski on Lake Thun in the summer.

1 EXPLORING THE BERNESE OBERLAND

To compensate for the region's almost impossible geography, Swiss engineers have criss-crossed the Oberland with cogwheel railways (some of them still driven by steam), aerial cableways, and sinuous mountain roads. Though often a confusing experience, getting to a particular resort can be part of the fun. The region's busiest railroad junction, and the point where most travelers change trains for local railways, is **Interlaken.**

You can buy a **transportation pass** for the Bernese Oberland from the Swiss Rail System. The train ticket is valid for 7 days and costs 230F in second class and 279F in first class. Another pass, valid for 15 days, costs 277F in second class and 332F in first class. With the 7-day pass, you'll travel free for 3 days and pay a reduced fare for the final 4 days. With the 15-day pass, you'll travel free for 5 days and pay reduced fares for the rest of the time. Children travel at half price. The pass is valid on most railroads; all mountain trains, cable cars, chairlifts, and steamers on Lakes Thun and Brienz; and most postal-bus lines in the area. The ticket also qualifies you for a 25% reduction on the Kleine Scheidegg-Eigergletscher-Jungfraujoch railway, the Mürren-Schilthorn aerial cable line, and the bus to Grosse Scheidegg and Bussalp. You must purchase the pass at least 1 week before you arrive. For information about the pass, call ℂ **058/327-32-71.**

Since Interlaken is the focal point of one of the most complicated networks of ski lifts in the world, most visitors opt to buy a comprehensive pass that allows unlimited access to the cog railways, buses, cable cars, chairlifts, and gondolas (incorporating every mechanical lift in and around Interlaken, Wengen, Grindelwald, and Mürren). Sold at the Interlaken tourist office (see "Interlaken," below) and tourist offices at the other leading resorts, it's called the **Jungfrau Top Ski Region Pass.** You can buy the 2-day pass for 126F, the 5-day pass for 265F, or the 7-day pass for 334F. Discounts of 10% are offered to seniors 62 and older, discounts of 20% to youths ages 16 to 20, and discounts of 50% to children 6 to 15. Kids 5 and under travel for only 10% of the above rates. This pass incorporates access to 44 ski lifts, 204km (127 miles) of well-groomed downhill runs,

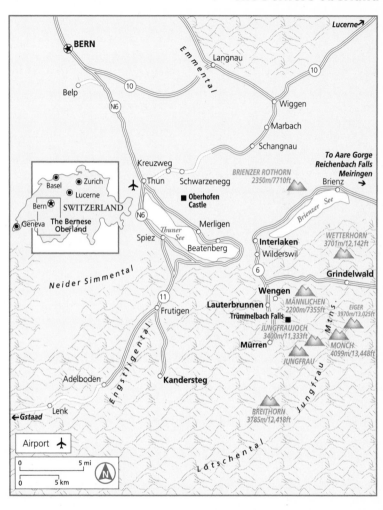

99km (60 miles) of prepared walking and cross-country ski paths, and 50km (31 miles) of tobogganing runs. It covers the region around Grindelwald, Wengen, and Mürren.

Other passes include the following:

- **First Region Ski Pass** is a small-scale cluster of ski lifts, favored by beginners and intermediates, that includes six lifts and a gondola. It's available only for the region immediately around Grindelwald and does not include Wengen. A 1-day pass costs 62F, a 2-day pass 112F.
- **Kleine Männlichen and Scheidegg Pass** offer the same scale of difficulty as the First Region Ski Pass, as well as the same price (1- and 2-day passes are the only offerings).

Unlike the First Region Ski Pass, it's available to residents of either Wengen or Grindelwald, but residents of Mürren are not invited to this particular cluster of runs.

BY MOUNTAIN BIKE   Hundreds of miles of cycling paths riddle the Bernese Oberland, and most of them begin in Interlaken. Separate from the network of hiking paths, the bike routes are signposted and marked on rental maps distributed at bike-rental agencies; it's the law to use only specially signposted routes and not destroy plant and animal life or ride across private fields. Hikers, incidentally, are given the right of way over bikers. To make arrangements to rent a bike, call © **033/823-15-34.** Rates usually begin at 45F per day, going up.

ON FOOT   The Bernese Oberland is ideal for walkers and hikers. The natural terrain here will satisfy everyone from the most ambitious mountain hiker to the casual stroller.

Trails designed for walkers branch out from almost every junction. Most are paved and signposted, showing distances and estimated walking times. Tourist offices can suggest itineraries for walkers.

For the more athletic, itineraries include long hikes far afield in the mountains, with suggestions for overnight accommodations en route.

Even if you don't feel up to scaling alpine peaks, you can still go on walks. Take one of the Swiss postal-bus rides uphill to a village, then stroll back down to Interlaken, for example. Be warned, however, that walking downhill in Switzerland can still strain your calf muscles.

2 INTERLAKEN ★★★

54km (34 miles) SE of Bern; 130km (81 miles) SW of Zurich

Interlaken is the tourist capital of the Bernese Oberland. Cableways and cog railways designed for steeply inclined mountains connect it with most of the region's villages and dazzling sights, including the snowy heights of the Jungfrau, which rises a short distance to the south. Excursion possibilities from Interlaken are both numerous and dazzling.

This "town between the lakes" (Thun and Brienz) has been a vacation resort for over 300 years. Although it began as a summer resort, it developed into a year-round playground, altering its allure as the seasons change. During the winter skiers take advantage of the town's low prices. Interlaken charges low-season prices in January and February, when smaller resorts at higher altitudes are charging their highest rates of the year. The most expensive time to visit Interlaken is during midsummer, when high-altitude and snowless ski resorts often charge their lowest rates.

An Augustinian monastery was founded in Interlaken in 1130 but was later closed during the Reformation; the ruins can still be seen in a park in the center of town. Tourism to the area is said to have begun in 1690, when Margrave Frederic Albert of Brandenburg journeyed into the snow-covered rocks of the Jungfrau massif. However, tourism as we know it today dawned at the beginning of the 19th century, when artists and writers—many of them British—were drawn to the town by its scenery. As the country's railroad and steamer services improved, a steady stream of visitors followed, including such notables as Mark Twain, Goethe (who seems to have lived everywhere), Wagner, Mendelssohn, and representatives of European royal families.

GETTING THERE   There are several trains daily between Zurich and Interlaken (2 hr.) and between Bern and Interlaken (40 min.). Frequent train service also connects Geneva with Interlaken (2½ hr.). For additional **rail information,** call ✆ **0900/300-300.**

Note: Although the town has two different railway stations, Interlaken East and Interlaken West, West is more convenient to the city's center.

If you're **driving** from Bern, head south on N6 to Spiez, then continue east on N8 to Interlaken.

GETTING AROUND   **Train** arrivals are at either Interlaken East or Interlaken West. If you're loaded with luggage, you'll want to grab a taxi. However, after you've been deposited at one of the local hotels (nearly all of which are in the city center), you'll rarely need a taxi—the town is closely knit and best explored on foot. Buses are convenient for connections to the satellite towns and villages or heading to the outskirts. The **bus station** is at Areckstrasse 6 (✆ **033/828-88-28**).

VISITOR INFORMATION   The **Tourism Organization Interlaken** is in the Hotel Metropole at Höheweg 37 (✆ **033/826-53-00;** www.interlaken.ch). It's open July to mid-September Monday to Friday 8am to 7pm, Saturday 8am to 5pm, and Sunday 10am to noon and 5 to 7pm. From mid-September to October, hours are Monday to Friday 8am to 6pm and Saturday 9am to 1pm. Hours November to April are Monday to Friday 8am to noon and 1:30 to 6pm, and Saturday 9am to noon. May to June the office is open Monday to Friday 8am to 6pm and Saturday 8am to 4pm.

A **visitor's card** is granted to persons registered at local hotels and confers certain discounts to some of the local attractions.

EXPLORING THE AREA

It's very simple: The best way to see everything in Interlaken is to walk. You can either randomly stroll around, enjoying the panoramic views in all directions, or follow a more structured walking tour. If you'd like some guidance, go to the tourist office (see above) and ask for a copy of *What a Wonderful World,* providing maps and listing hotels and local attractions.

The **Höheweg** ★★ covers 14 hectares (35 acres) in the middle of town between the two train stations. Once the property of Augustinian monks, it was acquired in the mid–19th century by the hotel keepers of Interlaken, who turned it into a park. As you stroll along Höhenpromenade, admire the famous view of the Jungfrau mountain. Another beautiful sight is the flower clock at the Casino Kursaal. You're also sure to see some *fiacres* (horse-drawn cabs). The promenade is lined with hotels, cafes, and gardens.

Cross over the Aare River to **Unterseen,** built in 1280 by Berthold von Eschenbach. Here you can visit the parish church, with its late-Gothic tower dating from 1471. This is one of the most photographed sights in the Bernese Oberland. The Mönch appears to the left of the tower, the Jungfrau on the right.

Back in Interlaken, visit the **Touristik-Museum der Jungfrau-Region,** am Stadthausplatz, Obere Gasse 26 (✆ **033/822-98-39**), the first regional tourism museum in the country. Exhibitions show the growth of tourism in the region throughout the past 2 centuries. The museum is open from May to mid-October Tuesday to Sunday from 2 to 5pm. Admission is 5F, or 4F with a visitor's card. Children are charged 3F.

To see the sights of Interlaken, Matten, and Unterseen by *fiacre,* line up at the Interlaken West train station. The half-hour round-trip tour costs 40F for one or two, plus 12F for each additional person; children 7 to 16 are charged half fare, and those 6 and under ride free.

Other attractions in the area include animal parks, afternoon concerts, and steamers across Lakes Brienz and Thun. During the summer visitors can sit in covered grandstands and watch Schiller's version of the William Tell story and the formation of the Swiss Confederation. We also recommend the delectable pastries sold in the local cafes.

OUTDOOR ACTIVITIES

If you're feeling energetic, or just looking to work off an excess of fondue dipping, Interlaken offers many opportunities for sports—sailing, windsurfing, rowing, fishing, golf, tennis, mountain trekking, and glider flying. There's also a swimming pool in town. More information is available at the tourist office.

GOLF   You can play at the **Interlaken-Unterseen course** (✆ **033/823-60-16;** www.interlakengolf.ch) from April to October. The cost is 100F Monday to Friday and 120F Saturday and Sunday. With a visitor's card, the cost is reduced to 90F on weekdays and 110F on weekends.

HORSEBACK RIDING   There are several bridle paths between Lake Thun and Lake Brienz. The **Voegeli Riding School,** Scheidgasse 66, in Unterseen (✆ **033/822-74-16;** www.reitschulevoegeli.ch), offers 1-hour riding lessons for 50F.

SWIMMING   There's a public **indoor pool** and a public open-air pool, **Bödeli** (✆ **033/827-90-90;** www.boedelibad.ch), behind the Kursaal. The indoor pool has a sauna and a solarium as well as a fitness room. This pool is open year-round Monday 9am to 9pm, Tuesday to Friday 9am to 9:45pm, and Saturday and Sunday 9am to 6pm. Entrance is 8F for adults, 4.80F for children 6 to 16, and free for children 5 and under. The outdoor pool, with its changing cabins and 9.9m (32-ft.) diving board, is open mid-May through September daily from 9am to 7pm. Keep in mind, though, that even July and August might be too chilly for you. Entrance is 6.50F for adults and 3.50F for children.

TENNIS   Use of a court at the **Höhematte** costs 25F per hour for visitors. If you're alone and willing to be matched up with another person, it will cost you half the court fee. For reservations, phone ✆ **033/822-14-72.** The courts are open from mid-April to mid-October daily from 8am to 8 or 9pm.

SHOPPING

True to its role as the nerve center of the entire Oberland region, Interlaken stocks an ample supply of souvenirs and sports equipment. You'll find all the handicrafts and art objects you could possibly need beside the resort's main street, Höheweg, and around the Interlaken West railway station. One of the best shops, which has been a fixture for tourists since the turn of the 20th century, is **Heimatwerk Interlaken,** Höheweg 115 (✆ **033/822-16-53**). It stocks only goods manufactured in Switzerland, including a wholesome and comprehensive roster of woodcarved children's toys, tablecloths and linens, cutting boards and cheese boards, ceramics, and glass. Since Interlaken has higher-altitude ski and hill-climbing resorts stretching upward on virtually all sides, you won't lack for purveyors of sporting-goods equipment. Two of the best are **Intersport,** Postgasse 16 (✆ **033/822-06-61**), and **Score Sport,** Bahnhofstrasse 8 (✆ **033/822-73-22**).

WHERE TO STAY

Very Expensive

Lindner Grand Hotel Beau-Rivage ★★★   This government-rated five-star and reconstructed Belle Epoque–style hotel between Höheweg and the Aare River is one of Interlaken's grand hotels. Only Victoria-Jungfrau is better. The Beau-Rivage sells luxury on a smaller, more intimate scale than its competitors, and is located in a very tranquil spot. It's only a short distance from the Interlaken East rail station, which makes it a good center for excursions in all directions. The central tower has an ascending series of covered loggias decorated with carvings and flowers, a triangular pediment, and a mansard roof. There are two wings with gables and wrought-iron balconies. The renovated rooms are conservatively modern with excellent beds and nicely kept bathrooms. The front rooms open onto the Jungfrau, and the rooms in the rear are not only quieter but face the river.

Höheweg 211, CH-3800 Interlaken. © **033/826-70-07.** Fax 033/823-28-47. www.lindner.de. 101 units. 359F–419F double; 499F–1,199F suite. Rates include buffet breakfast. AE, DC, MC, V. Free parking outdoors. **Amenities:** Restaurant; bar; babysitting; concierge; exercise room; indoor heated pool; room service; sauna. *In room:* TV, hair dryer, minibar, Wi-Fi (30F per 24 hr.).

Victoria-Jungfrau Grand Hotel & Spa ★★★ (Kids)   Since 1865, this grand hotel has reigned as one of the most important resort properties in Switzerland. The owner of the Victoria Hotel, Edouard Ruchti, united it with the Jungfrau Hotel in 1895, and the landmark property has stood ever since. Everyone from the emperor of Brazil to the king of Siam to Mark Twain has passed through its corridors. During World War II the hotel served as headquarters of the Swiss ·commander in chief, General Henri Guisan. Designed in a richly ornate Victorian style, it sits right in the town center at the foot of rigidly symmetrical gardens. The hotel boasts valuable antiques and one of the best-trained staffs in Interlaken. The most expensive rooms open onto views of the Jungfrau. The midsize to spacious accommodations are luxurious.

Höheweg 41, CH-3800 Interlaken. © **800/223-6800** in the U.S. or 033/828-28-28. Fax 033/828-28-80. www.victoria-jungfrau.ch. 212 units. 696F–796F double; 836F–900F junior suite; from 1,556F suite. Half board 150F per person. AE, DC, MC, V. Free parking outside, 30F in garage. **Amenities:** 3 restaurants; 2 bars; babysitting; children's center; concierge; exercise room; indoor heated pool; room service; spa; 5 tennis courts (lit). *In room:* TV, hair dryer, minibar, Wi-Fi (30F per 24 hr.).

Expensive

Hotel Interlaken ★   This is the resort's oldest hotel, receiving overnight guests since 1323, first as a hospital, later as a cloister, and, beginning in the early 1400s, as a tavern and inn. Guests have included Byron and Felix Mendelssohn. The hotel, directly east of the casino, has been gutted and rebuilt since, with a salmon-colored facade sporting baroque touches. The most expensive rooms have a few 19th-century antiques; the rest have conservative, modern furnishings with excellent beds and well-maintained bathrooms.

Höheweg 74, CH-3800 Interlaken. © **033/826-68-68.** Fax 033/826-68-69. www.interlakenhotel.ch. 60 units. 220F–330F double. Rates include buffet breakfast. Half board 45F per person. AE, DC, MC, V. Free parking. **Amenities:** Restaurant; bar; room service; sauna. *In room:* TV, hair dryer, minibar, Wi-Fi (30F per 24 hr.).

Hotel Metropole ★★   Americans often prefer this sleek, modern hotel in the city center (the only skyscraper in the Bernese Oberland), to the aging palaces of Interlaken. The 18-story building was built in 1976 and has since been stylishly renovated. It's the most up-to-date and best-managed hotel in town. The small, standardized rooms have plush carpeting, modern furniture, and balconies. All units have neatly kept bathrooms. Those facing south have a panoramic view of Interlaken and the towering mountains. Try to steer clear of the 18 units in the annex, as they are a bit lackluster and have no views.

Höheweg 37, CH-3800 Interlaken. © **800/223-5652** in the U.S. or 033/828-66-66. Fax 033/828-66-33. www.metropole-interlaken.ch. 95 units. 142F–363F double; 386F–593F suite. Half board 55F per person.

AE, DC, MC, V. Parking 8F outside, 14F in garage. **Amenities:** 2 restaurants; bar; babysitting; indoor heated pool; room service; sauna. *In room:* TV, hair dryer, minibar, Wi-Fi (29F per 24 hr.).

Moderate

Alpenblick ★ (Finds) Instead of staying in Interlaken itself, consider a retreat to the neighboring village of Wilderswil, 4km (2½ miles) from the center, to this small inn with the area's most outstanding restaurant, Gourmetstübli (see below). Bedrooms are cozy, comfortable, and well furnished, and housekeeping is first-rate, as is the welcome from the friendly owners. There is a rustic aura about the place, and an escape to this alpine retreat allows motorists to avoid the congestion of Interlaken.

Oberdorfstrasse 3, CH-3812 Wilderswil. ☎ 033/828-35-50. Fax 033/828-35-51. www.hotel-alpenblick.ch. 37 units. 200F–250F double; 260F–310F suite. MC, V. **Amenities:** Restaurant; bar; room service. *In room:* TV, hair dryer, Wi-Fi (15F for 1 hr.).

Hotel Weisses Kreuz This safe and tranquil hotel is located on the famous Höheweg, right in the center of Interlaken. The interior is pleasantly decorated yet simple, and the bedrooms are newly renovated. Each has a well-maintained bathroom. Owned and managed by the Bieri family since 1911, the hotel offers a brasserie-style restaurant with Italian/Swiss cuisine. In summer, guests gravitate to its boulevard terrace for people-watching, drinks, and pastries.

Höheweg (at Jungfraustrasse), CH-3800 Interlaken. ☎ 033/826-03-50. Fax 033/823-35-55. www.weisses kreuz.ch. 56 units. 170F–230F double. Rates include buffet breakfast. AE, DC, MC, V. Parking 10F (nearby). **Amenities:** Restaurant; Internet (free, in lobby). *In room:* TV.

Park-Hotel Mattenhof ★ This large, old-fashioned, government-rated four-star hotel is in a secluded area at the edge of a forest 2km (1¼ miles) south of the town center; you can reach it by heading away from the center toward Wilderswil. The exterior looks like a private castle, with its high, pointed roof, tower, loggias, and balconies. It was originally built as a simple and sedate pension in 1897, but adopted most of its mock-medieval form after a massive enlargement in 1906. During World War II it functioned as a hospital for injured soldiers, but for the past 30 years it has been managed by Peter Bühler and his family. They offer a calm retreat with terraces, manicured lawns, and panoramic views of the Alps. The salons are warmly decorated and sunny, and some of the small, well-furnished bedrooms have a view of the Jungfrau and the Niederhorn. All have well-kept bathrooms, and several also are equipped with a balcony.

Hauptstrasse, Matten, CH-3800 Interlaken. ☎ 033/828-12-81. Fax 033/822-28-88. www.park-mattenhof. ch. 76 units. May–Sept 200F–260F double; off season 140F–170F double. AE, DC, MC, V. Free parking. **Amenities:** 2 restaurants; 2 bars; outdoor pool. *In room:* TV, hair dryer, minibar.

Royal St. Georges ★ Built in 1907, this oft-restored hotel is a historical landmark structure. In spite of several renovations, it has retained its traditional character. In contrast to the old-style architecture, the bedrooms are as up-to-date as tomorrow, ranging in size from small to exceedingly spacious. Some of the suites are in the Victorian style. Bathrooms are generous in size and often stylized, such as a special Art Nouveau bathroom. The hotel is divided into two parts, the Royal Wing and the St. Georges Wing, both linked to each other through a gangway. Unlike most peas-in-a-pod hotel rooms, this government-rated four-star choice offers individualized bedrooms—you'd be hard-pressed to find two rooms that are identical.

Höheweg 139, CH-3800 Interlaken. ☎ 033/822-75-75. Fax 033/823-30-75. www.royal-stgeorges.ch. 95 units. 230F–330F double; 300F–430F suite. Rates include buffet breakfast. AE, DC, MC, V. **Amenities:** Restaurant; bar; Jacuzzi; room service; sauna. *In room:* TV, hair dryer, minibar, Wi-Fi (30F per 24 hr.).

Inexpensive

Hotel Alphorn ★ This bed-and-breakfast oozes charm the old-fashioned way. From the flower boxes that adorn the ground-floor windows to the vibrant colors of the breakfast room, this place has an inviting ambience. The rooms are small but have a private bathroom with shower and toilet, as well as cable TV—which the host is proud to tell you includes CNN. There is a bar where patrons go after a long day, but don't expect a rowdy crowd; this is a family-oriented and family-operated type of place.

Rugenaustrasse 8, CH-3800 Interlaken. ℭ **033/822-30-51.** Fax 033/823-30-69. www.hotel-alphorn.ch. 10 units. 110F–150F double. Rates include buffet breakfast. AE, MC, V. Free parking. **Amenities:** Bar. *In room:* TV, Wi-Fi (free).

Hotel Lötschberg ★ (Finds) A hotel that's sure to transmit an old-fashioned sense of Swiss charm, this sprawling villa-style building rises from the city's commercial core, a 3-minute walk from the railway station. Originally built in 1906 as a cost-conscious pension, and painted a striking shade of blue, it has been frequently improved, repaired, and renovated. All but three of the units have a TV set, and the three that don't are located within a simple, century-old guesthouse a short walk away. Rooms come in a wide variety of sizes, ranging from small units to medium-size ones (two to three guests), and even very spacious ones, each comfortable enough for four persons. Breakfast is the only meal served within this hotel, but on the premises, under separate management, is an Asian restaurant that serves lunch and dinner. You can rent mountain bikes from the Hutmachers or even check your e-mail for a small fee. Rates in the apartments do not include breakfast.

Général Guisanstrasse 31, CH-3800 Interlaken. ℭ **033/822-25-45.** Fax 033/822-25-79. www.lotschberg. ch. 19 units. 142F–210F double; 95F–130F apt. Rates include buffet breakfast. AE, DC, MC, V. Free parking. Closed Jan. **Amenities:** Bikes. *In room:* TV, Wi-Fi (free).

The Swiss Inn (Value) This small Edwardian inn with balconies and gables offers good value. Mrs. Vreny Müller Lohner rents tasteful, simply decorated one- to three-room apartments equipped with comfortable beds and well-kept bathrooms. They accommodate two to six guests, and children's beds or cots are available. The inn has a lounge, a sitting area with a fireplace, and a grill for barbecues in the garden.

Général Guisanstrasse 23, CH-3800 Interlaken. ℭ **033/822-36-26.** Fax 033/823-23-03. www.swiss-inn. com. 9 units. 100F–160F double; 140F–200F apt for 2; 230F–250F apt for 4. AE, MC, V. Free parking. *In room:* TV, kitchenette (in some).

WHERE TO DINE

Most guests dine at their hotels, which partially explains why such a world-famous resort as Interlaken has so few independent restaurants worth noting.

Expensive

Gourmetstübli ★★★ SWISS/INTERNATIONAL In the village of Wilderswil, at the Alpenblick hotel (see above), is the region's most outstanding restaurant. At this gourmet citadel, the chefs marry traditional cooking with modern flair. Menus are sometimes composed and dedicated to a season, as in the case of a Summer Symphony: Start with a mousse of eggplant (aubergine), fresh tomato, and whitefish, and follow with such sublime dishes as tartar and filet of beef in an olive sauce and another sauce composed of radishes, or else whitefish filet with couscous and a cucumber curry sauce. Sorbets and homemade ice creams top the dessert menu, or else you can make a selection from the cheese wagon, featuring lots of Swiss alpine choices. A fine wine list enhances the experience.

In the Hotel Alpenblick, Oberdorfstrasse 3. ☎ **033/828-35-50.** Main courses 60F–65F; fixed-price menus 119F for 4 courses, 169F–220F for 7 courses. AE, DC, MC, V. Daily noon–2pm and 5:30–9pm.

Moderate

Gasthof Hirschen (Value) SWISS   This hotel restaurant serves some of the best and most reasonably priced meals in town. The menu is varied; the potato soup with mountain cheese is the finest we've ever tasted. Another tasty appetizer is the ravioli filled with salmon. For a main dish, we recommend sautéed calves' liver, filet of beef bordelaise, beef goulash, broiled trout, or chateaubriand. The Hirschen also operates its own farm, which supplies Bio-Angus beef, veal, cheese, fresh vegetables, and herbs. Fresh berries and honey are also brought in from the farm during summer.

Hauptstrasse 11, Matten. ☎ **033/822-15-45.** www.hirschen-interlaken.ch. Reservations recommended. Main courses 19F–38F. AE, DC, MC, V. Tues–Sat 11am–1:30pm and 4:30–11pm; Sun 9am–11pm.

Il Bellini ★★ INTERNATIONAL   This is one of the finest restaurants in the Bernese Oberland. Established in 1994, it sits one floor above the lobby in the tallest hotel in Interlaken, the Metropole, and is outfitted in a graceful 19th-century rendition of pale pinks and greens. The fresh, good-tasting food is served with a discreet panache you might have expected in Italy, and includes an assortment of antipasti. You can order individual selections of hors d'oeuvres, including prosciutto with melon or smoked salmon and carpaccio. The soups, especially the homemade minestrone, are tasty, and the main courses include such delectable specialties as tender beefsteak Florentine, saltimbocca, and chicken breast grilled with tomatoes and mozzarella. The fish selections are limited but well chosen.

In the Hotel Metropole, Höheweg 37. ☎ **033/828-66-66.** www.metropole-interlaken.ch. Reservations recommended Fri–Sun. Main courses 22F–49F. AE, DC, MC, V. Daily 6:30–11pm.

Schuh SWISS/CHINESE/THAI   This attractive restaurant and tearoom in the center of town has been known for its pastries since 1885. They are still the town's finest. The alpine building has a thick roof arched over the fourth-floor windows and, in back, a sunny terrace with a view of the Jungfrau and a well-kept lawn. The dining room has large windows and a Viennese ambience. A pianist provides music. The menu changes with the season, but Swiss regional dishes are a feature, along with several Asian dishes, notably from Thailand and China.

Höheweg 56. ☎ **033/888-80-50.** www.schuh-interlaken.ch. Main courses 15F–46F. AE, DC, MC, V. Apr–Sept Sun–Thurs 9am–11:30pm, Fri–Sat 9am–12:30am; Oct–Mar Sun–Thurs 9am–10pm, Fri–Sat 9am–11pm.

Spice India ★ INDIAN   The Mathur family waited a long time for a restaurant of their own, and when they got it, they didn't disappoint. Ideally located in between the Hotel Metropole and the Chalet Hotel Oberland, this is a place where anyone who likes Indian food can enjoy a good meal served by people who are passionate about their restaurant. Among the top menu options are the Barrah kabobs (oven-grilled lamb marinated in yogurt with garlic and ginger paste), fish curry, filets of chicken, and basmati rice. There is also a vegetarian section from the menu and from that we recommend the *baingan ka bharta* (chargrilled eggplant with yogurt and cheese) and the *aloo ghobi,* a potato-and-cauliflower dish. The decor is a little bland for an exotic restaurant, but the food makes up for it.

Postgasse 6. ☎ **033/821-00-91.** www.spice-india.net. Reservations required for large groups only. Main courses 22F–38F. AE, DC, MC, V. Tues–Sun noon–2:30pm; daily 6–10:30pm.

Sternen da Mario PIZZA/ITALIAN   This is the best pizzeria in town, lying in a district of shops in an all-pedestrian section of Interlaken. You'll also find a complete menu of savory Italian dishes, including a tasty array of antipasti, ranging from shrimp cocktail to carpaccio. The salads are fresh and crisp, and the homemade soups, including a delectable minestrone, are made fresh daily. The pastas are also exceptional, especially the *fusilli alla Sorrentina,* inspired by recipes along the Amalfi Drive in Italy. A select array of fish and meat dishes, including scaloppini, is also served daily. Pizza margherita, based on a recipe created in Naples in 1889, is a specialty.

Jungfraustrasse 27. © 033/822-34-25. Reservations not needed. Pizza 15F–23F; main courses 24F–39F. MC, V. Tues–Sat 11am–midnight; Sun 2pm–midnight.

Zum Bären SWISS   Set within a richly folkloric setting whose origins go back to 1674, this is a worthwhile excursion for clients who want to escape the restrictions of their in-house dining plan for a view of old-fashioned alpine folklore. Expect lots of weathered and congenially battered paneling, dented wooden tables, chairs that have borne the weight of thousands of previous diners, and a standardized, mostly Swiss menu that's redolent with *rösti,* schnitzels of both pork and veal, grilled filet of beef with peppercorn or béarnaise sauce, and minced veal in cream sauce, Zurich style. It all goes well with beer that's served here in foaming mugfuls.

Seestrasse 2, Unterseen. © 033/822-75-26. Reservations recommended. Main courses 28F–46F. AE, MC, V. Oct–Apr Tues–Sun 8:30pm–midnight; May–Sept daily 8:30pm–midnight.

INTERLAKEN AFTER DARK

Merchants in Interlaken have always known how to inject their town with enough razzle-dazzle to keep visitors coming back. As such, Interlaken boasts one of the highest per-capita rates of nightclubs of any town its size in Switzerland. The town's business is so transient—composed mostly of short-term visitors on their way to somewhere else—the clientele of any particular bar or club is likely to change virtually every week. Keeping that in mind, here's a roster of those that, at this writing, were the most animated and/or fun.

You'll usually find a drinking buddy in the folksy, amiably kitschy **Victoria Bar** in the town's stateliest hotel, the Victoria-Jungfrau, Höheweg 41 (© 033/828-28-28). **Buddy's Pub,** in the Hotel Splendid, Höheweg 33 (© 033/822-76-12; www.splendid.ch), provides a cozy, richly paneled setting that evokes an upscale version of a smoke-stained pub in Ireland.

If you want to combine drinking with dancing, head to **Johnny Carlton's Club,** in the Hotel Carlton, Höheweg 94 (© 033/826-01-60). Although the dance floor is comically small, the music is danceable. Because there are never enough banquettes and chairs for the crowd, everyone seems to mingle extra freely. **Metro Bar,** in the Hotel Metropole, Höheweg 37 (© 033/828-66-66), draws a crowd in their 30s and 40s who mingle happily together.

Access to virtually every disco in Interlaken costs 7F on Friday and Saturday nights, and is free other nights. Things begin happening a bit earlier than you might expect—many are rocking by 11pm.

Despite its allegiance to the music coming out of London and Los Angeles, Interlaken also places a lot of emphasis on alpine folklore. The **Casino Kursaal,** Höheweg at Strandbadstrasse (© 033/827-61-00; www.casino-kursaal.ch), is the venue for the dinner-and-entertainment **Swiss Folklore Show,** a somewhat self-conscious duplication of the quirks and yodels that made alpine Switzerland so unique. The show is in a cavernous convention hall, Monday to Saturday beginning at 7:30pm during July and August, with a less dependable schedule during May and June and again in September and October. Access to the show, which at its most fun can be sudsy and the teeniest bit raucous, costs 34F; access to the show that includes a fixed-price menu ranges from 60F to 110F, depending on the meal you order.

Interlaken's most intense doses of folk schmaltz take the form of the *tellfreilichtspiele,* a secular version of a Teutonic morality play that's presented in an open-air amphitheater in Interlaken's suburb of Matten, a village en route to Grindelwald, reached after a brisk 15-minute walk from Interlaken's center. A sweeping cast of as many as 250 presents Schiller's pageant play *William Tell,* complete with galloping horses, flaming torches, flower-draped cows, apple-shooting scenes, and an all-German text delivered in the lilting diphthongs of the Schwyzerdeutsch accent. Tickets for the 2½-hour show cost 26F to 48F, and are available from **Tellbüro,** Bahnhofstrasse 5 (© **033/822-37-22**). The play is presented at 8pm every Thursday and Saturday between mid-June and early September. Bring a jacket or sweater, or rent one of the blankets from an on-site kiosk, as the alpine chill seems to enhance this epic tale of the struggle for Swiss independence from the tyranny of neighboring Austria.

EASY EXCURSIONS FROM INTERLAKEN

By making the mountains of the Bernese Oberland accessible by train and cable car, Swiss engineers paved the way for visitors to this popular region to explore some of the most scenic and enjoyable spots in the country. There are many organized excursions, as adventurous as they are varied, and Interlaken is the most sensible starting point.

Jungfraujoch ★★★

A train trip to Jungfraujoch, at 3,400m (11,152 ft.), is often considered a trip highlight by visitors. For more than a century, it's been the highest railway station in Europe. It's also one of the most expensive: A round-trip tour costs 193F in first class, 181F in second class. However, families can fill out a Junior Card form, available at the railway station, which allows children 16 and under to ride free. Departures are usually daily at 8am from the east station in Interlaken; expect to return around 4pm. To check times, contact the sales office of **Jungfrau Railways,** Höheweg 37 (© **033/828-71-11** or 828-72-33; www. jungfraubahn.ch).

With luck, you'll get good weather for your day trip; you should always consult the tourist office in Interlaken before boarding the train. The trip is comfortable, safe, and packed with adventure. First you'll take the Wengernalp railway (WAB), a rack railway that opened in 1893. It will take you to Lauterbrunnen, at 784m (2,572 ft.), where you'll change to a train heading for the Kleine Scheidegg station, at 2,029m (6,655 ft.)—welcome to avalanche country. The view includes the Mönch, the Eiger Wall, and the Jungfrau, which was named for the white-clad Augustinian nuns of medieval Interlaken (*jungfrau* means "virgin").

At Kleine Scheidegg you'll change to the highest rack railway in Europe, the Jungfraubahn. You have 9.6km (6 miles) to go; 6.4km (4 miles) of that will be spent in a tunnel carved into the mountain. You'll stop briefly twice, at Eigerwand and Eismeer, where you can view the sea of ice from windows in the rock (the Eigerwand is at 2,830m/9,282 ft. and Eismeer is at 3,110m/10,201 ft.). When the train emerges from the tunnel, the daylight is momentarily blinding, so bring a pair of sunglasses to help your eyes adjust. Notorious among mountain climbers, the Eigernordwand ("north wall") is incredibly steep.

Once at the Jungfraujoch terminus, you may feel a little giddy until you get used to the air. There's much to do in this eerie world high up Jungfrau, but take it slow—your body's metabolism will be affected and you may tire quickly.

Behind the post office is an elevator that will take you to a corridor leading to the famed **Eispalast (Ice Palace)** ★. Here you'll be walking inside "eternal ice" in caverns hewn out of the slowest-moving section of the glacier. Cut 19m (62 ft.) below the glacier's surface, these caverns were begun in 1934 by a Swiss guide and subsequently enlarged and embellished with additional sculptures by others. Everything in here is made of ice, including full-size replicas of vintage automobiles and local chaplains.

After returning to the station, you can take the Sphinx Tunnel to another elevator. This one takes you up 107m (351 ft.) to an observation deck called the **Sphinx Terraces,** overlooking the saddle between the Mönch and Jungfrau peaks. You can also see the Aletsch Glacier, a 23km (14-mile) river of ice—the longest in Europe. The snow melts into Lake Geneva and eventually flows into the Mediterranean.

Astronomical and meteorological research is conducted at a scientific station here. There's a research exhibition that explains weather conditions, and a video presentation.

There are five different **restaurants** from which to choose. The traditional choice is Jungfraujoch Glacier Restaurant. Top of Europe, opened in 1987, offers several different dining possibilities, and there's also a self-service cafeteria. As a final adventure, you can take a **sleigh ride,** pulled by stout huskies.

On your way back down the mountain, you'll return to Kleine Scheidegg station, but you can vary your route by going through Grindelwald, which offers panoramic views of the treacherous north wall.

Harder Kulm ★★

For a somewhat less ambitious excursion, set out from Interlaken East for this belvedere at 1,301m (4,267 ft.). The funicular ride takes 15 minutes and costs 25F round-trip for adults and 12F for children. From the lookout, you can see Interlaken, the Bernese Alps, and the two lakes, Thun and Brienz, that give Interlaken its name. Departures are every half-hour daily from May until the end of October. The first funicular departs at 9:10am, the last one back leaving at 6pm (6:30pm July–Aug). There's a mountain restaurant at Harder Kulm, with observation terraces. For details, call ✆ **033/828-72-03.**

Wilderswil/Schynige Platte ★★★

Less than 3km (2 miles) south of Interlaken, Wilderswil stands on a plain between lakes Brienz and Thun, at the foot of the Jungfrau Mountains. It's both a summer resort and a winter resort, as well as the starting point for many excursions. The resort has 16 levels of accommodations, ranging from hotels to guesthouses, but most tourists stay in Interlaken and visit Wilderswil to take the excursion to **Schynige Platte** (✆ **033/822-34-31;** www.schynigeplatte.ch). To get to Wilderswil, take the 6-minute train ride from the Interlaken East station. Switch to a cogwheel train for the harrowing, steep ascent to the Schynige Platte, at 1,936m (6,350 ft.). The rack railway, which opened in 1893, climbs the 7km (4½-mile) slope in less than an hour, with gradients of up to 25%. There are more than a dozen trips a day in season, June to October, costing 69F round-trip.

There's an alpine garden in Schynige Platte, containing some 600 species of plants; admission is 4F. From a nearby belvedere, visitors command a splendid view of the Eiger, Mönch, and Jungfrau. The resort's restaurant serves good food and drink.

Lake Thun ★ ★

Occupying an ancient terminal basin of a glacier, Lake Thun (Thunersee) was once connected to Lake Brienz (Brienzersee). The Lutschine River deposited so much sediment at Interlaken that the one body of water eventually became two. Lake Thun, once beloved by Brahms, is 21km (13 miles) long and 3km (2 miles) wide. The lake is 27km (17 miles) south of Bern and there is frequent rail service, which continues east to Interlaken.

Because of its mild climate, Lake Thun is known as the Riviera of the Bernese Oberland. Popular lake sports include water-skiing, yachting, and windsurfing. Onshore are excellent swimming pools (indoor and outdoor), windsurfing schools, golf courses, tennis courts, horse stables, and caves.

The lake's major resort is **Thun,** a small city that was founded on an island where the Aare River flows out of Lake Thun. The city has since expanded onto the banks of the river to become the political and administrative center of the Bernese Oberland and the gateway to the Bernese mountains.

The most interesting part of the city is on the Aare's right bank. The busy main street, **Hauptgasse,** has walkways built above the arcaded shops. There's a 17th-century town hall on Rathausplatz, where you can climb a covered staircase up to the formidable **Schloss Thun (Castle Kyburg)** ★. The castle is now a historical museum (✆ **033/223-20-01;** www.schlossthun.ch). It was built by the dukes of Zähringen at the end of the 12th century. Later it was the home of the counts of Kyburg, as well as the Bernese bailiffs. The massive residential tower has a large Knights' Hall, which contains a Gobelin tapestry from the time of Charles the Bold and a fine collection of halberds and other weapons. Other rooms have important archaeological finds, an exhibit of military uniforms, period furniture, and toys. From the turrets, there's a panoramic view of the surrounding area. The museum is open daily April to October from 10am to 5pm and November to March from 10am to 4pm. Admission is 8F for adults, 2F for children.

Meiringen ★

This resort lies about 13km (8 miles) from Brienz and can be easily visited on a day trip from Interlaken. Several trains headed to Meiringen stop at Interlaken's two railway stations every day. Travel time each way is about 50 minutes.

Strategically centered between three alpine passes (the Grimsel, the Brunig, and the Susten), this old town is a suitable base from which you can explore the eastern sections of the Bernese Oberland and the wild upper reaches of the Aare River. Classified as the major town in the Haslital district and set above the waters of Lake Brienz, Meiringen is famous throughout Europe for its meringue, a dessert that was supposedly invented here.

Lake Tours

A fleet of ships with a total capacity of 6,720 passengers operates on **Lake Thun** daily from April to October. A 4-hour voyage from Interlaken West to Beatenbucht, Spiez, Overhofen, Thun, and back costs 80F in first class, 53F in second class.

Boat trips on **Lake Brienz** are also available daily from June to September. There are five motor ships and one steamship, with a total capacity of 3,160 passengers. A 3-hour voyage from Interlaken East to Iseltwald, Giessbach, Brienz, and back costs 60F in first class and 40F in second class. For details, call **B.L.S.** (✆ **033/334-52-11;** www.bls.ch).

Rich in scenery and wildlife, the district attracts mountaineers, rock climbers, and hikers. Surrounding the town, you'll find around 300km (186 miles) of marked hiking trails through unspoiled natural settings, with a complicated network of lifts to reach panoramic vantage points. Destinations for excursions include the Aare Gorge, the Rosenlaui Glacier, and the Reichenbach Falls. The district also has a folklore museum, a crystal grotto, an antique water mill, and a pathway across a glacier. Almost everyone visits the parish church in the upper part of the village. Its crypt was built during the 11th century.

From Meiringen, you can set out for Grindelwald, a distance of some 27km (17 miles) and one of the great walks in the Jungfrau region. Along the way you can absorb the stunning panoramas of the massif, the Eiger, with its massive gray rock walls. Soaring summits and white glaciers form your backdrop as you walk along. If you get tired along the way, there are bus stops where you can board public transportation to take you into Grindelwald. This is also an option should the weather turn bad. Otherwise, depending on your stamina, the walk takes from 6½ to 9 hours.

If you're in the mood for meringue, you can buy one or two at a local bakery. According to legend, the dessert was created when Napoleon visited the town and the local chef in charge of the welcoming banquet had a lot of leftover egg whites. Inspired, he created the puffy mounds and served them in a saucer brimming with sweet mountain cream, much to the general's delight.

Aare Gorge ★★ is full of recesses, grottoes, precipices, and arches—all fashioned by the Aare's waters over centuries. The cleft is 1,400m (4,500 ft.) long and 195m (640 ft.) deep, carved in the Kirchet, a craggy barrier left over from the ice age. In some places the towering rock walls of the gorge are so close together that only a few rays of sunshine can penetrate, just before noon. A unique natural wonder of the Swiss Alps, the gorge can only be reached by car, via the Grimsel-Susten road along the Kirchet. Admission is 9F for adults and 5F for children. The gorge is open May to October daily from 10am to 5pm; in July and August its extended hours are from 8am to 6pm.

If you're a fan of Sherlock Holmes, you'll enjoy an excursion to **Reichenbach Falls** ★, where the rivers of the Rosenlaui Valley meet. The impressive beauty of the falls has lured many visitors, beginning with the British in the 19th century. One visitor, Sir Arthur Conan Doyle, creator of Holmes, was so impressed with the place that he used it as the setting for the scene in *The Final Problem* in which the villain, Professor Moriarty, struggles with the detective and tosses Holmes into the falls. You can see a Sherlock Holmes commemorative plaque near the upper station of the funicular. The falls can be visited from mid-May to mid-September. The funicular takes you to a point at 834m (2,735 ft.) near terraces overlooking the water. Handrails provide safety. Departures are every 10 minutes daily from 8:15 to 11:45am and 1 to 6pm. The cost of admission is 10F for adults and 8F for children. The price includes the cost of the funicular. It's a 10-minute walk from Meiringen to the base of the funicular. If you're driving from Meiringen, take the road to Grimsel and turn right toward Reichenbach Falls and Mervenklinik. For more information, call ℂ **033/972-90-10.**

After admiring the cascade, you can hike through the river valley. The footpath through the **Rosenlaui Valley** is marked. After 90 minutes you'll arrive at the entrance to Rosenlaui Gorge. The surfaces of the sheer rock faces echo the sounds of the many small waterfalls within. The **glacier gorges** ★, which have been hollowed out by the waters from the melting ice of the Rosenlaui Glacier, are a spectacular sight. You can walk from one end of this gorge to the other in about 30 minutes. A small hotel and seasonal

The Murder of Sherlock Holmes

In 1891 the English writer Sir Arthur Conan Doyle, creator of the most famous detective in all fiction, Sherlock Holmes, acted too hastily in killing off his fictional hero. In a story entitled *The Final Problem,* after a battle with Professor Moriarty (called "the Napoleon of Crime"), Holmes and the fiendish villain were sent plunging to their deaths into Reichenbach Falls at Meiringen.

Although the Sherlock Holmes stories had proven successful, Conan Doyle apparently decided that he'd had enough of Sherlock's sleuthing. His rather outraged public disagreed, so Conan Doyle was forced to virtually call back Sherlock Holmes from the dead, and the detective went on to solve at least 60 more crimes.

The wonder of the falls is reason enough to visit the site, but Holmes devotees wanted more, so in May 1991 the town leaders opened a **Sherlock Holmes Museum,** Bahnhofstrasse 26 (© **033/971-41-41**), in an old Anglican church at Meiringen. There, you can visit a re-creation of Sherlock Holmes's sitting room at 221B Baker St. in London, with exhibits donated by fans from around the world. The museum is open May through September Tuesday to Sunday from 1:30 to 6pm, and October to April Wednesday and Sunday 4:30 to 6pm. Admission costs 4F for adults and 3F for children.

restaurant are near the entrance. Most visitors turn around at the uppermost reaches of the gorge and make the 2-hour trek back to Reichenbach Falls to pick up the funicular back to Meiringen. The gorge can be visited May to October daily from 9am to 5pm. The cost is 7F for adults and 3.50F for children.

3 MÜRREN ★★

11km (7 miles) S of Lauterbrunnen; 30km (19 miles) S of Interlaken

This village has a stunning location, high above the Lauterbrunnen Valley. At 1,624m (5,327 ft.), Mürren is the highest year-round inhabited village in the Bernese Oberland. It's an exciting excursion from Interlaken in the summer and a major ski resort in the winter. Downhill and slalom skiing were developed here in the 1920s. Mürren is also the birthplace of modern alpine racing.

ESSENTIALS

GETTING THERE   Take the mountain **railway** from the Interlaken East rail station to Lauterbrunnen (trip time: 1 hr.). Once at Lauterbrunnen, you can take a cogwheel train the rest of the way to Mürren. Departures from Lauterbrunnen are every half-hour from 6:30am to 8:30pm daily, costing 10F one-way.

A regular **postal-bus** service goes once an hour from Lauterbrunnen to Stechelberg; the rest of the way you must travel by cable car, costing 8F round-trip. Departures are every half-hour, and the trip takes about 10 minutes.

Mürren is not accessible to traffic. You can **drive** as far as Stechelberg, the last town on the Lauterbrunnen Valley road, and switch to the cable car discussed above.

VISITOR INFORMATION The **Mürren Tourist Information Bureau** is at the Sportzentrum (✆ **033/856-86-86**). There is no street plan—follow the clearly indicated signs to the various hotels and commercial establishments. The office is open Monday to Friday 9am to noon and 2 to 7pm, Saturday and Sunday 2 to 6:30pm.

OUTDOOR FUN
In Town
There are miles of downhill runs in the area. Mürren, one of the finest ski resorts of Switzerland, provides access to the Schilthorn at 2,923m (9,587 ft.), the start of a 15km (9-mile) run that drops all the way to Lauterbrunnen. It also has one funicular railway, seven lifts, and two cable cars. A 1-day ski pass that includes the area around Schilthorn costs 59F, while a 6-day pass goes for 256F. For cross-country skiers, there's a 12km (7½-mile) track in the Lauterbrunnen Valley, 10 minutes by railway from Mürren.

The alpine **Sportzentrum (Sports Center),** in the middle of Mürren (✆ **033/856-86-86**), is one of the finest in the Bernese Oberland. The modern building has an indoor pool, a lounge, a snack bar, an outdoor skating rink, a tourist information office, and a children's playroom and library. There are facilities for squash, tennis, and curling. Hotel owners subsidize the operation, tacking the charges onto your hotel bill. Supplemental charges include 33F to 39F per hour for tennis, 25F per 45-minute session for squash, 19F per 2 hours use of the sauna. The facility is usually open Monday to Friday from 9am to noon and 1 to 6:45pm, and from Christmas to April and July to mid-September also on Saturday from 1 to 6:30pm and Sunday from 1 to 5:30pm; but check locally as these times can vary.

Nearby
The famous **Mürren-Allmendhubel Cableway** leaves from the northwestern edge of Mürren. From the destination, there's a panoramic view of the Lauterbrunnen Valley as

On the Trail of James Bond

The **Schilthorn,** with its aerial cableway and steep snow slopes, was the setting for the most exciting scenes in the film *On Her Majesty's Secret Service,* one of the classic Bond thrillers. The incomparable location, the dramatic view of ice-covered peaks, and the fact that the imposing summit house is accessible only by aerial cableway convinced United Artists to select the Schilthorn as the film site.

Between October 1968 and April 1969, an army of volunteers transformed the Schilthorn into the film's "Piz Gloria." A landing pad for helicopters was constructed that was also used as a curling rink in the film and now serves as a sun terrace. The film was the breakthrough that made Schilthorn the world-famous attraction it has become. Today the imitation-blood trails have long been washed away, the fake bodies carted off, and the revolving restaurant never really exploded. A James Bond video in the Touristorama reminds visitors of this spectacular scenic film adventure.

far as Wengen and Kleine Scheidegg. Between mid-June and late August, the alpine meadows are covered with wildflowers. A walk in this hilly region could easily be a highlight of your trip to Switzerland. The cable car operates daily throughout the year from 9am to 5pm. However, there are annual closings for maintenance in May and November. It costs 12F per person round-trip. For information, call ☎ **033/855-20-42.**

The most popular excursion from Mürren is a cable-car ride to the **Schilthorn ★★★**, famous for its 360-degree view. The panorama extends from the Jura to the Black Forest, including the Eiger, Mönch, and Jungfrau. The Schilthorn is also called "Piz Gloria" after the James Bond film *On Her Majesty's Secret Service* (the most dramatic scenes in the movie were filmed here). Today Piz Gloria is the name of the revolving restaurant on-site. The summit is the start of the world's longest downhill ski race. The cable car to Schilthorn leaves every 30 minutes, and the round-trip costs 92F. The journey to the top takes 20 minutes. For details, call ☎ **033/856-21-41.**

SHOPPING

Commercial real estate in Mürren is expensive, particularly since the terrain is so inhospitable and supplies have to be hauled up by cable car or helicopter. Consequently, many of the resort's store owners make it a point to cram as much as possible into their shops, hoping to catch impulse buyers during shopping sprees. Therefore, the rule is, don't make any assumptions that shops here won't have what you want, as they're deceptively all-encompassing. Two of the resort's most interesting shops combine displays loaded with both sporting equipment and handicrafts. These are **Sporthaus Abegglen** (☎ **033/855-12-45**) and **Sporthaus Stäger** (☎ **033/855-23-55**).

WHERE TO STAY
Expensive

Hotel Bellevue   This is one of the earliest hotels to be built in Mürren, dating from the first part of the 20th century when it attracted mainly British visitors. On the outside, its buttercup yellow-and-brown facade is not particularly distinctive, but once inside, its much-renovated decor is more welcoming, as it's in the rustic alpine "farmer's style." The owners pride themselves on having one of the best views of the major peaks in the area, including Jungfrau. The bedrooms are warmly decorated, well maintained, and comfortable. The on-site restaurant focuses on game dishes, often trapped by or shot by the owners themselves, including venison and quail.

Obere Dorfstrasse, CH-3825 Mürren. ☎ **033/855-14-01.** Fax 033/855-14-90. 19 units. 170F–190F double; 255F triple; 280F junior suite. Breakfast and dinner 35F extra. MC, V. **Amenities:** Restaurant; bar. *In room:* Hair dryer.

Hotel Eiger ★   Founded in the 1920s, this chalet is the longest-established hotel in Mürren. The public rooms are warmly decorated, and many of the windows have panoramic views. The bedrooms are small, cozy, and comfortable and decorated in a typical alpine style. The hotel, managed by the Stähli family, lies across the street from the terminus of the cable car from Lauterbrunnen.

Bahnhofplatz CH-3825 Mürren. ☎ **033/856-54-54.** Fax 033/856-54-56. www.hoteleiger.com. 44 units. 275F–335F double; 400F–530F suite. Rates include buffet breakfast. AE, DC, MC, V. Closed Easter to early June and mid-Sept to mid-Dec. **Amenities:** Restaurant; bar; babysitting; Jacuzzi; indoor heated pool; room service; sauna. *In room:* TV, hair dryer.

Hotel Jungfrau/Haus Mönch   This government-rated three-star, 19th-century building, located a 3-minute walk from the Mürrenbahn, lies under gables behind green shutters, stucco, and brick walls. A comfortable annex was constructed in 1965; both buildings have an inviting, modern decor with open fireplaces, clusters of armchairs, and a shared dining room. The small bedrooms are bright and appealing. Twenty of the rooms are in the Hotel Jungfrau and 29 are across the street in the lodge. Units are equal in comfort.

Im Gruebi, CH-3825 Mürren. (℃) **033/856-64-64.** Fax 033/856-64-65. www.hoteljungfrau.ch. 49 units. 220F–240F double. Rates include buffet breakfast. AE, DC, MC, V. Closed mid-Apr to late May and mid-Oct to mid-Dec. **Amenities:** Restaurant; bar. *In room:* TV, Wi-Fi (free).

Moderate

Hotel Alpenruh   Set in the most congested yet charming section of the village, the Alpenruh possesses an interior that's plusher than its chalet-style facade implies. The old building was upgraded in 1986 to government-rated three-star status without sacrificing any of its charm. The small rooms have pine paneling and a mix of antique and contemporary furniture, and most of them open onto a view of the Jungfrau. The hotel is owned by the company that operates the aerial cable cars to the Schilthorn's Piz Gloria, and you can get a voucher to have breakfast there.

CH-3825 Mürren. (℃) **033/856-88-00.** Fax 033/856-88-88. www.alpenruh-muerren.ch. 26 units. 160F–270F double. Rates include buffet breakfast. Half board 40F per person. AE, DC, MC, V. **Amenities:** Restaurant; bar; sauna. *In room:* TV, hair dryer, minibar.

WHERE TO DINE

Eiger Stübli ★ SWISS   The best food in Mürren is served here in a festive ambience. The Eiger Stübli's cuisine includes fondue and an international range of hearty and well-prepared specialties well suited to the alpine heights and chill. Main dishes include a delectable roast lamb shoulder with lentils, a whole sole from the grill, beef Stroganoff, a savory cheese fondue, a perfectly prepared roast breast of duck with orange sauce, or poached filet of trout. All main dishes may be ordered with *rösti* (Swiss hash browns). Dessert specialties include vodka sherbet and iced soufflé Grand Marnier.

In the Hotel Eiger. (℃) **033/856-54-54.** Reservations recommended. Main courses 21F–50F. AE, DC, MC, V. Daily 11:30am–2pm and 6–9pm. Closed Easter to mid-June and mid-Sept to mid-Dec.

Hotel Alpenruh ★ FRENCH   This small hotel contains one of the finest restaurants in Mürren, offering a large and varied menu. The place is always a reliable bet for lunch or dinner, even during the rainy months of April and May and again in November when many of the other restaurants and hotels in Mürren are closed. Both its dining rooms have attractive alpine themes and wide terraces with panoramic views of the surrounding mountains. Appetizers include dried tomato strips with sage butter and tortellini with ricotta. You can dive enthusiastically into such dishes as veal steak with a Dijon mustard sauce or lamb cutlet with a garlic-herb sauce. The steaks are delectable. The fish courses may include sole Colbert and anglerfish medallions with jumbo shrimp. For dessert, try the fresh pineapple with caramel mousse or a gratiné of kiwi and oranges.

In the Hotel Alpenruh. (℃) **033/856-88-00.** Reservations recommended in winter. Main courses 20F–45F. AE, DC, MC, V. Daily 7am–11pm.

Restaurant im Gruebi SWISS   This popular restaurant offers a sunny outdoor terrace on the lobby level of the Hotel Jungfrau. The large hexagonal dining room has views of the mountains and ski slopes. You get authentic Swiss flavor and first-rate ingredients here. Some specialties are prepared for two, including chateaubriand, New York steak, rack of lamb flavored with herbs, and veal filets with fruit in a cognac sauce. It also offers the classic fondue bourguignon. Ten different types of *rösti* are served, including the classic Jungfrau version—ham, tomatoes, and raclette cheese. The chef also features what he calls "week-hits," a different specialty every night. One night may feature a salad and an all-you-can-eat array of meat fondues. Another night may be pasta night, grill night, and so on. There's even a cheese night, featuring raclette, fondues, and various types of Swiss cheese preparations.

In the Hotel Jungfrau im Gruebi. (✆ 033/856-64-64. Reservations recommended in midwinter. Main courses 24F–36F; fixed-price menu 40F. AE, DC, MC, V. Daily 7:30am–9:15pm. Closed mid-Apr to mid-June and mid-Oct to mid-Dec.

Restaurant Piz Gloria ★ (Finds) SWISS   Piz Gloria is the most dramatically located restaurant in Europe, with a setting so inhospitable and an architecture so futuristic that it was used as the setting for the James Bond film *On Her Majesty's Secret Service.* Designed like a big-windowed flying saucer and anchored solidly to the alpine bedrock, it was built at staggering expense in one of Switzerland's highest locations, the Schilthorn. Closed during blizzards, the restaurant has a terrace where newcomers should beware of becoming seriously sunburned by the rays of the high-altitude, unfiltered sunlight. You'll dine inside at long wooden tables, each with a wraparound view. The menu includes hearty dishes suited to the climate. There are both weekly and daily specials, ranging from chicken *cordon bleu* to filet of codfish with rice and vegetables. One spaghetti dish is named for James Bond; it's made with peppers, mushrooms, bacon, and Italian veal sausages. Another dish often served is puff pastry filled with veal and served with a white sauce. The 007 dessert is a bowl of five different scoops of ice cream topped with fruit.

Schilthorn. (✆ 033/856-21-40. Main courses 20F–42F. AE, DC, MC, V. Daily from the 1st cable car's arrival until the last cable car's afternoon departure. The first departure from Stechelberg is at 7:25am in summer and at 7:55am in winter. The cable car's last departure from Schilthorn's summit is at 6pm in summer and 5pm in winter. Closed mid-Nov to early Dec and 1 week after Easter. The only access is via the Schilthorn cable car, which departs from the relatively low-lying town of Stechelberg and stops at 3 way stations, the most prominent of which is Mürren. Round-trip fare from Stechelberg 92F, round-trip fare from Mürren 71F.

MÜRREN AFTER DARK

Every hotel in Mürren contains a bar offering maximum amounts of alpine coziness. Two that deserve special mention, however, are the **Bliemlichäller,** a sudsy, popular, and sometimes raucous disco in the Hotel Blumental (✆ **033/855-18-26**); and an equivalent disco, the **Inferno-Bar,** in the Hotel Palace (✆ **033/856-99-99**). Both open in the late afternoon, then crank up in midwinter and midsummer around 10:30pm into roaringly high-energy discos. More correctly perceived as a pub for après-skiing or après–hill climbing is the winter-only **Tächibar** in the Hotel Eiger (✆ **033/856-54-54**).

---

4 WENGEN ★★★

26km (16 miles) S of Interlaken; 5km (3 miles) NE of Mürren

The Mönch, Jungfrau, and Eiger loom above this sunny resort town built on a sheltered terrace high above the Lauterbrunnen Valley, at about 1,250m (4,100 ft.). Wengen (pronounced *Ven*-ghen) is one of the more chic and better-equipped ski and mountain resorts in the Bernese Oberland. It has 30 hotels in all price categories, as well as 500 apartments and chalets for rent.

In the 1830s, the International Lauberhorn Ski Race was established here. At that time Wengen was a farm community. The British were the first to popularize the resort, after World War I. Today parts of the area retain their rural charm. The main street, however, is filled with cafes, shops, and restaurants welcoming tourists. Robert Redford is a frequent visitor. No cars are allowed in Wengen, but the streets are still bustling with service vehicles and electric luggage carts.

ESSENTIALS

GETTING THERE   Take the train from Interlaken West to Wengen with a change of train at Lauterbrunne. Departures are every 45 minutes from 6:30am to 11pm, costing 16F one-way. After a stopover at Wengen, the train goes on to Kleine Scheidegg and Jungfraujoch. For **rail information,** call ℂ **0900/300-300.**

If you're driving, head south from Interlaken toward Wilderswil, following the minor signposted road to Lauterbrunnen, where you'll find garages and open-air spaces for parking. You cannot drive to Wengen—you must take the train. You can park in one of the garages at Lauterbrunnen for 12F to 18F a day. Trains from Lauterbrunnen to Wengen leave at the rate of one every 15 minutes from 6am to midnight, costing 8F one-way.

VISITOR INFORMATION   There are no street names; hotels, restaurants, and other major establishments are signposted with directional signs, which make them relatively easy to find. The **Wengen Tourist Information Office** (ℂ **033/855-14-14;** www.mywengen.ch) is in the center of the resort. It's open mid-June to mid-September and mid-December to Easter only, Monday to Saturday 9am to noon and 2 to 5pm.

EXPLORING THE AREA

The **ski area** around Wengen is highly developed, with ski trails carved into the sides of Männlichen, Kleine Scheidegg, Lauberhorn, and Eigergletscher. A triumph of alpine engineering, the town and its region contain three mountain railways, two aerial cableways, one gondola, 31 lifts, and 250km (155 miles) of downhill runs. You'll also find a branch of the Swiss Ski School, more than 11km (7 miles) of trails for cross-country skiing, an indoor and outdoor skating rink, a curling hall, an indoor swimming pool, and a day nursery.

During the summer the district attracts hill climbers from all over Europe. The **hiking trails** are well maintained and carefully marked, with dozens of unusual detours to hidden lakes and panoramas. Wengen also has five public tennis courts available through the tourist office (see above), a natural skating rink *(natureisbahn),* and a partially sheltered indoor rink *(kunsteisbahn).* The hours these rinks keep are subject to change, so check with the tourist office for details.

Nearby Attractions

From Wengen and Grindelwald, a number of excursions take you up and down the Lauterbrunnen Valley. You can visit **Trümmelbach Falls** ★★★, which plunges in five powerful cascades through a gorge. You can take an elevator built through the rock to a series of galleries (bring a raincoat). The last stop is at a wall where the upper fall descends. The falls can be visited from the end of May through June and in September and October daily from 9am to 5pm; in July and August daily from 8:30am to 6pm. They're closed during other months. Admission is 11F for adults, 4F for children 6 to 16, and free for children 5 and under. It takes about 45 minutes to reach the falls on foot. For information, call ℂ **033/855-32-32.** A postal bus from Lauterbrunnen (only 15 min. from Wengen by train) stops at Trümmelbach Falls. It costs only 4F for adults, 3F for children, and departs once an hour from Lauterbrunnen. For information, call ℂ **033/828-70-38.**

You might also want to visit the base of the **Staubbach Waterfall** ★★, which plunges nearly 300m (984 ft.) in a sheer drop over a rock wall in the valley above Lauterbrunnen. Lord Byron compared this waterfall to the "tail of the pale horse ridden by Death in the Apocalypse." Staubbach can be reached from the resort village of Lauterbrunnen, which lies only 15 minutes from Wengen by train (see "Essentials," above). From the center of Lauterbrunnen, follow the signposts along a walkway running along a creek and then be prepared for some steep stairs to reach the viewing point for the falls.

SHOPPING

Despite its proximity to the wide-open spaces of the big-sky Alps, don't be disappointed by the distinctly nonalpine-looking shops here. The well-recommended **Swiss Made Shop,** Dorfstrasse (ℂ **033/855-26-27**), offers fragile and exquisite cutlery, porcelain, and flatware. Two of the town's most successful shops for ski and other sports equipment are **Alpia Sport,** Dorfstrasse (ℂ **033/855-26-26**), and **Central Sport,** Chalet Lauberhorn (ℂ **033/855-23-23**). If you're interested in capturing the scenery that unfolds on all sides, head for **Foto-Haus,** Dorfstrasse (ℂ **033/855-11-54**). In addition to film and cameras, it also sells one of the town's widest rosters of handcrafted souvenirs to commemorate your stay in the Oberland.

WHERE TO STAY

All the hotels in Wengen are mobbed most of the winter, so make reservations well in advance if you plan to arrive during ski season.

Hotel Alpenrose ★★ A longtime favorite of ours, this hotel is invitingly traditional, with a family atmosphere. Most of the cozy, well-furnished bedrooms have views over the Lauterbrunnen Valley, lots of light, and plenty of pine paneling. Accommodations facing south are more desirable because they get more sunlight and so they're slightly higher in price. The hotel is efficiently run and filled with cozy public rooms and a large formal dining area where, if you've been gathering wildflowers that day, you'll probably find them in a vase at your supper. In ski season, fans of this hotel, all sports lovers, fill up the rooms. Staying on-site for your meals is hardly a hardship, as the food is well prepared with fresh ingredients whenever possible. Old favorites pepper the menu, including fondue bourguignon, trout with almonds, and terrine maison.

CH-3823 Wengen. ℂ **033/855-32-16.** Fax 033/855-15-18. www.alpenrose.ch. 50 units. Winter 272F–424F double; summer 232F–368F double. Rates include half board. AE, DC, MC, V. **Amenities:** Restaurant; bar. In room: TV.

Hotel Eiger ★ Rustic timbers cover the walls and ceilings of this attractive hotel behind the railway station. Karl Fuchs and his family offer spacious, attractive rooms with balconies. The suites, which are rented on a weekly basis only, are often sold out a year in advance. There's a modern dining room with views of the Jungfrau massif and the Lauterbrunnen Valley. In the hotel lobby you'll find an inviting sitting area with a fireplace.

CH-3823 Wengen. ℂ **033/856-05-05.** Fax 033/856-05-06. www.eiger-wengen.ch. 33 units. Winter 260F–350F double; summer 230F–290F double. Rates include buffet breakfast. Half board 30F per person. AE, DC, MC, V. Closed mid-Apr to June 1 and Nov. **Amenities:** Restaurant; bar. In room: TV.

Hotel Regina ★★ Wengen's most time-honored hotel lies in an embellished Victorian elephant of a building with balconies and lots of charm. Guido Meyer has been known to arrange unusual concerts for his guests (once, during our stay, a group of Oklahoma high school students gave a concert on the front lawn). One of the public rooms has a baronial carved-stone fireplace. The midsize to spacious bedrooms are comfortable and cozy, each well furnished and immaculately maintained. Maintenance is high, as is the level of service.

CH-3823 Wengen. ✆ **033/856-58-58.** Fax 033/856-58-50. www.hotelregina.ch. 90 units. Winter 300F–460F double, 400F–500F junior suite; summer 260F–360F double, 340F–400F junior suite. Rates include half board. AE, DC, MC, V. Closed mid-Oct to mid-Dec. **Amenities:** 2 restaurants; bar; babysitting; exercise room; room service; sauna. *In room:* TV, hair dryer, minibar, Wi-Fi (free).

Hotel Silberhorn ★ Famous for the cluster of restaurants and nightclubs located on its first two floors, this first-class family-owned hotel also offers comfortable modern rooms filled with pine and chintz, many with wooden balconies, and a few with kitchenettes. The simple Victorian building has been modernly equipped. The most spacious, most comfortable, and most attractive rooms are in the older wing. The restaurants located here shine in midwinter. Apartment rates include breakfast, and a minimum of 7 nights is required in winter.

CH-3823 Wengen. ✆ **033/856-69-69.** Fax 033/856-69-70. www.silberhorn.ch. 71 units. Winter 360F–492F double, 446F–556F apt for 3, 538F–698F apt for 4; summer 302F–352F double, 380F–410F apt for 3, 430F–470F apt for 4. Children 5 and under stay free in parent's room. Rates include half board. AE, DC, MC, V. **Amenities:** 3 restaurants; bar (in winter only); babysitting; Jacuzzi; room service; sauna. *In room:* TV, hair dryer, kitchenette (in some), minibar.

Sunstar Hotel Originally constructed in 1910 as the Metropole Hotel, the present incarnation has been around since the mid-1970s. Today it's a government-rated four-star hotel in the heart of the village, with wraparound balconies and a modern design inspired by traditional alpine architecture. The Kirche family are the helpful hosts. The nice-size rooms are well furnished and comfortable, many opening onto balconies with panoramic views of the Alps. Guests can relax in the spacious lounge with a fireplace or retreat to the hotel's cozy bar.

CH-3823 Wengen. ✆ **033/856-52-00.** Fax 033/856-53-00. www.sunstar.ch. 76 units. Winter 244F–416F double, from 320F junior suite; summer 246F–324F double, from 302F junior suite. Rates include buffet breakfast. AE, DC, MC, V. Closed Easter to end of May and mid-Oct to mid-Dec. **Amenities:** Restaurant; bar; babysitting; indoor heated pool; room service; sauna. *In room:* TV, hair dryer, minibar.

Zum Bären (Value) Looking for comfortable lodging and good views near the city center of Wengen? This cozy chalet inn, popular with families and backpackers alike, fits the bill. There are no fancy amenities here, but the accommodations are clean, and most look out over the Swiss mountains. A buffet-style breakfast is served before guests depart to ski or take in the sights.

CH-3823 Wengen. ✆ **033/855-14-19.** Fax 033/855-15-25. www.baeren-wengen.ch. 14 units. Winter 180F–240F double; summer 140F–180F double. Rates include buffet breakfast. AE, DC, MC, V. Closed mid-Oct to mid-Dec. **Amenities:** Restaurant. *In room:* No phone, Wi-Fi (free).

WHERE TO DINE

Arvenstube SWISS This is a local favorite, with pine-wood panels and a polite crew ready to serve you. The well-prepared menu may include smoked trout with horseradish, air-dried alpine beef, smoked breast of goose, Bernese-style beef with mushrooms, filet of fera (a lake fish), and veal steak Alfredo and morels. Three kinds of fondue are also offered. The fondue bourguignon is particularly stunning with 40 garnitures—you must order it a day in advance. The Valais-style braserade of beef cooks over a small flame at your table.

In the Hotel Eiger. (📞 **033/856-05-05.** Reservations recommended. Main courses 20F–56F. AE, DC, MC, V. Daily 11am–2pm and 6–9:30pm (all day in winter). Closed May.

Hotel Bernerhof Restaurant SWISS/ITALIAN   The Schweizers run this old family favorite. There's an alpine-themed bar, which fills up in the early evening with beer drinkers returning from the slopes. Hearty alpine food, including raclette and fondue, is served in the dining room. Several savory Italian dishes are also featured. Favorite dishes include grilled trout with horseradish sauce, Burgundy-style snails, and a delectable fondue bourguignon.

CH-3823 Wengen. (📞 **033/855-27-21.** Reservations recommended (and sometimes required). Main courses 17F–44F. MC, V. Daily 11:30am–2pm and 6–9:30pm.

Hotel Hirschen Restaurant (Finds) SWISS   This quiet retreat at the foot of the slopes has true alpine flavor. The rear dining room is decorated with hunting trophies, pewter, and wine racks. Johannes Abplanalp and his family offer a dinner special called Galgenspiess—filet of beef, veal, and pork flambéed at your table. Other dishes include filet of breaded pork, rump steak Café de Paris, and fondue Bacchus (in white-wine sauce), *bourguignon* (hot oil), or *chinoise* (hot bouillon). A hearty lunch is *Winzerrösti*, consisting of country ham, cheese, and a fried egg with homemade *rösti*.

CH-3823 Wengen. (📞 **033/855-15-44.** Reservations recommended. Main courses 14F–47F. MC, V. Fri–Mon 6–11pm. Closed mid-Apr to May and late Sept to mid-Dec.

WENGEN AFTER DARK

Wengen has only one disco, the popular **Disco Tiffany.** Set in the cellar of the Hotel Silberhorn (📞 **033/856-69-69**), near the arrival point for the cog-railway cars from Lauterbrunnen, it's small, crowded, and painted in tones of navy blue and black. Look for nightly openings between mid-December and early April, and openings on Friday and Saturday nights the rest of the year. No cover; show up after 10:30pm.

More reliable and prevalent than discos in Wengen are the resort's hard-drinking bars and sudsy pubs. The two wildest are the **Tanne Bar,** Dorfstrasse (no phone), across the street from the Sunstar Hotel; and **Sina's Pub,** Dorfstrasse (📞 **033/855-31-72**), where karaoke mics and monitors are pulled out from storage whenever things begin to look dull. An enduring favorite is the **Pickel Bar,** in the Hotel Eiger (📞 **033/856-05-05**). Set in a trapezoidal room lined with thick unfinished planks and stout timbers, it's illuminated with candlelight and can take all the punishment a rowdy core of skiers can dish out.

5 GRINDELWALD ★★★

22km (14 miles) S of Interlaken; 192km (120 miles) SW of Zurich

The "glacier village" of Grindelwald, at 1,033m (3,388 ft.), is set against a backdrop of the Wetterhorn and the towering north face of the Eiger. It's both a winter and a summer resort.

Unlike Wengen and Mürren, it's the only major resort in the Jungfrau region that can be reached by car. Because of its accessibility, Grindelwald is often crowded with visitors, many of whom come just for the day.

Grindelwald is surrounded by folkloric hamlets, swift streams, and as much alpine beauty as you're likely to find anywhere in Switzerland. Although at first the hiking options and cable-car networks might seem baffling, the tourist office will provide maps of the local peaks and valleys and help clear up any confusion.

ESSENTIALS

GETTING THERE   The **Bernese Oberland Railway (BOB)** leaves from the Interlaken East station. The trip takes 35 minutes. Call ✆ **0900/300-300** for information.

If you're **driving,** take the Wilderswil road south from Interlaken and follow the signs all the way to Grindelwald.

VISITOR INFORMATION   The resort doesn't use street names or numbers; instead of street names, hotel direction signs are used to locate places. If you're booked into a hotel or tourist home in Grindelwald, request a pass at your hotel that will entitle you to many discounts, especially on mountain rides.

The tourist office is at the **Sportszentrum,** on Hauptstrasse (✆ **033/854-12-12**). It's open Monday to Friday 8am to noon and 1:30 to 6pm, and Saturday and Sunday 8am to noon and 1:30 to 5pm.

THE GREAT OUTDOORS

For details about the tours below, including seasonal changes, consult the tourist office (see above).

GLACIER TOURS   The town maintains a sheltered observation gallery, adjacent to the base of the **Lower Grindelwald Glacier (Untere Gletscher),** which offers a close look at the glacier's ravine. The half-mile gallery stretches past the deeply striated rocks, which include formations of colored marble worn smooth by the glacier's powers of erosion. The gallery is easy to reach on foot or by car. Round-trip bus service is available from Grindelwald for 15F, and a parking lot and restaurant are nearby.

HIKING & MOUNTAIN CLIMBING   If you've come to Switzerland to see the Alps, Grindelwald and its surroundings offer dozens of challenging paths and mountain trails that are well marked and carefully maintained. Outdoor adventures range from an exhilarating ramble across the gentle incline of an alpine valley to a dangerous trek with ropes and pitons along the north face of Mount Eiger. The choice depends on your inclination and your skills. A map showing the region's paths and trails is available at the town's tourist office.

If you're adventurous enough to be tempted by peaks 3,900m (12,792 ft.) high or higher, or if you'd like to learn the proper way to climb rocks and ice, contact the **Bergsteigerzentrum** (✆ **033/854-12-90**), which lies adjacent to the Sunstar Hotel in Grindelwald. The Bergsteigerzentrum can also provide information on a modest 1-day hiking tour suitable for anyone capable of hiking in boots for 2 or 3 hours. After a scenic mountain train ride from Grindelwald to Eigergletscher, you'll be led by a local mountain guide to the Bergsteigerzentrum Grindelwald, a husky-breeding center. Then you'll hike along the foot of the north face of Mount Eiger. Along the way, your guide will narrate the history of this famous wall, providing interesting stories. Back down in Alpiglen, you can rest and enjoy a lunch of toasted cheese sandwiches. The train will transport you back to Grindelwald. Try to make reservations 2 to 3 days in advance.

Faulhorn, at 2,639m (8,656 ft.), is a historic vantage point from which you can view a panorama of untouched alpine beauty. Near the summit is the mountain hotel **Faulhorn**

Hotel (📞 033/853-27-13), which has been here for over 150 years and can be reached in a 7-hour hike from Grindelwald. Less committed hikers usually opt for cable-car or bus transfers to Bussalp, to First, or to Schynige Platte, and then continue their hike on to Faulhorn from any of those three points. Hikes to Faulhorn from Bussalp take 2¾ hours; from First, 2½ hours; and from Schynige Platte, 4 hours.

A 30-minute ride on a six-passenger gondola ("bubble car") will take you to **First Mountain** ★★, at 2,134m (7,000 ft.). You can stop at the intermediate stations of Bort and Grindd as you cross the alpine meadows to the First Mountain terminal and sun terrace. You'll have many hiking possibilities into the neighboring Bussalp or Grosse Scheidegg area, and you can return by bus. An hour's brisk hike will take you to idyllic Lake Bachalp. Besides the 2½-hour trek to Faulhorn, you can trek on foot to the Schynige Platte in 6 hours. A round-trip gondola ride between Grindelwald and First costs 65F. There's a large restaurant at First, **Bergrestaurant First** (📞 033/853-12-84), where you can order lunch.

Grosse Scheidegg ★, at 1,930m (6,330 ft.), is a famous pass between the Grindelwald and Rosenlaui valleys. You can hike here in 3 hours from Grindelwald, or take the bus for 40 minutes. Our preference is usually to take a bus to Grosse Scheidegg and then begin our hill walking away from the village traffic and crowds. Round-trip bus passage from Grindelwald to Grosse Scheidegg is 43F per person.

If you want to climb in the upper regions of the Oberland, you might consider this itinerary: Take a bus from Grindelwald to Grosse Scheidegg. Walk for 2½ hours from Grosse Scheidegg to **Schwartzwaldalp.** The peaks of the First and Wetterhorn will loom on either side of you. After a panoramic respite in Schwartzwaldalp, you can take a bus, which will retrace your steps back to Grindelwald via Grosse Scheidegg. This excursion is only possible in the summer; the total bus fare is 48F per person. Also only in the summer, a short aerial cable-car ride will take you to **Pfingstegg,** at 1,369m (4,490 ft.), from which you can hike to the Lower and Upper Grindelwald glaciers. The round-trip cost is 18F. A hike to **Baregg-Stieregg** (1 hr.) is highly recommended as a 1-day journey, as is the trek to **Banisegg** (2 hr.). You'll get a view of the Eismeer and the Fiescherwand, and they're both worth the hike.

From Grindelwald, it's also easy to visit **Kleine Scheidegg** ★★, which is the departure point for the final ascent to Jungfraujoch by train. The rack-and-pinion railway from Grindelwald to Kleine Scheidegg costs 53F round-trip or 32F each way. For information on this and all trains departing from Grindelwald, call the **Grindelwald railway station** (📞 033/828-75-40).

SKIING In winter Grindelwald is one of the major ski resorts of Europe, perfect as a base for skiing in the Jungfrau ski region. It has 22 lifts, 8 funiculars, a trio of cable cars, and more than 160km (100 miles) of downhill runs. Snowboarders and novice skiers are also welcome. It's a ski circus for all ages and various skills.

In the winter skiers take the cableway to **Männlichen,** at 2,200m (7,216 ft.), which opens onto a panoramic vista of the treacherous Eiger. From here there is no direct run back to Wengen; however, skiers can enjoy an uninterrupted ski trail stretching 7.2km (4½ miles) to Grindelwald. The cost of the Männlichen cable car (Grindelwald-Grund to Männlichen) is 35F each way, or 58F round-trip. For information, call the departure point for the **Männlichen Bahn** in Grindelwald (📞 033/854-80-80).

SHOPPING

There are a lot more shops in Grindelwald than the seasonal local economy can sometimes support (many shops, hastily opened to capitalize on the influx of tourists, last for only one season). Most of them line the crowded edges of the resort's main thoroughfare, a sometimes traffic-clogged highway. A half-dozen of these shops specialize in sporting goods and ski equipment, many stockpiling inventory from prestigious, high-tech manufacturers from around Europe and North America. The best of them include **Buri-Sport,** Hauptstrasse (✆ **033/853-14-27**), and **Bernet Sport,** Hauptstrasse (✆ **033/853-13-09;** www.bernet-sport.ch). If you're in the market for a timepiece, **Casa Grande,** Beim Bahnhof (✆ **033/853-50-15**), has a wide inventory of all kinds of Swiss watches and—to a much lesser extent—simple jewelry.

WHERE TO STAY
Very Expensive
Grand Hotel Regina ★★★ Across from the Grindelwald train station, this hotel is part rustic and part urban slick and dates from the turn of the 20th century. It became a hotel in 1953 and still evokes the glamour of that era. The facade of the oldest part has an imposing set of turrets with red-tile roofs. One of the salons has Victorian chairs clustered around bridge tables, with sculpture in wall niches. The collection of art includes etchings, gouaches, and oil paintings. The large bedrooms, done in various styles, are comfortable and contain well-maintained bathrooms. These elegantly furnished rooms are your finest choice for a vacation here in either summer or winter. Most bedrooms enjoy panoramic views.

CH-3818 Grindelwald. ✆ **800/223-6800** in the U.S. or 033/854-86-00. Fax 033/854-86-88. www.grand regina.ch. 90 units. 630F–740F double; 760F–2,690F suite. AE, DC, MC, V. Free parking outside, 20F in garage. Closed mid-Oct to mid-Dec. **Amenities:** 2 restaurants; 2 bars; babysitting; exercise room; 2 pools (1 heated indoor); room service; spa. *In room:* TV, minibar, Wi-Fi (5F per 30 min.).

Romantik Hotel Schweizerhof ★★ Originally built in 1912 on the former site of an ironmonger's and blacksmith's shop, this spacious and gracious hotel sits on the main street of Grindelwald, close to the railway station, behind a facade of very dark wood that resembles an oft-expanded chalet. The public areas are comfortably outfitted with deep upholstered wing chairs and sofas, and bedrooms have tile-sheathed bathrooms, carved-pine panels, comfortable furniture, and lots of folkloric charm. Staff is helpful and friendly.

CH-3818 Grindelwald. ✆ **033/854-58-58.** Fax 033/854-58-59. www.hotel-schweizerhof.com. 52 units. 400F–550F double; 570F–1,142F suite. Rates include half board. AE, DC, V. Closed Oct to mid-Dec and Apr 6 to late May. **Amenities:** 2 restaurants; bar; babysitting; exercise room; indoor heated pool; room service; spa; Wi-Fi (free, in lobby). *In room:* A/C, TV, hair dryer, minibar.

Expensive
Belvedere ★ This is a vastly renovated government-rated four-star superior hotel dating from 1907. It once declined the offer of a higher rating from the Swiss government so that it could keep its prices within reason. It has the most spectacular view in Grindelwald, and its luxurious public rooms include a fireplace and comfortable armchairs. There's also a lounge for nonsmokers decorated in the antique Louis Philippe style with well-preserved old pieces and Bohemian crystal chandeliers. The attractive and spacious bedrooms all have balconies and private bathrooms. Twenty-two of the double rooms are classified as luxury twins or junior suites. The hotel is a 5-minute walk from the center of the resort and easily accessible by the mountain railway systems.

CH-3818 Grindelwald. ✆ **033/854-57-57.** Fax 033/853-53-23. www.belvedere-grindelwald.ch. 55 units. 225F–315F per person double; 255F–345F per person junior suite. Rates include breakfast and 6-course dinner. AE, DC, MC, V. Free parking. **Amenities:** 2 restaurants; bar; babysitting; exercise room; Jacuzzi; indoor heated pool; room service; sauna. *In room:* TV, hair dryer, minibar, Wi-Fi (25F per hour).

Parkhotel Schoenegg   This hotel, established by the Stettler family in 1890, has become a modern expansive property. The bedrooms are cozy and comfortable, some with private balconies. Each is furnished in an alpine decor, and beds are excellent, as is the housekeeping. The hotel's dining room serves French cuisine. Various local ski runs terminate at the hotel; a lift to the ski school is close to the front door.

CH-3818 Grindelwald. ✆ **033/854-18-18.** Fax 033/854-18-19. www.parkhotelschoenegg.ch. 50 units. 300F–400F double. Rates include half board. AE, MC, V. Parking 8F–14F. Closed Apr to mid-June and late Oct to mid-Dec. **Amenities:** Restaurant; bar; babysitting; exercise room; Jacuzzi; indoor heated pool; room service; sauna. *In room:* Hair dryer, Wi-Fi (free).

Moderate

Hotel Derby   Peter and Christiane Märkle carry on the century-old family tradition at this large and modernized mountain chalet, which is rated three stars by the government. The present building, with a twin-peaked roof and several irregularly shaped balconies, dates from 1973. The pine-paneled bedrooms are brightly furnished and comfortable, if a bit small. The Derby offers some of the best restaurant and bar options in town.

CH-3818 Grindelwald. ✆ **033/854-54-61.** Fax 033/853-24-26. www.derby-grindelwald.ch. 70 units. 184F–272F double; 262F–312F junior suite. Rates include buffet breakfast. Half board 35F per person. AE, DC, MC, V. Free parking. **Amenities:** 3 restaurants; bar; room service; sauna. *In room:* TV, hair dryer, minibar, Wi-Fi (5F per hour).

Hotel Eiger   This hotel looks like a collection of interconnected balconies from the outside, each on a different plane and built of contrasting shades of white stucco and natural wood. The interior is attractive, simple, and unpretentious, with lots of warmly tinted wood, hanging lamps, and contrasting lights. The small to midsize bedrooms are comfortable, well furnished, and alpine cozy. Maintenance is high, and the hotel staff is extremely inviting and hospitable.

CH-3818 Grindelwald. ✆ **033/854-31-31.** Fax 033/854-31-30. www.eiger-grindelwald.ch. 50 units. Winter 124F–194F double; 154F–269F per person suite; summer 154F–184F per person double, 179F–264F per person suite. Rates include buffet breakfast. Half board 35F per person. AE, DC, MC, V. Free parking outdoors, 6F–12F in garage. **Amenities:** 2 restaurants; 2 bars; babysitting; exercise room; spa; Wi-Fi (free). *In room:* TV, hair dryer, minibar.

Hotel Gletschergarten ★ (Finds)   One of the oldest and most evocative hotels in town is this family-run (by the Breitensteins) hotel that originally opened in 1899 as a cafe and restaurant, and which by 1906 had become a full-fledged, full-service hotel. Ongoing renovations since then have kept the place looking spiffy. It sits at the eastern edge of the main street of Grindelwald, nearly adjacent to the town's church, behind a time-blackened wooden facade with lots of folkloric detailing. Bedrooms are tasteful and cozy, with views over the mountains and their permanent snowfields. Those on the corners of the building tend to be a bit larger than the others. Each has access to a balcony, which in midsummer is likely to be festooned with flowering plants. Expect goodly doses of cozy comfort at this place, as well as a gracious welcome. The food is very good and reasonably priced.

CH-3818 Grindelwald. ✆ **033/853-17-21.** Fax 033/853-29-57. www.hotel-gletschergarten.ch. 26 units. 200F–300F double. AE, DC, MC, V. Closed Apr to late May and early Oct to mid-Dec. **Amenities:** Restaurant and bar (open to hotel residents only); sauna. *In room:* TV, hair dryer, Wi-Fi (free).

Hotel Kreuz & Post ★   This angular, modern hotel is ideally located on the main square of town, across from the Sports Center. The Konzett family takes advantage of the location by setting up an outdoor cafe on the sidewalk in front. The interior is decorated in part with 18th-century antiques and engravings. Many of the rooms have balconies. Ranging from small to midsize, the tidy units are traditionally furnished and equipped with neatly kept bathrooms. The welcome here is warm in any season. There's a sun terrace on the roof with a panoramic view of the mountains.

CH-3818 Grindelwald. ℰ **033/854-54-92.** Fax 033/854-54-99. www.kreuz-post.ch. 42 units. Winter 160F–215F per person double, 180F–300F per person suite; summer 115F–175F per person double, 150F–225F per person suite. Rates include buffet breakfast. Half board 45F per person. AE, DC, MC, V. Free parking. **Amenities:** 2 restaurants; bar; babysitting; exercise room; Jacuzzi; sauna; Wi-Fi (free). *In room:* TV, hair dryer, minibar.

Hotel Restaurant Steinbock (**Value**) Mentioned as a tavern for the first time in chronicles in 1798, the rebuilt Steinbock basks in tradition. It's a cozy, chalet-style, government-rated three-star hotel, just opposite the Sunstar Hotel and lying near the bottom of the gondola leading to the First skiing area in winter or a hiking Valhalla in summer. The ski bus stop for Klein Scheidegg/Männlichen areas is located just next to the Steinbock. Completely rebuilt in 1992, the hotel is run by the Ponzio family, who also operate the on-site Pizzeria da Salvi, where the best pies in town emerge piping hot from a woodstove. Bedrooms are small but handsomely and comfortably furnished in a modern alpine style. The hotel's Grappa Bar offers 100 different kinds of grappas.

CH-3818 Grindelwald. ℰ **033/853-89-89.** Fax 033/853-89-98. www.steinbock-grindelwald.ch. 22 units. 210F–360F double. Rates include buffet breakfast. MC, V. **Amenities:** Restaurant; bar. *In room:* TV, hair dryer.

Inexpensive

Central Hotel Wolter It's more modern and boxy than the other hotels in town, but its central location just a few steps from several more expensive hotels makes it a solid and reliable choice. On the ground floor there's a popular outdoor cafe and a substantial restaurant. Upstairs are the reception area and a salon that resembles a room in a private home. It has armchairs, a few antiques, and a compact bar. The small bedrooms are simply decorated, all with comfortable beds and well-kept bathrooms.

CH-3818 Grindelwald. ℰ **033/854-33-33.** Fax 033/854-33-39. www.central-wolter.ch. 35 units. 170F–240F double. Rates include buffet breakfast. Half board 30F per person. AE, DC, MC, V. Parking 5F. Closed mid-Nov to mid-Dec. **Amenities:** Restaurant; bar; room service; free entrance to nearby sports center. *In room:* TV, hair dryer, minibar.

Hotel Hirschen (**Value**) In the government-rated three-star Hirschen, the Bleuer family offers one of the best values in town. The hotel, which has an attractive modern facade, is both comfortable and affordable with rooms in a variety of styles. Each is well furnished with good beds and equipped with neatly kept bathrooms.

CH-3818 Grindelwald. ℰ **033/854-84-84.** Fax 033/854-84-80. www.hirschen-grindelwald.ch. 28 units. 150F–280F double. Rates include continental breakfast. Half board 33F. AE, DC, MC, V. Free parking outside, 8F in garage. Closed Nov to mid-Dec. **Amenities:** Restaurant; bar; room service. *In room:* TV, Wi-Fi (in most units; free).

Hotel Jungfrau Swiss Mountain Lodge This establishment consists of two hotels, the Jungfrau (with 18 rooms, built in 1903) and the Crystal (with 29 rooms, built in 1972), located across the street from one another at the edge of the village, a 3-minute walk from the railway station. Both the reception area and the dining room, called "Mr. Chicken," are in the Jungfrau, but both hotels offer clean, comfortable rooms at favorable prices. The lounge has a view of the fierce north face of the Eiger, and it expands onto an outdoor terrace during warm weather. The bedrooms were recently renovated in a Canadian mountain-lodge style.

CH-3818 Grindelwald. (C) **033/854-41-41.** Fax 033/854-41-42. www.jungfraulodge.ch. 47 units. Summer 140F–190F double; winter 120F–220F double. Rates include buffet breakfast. AE, DC, MC, V. Free parking. Closed Nov. **Amenities:** Restaurant; bar; room service. *In room:* TV.

WHERE TO DINE
Expensive
La Pendule d'Or/Jägerstube ★ SWISS/FRENCH   Some of the best cuisine in Grindelwald is served in these two dining rooms. Men must wear jackets and ties in La Pendule d'Or, but not in Jägerstube, an elegant version of a hunter's retreat, and our preferred choice. Some special dishes include crayfish tails in puff pastry with a green asparagus salad with stuffed morels, or medallions of ox gratinated with tomatoes and mozzarella. The cooking, if not always sublime, is exceedingly professional. Flavors are balanced and ingredients are first-rate. Both restaurants serve the same menu, but fondue is offered only in the Jägerstube. Service is formal.

In the Grand Hotel Regina. (C) **033/854-86-00.** Reservations recommended. Main courses 53F–65F. AE, DC, MC, V. La Pendule d'Or daily noon–2pm and 7–10pm. Jägerstube daily 7–10pm. Closed mid-Oct to mid-Dec.

Restaurant Français ★★ INTERNATIONAL   This is the best restaurant in Grindelwald. The owner, Urs Hauser, is always in the dining room during meal hours to aid and advise diners. Special buffets are a feature of the restaurant. As you listen to the soothing sounds of a live pianist, you can study the menu, which changes frequently. Just to give you an idea, you may be served an appetizer of game terrine, Grindelwald air-dried meat, or thinly sliced lamb carpaccio. Fish dishes may include poached filet of turbot served on zucchini and potato rounds with a yellow-red pepper sauce, or fried filet of salmon with a truffle-butter sauce. Main dishes are likely to include lamb entrecôte in a coating of peppercorns, or breast of guinea fowl with red wine and prunes. The cuisine intelligently blends flavors with imagination and zest. The cooks in the kitchen really know their stuff, and the wine list is among the finest in the area.

In the Hotel Belvedere. (C) **033/854-54-54.** Reservations recommended. Main courses 36F–41F; 6-course gourmet menu 69F. AE, DC, MC, V. Daily noon–1pm and 6:45–9pm.

Moderate
Il Mercato ITALIAN/SWISS   The decor is elegant and alpine, with Italian touches you might expect in the Ticino. The dining room's visual centerpiece is a large window with a sweeping view over the mountains. During warm weather, tables are set out on a flower-dotted terrace. Menu items include virtually everything from the Italian repertoire, with an emphasis on cold-weather dishes from the Val d'Aosta (northern Italy's milk and cheese district). There's a tempting array of salads, pizzas, pastas, risottos, and grilled veal, beef, and chicken dishes, always with fresh ingredients.

In the Hotel Spinne. (C) **033/854-88-88.** www.spinne.ch. Reservations recommended. Main courses 18F–54F. AE, DC, MC, V. Daily noon–2pm and 6–9:30pm. Closed Oct to mid-Dec.

Restaurant Alte Post ★ (Finds SWISS   Often fully booked at least a day in advance, this Swiss, pine-paneled charmer serves traditional specialties, often to local residents of Grindelwald, with efficient service. Typical dishes include a terrine of morels, smoked filet of trout, asparagus with air-dried ham, filet steak with green peppers, scallop of veal *cordon bleu,* and beef Stroganoff. Because of the first-rate cooking and the quality ingredients, this is one of the most satisfying choices in town.

CH-3818 Grindelwald. ✆ **033/853-42-42.** Reservations required. Main courses 17F–50F. AE, MC, V. Thurs–Tues 11:30am–2pm and 6:30–9pm. Closed end of Oct to mid-Dec.

Restaurant Kreuz & Post SWISS/INTERNATIONAL   Explore this alpine restaurant before choosing a table. Tucked away in the corner is an attractive room, the Challi-Stube; the ceiling and paneling are especially well crafted. Everything in here is made of wood from a farmhouse that was torn down in 1748. The menu is in English, and hearty alpine flavor and first-class ingredients characterize the cuisine. Typical appetizers are smoked salmon and oxtail soup. For a main course, steak, pork, and fish are offered, including blue trout sautéed in butter. For a traditional Swiss dish, try sliced veal Zurich style with *rösti,* or veal steak with a morel-cream sauce. The chef specializes in the two classic fondues, *chinoise* and bourguignon, served for two.

In the Hotel Kreuz & Post. ✆ **033/854-54-92.** Reservations recommended. Main courses 15F–56F; 2-course fixed-price lunch 19F; 5-course fixed-price dinner 48F. AE, DC, MC, V. Tues–Sun noon–2pm and 6:30–8:45pm. Closed mid-Apr to mid-May

Restaurant Sportzentrum SWISS   This rustic, timbered dining room in the modern Sports Center is in the middle of the resort. Windows look down over an indoor swimming pool on one side and an enormous ice-hockey rink on the other. It opens early in the morning and serves snacks and drinks until late. The menu offers many Swiss specialties, including cheese fondue, beef bourguignon, and Wiener schnitzel. Come here for typically soul-satisfying Swiss food, each dish well prepared and reasonably in priced.

CH-3818 Grindelwald. ✆ **033/853-32-77.** Reservations not accepted. Main courses 18F–45F. MC, V. Daily 7:30am–11:30pm.

Inexpensive

Onkel Tom's Hütte PIZZAS & SALADS   Set within a rustic-looking A-frame house whose indestructible furniture and plank floors have seen thousands of snow-and-mud-covered boots tramping across its surface, this is Grindelwald's most visible and popular pizza place. There's a wide selection of beer and wine available, and a multilingual staff member will bring any of the three sizes of pizza to your amiably scarred and battered table. Varieties of pizza include the Onkel Tom (tomatoes, cheese, pepperoni, and assorted vegetables), the Rustica (tomatoes, cheese, broccoli, and garlic), and an Al Capone (tomatoes, cheese, braised leeks, bacon, and onion).

At the top of Hauptstrasse, near the Firstbahn cable-car station. ✆ **033/853-52-39.** Reservations not accepted. Pizzas 12F–30F; salads 8F–15F. MC, V. Thurs 6–10:30pm; Fri–Tues noon–2pm and 4–10:30pm. Closed Nov and June.

GRINDELWALD AFTER DARK

After sundown Grindelwald transforms itself into one of the liveliest towns in the Bernese Oberland. In addition to the following choices, many of the hotels sponsor get-together parties at least once a week for residents, and each contains at least one bar. Bars that aggressively seek the patronage of nonresidents include the **Cava Bar,** in the Derby Hotel (✆ **033/854-54-61**), which is located near the railway station and throws in the occasional live band, and the **Challi Bar,** in the Hotel Kreuz & Post (✆ **033/854-54-92**), which does a roaring business—mostly from drinkers, less so from dancers—inside what looks like the re-creation of an alpine barnyard lined with roughly textured planks. Both bars are only open in the winter.

Don't be fooled by the name of the **Espresso Bar,** in the Hotel Spinne (© **033/854-88-88**), a cramped, hot, and crowded venue with the inner walls of a log cabin and a penchant for suds and schnapps. Only a handful of its clients actually opt for coffee. The same hotel is the site of everybody's favorite ethnic hideaway, the **Disco Mescalero.** Here, tacos, tortillas, and refried beans are served until around 10pm, after which lots of very danceable music is unleashed. Over the summer, the Mexican restaurant is closed; the disco, however, still opens 3 days a week. Offhandedly elegant is **Regina Bar,** the entertainment focal point of the Grand Hotel Regina (© **033/854-86-00**), and **Le Plaza-Club,** a prosperous-looking disco favored by prosperous-looking people in the Hotel Sunstar (© **033/854-77-77**). Finally, the **Gepsi-Bar,** in the Hotel Eiger (© **033/844-31-31**), is appealingly conducive to dialogue and flirtation. There's no dancing here, but musicians sometimes arrive to perk things up a bit.

6 GSTAAD ★★

61km (38 miles) SW of Thun; 42km (26 miles) SE of Bulle

Against a backdrop of glaciers and mountain lakes, Gstaad is a haven for the rich and famous. Frequent visitors include King Juan Carlos II of Spain, Elizabeth Taylor, and Julie Andrews.

Built at the junction of four quiet valleys near the southern tip of the Bernese Oberland, Gstaad was once only a place to change horses during the grueling voyage through the Oberland. But as the railroad lines developed, it grew into a resort. After the opening of the deluxe Alpina Grand Hotel, wealthy Russian and Hungarian families started coming, bringing their entourages of valets, nannies, and translators. In 1912, 2 years before the outbreak of World War I, a hotel that was to become one of the most legendary in Switzerland, the Palace, opened, promising the ultimate in luxury. In 1916 Le Rosey school (listed in the Guinness Book of World Records as "the most expensive prep school in the world") opened its doors in the satellite town of Tolle. The school contributed to the fame of Gstaad, as prestigious visitors, including King Leopold of Belgium, came to see their children.

The town, by far the most chic in the Bernese Oberland, retains much of its turn-of-the-20th-century charm. Some first-time visitors, however, say that the resort is a bore if you can't afford to stay at the Gstaad Palace or mingle with the stars in their private chalets. Yet the town has many moderately priced hotels, taverns, and guesthouses with an allure of their own. Many of the bistros and cafes close from late April to mid-June and from October to mid-December.

ESSENTIALS

GETTING THERE Gstaad is on the local train line connecting Interlaken with Montreux and several smaller towns in central-southwest Switzerland. About a dozen trains come into Gstaad every day from both of those cities, each of which is a railway junction with good connections to the rest of Switzerland. Travel time from Montreux can be as little as an hour and 20 minutes; from Interlaken, about 30 minutes, sometimes with a change of train at the hamlet of Zweisimmen. Call © **0900/300-300** for **rail schedules** and information.

If you're **driving** from Spiez, head southwest on Route 11; from Bulle, head south and then east on Route 11.

plans, but there are directional signs to lead you to hotels and restaurants. The **Gstaad-Saanenland Tourist Association,** CH-3780 Gstaad (© **033/748-81-81;** www.gstaad. ch), is a useful source of information, open July and August Monday to Friday from 8:30am to 6:30pm, Saturday 9am to 6pm, and Sunday 10am to 5pm; September to June, hours are Monday to Friday 8:30am to noon and 1:30 to 6pm, and Saturday 10am to noon and 1:30 to 5pm.

FUN IN THE OUTDOORS

Gstaad is a resort rich in entertainment and sports facilities. Many skiers stay in Gstaad by night and venture to one of the nearby ski resorts during the day. Cable cars take passengers to altitudes of 1,500m and 3,000m (4,920 ft. and 9,840 ft.)—at the higher altitudes there's skiing even in the summer. Other facilities include tennis courts, heated indoor and outdoor swimming pools, and about 320km (200 miles) of hiking trails. Many of these scenic trails are possible to walk or hike year-round (the tourist office will advise). The **Gstaad International Tennis Tournament,** beginning the first Saturday in July, is the most important tennis event in Switzerland.

Skiers setting off from Gstaad have access to 70 lifts, mountain railroads, and gondolas. The altitude of Gstaad's highest skiable mountain is 1,965m (6,445 ft.), with a vertical drop of 1,066m (3,496 ft.). Most beginner and intermediate runs are east of the village in Eggli, a ski area reached by cable car. Eggli has a sunny, southern exposure. Wispellan-Sanetch is favored for afternoon skiing, with lots of runs down to the village. At its summit is the Glacier des Diablerets, at a height of 2,970m (9,741 ft.). Wassergrat, reached from the south side of the resort, is yet another skiing area. Advanced skiers prize Wasserngrat for its powder skiing on steep slopes.

Swiss Ski School at Gstaad (© **033/744-18-65;** www.gstaadsnowsports.ch) has first-class teachers and qualified mountain and touring guides, with special classes available for children. Some 100 private instructors are available. It receives stiff competition from the **Schweizer Schi Schule (Swiss Ski School;** © **033/744-36-65;** www.snow-sports. ch) in the nearby satellite resort of Schönried.

Gstaad has several satellite resorts, which many visitors prefer. Saanen and Schönried are both summer and winter resorts, with excellent accommodations. **Saanen,** at 1,051m (3,447 ft.), is east of Gstaad; some of its wooden chalets date from the 1500s. The **Menuhin Festival** draws an international music-loving crowd from late July to mid-September. The resort can be reached easily by car or by the Montreux-Oberland railway; there's also a small airfield at Saanen for visitors who fly in. **Schönried,** some 4km (2½ miles) northeast of Gstaad, is appreciated for its arguably better snowfall and accommodations, notably the Alpenrose Hotel.

Whichever resort you choose—Gstaad, Saanen, or Schönried—you'll be surrounded by dramatic glaciers and bucolic alpine pastures. This part of the country, called **Saanenland,** is one of the most beautiful parts of Switzerland.

The funiculars and chairlifts around Gstaad are configured into a system that services the slopes of at least six other resorts scattered over four valleys of the Bernese Oberland. In addition to Gstaad, the region's star, the resorts include Saanen, Saanen-Möser, Schönreid, and Sankt Stephan.

An all-inclusive ski pass—known locally as the **Ski Gstaad Pass**—is sold at the departure point of any of the region's funicular stations, and allows access to 250km (155 miles) of downhill slopes and 70 chairlifts and gondolas. The all-inclusive passes may vary depending on what point in the season you buy them, but generally cost 118F for 2 days, 259F for 5 days, and 333F for 7 days, with a complicated set of discounts for children depending on their age and to what degree they're traveling as part of a family unit.

If you're in Gstaad for only 1 day, it's probably smarter to buy a limited pass for access to just a few slopes and chairlifts. The less comprehensive pass (known as a pass for Eggli-La Vide Manette) is sold only in 1-day increments for a price of 62F. Frankly, for anyone planning on 2 or more days of skiing, it's a lot more appealing, and not that much more expensive, to go for the more comprehensive pass.

SHOPPING

Stores along Gstaad's main shopping street, **Hauptstrasse,** seem more upscale, more lavish, and more aggressively tuned to the big-city affluence of Paris, London, and Munich than in virtually any other ski resort in Switzerland. Most of the shops that sell sporting goods in Gstaad inventory other sorts of casual and formal clothing as well, allowing buyers one-stop shopping for the layered look that keeps you warmer on the slopes. Two worthy outlets are **Brand,** Palace Strasse (✆ 033/744-17-75; www.brandsport.ch), and **HermenJat,** Hauptstrasse (✆ 033/744-15-47; www.hermenjat-gstaad.com). If you want to check out the kinds of jewelry bought by the resort's most glamorous clients, consider a visit to **Villiger,** Promenade (✆ 033/744-11-22). Barring that, you can always visit any of the aggressively upscale, relentlessly chic luxury boutiques in the Palace Hotel.

Von Siebenthal, Promenade (✆ 033/744-12-81), is a three-story housewares emporium filled with high-performance Swiss-made gadgets, ranging from wooden molds for making anise cookies to fondue sets.

The best bookstore for reading on a cold alpine night is **Media Treff Gstaad,** Lauenenstrasse (✆ 033/744-39-90).

WHERE TO STAY

Gstaad is not known for its inexpensive hotels. Prices soar in the winter. When business is slow, many of the hotels close; the dates of these closings can vary from year to year.

Very Expensive

Grand Hotel Park ★★★   This landmark hotel lives again. In 1990 one of the Oberland's most venerable hotels was demolished and rebuilt in a style that reflects the 1910 original. Associated with, and partially owned by, investors in the Palace Hotel, it sits astride a hill overlooking the center of the town and across from the Palace. Its design, including the bedrooms, evokes a mixture of the Edwardian age with a posh ski resort you might find in Vail, Colorado. Standard rooms measure a generous 35 sq. m (377 sq. ft.), and the more expensive rooms facing south open onto views of the Wispile, Eggli, and Glacier des Diablerets. Each room comes with an immaculately kept bathroom. Although some of the original turn-of-the-20th-century furniture was incorporated into the new design, much of the interior is sleekly modern and richly accessorized with decorative and structural bands of chiseled granite, polished marble, and burnished pine. It's also home to the first Louis Vuitton boutique in a European hotel.

Wispilenstrasse CH-3780 Gstaad. ✆ 033/748-98-00. Fax 033/748-98-08. www.grandhotelpark.ch. 99 units. Winter 690F–990F double, from 1,540F suite; summer 395F–920F double, from 1,200F suite. Rates include buffet breakfast. AE, DC, MC, V. Parking 20F in winter, free in summer. Closed mid-Mar to mid-June and mid-Sept to mid-Dec. **Amenities:** 5 restaurants; 3 bars; babysitting; concierge; exercise room; 2 pools (1 indoor heated saltwater); room service; spa. *In room:* TV/DVD, hair dryer, minibar, Wi-Fi (25F per 24 hr.).

Hotel Olden ★★ This is one of the most low-key and gracefully unpretentious hotels in Gstaad, a sort of Victorian country inn set amid a sometimes chillingly glamorous landscape—or at least a chillingly expensive landscape. The Olden has a facade painted with regional floral designs and pithy bits of folk wisdom. Embellishments are carved or painted into the stone lintels around many of the doors. The small to midsize rooms are generally furnished in a typical alpine style, although the bathrooms have been modernized. Some guests are housed in the adjacent chalet wing (the comfort level and amenities are the same).

Hauptstrasse, CH-3780 Gstaad. ℂ **033/748-49-50.** Fax 033/748-49-59. www.hotelolden.ch. 16 units. Winter 500F–680F double, 680F–850F junior suite, 780F–1,680F suite; summer 350F–550F double, 550F–690F junior suite, 650F–1,500F suite. Rates include continental breakfast. AE, DC, MC, V. Parking 20F. Closed late Apr to late May. **Amenities:** Restaurant; bar; room service. *In room:* TV, minibar, Wi-Fi (free).

Palace Hotel Gstaad ★★★ This other landmark hotel on a wooded hill overlooks the center of Gstaad. Opened in 1912, the Palace has mock-fortified corner towers and a neomedieval facade. The designer, Valentino, called the architecture a "brutal Sleeping Beauty castle." It's one of the most sought-after luxury hideaways in the world, attracting corporation heads, movie stars, and fashionable aristocrats, many of whom return every winter and stay a long time, earning the Palace the reputation as "Switzerland's largest family boardinghouse." Owner and manager Ernst Scherz's motto is: "Every king is a client, and every client is a king." It's true—if you can afford it.

The nerve center of this chic citadel is an elegantly paneled main salon, with an "eternal flame" burning in the baronial stone fireplace (though this flame isn't so eternal—it burns only in winter). Radiating hallways lead to superb restaurants, bars, discos, and sports facilities. The plush, spacious rooms are tastefully furnished and very distinguished.

Palacestrasse 1, CH-3780 Gstaad. ℂ **800/223-6800** in the U.S. or 033/748-50-00. Fax 033/748-50-01. www.palace.ch. 104 units. Winter 720F–1,890F double, 1,350F–2,390F junior suite, 2,350F–6,100F suite; summer 650F–1,210F double, 1,130F–1,480F junior suite, 2,050F–4,600F suite. Rates include half board. AE, DC, MC, V. Free parking outside, 20F in garage. Closed end of Mar to mid-June and late Sept to shortly before Christmas (dates vary). **Amenities:** 5 restaurants; 2 bars; babysitting; children's center; concierge; exercise room; health club and spa; 2 pools (1 heated indoor); room service; 4 outdoor tennis courts (lit). *In room:* TV, hair dryer, minibar, Wi-Fi (25F per 24 hr.).

Expensive

Grand Hotel Bellevue ★ A venerable favorite still holding its own, this hotel opened in 1912. It stands in a serene park with tall, old trees in the midst of the town. The rooms are spacious and well lit, in a calming color palette. The furnishings are traditional and exceedingly comfortable, as reflected by the deluxe beds and the well-maintained bathrooms. When you check in, you get government-rated five-star luxury in the standard doubles, junior suites, or deluxe suites. The Michelin-star rated restaurant Coelho serves acclaimed cuisine in its dining room and on a sunny terrace. For entertainment, the hotel bar has its own pianist, and in the basement is a private cinema surrounded by a wine cellar. The on-site spa is one of the best in the area, many of its bath facilities inspired by Japan.

Hauptstrasse, CH-3780 Gstaad. ℂ **033/748-00-00.** Fax 033/748-00-01. www.bellevue-gstaad.ch. 52 units. 450F–790F double; 750F–990F junior suite; 950F–2,500F suite. Rates include buffet breakfast. AE, DC, MC, V. Free parking outside. Closed mid-Oct to mid-Dec. **Amenities:** 2 restaurants; 2 bars; concierge; exercise room; indoor heated pool; room service; spa. *In room:* TV/DVD, CD player, fax, hair dryer, minibar, Wi-Fi (free).

Hostellerie Alpenrose ★★★ (Finds) For those who seek the charm of a small inn, this is the preferred choice in the area—it's the only Relais & Châteaux listing within

48km (30 miles). The pine-paneled rooms are exquisitely decorated with rustic furnishings, and the small bedrooms are comfortable and tastefully appointed. Its kindly host, Michel von Siebenthal, is a memorable fellow, setting the fashionable tone of the chalet, which is famous for its restaurant (see below).

Saanenmöserstrasse, CH-3778 Schönried-Gstaad. ✆ **033/748-91-91.** Fax 033/748-91-92. www.hotel alpenrose.ch. 19 units. 390F–630F double; 420F–830F suite. Rates include half board. AE, DC, MC, V. Free parking. Closed mid-Oct to mid-Dec. **Amenities:** 2 restaurants; 2 bars; bikes; Jacuzzi; room service; sauna. *In room:* TV, minibar, Wi-Fi (free).

Hotel Bernerhof ★ (Kids)

This hotel lies in the center of the resort town, about half a block from the rail station. Built on the site of a hotel dating from 1904, it offers modern comforts and attracts a loyal clientele that keeps in touch via a hotel newsletter. Wooden balconies extend across the front. Thomas and Claudia Frei offer well-furnished rooms with neatly kept bathrooms. Children are catered to at the hotel, and many activities are planned for them. The restaurant is recommended below. The Stöckli Bar is a popular place for drinks.

Bernerhofplatz CH-3780 Gstaad. ✆ **033/748-88-44.** Fax 033/748-88-40. www.bernerhof-gstaad.ch. 47 units. 260F–440F double; 310F–550F suite. Rates include buffet breakfast. Half board 45F per person. AE, DC, MC, V. Free parking outside, 15F in garage. **Amenities:** 3 restaurants; bar; babysitting; bikes; children's playground; exercise room; Jacuzzi; indoor heated pool; room service; sauna. *In room:* TV, CD player, hair dryer, minibar, Wi-Fi (free).

Hotel Le Grand Chalet ★★

Tucked away near the mountains in Gstaad is this cozy and distinctly Swiss family-run hotel. The rooms use light-wood furniture and moldings, white walls and linens, and strategically placed lights to make the accommodations elegant and seemingly spacious. Every room has a desk and a plethora of closet space. The double rooms here are much nicer than the suites, which tend to be on the gaudy and dim side. However, the views from their balconies are panoramic, so it's a trade-off.

Le Grand Chalet, CH-3780 Gstaad. ✆ **033/748-76-76.** Fax 033/748-76-77. www.grandchalet.ch. 25 units. 270F–570F double. Rates include buffet breakfast. AE, DC, MC, V. **Amenities:** 2 restaurants; exercise room; room service; sauna. *In room:* TV, kitchenette (in some), hair dryer, minibar.

Wellness & Spa Hotel Ermitage-Golf ★★

This is a government-rated five-star hotel designed and built in 1958. Its developers intended for a golf course to surround it on all sides. Although the building permit for the golf course was eventually refused by the city, the name remained in place. There's a 9-hole golf course about 3km (2 miles) away, however. Today this is a large and comfortable hotel, with a helpful staff and lots of alpine warmth. In the winter it's a toasty, cozy retreat; in the summer it's a pleasure chalet, as red geraniums bloom on its balconies and chaise longues are set up on its lawns. Heiner Lutz and Laurenz Schmid offer paneled bedrooms, each individually furnished. Some have Oriental rugs and offer grand comfort.

Hauptstrasse, CH-3778 Schönried-Gstaad. ✆ **033/748-60-60.** Fax 033/748-60-67. www.ermitagegolf.ch. 69 units. 350F–640F double; 470F–740F junior suite; from 540F suite. Rates include half board with a minimum stay of 3 nights. AE, DC, MC, V. Parking 10F–18F. **Amenities:** 3 restaurants; 2 bars; babysitting; exercise room; Jacuzzi; 2 pools (1 heated indoor); room service; sauna; 2 outdoor tennis courts (lit). *In room:* TV, hair dryer, minibar.

Moderate

Hotel Alphorn (Finds)

Located at the base of the Wispile cable car, this intimate chalet is a small, relatively unpublicized hotel owned by the Bruriswill family. The hotel, built in 1970 and enlarged and upgraded in 1992, has a ski shop on the premises. The small rooms are comfortable and snug, each fitted with a well-kept private bathroom.

Steigstrasse, CH-3780 Gstaad. ⓒ **033/748-45-45.** Fax 033/748-45-46. www.gstaad-alphorn.ch. 30 units. 166F–286F double. Rates include buffet breakfast. Half board 33F per person. AE, DC, MC, V. Free parking. **Amenities:** Restaurant; babysitting; sauna. *In room:* TV, hair dryer, minibar, Wi-Fi (7F per 24 hr.).

Posthotel Rössli (**Value**) The Rössli is an authentic and traditional chalet in the center of Gstaad. Often attracting a young crowd, it's well heated and furnished with modern conveniences in its small but cozy and comfortable bedrooms. All are equipped with neatly kept bathrooms. Every week Ruedi Widmer, mountain guide, ski teacher, and owner of the hotel, organizes walks and grill parties in summer or skiing days in winter. Guests are invited to participate at no extra charge. Locals mix with guests in the *bierstube* (beer tavern), the Stübli.

Promenade, CH-3780 Gstaad. ⓒ **033/748-42-42.** Fax 033/748-42-43. www.posthotelroessli.ch. 36 units. 196F–352F double. Half board 36F per person. Rates include buffet breakfast. AE, DC, MC, V. Free outdoor parking, 10F in garage. **Amenities:** Restaurant. *In room:* TV, hair dryer, minibar, Wi-Fi (free).

WHERE TO DINE

Most visitors dine at their hotel, so there are few independent restaurants in Gstaad. The following choices include some worth venturing out for, as well as others in previously recommended hotels.

Very Expensive

Hostellerie Alpenrose ★★ SWISS/FRENCH During the summer the paneled dining rooms are full of local residents and guests from the surrounding chalets. Michel von Siebenthal is your chef; his father built the first ski lift in the region in 1935. He has elevated a modest pension into a culinary citadel known throughout Switzerland for its cuisine. The varied menu changes every 3 weeks. Lobster is almost always on the menu, but look for marinated salmon, which remains a delectable house specialty. Begin with the duck-liver terrine or a velvety-smooth imaginative soup made of nettles. One savory dish is a cassoulet of mushrooms. The grilled turbot is prepared with several different sauces, including an unusual carrot sauce, and you can also order a superb wild duck in a juniper-berry sauce. Consider having an after-dinner drink in the nightclub, Sammy's.

Saanenmöserstrasse. ⓒ **033/748-91-91.** Reservations recommended. Main courses 48F–75F. AE, DC, MC, V. Daily 6:30–10pm; Wed–Thurs noon–2pm; Fri–Sun noon–2:30pm. Closed mid-Nov to mid-Dec.

The Restaurant ★★★ FRENCH/INTERNATIONAL The Palace Hotel opens up to three different dining rooms, each elegantly paneled and boasting impeccable service and the finest haute cuisine. Some of the finest chefs in the Bernese Oberland create dishes here for an extremely demanding clientele. Formal attire is essential—men without ties or jackets will be asked to dine in the Sans-Cravatte.

For an appetizer, caviar and foie gras abound, but there are also superb hors d'oeuvres, including beefsteak tartare, and delicate soups and consommés. Some especially delectable dishes include crisp rack of Scottish lamb with eggplant lasagna, grilled sole flavored with oregano, crispy duck for two, and chicken Taj Mahal with curry and many side condiments. This wide repertoire includes imaginative interpretations of old favorites. Most desserts are elaborate, but if you wish, you can order a simple sorbet.

In the Palace Hotel. ⓒ **033/748-50-00.** Reservations required. Main courses 38F–72F. AE, DC, MC, V. Daily 12:30–3pm and 7:30–11pm. Closed end of Mar to mid-June and mid-Sept to shortly before Christmas.

Restaurant Chesery ★★★ FRENCH/SWISS At an elevation of 1,097m (3,598 ft.), this is one of the 10 best restaurants in Switzerland. The floors are pink marble and the walls are polished pine. The menu changes daily, based on the freshest ingredients available. The chef is a perfectionist and shops far and wide for only the finest of produce with which to dazzle his clients—grouse from Scotland, Charolais beef from France, truffles from Umbria. You may sample his salt-crusted sea bass with wild rice, chicken Houban (a very special breed from France), Scottish lamb with a crust of fresh herbs, or rack of venison with whortleberries. In the basement bar, Casino, a piano player entertains nightly, and the bar is open from 6pm to 3am, when the last ski bunny departs.

Lauenenstrasse. (☎ **033/744-24-51**. www.chesery.ch. Reservations required. Main courses 37F–68F; fixed-price lunch 78F–82F, dinner 168F. AE, DC, MC, V. Tues–Sun 11:30am–2:30pm and 7pm–midnight. Closed mid-Oct to mid-Dec, Easter to mid-June, and in winter (Tues–Fri) for lunch.

Moderate

Olden Restaurant ★★ MEDITERRANEAN/FRENCH This is the most formal restaurant of the several dining choices available in the Hotel Olden. On the street level, it attracts the latest visiting celebrity with its country charm. Meals are formally served in the pine-paneled dining room. The always-tempting menu might include smoked salmon, fresh gooseliver terrine, shrimp bisque with green peppercorns, house-style tagliatelle, raclette, veal cutlet Milanese, Scottish lamb, or sea bass with olives, potatoes, tomatoes, and onions. Although there are grander restaurants in Gstaad, as well as dining rooms serving a more haute cuisine, the Olden remains our most satisfying choice year after year.

In the Hotel Olden, Hauptstrasse. (☎ **033/744-34-44**. Reservations recommended. Main courses 27F–73F. AE, DC, MC, V. Tues–Sun noon–2:30pm and 6:30–10:30pm. Closed mid-Apr to mid-May and 2 weeks in Nov.

Posthotel Rössli SWISS Set within a 150-year-old chalet in the heart of town, nearly adjacent to the Stadtkirche, with a paneled interior, small windows, and agrarian artifacts scattered throughout, this restaurant welcomes many generations of diners. Menu items—most of which are on the lower end of the price scale—are hearty, alpine inspired, and served in generous portions. Examples include pork and veal schnitzels, tender beefsteaks in a mushroom-flavored cream sauce, velvety fondues, chicken roulades layered with ham and cheese, and several variations on Italian pastas. Salads are fresh, and the beer is cold.

Hauptstrasse 1. (☎ **033/748-42-42**. Reservations not accepted. Main courses 13F–43F. AE, MC, V. Daily 11:30am–2:30pm and 4:30–10pm.

Restaurant Stafel (Kids INTERNATIONAL This tavern-style restaurant at the previously recommended Hotel Bernerhof attracts plenty of discerning devotees. A long-time family favorite, it serves a menu so wide-ranging there's something to please just about anyone. Along with the standard international dishes, it also offers a selection of excellent Swiss regional specialties, including a fondue with veal liver. Asian culinary delicacies are featured in the *blun-chi* section, and every day a large variety of succulent fresh pasta dishes are prepared. The hotel also houses the popular après-ski Stöckli Bar.

In the Hotel Bernerhof. (☎ **033/748-88-44**. Reservations recommended. Main courses 30F–46F. AE, DC, MC, V. Daily 11:30am–2:30pm and 6:30–10:30pm.

Ristorante Rialto ITALIAN One of the finest Italian restaurants in the Bernese Oberland, the Rialto lies in the heart of Gstaad. The proprietors use only the freshest ingredients, and the menu changes with the season. You may begin with a selection of always-tempting antipasti, followed by the luscious salmon carpaccio with a truffle-cream sauce or one of the pasta dishes, including pappardelle. The flavor-filled risotto with fresh asparagus and the chef's sea bass Mediterranean style are both excellent.

GSTAAD AFTER DARK

Much more than its competitors, Gstaad has been accused of attracting glamorous folk who care more about the resort's social scene than they do about skiing. As such, the resort supports a healthy roster of nightspots that range from boozy to glamorous. In midwinter your options include alpine coziness in at least two mountain huts accessible only by cable car, the **Berghaus Eggli,** on the Eggli ski slopes (*©* **033/748-96-12**), and the **Berghaus Wispile,** on the Wispile ski slopes (*©* **033/748-96-32**). Access to either requires an 8-minute ascent on the Eggli (south of the center) and Wispile (north of the center) cable cars *(Gondelbahns).* Both are infused with the odors of simmering raclette and fondues, are open only during the height of the winter season, and encourage guests to ski home after a night of alpine *Gemütlichkeit* (a Swiss term for cozy, good times shared with sympathetic souls). Don't even think of riding the cable car uphill for a meal or drink at either of these places after dark without a reservation, as their scheduling and priorities are as haphazard as anything at the resort.

More conventional evening diversions include the **Palace Hotel** (*©* **033/748-50-00**), which contains a supremely upscale bar adjacent to the pine-sheathed lobby where the comings and goings could fill any Robin Leach production. The hotel also contains the most exclusive—and occasionally stuffy—disco in Gstaad, the **Green Go Disco,** where pinpricks of light illuminate a mysterious semipsychedelic decor of orange, green, and black. Call ahead, as it operates only during midwinter and selected weekends in the peak of midsummer.

In the heart of Gstaad, there's a bar, the **Hostellerie Chesery,** Lauenenstrasse (*©* **033/ 744-24-51**), that hosts both piano music and dance music (later in the evening). Its main focus, its restaurant, is separately recommended above. An appealingly battered hangout reminiscent of England is **Richie's Pub,** Hauptstrasse (*©* **033/744-57-87**). Nobody dances here, but the place is a town favorite. A few steps away is a worthy and much more elegant competitor, the **Rialto Bar,** in the Ristorante Rialto, Promenade (*©* **033/744- 34-74**). There is a large terrace in the summer, and in the winter there's sometimes live music in the restaurant.

THE BERNESE OBERLAND

9

GSTAAD

The Valais

The Valais is a region in southern Switzerland that borders on Italy and consists mostly of the valley around the upper Rhône River. The valley was called Vallis Poenina by the Romans, and the Germans refer to it as Wallis. The main attractions here include the Matterhorn, the Great St. Bernard Pass, and Zermatt. The area offers excellent skiing and other winter sports (Zermatt has one of the longest ski seasons in Switzerland).

The Valais is surrounded by the Alps, with more than 50 major mountain peaks, but the Matterhorn, at 4,410m (14,465 ft.), is by far the most majestic. The Valais contains the largest glacier in Switzerland as well as several others that send tributaries to feed the Rhône, which flows northwest to Lake Geneva, then on through France to the Mediterranean. The Valais also contains about 8 sq. km (3 sq. miles) of lakes.

Often called the hiking capital of Switzerland, the Valais is riddled with well-maintained and well-marked mountain paths. Some of this former network of alpine mule paths are called Roman roads, because in ancient times the Simplon and Great St. Bernard passes were the gateways to the Valais from Italy. Walks along irrigation channels—called *bisses*—are among the most intriguing for nature lovers.

For centuries the Rhône Valley has been a major route through the Alps. The Celts used the Great St. Bernard Pass and Simplon Pass, and then the Gauls held the territory for 500 years. Hannibal and Napoleon both passed through on their way to conquest. Today wide highways and tunnels provide a direct route to Italy.

Protected by mountains, the Valais enjoys a sunny, stable climate, with weather comparable to that of northwestern Spain and France's Provence. The vineyards are second only to those of the Vaud, and the local wine is known for its fruity bouquet and delicate flavor. Dairy farming is widespread. Raclette, the classic Swiss dish, is usually made of the rich, unskimmed milk from the Bagnes Valley, near the Great St. Bernard Pass. Just outside most of the regional towns, you'll see *mazots* or *raccards* (small, elevated grain-storage barns).

Most residents in the western part of the Valais, from Lake Geneva to Sierre, speak French, while those living to the east speak a German dialect. Many people speak both languages as well as some English. Most residents of the Valais are Roman Catholic, evident in the number of churches, abbeys, and monasteries.

The Valais is an increasingly popular year-round travel destination, but not to worry: The growth of resorts and recreation facilities has not disturbed the natural splendor and tranquillity of the alpine countryside.

Chances are if you're visiting the Valais by train you'll land at the major rail terminus of Martigny, which attracts visitors heading across the Great St. Bernard Pass. Visitors going to the ski resort of Verbier also pass through here. Frequent trains arrive in Martigny from Lausanne every hour, taking 30 minutes; from Montreux, every half-hour, taking 30 minutes; and from Sion, every 15 minutes, taking 30 minutes.

If you'd like to take one of the most scenic **bike trips** in the Valais, rent a bike at the kiosk at the **train station** (© **0900/300-300**), costing 33F per day.

From Martigny you can cycle through a beautiful region of the lower Valais, heading across the Rhône River to the villages of Fully, Chataigner, Mazembroz, and Saillon. The Rhône Valley route cuts through some of the most magnificent mountain scenery in all of Switzerland. You pass the promenades of Lake Geneva, which, surprisingly, are lined with palm trees and go along miles of Lavaux vineyards. The Alpine pastures in the Urserental are without trees but are filled with beautiful meadows that burst into spring bloom. Many cyclists plan their routes to pass the ice towers of the Rhône Glacier. Always in the distance you can view snow-capped alpine peaks.

1 VERBIER ★

128km (80 miles) E of Geneva; 40km (25 miles) N of Great St. Bernard Tunnel; 29km (18 miles) E of Martigny; 58km (36 miles) SW of Sion

Verbier sits on a vast, sunny plateau in the Bagnes Valley in Switzerland's southernmost Alps. It looks toward the Combin and Mont Blanc mountains, which are covered with snow year-round, even when the town is bursting with leafy trees and flowers. At 1,500m (4,920 ft.), Verbier was a pastureland before developing into an outstanding sports center. The area is protected from harsh winds by the surrounding mountains. The predominant language of the resort is French.

Verbier doesn't have the architectural distinction of Zermatt. Everything from souvenir shops to the fast-food joints to the chalets is modern. But you don't concentrate on the man-made architecture—the draw is the panoramic site of the resort itself, as its buildings are scattered over a slope of the Bagnes Valley surrounded by snow-covered mountains.

ESSENTIALS

GETTING THERE   From the railway junction of Martigny, take the train along a secondary spur route to Le Châble. Call ✆ **0900/300-300** for **train schedules.** At Le Châble you can transfer to a postal bus. Le Châble is also the departure point for an aerial cableway leading directly to Verbier. The cost of one-way transport on the cable car is 8F per person.

During the peak of the ski season, a consortium of hotels operates a shuttle **bus** that travels directly from Martigny to Verbier that's timed to coincide with the arrival of important trains into Martigny. The one-way cost is 17F. Regrettably, it operates only during winter, and only on Friday afternoon (one bus) and on Saturday (three buses). For **shuttle bus information** and reservations, call ✆ **0900/300-300.**

If you're **driving,** take N9 as far as Martigny on the Great St. Bernard route. Turn left for Verbier at Sembrancher.

VISITOR INFORMATION   Some areas have no street names, so many establishments are signposted. The **Verbier Tourist Office,** Place Centrale (✆ **027/775-38-88;** www.verbier.ch), dispenses information. It's open July to August Monday to Saturday 8am to 12:30pm and 2 to 6:30pm, and Sunday 9am to noon and 3 to 6:30pm. In May and June and from September to mid-December hours are Monday to Friday 8am to noon and 2 to 6:30pm, Saturday 9am to noon and 4 to 6:30pm, and Sunday 9am to noon. Winter hours are Monday to Friday 8am to 12:30pm and 2 to 6:30pm, Saturday 8:30am to 7pm, and Sunday 9am to noon and 3 to 6:30pm.

Skiing tops the list of attractions. The area offers 306km (190 miles) of ski runs, serviced by 47 lifts. Téléverbier, a company founded in 1950, oversees one of the biggest conveyance systems in all of Switzerland. A recent addition, a heavy-duty cable car ("Le Jumbo"), whose cables are strung between the region of La Chaux and the Col des Gentianes, is the largest lift in the country.

In cooperation with neighboring regions, visitors can use their Téléverbier passes on more than 98 additional lifts in the area known as Les 4 Vallées (valleys) and L'Entremont. From Verbier, a single lift ticket can take skiers as high as 3,300m (10,824 ft.). The permit also authorizes cross-country skiing, and several circuits are possible. One goes from Verbier to Mont-Gelé, Mont-Fort, and La Chaux, and then back to Verbier. Another circuit goes from Verbier to Tortin, Mont-Fort, and La Chaux. For information on skiing in the Téléverbier network, contact **Téléverbier S.A.,** CP 419, CH-1936 Verbier (② **027/775-25-11;** www.televerbier.ch).

Throughout the winter, comprehensive passes that entitle skiers to access on all the ski lifts and slopes in the 4 Vallées region cost 126F for 2 days, 289F for 5 days, and 382F for a full week. Children ages 6 to 16 and seniors 63 or older pay only 60% of these rates.

The **Swiss Ski School (Schweizer Schi Schule;** ② **027/775-33-63)** has 170 instructors and in winter offers group lessons daily from 9:15 to 11:45am and more individualized lessons every day in winter from 2:10 to 4:30pm. Private lessons can be arranged as well.

The inauguration of **Le Centre Sportif (Verbier Polysports Center;** ② **027/771-66-01)** has greatly expanded sports offerings in all seasons. Facilities include a covered swimming pool, 10 indoor curling lanes, an indoor ice rink, 9 tennis courts, squash courts, saunas, whirlpools, a solarium, and a games area. The center, open daily 10am to 9pm, also contains a simple restaurant.

Besides sports, Verbier abounds in alpine beauty. The **Haut Val de Bagnes Nature Reserve (Haut Val de Bagnes Réserve Naturelle)** ★★, whose terrain can be safely visited only between mid-May and early October, has a rich variety of flora and fauna, including some rare species of plants. You might see alpine aquilegia, white gentian, yellow pond lily, edelweiss, and several kinds of orchids. Botanical walks are organized in the summer; inquire at the tourist office. There's a sweeping view of the Bagnes Valley from the Combe des Violettes. In the distance you can see Mont-Pleureur, with Italy in the blue mist on the horizon.

There are about 21km (13 miles) of footpaths in and around Verbier that are open for **hiking** in summer and hiking or cross-country skiing in winter. These are carefully maintained and signposted by the municipality. A bit farther afield from Verbier, you'll find almost 402km (250 miles) of hiking trails of varying degrees of difficulty. Maps are available (see the tourist office, under "Essentials," above). There are usually signs posted to indicate the estimated time it takes the average hiker to reach each destination.

If you'd prefer to participate in activities more strenuous than mere walking and hiking, you can try one of several alpine adventures. Trained mountain guides lead jaunts in rock climbing, mountaineering, and cliff climbing, often on excursions of 3 days or more. Call the **Bureau des Guides de Verbier,** a branch of the above-recommended ski school (② **027/775-33-63;** www.guide-verbier.ch), or one of its competitors, **La Fantastique** (② **027/771-41-41;** www.lafantastique.com), for more information about hiring a mountain guide.

Golf Club de Verbier (② **027/771-53-14;** www.verbiergolf.com) is an 18-hole course open from June to October. It is one of the finest in the Valais, set against a scenic alpine backdrop, at an altitude of 1,574m (5,163 ft.). In July and August greens fees are

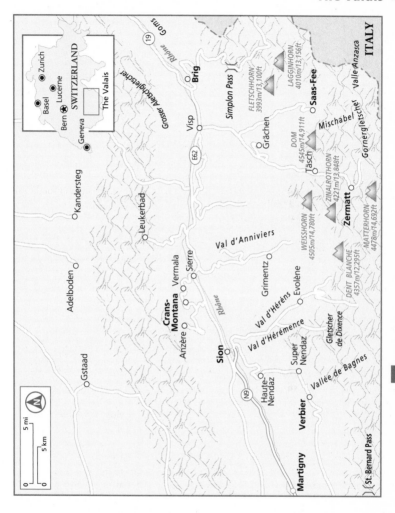

90F daily; otherwise, they are 65F Monday to Friday, rising to 75F Saturday and Sunday. Every hole provides stunning views of such mountain ranges as Combin, Rogneux, and even Mont-Blanc.

SHOPPING

Much of the merchandising that keeps Verbier's economy pumping involves alpine sports, summer or winter, and as such, you'll find half a dozen sporting-goods stores in town. Three of the best are **Philippe Roux Sport,** place Centrale (② 027/771-47-12; www.philippe-roux.ch); its nearby competitor, **Médran-Sport,** route de Verbier (② 027/ 771-60-48); and, located close to the departure point for most of the cable cars and ski lifts, **La boit'askis,** rue de Médran (② 027/771-34-87; www.boitaskis.com).

In the peak of the winter season, hotels often require Saturday-to-Saturday bookings.

Expensive

Hôtel Les 4 Vallées ★★ The hotel stands near the main square and the Médran lift station, and was built in the early 1980s in a contemporary chalet style. Each of its often sunny rooms has pine paneling, plush carpeting, and a balcony (many of which look southward toward the mountains). A copious breakfast buffet is served in a room with large windows and paneling.

Rue de Médran, CH-1936 Verbier. ✆ **027/775-33-44.** Fax 027/775-33-45. www.les4vallees.com. 20 units. Winter 295F–610F double; summer 270F–470F double. Rates include buffet breakfast. AE, DC, MC, V. Parking 25F. Closed May–June and Sept–Nov. **Amenities:** Bar; free use of nearby indoor swimming pool; sauna. *In room:* TV, hair dryer, minibar, Wi-Fi (free).

Hôtel Rosalp ★★★ This Relais & Châteaux establishment is the plushest resort here, and it underwent a top-to-bottom renovation in 2007. Roger and Anita Pierroz built the Rosalp in 1945, and Anita's cooking brought early fame to the place. But their son, Roland, put it on Europe's gastronomic map. Today first-class rooms and refined cuisine are available, the suites are excellent, and the small public salon is a tranquil retreat. The bedrooms are decorated with flair and filled with modern comforts. Many have dark paneling and some contain a sun deck. Suites for four contain two rooms, two bathrooms, and a private salon. The hotel has the area's premier restaurant, Le Restaurant Pierroz (see below).

Rte. de Médran, CH-1936 Verbier. ✆ **027/771-63-23.** Fax 027/771-10-59. www.rosalp.ch. 18 units. Winter 450F–625F double, 1,150F suite for 4; summer 355F–400F double, 910F suite for 4. Rates include continental breakfast. Half board 75F per person. AE, DC, MC, V. Parking free outside, 15F in garage. Closed May–June and Oct–Nov. **Amenities:** 2 restaurants; bar; exercise room; Jacuzzi; sauna. *In room:* TV, hair dryer, minibar, Wi-Fi (free).

Hôtel Vanessa ★ One of the biggest hotels in Verbier is also one of the resort's finest. This government-rated four-star, six-floor hotel dating from 1980 has comfortable and modern midsize rooms; most resemble suites and offer bright upholstery and balconies. The beds are exceedingly comfortable, and the maintenance is among the finest in town. Each unit is fitted with a well-maintained bathroom.

Place Centrale, CH-1936 Verbier. ✆ **027/775-28-00.** Fax 027/775-28-88. www.hotelvanessa.ch. 56 units. Winter 380F–425F double, 390F–480F duplex, 490F–900F suite; summer 280F double, 315F–345F duplex, 450F–560F suite. Rates include breakfast. Half board 65F per person. AE, DC, MC, V. Parking 15F. Closed Apr to mid-July and Sept to mid-Dec. **Amenities:** Restaurant; babysitting; exercise room; Jacuzzi; room service; sauna. *In room:* TV, hair dryer, minibar, Wi-Fi (free).

Le Chalet d'Adrien ★★★ Brigitte and Eric Cachart operate one of the most spectacular resorts in the Valais. They took an old chalet and modernized it with sensitivity. For some, it is now the most elegant way to stay in Verbier. The chalet lies only 30m (98 ft.) from a lift that hauls skiers to the top of the Savoleyres *pistes.* Each guest has a personal changing room with heated boot benches and exclusive ski lockers. The hotel stands on a promontory overlooking the resort, and most bedrooms have a private terrace with a panoramic view of the Alps. Each luxurious room is individually decorated, but all of them have wood paneling, coordinated fabrics, and period furnishings. In the suites a wood fire crackles in winter. With an old oven and copper cauldrons in the fireplace, the chefs turn out a superb cuisine, including hot stews, fondues (with truffles), and old-fashioned pies and tarts.

Chemin des Creux, CH-1936 Verbier. © **027/771-62-00.** Fax 027/771-62-24. www.chalet-adrien.com. 20
units. 510F–750F double; 850F junior suite; 1,150F suite. Half board 85F per person. AE, MC, V. Closed
Oct–Nov and May–June. **Amenities:** 2 restaurants; bar; room service; spa. *In room:* TV, hair dryer, minibar,
Wi-Fi (free).

Moderate

Ermitage   Next to the tourist office, in the heart of the resort, this is a durable choice
with comfortable beds and a welcoming family atmosphere. Rooms are midsize and
tastefully furnished in a chalet style, each with private bathroom with tub or shower. The
most desirable rooms open to the south with the Combins mountains in the distance;
rooms on the north are less desirable, fronting the heavy traffic along the main street.
Most of the rooms have twin beds, and there's only a handful of singles. Guests gather in
the lobby, where there is an Internet hookup. On the ground floor is the separately recommended Restaurant l'Ecurie (see below).

18, Carrefour Central, CH-1936 Verbier. © **027/771-52-64.** www.ermitage-verbier.ch. 25 units.
180F–360F double; 320F–670F family unit. Rates include buffet breakfast. AE, DC, MC, V. Free parking.
Closed mid-Sept to mid-Oct and mid-Apr to mid-May. **Amenities:** Restaurant; bar; Wi-Fi (free, in lobby).
In room: TV, hair dryer, minibar.

Hôtel de la Poste (Kids)   This red-shuttered chalet on the main street near the central
square has long been a family favorite. Despite its lack of special facilities or program-
ming for children, this family-owned and -run resort stands out against the other more
upscale, adult-oriented hotels in the market as a great spot for families. Constructed in
1955, it was rebuilt in 1962 and then drastically altered in 1980, which accounts for its
present look. The small rooms are snug and comfortable with a modern alpine decor, and
each comes with an adequate tiled bathroom. The hotel restaurant, La Tana, serves typical Swiss alpine cuisine.

Rue de Médran, CH-1936 Verbier. © **027/771-66-81.** Fax 027/771-34-01. www.hotelposteverbier.ch. 30
units. Winter 250F–454F double; summer 170F–340F double. Rates include half board. AE, DC, MC, V. Free
parking. Closed mid-Apr to mid-June and mid-Sept to mid-Dec. **Amenities:** Restaurant; bar; indoor
heated pool. *In room:* TV, minibar.

WHERE TO DINE

Verbier has several excellent restaurants, many serving traditional Swiss dishes and Continental cuisine. Most of the best restaurants are connected with hotels.

Expensive

Le Restaurant Pierroz ★★★ FRENCH   The finest food in the Valais is served at
this Relais & Châteaux selection. Roland Pierroz is one of the great chefs of Switzerland;
gourmets drive across national borders to sample his light cuisine moderne and regional
specialties. The menu changes frequently but could include roulades of carpaccio of sea
bream with tomatoes *en confit;* a theatrical but delicious version of fried foie gras in a
beet-and-onion "cage"; red-mullet soup studded with shellfish; a divine poached chicken
with truffles and baby vegetables (for two); and tournedos of lamb with a mousseline of
local potatoes *(rattes),* garlic, and crispy sauerkraut. The cheese trolley emerges with at
least 35 selections, followed by desserts such as a crisp and tasty apple tart with ice cream
that is celestial. The finest meal we've ever had in Switzerland was had here.

In the Hôtel Rosalp, rue de Médran. © **027/771-63-23.** Reservations required at least a day ahead. Main
courses 68F–82F. AE, DC, MC, V. Daily noon–2pm and 7–9:30pm. Closed May–June and Oct–Nov.

Au Vieux Verbier SWISS   One of the few restaurants in Verbier not affiliated with any hotel, the Old Verbier is on a hillside a few paces from the town's ski slopes. It's set in a building that functions as the nerve center for the surrounding hillside cable cars. Its decor features brightly polished brassware, ceiling beams, and stone. The kitchen defines its cuisine as *bonne cuisine bourgeoise,* which is rich, traditional, and filling, exemplified by such featured dishes as La Potence—a grilled steak flambéed at your table with a red-wine sauce. Grilled fish and roasted rack of lamb are among the more delectable items to order. The specialty of the house—and it's a delight for connoisseurs—is pigs' feet in Madeira with *rösti,* but it's only served in autumn.

Gare de Médran. ✆ 027/771-16-68. Reservations required for dinner. Main courses 22F–48F; fixed-price menus (summer only) 40F. AE, DC, MC, V. Daily noon–3pm and 6:30pm–midnight. Closed early May to mid-July and Mon in summer and fall.

La Pinte ★ (Finds) SWISS   This is master chef Roland Pierroz's second, more reasonably priced restaurant, on the ground floor of the Hôtel Rosalp. The 19th-century paneling is decorated with painted flowers; in the back a snug room displays hunting trophies. The cuisine features simmered and grilled specialties. A typical meal includes a to-die-for tart made with leeks or Gruyère cheese. Meats, ranging from a brochette of lamb to tournedos, are grilled over an open fire. Several regional dishes are available, including a savory sausage with lentils. Specials change daily.

In the Hôtel Rosalp, rue de Médran. ✆ 027/771-63-23. Reservations required. Main courses 32F–55F. AE, DC, MC, V. Daily noon–2pm and 7–9:30pm. Closed May to mid-Dec.

Le Sonalon ★ (Finds) SWISS/CONTINENTAL   Some 4km (2½ miles) northwest of Verbier's center, this discovery lies near the edge of one of Verbier's less frequently used ski slopes *(la piste de Savolère).* This wood-sided chalet was built in the mid-1980s and has been known as a warm, comfortable dining spot ever since. You can reach it by car, following the directions listed below, or take the cable car to the Savolère station, then trek downhill on a steeply inclined 10-minute walk. In a dining room sheathed in light-colored wood paneling, or on an outdoor terrace with panoramic views encompassing the entire village of Verbier, you'll enjoy well-prepared meals whose gusto seems enhanced by the high altitudes. Menu items include raclette (available at dinner but not at lunch), several kinds of fondue, grilled lamb chops with aromatic herbs, filets of beef prepared with pepper sauce or mushrooms, and such palate-pleasing fish as pikeperch, filet of sole, and salmon. Calorie-conscious dishes such as grilled chicken in a sweet-and-sour sauce are classified as "fitness platters," although their weight-reducing benefits are usually offset by such desserts as crème brûlée, tiramisu, or a particularly succulent version of pears marinated in red wine and spices, served with cinnamon-flavored ice cream.

Rte. de la Marlenaz. ✆ 027/771-72-71. Reservations recommended. Main courses 18F–58F. AE, DC, MC, V. Daily 11:30am–2pm and 7–10pm. Closed Mon–Tues May–June and Oct–Nov. From place Centrale in Verbier, follow the signs to Savolère and Carrefour, then branch off on a dirt road signposted LE SONALON.

Restaurant l'Ecurie ★ SWISS/FRENCH   On the ground floor of the Ermitage (see above), this restaurant appeals to hikers in summer, skiers in winter, and expats occupying the nearby chalet clusters year-round. They come for the mountain specialties, the rustic atmosphere, the affordable regional wines, and the grilled meats done to perfection on the wood-fired grill. The cozy ambience here is especially heartwarming on a cold winter night. Many diners like the country-style section of the restaurant, with its rough wooden tables and chairs, although there is another section with more formal service at candlelit tables covered in white starched linen. The homemade pastas have long been a feature of the kitchen, and chefs also make a series of Italian-inspired risottos. Fish is grilled as you like it, and scampi appears in a range of dishes along with other seafood. Another specialty is roast chicken served with crisp fries. The owners run the restaurant, with Lisette out front welcoming you, and her husband Jean-Marc (nicknamed Babouin), in the back doing the superb cooking.

Place Centrale. ✆ **027/771-27-60.** Reservations recommended. Main courses 25F–52F. AE, DC, MC, V. Mon–Sat 10:30am–4pm and 5:30–10pm.

Inexpensive

Pizzeria Fer à Cheval (Value) PIZZA/GRILLS   Although it defines itself as a pizzeria, this is one of the best cost-conscious restaurants in Verbier, offering more than the dozen types of pizza for which it's best known. Crowded and friendly, with additional seating on another floor, it lies a short walk uphill from the resort's main square. It has an outdoor terrace that's used throughout the summer and on nice days the rest of the year, and an interior with large windows and pine-wood paneling. The menu includes pizzas, pastas like lasagna and spaghetti, all sorts of salads, and grills such as tenderloin of pork and filet steaks. A great between-meals snack is a *croûte au fromage*—a slice of bread covered with melted Gruyère and white-wine sauce, garnished with sliced ham or a fried egg.

Rue de Médran. ✆ **027/771-26-69.** www.feracheval.ch. Reservations recommended. Salads 7F–19F; pizzas and pastas 15F–28F; platters 28F–42F. AE, DC, MC, V. Daily 8am–midnight. Closed May–June and Sept to early Nov.

VERBIER AFTER DARK

Partly because of its cosmopolitan mixture of English, French, and Swiss clients, many of whose youthful high spirits rise to alpine levels during ski and hill-climbing vacations, Verbier has more discos (at least four, all open only in the winter) and bars than you'd expect. The disco most popular with English-speaking tourists is the **Farm Club,** route de Verbier (✆ **027/771-42-77**). Here, amid weathered beams, sturdy and amiably battered furniture, and a modern decor that includes several fireplaces, you can drink and dance to your heart's content. It's open every night between December and April, and things really get going after 10:30pm.

Even if you arrive during the off season when the discos are closed, you can always drink in any of the dozen or so bars and pubs. The most English of the lot is the neo-Victorian **Nelson Pub,** rue de Verbier (✆ **027/771-31-51**). Look for cheeseburgers, croque-monsieur, and platters of air-dried alpine beef, along with at least 40 brands of beer from virtually everywhere. A less theme-ish, less aggressively Olde English venue is **Le Crok,** route des Creux (✆ **027/771-69-34**), with tiny tables, leather-upholstered banquettes, and a modern decor. The place offers stiff drinks and frequent live music. The **Bar New Club,** rue de la Poste (✆ **027/771-22-67**), re-creates the glossy, comfortable living room of an affluent bachelor, with couches perfect for conversation and comfortable drinking. **Bar L'Auin,** in the Hotel Rosalp, rue de Médran (✆ **027/771-63-23**), is the most conservative, discreet, elegant, and comfortable bar in town. The fireplace here gives a warm glow.

GREAT ST. BERNARD PASS ★★★: AN EASY EXCURSION FROM VERBIER

Because of the danger of avalanches and road blockage, most winter drivers headed between the Valais and northern Italy travel through the 6km (4-mile) Great St. Bernard

St. Bernards Put Out to Pasture

The fabled rescue dogs, the St. Bernards, have been sold. Big and bulky, an adult male can weigh up to 220 pounds and eat more than 4 pounds of meat a day; the monks who owned them could no longer afford them. There's no record of when the St. Bernards started rescuing people, but they're credited with saving some 2,000 travelers over the past 2 centuries. Obsolete with the advent of modern technology (helicopters and heat sensors have replaced these proud dogs), they will be sadly missed.

Tunnel instead of negotiating overland roads that are treacherous or impassable. In the summer, however, many visitors make the pilgrimage over the St. Bernard Pass instead, often to conclude that the drive is one of the highlights of their trip. The overland road is usually open only from mid-June to early October; its highest point lies about an hour's drive from Martigny, 40km (25 miles) away. If you're staying in Verbier and you'd like to visit the pass, you can drive east from Verbier along a winding road until you come to the village of Sembranchen. From here, E21 leads directly south to this historic pass. Follow the signs pointing uphill to Hospice St-Bernard. Travel time by car from Verbier is about 1¼ hours.

St. Bernard dogs used to be bred by Augustinian monks in one of the oldest monasteries in Europe, the **Great St. Bernard Hospice,** Le Grand-St-Bernard, 1946 Bourg-Saint-Pierre (© **027/787-12-36;** www.gsbernard.net). Set on the Swiss side of the vertiginous Swiss-Italian border, it was founded in 1050 and was mostly rebuilt of somber-looking gray stone in the 1600s. Year-round, the hospice houses only four or five Franciscan monks, many native to the Valais, as well as monks from other parts of Europe who stay for short-term bouts of meditation and prayer. Visitors can arrive by car only between June 15 and early October; the rest of the year, all roads are snowbound and transit is possible only via special skis. (See below for details.)

The monastery shelters a treasury of religious artifacts, a museum showcasing the often-tragic history of the pass, and historic kennels that used to be devoted to the perpetuation of the bloodlines of the St. Bernard breed of dog. During the winter visitors are forced to make a strenuous 6km (4-mile) uphill trek, on specially accessorized skis, from a parking lot near the Swiss entrance to the St. Bernard Tunnel. Don't even think of trying this without warning the monastery of your plans in advance, as the brothers will discourage you in the event of impending storms or avalanches. Proper equipment is required, including sealskin sheathing for your skis for traction during the uphill trek. In the event of an emergency, midwinter guests can be evacuated by snowmobile or helicopter.

In June and September hours are daily 9am to noon and 1 to 6pm; July and August hours are daily 9am to 7pm. Admission to the public areas of the monastery and its chapel is free; admission to the museum and the former kennels costs 8F per person. The rest of the year, visits can be made only by special arrangement.

During limited warm-weather periods, you can stay in the wood-sheathed interior of the **Hôtel de l'Hospice du Grand-St-Bernard,** Le Grand-St-Bernard, 1946 Bourg-Saint-Pierre (© **027/787-11-53;** fax 027/787-11-92; www.hotelhospice.ch). The four-story, gray-stone building was built in 1899. It's owned by the monastery, leased to a private entrepreneur, and contains 33 rooms. None has a TV or phone, and furnishings **259** are simple and vaguely monastic. But views sweep out over both the Swiss and Italian Alps, and the food in the in-house restaurant is plentiful and reasonably priced. The hotel is open only between early June and mid-October, when it welcomes hill climbers, nature lovers, and members of religious organizations. The rest of the year it's locked tight, and the intrepid visitors who make the uphill trek on skis are housed, space and circumstances permitting, in the monastery itself. Per-person rates are 59F, single or double occupancy, with breakfast and dinner included. MasterCard and Visa are accepted.

Where to Stay & Dine

Auberge du Vieux-Moulin (Finds) This is a remote oasis. Part of a rocky hill was blasted away to make room for this small roadside inn in the hamlet of Bourg-Saint-Pierre, which lies on the way to the monastery (see above). Built in 1964 and completely renovated since, the small rooms are streamlined and comfortable, with good beds. Guests in a room without private bathroom will find clean corridor facilities. Private bathrooms are small but neat.

CH-1946 Bourg-Saint-Pierre. ℭ **027/787-11-69.** Fax 027/787-11-92. 19 units, 9 with bathroom. 60F double without bathroom, 95F with bathroom. Rates include continental breakfast. AE, DC, MC, V. **Amenities:** Restaurant. *In room:* No phone.

2 SION ★★

27km (17 miles) E of Martigny; 53km (33 miles) W of Visp

The capital of the Valais, the ancient city of Sion is known for its glorious springs and autumns and for its ancient status as a trading post on the trails between France and Italy. Dating from Roman times, the town is dominated by the silhouettes of the castles of Valère and Tourbillon. The majority of its population speaks French.

Most of the towns of the Valais are sports oriented, but Sion is one of the exceptions. Come here if you want to see a beautifully preserved old Swiss town with a lot of history and plenty of impressive walks in all directions. It's not as tourist oriented as such cities as Verbier, and even though it's a capital, it's still off the beaten path for most visitors. The stone streets of the Vieille Ville (Old Town) are flanked with cafes and restaurants.

ESSENTIALS

GETTING THERE Sion lies on the major rail lines that connect Milan and Turin (via the Simplon Tunnel) with Geneva and Paris. Trains arrive from both directions every day. Call ℭ **0900/300-300** for **rail schedules.** If you're driving, head east from Martigny, and from Visp go west, on E2.

VISITOR INFORMATION The **Sion Tourist Information Office** is on place de la Planta (ℭ **027/327-77-27;** www.siontourism.ch). It's open mid-July to mid-August Monday to Friday 8:30am to 6pm, Saturday 10am to 4pm, Sunday 9am to noon; off season, hours are Monday to Friday 8:30am to noon and 2 to 5:30pm, Saturday 9am to noon.

SEEING THE SIGHTS

Château de Tourbillon (ℭ **027/606-47-45**) is perched on a steep rock on a hill overlooking the northern periphery of the town. It's the broodingly impressive ruin of a medieval stronghold built by a 13th-century bishop to defend Sion against the House of

THE VALAIS

10

SION

Savoy. Destroyed by a fire in 1788, it has never been reconstructed, but you can still make out the remains of a keep, watchtower, and chapel. There's a **panoramic view** ★ of the Rhône Valley from its base, which sits at an elevation of 645m (2,116 ft.). Admission is free.

Atop the town's other steep hill are the deeply weathered walls of an unusual Gothic church, the **Eglise-Fortresse de Valère** ★ (also known as the Château de Valère), whose foundations were built as a fortress by the ancient Romans. In much better shape than the previously mentioned castle, the three-aisle basilica dates from the 12th and 13th centuries. It contains 17th-century choir stalls and what has been called "the oldest playable organ in the world," dating from the 14th century.

Valère Museum ★, in the Eglise-Fortresse de Valère (✆ **027/606-47-10**), is in the former residence of the cathedral chapter and is now the cantonal museum of history and ethnography. It contains fine works of medieval religious art, ancient arms and armor, uniforms, Roman and Gothic chests, and interesting ethnological collections. Both the museum and the fortified church that contains it are open Tuesday to Sunday from 10am to noon and 2 to 6pm (to 5pm Oct–Apr). Admission to both the church and museum costs 7F for adults and 5.50F for children 12 and under. A family pass costs 16F. *Note:* There's a steep uphill climb between the parking lot and the church.

Back in town, the **Hôtel de Ville (town hall),** rue du Grand-Pont, whose inner chambers cannot be visited, has a facade embellished with 17th-century doors and columns. The foundations were laid by the ancient Romans in A.D. 377. On Sion's main street, rue du Grand-Pont, is an **astronomical clock.**

Northeast of the Hôtel de Ville is the **Cathédrale Notre-Dame-du-Glarier,** 13, rue de la Cathédrale (✆ **027/322-80-66**). It was reconstructed in the 15th century, although the original **Romanesque belfry** ★ remains, dating from the 11th and 13th centuries. Inside, look for the triptych in gilded wood, called *The Tree of Jesse.*

Although Sion has the monuments mentioned above, you can connect more intimately with regional life by taking an organized **wine-tasting excursion** (the tourist office—see "Visitor Information," above—will provide details). A long marked **footpath,** the most impressive walk in the area, is called *le chemin du vignoble,* and it passes through vineyards on the outskirts of the city. Our favorite vintner is the **Varone Vineyard,** a *centre de dégustation* at 30, av. Grand-Champsec (✆ **027/203-56-83**; www.varone.ch), across the river. It is open Monday from 2 to 6:30pm, Tuesday to Friday 10am to noon and 2 to 6:30pm, and Saturday 10am to noon and 2 to 5pm. Before beginning your hike, pick up the makings of a picnic at **Co-op City,** place du Midi, right off avenue de la Gare.

WHERE TO STAY

Hôtel Castel   Modern and boxy, this government-rated three-star hotel is at the edge of the road to Simplon at the northeast edge of town. Built in 1968, it was recently renovated. The small rooms have modern furniture and soundproof windows, and each comes with a good bed and tidy bathroom. Many units have views of the jagged cliffs that support the medieval château.

36, rue du Scex, CH-1950 Sion. ✆ **027/322-91-71.** Fax 027/322-57-24. www.hotel-castel.ch. 30 units. 125F–160F double; 165F–185F triple. Rates include buffet breakfast. AE, DC, MC, V. Free parking. **Amenities:** Restaurant. *In room:* TV, minibar.

Hôtel du Rhône   This cinder-block hotel allows you to escape the traffic congestion of the Old City, lying at its outer border. The small rooms are furnished with angular contemporary furniture and full bathrooms. In spite of its no-frills atmosphere, the hotel is the best place to stay in town.

10, rue du Scex, CH-1950 Sion. ℰ **800/780-7234** in the U.S. or 027/322-82-91. Fax 027/323-11-88. www. bestwestern.ch/durhonesion. 45 units. 170F–190F double. Children 12 and under stay free in parent's room. Rates include buffet breakfast. AE, DC, MC, V. Parking 15F. **Amenities:** Restaurant; bar; room service. *In room:* TV, hair dryer, minibar, Wi-Fi (5F per 24 hr.).

WHERE TO DINE

Caves de Touts-Vents (Finds) SWISS/FRENCH   This restaurant occupies several levels of a 13th-century cellar, whose vaultings were originally built to store wine. You descend a steep flight of stairs to reach the first room, much of which is devoted to a well-stocked bar. Claustrophobics may elect to go no farther. The lack of windows, the ancient stones, the flickering candles, and the effect of the wine work together to make the room cozy. The specialties—and good-tasting ones at that—include tagliatelle with salmon, mushrooms in puff pastry, calves' liver with shallots, and, of course, fondue and raclette.

16, rue des Châteaux. ℰ **027/322-46-84.** www.cave-tous-vents.ch. Reservations recommended. Main courses 15F–35F. AE, MC, V. Restaurant daily 7–10:30pm. Cafe and bar Tues–Sat 5pm–midnight. Closed mid-July to Aug.

La Sitterie ★ FRENCH   In this restaurant with its elegant table appointments, you dine on a refined French cuisine, inspired by that country right beyond the border. Jacques Bovier is an inspired chef, turning out creative dishes based on market-fresh ingredients. Start, perhaps, with his chervil soup with hard-boiled eggs and lardoons, or else a rabbit pâté. You might follow with a spring meadow alpine lamb with fresh herbs served with an organic polenta Ticino style. Desserts are rich and luscious here, including homemade vanilla ice cream with leaves of chocolate, with a side of kirsch-laced cherries, perhaps a crème brûlée with fried strawberries.

41, rte. du Rawyl. ℰ **027/203-22-12.** www.lasitterie.chi. Reservations required. Main courses 24F–48F; fixed-price lunch 39F, dinner 62F for 4 courses, 78F for 5 courses. AE, DC, MC, V. Tues–Sat 11am–3pm and 6pm–midnight.

Le Jardin Gourmand ★★★ SWISS/FRENCH   Established in 1996, this is the town's finest restaurant. Set near the railway station, it occupies a trio of rooms outfitted in Louis XVI furniture, with complicated wooden ceilings, floors of Carrara marble, and a glassed-in winter garden that's air-conditioned in summer. If you're absolutely committed to cutting costs, you may opt to dine in the cafe-style brasserie near the entrance, where lunchtime fixed-price menus are rock-bottom inexpensive. It's much more appealing, however, to pass into the inner sanctum, where chef/owner Pascal Fantoli prepares food equivalent to what you'd expect from a culinary citadel in Lausanne or Geneva. Examples include a crawfish-and-scallop-studded couscous infused with saffron and served with an aromatic court bouillon, a salad of wild greens with quail meat and foie gras, baby turbot with an anisette-flavored cream sauce, strips of filet of lamb with Provençal-derived aioli (garlic mayonnaise), and a particularly succulent dessert with frozen nougat, almonds, caramel, and rum sauce.

22, av. de la Gare. ℰ **027/323-23-10.** www.lejardingourmand.ch. Reservations recommended. Main courses 18F–38F. AE, DC, MC, V. Mon–Sat 11:30am–2pm and 7–10pm. Closed 4 weeks in July–Aug.

L'enclos de Valère ★★ FRENCH   It's sometimes unnerving to drive a car up the steep and narrow street leading to this restaurant, but once you reach it, you'll find a site loaded with charm and one of the best-regarded restaurants in Sion. Located near the edge of the gardens that surround the Eglise-Fortresse de Valère, the restaurant is small and intimate, with an outdoor dining area. The dining room has a regional decor, with flagstone floors and a beamed ceiling. The menu changes monthly and may include lamb with garlic and thyme; crawfish salad; filets of perch with white-butter sauce; magret of duckling with raspberry-vinegar sauce; and an *assiette Clos de Valérie* loaded with dried meats, pâtés, shredded duck meat, and salads. Dessert may include a slice of lemon tart or a crème brûlée.

18, rue des Châteaux. (✆ **027/323-32-30.** www.enclosdevalere.ch. Reservations recommended. Main courses 32F–48F. DC, MC, V. Daily 9am–midnight (till 6pm on Sun). Closed Jan–Feb 15 and Mon in Sept–Oct.

3 CRANS-MONTANA ★★

14km (9 miles) N of Sierre; 21km (13 miles) E of Sion; 158km (98 miles) E of Geneva

Crans and Montana-Vermala, at 1,494m (4,900 ft.), are twin ski resorts; both are modern and fashionable and long associated with an upscale Italian clientele. Set on a handsome plateau where the air is said to be "lighter than champagne," they enjoy excellent snowfall and views as far as the Rhône Valley. Crans, whose hotel construction began in 1912, is composed for the most part of colonies of apartments and hotels, many in the half-timbered mountain style. Montana, clustered around the shores of Lac Grenon, is the older section, begun in 1892. Connected to them both, at a slightly lower altitude, is Aminona, still an infant resort but rising rapidly.

Note that the lack of street names in many cases is confusing, although restaurants and hotels often have directional signs. It seems that all the residents want to erase the distinctions between Crans and Montana, as the resort has become virtually one over the years.

ESSENTIALS

GETTING THERE From Geneva, take a direct train to Sierre; call (✆ **0900/300-300** for **rail information.** At Sierre, change to a funicular or bus, each of which charges around 13F per person each way to Crans-Montana. Call the **Crans-Montana Service des Buses et Funiculaires** (✆ **027/481-33-55;** www.cie-smc.ch) for departure times.

A postal **bus** from Sion makes the run up the mountain to Crans-Montana.

If you're **driving,** the resorts are accessible by good roads from Sion or the market town of Sierre. From Sion, take E2 east to Sierre; from here, follow the signs up the winding mountain road until you reach Crans-Montana.

VISITOR INFORMATION Not all thoroughfares have street names; to find establishments that lie off the street plans, you should look for directional signs. The **Tourist Information Office** is at Immeuble Scandia, in Crans. In Montana an equivalent organization is on avenue de la Gare. Both offices have the same phone number: **027/485-04-04** (www.crans-montana.ch). Hours are Monday to Friday from 8:30am to noon and 2 to 5:30pm, and Saturday from 9am to noon. During high season it's open till 6:30pm Monday to Friday, Saturday 9:30am to noon and 2 to 4pm, and Sunday 9am to noon.

FUN IN THE OUTDOORS

Neither resort limits its allure to wintertime diversions. During the summer Montana tends to focus on spa cures and general health and well-being, and Crans transforms itself into a golf center. Nearby facilities include the 18-hole Plan-Bramois course, on the western outskirts of town, and the 9-hole Jack Nicklaus (formerly known as the Xires) course, on the resort's southern perimeter. For golf information, call 𝓒 027/485-97-97. The Omega European Masters, held at Crans each year in September, draws top golfers from all over the world. Tennis, hiking, and mountain climbing are the main summer sports at Crans-Montana; others include horseback riding, hiking, and fishing. Winter sports include skating, ski-bobbing, and ice-hockey matches. Skiing is available year-round.

There's a spectacular ascent to **Point Plaine-Morte** ★★, at nearly 3,000m (9,840 ft.); but even at such a great height, there are still runs suitable for novice skiers. To get here, take the gondola from Montana-Barzettes to the east of Montana, stopping at Les Violettes first. There's a restaurant at Plaine-Morte.

Cry d'Err, which looms north of the resort, rises to 2,264m (7,426 ft.) and has a large restaurant and a sunbathing terrace. To get here, take the Grand Signal gondola from Montana or the Crans-Cry d'Err gondola from Crans.

Piste Nationale is known for its steep, narrow runs, which attract many skiers. **Mount Tubang,** especially its La Toula run, is another slope only for the advanced skier.

All-inclusive ski passes that provide access to all the cable cars and chairlifts in the Crans-Montana district cost 119F for 2 days and 270F for 5 days. Children between the ages of 6 and 15 are charged 72F for 2 days and 162F for 5 days. A passport-size photo is required for anyone who wants to buy a ski pass.

SHOPPING

The crisp air and the dozens of outdoor diversions here might inspire purchases of sporting equipment rather than kitschy souvenirs. The accessories and paraphernalia you'll need to do anything in the Alps will jump out at you from virtually every local shop. Two of the best, however, are **Alex Sports,** rue du Prado, in Crans (𝓒 027/481-40-61; www.alexsports.ch), and **Ski Rinaldo,** route de Rawyl, in Montana (𝓒 027/481-89-17; www.ski-rinaldo.ch).

WHERE TO STAY

Very Expensive

Grand Hôtel du Golf ★★★   This elegant retreat attracts the celebrity crowd and others, especially golfers, who demand the very best. Altered and rebuilt many times, it dates from 1906 when Sir Arnold Lunen first introduced golf here, attracting English visitors. In time the hotel attracted many royal families, including those from the Netherlands, Portugal, and Belgium. Today, instead of kings, you get CEOs and the like. The spacious bedrooms are elegantly furnished, tasteful, comfortable, and traditional. Each of the rooms opens onto panoramic views and contains state-of-the-art bathrooms. Soft music and an intimate atmosphere attract patrons to the Green Bar before they head for the restaurant-grill, Le Relais, offering a classical continental cuisine, with many Swiss specialties. The hotel also has the finest recreational facilities at the resort.

CH-3963 Crans. 𝓒 027/485-42-42. Fax 027/485-42-43. www.grand-hotel-du-golf.ch. 88 units. Winter and mid-July to mid-Sept 340F–720F double, 830F suite for 2; off season 1,270F suite for 2. Rates include half board. AE, DC, MC, V. Free parking. Closed Apr 15–May and end of Sept to mid-Dec. **Amenities:** 2 restaurants; bar; babysitting; exercise room; golf course; indoor heated pool; room service; spa. *In room:* TV, hair dryer, minibar, Wi-Fi (free).

Expensive

Aïda-Castel ★★   Known for its Valaisian decor, this government-rated four-star hotel is composed of two separate chalet-style buildings united during a series of massive renovations in the early 1990s. They lie on either side of the hotel's driveway, connected by a quiet passageway that passes above the underground piano bar. Set midway between

Montana and Crans, near the flashier Hôtel Crans-Ambassador, it offers spacious bedrooms with lots of exposed wood and small seating areas that give the fleeting impression that the rooms are equivalent to small suites. Most accommodations have private balconies, and each comes with a bathroom. This is one of the few hotels of Crans-Montana that remains open the entire year.

CH-3962 Crans-Montana. ✆ **027/485-41-11.** Fax 027/481-70-62. www.aida-castel.ch. 61 units. Winter 350F–500F double; summer 270F–360F double. Rates include half board. AE, DC, MC, V. Free parking. **Amenities:** 3 restaurants; bar; outdoor pool; room service; sauna. *In room:* TV, hair dryer, minibar, Wi-Fi (30F per 24 hr.).

Hôtel Alpina & Savoy ★ This is the oldest hotel in Crans, built in 1912. Owned by three generations of the Mudry family, it has been frequently modernized and expanded. The hotel remains consciously unfashionable but venerable, lying a short walk from the departure point for the Cry d'Err gondola. The bedrooms come in different shapes and sizes, but each is exceedingly comfortable with alpine decor, excellent plumbing, and a tidy bathroom.

Rte. touristique de Crans, CH-3963 Crans. ✆ **027/485-09-00.** Fax 027/485-09-99. www.alpina-savoy.ch. 45 units. Winter 250F–350F double, 440F–660F suite; summer 175F–250F double, 275F suite. Rates include half board. AE, DC, MC, V. Parking 20F. Closed mid-Apr to mid-June and mid-Sept to mid-Dec. **Amenities:** Restaurant; indoor heated pool; room service; sauna. *In room:* TV, minibar, Wi-Fi (30F per 24 hr.).

Moderate

Hôtel de la Forêt (Value) This is one of the better bargains in the area. A hotel of one kind or another has stood on this site, about half a mile east of Montana's center, since the turn of the 20th century. Skiers appreciate the hotel's proximity to the slopes—only 180m (590 ft.) from the cable car of Les Violettes-Plaine Morte. Alain and Serge Morard throw weekly raclette parties for their guests. The midsize bedrooms facing south have balconies and some barely perceptible noise from the road; those rooms facing north don't have balconies and get less sun but are quiet and offer views of the forest. Each unit comes with an efficiently organized bathroom.

CH-3962 Montana. ✆ **027/480-21-31.** Fax 027/481-31-20. www.delaforet.ch. 60 units. Winter 180F–310F double; summer 156F–276F double. Rates include half board. MC, V. Parking 15F. Closed mid-Apr to May and mid-Oct to mid-Dec. **Amenities:** Restaurant; bar; exercise room; indoor heated pool; room service; sauna. *In room:* TV, hair dryer.

Le Mont-Paisible ★ In a rustic setting with panoramic views in all directions, this chalet offers private viewing balconies from all its accommodations. The rooms facing south have panoramas of the Valaisan Alps from the Simplon to Mont Blanc. Each midsize bedroom is furnished in a traditional Swiss style, with comfortable beds and private bathrooms with tub or shower. An elegant French cuisine is served in the restaurant, its windows opening onto views of the mountains. In winter, guests gather in the lounge with an open fireplace.

Rte. d'Aminona, CH-3963 Crans-Montana. ✆ **027/480-21-61.** Fax 027/481-77-92. www.montpaisible.ch. 40 units. 130F–200F double. DC, MC, V. **Amenities:** Restaurant; bar; room service; outdoor tennis court (lit); Wi-Fi (free, in lobby). *In room:* TV.

WHERE TO DINE

Expensive

Hostellerie du Pas de l'Ours ★★★ SWISS/FRENCH Go here for the finest cuisine served in Crans-Montana. The talented chef, Franck Reynaud, betrays his Provençal roots in many of his dishes, each based on the best shopping in any season. His

foie gras is homemade, and he makes savory soups the way his grandmother did—that
is, with truffles. In inland Crans, he manages to get fresh seafood and lobster, which he
concocts into tempting dishes. He has a certain magic with sea bream and red mullet.

The stone in the lobby dates from the 16th century. In the lobby you'll also find a cozy
arrangement, perhaps a table near the fireplace, which blazes in winter. The hostellerie
also rents 14 well-furnished bedrooms, costing two persons 400F to 810F nightly.

14, rue du Pas de l'Ours. ✆ **027/485-93-33.** www.pasdelours.com. Fixed-price 3-course lunch 45F–65F;
fixed-price dinners 78F–125F for 5 courses, 84F–135F for 6 courses, 97F–155F for 7 courses, 109F–175F
for 8 courses. AE, DC, MC, V. Tues–Sat noon–1:30pm and 7–9:30pm. Closed May and Nov.

Le Cervin/La Bergerie ★ SWISS/FRENCH Set in a meadow above the twin
resorts, this red-shuttered, barnlike restaurant offers two different sections, both simply
decorated. The more formal Le Cervin, on the street level, is a well-upholstered *maison
bourgeoise* with lots of emphasis on the nuances of gastronomy. Here the French and
Swiss specialties are likely to include salmon steak with fresh mushrooms, tournedos with
onions, and salads studded with quail eggs and foie gras. La Bergerie, in the building's
basement, features *la cuisine valaisanne* and platters of raclettes, fondues, grilled steaks,
salads, and brochettes. The daily buffet in the brasserie is especially appealing.

Quartier Vermala, Crans. ✆ **027/481-21-80.** Reservations required in the evening. Le Cervin main
courses 35F–65F. La Bergerie platters 28F–38F. AE, DC, DISC, MC, V. Daily noon–2:30pm and 7:30–10pm.
Closed mid-Oct to mid-Dec.

Moderate

Auberge de la Diligence ⟨**Value**⟩ REGIONAL/LEBANESE This relatively inexpensive alpine tavern is on the highway beside the road leading in from Sierre. It specializes
in flavor-filled combinations of cuisine from both the Valais and faraway Lebanon, whose
spices and succulent flavors are much appreciated in the cold alpine air. The outdoor
terrace is popular on fine days, and there's ample parking nearby. Dishes include couscous and fondues, grilled fish and steaks, well-spiced kabobs of chicken and lamb, and a
succulent platter of Lebanese appetizers.

The hotel housing the tavern maintains nine bedrooms upstairs, five with a bathroom
and all with TV and phone. Each has a balcony and, although they're larger than you
might have expected, they come with almost no amenities or extra services. That fact
contributes to their reasonable value at 150F for a room with a bathroom, and 110F for
a room with shared facilities. Rates include breakfast. Both the hotel and its restaurant
are open year-round.

Quartier La Combaz, CH-3963 Crans-Montana. ✆ **027/485-99-85.** Fax 027/485-99-88. www.ladiligence.
ch. Reservations recommended in the evening. Main courses 18F–58F. AE, DC, MC, V. Restaurant daily
11:30am–2pm and 7–9:30pm. Cafe daily 8am–11:30pm.

Le Pavillon ★ SWISS Graced with a delightful lakeside locale—a verdant setting
near the Migros grocery store in the lowlands of "downtown" Montana—and an expansive terrace, Le Pavillon is popular in both winter and summer. You can drop in for
snacks and drinks at any time; at mealtimes, the chef presents a *cuisine du marché,* featuring fresh ingredients from the marketplace. Perfectly prepared menu items are likely to
include grilled filet of lamb with Provençal sauce, magret of duckling with orange sauce,
filet of beef with green peppercorns, a savory version of fondue *chinoise,* and trout and
perch from nearby lakes. Dessert includes a sorbet *valaisan,* flavored with apricots and
locally distilled apricot liqueur.

Montana. ☎ **027/481-24-69.** Reservations recommended. Main courses 28F–52F. AE, DC, MC, V. Daily noon–2pm and 7–10pm. Closed Mon–Tues in Apr–May and Oct, and 2–3 weeks in Nov.

Le Thai Restaurant ★ THAI   Chef Niyaka Faust arrived in Switzerland nearly 2 decades ago, and she learned to accommodate her native cooking to European tastes. And she has succeeded brilliantly. Her food is also influenced by Chinese recipes, especially stir fries, and Indian, especially curries. Her cuisine uses fresh herbs and spices instead of dried ingredients. The array of appetizers is among the tastiest at the resort, ranging from fried shrimp wraps to a vegetable–lemon grass salad. Chicken is a special treat here, especially the red chicken curry or the chili-jam chicken. Magret duck with Thai spices is another specialty. Fish can be fried crispy Thai style, or else you can enjoy one of several beef dishes. All dishes are served with a jasmine-perfumed rice.

12, rte. du Rawyl. ☎ **027/481-82-82.** Reservations required. Main courses 26F–42F. AE, DC, MC, V. Wed–Sat noon–2:30pm and 6–10pm; Sun 6–10pm.

CRANS-MONTANA AFTER DARK

Here's how the night scene works in the twin playgrounds of Montana and Crans: Head for a pub both before and after dinner. Suitably rowdy choices with a bit of flair and humor include **Amadeus Pub,** rue Centrale, in Crans-Montana (☎ **027/481-24-95**). After your obligatory pints of beer, which cost around 6F each, head off to any of the resort's discos, preferably after midnight. The best of them is **Xellent Club,** rue Centrale, in Crans (☎ **027/481-65-96**). The cover is around 20F, which includes the first drink, and both mingle—in ways that can be a lot of fun—electronic dance music with bouts of folkloric evergreen.

4 ZERMATT ★★★ & THE MATTERHORN ★★★

66km (41 miles) SE of Sierre; 48km (30 miles) SW of Brig; 242km (151 miles) E of Geneva

Zermatt, 1,594m (5,228 ft.) above sea level, is a small village at the base of the Matterhorn. It made its debut as a hiking and hill-climbing resort more than 150 years ago when it was discovered by English tourists. World attention was turned on the **Matterhorn** in the 1860s, when Edward Whymper, the English explorer and mountaineer, made a series of attempts to ascend it. Approaching the Matterhorn from the Italian side, he tried six times to climb it and failed. Then, on July 14, 1865, after changing his strategy and approaching the mountain from the Swiss side (using Zermatt as his departure point), he succeeded, and—accompanied by two of his guides—became the first person to reach the summit of the Matterhorn. During the process, however, four climbers in his team had fallen to their deaths.

Three days later, an Italian guide, Jean-Antoine Carrel, spurred on by the acclaim of Whymper's feat, successfully made the climb from the Italian side. Since then, the Matterhorn (known as Mont Cervin to the French-speaking Swiss) still lures mountain climbers, although only a few of them attempt to reach its summit. Two of the most memorable hikes are the climb up to the **Mettelhorn** (3,300m/10,824 ft.) and the hike up to the **Matterhorn Hut,** a few thousand feet below the wind-blasted cliffs that surround the summit.

Zermatt is a world-renowned resort with many luxurious accommodations and dozens of fashionable boutiques. You can walk from one end of the town to the other in about 15 minutes, which is handy because no cars are allowed on the local streets. The town does, however, have one of the best networks of alpine cable cars, gondolas, and cog railways in Switzerland—36 of them operating in the winter and 21 in the summer. In the peak season it's mobbed with hundreds of tourists.

Because more snow falls on Zermatt than on many other winter resorts in Europe, high-altitude skiing—especially at the Théodul Pass—continues throughout the spring and early summer. As for winter skiing, skiers can choose between wide, gentle slopes and difficult runs only for world-class champion skiers. Zermatt's **ski school** (© **027/966-24-66**) offers certified instruction and mountain guides.

From Zermatt, you can take one of the grandest and most scenic train rides in Europe. The **Glacier Express** (www.glacierexpress.ch) might be the slowest express train in the world, taking 7½ hours to pass through southeastern Switzerland, but it's the most panoramic. A stunning feat of mountain engineering, the train begins its daily run in Zermatt, heading for the resort of St. Moritz in the Engadine. Along the way it crosses 291 bridges and goes through 91 tunnels. Windows on the train are designed to take in these stunning mountain panoramas. There's also a dining car on board. Make advance reservations by calling **Rail Europe** at © **877/272-RAIL** (272-7245), or see their website at www.raileurope.com.

ESSENTIALS

GETTING THERE   Take a train to Visp or Brig, where you can transfer to a narrow-gauge train to Zermatt. Departures are every 20 minutes daily between 6am and 11:30pm. It's about a 4-hour trip from Geneva. For Swiss **rail information,** call © **0900/300-300.**

In addition, **buses** run from Visp and Brig to Täsch hourly, which is the departure point for the cog railway that ascends frequently to Zermatt. Call the tourist office (see below) for more information.

If you're **driving,** head to Täsch, 4.8km (3 miles) from Zermatt, and park your car in an open lot or a garage. A rail shuttle in the center of the village will then take you to the resort for 16F per person round-trip.

VISITOR INFORMATION   The **Zermatt Tourist Office** is on Bahnhofplatz (© **027/966-81-00;** www.zermatt.ch) and is open mid-June to September Monday to Saturday 8:30am to 6pm, and Sunday 8:30am to noon and 1:30 to 6pm. The rest of the year hours are Monday to Saturday 8:30am to noon and 1:30 to 6pm, and Sunday 9:30am to noon and 4 to 6pm.

Only a few of Zermatt's streets, notably Bahnhofstrasse, have names—most don't. To find your way around, you can rely on the dozens of signs pointing the way to the various hotels and restaurants at the resort.

SEEING THE SIGHTS

There are many diversions in Zermatt, including a popular curling center, with eight rinks, each equipped with precision-crafted curling stones. There are also two natural ice-skating rinks, unusual shops, and a variety of bars and restaurants.

SKIING & HIKING

There are a number of ski-lift passes sold in various combinations, but there isn't much savings regardless of the plan you select. A 2-day pass covering all the lifts in the Zermatt area costs 155F, while day passes cost 80F. The one break that ski-pass holders get is free rides on the ski bus linking all ski areas. To purchase tickets, visit the tourist office (see above).

GORNERGRAT ★★★ Gornergrat is perched at a lofty altitude of 3,099m (10,165 ft.). To get here, take a cogwheel train, the highest open-air railway in Europe, to its terminus. En route, you'll stop at **Riffelberg,** which offers a panoramic view of both the Matterhorn and Mount Rosa. The complete ride from Zermatt to Gornergrat is 76F round-trip in summer, 80F round-trip in winter. At Gornergrat an observatory looks out on the bleak expanses of the Gorner glacier and over the heights of the Dom, which, at nearly 4,572m (14,996 ft.), is the highest mountain entirely within Switzerland.

At Gornergrat you can take a cable car to other elevations. A two-stage cable car reaches a point near the top of the **Stockhorn,** at 3,407m (11,175 ft.); the cost is an additional 30F round-trip from Gornergrat.

BLAUHERD–UNTER ROTHHORN ★★ To get to Blauherd–Unter Rothorn, take a cog railway through a tunnel from Zermatt to the alpine meadows of Sunegga, and then transfer to a cable car. After changing cable cars at Blauherd (which offers many hiking and skiing options of its own), you'll continue by cable car to the flat, rocky summit of the Unter Rothorn, where possibilities for alpine rambles or ski descents abound.

SCHWARZSEE-THEODUL To reach Zermatt's third major ski area, take a cable car from Zermatt to **Furi-Schweigmatten** (usually abbreviated to Furi). Here you'll find a variety of cross-country skiing and hiking trails, and downhill skiing even in midsummer across the Théodul Pass and the border into Italy. In the winter you can continue downhill on skis to the Italian ski resort of Breuil-Cervinia for lunch, on the opposite side of the Matterhorn from Zermatt. At Furi a cable car carries you downhill to the calm waters of Schwarzsee (Black Lake) at 2,584m (8,476 ft.). Here the **Schwarzseehotel** (✆ **027/ 967-22-63**) offers vistas plus a terrace for lunch or a drink. Some skiers depart from Schwarzsee for another series of lonely but spectacular downhill runs. The round-trip excursion from Zermatt via Furi to Schwarzsee costs 47F.

KLEIN MATTERHORN ★★★ To reach the "Little Matterhorn" from Furi, you must take two additional cable cars (the first of which will transfer at an alpine junction named Trockenersteg) before reaching an elevator that will carry you up to one of the highest mountain terraces in the world (3,760m/12,333 ft.). If the sky is clear, you'll be able to see both the French and the Italian Alps and breathe a rarefied air usually reserved for the hardiest of alpine climbers. The excursion to Klein Matterhorn from Zermatt costs 90F round-trip.

SHOPPING

Zermatt's critics accuse it of combining a hard-nosed commercialism, shrewdly calculating the value of every snowflake, with a less harsh obsession with Swiss folklore. Consequently, the town's main shopping thoroughfare, **Bahnhofstrasse,** contains branches of stores you might have expected only in much larger cities, with an emphasis on luxury goods, alpine souvenirs, and sporting goods. Ski and mountaineering equipment here tends to be state of the art. Stores selling the stuff appear virtually everywhere, but one worthwhile example is **Slalom Sport,** Steinmatt (✆ **027/966-23-66;** www.slalom-sport. ch), close to the village church. Well-recommended competitors, both on Bahnhofstrasse near the Gornergrat cable car, include **Glacier Sport** (✆ **027/967-27-19**) and **Bayard Sport** (✆ **027/966-49-50**).

Local souvenirs in Zermatt include everything from the genuinely artful to the hopelessly kitschy. One outlet is **WEGA,** on Bahnhofplatz (✆ **027/967-21-66**).

Snow and ice aren't the only things that sparkle in Zermatt, so if you're susceptible to
impulse purchases of jewelry, one of the best places to browse is **Bijouterie Schindler,** Bahnhofstrasse 5 (✆ **027/967-11-18**), which stockpiles both Swiss watches and gemstones.

WHERE TO STAY

Zermatt has something for most budgets. It contains more than 120 hotels and guesthouses, plus a growing array of private apartments and condominiums. Some hotels
make arrangements to meet clients at the cog-railway station if you inform them in
advance of your arrival.

Very Expensive

Grand Hotel Zermatterhof ★★★   This white-walled 1879 hotel, Zermatt's
grandest resort, pointedly refuses to imitate a chalet. Rated five stars by the Swiss government, it's more plush and comfortable than anything in town. The bedrooms are paneled
and well upholstered, with vivid colors. Alpine-style furnishings add a warm, cozy ambience, and each room is equipped with deluxe beds, plus marble and tile bathrooms
boasting dual basins, robes, and heated towel racks. In summer, a carriage awaits guests
at the rail station at Täsch.

Bahnhofstrasse, CH-3920 Zermatt. ✆ **027/966-66-00.** Fax 027/967-66-99. www.zermatt.ch/zermatterhof.
84 units. Winter 640F–830F double, 1,235F–2,320F suite; off season 460F–660F double, 780F–1,930F
suite. Rates include half board. AE, DC, MC, V. **Amenities:** 2 restaurants; 2 bars; babysitting; children's
center; exercise room; Jacuzzi; outdoor pool; room service. *In room:* TV, hair dryer, minibar, Wi-Fi (free).

Mont Cervin Palace ★★★   This has remained one of Zermatt's leading hotels since
it was established in 1872. The rooms are often sunny and spacious, with fine craftsmanship. Units in the old quarter are more old-fashioned and still preferred by traditionalists.
Accommodations in the newest wing have a restrained classic decor, and some are decorated in regional stucco along with hand-carved blond-wood pieces. You and your bags
will be picked up at the rail station by a horse-drawn sleigh in the winter or by an old-
fashioned horse-drawn carriage in the summer.

Bahnhofstrasse 31, CH-3920 Zermatt. ✆ **800/223-6800** in the U.S. and Canada or 027/966-88-88. Fax
027/966-88-99. www.seiler-hotels.ch. 133 units. Winter 600F–950F double, from 1,000F suite; summer
330F–685F double, from 695F suite. Rates include buffet breakfast. AE, DC, MC, V. Closed mid-Apr to mid-
June and mid-Oct to end of Nov. **Amenities:** 2 restaurants; bar; babysitting; exercise room; 2 heated
pools (1 indoor, 1 outdoor); room service; spa. *In room:* TV, hair dryer, minibar, Wi-Fi (free).

Riffelalp Resort 2222 ★★ **(Finds)**   Set within a 20-minute cog-railway ride north of
Zermatt, this resort sits on sloping terrain midway up the mountain, in the midst of
some of the region's most venerated skiing. It originated in 1884, when ancestors of the
present owners (the Seiler family) erected a Victorian-style summer-only hotel, which
was eventually damaged in a disastrous fire in 1961. Since then, the original building (the
"Nostalgia wing") has been repaired and enlarged with a modern annex ("the Chalet").
This government-rated five-star resort offers quick access to the region's spectacular hiking, skiing, and views. The Gornergrat cable car will carry you even higher into the Alps
(all the way to the Stockhorn) if you want more altitude, or down into Zermatt if you're
looking for a rowdy good time in the town's bars, discos, or restaurants.

Riffelalp, 3920 Zermatt. ✆ **027/966-05-55.** Fax 027/966-05-50. www.riffelalp.com. 72 units. Winter
630F–1,050F double, 920F–2,500F suite; summer 410F–620F double, 690F–1,300F suite. Rates include
buffet breakfast in summer, half board in winter. AE, DC, MC, V. Closed mid-Oct to mid-Dec and mid-Apr
to mid-June. From Zermatt, take the Gornergrat cable car to its halfway point, Riffelalp. **Amenities:**

2 restaurants (1 w/outdoor terrace); bar; fitness room; Jacuzzi; 2 heated pools (1 indoor, 1 outdoor); room service; sauna. *In room:* TV, minibar, Wi-Fi (free).

Expensive

Hotel Butterfly   This Best Western hotel lies under a peaked roof, with large windows and flower boxes. The Alps loom in the distance. The interior is warm and cozy, with arched windows, Oriental rugs, and knotty-pine furniture. Mrs. Gunda Woischnig offers small to midsize rooms with balconies facing south, all of them renovated in the late 1990s. The well-stocked hotel bar serves as an intimate rendezvous point, and a buffet breakfast is served.

CH-3920 Zermatt. ✆ **027/966-41-66.** Fax 027/966-41-65. www.hotelbutterflyzermatt.com. 61 units. 190F–350F double. Rates include buffet breakfast. Half board 35F per person. AE, DC, MC, V. Closed mid-Oct to mid-Dec. **Amenities:** Restaurant; bar; exercise room; room service; sauna. *In room:* TV, hair dryer, minibar, Wi-Fi (free).

Hotel Riffelberg   Set in an alpine meadow 2,460m (8,069 ft.) above sea level, a 90-minute trek or a 30-minute cog-railway ride from Zermatt, this isolated hotel sits amid natural splendor in the shadow of the Matterhorn. Built in 1853 by a local clergyman and purchased by the city of Zermatt in 1873, it has served as a well-maintained hotel and restaurant ever since, with the kind of views that restore health to bodies and minds. Because of its altitude, the area gets 8 full hours of sunlight in December, and even more in midsummer. Skiing between December and April, thanks to the nearby Gornergrat cableway, is excellent. Despite several recent renovations, the Riffelberg retains a simple alpine decor in its comfortable but small bedrooms. Round-trip transit from Zermatt on the cog railway costs 76F per person, and the last train from Zermatt departs at 6pm. The Riffelsee is not far from the train stop; an ibex colony lives nearby as well.

CH-3920 Zermatt-Umgebung. ✆ **027/966-65-00.** Fax 027/966-65-05. www.matterhorn-group.ch. 29 units. Winter 350F–400F double, 540F–580F quad; summer 350F double, 370F quad. Rates include half board. AE, DC, MC, V. Closed mid-Oct to mid-Dec. **Amenities:** 2 restaurants; bar; exercise room; Jacuzzi; room service; sauna; Wi-Fi (free, in lobby). *In room:* TV, minibar.

Hotel Walliserhof ★★ (Finds)   Originally a Valaisian farmhouse, this hotel is one of the most successful conversions in town. It enjoys much German patronage, ever since the German newspaper *Bunte* named it "Swiss Hotel of the Year" a few years back. Renovations have made it worthy of a four-star government rating. In the center of town, with its red shutters and balconies, it's easy to spot. It offers a large terrace out front, and inside you'll find stone fireplaces, thick walls, masonry columns, and flagstone floors. The midsize carpeted bedrooms have wooden furniture and good beds, plus neat bathrooms.

Bahnhofstrasse, CH-3920 Zermatt. ✆ **027/966-65-55.** Fax 027/967-65-50. www.reconline.ch/walliserhof. 30 units. Winter 300F–470F double, 350F–580F suite; summer 340F–370F double, 390F–480F suite. Rates include half board. AE, MC, V. **Amenities:** 2 restaurants; bar; room service. *In room:* TV, hair dryer, minibar.

Romantik Hotel Julen ★★   Across the river from Zermatt's historic cemetery, this hotel (ca. 1937), with its weathered balconies, is Zermatt's most romantic. The midsize bedrooms are furnished in mountain-resort style with carved pine beds and ceramic-tile bathrooms. Try for one on the south side—they have balconies with views of the Matterhorn. The main dining room features French cuisine and has an ornate ceiling and paneled walls. In addition, the Schäferstübli offers more informal fare in a setting of pine wood, ceiling beams, and the inevitable cowbells. The hotel has installed an entire spa, and on the third floor is a "dreamshower" (you select what you want, from warm tropical to ice-cold glacier).

CH-3920 Zermatt. 𝄡 **027/966-76-00.** Fax 027/966-76-76. www.zermatt.ch/julen. 32 units. Winter 530F–608F double, 672F–800F suite; summer 350F–456F double, 410F–660F suite. Rates include half board. AE, DC, MC, V. **Amenities:** 2 restaurants; bar; babysitting; exercise room; indoor heated pool; room service; spa. *In room:* TV, hair dryer, minibar, Wi-Fi (free).

Schlosshotel Tenne ★

The chiseled stonework and baroque-style stepped roofs, coupled with the Art Nouveau decor of its bedrooms and public rooms, make this hotel a welcome change from the many chalet-style hotels that surround it. Comfort and service are key here, and you live well in alpine surroundings, with stunning views in most directions. Beds are exceedingly comfortable, and the private tiled bathrooms are of a good size. Each of its junior suites contains a whirlpool bathtub and a separate sitting room with fireplace. All south-facing rooms have private balconies.

Bahnhofplatz 18, CH-3920 Zermatt. 𝄡 **027/966-44-00.** Fax 027/966-44-05. www.schlosshotel-tenne.ch. 38 units. Winter 320F–400F double, 400F–440F junior suite for 2; summer 230F–340F double, 340F–380F junior suite for 2. Rates include buffet breakfast. AE, MC, V. Closed May and Oct–Nov. **Amenities:** Restaurant; bar; exercise room; Jacuzzi; room service; sauna. *In room:* TV, hair dryer.

Seiler Hotel Monte Rosa ★

According to Edward Whymper, the Englishman who conquered the Matterhorn, this is the best hotel at Zermatt. Of course, he made that pronouncement back in 1865. Monte Rosa has long since lost that position but still holds its own as one of the most welcoming and traditional hotels in the Valais. Located on the main street, the Monte Rosa has stone posts, lintels, and red shutters around its windows. The lounges have parquet floors, thick rugs, and crackling fireplaces; the antique armchairs are beautifully upholstered in stripes and patterns. The midsize to spacious bedrooms, decorated with Victorian prints and cabinetry, are among the most comfortable in Zermatt. Rooms facing south are the most desirable, the most expensive, and the hardest to come by. Each unit comes with a good-size, immaculately kept private bathroom.

Bahnhofstrasse 80, CH-3920 Zermatt. 𝄡 **800/223-6800** in the U.S. or 027/966-03-33. Fax 027/966-03-30. www.seiler-hotels.ch. 47 units. Winter 405F–800F double, 880F–2,370F suite; summer 280F–520F double, 620F–1,560F suite. Rates include breakfast in summer, half board in winter. AE, DC, MC, V. Closed mid-Sept to mid-Dec. **Amenities:** Restaurant; bar; babysitting; room service. *In room:* TV, hair dryer, minibar, Wi-Fi (free).

Moderate

Hotel Post ★ (Finds)

Built in 1880, and extensively rebuilt in the 1950s when American-born Karl Ivarsson and his family acquired it, this hotel is better known for its sprawling restaurant and nightlife facilities than for its bedrooms. There's a definite Anglo influence here, not only from the Americans attracted to the place but the increasing numbers of Brits as well. The small to midsize bedrooms have unusual floor plans, deliberately mismatched pieces of antique furniture, modern plumbing, and in some cases a TV. By no means should you assume that the Hotel Post falls into the predictable mold of the typical Swiss hotel. Its clients tend to be the most iconoclastic in Zermatt, and have included many of the great names in British rock 'n' roll, including David Bowie. Fittingly, the Post's labyrinth of nightlife facilities are the loudest, the most irreverent, and the most fun in Zermatt.

Bahnhofstrasse, CH-3920 Zermatt. 𝄡 **027/967-19-32.** Fax 027/967-41-14. www.hotelpost.ch. 21 units. Winter 206F–292F double, 328F–360F deluxe double; summer 199F–299F double, 299F–399F deluxe double. Rates include buffet breakfast. AE, DC, MC, V. **Amenities:** 3 restaurants; 5 bars; babysitting; room service; spa. *In room:* TV/DVD, CD player, hair dryer, MP3 docking station, Wi-Fi (free).

Inexpensive

Hotel Alphubel (**Value**) Located near the train station, this is a large chalet with a solid stone foundation and curved stairs leading to the entrance. The Julen family named it after a local mountaintop. The small rooms are decorated in a functional, modern style with well-maintained bathrooms. The restaurant is open for half-board guests only and serves good, moderately priced dishes.

CH-3920 Zermatt. 🕿 **027/967-30-03.** Fax 027/967-66-84. www.zermatt.ch/alphubel. 30 units. 144F–246F double. Rates include buffet breakfast. AE, MC, V. Closed mid-Oct to mid-Nov. **Amenities:** Restaurant; bar; sauna. *In room:* TV, hair dryer.

Hotel Antika ★ Set behind an attractive chalet facade, each of the bedrooms of this hotel opens onto its own covered loggia with flower boxes and wooden trim. Making use of wood furnishings, rooms have an alpine charm and cozy comfort, with excellent beds. Most offer mountain views. The interior is accented with Oriental carpets and a partial sheathing of weathered planks. A large garden behind the hotel is great for quiet contemplation of the Matterhorn.

CH-3920 Zermatt. 🕿 **027/967-21-51.** Fax 027/967-57-83. www.antika.ch. 28 units. Winter 106F–245F double; summer 106F–185F double. Rates include buffet breakfast. AE, DC, MC, V. Closed May and mid-Oct to mid-Nov. **Amenities:** Restaurant; Jacuzzi; room service; sauna. *In room:* TV, hair dryer.

Hotel Darioli ★ This five-story, balconied hotel is on the main street near the train station. Built in 1964, the hotel was completely overhauled in 1979 and has been renovated often since. It's one of the few hotels in Zermatt to remain open all year, although its restaurant closes in November. This is one of the best government-rated three-star hotels in town; many guests prefer it to some hotels with higher ratings. The reception area is upstairs. The hotel has Oriental rugs and an attractive wooden bar. The Darioli family offers comfortable midsize rooms with regional furniture, usually painted in vivid colors with stenciled floral patterns. Most of the rooms have private bathrooms. One of the most consistently popular restaurants in Zermatt, Le Gitan (see below), is on this hotel's street level.

Bahnhofstrasse, CH-3920 Zermatt. 🕿 **027/967-27-48.** Fax 027/967-12-37. www.darioli.ch. 12 units, 8 with bathroom. 100F–210F double. Rates include buffet breakfast. AE, MC, V. **Amenities:** 2 restaurants; 2 bars; room service. *In room:* TV (in some).

Hotel Tannenhof (**Value**) The hotel is located in the center of the village, just a 3-minute walk from the train station and lying just off the Bahnhofstrasse (follow the signposts onto a pathway). The atmosphere is rustic and the rooms are simple and a bit small, but the place fills up quickly in winter. The hotel has simple alpine furnishings, including good beds, along with thick, cozy rugs.

Bahnhofstrasse, CH-3920 Zermatt. 🕿 **027/967-31-88.** Fax 027/967-21-73. www.rhone.ch/tannenhof. 23 units, 14 with bathroom. 90F–120F double without bathroom, 110F–160F with bathroom. Rates include buffet breakfast. AE, DC, MC, V. Closed Oct to mid-Dec.

Hotel Weisshorn Convenient for frugal travelers arriving at the train station, this is a bargain in this otherwise high-priced resort area. However, if you're planning a winter visit, make reservations as far in advance as possible, as the hotel fills up quickly. You don't get luxury here, but you're provided with alpine comfort in a setting of low-paneled ceilings and winding staircases. The place is snug and cozy as the blizzards rage outside.

The bedrooms are small but adequate, with plush comforters and, in some cases, small balconies.

Am Bach 6, CH-3920 Zermatt. ☎ **027/967-11-12.** Fax 027/967-38-39. www.holidaynet.ch/weisshorn. 16 units, 7 with bathroom. 122F–160F double with bathroom, 98F–122F without bathroom. Rates include buffet breakfast. MC, V. **Amenities:** Restaurant. *In room:* TV.

WHERE TO DINE
Expensive
Alex Grill ★ SWISS   This stylish basement restaurant is decorated with carved paneling, leaded windows, flagstone floors, bright upholstery, and rich accessories. The chefs concoct appetizing dishes based on regional and Swiss recipes prepared with market-fresh ingredients. As an appetizer, try a platter of three kinds of smoked fish or fresh Atlantic oysters. The main courses include grilled lobster, grilled salmon scallop, and giant shrimp with a chive-flavored cream sauce. The meat dishes include veal kidneys in mustard sauce, grilled rack of lamb, chicken breast filled with a salmon-and-herb mousse, and a variety of game in season.

In the Hotel Alex, Bodmenstrasse. ☎ **027/966-70-70.** Reservations recommended. Main courses 40F–55F. AE, MC, V. Daily noon–2pm and 7–9:30pm. Closed May to mid-June and mid-Oct to mid-Nov.

The Grill Room/the Stübli ★ ITALIAN/SWISS   In what was originally built as a farmhouse, in the heart of town, these restaurants—unlike many of their competitors—remain open every day throughout the year. The Grill Room is the more elegant of the two, serving French, German, and Italian fare. There's an especially elegant collection of hors d'oeuvres, including smoked salmon, and main courses, such as veal cutlets and brook trout with almonds or veal piccata with risotto. The commendable regional dishes are filled with rich, subtle flavors. The less formal Stübli serves basically the same menu but concentrates on alpine Swiss specialties, such as fondues, raclettes, and grilled meats, in a cozy setting.

In the Hotel Walliserhof, Bahnhofstrasse. ☎ **027/966-65-55.** Reservations recommended. Main courses 23F–50F. AE, DC, MC, V. Daily 11am–2pm and 7–11pm.

Le Gitan ★ SWISS   This is neither the most formal restaurant in town nor the most glamorous. Despite that, reservations during the winter ski season are sometimes booked a week in advance, and virtually everyone in town seems to pick Le Gitan as his or her favorite restaurant. Set on the street level of a well-managed three-star hotel, the interior is very cozy, with an open fireplace and room for no more than 50 diners. With a wide selection of Swiss and regional specialties available, the array of grilled meats is the house specialty. The grilled beef, veal, game, and pork dishes are all richly garnished and impressively presented. Of special note is an excellent *gigot d'agneau* (lamb) with garlic, and a selection of savory fondues served in the bistro in front of the restaurant.

In the Hotel Darioli, Bahnhofstrasse. ☎ **027/968-19-40.** www.darioli.ch. Reservations required. Main courses 19F–45F. AE, MC, V. Daily 6:30–10pm.

Schlosshotel Tenne ★ SWISS/INTERNATIONAL   In the lobby level of the previously recommended hotel of the same name, this duplex restaurant includes an upper wraparound gallery and a ceiling fresco covered with a representation of the zodiac. The kitchen continues to steer a steady course between rich, regional specialties and the subtler flavors of an international repertoire. Ingredients are first-rate, and the restaurant is known for its grill specialties. The menu may include herb-flavored shrimp soup, whole-meal

ZERMATT & THE MATTERHORN

noodles, roast salmon in a white-wine sauce, or rack of lamb from the grill. For dessert, try cherries flambé with a honey parfait.

In the Schlosshotel Tenne. ✆ **027/966-44-00.** Reservations required in winter. Main courses 22F–60F. AE, MC, V. Daily 7–9:30pm. Closed mid-Oct to mid-Dec.

Moderate

Arvenstube SWISS/INTERNATIONAL   A tempting variety of international and Swiss dishes is served in this paneled dining room with a corner bar. The chefs here continue to please visitors year after year with their skill. As an appetizer, try the *assiette valaisanne,* a plate of air-dried meats from the Grisons. Other specialties include *riz Casimir* (a curry rice dish), tournedos in a savory-mustard sauce, and sliced veal in a mushroom-cream sauce. These dishes are often served with *rösti* (Swiss hash browns). Trout with almonds is another favorite.

In the Hotel Pollux, Bahnhofstrasse. ✆ **027/966-40-00.** Reservations recommended. Main courses 23F–68F. AE, DC, MC, V. Daily 11:30am–2pm and 6–9pm. Closed 2 or 3 weeks in Nov.

Findlerhof ★★ (Finds) SWISS/ITALIAN   The Findlerhof is the best mountain restaurant near Zermatt. Despite its remote location—in the small hamlet of Findeln, on a steep mountainside—the place is very popular. It has a sun terrace and a roof terrace facing the Matterhorn. Your hosts are Franz and Heidi Schwery, who offer such delights as meat and salmon carpaccio, salads laced with salmon and scampi, and excellent pasta dishes.

Findeln. ✆ **027/967-25-88.** www.findlerhof.ch. Reservations required. Main courses 23F–49F. MC, V. Daily 11am–6pm. Take the Sunnegga chairlift to the 1st stop, then hike across the fields; leave your skis in the snow and head down the steep, winding pathway, past the plastic palm trees.

Grillroom Stockhorn ★ SWISS   This restaurant is one of the two or three best dining rooms in town. A fireplace extends into the dining room of this elegant chalet owned by Michel Julen. The decor includes an alpine wedding chest and regional chairs, as well as travertine floors, heavy beams, varnished pine, earth-tone accents, and stained stucco walls. The savory, rib-sticking specialties include raclette, piccata with spaghetti, fondue bourguignon, and grilled meats. Chocolate fondue is recommended for dessert. There's also a bar. The restaurant lies in the Hotel Stockhorn, which has only four bedrooms, each with a private balcony and shower, costing 115F to 150F for a double.

Riedstrasse. ✆ **027/967-17-47.** www.grill-stockhorn.ch. Reservations required. Main courses 22F–43F. AE, MC, V. Daily 6:30–10pm. Closed May to mid-June and Oct to mid-Nov.

Portofino Grill INTERNATIONAL   Decorated in tones of marine blue with lots of highly varnished wood, this is the most elegant of the several dining choices in the Hotel Post. A fresh antipasto buffet is laid out in what used to be a boat, and the cuisine—which some visitors consider a welcome change from a constant diet of Swiss alpine food—features seafood and Italian choices. Menu items include a selection of homemade pastas with savory sauces, and freshly prepared veal, poultry, and meat dishes. Many diners opt for a before- or after-dinner drink in the Boathouse Bar. Crafted from the cabin of a once-glamorous three-masted schooner, it seats only a dozen drinkers in cozy, knee-rubbing proximity. The spillover from the main bar moves into what's affectionately known as "the Disaster Room," where photos of the 20th century's greatest marine disasters are prominently displayed.

In the Hotel Post. ✆ **027/967-19-32.** Reservations recommended. Main courses 20F–45F. AE, DC, MC, V. Dec–Apr daily 7–11pm. Closed Easter–Nov.

Schäferstübli SWISS   This moderately priced restaurant offers atmospheric dining amid plank-covered walls, heavy beams, flickering candles, and leaded-glass windows. If you're not already a convert of Swiss cuisine, you may easily become one after a meal here. The house specialty is lamb, served in a variety of styles. You can also order grilled veal and beef dishes, traditionally prepared. The restaurant is part of the Romantik Hotel Julen but has its own separate entrance.

In the Romantik Hotel Julen. ✆ **027/966-76-00.** Reservations required. Main courses 14F–35F; lamb fondues 45F per person; cheese fondues 25F per person; all-you-can-eat raclette 45F per person. AE, DC, MC, V. Daily 6–9:30pm. Closed May and 2 weeks in Nov.

Walliserkanne SWISS/ITALIAN   This rustic family restaurant is 2 minutes from the Zermatt train station. Walliserkanne is divided into three main dining rooms and a second restaurant in the basement. The elegant rooms are large and feature paintings by local artists on the walls. The restaurant offers a delectable menu of Italian dishes such as antipasto *misto della casa* (variety of Italian starters), carpaccio *d'agnello con rucola e parmigiano* (thin slices of raw lamb served with arugula and Parmesan), or *vitello tonnato* (slices of roast veal with tuna fish sauce). Pizzas and pastas round out the succulent fare. The menu also offers a wide choice of desserts.

Bahnhofstrasse 32. ✆ **027/966-46-10.** www.walliserkanne.ch. Reservations recommended. Main courses 23F–38F. AE, MC, V. Daily 11:30am–2pm and 6–10pm.

ZERMATT AFTER DARK

Zermatt is known for its après-ski activities, which include tea dances, restaurants, bars, nightclubs, and discos. It has more nightclubs than any other resort in the Valais.

An Entertainment Complex

Hotel Post (✆ **027/967-19-31;** www.hotelpost.ch; see review above), where everybody shows up after recovering from Elsie's Irish coffee (see below), has a virtual monopoly on nightlife in Zermatt. The owner, Karl Ivarsson, an American, has gradually expanded it into one of the most complete entertainment complexes in Zermatt, with a number of restaurants and nightspots under one roof. Photographs of former guests, including famous athletes and models, are displayed under glass at the reception desk. On the way to the restaurant, in the basement, you'll pass a series of murals telling the story of a lonely tourist looking for love in Zermatt.

Take your pick of the various venues, including the **Jazz Bar,** open December to Easter and 1 month in summer. In winter they import a different band every year, although there's only a piano player in summer. The **Broken Bar,** located in the basement, is where the most hardened ski bums listen to hard-rock music at very high volumes, drink heavily, and generally raise hell. For hunger pangs, head for the **Brown Cow** at street level, a rustic room with 19th-century farm implements hanging from the ceiling. The menu includes hamburgers, goulash soup, sandwiches, and salads.

The Bar Scene

Elsie's Bar, at Kirchplatz (✆ **027/967-24-31;** www.elsiebar.ch), is a small house, dating from 1879, that packs in a large crowd around 6pm. It's comfortable, sedate, and bourgeois. Skiers show up for hot chocolate or Elsie's famous Irish coffee. The house is on the main street, near the Zermatterhof Hotel. During the day the menu includes ham and eggs, hot dogs, and even escargots. They also serve caviar and oysters (a special luxury in this area). The cafe is open in the winter daily from 11am to 2am and in the summer daily from 4pm to 2am.

One of the most animated and energetic bars is **Grampy's Pub,** Bahnhofstrasse (② 027/967-77-88), across from the Hotel Post, a pub and disco favored by the resort's army of off-duty waiters, bartenders, chambermaids, and ski instructors. A roughly equivalent competitor is the **Papperla Pub** (② 027/967-40-40; www.papperlapub.ch), near the Hotel Julen, where live music produced by Swiss folk and North American country-and-western bands gets your blood pumping.

Hotels that contain relatively animated pubs include the Hotel Bristol, the Schlosshotel Tenne, and the Hotel Excelsior. The least pretentious of the lot is the **Kegelstube** (**"Bowling Alley Bar"**) in the Hotel Bristol (② 027/966-33-80), where the resort's only bowling alley adds visual distraction to the large bar area. Upstairs, the more formal **Bristol Bar** has a dance floor, a fireplace, and a view of the attached restaurant. The Schlosshotel Tenne's most appealing after-dark spot is the **Bar Tenne** (② 027/966-44-00), whose Art Nouveau decor is a welcome change from the relentless emphasis on Swiss chalets everywhere else. Here, near a bar that resembles an ambulatory in a monastery, and a DJ booth that might have been a church pulpit, you can relax on comfortable sofas or dance beneath the klieg lights of a circular dance floor. In the Hotel Excelsior (② 027/966-35-00), you can head for the sometimes rowdy and garrulous **Ex-Bar,** or seek refuge in the somewhat calmer, somewhat more upscale, winter-only **Luna Bar,** which is shielded from the noise nearby by thick doors and masonry walls.

Hotel Simi (② 027/966-46-00), with its Dancing Simi, combines a regime of Swiss folklore and oompah music with alpine warmth, a busy bar area, platters of food, and some emphasis on disco. You'll find a rough approximation of big-city, urban life in the form of the **Scotch Corner Bar,** in the Hotel Aristella (② 027/967-20-41). You can always grab a beer and a shot or two of schnapps in the cozy setting of the Hotel Walliserhof's **Stübli** (② 027/966-65-55).

11

Lausanne & Lake Geneva

For decades, visitors have sought out the scenic wonders of Lake Geneva (Lac Léman) in the southwestern corner of Switzerland. Native son Jean-Jacques Rousseau popularized the lake among the Romantics, and Lord Byron and Shelley both made pilgrimages here.

Formed by the Rhône, Lac Léman is the largest lake in central Europe. It consists of the Grand Lac to the east and the Petit Lac to the west, near Geneva (for a description of Geneva and its environs, see chapter 12). The lake covers 582 sq. km (225 sq. miles); more than half belongs to Switzerland, the rest to France. The French own most of the southern shore, except for Geneva in the west and the Valais in the east; the Swiss hold the entire northern shore, which forms a large arc. The water is limpid blue, except where the muddy Rhône empties into it.

Famous people who chose to live on the lake's shores have included the historian Edward Gibbon; writers Honoré de Balzac, George Eliot, and André Gide; composers Richard Wagner and Franz Liszt; the aviator Charles Lindbergh; and actors Charlie Chaplin, Yul Brynner, Audrey Hepburn, James Mason, Noel Coward, William Holden, David Niven, and Sophia Loren (many of whom went here originally for tax reasons but liked the area so much that they stayed on until their deaths). Some of these actors, such as Chaplin and Hepburn, adopted Switzerland as their permanent home and were buried here.

Since 1823 steamer trips have been the most popular way to tour the lake. Nearly all the cities, hamlets, and towns along the lake have schedules posted at the landing quays, and service usually runs from Easter to October. If possible, though, we recommend touring by car or bus so that you can stop and visit sights along the way. Railways also run along both shores. Our exploration will begin with Lausanne.

1 LAUSANNE ★★

66km (41 miles) NE of Geneva; 214km (133 miles) SW of Zurich

Lausanne, whose 140,000 inhabitants make it the second-largest city on Lake Geneva and the fifth largest in Switzerland, is built on three hills overlooking the lake. The upper and lower towns are connected by a small metro (subway).

Lausanne has been inhabited since the Stone Age (it was the ancient Roman town of Lousanna). In 1803 the canton of Vaud, of which Lausanne is the capital, became the 19th to join the Swiss Confederation.

For centuries Lausanne has been a favorite spot for exiles and expatriates, attracting, among others, deposed monarchs. Lausanne flourished particularly in the Age of Enlightenment, when it was associated with Rousseau and Voltaire, two of the leading writers in the 18th century. Even today the city is cited by many French-speaking Swiss as the place they would most like to live because of its low-key elegance and sense of grace. Regrettably, it's no longer a center of the intellectual or artistic elite. Voltaire and the likes have given way to water-skiers, swimmers, and "Sunday sailors," most of whom have never heard of Rousseau, much less read him. Even so, Lausanne retains an aesthetic charm and a cultural tradition—today it's the headquarters of the International Olympic Committee.

ESSENTIALS

GETTING THERE   Lausanne doesn't have a major airport (just a small airport reserved just for private aircraft), so most visitors fly to Cointrin Airport in Geneva (see chapter 12) and then travel on to Lausanne. The **train** from Geneva leaves for Lausanne every 20 minutes and the trip takes between 30 and 45 minutes, depending on the individual train. Call ✆ **0900/300-300** for **train** schedules.

In addition, between late May and late September, a lake steamer cruises several times a day in both directions between Geneva and Saint-Gingolph, Lausanne, Vevey, Montreux, and Nyon. Sailing time from Geneva is about 3½ hours. Round-trip transit from Geneva costs 91F in first class and 67F in second class, with 50% discounts for children 16 and under. For information, contact the **Compagnie Générale de Naviga-tion (CGN),** 17, av. de Rhodanie (✆ **0848/811-848;** www.cgn.ch).

If you're **driving,** Lausanne is connected by freeway (N1) to Geneva. The Great Saint Bernard road tunnel is 113km (70 miles) to the southeast, reached along E2, which becomes E21 during your final approach. The speed limit on most of the highways lead-ing into Lausanne, and throughout the rest of Switzerland as well, is 120kmph (75 mph).

VISITOR INFORMATION   There are two branches of the **Office du Tourisme et des Congrès** in Lausanne. The larger of the two faces the lakefront in Ouchy, at 2, av. de Rhodanie (✆ **021/613-73-21** or 613-73-73; www.lausanne-tourisme.ch). Hours are Monday to Friday 8am to 5pm, Saturday and Sunday 9am to 5pm. The tourist office in the railway station (✆ **021/321-77-66**) is open daily, year-round, 9am to 5pm.

CITY LAYOUT

Lausanne is spread out along the shore of Lake Geneva, surrounded by suburbs. There are two sections in particular that attract the most visitors—the **Upper Town (Haute Ville)** and the once-industrial neighborhood of Flon, which collectively comprise the oldest parts of the city, and the **Lower Town (Basse Ville),** and its lake-fronting district of **Ouchy;** the two sections are connected by a small subway (metro). The metro features 14 separate stations instead of its previous 4, thereby incorporating Lausanne with many of its outlying suburbs. This is the only underground (metro) in Switzerland.

Haute Ville ★★

Lausanne's Upper Town still evokes the Middle Ages—a night watchman calls out the hours from 10pm to 2am from atop the cathedral's belfry. A visit to the Haute Ville takes about 2 hours and is best done on foot. In fact, walking through the old town of Laus-anne is one of its major attractions. It's easy to get lost—and that's part of the fun. This area is north of the railroad station; you can reach it by proceeding uphill along rue du Petit-Chêne. The focal point of the Upper Town, and the shopping and business heart of Lausanne, is **place Saint-François.** The Church of St. François, from the 13th century, is all that remains of an old Franciscan friary. Today, the square is filled with office blocks and the main post office; regrettably, La Grotte, the villa with the terrace on which Edward Gibbon completed *The History of the Decline and Fall of the Roman Empire* in 1787, was torn down in 1896 to make room for the post office. While vehicles are

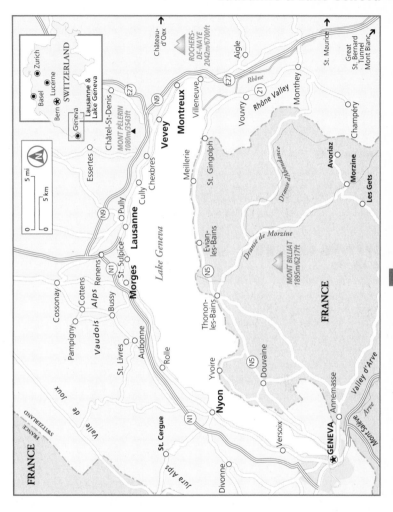

permitted south of the church, the historic area to the north of the church is a pedestrian-only zone; it has more than 2km (1¼ miles) of streets, including **rue de Bourg,** northeast of the church, the best street for shopping. Rue de Bourg leads to the large, bustling rue Caroline, which winds north to **Pont des Bessières,** one of the three bridges erected at the turn of the 20th century to connect the three hills on which Lausanne was built. From the bridge, you'll see the Haute Ville on your right, with the 13th-century **cathedral of Lausanne,** opening onto place de la Cathédrale. From the square, rue du Cité-de-Vant goes north to the 14th-century **Château Saint-Maire,** on place du Château—once the home of bishops and now containing the offices of the canton administration.

From here, avenue de l'Université leads to **place de la Riponne,** the site of Lausanne's biweekly food and produce markets (Wed and Sat May–Oct 8am–1pm), where stalls loaded with the agrarian bounty of the district are set up within the square and the streets around its perimeter. The **Palais de Rumine** rises from the place de la Riponne's east side. From place de la Riponne, rue Pierre-Viret leads to the **Escaliers du Marché,** a covered stairway dating back to the Middle Ages. You can also take rue Madeleine from the place de la Riponne, continuing south to place de la Palud. On the side of place de la Palud is the 17th-century **Hôtel de Ville (town hall).**

South of place de la Palud is rue du Pont, which turns into rue Saint-François (after crossing rue Centrale). Nearby, at **place du Flon,** you can catch the subway to Ouchy. Place du Flon, with its cafes and bars, has become a favorite evening hangout.

Ouchy ★★

Ouchy, once a sleepy fishing hamlet, is now the port and hotel resort area of Lausanne. The lakefront of Lausanne consists of shady quays and tropical plants spread across a lakefront district of about half a mile. Adjoining place de la Navigation is place du Port immediately to the east. **Quai de Belgique** and **quai d'Ouchy** are lakefront promenades bursting with greenery and offering the best views of the lake.

GETTING AROUND

BY METRO To avoid the crawling pace of the city's trams, take the metro. The trip between the heart of the Haute Ville and Ouchy takes 6 minutes. Departures are every 7½ minutes Monday to Friday from 6:15am to 11:45pm. During off hours and on weekends and holidays, trains run every 15 minutes. A one-way ride from the town center to Ouchy costs 2.60F; a 24-hour ticket sells for 7.60F for rides within the inner city (zone 1), 8.60F for rides within the inner city plus zone 2, and 12F for a day ticket valid for travel within all three of Lausanne's far-flung zones.

Children (6–16 years) pay 6F for a day ticket within zones 1 or 2, or 7F for a day ticket valid for all three zones. Holders of Swiss Passes ride the metro for free.

BY BUS & TRAM The TL (Lausanne Public Transport Company) has a well-designed network of trams and buses whose routes complement the city's subway line. The tram or bus fare is 2.60F, regardless of the distance, for a single trip completed within 60 minutes on lines 1 to 50 of the TL urban network on the Lausanne-Ouchy metro. You can purchase your tickets at the automatic machines installed at most stops.

BY TAXI Lausanne contains dozens of taxi stands, where you'll usually find a line. Alternatively, you can telephone Allô Taxis (✆ **0800/870-872**), Taxi-Service (✆ **0844/ 814-814**), or **Taxiphone** (✆ **0800/801-802;** www.taxiphone.ch) for a cab. The meter starts at 8F; each kilometer traveled adds 3.50F during daylight hours in town, or 4F in town on weekends or at night between 8pm and 6am. For trips outside the town limits, each kilometer traveled costs 5F, regardless of the time of day. The first 10 kilograms (22 lb.) of luggage are free, with 1F charged for every suitcase thereafter.

BY CAR If you drive to Lausanne or rent a car here, wearing seat belts is required, and children 11 and under are not allowed to ride in the front seat. In Lausanne there are four types of parking zones: a white zone, in which parking is free and unlimited; a red zone and a blue zone, in which parking is free but variously limited (15 hr. in the red zone and 90 min. in the blue zone); and a fourth zone with parking meters. To park, you must display a parking disk on the dashboard of your car; parking disks are free and can

To France by Lake Steamer

With its scenic beauty, it's hard to beat Switzerland. But for a change of pace, you can visit **Evian-les-Bains** in France. It lies on one of the southern shores of Lake Geneva and is the leading spa resort in eastern France, its lakeside promenade fashionable since the 19th century. Bottled Evian is, of course, one of the great French table waters.

Lake steamers to Evian are operated by **CGN** (**Compagnie Générale de Navigation;** ℂ **0848/811-848;** www.cgn.ch). They depart from the lakefront quays of Lausanne every hour in summer (mid-May to mid-Sept), and about three times per day in the dead of winter. Transit takes only 35 minutes each way. Once you get to Evian, you can wander, lunch, and kibitz on your own, as there are no guided tours available. Round-trip cost of passage from Lausanne to Evian is 31F in second class or 42F in first class. Note that the midsummer departures that leave either city around noon (there's usually a 12:30pm departure from Lausanne) offer more comprehensive restaurant service than what's available at other times, when there's just a snack bar operational.

be obtained at police stations, automobile clubs, and most gas stations. *Note:* Anything identified as a "yellow zone" is strictly private and reserved only for cars with special plates—if in doubt, don't park there under any circumstances, or else you will risk a fine.

BY BIKE   The city of Lausanne maintains a program wherein visitors, upon presentation of a passport or ID card and a (refundable) deposit of 20F, can rent a bicycle for free for a period of 1 day. For these free 1-day rentals, go to **Lausanne** Roule, place de l'Europe 1B (ℂ **021/533-01-15**), open daily April to November 7:30am to 9:30pm. Bikes can be transported by train from Lausanne to any of the region's outlying districts (or anywhere in Switzerland) for an extra fee. But be aware that to avoid additional penalties, bicycles must be returned the same day before 9:30pm. Like an overdue library book, fees and penalties build up quickly at a rate of between 10F and 20F a day for every day that a user doesn't return his or her bike. Reservations are accepted, but only for groups of five or more cyclists traveling together. For additional information about this program, click on www.lausanneroule.ch.

BY BOAT   To rent boats or *pédalos* (pedal boats), try various rental kiosks at Ouchy and Parc Bourget at Vidy.

ON FOOT   This is the only way to see the old Upper Town effectively. Afterward, you can take the subway to Ouchy and resume your walk along the lakefront quays. Between May and September, Lausanne's civic authorities conduct a **guided walking tour** of their city, lasting 2 hours, Monday through Saturday. Departure is from place de la Palud, adjacent to the city hall, at 10am and 2:30pm. The cost is 10F for adults, 7F for seniors and students, and free for children. For more information on this, or on any of the "specialty tours," which require a minimum, prearranged group of five participants, and which focus on in-depth explications of specific buildings or specific minidistricts within

Lausanne, call the city's tourist office (see "Essentials," above) or click on www.lausanne-tourisme.ch.

SEEING THE SIGHTS

The **cathedral of Lausanne,** place de la Cathédrale, is the focal point of the Upper Town and one of the finest medieval churches in Switzerland. North of the cathedral, at the end of the Upper Town, is the **Château Saint-Maire.** It was built of brick and stone in the 14th and early 15th centuries. Powerful bishops lived here until they were replaced by the Bernese bailiffs, who turned Lausanne into a virtual colony of Bern. Today, the château is used for the canton's administrative offices.

In the center of town is **place de la Palud.** Located on the square is the **Hôtel de Ville (town hall),** which has a 17th-century Renaissance facade; it was completely restored in the late 1970s. Today it's the headquarters of the Communal Council. Also on the square is the **Fountain of Justice,** dating from 1726. A clock with animated historical scenes presents a drama every hour on the hour from 9am to 7pm daily. To visit the cathedral, take the **Escaliers du Marché,** a covered flight of medieval stairs on one side of the square.

North of place de la Palud is **place de la Riponne,** at the edge of which sits the Italianate **Palais de Rumine,** built in 1906. It contains several museums, a university founded in 1537, and the university and cantonal library with some 700,000 volumes.

On the east side of town, **Mon Repos Park** contains landscaped gardens and the **Empire Villa,** where Voltaire performed his work *Zaïre* for a group of friends. The **Tribunal Fédéral** is in the northern area of the park; it was constructed in the 1920s and today houses Switzerland's highest court.

To the north, the mostly timber-built **Tour de Sauvabelin,** which stands very close to a panoramic lookout known simply as *le signal,* rises above the town. At 637m (2,089 ft.), both the tower and its nearby belvedere overlook Lac Léman with the Fribourg Alps rising in the distance. Some high-energy travelers make it a point to climb to the belvedere from the center of Lausanne, a trek that takes—for very fit hill climbers—about 25 minutes along clearly signposted trails.

Ouchy is the lakeside resort and bustling port of Lausanne. Its tree-shaded quays have flower gardens that are nearly half a mile long. The small harbor contains a 700-boat marina, and the Savoy Alps are visible on the opposite shore. The **Château d'Ouchy** is now a hotel and restaurant. The Allies, Greece, and Turkey signed a peace treaty here in 1923. The 13th-century keep is still standing. In the **Hôtel d'Angleterre,** formerly the Auberge de l'Ancre, is a plaque commemorating the stay of Lord Byron, who wrote *The Prisoner of Chillon* here. In the **Beau-Rivage,** the Treaty of Lausanne was ratified in 1923; it settled the final reparations disputes after World War I.

THE TOP ATTRACTIONS

Cathédrale de Lausanne ★★ One of the most beautiful Gothic structures in Europe, the cathedral stands 150m (492 ft.) above Lake Geneva. Construction began in 1175; in 1275 the church was consecrated by Pope Gregory X. While in Lausanne, the pope met Rudolph of Habsburg, emperor of Germany and the Holy Roman Empire. The doors and facade of the cathedral are luxuriously ornamented with sculptures and bas-reliefs. The architect Eugène Viollet-le-Duc began a restoration of the cathedral in the 19th century—and it's still going on! The interior is relatively austere except for some 13th-century choir stalls; the rose window also dates from the 13th century. The cathedral has two towers, with an observation deck 225 steps up one of the towers.

Place de la Cathédrale. 📞 021/316-71-61. Free admission to cathedral; tower 2F. Apr–Sept Mon–Fri **283**
7am–7pm, Sat 8am–7pm, Sun 2–7pm; Oct–Mar Mon–Fri 7:30am–6pm, Sat 8:30am–5pm, Sun 2–5:30pm.
Visits not permitted Sun morning during services. Bus: 7 or 16.

Château de Beaulieu et Musée de l'Art Brut ★ Located on the northwestern side of town, this château dates from 1756 and was once occupied by Madame de Staël. The museum displays what the artist Jean Dubuffet called *art brut* in the 1940s. This curious mélange of artwork was collected by the painter from prisoners, the mentally ill, and the criminally insane. It's like a bizarre twilight zone of art, often dubbed "psycho-pathological," especially the art by schizophrenics. Dubuffet despised the pretentiousness of the avant-garde art scene around him, and as a form of protest decided to begin this collection of the works of "nonartists," many of whom he found superior to the more established artists of his day.

11, av. des Bergières. 📞 021/315-25-70. www.artbrut.ch. Free admission. Tues–Sun 11am–6pm. Bus: 2 to Beaulieu.

Musée Cantonal des Beaux-Arts (Cantonal Museum of Fine Arts) The chief city museum is devoted to the works of artists who painted in western Switzerland from the 18th to the 19th centuries. This complex also houses the Geological Museum, the Museum of Paleontology, the Archaeological and Historical Museum, and the Zoological Museum.

In the Palais de Rumine, 6, place de la Riponne. 📞 021/316-34-45. Free admission. Tues–Wed 11am–6pm; Thurs 11am–8pm; Fri–Sun 11am–5pm. Bus: 5, 6, or 8.

Musée Historique de Lausanne/Ancien-Evêché A bishop's palace until the early 15th century, the Ancien-Evêché has a 13th-century fortified tower and a collection of historical studies of Old Lausanne. You can see a 23-sq.-m (248-sq.-ft.) scale model depicting the old city as it was in the 17th century.

4, place de la Cathédrale. 📞 021/315-41-01. Admission 8F adults, 5F seniors, free for students and children 16 and under. Sept–June Tues–Thurs 11am–6pm, Fri–Sun 11am–5pm; July–Aug daily 11am–6pm. Bus: 7 or 16.

Musée Romain de Lausanne-Vidy At Vidy, west of Ouchy, lying off the Lausanne-Maladière exit from N1/E25, is one of the more intriguing Roman museums of Switzerland. This museum of antiquities is filled with findings from excavations at the site of Lousonna, a Roman settlement that lasted from about the 15th century B.C. into the 4th century A.D. Once a private home, this place now shows Roman treasures—everything from votive figures to ancient coins, even the tools of daily life, right down to the pins that held up those togas. Guided tours of nearby archaeological digs are conducted on the last Sunday of every month for another 3F.

24, chemin du Bois-de-Vaus. 📞 021/625-10-85. Admission 8F, 5F seniors and students, free for children 16 and under. Tues–Sun 11am–6pm. Free admission 1st Sat of each month. Bus: 1, 2, or 4.

Olympic Museum Seeing that the Comité International Olympique has been installed in Lausanne since 1915, the city decided in 1993 to open a museum recalling the history of the games since ancient Greece. The largest information center for the Olympic movement in the world, it's a tribute to the union of sport, art, and culture, with a coin and stamp collection, an Olympic Study Center, a library, an information center, and a video library recalling some of the games' most historic moments. There's even a scattering of artifacts commemorating the sporting triumphs of South America's

Aztec empire. Advanced audiovisual, computer, and robotic technology allows visitors to share in the great feats and the emotions of the athletes. An Olympic flame burns alongside a column that lists the venues where the games have been held.

1, quai d'Ouchy. ℂ **021/621-65-11.** www.olympic.org. Admission 15F adults; 10F seniors, students, and children 6–16; free for children 5 and under; 35F family ticket. Apr–Oct daily 9am–6pm (till 8pm Thurs); Nov–Mar Tues–Sun 9am–6pm. Closed Jan 1 and Dec 25. Take bus no. 8 from the center of Lausanne or the metro from the rail station to Ouchy, then walk for 15 min. with the lake on your right, passing the Beau-Rivage Palace hotel en route.

THE ACTIVE VACATION PLANNER

The Lausanne tourist office (see "Essentials," earlier in this chapter) can tell you the best places to **jog** in and around the city. *Vita parcours* (that is, jogging) trails, broken up by various stops for exercising, are found at Vidy, at Chalet-à-Gobet, and above Pully, the last lying between Lausanne and Montreux. The tourist office will also advise about the best transportation connections to reach starting points, and provide maps showing their various locations.

You can go **hiking**—some call it strolling—through vineyard and château country along the north shore of Lake Geneva. The Lausanne tourist office, as well as various town and village offices, will advise you of the best itineraries and supply detailed maps to guide you on your way. If you enjoy planning this sort of thing even before your arrival in the Vaud, consider contacting the **Association Vaudoise de Tourisme Pédestre (Vaudois Association of Trekkers and Hill Climbers),** 23, Grand St-Jean, CH-1003 Lausanne (ℂ **021/323-10-84;** www.avtp.ch).

For more vertiginous and higher-altitude adventures, you can take **mountain wilderness trails** cutting into the Alps Vaudoises. You can explore the canyons and heavily wooded areas around Château-d'Oex, or the alpine meadows above Villars.

SHOPPING

Shoppers in Lausanne tend to be much more concerned with the commercialized glamour of Paris than with kitschy mountain souvenirs. That being the case, you'll find lots of emphasis on high-profile outfits such as luggage and leather maker **Louis Vuitton,** 30, rue de Bourg (ℂ **021/312-76-60**); or haute jeweler **Cartier,** 6, rue de Bourg (ℂ **021/320-55-44**).

But if handmade souvenirs from the Vaud region appeal to you, head for **Heidi's Shop,** 22, rue du Petit-Chêne (ℂ **021/311-16-89**). The biggest and best bookstore in Lausanne is **Librairie Payot,** 4, place Pepinet (ℂ **021/341-33-31**), which carries English-language titles. The biggest jeweler in Lausanne, with a well-established international reputation, is **Bucherer,** 15, place St-François (ℂ **021/312-36-12**). Competitors, especially for Swiss watches, include **Roman Mayer,** 12, place St-François (ℂ **021/312-23-16**), which has good buys in Omega watches, and **Junod,** 8, place St-François (ℂ **021/312-27-45;** www.junod-lausanne.ch), carrying Blancpain watches among others.

The major tobacco outlet is **Besson,** 22, rue de Bourg (ℂ **021/312-67-88**), known for its Davidoff cigars.

WHERE TO STAY

The luxury and elegance of the top hotels in Lausanne have made the city a favorite destination of the wealthy, and trade fairs and conventions also keep the better hotels booked. In the summer space is especially tight, so be sure to make a reservation. The

A Dramatic Ascent to Les Diablerets

For a high-alpine view of Switzerland's highest heights, consider a day trip from Lausanne to the high-alpine village of **Les Diablerets,** which is rather confusingly designated as the geographical and spiritual centerpiece of a high-altitude and rocky **Les Diablerets region** ★★. To reach Les Diablerets, visitors take a conventional train from Lausanne to the town of Aigle—a 30-minute, relatively high-speed ride, priced at 30F per person round-trip. In Aigle they transfer onto a relatively slow narrow-gauge train that carries them to the village of Les Diablerets—a 46-minute ride priced at 24F per person round-trip.

In Diablerets you can wander around the alpine village, site of about 10 hotels, including 2 in the government-rated four-star category. There's an attempt to maintain old-fashioned aesthetics in this town, and it does have some alpine charm. Diablerets village is the centerpiece of three distinct regions: the D'Ifenau ski region, the Le Meilleret ski region (which funnels into yet another ski region known as the Villarf region), and the Glacier region (Les Diablerets Glacier 3000). It's also the site of a 7.2km (4½-mile) bobsled ride *(piste de luge)* that's among the most thrilling (terrifying?) in the region.

After visiting Les Diablerets village, you can return to Lausanne or continue on to see the **Glacier des Diablerets** at 2,997m (9,830 ft.). In winter a free minibus hauls you to the door of most of the hotels in Les Diablerets Village. Then continue to the base of one of Switzerland's newest (inaugurated in 1999) cable cars at Col du Pillon, which will carry you on to the Glacier des Diablerets. The minibuses take 15 minutes for the ride. In summer there are no free minibuses; instead, you'll board any of five daily departures aboard a Swiss Postal Bus for the 15-minute ride to the base of the cable car at Col du Pillon, and pay 15F per person each way. Or if you want to walk through the village, it will take you about 90 minutes from the railway station to the base of the cable car.

Once you reach Col du Pillon, departures on the cable car to the glacier are continuous between 8:30 and 9am, and ending between 4 and 5:30pm (times depend on the season). The 15-minute uphill ride (very steep, very dramatic) requires one change of car at a midway point up the mountain. The cost is 60F per person round-trip. For **cable car information** and confirmation that the car is running, call ✆ **024/492-33-77.**

The summit is the site of a futuristic-looking aerie designed by Mario Botta, resembling an angular Inca temple or a spacecraft, depending on your point of view. Inside, there are two eateries: a self-service restaurant and a more formal sit-down restaurant. The aerie is also the departure point for winter skiing (Dec to mid-Apr), summer skiing (late June to late July), and lots of hiking trails on or near the edges of the glaciers. There's also a snow-bus excursion, priced at 18F for a 30-minute outing, in a vehicle with very big snow tires and big windows. There *might* be a group of husky dogs on-site practicing dog sledding, Alaskan style, but don't count on it. The entire site, including the cable car, is closed during May for annual maintenance.

tourist office can also help you find a hotel. If you want to stay directly on the lake, we recommend a hotel in Ouchy.

Very Expensive

Beau-Rivage Palace ★★★   This Beaux Arts, government-rated five-star hotel sits directly beside Lac Léman, surrounded by 4 hectares (10 acres) of lush gardens that include rare cedars, masses of seasonal flowers, neoclassical sculptures, and even a small plot devoted to burial grounds for the pets of the sometimes spectacularly famous guests who stayed here. Built in 1861, and enlarged in 1908, the hotel has been frequently renovated, but always with a sense of respect (reverence, even) for its original architecture. Set downhill from the rest of Lausanne, in the lake-fronting residential neighborhood of Ouchy, the hotel is among the last bastions of formal Europe. Rooms come in a wide range of styles. The least expensive of these are somewhat sparsely furnished and open onto the parking area. The more expensive units have Oriental carpets, a mixture of genuine antiques and convincing reproductions, often in one of the French Louis styles, and private balconies overlooking Lake Geneva.

17–19, place du Port, Ch-1006 Lausanne-Ouchy. ✆ **800/223-6800** in the U.S. or 021/613-33-33. Fax 021/613-33-34. www.brp.ch. 169 units. 520F–830F double; from 1,150F suite. AE, DC, MC, V. Parking 30F. Metro: Ouchy. **Amenities:** 3 restaurants; 2 bars; babysitting; concierge; exercise room; 2 pools (1 indoor, 1 outdoor); room service; 2 outdoor tennis courts (lit). *In room:* A/C, TV, hair dryer, minibar, Wi-Fi (30F per 24 hr.).

Château d'Ouchy ★   Built around 1900, this deluxe hotel uses a medieval (12th century) tower as its core. It enjoys the best location in all of Lausanne, across from the flower-bedecked pedestrian quay along the lake. Its once fortified tower, ideal for a honeymoon, is capped by a tiled roof and surrounded by a Renaissance style gables. Massive renovations have upgraded the entire hotel. After years of decline, all of the individually decorated bedrooms—spacious for the most part—have elegance, character, comfort, and charm, with modern conveniences. The château remains the most nostalgic and evocative choice for a hotel in Lausanne.

2 place du Port, CH-1006 Lausanne-Ouchy. ✆ **021/331-32-32.** Fax 021/331-34-35. www.chateau douchy.ch. 43 units. 495F-655F double. AE, DC, MC, V. **Amenities:** Restaurant; bar; exercise room; room service. *In room:* A/C, TV, hair dryer, minibar, Wi-Fi (free).

Lausanne Palace ★★★   The Palace is as grand and elegant a hotel as you'll find anywhere in Europe. The columns, plaster details, and marble floors date from the 19th century; the public rooms are decorated with tapestries, crystal chandeliers, and gilded Empire or Louis XVI furniture. In distinct contrast to its nearest rival, the above-noted Beau-Rivage Palace, which sits within gardens directly beside the lake, it occupies a location in the commercial heart of Lausanne, just above the railway station but below the cathedral, with views that sweep out over the lake. Many of the rooms reflect the hotel's turn-of-the-20th-century style; others are in a more contemporary mode. The best units have marble fireplaces. The front rooms open onto urban streets; the accommodations to the rear face the lake, and most have private balconies. All come with luxurious marble bathrooms.

7–9, rue du Grand-Chêne, CH-1002 Lausanne. ✆ **800/223-6800** in the U.S. or 021/331-31-31. Fax 021/323-25-71. www.lausanne-palace.ch. 146 units. 540F–750F double; 1,250F–2,990F suite. AE, DC, MC, V. Parking 20F. Metro: Flon. **Amenities:** 4 restaurants; 5 bars; babysitting; exercise room; indoor heated pool; room service; spa; Wi-Fi (free, in lobby). *In room:* TV, hair dryer, minibar.

Hotel Angleterre & Résidence ★   At the edge of Lake Geneva, a trio of elegant villas from the 18th and 19th centuries combines to form this stylish boutique hotel on the Ouchy waterfront, immediately adjacent to the more luxurious Beau-Rivage, with which it is associated as a kind of kid sister, and with whom it shares many of its dining, drinking, and spa facilities. The famous Beau-Rivage hotel in fact owns La Residence, but this hotel is less expensive, with a very contemporary-looking decor and a location that's even closer to the water. Many guests who can afford the grander palace actually prefer to stay here. There are intimate and cozy touches, including a lounge, with bright colors and dining in summer on a deck that stretches toward the water. One part of the hotel, L'Angleterre, housed Lord Byron when he was writing *The Prisoner of Chillon.*

15, place du Port, CH-1006 Lausanne. 𝄞 **021/613-34-34.** Fax 021/613-34-35. www.angleterre-residence. ch. 75 units. 425F double; 460F–495F junior suite. Children 11 and under stay free in parent's room. AE, DC, MC, V. Parking 25F. **Amenities:** 2 restaurants; bar; exercise room; 2 heated pools (1 indoor); room service; spa. *In room:* A/C, TV, hair dryer, minibar, Wi-Fi (18F per hour).

Hôtel de la Paix ★   Opened in 1910, this is a landmark and has seen a lot of changes in the past decades, including recent renovations. With its elaborate balconies and log-gias, many with wrought-iron details, the hotel retains its original facade, although the interior has been vastly renewed. In the heart of the city, it faces the lake and the Alps beyond, and is convenient for shopping in the Old Town. A favorite with business cli-ents, it offers completely modern midsize bedrooms, either opening onto the lake or, less desirably, onto one of the city's urban landscapes. About one-quarter of the bedrooms are refurbished each year.

5, av. Benjamin-Constant, CH-1002 Lausanne. 𝄞 **800/528-1234** in the U.S. and Canada or 021/310-71-71. Fax 021/310-71-72. www.hoteldelapaix.net. 109 units. 385F–470F double; 550F–1,300F suite. Rates include buffet breakfast. AE, DC, MC, V. Parking 27F. Metro: St-François. **Amenities:** 2 restaurants; bar; babysitting; room service. *In room:* TV, hair dryer, minibar, Wi-Fi (30F per 24 hr.).

Moderate

Hôtel Agora ★   Set just 270m (900 ft.) from the railroad station, this is a govern-ment-rated family-owned, four-star, six-story hotel that opened in 1987 after a total renovation of an older hotel on the site. The look is startlingly unique to Lausanne. Locals often compare its architecture, with a facade of sculpted marble, to a spaceship. "ET has landed," wrote one columnist. The small to midsize bedrooms are comfortable and contain modern furniture and firm beds. Amenities include soundproof windows. The accommodations often have a futuristic aura, with glowing silver or glittering metal-lic appointments.

9, av. du Rond-Point, CH-1006 Lausanne. 𝄞 **021/555-59-55.** Fax 021/555-59-59. www.fhotels.ch. 82 units. 145F–390F double; 430F junior suite. AE, DC, MC, V. Free parking. Bus: 1, 3, or 5. *In room:* A/C, TV/ DVD, CD player, hair dryer, Wi-Fi (30F per 24 hr.).

Hôtel Continental   Opposite the main rail station, this hotel is ideally located for both business travelers and visitors. A modern, government-rated four-star hotel, it's convenient and practical, although not as prestigious as some of the earlier recommenda-tions noted above. Midsize to spacious rooms, all just renovated, contain modern fur-nishings, appointed with blonde wood and color-coordinated fabrics. While it doesn't have the grand style of some of the palaces recommended, it's most affordable and up-to-date in its amenities. Bedrooms are midsize to spacious, each with an efficiently orga-nized private bathroom.

2, place de la Gare, CH-1001 Lausanne. ✆ **021/321-88-00.** Fax 021/321-88-01. www.hotelcontinental.ch. 116 units. 335F–390F double; 550F junior suite. Rates include buffet breakfast. AE, DC, MC, V. Parking 20F (nearby). **Amenities:** 2 restaurants; bar; babysitting. *In room:* TV, hair dryer, minibar, Wi-Fi (35F per 24 hr.).

Hôtel Nash Carlton   In the summer, awnings decorate the arched windows of this white Mediterranean-style four-story villa with a red-tile roof, located in a park near the lake. Built in 1909, it offers soundproof, midsize bedrooms that are comfortable, each with a conservatively modern decor. Try for a room with a balcony, even though they don't open onto the lake. There's no restaurant on-site, but in view of the many nearby dining options, no one seems to mind.

4, av. de Cour, CH-1007 Lausanne. ✆ **021/613-07-07.** Fax 021/613-07-10. www.nashcarlton.com. 44 units. 168F–330F double; 445F–480F junior suite. Rates include buffet breakfast. AE, MC, V. Parking 10F. Bus: 2 or 5. **Amenities:** Restaurant; bar; babysitting; concierge; room service. *In room:* A/C, TV, hair dryer, minibar, Wi-Fi (10F per hour).

Inexpensive

Hôtel Aulac (**Value**)   This lakefront Ouchy hotel has a baroque yellow facade with white trim and a three-story Renaissance porch flanked by two elaborate columns. Originally built around the turn of the 20th century, this up-to-date hotel has been recently renovated. The mansard roof is inlaid with tiles in a geometric design and topped with a tall Victorian clock tower. Sailboats bob in the lake nearby. This is the least expensive hotel right on the water in Lausanne, but it's hardly the best, and most of its bedrooms rarely rise above a standard motel offering. The standardized accommodations are somewhat tacky and battered, but reasonably comfortable and are priced at the lower end of the scale below. Request a room with a lake view and balcony. In spite of its drawbacks, this hotel is a favorite and is often heavily booked because of its location. It's pleasant lake-fronting restaurant, Le Pirate, specializes in fish.

4, place de la Navigation, CH-1000 Lausanne-Ouchy. ✆ **021/613-15-00.** Fax 021/613-15-15. www.aulac. ch. 84 units. 210F–270F double; 360F suite. Rates include continental breakfast. AE, DC, MC, V. Metro: Ouchy. Parking 15F (nearby). **Amenities:** Restaurant; room service. *In room:* TV, hair dryer, minibar, Wi-Fi (35F per 24 hr.).

Hôtel Elite ★ (**Finds**)   The large, illuminated sign on the front lawn obscures the neo-classical details of this white, five-story hotel with balconies, a flat roof, and a strong dose of regional charm. You'll find this midcity location just uphill from the rail terminal, on a very small street that conveys a spirit of country living. Originally built at the turn of the 20th century, it's been operated by the same family since 1938. Fruit trees and a garden add the grace note, and some of the bedrooms are air-conditioned. One room has a kitchenette, and all units contain midsize bathrooms. Fourth-floor units open onto lakeside views.

1, av. Sainte-Luce, CH-1003 Lausanne. ✆ **021/320-23-61.** Fax 021/320-39-63. www.elite-lausanne.ch. 33 units. 180F–240F double; 405F–500F junior suite. Rates include buffet breakfast. AE, DC, MC, V. Free parking. Bus: 1, 3, or 5. *In room:* A/C (in some), TV, hair dryer (in some), Wi-Fi (25F per 24 hr.).

Minotel AlaGare   A government-rated three-star stucco hotel a block from the rail station, this building dates from the turn of the 20th century but has been recently renovated. Access to the hotel is via a pedestrians-only street in the town center, but any resident can drive up to the front door of the hotel and deposit luggage. In summer, flowers bloom in the window boxes of the hotel, adding an inviting touch. The interior has pine paneling stained in several different tones. The well-maintained bedrooms have sleek modern styling and are generally small.

14, rue du Simplon, CH-1006 Lausanne. ✆ **021/617-92-52.** Fax 021/617-92-55. www.alagare.com. 45
units. 150F–200F double. Children 11 and under stay free in parent's room. Rates include buffet breakfast.
AE, DC, MC, V. Closed Jan–Mar. Bus: 1, 3, or 5. **Amenities:** Restaurant. *In room:* TV, hair dryer, Wi-Fi (free).

Minotel Crystal Within walking distance of the Palais de Beaulieu, a congress center, this unpretentious government-rated three-star hotel is often the favorite of visiting business clients. Monsieur and Madame Fiora welcome guests to their location on a quiet pedestrian street. The bedrooms are standardized, with tidy bathrooms. There's an underground parking facility a short walk from the hotel.

5, rue Chaucrau, CH-1003 Lausanne. ✆ **021/317-03-03.** Fax 021/320-04-46. www.crystal-lausanne.ch.
40 units. 174F–244F double; 270F triple; 324F suite. Rates include breakfast. AE, DC, MC, V. Parking 20F.
Bus: 1 or 5. **Amenities:** Restaurant; bar; Internet. *In room:* TV, hair dryer, minibar, Wi-Fi (25F per 24 hr.).

WHERE TO DINE

Lausanne offers a wide range of restaurants where you can find the specialties of Switzerland and the Vaud, as well as those of France, Greece, Italy, and China. Typical Swiss food is served in the Upper Town.

Try the Geneva lake fish, omble chevalier. Trout and perch from the lake are also popular; in autumn many restaurants feature game dishes.

Expensive

Café Beau-Rivage ★ SWISS This grand and elegant *brasserie de luxe* is in a lakeside pavilion, the dining room resembling a Paris cafe, with mirrors, pillars, cheerfully striped banquettes, bay windows, a flowery terrace, and a bustling environment that's less chillingly formal than you might have expected. Typical tasty dishes, made only with the freshest ingredients, include a superb version of steak tartare prepared on a trolley directly at table; a very fresh salad of wild mesclun greens with *chèvre* (goat cheese); filets of sole, either grilled or breaded and fried meuniere style; fricassee of chicken flavored with vinegar and tarragon; a satay of red tuna, skewered and served with peanut sauce; and tagliatelle with seafood. Sumptuous desserts can be ordered from the trolley.

In the Beau-Rivage Palace, 18, place du Général-Guisan, Ouchy. ✆ **021/613-33-39.** Reservations recommended. Main courses 39F–62F; fixed-price lunch 52F, dinner 88F. AE, DC, MC, V. Cafe daily 9am–1am.
Restaurant daily noon–11:30pm. Metro: Ouchy.

Moderate

A la Pomme de Pin ★★ TRADITIONAL FRENCH/SWISS Our favorite restaurant in Lausanne's old town lies between the back side of the cathedral and the château, within a 17th-century setting that most local residents remember from their childhood: It's nourished local hunger pangs since around 1935. There are actually two restaurants on-site here, including a brasserie with bordeaux-colored leather banquettes, and a more expensive, and more formal restaurant. Main courses in the brasserie are likely to include filet of fera (a whitefish from the nearby lake) prepared with white wine, parsley, and tomatoes; and roasted pigs' trotters served with *rösti* and salad. Main courses in the restaurant might include rack of Emmenthaler valley veal with a mousseline of potatoes and foie gras, or a roasted rack of alpine lamb with potatoes and mountain herbs.

11–13, rue Cité Derrière. ✆ **021/323-46-56.** Reservations recommended. Brasserie main courses 22F–34F; restaurant main courses 42F–54F. AE, DC, MC, V. Mon–Fri 8am–midnight; Sat 4pm–midnight. Closed 4 weeks every year beginning in late July. Bus: 7 or 16.

Buffet de la Gare CFF SWISS/FRENCH Inside Lausanne's main rail station, the brasserie is large and bustling, while the restaurant offers a secluded series of cubbyholes and nooks and more upscale service. There's little difference in price between the brasserie and the restaurant. Many find the brasserie more fun, the restaurant more sedate. Dishes available at both include vol-au-vent with mushrooms, filets of sole "Uncle Charles," poached turbot in hollandaise sauce, veal sausages, and mignons of pork in cream sauce.

In the train station, 11, place de la Gare. ℂ **021/311-49-00.** www.buffetdelagare.ch. Reservations recommended in the restaurant only. Main courses 21F–36F; fixed-price menus 18F–38F. MC, V. Restaurant daily 7am–midnight. Brasserie daily 11am–midnight. Bus: 1, 3, or 5.

Le Jardin d'Asie ★ CHINESE/JAPANESE   The finest Asian restaurant in Lausanne, Le Jardin celebrates the cuisine of China, Japan, and to a lesser degree, Malaysia. The setting is a pale-green-and-pink representation of a garden, with enough space between tables to permit the broadly international clientele discreet conversations. Menu items include a choice of foods from the major culinary traditions of China, as well as sushi, sashimi, and *teppanyaki* (Japanese cuisine prepared by a uniformed chef in front of your table). There's even a choice of Malay dishes, including shrimp or chicken in peanut sauce and beignets of shrimp.

7, av. du Théâtre. ℂ **021/323-74-84.** www.jardindasie.ch. Reservations recommended. Main courses 22F–34F; fixed-price Chinese menu 44F–75F; fixed-price Japanese menu 45F–80F. AE, DC, MC, V. Mon–Sat noon–2:30pm and 7–10pm; Sun 7–9:30pm. Bus: 7 or 16.

Nomade Vinothèque, Resto & Bar ★ INTERNATIONAL   Set directly on Place de l'Europe, a low-lying valley in the heart of Lausanne's commercial core, midway between the cathedral and the Lausanne Palace Hotel, this is one of the best restaurants in Lausanne, with one of the most imaginative and hip wine bars. Inside, you'll find long communal tables and a labyrinth of warmly decorated rooms, many accented with racks of wine and contemporary paintings. Specialties include a platter piled high with veal kidneys and veal sweetbreads, each cooked with Noilly Prat; magret of duck with wild mushrooms; beef tartare that's prepared with just the right amount of spiciness; filet of sea bass in a sesame-coated crust; and brochettes of giant shrimp with a spicy citrus and tamarind sauce. There's also an array of tapas for lighter, predinner appetites.

9, place de l'Europe. ℂ **021/320-13-13.** www.restaurantnomade.ch. Reservations not necessary. Main courses 24F–48F; glasses of wine 6.50F–11F; tapas 7.50F–14F per portion. AE, DC, MC, V. Mon–Wed 9am–midnight; Thurs 9am–1am; Fri 9am–2am; Sat 10am–2am; Sun 4:30pm–midnight. Bar daily until 1am. Bus: 7 or 16.

Pinte Besson ★ (Finds) SWISS/REGIONAL   This is a tiny restaurant with a smoke-stained vault of hand-chiseled masonry dating from 1780. It's celebrated locally for its cheese fondues, cheese on toast, and seasonal specialties, along with dried alpine beef. Beef or horse steak is grilled and served on a slate stone. There are sidewalk tables in summer, and benches are placed outside on sunny days.

4, rue de l'Ale. ℂ **021/312-59-69.** www.pinte-besson.com. Reservations recommended. Main courses 16F–39F. MC, V. Mon–Sat 8am–midnight. Closed Aug. Bus: 1 or 9.

Pur CONTINENTAL   There's lots of emphasis on the young, the restless, and the emotionally available at this restaurant and bar. As such, you'll find a venue that seems to change radically throughout the day and night. At least some of this results from long communal tables illuminated at night with lots of candles artfully shoved into candelabras. There's an impressive list of cocktails, and a winning, and rather large, selection of wines from around Europe, each sold by the glass, which taste especially good when

accompanied with menu items which seem designed to be shared with other diners.
Examples include a *panna cotta* of foie gras with port-flavored cream sauce; cabbage rolls
with enoki mushrooms and satay (peanut) sauce; a crostini (broiled sandwich) *brillat-
savarin* with smoked salmon and melon; roasted strips of duck with truffled potato slices
and stewed eggplant; and a well-prepared version of Norwegian salmon with a gratin of
pistachios, basil, and mushroom-stuffed crepes. Be warned in advance that if you miss
mealtime at this place, by even as much as a minute or two, the staff will have made a
stampede to shut the kitchens down tight, like a drum, and no amount of coaxing will
prompt the strong-willed staff here to change its mind and actually bring out any food.
That lack of hospitality aside, you still might meet some counterculture city residents
here, albeit with lots of emphasis on 20- and 30-somethings.

17, Port-Franc (Place de l'Europe). ⓒ **021/311-99-33.** www.pur-flon.ch. Main courses 19F–41F. AE, DC,
MC, V. Mon–Fri 7am–11pm; Sat–Sun 9am–midnight. Bus: 7 or 16.

NEARBY DINING

Auberge du Raisin ★★ SWISS/FRENCH It's set in its ways and its staff is a bit
rigid, but despite these minor drawbacks, a stopover at this verdant property will offer
impeccable food and insight into upscale, *grand bourgeois* life within French-speaking
Switzerland. Set on 13th-century foundations, in the center of the town of Cully, it's
most famous for its restaurant, where delicate flavorings are a hallmark of chef Peter
Hasler. Within a setting accented with antique paneling and an elegant sense of alpine
rusticity, you can order such classic dishes as steamed supreme of pigeon with truffles, a
cold consommé of lobster with fresh tarragon, ravioli stuffed with scallops and served
with a caviar-enriched champagne sauce, and a poached filet mignon of veal with summer vegetables.

Nine comfortable, somewhat frilly-looking bedrooms are on-site (220F double;
310F–380F suite). Rates include buffet breakfast.

1, place de l'Hôtel de Ville, CH-1096 Cully. ⓒ **021/799-21-31.** Fax 021/799-25-01. www.aubergeduraisin.
ch. Reservations required. Main courses 35F–60F; fixed-price dinner 130F–180F, lunch 55F. AE, DC, MC, V.
Mon–Sat noon–2pm and 7–9:30pm. From Lausanne, take Rte. Cantonale, which borders the edge of the
lake, following the signs to Vevey, then turn off to follow the signs to Cully.

Hotel de Ville—Philippe Rochat ★★★ SWISS/FRENCH For years, Philippe
Rochat dutifully followed in the footsteps of the founder of this legendary restaurant
(Frédy Girardet), quietly helping the grand patriarch of French cuisine prepare the thousands of upscale platters that contributed to this establishment's fame. Since 1996 and
the retirement of his mentor, Switzerland's culinary patriarch, Rochat has taken over,
doing a masterful job of keeping Girardet's legend alive while simultaneously updating
the menu with some creations of his own. The venue for this minidrama, which has been
avidly watched by gastronomes throughout the region, is within the solid stone walls of
what was originally conceived in 1929 as Crissier's Town Hall (Hôtel de Ville). He prepares succulent meals for tables of culinary aficionados who sometimes make reservations
many months in advance. Specialties change frequently, according to the availability of
ingredients and the inspiration of Rochat himself. Recent successes have included a
ragout of fresh quail with young vegetables, crawfish in caviar butter, duckling from the
wetlands around Nantes cooked pink and prepared with Brouilly wine, preserved duckling in lemon and spices, and glazed sweetbreads with wild mushrooms. The cheese
trolley that's wheeled around after the main course is absolutely spectacular.

In the Hotel de Ville, 1, rue d'Yverdon, Crissier. (℗ **021/634-05-05.** www.philippe-rochat.ch. Reservations essential. Main courses 60F–120F; fixed-price dinner 295F–360F, lunch (Tues–Fri) 175F. AE, DC, MC, V. Tues–Sat noon–2pm and 7–9pm. Closed last week of July and 1st 2 weeks of Aug.

LAUSANNE AFTER DARK

Few other cities in Switzerland manage to remain as cosmopolitan but relentlessly conservative as Lausanne. Consequently, you'll find lots to do, often with a Gallic insouciance, after dark. You may begin your evening hanging out in any of the cafes and bars ringing the **Espace Flon,** a cluster of restaurants and shops at place Flon. Lots of hideaways, frequented by strollers of all ages, will be here to tempt you, but one of the most appealing is **Le Grand Café,** 3, allée Ernest-Ansermet (℗ **021/320-40-30**). Here, in an American-inspired space that contains some of the glitter and razzmatazz of a Planet Hollywood (though it's not connected), you can meet a cross section of virtually every night owl in town. The cafe lies inside the Casino of Lausanne.

Attractive and popular discos include **Le Mad,** 23, rue de Genève (℗ **021/340-69-69;** www.mad-geneve.ch), where the fads and preoccupations of nocturnal Paris filter quickly in from the west via an under-30 crowd. You'll recognize this place instantly, since its exterior is covered with an artist's rosy rendition of street graffiti as it might have been applied by a supremely talented French-speaking artist.

Ouchy White Horse Pub, 66, av. d'Ouchy (℗ **021/616-75-75;** www.whitehorse.ch), draws the crowds at night, who in summer enjoy the terrace with views of the water. Beer is on tap, and a range of tapas and burgers is sold. It's the most authentic pub atmosphere in town.

Lausanne is also a city of culture. It shares the Orchestre de la Suisse Romande with Geneva and also occasionally hosts the legendary ballet company of Maurice Béjart. The local tourist office will advise on what's available at the time of your visit. Most performances of major cultural impact take place at the **Théâtre-Municipal Lausanne,** avenue du Theatre (℗ **021/310-16-00). Le Théâtre de Beaulieu,** at 10, av. des Bergières (℗ **021/643-21-11;** www.theatredebeaulieu.ch), is also a venue for dance concerts, operas, and orchestral music presentations. Tickets can be purchased at **Ticket Corner (www.ticket corner.ch),** which has various locations throughout Lausanne, including one that's prominently positioned within Lausanne's railway station. Tickets can also be bought at one of Lausanne's large department stores, la FNAC, 6, rue de Genève (www.fnac.ch). For more information, contact the Théâtre-Municipal Lausanne.

2 MORGES ★

11km (7 miles) W of Lausanne; 26km (16 miles) E of Geneva

Set against a backdrop of the Savoy Alps, the small town of Morges on Lac Léman is headquarters for the region's vineyards. Its port was built on an ancient site inhabited by prehistoric lake dwellers. Because of its elegant lakeside setting, and because of its stellar hotels and restaurants, Morges became one of the premier stopovers along Lake Geneva. Today the town is a favorite stop for a chic set of international yachters. In June of 2007, UNESCO designated most of the vineyards within this region of the Vaud as a site of major importance to the world patrimony—the first area in French-speaking Switzerland to receive this distinction. Under protection is the Lavaux region, including vineyards that are spread over 14 villages on steep hillsides east of Lausanne. The vineyards, laced with rock walls and pathways, slope down to Lake Geneva's waterfront. With a landscape

shaped by generations of winegrowers for more than 8 centuries, the area produces eight
different wines protected with an AOC label *(appellation d'origine contrôlée).*

ESSENTIALS

GETTING THERE Trains run almost every 30 minutes throughout the day between Geneva and Lausanne, and most of them stop at Morges. For **rail information,** call 🕿 **0900/300-300.**

Bus no. 57 runs from Lausanne to Morges. Call 🕿 **0900/300-300** for **bus schedules.** One-way transit costs 26F from Geneva and 3.50F from Lausanne.

If you're **driving** from Lausanne, head west toward Geneva along N1.

In addition, between late May and September, several **lake steamers** stop at Morges every day on their way between Geneva and Lausanne; depending on their schedule, some require a boat change at Yvoire. For information, contact the **CGN (Compagnie Générale de Navigation),** 17, av. de Rhodanie, in Lausanne (🕿 **0848/811-848;** www. cgn.ch), or **Jardin Anglais,** in Geneva (🕿 **021/614-62-00).**

VISITOR INFORMATION The **Morges Tourist Information Office,** on rue du Château (🕿 **021/801-32-33;** www.morges.ch), is open April to September Monday to Friday 9am to 6pm and Saturday 9:30am to 5pm. From October to March hours are Monday to Friday 9:30am to 4:30pm and 1:30 to 5:30pm.

SEEING THE SIGHTS

Baron Louis of Savoy built the **Castle of Morges** in 1286 to defend himself against the bishopric of Lausanne. The imposing bastion, which originally had a moat, was the residence of a Bernese bailiff from 1536 to 1798. It eventually passed to the canton of Vaud, which used it as an arsenal. Today it contains the **Vaud Military Museum (Musée Militaire Vaudois;** 🕿 **021/316-09-90;** www.musees-vd.ch). The weapons and uniforms on display date from the late 15th century to modern times. The museum is open February to June and September to November, Tuesday to Friday from 10am to noon and 1:30 to 5pm and on Saturday, Sunday, and holidays from 1:30 to 5pm; in July and August, hours are Tuesday to Sunday 10am to 5pm. Admission is 10F.

Calling on Audrey Hepburn

What movie fan can ever forget the pencil-thin, doe-eyed, ravishingly beautiful Audrey Hepburn? She wowed us in *Roman Holiday, Breakfast at Tiffany's,* and *Wait Until Dark.* She was the epitome of class without snobbery, and the ultimate performer yet an artist without pretensions. For years she made her home in the neighboring hamlet of Tolochenaz, 1.6km (1 mile) east of Morges. It was in this village where the star spent long hours as an ambassador for UNICEF. Born in Brussels in 1929, Hepburn died here in 1993. You can walk here or take TPM bus no. 2 to reach the village cemetery, **Cimetière de Tolochenaz,** where she was buried. Fans still call on her gravesite, often bringing flowers. The stone-sided chalet that Hepburn occupied for the last 40 years of her life is not open to the public, though, and a pavilion that once housed some of her memorabilia is now closed (her son, Sean Ferrer, decided to take back the objects of hers which had been on public display).

Musée Alexis Forel ★, in a 15th-century patrician house at 54, Grand-Rue (✆ **021/ 801-26-47;** www.museeforel.ch), contains a collection of engravings, 17th- and 18th-century furniture, 18th-century silver and glassware, ancient ceramics, and antique dolls—all exhibited in the intimate setting of a former private home. The museum is open March to November Wednesday to Sunday from 2 to 6pm. Admission is 8F for adults, 3F for ages 6 to 16.

If the day is sunny, you can take one of the most lovely **bike rides** in western Switzerland beginning at Morges train station, where you can rent a bike for 32F a day. The tourist office (see above) will provide a map and help you plot your route. The trail leads from Morges to the village of Lully and goes via Bussy and Ballens to Biere. This takes you through some of the most scenic vineyards of Lake Geneva. From Biere you continue down a small valley to Begnins and then Fechy, the latter a panoramic lookout point. Eventually you reach Aubonne, where you can take a second-class road via Lavigny, Villars-sous-Yens, and Lully back to Morges. The 56km (35-mile) trip takes about 5½ hours.

WHERE TO STAY & DINE

La Fleur du Lac ★★ SWISS/FRENCH   Many residents of Geneva make weekend excursions to taste the unusual and imaginative food served at this beautiful restaurant on the quay beside the lake. Famous specialties include Lake Geneva perch in a salt crust plus imported seafood. The menu, which changes with the seasons, includes an unusual version of medallions of foie gras served with pistachio nuts and a sweet-and-sour sauce inspired by Asia, filet of lake perch with butter sauce and tartar sauce, and poached supreme of turbot with wine/herb sauce and shellfish. Dessert might be a "fantasy of coconut." More than 250 domestic and foreign wines are available. There's an outdoor terrace facing the lake. The bus from Lausanne stops in back of the hotel.

This establishment also rents 30 rooms, and no two are alike. All units face south, with a view across the lake to the French Alps and snowcapped Mont Blanc. Most of the rooms have large balconies or terraces, along with phones, TVs, and such amenities as combination tubs/showers, hair dryers, and trouser presses. For room and breakfast, doubles cost 338F to 402F, suites 388F to 518F.

Quai Igor-Stravinsky, 70, rue de Lausanne, CH-1110 Morges. ✆ **021/811-58-11.** Fax 021/811-58-88. www.fleur-du-lac.ch. Reservations required. Main courses 32F–78F; fixed-price menus 50F–78F. AE, DC, MC, V. Daily noon–2pm and 7–9:30pm. Bus: 57 from Lausanne.

Restaurant de l'Union FRENCH   Set between two historic and central streets of Morges's Old Town, this well-recommended, appealingly old-fashioned restaurant offers well-prepared cuisine that's neither expensive nor pretentious. Prepared by members of the von Kaenel family, the food choices include a succulent version of fricassee of chanterelles. The best beef selection is *tournedos vaudois,* which is grilled on a hot stone set directly atop your table. Also look for an unusual version of horse meat with sweet peppers (a favorite with the lunch crowd eager for a quick platter of very traditional food), and grilled filet of lamb with rosemary. Everybody's favorite dessert is an idiosyncratic and very popular version of *tarte à la raisinée,* which combines the texture of a flan with that of a pastry.

The restaurant is in a hotel that contains 14 simple bedrooms, all with private bathroom, TV, and phone. With breakfast included, doubles cost 150F to 190F.

In the Hôtel de Savoie, 7, Grand-Rue, CH-1110 Morges. ✆ **021/801-21-55.** www.hotelsavoie.ch. Reservations recommended. Main courses 28F–41F; fixed-price menu 35F. AE, DC, MC, V. Mon–Sat 11:30am–2:30pm and 6:30–11pm.

3 NYON ★

22km (14 miles) E of Geneva; 27km (17 miles) SW of Lausanne

Unhurried and peaceful, Nyon has been a popular lakefront resort since the Victorian era; masses of flowers decorate its waterfront quays. In Roman times Julius Caesar used the settlement here as a military outpost for his soldiers. Between 1781 and 1813, Nyon was famous for its delicate, almost translucent porcelain.

A major stopover on the lake-steamer route, Nyon is ideal for walks. You can, in fact, take a walk around the town walls known as **Promenade des Vieilles Murailles.** The walk goes along the 19th-century town walls until the promenade broadens into the **Esplanade des Marronniers,** from which the most stunning panorama unfolds. You can also wander around at leisure, enjoying the flower-filled park and quays bordering the yachting harbor.

ESSENTIALS

GETTING THERE   Nyon lies directly on the rail lines that connect Geneva with Lausanne. Trains depart from both those larger cities for Nyon every 30 minutes throughout the day. Call ✆ **0900/300-300** for **train schedules.**

Nyon is connected by bus to a handful of other French-speaking towns to its northwest, few of which have railway junctions of their own. There are also **bus** connections from Nyon's railway station to Geneva several times throughout the day. Despite these buses, most travelers arrive in Nyon by train. For bus schedules, contact the tourist office (see below).

If you're **driving,** head west from Lausanne, or east from Geneva, along N1.

In addition, there are a handful of **lake steamers** that travel in summer (May–Sept) between Geneva and Lausanne, stopping briefly in Nyon. Trip time by boat from Lausanne to Nyon is 2½ hours. For information and reservations, contact **CGN (Compagnie Général de Navigation),** 17, av. de Rhodanie, in Lausanne (✆ **0848/811-848;** www.cgn.ch).

VISITOR INFORMATION   The **Nyon Tourist Information Office,** at 8, av. Viollier (✆ **022/365-66-00;** www.nyon-tourisme.ch), is open mid-May to mid-September Monday, Tuesday, Thursday, and Friday 8:30am to noon and 2 to 5:30pm; off season, on the same days, hours are 8:30am to 12:30pm and 1:30 to 5:30pm.

SEEING THE SIGHTS

For an adventure off the beaten path, you can rent a **bike** for 33F at the Nyon rail station and cycle to Céligny, lying midway between Coppet and Nyon. You can go all the way to Coppet in 10km (6 miles) by heading south. But spend what time you can at **Céligny,** one of the most enchanting of all lakeside villages.

Richard Burton called Céligny home during the last years of his life. A small port here is filled with yachts and grassy lawns ideal for sunbathing. In fact, the swimming here is the best along the lake. Later you can wander over to the village cemetery to visit the grave of the great actor and former resident. Elizabeth Taylor has told friends that she has purchased the plot next to the man she married and divorced twice.

Musée du Léman, 8, quai Louis-Bonnard (✆ **022/361-09-49;** www.museeduleman. ch), is devoted exclusively to the geography, history, marine culture, arts, and ethnography of Lake Geneva. It also contains three large aquariums, plus flora and fauna of the largest lake of western Europe.

Musée Romain, rue Maupertuis (*C* **022/361-75-91;** www.mrn.ch), displays speci-mens of Roman architecture, as well as Roman statuary, inscriptions, mosaics, crafts, amphorae, glasswork, and coins. The basilica, which stands at one end of the forum of the Roman colony (Colonia Julia Equestris), was a public building for justice and com-merce.

Entrance to either museum costs 8F for adults, 4F for children and students. Both museums maintain the same hours: April to October Tuesday to Sunday 10am to 5pm (also Mon July–Aug); November to March, Tuesday to Sunday 2 to 5pm.

WHERE TO STAY & DINE

Hostellerie du XVI Siècle ★ Finds SWISS   This is a charming old inn with good food and affordable bedrooms. The building that gives this place its name was built dur-ing the 16th century on ancient Roman foundations. After a disastrous fire in the early 1990s, this place reopened as a simple, unpretentious restaurant. The delightful cuisine may include filets of perch sautéed with almonds, an array of grilled meats, and salads. The most popular offering is a two-course *menu du jour,* which includes an appetizer and a well-stocked main course, which changes daily. The most prevalent specialties are game hen with rosemary and entrecôte XVI Siècle, a hefty chunk of beefsteak seasoned with local herbs and served with matchstick potatoes. This is not a site for *grande gastronomie—* instead, the food is straightforward, generous in its portions, and geared to popular tastes.

The property also houses 19 simple but pleasantly furnished bedrooms, 13 with pri-vate bathroom. Doubles without bathroom rent for 100F, going up to 180F with bath-room. Breakfast is included.

Place du Marché, CH-1260 Nyon. *C* **022/994-88-00.** www.16eme.com. Reservations recommended. Main courses 30F–40F. AE, MC, V. Mon–Sat 11:30am–2pm and 6:30–10pm.

Hôtel Beau-Rivage ★   This is your best bet. Sections of this hotel were built in 1481, when an inn stood on the site welcoming pilgrims and merchants. Most of the building seen today, however, dates from around 1900. Cozy and old-fashioned, the Beau-Rivage, 7 minutes from the railroad station, was built directly on the quays in the heart of the Old Town. Sweeping views of the lake are available from any of the many balconies. The public rooms have been tastefully modernized in a summertime motif, which includes a series of brightly colored modern paintings. The midsize bedrooms are traditionally furnished, some with four-poster beds.

49, rue de Rive, CH-1260 Nyon. *C* **022/365-41-41.** Fax 022/365-41-65. www.hotel-beau-rivage-nyon.ch. 50 units. 240F–380F double; from 480F suite. Rates include buffet breakfast. AE, DC, MC, V. Free parking outside, 25F in garage. **Amenities:** Restaurant; bar; room service; Wi-Fi (5F per 30 min.). *In room:* TV, hair dryer, minibar.

4 VEVEY ★

18km (11 miles) E of Lausanne; 6km (4 miles) NW of Montreux

Home of Nestlé chocolate, the resort of Vevey has been popular with British visitors since the 19th century. It's at the foot of Mount Pélerin, which you can ascend by funicular. The town, dating from Roman times, was built at the mouth of the Veveyse River and is the center of the Lavaux vineyards. In the Middle Ages it was known as an important trading post on the route from Piedmont, in Italy, to Burgundy, in France.

Rousseau's descriptions of his "sentimental rambles" in the lake district lured the first Romantic visitors. In time, English and Russian aristocrats selected the sheltered Swiss Riviera for long winter sojourns. Famous exiles to the area have included the English regicide Edmund Ludlow, the French painter Gustave Courbet, the Polish pianist Ignace Paderewski, and the Polish novelist Henryk Sienkiewicz.

As former visitors Henry James, Oskar Kokoschka, and even Dostoyevsky could tell you, Vevey is a great town for walks, especially Old Town, with its interesting restaurants, bars, and shops. You can no longer see Graham Greene or Victor Hugo on the streets, but you'll still find much that is rewarding. Stop in at the tourist office and pick up a free brochure, *On the Trail of Hemingway,* that will direct you to not only the former residences of Papa but also to places frequented by dozens of celebrities.

ESSENTIALS

GETTING THERE Vevey lies on the major rail link between Lausanne and (via the Simplon Tunnel) the great cities of northern Italy. Dozens of **trains** stop here every day. Trip time from Lausanne is 15 minutes and the round-trip fare costs around 13F. Call the tourist office (see below) for more information.

If you're **driving** from Lausanne, head south along N9; from Montreux, drive northwest on N9 along the edge of the lake.

Daily from May through mid-October, about half a dozen lake steamers transit the length of Lake Geneva, stopping at Lausanne, Vevey, Geneva, and several other cities along the way. Travel time to Vevey from Geneva is almost 5 hours; from Lausanne, about 1 hour. For information, contact the **CGN (Compagnie Générale de Navigation),** 17, av. de Rhodanie, Lausanne (© **0848/811-848;** www.cgn.ch).

VISITOR INFORMATION The **Vevey Tourist Office,** 29, Grand-Place (© **021/962-84-84;** www.montreux-vevey.com), is open June to mid-September daily from 9am to 6pm; the rest of the year, hours are Monday to Friday 9am to noon and 1 to 5:30pm, Saturday and Sunday 10am to 3pm.

SEEING THE SIGHTS

Begin by exploring the **Grand-Place,** a mammoth market plaza, the town's nerve center and largest parking lot, facing Lac Léman. The corn exchange on the north dates from the early 19th century. As you walk in this area and along the quay, you'll enjoy views of the Savoy Alps.

For a slice of local life, head for the **Café de La Clef,** 25 rue de Conseil (© **021/921-22-45;** www.clefdesol.ch), where Jean Jacques Rousseau stayed in 1730. This is the landmark cafe of Vevey, and over the years it's seen a parade of who's who from Oona Chaplin to Le Corbusier. As you drink your libation, you can enjoy views of the pillared marketplace out front. The decor is dowdy and unfashionable, just how the habitués like it. If you're around at lunchtime, drop in for local Swiss specialties including lake fish such as perch or even a fondue in winter.

Church of St. Martin, boulevard St-Martin (no phone), dating from the 10th century, is on a belvedere overlooking the resort. It has a large rectangular tower with four turrets, and there's a good view of Vevey from the tower. Its interior has a dusty-looking collection of excavations that, along with the church itself, is always open.

A statue by John Doubleday on the new **square Chaplin,** quai Perdonnet, commemorates the area's most illustrious former resident, Charlie Chaplin. Chaplin moved here from the United States in 1952 with his young wife, Oona O'Neill, in part to escape accusations of Communist sympathies. Except for brief interludes, he remained in Vevey until his death in 1977. When he died, he was considered a popular, unpretentious (and fabulously wealthy) local citizen. The life-size statue erected in his honor represents the little tramp in baggy pants—the character Chaplin made famous—gazing out at his favorite view of Lake Geneva and the Alps in the distance.

Chaplin actually lived in the little village of **Corsier,** above Vevey, which dates from the 2nd century. Its church is thought to have been established by the Abbey of St. Maurice; inside you can see some 15th-century paintings. Villagers dedicated a park to their famous resident. Although the stately villa he occupied cannot be visited, the comedian is buried in the cemetery (Cimetière de Corsier), a 3-minute walk downhill from the village. Bus nos. 11 and 12 go from Vevey to Corsier.

Musée de l'Alimentarium   Established in the 1980s with funds derived mostly from the charitable foundations associated with the Nestlé organization, this museum celebrates the development of foodstuffs around the world. Set near the statue of Chaplin, it's the most interactive museum in Vevey, containing lots of buttons that children (and adults) can push to release odors of sizzling foods, activate dioramas and computerized exhibitions, and begin film clips that show the preoccupation of the human race with its own survival.

Quai Perdonnet. ✆ **021/924-41-11.** www.alimentarium.ch. Admission 12F adults, 8F students and seniors, free for children 16 and under. Tues–Sun 10am–6pm.

Musée Historique de Vevey   This stately château contains two museums: the Musée Historique de Vevey and the Musée de la Confrérie de la Vigneron (Winemakers' Museum). Exhibits include 18th-century antiques and mementos of the vintners' trade, wrought-iron work, arms, pewter, tools, and some of the paraphernalia associated with the region's wine festivals. Paintings by local artists are also displayed, as well as ancient and medieval artifacts once excavated from the area around Vevey.

2, rue du Château. ✆ **021/921-07-22.** www.museehistoriquevevey.ch. Free admission. Apr–Oct Tues–Sun 11am–5pm; Nov–Mar Tues–Sun 2–5pm.

Musée Suisse de l'Appareil Photographique (Swiss Camera Museum)   The only museum of its kind in Switzerland, this five-story celebration of the printed image contains examples of the machines that recorded human history from the earliest daguerreotypes to the present. The uppermost floor is devoted to a changing exposition of modern photographic art, but for aficionados of photography, the fascination here is the amazing range of cameras from the 1920s to today.

6, rue des Anciens-Fossés. ✆ **021/925-21-40.** www.cameramuseum.ch. Admission 8F adults; 6F students, seniors, and children 16 and under. Tues–Sun 11am–5:30pm.

WHERE TO STAY

Hôtel des Négociants   Built close to Vevey's main square in 1974, this government-rated two-star, four-story, brick-sided hotel does a thriving business in its street-level brasserie. The members of the Schoellkopf-Dorsaz family are your hosts, working hard to carefully maintain the hotel when they're not catering to hungry guests in their dining room. The small guest rooms are functionally furnished but well maintained, each outfitted with a small bathroom.

27, rue du Conseil, CH-1800 Vevey. ✆ **021/922-70-11.** Fax 021/921-34-24. www.hotelnegociants.ch. 23 units. 143F–182F double. Rates include buffet breakfast. MC, V. **Amenities:** Restaurant. *In room:* TV, Wi-Fi (free).

Hôtel des Trois Couronnes ★★★ This hotel is famous as the setting of Henry James's first popular success, *Daisy Miller;* the film version, by the director Peter Bogdanovich, was also made here. The Daisy Millers still arrive today, although perhaps not as innocent as the subject of James's novella. The hotel sits in the center of town, in a white-stucco-and-gray-stone building with noble details. Built in 1842, it still remains the grande dame, as it's so often called, of Vevey hotels. Rated five stars by the government, it has been progressively renovated over the years. The lobby has an elegant gallery with white balustrades three floors tall. The midsize to spacious rooms retain their 19th-century charm, the more expensive units with attractive antiques. Each unit comes with a luxurious private bathroom.

49, rue d'Italie, CH-1800 Vevey. ✆ **800/223-5652** in the U.S. or 021/923-32-00. Fax 021/923-33-99. www.hotel3couronnes.ch. 55 units. 220F–550F double; 750F–2,500F suite. Rates include buffet breakfast. AE, DC, MC, V. Parking 25F. **Amenities:** Restaurant; bar; concierge; exercise room; indoor heated pool; room service; spa. *In room:* A/C, TV/DVD, hair dryer, minibar, Wi-Fi (free).

Hôtel du Lac ★ This well-established hotel is popular because of its lakeside view and its distinct sense of old-fashioned charm. A government-rated four-star choice, it was built in 1864 but has been renovated bit by bit ever since, most recently in 2006. It has a swimming pool and a flower-studded lakeside terrace. Appropriate for a relaxing vacation beside the lake, the hotel is mostly patronized by foreign, especially British, visitors. If you read Anita Brookner's novel *Hôtel du Lac,* you may expect a grander place. Brookner took poetic license in describing its formality and refinement. The hotel restaurant, Les Saisons, deserves its excellent reputation for Swiss and French specialties.

1, rue d'Italie, CH-1800 Vevey. ✆ **800/780-7234** in the U.S. or 021/925-06-06. Fax 021/925-06-07. www.hoteldulac-vevey.ch. 50 units. 420F–580F double; 570F–760F junior suite. Rates include buffet breakfast. AE, DC, MC, V. Free parking outdoors, 33F in garage. **Amenities:** Restaurant; bar; babysitting; concierge; exercise room; outdoor pool; room service; spa. *In room:* A/C, TV, hair dryer, minibar, Wi-Fi (10F per hour).

On the Outskirts

Le Mirador-Kempinski ★★★ Evocative of an elegant manor house, Le Mirador is one of the grandest spas in western Switzerland. Lying 400m (1,312 ft.) above Lake Geneva in the heart of Swiss wine county on Mont-Pélerin, 13km (8 miles) north of Vevey, the hotel is composed of a four-story chalet and an equally luxurious balconied annex. This retreat is deluxe living in grand style, with luxurious furnishings and fine paintings. Although a favorite venue for conferences, the resort is also ideal for the spa devotee, drawn to such treatments as cellular therapy. There is no better example in Switzerland of a 21st-century resort than Le Mirador.

5, chemin du Mirador, CH-1801 Mont-Pélerin. ✆ **021/925-11-11.** Fax 021/925-11-12. www.mirador.ch. 62 units. 750F double; from 950F suite. AE, DC, MC, V. Free parking. **Amenities:** 3 restaurants; bar; exercise room; indoor/outdoor heated pool; spa. *In room:* A/C, TV, hair dryer, minibar, Wi-Fi (9F per hour).

WHERE TO DINE

Auberge de la Veveyse SWISS The bracing air and high altitudes might stimulate your appetite as you head for this century-old inn on the outskirts of St-Légier, 10km (6¼ miles) north of Vevey. Be aware that the ground floor of this sprawling inn contains both a modest but modern brasserie as well as a more formal and more pretentious *restaurant gastronomique,* wherein a half-dozen round tables create a coziness that's especially appreciated during the winter cold. Expect a rough-and-ready charm and simple platters of grilled steaks and fish in the brasserie. In the restaurant, menu items change with the season, and might include a tartare of partially smoked salmon with chives and citrus sauce, fried snails with cherry tomatoes on toast, fried sweetbreads with mustard sauce, and a confit of duck with green beans.

212, rte. De Châtel, 1806 St-Légier. ☎ **021/943-67-60.** Reservations recommended. Restaurant fixed-price menus 72F–145F; brasserie main courses 12F–45F, fixed-price menus 18F–52F. AE, DC, MC, V. Tues 5–10pm; Wed–Sat 9:30am–3pm and 5–10pm. Closed 3 weeks over New Year's and 2 weeks in July–Aug.

Bistro de l'Hotel de Ville SWISS   Very unpretentious and small, this landmark cafe overlooks the trees and cobblestones of an old square across from the city hall, and outside tables are available in fair weather. The food is simple but good. Appetizers include *assiette valaisanne* (air-dried beef); typical main courses are steak maison, steak with mushroom sauce, and couscous. It also offers sandwiches and three kinds of fondue. No food is served after 4pm.

19, rue de l'Hôtel-de-Ville. ☎ **021/921-78-80.** www.lebistro.ch. Reservations recommended. Main courses 15F–25F. MC, V. Mon–Thurs 7am–10pm; Fri 7:30am–midnight; Sat 9am–midnight.

Le Montagne ★ CONTINENTAL   Set high in the hills above Vevey, 4km (2½ miles) north of the center, this restaurant, built in 1906, perches on sloping terrain whose views sweep out over the French and Swiss Alps. Inside, hardworking owner/chef David Tarnowski offers a cozy dining room outfitted in tones of spring green and vineyard-inspired browns and russets, and a cuisine that many of the nearby über-rich residents travel for miles to taste. Menu items are artfully presented and much fussed over. Examples include sophisticated variations on fera, a local freshwater whitefish, which is served with a compote of fresh tomatoes. Especially artful is a marinated version of perch that has been surgically deboned and reassembled on a platter, and served with pulverized broccoli and perch tempura. Our favorite dessert is the chef's cherry platter, a dessert plate sculpted together from cherries transformed into marmalade, soup, ice cream, and mousse.

Rue du Village 21, 1803 Chardonne. ☎ **021/921-29-30.** Reservations recommended. Main courses 44F–65F; fixed-price lunch 58F, dinner 98F–148F. AE, MC, V. Wed–Sun 11:45am–2pm and 7–9:30pm. Closed 3 weeks in Aug and 3 weeks in Jan.

Restaurant Denis Martin "Le Château" ★★ CONTINENTAL   One of the most spectacular restaurants of Vevey occupies the street level of the town's oldest building—a baronial villa built in 1599. Inside, a pair of dining rooms offer soaring vaults composed of stone, contemporary accessories, and a noteworthy collection of modern sculpture by well-known Swiss artist André Raboud. During clement weather a flower-studded outdoor terrace offers sweeping views over lawns and the nearby lake. Menu items change frequently, according to the inspiration of chef and owner Denis Martin, but two representative, consistently excellent specialties include duck liver served with apple chutney and spice bread, and line-caught sea bass with basil-flavored olive oil and sweet peppers. If you prefer to leave the composition of your meal to the experts, consider one of the fixed-price menus, the most elaborate of which is composed of 15 artfully presented minicourses.

2, rue de Château, on the street level of the Musée Historique de Vieux Vevey. ☎ **021/921-12-10.** www.denis-martin.com. Reservations required. Main courses 48F–98F; fixed-price menus 160F–310F. AE, DC, MC, V. Tues–Sat 7–10pm. Closed mid-Dec to mid-Jan.

VEVEY AFTER DARK

At the columned marketplace in the center of town, **Café de La Clef Chez Manu,** 1, rue du Conseil (☎ **021/921-22-45**), was made famous in 1730 when Jean-Jacques Rousseau used to hang out here. As for decor, the place looks lost in a time capsule back somewhere in the early part of the 20th century, but it remains Vevey's enduring favorite as a worthy hangout at all times of the day or night. The place fills up for lunch with locals devouring such dishes as perch from Lake Geneva. The other much frequented spot is **Les Temps Modernes,** 6B, rue des Deux Gares (© **021/922-27-20;** www.lestempsmodernes.ch), both a restaurant and a club. It's the French name for *Modern Times,* one of the most famous films made by Vevey's most famous resident, the late Charlie Chaplin. This club attracts the most diverse group of patrons, from skiers to bankers. With its junky furniture, the club occupies a warehouselike building. If you stay for dinner, the food is excellent, although many visitors come here to enjoy live music performances—everything from hot salsa nights to concert jazz. There's no cover unless the performers are well known; if they are, you'll pay 25F. It's closed in July and August.

5 MONTREUX ★★

3km (2 miles) E of Vevey; 24km (15 miles) E of Lausanne; 100km (62 miles) E of Geneva

The chief resort of the Swiss Riviera, Montreux rises in the shape of an amphitheater from the shores of Lac Léman. An Edwardian town with a distinct French accent, it has long been a refuge for expatriates, including the novelist Vladimir Nabokov. Known for its balmy climate, it sports a profusion of Mediterranean vegetation, which grows lushly in the town's many lakeside parks. The mountains at the town's back protect it from the winds of winter, allowing fruit trees, cypresses, magnolias, bay trees, almonds, and even palms to flourish.

The city has expanded greatly from its original 19th-century core, incorporating several former villages along the shoreline. One of these, Clarens, was used by Rousseau as the setting for his epistolary novel *La nouvelle Héloïse.* The resort enjoyed its heyday in the years just before World War I, when it had only 85 hotel beds. It hosted such distinguished visitors as Tolstoy, Flaubert, Dostoyevsky, and Ruskin. In recent times the town has revived, and today about three-fourths of the resort's 20,000 inhabitants are engaged in some touristic capacity or another.

Though the resort is favored year-round, it's most densely crowded in summertime, when traffic clogs most of the streets.

ESSENTIALS

GETTING THERE Montreux not only lies on the famous Orient Express line linking Paris to Milan, but it's also connected to the link between Geneva and the Simplon Tunnel. Dozens of trains stop at Montreux every day headed in both directions. The most famous is the *Train Panoramique,* a big-windowed train with a transparent roof that links Montreux to Interlaken. Passengers who take this conveyance often continue, after a change of train, on to Lucerne in a conventional railway car. For bookings, contact **M.O.B. (Société Montreux-Oberland-Bernois),** Gare de Montreux (© **021/964-55-35;** www.mob.ch). For more Swiss **rail information,** dial © **0900/300-300.**

If you're **driving,** Montreux sits in the middle of a network of superhighways linking Germany, France, and Italy with Switzerland. The divider of the traffic coming from Germany via Bern is just outside Montreux. From that vantage point, you can go either east or west across Switzerland.

In addition, Montreux is one of the stops on the east-west steamer route between Villeneuve and Geneva. Travel by **lake steamer** from Lausanne is about 1 hour, or about

3 hours from Geneva. Most boats depart between May and September, with limited service throughout the rest of the year. For information and bookings, contact **CGN (Compagnie Générale de Navigation)** in Lausanne (✆ **0848/811-848;** www.cgn.ch).

VISITOR INFORMATION The **Montreux Convention & Tourist Information Office,** rue du Théâtre (✆ **021/962-84-84;** www.montreuxtourism.ch), is opposite the boat-landing pier. Throughout the year it's open daily from 9am to 6pm.

SEEING THE SIGHTS

Explore the old houses and crooked streets of Old Montreux. Later, stroll along the quayside promenade by the lake. The only way to discover the charms of far-flung and widely scattered Montreux is by using up a lot of shoe leather.

The most impressive castle in Switzerland, the **Château of Chillon** ★★ (✆ **021/966-89-10;** www.chillon.ch) is on the lake 3.2km (2 miles) south of Montreux. To reach it, you can ride trolley bus no. 1 for 3F each way. But for many, the most enthralling way to reach Chillon from Montreux is to walk along the scenery-studded 3km (2-mile) lake path; it's the grandest promenade you can take in Montreux. Most of the castle dates from the 13th century, but its oldest section is thought to be 1,000 years old. The castle was built by Peter II of Savoy and is one of the best preserved, and most frequently photographed, medieval castles of Europe. So-called sorcerers were tried and tortured here. The most famous prisoner, François Bonivard, was described by Byron in *The Prisoner of Chillon.* Bonivard was the prior of St. Victori in Geneva, and when he supported Geneva's independence in 1532, the Catholic duke of Savoy chained him in the dungeon until 1536, when he was released by the Bernese.

The château is open April to September daily from 9am to 6pm, March and October daily from 9:30am to 5pm, and November to February daily from 10am to 4pm. It's closed Christmas and New Year's. Admission costs 12F for adults, 6F for children 6 to 16.

Rochers-de-Naye ★★★ at 2,042m (6,698 ft.) is one of the most popular tours along Lake Geneva. From Montreux, a cogwheel train takes visitors up to Rochers-de-Naye in less than an hour. The train ascends the slopes over Lac Léman, passing **Glion,** a little resort on a rocky crag almost suspended between lake and mountains. You come to **Caux** at 1,097m (3,598 ft.), lying on a natural balcony overhanging the blue bowl of the lake. Finally, the peak of Rochers-de-Naye rises high in the Vaudois Alps. In the distance you can see the Savoy Alps, including Mont Blanc and the Jura Alps. At the end is an alpine flower garden, the loftiest in Europe. The train departs from the railway station of Montreux every hour during the day, beginning at 7:30am, with the last departure between 5:30 and 7pm, depending on the season. The travel time to Caux is 20 minutes. The round-trip fare between Montreux and Rochers-de-Naye is 59F. Holders of Swiss Rail passes or Eurail passes pay half price. Call ✆ **084/024-52-45** for more information.

Villeneuve, the little port town at the end of the lake, is where Lord Byron wrote *The Prisoner of Chillon* in 1816. Mahatma Gandhi visited Romain Rolland when the French novelist and pacifist lived here. The town and its surrounding countryside have been painted by many artists, including Oskar Kokoschka, who once lived here. Villeneuve is a 25-minute walk from the Château of Chillon, which is visible from virtually every point in the village.

WHERE TO STAY

Many of the main hotels of Montreux have greatly improved in recent years. Unfortunately, good budget accommodations are lacking. Hotels tend toward the superexpensive. If you want to stay in the area more cheaply, seek lodgings in Vevey.

Montreux Jazz Festival

One of the biggest musical bashes in Europe occurs at the internationally known **Montreux Jazz Festival** (✆ **021/966-44-44;** www.montreuxjazz. com). Beginning the first week of July and running for 2 weeks, everyone from Bob Dylan to Buddy Guy is likely to show up for the music and festivities. Ticket prices are high. You pay from 65F to 300F for each individual ticket. The tourist office in Montreux provides advance information and even sells tickets. Tickets for many events, especially the top ones, often sell out early. If you show up and can't get a ticket, you can still enjoy Jazz Off, some 500 hours of admission-free open-air concerts, often staged by new or wannabe talent throughout the city. The tourist office keeps a schedule, but much of the fun is spontaneous.

Very Expensive

Le Montreux Palace ★★★   Facing the lake, this is an opulent palace that was built in 1906. Despite being the largest hotel in Montreux, a monument visible from miles away, frequent renovations have retained its embellished ceilings, parquet floors, and crystal chandeliers. Once a favorite of Russian czars, it later attracted Vladimir Nabokov—the author of *Lolita,* among other works—who spent long periods of creative time here. Architectural charm abounds—one room has an arched ceiling with an Art Nouveau stained-glass skylight ringed with statues of cupids and demigods. Each of the comfortably old-fashioned bedrooms, many quite spacious, has French doors and a balcony. The rooms in the rear, however, open onto the mountain and not the lake. All units come with luxurious marble bathrooms. In all, the place is elegant, bemused, blasé, and very historic. The Willow Stream Spa here is one of the finest in Europe, with 10 womblike salons with waterfalls and stone floors. Treatments range from an Indian head massage to Turkish scrubs.

100, Grand'Rue, CH-1820 Montreux. ✆ **021/962-12-12.** Fax 021/962-17-17. www.fairmont.com/ montreux. 235 units. 500F–978F double; from 1,098F suite. AE, DC, MC, V. Parking 40F. Bus: 1. **Amenities:** 2 restaurants; 2 bars; babysitting; concierge; exercise room; 2 pools (1 heated indoor); room service; spa; outdoor tennis court (lit). *In room:* A/C, TV, hair dryer, minibar, Wi-Fi (35F per day).

Royal Plaza ★★   This is the most architecturally avant-garde hotel in Montreux. Designed in a semifuturistic style in 1982, it rises eight floors above an enviable position beside the lake, amid gardens and pedestrian walkways accented with shrubs, lawns, and trees. Because of the slope of the hillside on which the hotel is built, the lobby is set on the hotel's third floor, but few visitors realize that until they begin to explore the hotel a bit. Most of the spacious rooms face the lake and are designed in a sleek modern decor that would suit any five-star hotel in the world. All the accommodations contain luxurious bathrooms.

97, Grand'Rue, CH-1820 Montreux. ✆ **800/327-0200** in the U.S. or 021/962-50-30. Fax 021/962-51-51. www.royalplaza.ch. 146 units. 495F–795F double; 995F–2,950F suite. AE, DC, MC, V. Underground parking 28F. Bus: 1. **Amenities:** 3 restaurants; 2 bars; exercise room; indoor heated pool; room service; spa. *In room:* A/C, TV, hair dryer, minibar, Wi-Fi (35F per day).

Grand Hôtel Excelsior ★★   A renowned Montreux landmark since 1903, this government-rated five-star lakeside hotel offers quiet opulence and discreet personal service. The elegant marble foyer has marquetry, a hushed sense of restraint, and Queen Anne antiques. The charm of this hotel is enhanced by oil paintings and baroque sculpture. The luxurious rooms are spacious, and all have lakefront balconies.

21, rue Bon-Port, CH-1820 Montreux. ℂ 021/966-57-57. Fax 021/966-57-58. www.hotelexcelsior montreux.com. 70 units. 250F–330F double. Rates include buffet breakfast. Half board 55F. AE, DC, MC, V. Parking 25F. Bus: 1. **Amenities:** 2 restaurants; bar; babysitting; exercise room; indoor heated pool; room service; sauna. *In room:* TV, hair dryer, minibar, Wi-Fi (30F per 24 hr.).

Hôtel Eden au Lac ★★   The lingering nostalgia and beautiful restoration of this hotel evoke scenes from the movie *Death in Venice*, based on a work by Thomas Mann. It's a favorite hotel in Montreux, and it's less expensive than the Palace. Situated on the lakeside promenade, it has a grand 19th-century style and a facade that resembles an Art Nouveau wedding cake. The pink-and-white neobaroque Gatsby Bar has stained-glass windows, and there's a garden terrace with magnolias. The owners offer well-appointed, spacious rooms. The junior and senior suites are among the most opulent in Montreux.

11, rue du Théâtre, CH-1820 Montreux. ℂ **021/966-08-00.** Fax 021/966-09-00. www.edenmontreux.ch. 105 units. 255F–460F double; 430F–650F suite for 2. Rates include buffet breakfast. AE, DC, MC, V. Parking 25F. Closed mid-Dec to end of Jan. Bus: 1. **Amenities:** Restaurant; bar; exercise room; outdoor pool; room service; sauna. *In room:* A/C (in some), TV, hair dryer, minibar, Wi-Fi (28F per day).

Hotel Victoria ★★   This Relais & Châteaux opens onto views of mountains and lakefront and is surrounded by extensive, manicured grounds. It truly lives up to Lake Geneva's reputation as an idyllic retreat for hedonists. Expect a lot of pampering at this mansion dating from 1869. Noel Coward, the playwright, stayed here some 4 decades ago and raved about it in letters sent back to his theatrical friends in London. Following in Coward's footsteps, the Victoria has witnessed a parade of other celebrities, even royalty. The most desirable bedrooms open onto a private balcony overlooking the lake. All the accommodations are good, however, with well-chosen furnishings, fine art, and luxurious bathrooms.

Rte. de Caux, CH-1823 Glion sur Montreux. ℂ **021/962-82-82.** Fax 021/962-82-92. www.victoria-glion. ch. 50 units. 270F–420F double; 480F–620F junior suite. Rates include buffet breakfast. AE, DC, MC, V. Parking 20F. **Amenities:** Restaurant; bar; exercise room; outdoor pool; sauna; outdoor tennis court (lit). *In room:* TV, hair dryer, minibar, Wi-Fi (30F per 24 hr.).

Moderate

Grand Hôtel Suisse et Majestic ★   This opulent landmark, originally built in 1870 and renovated frequently since then, is in the heart of Old Montreux, beside the lake. Take one of the three elevators past the *trompe l'oeil* murals to the Art Nouveau lobby on the top floor. From here you'll have access to a terrace with classical statuary and a panoramic view. Comfort and subdued elegance are the keys to the success of this hotel. Most of the spacious rooms have an updated Belle Epoque decor, each equipped with a luxurious bathroom. The average unit is priced at the lower end of the scale below.

43, av. des Alps, CH-1820 Montreux. ℂ **021/966-33-33.** Fax 021/966-33-00. www.suisse-majestic.ch. 140 units. 340F–390F double; 470F–800F suite. Rates include buffet breakfast. AE, DC, MC, V. Parking 30F. Bus: 1. **Amenities:** 2 restaurants; bar; room service. *In room:* TV, hair dryer, minibar, Wi-Fi (30F per day).

Inexpensive

Hotel Tralala This off-white building, originally erected in 1800, became a hotel in 1992. In a quiet neighborhood, 5 minutes from the center of town, this has become a popular spot for those on a short stay in Montreux. The rooms are small, with a slight Mexican decor, and are well maintained and comfortable. Many of the rooms open onto lake views, and each is dedicated to an artist who has appeared in Montreux. You might sleep with David Bowie, Aretha Franklin, Miles Davis, or even Igor Stravinsky.

2, rue du Temple, CH-1820 Montreux. © **021/963-49-73.** Fax 021/963-23-11. www.tralalahotel.ch. 35 units. 160F–240F double. Rates include buffet breakfast. AE, MC, V. Parking 20F. **Amenities:** Restaurant; bar; babysitting; bikes; concierge; Internet (free, in lobby). *In room:* TV, hair dryer, Wi-Fi (free).

WHERE TO DINE

Very Expensive

Le Pont de Brent ★★★ FRENCH/SWISS   The district's finest and best-known restaurant is in a turn-of-the-20th-century house near a historic bridge in the hamlet of Brent. Gérald Rabaey, the owner and chef, prepares a frequently changing array of seafood, including a soup made with mussels and leeks, Breton lobster with zucchini in a tarragon-flavored cream sauce, rabbit in mustard sauce, and roast pigeon with herbs. Succulent versions of trout, turbot, and sea bass are also featured, along with fresh mushrooms and the best fruit of any season. We could heap praise upon praise on this restaurant and still not do it justice. It is the grandest choice for dining along Lake Geneva. The combination of flavors is inspired. Inventiveness and solid technique reign supreme here.

In Brent. © **021/964-52-30.** www.lepontdebrent.com. Reservations required. Fixed-price menus 185F–285F; 3-course business lunch 85F Tues–Fri only. MC, V. Tues–Sat noon–2pm and 7–9:30pm. Closed 3 weeks in midsummer and 2 weeks Dec–Jan. From Montreux, follow the signs to Blonary-Brent, driving 3km (2 miles) northwest of the city.

L'Ermitage ★★★ FRENCH/SWISS   Set in Montreux's lakefront suburb of Clarens, this restaurant occupies the dignified premises of a *maison bourgeoise* built in the late 19th century and surrounded with a spacious park. The celebrated chef, Etienne Krebs, owns the place along with his charming wife, Isabelle, who handles the dining room, which has welcomed everyone from the president of Switzerland to Quincy Jones. You'll dine in one of three rattan-filled rooms painted "the colors of water and sun" or on a terrace overlooking the lake. Menu items change with the seasons but always reflect fresh ingredients. Palate-pleasing examples include a casserole of foie gras with celery; filet of fera (a fish from the nearby lake) with capers and artichoke hearts; a salad of baby crawfish in an emulsion of tomatoes and olive oil; rosettes of roast lamb with aromatic alpine herbs; and a supreme thigh of wild duckling in a sheathing of mashed potatoes with a sauté of exotic mushrooms.

The site also maintains four rooms priced at 300F to 390F and three suites at 410F to 510F, with breakfast included. Each has rattan furniture and is individually decorated with taste and flair.

75, rue du Lac, CH-1815 Clarens. © **021/964-44-11.** Fax 021/964-70-02. www.ermitage-montreux.com. Reservations recommended. Main courses 54F–70F; fixed-price meals 75F–225F. AE, DC, MC, V. Sept–May Tues–Sat 11:30am–2pm and 7–10pm; June–Aug daily 11:30am–2pm and 7–10pm. Drive .8km (½ mile) east of Montreux, following the lakefront road and signs pointing to Vevey.

Expensive

La Vieille Ferme ★ SWISS/INTERNATIONAL   This old stone-walled house is in the village of Chailly, in a building dating from the 13th century that functioned as a munitions warehouse for local monks and later as a farmhouse. As such, it's one of the oldest buildings in the region. Accompanying your meal will be regional background music, which is performed almost every night. Yvan Mabillard is clearly a master chef, as revealed by his offering of succulent beef dishes, aromatic alpine lamb, chicken, rabbit, frogs' legs, tender veal, lake perch, trout, crawfish, and a velvety gooseliver made into a terrine. The menu also includes gratiné of shrimp or grilled beef, and fondue bourguignon and cheese fondue. The chef grills fresh fish and meat better than anyone else in the area. The arrival of large tour groups may interrupt your intimate dinner.

40, rue de Bourg, Chailly-sur-Montreux. ✆ **021/964-64-65.** www.laferme.ch. Reservations required. Main courses 30F–63F. AE, MC, V. Wed–Sun 11:30am–2:30pm and 6pm–midnight. From Montreux, follow the signs to autoroute N1; then just before you reach the autoroute, follow the signs to Chailly-Village, a total of 3km (2¹/₂ miles) north of Montreux.

Les Magnolias ★ RHONE/PROVENÇAL   Despite its role as the showcase restaurant in one of the most elegant Beaux Arts hotels in Montreux, this is not a particularly expensive establishment—at least by Swiss standards. You'll reach it by passing through the hotel's marble lobby, but once you're inside you'll notice a subtle nautical decor in the comfortable bar off to one side, and an emphasis on the culinary traditions of the Rhône Valley. Menu items change with the season and may include delectable deep-fried zucchini flowers with a *mousseline* of sea wolf, a standard version of *pissaladière niçoise* (a kind of Provençal quiche), filets of perch or sole meunière, and a divine roasted salmon garnished with duck liver and herbs.

In the Grand Hôtel Excelsior, 21, rue Bon-Port. ✆ **021/966-57-57.** Reservations recommended. Main courses 30F–45F; fixed-price dinner 60F. AE, DC, MC, V. Daily noon–2pm and 7–10pm. Bus: 1.

Moderate

Caveau des Vignerons SWISS   At the corner of rue di Marché, this is a tavern that has long been a local favorite. A traditional Swiss cuisine is served in a candlelit cave that is elegantly decorated with wood paneling. In this unusual atmosphere, you can order some of the best-tasting dishes in town, all reasonably priced. True devotees flock here for the horse meat, which you can cook yourself at the table, although those from other cultures might prefer to stick to one of the delectable Swiss specialties instead. The Cave turns out some of the best cheese and meat fondues in town. You can also look for the constantly changing daily specials, and finish your selection with one of the creamy desserts.

30, rue Industrielle. ✆ **021/963-25-70.** Reservations recommended. Main courses 22F–38F; fixed-price menu 30F–40F. AE, DC, MC, V. Mon–Fri 9am–midnight; Sat 3pm–midnight. Bus: 1.

Restaurant Chinois Wing Wah (**Kids**) CANTONESE   Hearty portions of well-prepared Chinese food and relatively reasonable prices attract many families to this scarlet-and-gold dining room. The owner, originally from Hong Kong, prepares lacquered duck, twice-grilled beef, spicy shrimp, diced chicken with hot peppers, crispy roast chicken, and curried shrimp. The restaurant's name translates as "happiness."

17, av. du Casino. ✆ **021/963-34-47.** Reservations required. Main courses 29F–38F; fixed-price lunch 17F–30F, dinner 50F–80F. AE, DC, MC, V. Daily 11:30am–2pm and 6:30–10:30pm. Bus: 1.

MONTREUX AFTER DARK

The major action spins around the **Casino de Montreux,** 9, rue du Théâtre (✆ **021/ 962-83-83**), but don't expect a casino where fortunes are made and lost, or even a particularly impressive architectural monument. The casino here has almost no architectural interest, set in a dull modern building in the heart of town near the lake. Despite that, it can provide some nightlife diversion in an otherwise rather dull town. About 200 slot machines shake, rattle, and roll, along with a handful of roulette tables. There is a small disco open nightly till 4am.

Harry's New York Bar, in Le Montreux Palace, 100, Grand-Rue (© **021/962-12-12**), is the most convivial watering hole and the first Harry's to be established in Switzerland. There's a Harry's Bar in many European cities today, but this particular example—managed by one of the grandest hotels of Montreux—won't remind you of any of them. Once the home of an auto showroom, it underwent an elegant transformation with the installation of rich paneling and touches of brass and leather. The bartenders—a well-trained crew hailing from almost everywhere—mix cocktails the old-fashioned way (shaken, not stirred). Most clients come here to drink, but if you're hungry, they serve light but elegant meals.

Another after-dark hot spot is **Caesar's,** 57, Grand-Rue (© **021/963-75-59**), known for its lakeside terrace dances and occasional cabaret.

Geneva

If it's a toss-up between Geneva and the larger city of Zurich (and you have time for only one stopover), make it Geneva.

Switzerland's second-largest city has an idyllic setting on one of the biggest alpine lakes and within view of the pinnacle of Mont Blanc. Filled with parks and promenades, the city becomes a virtual garden in summer.

Geneva is located in the Rhône Valley at the southwestern corner of Lake Geneva (or Lac Léman, in French), between the Jura Mountains and the Alps. It's the capital of the canton of Geneva, the second-smallest canton in the Swiss Confederation.

Surrounded by French territory, Geneva is connected to Switzerland only by the lake and a narrow corridor. The city's strong French influence shows in its mansard roofs, iron balconies, sidewalk cafes, and French signs.

In fact, many patriotic French feel this French-speaking city of elegance and charm should belong in France. And though it does indeed sit on the doorstep of France, Geneva in some respects is

international, belonging to the world with its 250 international organizations based here, the most important being the European headquarters for the United Nations, the World Health Organization, and the International Red Cross.

It's the most orderly and serene of all major European cities (or most sterile, in the view of those who'd like more local color, nightlife, and excitement).

Because of its ideological and geographic isolation from Switzerland, Geneva almost feels like one of those old European "city-states." Locals here used to burn books by Rousseau until Voltaire arrived and set them straight. Those romantics Shelley and Byron came here seeking inspiration from the surrounding mountains, but Lenin failed to convert anyone to communism.

As one local and very wealthy lady told us, "Geneva is one of the few places on the planet I can walk around in my white sable without fear I'll be hit by a rotten tomato by an animal rights fanatic, or else have it stolen from me by some poor wretched down and out." She actually said that.

1 ORIENTATION

ARRIVING

BY PLANE The **Geneva-Cointrin Airport** (© 022/717-71-11; www.gva.ch), although busy, is quite compact and easily negotiated. **Swiss International Air Lines** (© 877/359-7947 from the U.S.; www.swiss.com) serves Geneva more frequently than any other airline and offers the best local connections, connecting Geneva with Lugano, Zurich, and Bern, plus flying in from several European capitals. Other international airlines flying into Geneva include **Air France** (© 800/237-2747 from the U.S.; www. airfrance.com), with 10 flights daily from Paris; and **British Airways** (© 800/217-9297; www.britishairways.com), with 8 daily flights from London.

To get into the center of Geneva, there's a train station linked to the air terminal with trains leaving about every 8 to 20 minutes from 5:25am to 12:25am for the 7-minute trip; the one-way fare is 13F in first class and 10F in second class. A taxi into town will cost between 30F and 40F, or you can take bus no. 10 for 12F.

BY TRAIN   Geneva's CFF (Chemins de Fer Fédéraux) train station in the town center is **Gare Cornavin,** place Cornavin (ℂ **0900/300-300** for ticket information). A small tourist office branch is at the train station.

Note: When the Lausanne-Geneva railroad line was extended to Cointrin Airport, a second "main" railroad station was built here with both long-distance and intercity trains. To avoid having to make the trip back to the center from the airport, be sure you get off the train at the Cornavin station.

BY CAR   From Lausanne, head southwest on N1 to the very end of southwestern Switzerland.

BY LAKE STEAMER   There are frequent daily arrivals by Swiss lake steamer year-round from Montreux, Vevey, and Lausanne (you can use your Eurailpass for the trip). If you're staying in the Left Bank (Old Town), get off at the Jardin Anglais stop in Geneva; Mont Blanc and Pâquis are the two Right Bank stops. For more information, call ℂ **0848/811-848** or visit www.cgn.ch.

VISITOR INFORMATION

Geneva's tourist office, the **Office du Tourisme de Genève,** is located at 18, rue du Mont-Blanc (ℂ **022/909-70-00;** www.geneve-tourisme.ch), and is open daily year-round from 9am to 6pm. The staff provides information about the city, and can also arrange hotel reservations both in Geneva and throughout Switzerland, and refer you to other establishments specializing in car and motorcycle rentals and excursion bookings. They can also give you details about audio-guided visits to the Old Town.

CITY LAYOUT

Geneva is a perfect city to explore on foot. It's divided by Lake Geneva (Lac Léman) and the Rhône River into two sections: the Right Bank and the Left Bank. In addition to taking our walking tour of the highlights (see "Attractions," later in this chapter), you may rent an audio-guided tour in English from the tourist office (see above) for 10F. This tour covers more than two dozen highlights in the Old Town, and comes complete with cassette, player, and map. Its estimated duration is 2 hours. A 50F deposit is collected prior to your receipt of a cassette player.

RIVE GAUCHE (LEFT, OR SOUTH BANK)   This compact and colorful area is the oldest section of the city. Here you'll find Old Town, some major shopping streets, the famous Flower Clock, the university, and several important museums.

Grand-Rue is the well-preserved main street of Old Town. It's flanked by many houses dating from the 15th and 18th centuries. The street winds uphill from the ponts de l'Ile; at place Bel-Air it becomes rue de la Cité, then Grand-Rue, and finally rue de l'Hôtel-de-Ville. (Rousseau was born in a simple house at no. 40 Grand-Rue.) Eventually it reaches **place du Bourg-de-Four**—one of the most historic squares of Geneva. South of this street is **promenade des Bastions,** a greenbelt area overlooking the Arve River, with a monument to the Reformation. Directly to the west, in the northern corner of promenade des Bastions, is **place Neuve,** which is the finest square in Geneva.

From place Neuve, you can take rue de la Corraterie, which was once surrounded by the city wall, to the Rhône and the **ponts de l'Ile.** On this bridge is the **Tour-de-l'Ile,** what's left of the 13th-century bishops' castle.

On the shore of Lake Geneva is the **Jardin Anglais (English Garden)** with its Flower Clock and, farther out, the **Parc La Grange** and the nearby **Parc des Eaux-Vives.**

RIVE DROITE (RIGHT, OR NORTH BANK)   You can cross to the other side of the Rhône on any of several bridges, including pont du Mont-Blanc, pont de la Machine, pont des Bergues, and ponts de l'Ile. The Right Bank is home to Gare Cornavin, the major international organizations, and several attractive parks.

Place St-Gervais is in the St-Gervais district; this has been the area for jewelers and watchmakers since the 18th century.

Along the northern shore of Lake Geneva is **quai du Président-Wilson,** named for the U.S. president who helped found the League of Nations.

The Right Bank is surrounded by parks, from the tree-shaded promenades along the Rhône to the **Parc de la Perle du Lac, Parc Barton,** and on the city outskirts, **Parc Mon-Repos.**

FINDING AN ADDRESS   In a system developed during the Middle Ages, all Swiss cities begin their street-numbering system with the lowest numbers closest to the old center of town. The numbers increase the farther out from Old Town you go. Even numbers are on one side of a street; odd numbers are on the other side.

MAPS   The tourist office (see above) presents visitors with a free detailed and easy-to-follow map of Geneva. That same map is available from most of the city's hotels as well.

NEIGHBORHOODS IN BRIEF

RUES BASSES

Rues Basses (translated either as "low streets" or figuratively as "lower town") is found between Old Town and the south bank of the Rhône. It's the major commercial and shopping district of Geneva. Its major street is rue du Rhône, although rue de la Confédération and rue du Marché are also important arteries.

OLD TOWN (VIEILLE VILLE)

At an altitude of 398m (1,305 ft.), Old Town is the most history-rich section of Geneva. This is Left Bank Geneva, with its narrow streets, flower-bedecked fountains, and architectural blends of Gothic, Renaissance, and 18th-century features. The twin towers of the Cathedral of St. Pierre dominate Old Town, whose geographical and spiritual center is place du Bourg-de-Four.

THE PROMENADES OF GENEVA

These streets almost constitute a "neighborhood" in themselves. This section of quays along both Lake Geneva and the Rhône is best experienced by walking. One of the most scenic walks is from the Parc des Eaux-Vives on the Left Bank to the Parc de Mon-Repos on the Right Bank. Along the way is a clear view of Geneva's most famous and visible monument, the Jet d'Eau. Set a few inches above the surface of the lake, this fountain spurts a plume of shimmering water that rises to heights, depending on the wind on the day it's being measured, of between 140m and 145m (459–476 ft.) tall. Except for a 2-week maintenance regime conducted every midwinter, Jet d'Eau operates year-round, except when winds blow hard down from the Alps, during which period it's shut off to avoid drenching the passersby on the nearby quais.

CAROUGE

Carouge, a suburb of Geneva, is a historic European town. It dates from the 18th century, when it was built by the king of Sardinia to rival Geneva.

Architects from Turin supplied the Piedmontese charm. At the Congress of Vienna, in 1815, Carouge was annexed to the canton of Geneva. Carouge was once the playground of smugglers and gold washers who panned for the precious metal in the Arve. The Genevese themselves—at least those who wanted to escape from the puritanical city—came here in search of decadence.

Switzerland considers Carouge a national landmark because of its architecture. It can be reached from Geneva by tram no. 12 or 13 from the center. Begin your exploration in the Market Square, with its old fountain, plane trees, and markets. A Roman stone was imbedded in the Church of the Holy Cross. As you walk around, you'll pass the court of the count of Veyrier's palace, dating from 1783; place du Temple, with a fountain from 1857; and a Louis XVI carved door at 18, rue St-Victor.

2 GETTING AROUND

Walking, of course, is the cheapest, most practical form of transportation in Geneva. It's also the most advantageous from a tourist's point of view. Tree-shaded promenades line the edges of the lake, and you can browse many chic shops walking at a moderate pace along streets that include rue du Rhône. Savor the measured tempo of life here that makes this city particularly alluring to the foreign visitor.

Nevertheless, if speed is the object, you may avail yourself of the public transportation system, which is reasonably priced and as dependable as a Swiss watch.

BY PUBLIC TRANSPORTATION

Most of Geneva's public tram and bus lines begin either at the very central place Cornavin in front of the main railroad station, or, to a lesser extent, on the opposite bank of the river, at the place du Bel Air. Local buses and trams operate daily from 5am to midnight, and you can purchase a ticket from a vending machine before you board. Instructions are also given in English. **Transport Publics Genevois** (✆ **0900/022-021;** www.tpg.ch), next to the tourist office in Gare Cornavin, offers free maps of local bus routings. Trips that stay within zone 10, enveloping most of Geneva, cost 3F, and unlimited use of all zones costs 10F for 1 day.

Guests who have proof that they are booked into a hotel, B&B, or hostel are granted free rides on public transportation. Ask at your hotel for a public transportation ticket.

BY TAXI

The meter on whatever cab you take in Geneva will automatically begin calculating your fare at 7F, and then add between 3F and 3.50F for every kilometer you travel, depending on the time of day or night. The fare from the airport to the center of town ranges from 30F to 40F. No tipping is required, but extra baggage may cost 1.50F. To call for a **taxi,** call ✆ **022/331-41-33** or 320-20-20.

BY CAR

Driving is not recommended; parking is difficult and the many one-way streets make navigation complicated. However, should you wish to rent a car and tour Lake Geneva (see chapter 11), you'll find many car-rental companies represented in the arrivals hall of the airport and in the center of the city. Major car-rental companies in Geneva include **Avis,** 44, rue de Lausanne (✆ **022/731-90-00,** or at the airport 929-03-30; www.avis. com); **Budget,** at the airport (✆ **022/717-86-75;** www.budget.com); **Hertz,** at the airport (✆ **022/717-80-80;** www.hertz.com); and **Europcar,** 37, rue de Lausanne (✆ **022/ 909-69-90;** www.europcar.com). If you absolutely insist on driving a car, and if your hotel doesn't offer parking facilities and valet parking, the best bet for parking within the city limits tends to be within any of the many underground parking garages, whose presence is indicated with large blue-and-white signs designated with a letter "P." Rates for underground parking average between 1.50F and 2F per hour.

BY BIKE

Touring the city by bicycle isn't particularly practical because of the steep cobblestone streets, speeding cars, and general congestion. However, you might want to consider renting a bike for touring the countryside around Geneva. The major rental outlet is at the baggage desk at **Gare Cornavin** (✆ **022/791-02-50**), where city bikes cost 33F. Another major outlet, charging from 24F to 34F per day, depending on the degree of sophistication of the bicycle, is **Genève Roule,** 17, place Montbrillant (✆ **022/740-13-43;** www.geneveroule.ch).

Fast Facts   Geneva

Babysitters A list of agencies is available at the tourist office. Most of the expensive hotels will also secure an English-speaking babysitter for you, or you can call **Chaperon Rouge** (✆ **022/304-04-82**), an organization associated with the Red Cross responsible for teaching young girls about child-care rituals. Some students make themselves available for babysitting in either a private home or a hotel room; the service is particularly pertinent for sick children.

Bookstore One of the largest in Geneva is the well-stocked **Payot,** 5, rue Chantepoulet (✆ **022/731-89-50;** www.payot.ch), with a good selection of books in French, German, and English.

Business Hours Most banks are open Monday to Friday 8:30am to 4:30pm (until 5:30pm Wed). Most offices are open Monday to Friday 8:30am to 5:30pm, although this can vary. It's always best to call first.

Car Rentals See "By Car," above.

Consulates If you lose your passport or have other business with your home government, go to your nation's consulate: **United States,** 7, rue Versonnex (✆ **022/ 840-51-60**); **Australia,** 2, chemin des Fins (✆ **022/799-91-00**); **Canada,** 5, av. de L'Ariana (✆ **022/919-92-00**); **New Zealand,** 2, chemin des Fins (✆ **022/929-03-50**); the **United Kingdom,** 58, av. Louis Casaï, Cointrin (✆ **022/918-24-00**).

Currency Exchange In a city devoted to banking and the exchange of international currencies, you'll find dozens of places to exchange money in Geneva. Three of the most visible outlets, however, are run by **UBS-SA,** one of the country's largest banking conglomerates. You'll find a branch at the **Gare Cornavin,** 12, place Cornavin (✆ **022/748-27-11**), that's open Monday to Friday from 8:30am to 4:30pm; a branch at the **Cointrin Airport** (✆ **022/306-14-88**) that's open

Monday to Friday from 8:30am to 4:30pm; and a downtown branch at 75, rue du Rhône (℡ **022/375-75-75**) that's open Monday to Friday from 8am to 4pm. The branches in the airport and in the railway station also house "money-automats"—you receive an equivalent amount of Swiss francs for every $20, $50, or $100 bill you insert into the machine.

Dentist English-speaking dentists are available at one of the *cliniques dentaires* at 5, chemin de Malombré (℡ **022/346-64-44;** www.malodent.ch), open daily from 8am to 7pm.

Doctor If you become ill and want to consult a doctor, including one who will travel to your hotel, call ℡ **022/322-20-20;** or arrange an appointment with an English-speaking doctor at the **Hôpital Cantonal,** 22, rue Micheli-du-Crest (℡ **022/372-33-11**).

Drugstores Each night a different set of four drugstores stays open either till 9 or 11pm. Call ℡ **144** or 111 to find out which drugstore will be open. One of the world's biggest drugstores, **Pharmacie Principale,** in Confédération-Centre, 8, rue de la Confédération (℡ **022/318-66-60**), sells everything from medicine to clothing, perfumes, optical equipment, cameras, and photo supplies. It's open daily from 9am to 9pm.

Emergencies In an emergency, dial ℡ **117** for the police, ℡ **144** for an ambulance, or ℡ **118** to report a fire.

Eyeglasses You can go to **Visi-Lab** in the Confédération-Centre, 8, rue de la Confédération (℡ **022/318-66-80**).

Hospitals A prime choice for medical aid is the **Geneva University Hospital,** 24, rue Micheli-du-Crest (℡ **022/372-60-19;** www.hug-ge.ch). Most physicians speak English and German.

Library The **American Library,** at 3, rue de Monthoux (℡ **022/732-80-97;** www.amlib.ch), has a subscription service open to those looking for a wide variety of the latest books in English. A month's membership, the minimum allowable, costs 40F. A refundable deposit of 50F is required before you can borrow your first book.

Lost Property Go to the **Service Cantonal des Objets Trouvés,** 5, rue des Glacis-de-Rive (℡ **022/546-09-00**), open Monday to Friday from 7:30am to 4pm.

Luggage Storage/Lockers Luggage can be stored and lockers rented at the main railroad station, **Gare Cornavin,** place Cornavin (℡ **0900/022-021**).

Newspapers & Magazines Newspapers in Geneva are printed in French, but the latest copies of the *International Herald Tribune, USA Today,* the *New York Times,* and the *Washington Post* are available at most newsstands and in large hotel newsstand kiosks. And if you're planning on moving to Geneva, or spending more than a month here, consider acquiring a copy of the *Guide to English-Speaking Geneva,* which is available free at the American Library (see above).

Police In an emergency, call ℡ **117.** For nonemergency matters, call ℡ **022/327-41-11.**

Post Office There's a limited **Office de Poste** at Gare Cornavin, 16, rue des Gares (℡ **0848/888-888**), open Monday to Friday from 6am to 10:45pm, Saturday from 6am to 8pm, and Sunday from noon to 8pm. A better bet is the city's main post office, **Bureau de Poste Montbrillant,** rue des Gares (✆ **022/739-23-58**), which offers a full range of telephone, telegraph, and mail-related services Monday to Friday from 8am to 10:45pm, Saturday 8am to 10pm, and Sunday noon to 8pm.

Safety Geneva is one of the safest cities in the world, but that doesn't mean you shouldn't take the usual precautions when traveling anywhere. Protect your valuables. Car thefts have been on the rise. High-class prostitutes and confidence swindlers proliferate in Geneva to prey on the well-heeled.

Shoe Repairs An outlet of **Mr. Minit** is located in the Metro-Shopping arcade, 30, rue du Mont-Blanc (✆ **022/732-42-59**). Most repairs can be performed while you wait.

Taxes There is no special city tax, other than the 7.6% value-added tax (VAT) attached to most goods and services throughout Switzerland.

Telegrams, Telex & Fax Virtually every post office in Geneva maintains a handful of *tele-cabines* where you can pay cash for a phone call to anywhere in the world, but the densest concentration of these phones lies within the main railway station, **Gare Cornavin,** place Cornavin (it's open 24 hr. a day). Within less than a block, you'll find additional phones in the **Office de Poste Montbrillant,** 16, rue des Gares (✆ **0848/888-888**), which is open Monday to Friday 8am to 8pm and Sunday noon to 8pm. Either site can send telegrams or faxes for you.

Tipping Most restaurants and hotels, even taxis, add a service charge of between 10% and 15% to your bill, so, strictly speaking, no further tipping is necessary. Tipping rituals have evolved recently, within Geneva to reflect practices within neighboring France, so today, many diners leave a few coins—we established guidelines of around 2F extra for each member of a dining party, merely as a sign of respect for your waitstaff, but only if the service was adequate.

Toilets You'll find public facilities at all rail and air terminals and on main squares. Otherwise, you can patronize those in cafes and other commercial establishments such as department stores.

Transit Information For **train information,** call ✆ **0900/300-300** from anywhere in Switzerland. Contact the **airport** at ✆ **022/717-71-11.** For **bus information** Monday to Friday from 8am to 9pm, dial ✆ **0900/022-021;** for information on Saturday and Sunday, call ✆ **022/308-34-34.**

3 WHERE TO STAY

A truly world-class city, Geneva has lots of hotels, most of which are clustered around the railway terminal or stretched along the lakefront. But be warned—Geneva hosts a number of international conferences and conventions, so many of its hotels are booked months in advance. And while it does incorporate dozens of expensive hotels in all different architectural styles (from the antique to the supermodern), it doesn't have very many intimate, family-run inns.

Note: Unless indicated otherwise, all rooms in hotels we've recommended below have a private bathroom.

Very Expensive

Four Seasons Hôtel des Bergues ★★★   This elegant, four-story hotel—designated a historic monument by the Swiss—once catered to the monarchs of Europe. After being conglomerated into a Four Seasons, the hotel underwent a massive renovation, downsizing from 122 rooms to 103 more spacious rooms. It is now the most ostentatiously elegant hotel in Geneva.

Stratospherically expensive, with an armada of uniformed, polite staff members, the Four Seasons is a favorite with the haute international business community, diplomats, and members of European society. Grandly memorable from its centrally located position at the edge of the Rhône, the hotel also hosted many meetings of the League of Nations.

The hotel's public rooms are among the most lavish in Switzerland. The bedrooms have Directoire and Louis Philippe furnishings. Accommodations ranked "superior" on the Bel Etage floor are the finest choices here, although all units are beautifully appointed. Lake-view rooms are more expensive.

33, quai des Bergues, CH-1211 Genève. ✆ **022/908-70-00.** Fax 022/908-74-00. www.hoteldesbergues. com. 103 units. 810F–1,040F double; from 2,250F suite. AE, DC, MC, V. Parking 40F. Bus: 1. **Amenities:** Restaurant; bar; airport transfers (110F); babysitting; children's programs; concierge; exercise room; room service; spa. *In room:* A/C, TV/DVD, CD player, hair dryer, minibar, Wi-Fi (30F per 24 hr.).

Hôtel Beau-Rivage ★★★   This grand old landmark 1865 hotel receives our highest recommendation for its traditional Victorian charm and impeccable service. The most tragic event in its history was the assassination of Empress Elisabeth ("Sissi") of Austria, who was stabbed on the nearby quays in 1898 by the anarchist Luigi Lucheni, and then carried back to her lodgings in the Beau-Rivage to die a few hours later. To this day, history buffs rent the pale-blue Empress Suite.

Its most striking feature is the open, five-story lobby. The hotel also became the first in Europe to install elevators. The rooms are individually furnished and frequently redecorated. All front rooms have views of the lake. Accommodations are categorized by size, with "romantic" rooms being more spacious and "classical" rooms being medium in size. Some of the romantic units contain ceiling frescoes teeming with cherubs and mythical heroes.

13, quai du Mont-Blanc, CH-1201 Genève. ✆ **022/716-66-66.** Fax 022/716-60-60. www.beau-rivage.ch. 94 units. 900F–1,400F double; from 1,900F suite. AE, DC, MC, V. Parking 40F. Bus: 1. **Amenities:** 2 restaurants; bar; babysitting; concierge; exercise room; room service. *In room:* A/C, TV/DVD, CD player, fax, hair dryer, minibar, Wi-Fi (free).

Hôtel d'Angleterre ★   Elegant and tasteful, this boutique hotel is the smallest of the grand palace hotels that line the edge of the lake, beside the waterfront promenade of Geneva. Set behind a stately looking facade that was originally erected in 1872, it has successfully competed with larger and equally grand hotels as the hotel of choice for visiting celebrities. Bedrooms are outfitted in tasteful renditions of what you might have expected in a British country house, with flower-patterned chintzes and deep upholsteries. Rooms have been systematically overhauled, several per year, keeping everything spiffy. Especially appealing is the street-level bar area, where a safari-inspired decor mixes what you might have expected in a country house in England with a scattering of antique trunks (which double as tables), animal hides–cum-upholsteries, and a sense of colonial adventure.

17, quai du Mont-Blanc, CH-1201 Genève. ✆ **022/906-55-55.** Fax 022/906-55-56. www.dangleterre hotel.com. 45 units. 680F–990F double; from 1,680F suite. AE, DC, MC, V. Parking 40F. Bus: 1. **Amenities:** Restaurant; bar; babysitting; exercise room; room service; sauna. *In room:* A/C, TV, hair dryer, Wi-Fi (free).

Basel · Zurich
Bern ★ SWITZERLAND
· Geneva

Best Western Strasbourg **3**
Four Seasons Hôtel
  des Bergues **15**
Hôtel Beau-Rivage **18**
Hôtel Bel'Espérance **13**
Hôtel Bernina **6**
Hôtel Central **12**
Hôtel d'Angleterre **19**
Hôtel de la Cigogne **14**
Hôtel de la Paix **16**
Hôtel des Tourelles **10**
Hôtel Edelweiss **2**
Hôtel International
  & Terminus **4**
Hôtel Lido **7**
Hôtel Moderne **8**
Hôtel Président Wilson **21**
Hôtel St-Gervais **9**
Hôtel Tiffany **11**
Kempenski Geneva **20**
Le Richemond **17**
Les Armures **1**
Le Warwick **5**

GENEVA

12

WHERE TO STAY

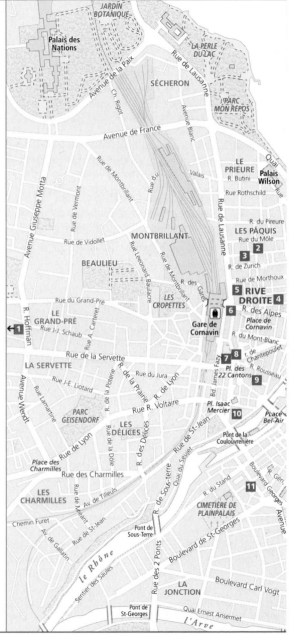

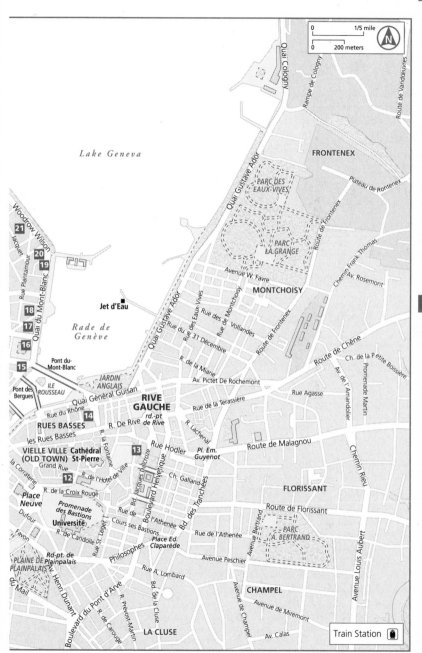

Hôtel de la Paix ★★ In terms of opulence, it's a notch down from the Beau-Rivage, but since its prices are less expensive and it's a lot less pretentious, many clients seek it out. It's grand and glamorous, and after a complete overhaul, it's better than it's ever been. Designed by an Italian architect, the building belonged to the kingdom of Sardinia for a long time, functioning for a period as a kind of unofficial residence and embassy. The main salon, a double-tiered arched extravaganza, with marble columns, Corinthian capitals, and a balustraded loggia overlooking a massive crystal chandelier, is in all the architectural guidebooks to Geneva. Bedrooms come with comfortably contemporary furnishings. On the lobby level of this hotel is a rather daringly decorated bar and restaurant, the **Nobel Bar and Restaurant Vertig'O** (p. 355), which evokes hip and quirky nocturnal Paris.

11, quai du Mont-Blanc, CH-1201 Genève. ✆ **800/223-6800** in the U.S. or 022/909-60-00. Fax 022/909-60-01. www.hoteldelapaix.ch. 84 units. 650F–900F double; from 925F–1,600F suite. AE, DC, MC, V. Parking 40F. Bus: 1. **Amenities:** Restaurant; bar; babysitting; concierge; room service. *In room:* A/C, TV, hair dryer, minibar, Wi-Fi (free).

Hôtel Président Wilson ★★★ This hotel is sprawling, extremely comfortable, and plush in a style that includes the kinds of details (leather upholstery, polished hardwoods, lots of airy space) that you might have associated with a private and very comfortable club in London. It's also one of the very few palace hotels of Geneva to boast its own outdoor swimming pool, which is positioned one floor above the lobby level. The hotel was named for Woodrow Wilson and the president's ill-fated attempt to get the United States to join the League of Nations. The hotel is across a busy boulevard from the lakefront, a 5-minute drive (or a brisk 12-min. walk) from the center of town. Each of the guest rooms and suites offers views of the lake, and each is furnished with classic European styling, with extensive use of wood and rich fabrics. Luxury extras are all in place, with bidets, robes, marble bathrooms, full-length mirrors, dual basins, and elegant carpeting. One of the galleries displays the hotel's collection of 17th-century Gobelin tapestries.

47, quai du Président-Wilson, CH-1211 Genève. ✆ **022/906-66-66.** Fax 022/906-66-67. www.hotelpwilson.com. 230 units. 890F–1,040F double; from 1,200F suite. AE, DC, MC, V. Parking 40F. Bus: 1. **Amenities:** 4 restaurants; 2 bars; babysitting; bikes; concierge; exercise room; indoor heated saltwater pool; room service; spa. *In room:* A/C, TV/DVD, CD player, hair dryer, minibar, MP3 docking station (in some), Wi-Fi (25F per 24 hr.).

Kempinski Geneva ★ Located at the edge of the lake, this hotel was built of gray concrete in a style that evokes a bunker with windows. From the restaurants, lounge, and bar a view opens onto the lake with the Alps as a backdrop. The decor manages to be both contemporary and rather cozy. Part of the lower ground floor was inspired by a Roman amphitheater. A suspended footbridge leads to the lobby, and a mammoth window curves up to the second floor. On three sides, the rebuilt structure sports two-story-high porticoes and a glass canopy, with two elevators offering panoramic views. The bedrooms are luxurious and spacious, with tasteful, comfortable furnishings. Many of the rooms open onto private balconies with panoramic views. A large luxury shopping arcade is on the ground floor of the hotel.

19, quai du Mont-Blanc, CH-1211 Genève. ✆ **022/908-90-81.** Fax 022/908-90-90. www.kempinski-geneve.com. 423 units. 400F–1,400F double; from 2,400F suite. AE, DC, MC, V. Parking 40F. Bus: 1. **Amenities:** 3 restaurants; bar; babysitting; concierge; exercise room; indoor heated saltwater pool; room service; sauna. *In room:* A/C, TV, hair dryer, minibar, Wi-Fi (30F per 24 hr.).

Le Richemond ★★★   Le Richemond has for years been identified as the greatest hotel in Geneva. Erected in 1875, the neoclassical, travertine building has wrought-iron balustrades, each emblazoned with the letter "R," and is situated across the quay-side boulevard from the lake, across from a small park. In the 19th century it was an unpretentious guesthouse. But its acquisition by the Rocco Forte chain catalyzed a radical re-examination of its decor. Accommodations range from the most spacious in the city to medium in size; nearly half of the units here are suites, attracting all of Europe, plus international CEOs. This is true Grand Hotel living, with elegant fabrics, tasteful upholstery, and luxurious beds, plus spacious marble bathrooms with robes and a basket of expensive toiletries.

Jardin Brunswick, CH-1201 Genève. ℂ **022/715-70-00.** Fax 022/715-70-01. www.lerichemond.com. 98 units. 720F–1,300F double; from 1,600F suite. AE, DC, MC, V. Parking 50F. Bus: 1. **Amenities:** Restaurant; bar; babysitting; concierge; exercise room; room service; spa; Wi-Fi (free, in lobby). *In room:* A/C, TV, DVD (in some), hair dryer, minibar, MP3 docking station (in some).

Le Warwick ★ (**Kids**)   This contemporary and solidly reliable hotel, located across from the train station, was built during the 1970s. The abstractly modern lobby contains sweeping staircases, loggias, balconies, marble floors, and Oriental rugs. On hand is a large but somewhat depersonalized and anonymous-looking staff in the kind of smart, upscale uniforms that evoke a hotel a bit grander than it really is. The refurbished, sound-proof bedrooms are often sunny, boldly patterned, and comfortable, with marble bathrooms. Le Warwick allows children up to 12 years of age to stay free in their parent's room. Its brasserie is open for light meals and snacks all day long.

14, rue de Lausanne, CH-1201 Genève. ℂ **800/203-3232** in the U.S. and Canada or 022/716-80-00. Fax 022/716-80-01. www.warwickgeneva.com. 167 units. 700F–850F double; from 1,500F suite. Children 12 and under stay free in parent's room. AE, DC, MC, V. Parking 18F. **Amenities:** Restaurant; bar; babysitting; concierge; room service. *In room:* A/C, TV, hair dryer, minibar, Wi-Fi (free in suites and business rooms; 30F per 24 hr. in other units).

Moderate

Best Western Strasbourg ★   Set close to the railway station on a tranquil dead-end street, this building was originally constructed around 1900 by a nostalgic entrepreneur originally from Strasbourg. Over the years many different renovations, both inside and out, have kept it looking fresh and new, albeit bland and uncontroversial. Some of the bedrooms have wooden surfaces and pastel colors; others are comfortably and traditionally conservative. The bedrooms, as befits a turn-of-the-20th-century hotel, range from spacious (usually on the lower floors) to a bit cramped. Each bedroom has fine linens, plus compact bathrooms with tile and decent plumbing.

10, rue Pradier, CH-1201 Genève. ℂ **800/528-1234** in the U.S. or 022/906-58-00. Fax 022/906-58-14. www.bestwestern.com. 51 units. 250F–270F double; 400F–500F suite. Rates include continental breakfast. AE, DC, MC, V. Bus: 1, 2, 3, 4, 8, 12, 13, or 44. **Amenities:** Concierge; room service. *In room:* TV, hair dryer, minibar, Wi-Fi (10F per hour).

Hôtel Edelweiss   This brown-and-white, eight-story hotel towers above its neighbors within the bustling, working-class Pâquis neighborhood, a short walk from the hyperexpensive quai du Président-Wilson. Inside, it has a rustic decor that contrasts with its modern exterior. The bedrooms are cozy and furnished with pine-wood furniture crafted in a country-Swiss style. Even though it's in the heart of Geneva, you get provincial comfort here and a sense of high-alpine Switzerland far from the moneyed, urban gloss of modern-day Geneva. (Fans praise it as a short-term substitute for a trip to Switzerland's mountainous interior.) Bedrooms are medium in size with sitting areas and desk space. Bathrooms, although small and plain, are neatly kept. Built in the early 1960s, the hotel is frequently spruced up.

2, place de la Navigation, CH-1201 Genève. ✆ **022/544-51-51.** Fax 022/544-51-99. www.manotel.com/ edelweiss. 42 units. 210F–400F double. Rates include buffet breakfast. AE, DC, MC, V. Bus: 1. **Amenities:** Restaurant; bar; room service. *In room:* A/C, TV, minibar, Wi-Fi (free).

Inexpensive

Hôtel Bel'Espérance (**Value**) Appealingly located at the gateway to Old Town, close to the lake, this is a decent, completely unpretentious budget hotel managed by the Salvation Army. It's not bare-bones, though: It has well-furnished, good-size bedrooms, accompanied by private bathrooms. Many rooms are suitable for up to four people, and the most desirable units open onto a private balcony with a view of the Cathédrale de St. Pierre. A homey, warm atmosphere prevails.

1, rue de la Vallée, CH-1204 Genève. ✆ **022/818-37-37.** Fax 022/818-37-73. www.hotel-bel-esperance. ch. 40 units. 154F–190F double; 186F–228F triple. Rates include breakfast. AE, DC, MC, V. Bus: 8. *In room:* TV, Wi-Fi (free).

Hôtel Bernina Set directly across from Gare Cornavin, this is an old-fashioned but worthy hotel with a reputation for fair prices and relatively comfortable accommodations. Just don't expect luxury; there's a Sputnik-era severity to the lobby, with furniture like what you'd expect in an airport waiting lounge, and a blasé, not particularly responsive staff. Rooms are high-ceilinged and sunny, albeit somewhat battered, but they're clean, filled with angular modern furniture, and soundproof against the noise of the traffic outside. The restaurant congestion of the railway station is just across the square.

22, place Cornavin, CH-1211 Genève. ✆ **022/908-49-50.** Fax 022/908-49-51. www.bernina-geneve.ch. 80 units. 240F–293F double. Rates include buffet breakfast. AE, DC, MC, V. Bus: 10. **Amenities:** Room service. *In room:* TV.

Hôtel des Tourelles (**Value**) Named after the twin towers that flank the edges of its turn-of-the-20th-century facade, this stone-sided, government-rated two-star hotel offers good value in simple, straightforward rooms that are made more palatable by high ceilings, small refrigerators, and, in some cases, balconies overlooking the Rhône and its quays. Some of the bedrooms have decorative marble fireplaces dating from the year of the hotel's construction. The staff is helpful and, in some cases, charming. Breakfast is the only meal served. The only drawback to this place involves traffic noise from the busy riverside avenues adjacent to the hotel, but shutting the double-glazed windows helps muffle most of it.

2, bd. James-Fazy, CH-1201 Genève. ✆ **022/732-44-23.** Fax 022/732-76-20. www.destourelles.ch. 22 units. 160F–180F double. Rates include buffet breakfast. AE, DC, MC, V. *In room:* TV, fridge, hair dryer, Wi-Fi (free).

Hôtel International & Terminus (**Kids**) This hotel lies across the street from the main entrance of Geneva's railway station and has been directed by three generations of the Cottier family. Originally built in 1900, it has been radically upgraded, with pairs of smaller rooms reconfigured into larger units especially good for families. Rated three stars by the local tourist board, the hotel offers exceedingly good value. The small to spacious bedrooms are fitted with first-rate furnishings and the maintenance level is high. Bathrooms seem to have been added as an afterthought in areas not designed for them, and are a bit cramped with shower stalls. The restaurant, La Veranda, serves some of the most reasonable meals in Geneva, and keeps the pizza ovens cauldron hot.

ch. 60 units. 170F–290F double. Rates include buffet breakfast. AE, DC, MC, V. **Amenities:** Restaurant. *In room:* TV, hair dryer, minibar, Wi-Fi (free).

Hôtel Lido   This durable choice 2 blocks from the rail station was built in 1963 and has been completely renovated several times since. This is a simple, government-rated two-star hotel with few if any frills—it's recommended for its bargain price. The small rooms are furnished in a no-nonsense functional style. All rooms come equipped with neatly kept bathrooms. The hotel has five floors with an elevator.

8, rue de Chantepoulet, CH-1201, Genève. ℂ **022/731-55-30.** Fax 022/731-65-01. www.hotel-lido.ch. 31 units. 170F–230F double. Rates include continental breakfast. AE, DC, MC, V. Parking 25F. **Amenities:** Breakfast room. *In room:* TV.

Hôtel Moderne   Near the railroad station and the lake, this is a seven-story, rectangular, white structure, with a low-lying, glassed-in extension containing the breakfast room. The public rooms are modern, with Nordic furniture and abstract angles and curves. The bedrooms, each with soundproof windows, have standardized furnishings and are well maintained, modern, and often sunny. You'll wish the bathrooms had more room to spread out your stuff, though you'll appreciate the tidy maintenance, up-to-date plumbing, and clean showers. The hotel's restaurant serves only breakfast, but there's an Italian restaurant under separate management in the same building.

1, rue de Berne, CH-1201 Genève. ℂ **022/732-81-00.** Fax 022/738-26-58. www.hotelmoderne.ch. 55 units. 215F double. Rates include buffet breakfast. AE, DC, MC, V. Parking (nearby) 25F. Bus: 10. **Amenities:** Restaurant; room service. *In room:* TV, Wi-Fi (9F per hour).

Hôtel St-Gervais   One of the simplest hotels we recommend in this guide, the St-Gervais is inside an old-fashioned, vaguely nondescript building in Geneva's medieval core, a 3-minute walk from Gare Cornavin. Although it has quirky idiosyncrasies that appeal to architects and historic renovators, some guests have expressed annoyance at having to navigate their way to the upper floors with a lot of luggage. Fortunately, there's a cramped elevator on-site. The place is minimalist but comfortable, with an emphasis on durable, functionalist furniture. You get routine rooms here, and well-worn but still comfortable beds. As for plumbing, you most often have to settle for just a sink, although the hotel maintains an adequate number of hallway bathrooms, which are kept very tidy.

20, rue des Corps-Saints, CH-1201 Genève. ℂ **022/732-45-72.** Fax 022/731-42-90. www.stgervais-geneva.ch. 24 units, 3 with bathroom. 119F double without bathroom, 145F with bathroom. Rates include breakfast. AE, DC, MC, V. **Amenities:** Bar; Wi-Fi (20F per 24 hr.).

ON THE LEFT BANK
Expensive
Hôtel de la Cigogne ★★★   Personalized and charming, this is our favorite Left Bank hotel, a chic, glamorous retreat for the discerning. This deluxe hotel was rebuilt after years of dilapidation and turned into an offbeat Relais & Châteaux that showcases designer and decorator talent. Combined with an adjoining building, the old hotel and its mate have the renovated facades of the original 18th- and 19th-century structures. With three sheltered courtyards overlooking a flowering plaza, this is one of the most tranquil hotels in Geneva. The bedrooms contain handmade mattresses, luxurious bathrooms, and bed linens embroidered with the hotel's coat of arms. Each bedroom is furnished differently, ranging from 1930s movie-mogul style to the "baron and baroness at their country place." Some units have working fireplaces.

17, place Longemalle, CH-1204 Genève. ✆ **022/818-40-40.** Fax 022/818-40-50. www.cigogne.ch. 52 units. 495F–620F double; 870F–970F suite. Rates include continental breakfast. AE, DC, MC, V. Parking 27F. **Amenities:** Restaurant; babysitting; room service. *In room:* A/C, TV, hair dryer, minibar, Wi-Fi (free).

Les Armures ★★★   Surpassed only by La Cigogne, this is one of the most elegant and prestigious hotels on Geneva's Left Bank. Positioned a few steps from both the cathedral and the medieval Maison Tavel, it lacks the late-19th-century grandeur of its five-star competitors across the river. Instead, you'll find a labyrinth of narrow corridors, and architectural gemstones that include beamed (and sometimes frescoed) ceilings and carefully preserved remnants of the building's 17th-century origins. Each unit is different from its neighbors, usually with exposed brick or stone, and each alternates modern plumbing with richly detailed tile work in its bathrooms. The ambience here is cozy and well upholstered, with an ostentation that's subtle and based for the most part on the building's sense of quirky, antique charm.

1, rue du Puits Saint-Pierre, CH-1204 Genève. ✆ **022/310-91-72.** Fax 022/310-98-46. www.hotel-les-armures.ch. 32 units. 635F–660F double; 870F–970F suite. Rates include buffet breakfast. AE, DC, MC, V. Parking 35F. **Amenities:** Restaurant; bar; babysitting; concierge; room service. *In room:* A/C, TV/DVD, hair dryer, minibar, Wi-Fi (25F per 24 hr.).

Moderate

Hôtel Tiffany ★ ⬭Value   This little charming five-story Belle Epoque boutique hotel lies on a Left Bank street 3 blocks south of the river and about a 12-minute stroll from the center and the lake. Although it can hardly match the style and glamour of the lakeside palaces, it's attractive in its own modest way, featuring touches like stained glass, Art Nouveau bed frames, leather-clad armchairs, and a summertime sidewalk cafe. In its category, it offers some of the most reasonable prices in Geneva, especially considering its style. Bedrooms are midsize with lots of extras, including soundproofing and spacious bathrooms. We prefer the rooms in the "attic," with their beams, rooftop vistas, and sloping walls.

1, rue des Marbriers, CH-1204 Genève. ✆ **022/708-16-16.** Fax 022/708-16-17. www.hotel-tiffany.ch. 46 units. 430F–480F double; from 650F suite. AE, DC, MC, V. Parking nearby 34F. **Amenities:** Restaurant; bar; exercise room; room service. *In room:* A/C, TV, DVD and CD player (in suites), hair dryer, minibar, Wi-Fi (10F per hour).

Inexpensive

Hôtel Central   Confusingly located on the fifth, sixth, and seventh floors of a prominent building erected in 1924, this hotel has been a haven for cost-conscious visitors to Geneva since 1928. You'll find a very modern format, with a minimalist interior, on a street lined with banks and upscale shops. You'll register in the sixth-floor reception area, containing carved antiques from Bali. (The establishment's Danish-born owner used to manage a five-star hotel there.) Know in advance that the smallest rooms have two-tiered bunk beds, toilets in alcoves off the hallway, and very little space. The more expensive rooms are bigger and more comfortable. Be alert that the reception staff is available only from 7am to 9pm, so if you're planning on a late-night check-in, make prior arrangements. Breakfast is served in the bedrooms.

2, rue de la Rôtisserie, CH-1204 Genève. ✆ **022/818-81-00.** Fax 022/818-81-01. www.hotelcentral.ch. 32 units, 28 with private toilet. 95F double without toilet; 115F–165F with toilet; 215F suite. Rates include continental breakfast. AE, DC, MC, V. Bus: 12. **Amenities:** Room service. *In room:* TV, Wi-Fi (free).

4 WHERE TO DINE

Geneva is one of the gastronomic centers of Europe, with an unmistakable French influence. Genevans today take their dining seriously, and practice fine eating with consummate flair and style. Meals are often long, drawn-out affairs and, in many cases, more expensive than many travelers are used to.

Naturally, Geneva serves all the typically Swiss dishes, such as filets of perch from Lake Geneva and fricassee of pork. In season many of its restaurants offer cardoon, which is similar to an artichoke and is usually served gratiné. By all means, try the Genevese sausage *longeole*. Omble chevalier comes from Lac Léman and is like a grayling, although some compare it to salmon.

Cheese is also a staple on the Genevese table, including such Swiss varieties as *tomme* and Gruyère, plus, in season, *vacherin* from the Joux Valley. Naturally, everything will taste better with the Perlan (white wine) and gamay (red wine) from Geneva's own vineyards.

ON THE RIGHT BANK
Very Expensive

Le Chat-Botté ★★★ FRENCH   This grand restaurant is in one of the fanciest hotels in Geneva. Suitably decorated with tapestries, sculpture, and rich upholstery, with a polite and correct staff, it serves some of the best food in the city. There are some critics who consider it among the best restaurants of Europe. If the weather is right, you can dine on the flower-bedecked terrace, overlooking the Jet d'Eau. The cuisine, although inspired by French classics, is definitely contemporary. Typical starters include delectable zucchini flowers stuffed with vegetables and essence of tomato; and lobster salad with eggplant "caviar," olive oil, and fresh herbs. Some of the most enticing items on the menu include carpaccio with black olives and Parmesan cheese, poached wing of skate in an herb-flavored sauce, and oven-roasted Sisteron lamb with stuffed vegetables. The chef's best-known dish is a delicate filet of perch from Lake Geneva, which is sautéed until it's golden.

In the Hôtel Beau-Rivage, 13, quai du Mont-Blanc. (*C* **022/716-69-20.** Reservations required. Main courses 60F–90F; fixed-price menus 185F–220F. AE, DC, MC, V. Daily noon–2pm and 7–9:45pm. Bus: 1.

Spices ★★ INTERNATIONAL   There's something yummy and mellow looking about the tawny decor of this restaurant, positioned off the sprawling lobby of the also-recommended Hôtel Président Wilson (p. 318). It's the best-decorated and most exciting hotel restaurant in Geneva, with big windows overlooking the lake. Menu items change with the season and the inspiration of the chef, but are likely to include warm marinated salmon with sage and a wasabi-flavored pistou; a sweet-and-sour combination of freshwater crayfish with Maine lobster; Chinese-style raviolis stuffed with foie gras of duckling with a ginger-flavored cream sauce; line-caught sea bass fried with Sicilian artichokes; and a superb version of breast of Bresse chicken where, on one platter, you'll find versions braised with teriyaki and stuffed with foie gras.

In the Hôtel Président Wilson, 47, quai Wilson. (*C* **022/906-65-52.** Reservations recommended. Main courses 75F–110F. AE, DC, MC, V. Mon–Fri noon–2pm; Mon–Sat 7:30–10pm.

Windows ★ CONTINENTAL   Flooded with sunlight from large panoramic windows, and permeated with an undeniably upscale but discreet and rather clubby sense of old-fashioned exclusivity, it attracts a clientele of French-Swiss politicians, film industry

GENEVA

12

WHERE TO DINE

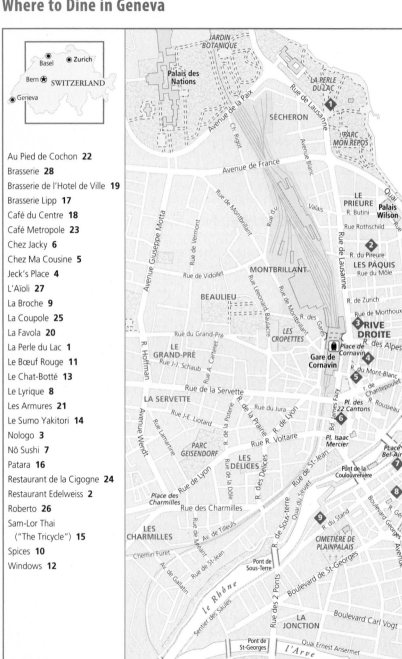

Au Pied de Cochon **22**
Brasserie **28**
Brasserie de l'Hotel de Ville **19**
Brasserie Lipp **17**
Café du Centre **18**
Café Metropole **23**
Chez Jacky **6**
Chez Ma Cousine **5**
Jeck's Place **4**
L'Aïoli **27**
La Broche **9**
La Coupole **25**
La Favola **20**
La Perle du Lac **1**
Le Bœuf Rouge **11**
Le Chat-Botté **13**
Le Lyrique **8**
Les Armures **21**
Le Sumo Yakitori **14**
Nologo **3**
Nô Sushi **7**
Patara **16**
Restaurant de la Cigogne **24**
Restaurant Edelweiss **2**
Roberto **26**
Sam-Lor Thai
  ("The Tricycle") **15**
Spices **10**
Windows **12**

personnel, writers, and the merely rich. Menu items change with the seasons, but are likely to include orange-marinated chicken cutlets with a yogurt-flavored avocado sauce and bulgur wheat; zucchini flowers stuffed with eggplant "caviar" and Provençal herbs; asparagus and Roquefort soup; roasted omble chevalier, a whitefish from the nearby lake, served with a reduction of carrot juice and a passion fruit–flavored butter sauce; and pan-fried veal cutlets served with a demi-glacé of veal drippings and green asparagus. And if you happen to be walking along the quais between 3 and 5pm, consider dropping into this place for high tea (30F per person), which includes finger sandwiches and pastries.

In the Hôtel d'Angleterre, 17, quai du Mont-Blanc. ✆ **022/906-55-55.** Reservations recommended. Main courses 49F–74F; fixed-price lunch 54F, dinner 70F–190F. AE, DC, MC, V. Daily noon–2pm and 7–10:30pm. Bus: 1.

EXPENSIVE

Brasserie ★ MEDITERRANEAN   In the Parc des Eaux-Vives, this is the less formal and more affordable part of the restaurants in this mansion that dates back to the 18th century. In the more formal restaurant, called Parc des Eaux-Vives (same phone as below), meals can run up to 230F or beyond. In this more modern brasserie section, a light and varied cuisine is offered, as you sit on a large summer terrace overlooking the lake. The chefs cook with energy and verve, and use pure, authentic ingredients to concoct memorable meals. Begin with such starters as a Maine lobster in a ravioli of cauliflower semolina, or else pan-fried duck foie gras with confit of apple and a beet chutney. All pastas are handmade, including tagliatelle carbonara.

Both the fish and meat courses are sublime, in flavors ranging from slow-cooked pig's cheek with a perfume of orange peel and creamy polenta to salmon in lemon butter with shellfish-studded black rice. Desserts are not only luscious but creative, including a caramel tartlet with caramelized popcorn.

82, quai Gustave. ✆ **022/849-75-75.** Reservations required. Main courses 35F–54F. AE, DC, MC, V. Daily noon–2pm and 7–9:30pm.

Chez Jacky ★ (Finds) SWISS   This provincial bistro should be better known, although it already attracts everyone from grandmothers to young skiers en route to Verbier. It's the domain of Jacky Gruber, an exceptional chef from the Valais. There's subtlety in Monsieur Gruber's cooking that suggests the influence of his mentor, Frédy Giradet, hailed as Switzerland's greatest chef before his recent retirement. The chef tirelessly seeks the most select produce for his imaginative and innovative dishes, and he continues to dazzle his regular clients year after year, winning new converts as well. You may begin with Chinese cabbage and mussels and continue with filet of turbot roasted with thyme, or perhaps beautifully prepared pink duck on a bed of spinach with a confit of onions. Be prepared to wait for each course, though.

11, rue Jacques-Necker. ✆ **022/732-86-80.** www.chezjacky.ch. Reservations recommended. Main courses 43F–46F; fixed-price lunch 28F–48F, dinner 67F–93F. AE, DC, MC, V. Mon–Fri 11:30am–2pm and 7–10pm. Closed 1st week of Jan and mid-July to mid-Aug. Bus: 5, 10, or 44.

La Perle du Lac ★ SWISS   Situated in a single-story pavilion owned by the city, this is the only restaurant in Geneva that's not separated from the waters of the lake by a stream of traffic. It's set beneath the venerable trees of Mon-Repos Park, not far from the United Nations complex. Although the candlelit interior is lovely, you may want to reserve a table on the outdoor terrace in warm weather. A talented French chef prepares a marvelous mousseline of sweetbreads and mushrooms. Other specialties, each delectable,

include line-caught grilled sea wolf with fresh fennel and olive oil, and braised strips of
fera (freshwater lake fish) flavored with saffron. Ravioli appears in an unusual version
stuffed with fresh watercress. The real allure here involves competent but not necessarily
inspired cuisine, and a location and lakeside setting that more than compensates.

128, rue de Lausanne. ✆ **022/909-10-20.** www.laperledulac.ch. Reservations required. Main courses
35F–65F; fixed-price menu 88F–130F. AE, DC, MC, V. Tues–Sun noon–2pm and 7:30–10pm. Closed mid-
Dec to mid-Jan. Bus: 4 or 44.

Moderate

Le Boeuf Rouge LYONNAIS Few other restaurants in Geneva's center work so hard
to bring you an authentic version of the brasserie-style cuisine of Lyon, and although the
place isn't as famous or as much talked about as it was during its 1980s heyday, it's still
a viable dining choice. You'll find such dishes as Lyonnais sausage with scalloped potatoes, chateaubriand in red-wine sauce, blood sausage, and quenelles of pikeperch—any
of which might be preceded by a delectable version of onion soup or green salad with
croutons and bacon. The decor is appealingly kitschy, complete with lots of Art Nouveau
posters and late-19th-century ceramics. The staff here is brusque but kind.

17, rue Alfred-Vincent (corner of rue Pâquis). ✆ **022/732-75-37.** www.boeufrouge.ch. Reservations
recommended. Main courses 17F–46F; fixed-price menus 44F–48F. AE, DC, MC, V. Mon–Fri noon–2pm
and 7–10:30pm; Sat 7–10pm. Bus: 1.

Patara ★★★ THAI This is the most elegant and prestigious Thai restaurant in
Geneva, occupying a street-level premises within the Hôtel Beau-Rivage, and a position
immediately adjacent to Le Chat Botté, one of the most elegant restaurants in town.
Within a decor of teak woodcarvings, Thai paintings, and soothing colors of blue-green,
an impeccably dressed, mostly Thai staff will serve flavor-filled examples of the best of
their country's cuisine. The best menu items include braised chicken in green curry with
coconut milk, steamed sea bass in lime sauce, giant prawns with garlic and cilantro, and
pan-fried filet of gilthead in a spicy basil sauce. There are also other interesting selections,
like asparagus and shiitake mushrooms in oyster sauce.

In the Hôtel Beau-Rivage, 13, quai du Mont-Blanc. ✆ **022/731-55-66.** www.patara-geneve.com. Reservations recommended. Main courses 22F–48F; fixed-price dinner 90F. AE, DC, MC, V. Mon–Fri noon–2pm;
daily 7–10pm. Closed last 2 weeks of Dec. Bus: 1.

Inexpensive

Jeck's Place ★ THAI/SINGAPOREAN Near the Gare Cornavin, this place is a
delight. It's like taking a culinary trip to Southeast Asia, with stopovers in such places as
China, Malaysia, Thailand, and India. Escaping from the traffic outside, you enter a
warm and friendly enclave, where Jeck Tan of Singapore will greet you. The cuisine of
Asian specialties provides temptation with every order, and the trays of delicacies are
brought out by waitresses in sarongs. The specials of the day will be seasoned with delicate blends of spices, notably lemon grass and curry, but also chili and ganlaga (from the
ginger family). It's not the dull beef sauté, for example, but a medley of delight in a sauce
flavored with cloves, curry, cinnamon, coconut milk, and lemon grass. We often make a
meal of the appetizers alone, including homemade steamed dumplings stuffed with a
blend of pork and vegetables flavored with coriander. The house specialty, and our favorite dish, is Jeck's chicken in green curry.

14, rue de Neuchâtel. ✆ **022/731-33-03.** www.jecksplace.ch. Reservations recommended. Main courses
22F–36F; special lunch platter 14F. AE, DC, MC, V. Mon–Fri 11:30am–2pm; daily 6:30–10:30pm. Bus: 4, 5, or 9.

Moderate

Brasserie de l'Hôtel de Ville ★ SWISS   This is one of the most deliberately archaic-looking restaurants in Geneva, with a reputation that dates from 1764 and a clientele that prefers that absolutely nothing changes in either its old-fashioned decor or its choice of dishes. In spite of its look, it's rather hip and popular with the Genevois. Be aware that this place doesn't have a lot of patience with diners who aren't familiar with dining rituals as practiced in an upscale brasserie, and the staff can be brusque. Nonetheless, we continue to recommend it as we would a time capsule to another era. The menu is more sophisticated and better than ever. Try the filets of freshwater lake perch meunière. Sometimes the prized fish of Lake Geneva, omble chevalier, is also served in a butter sauce. One old-fashioned dish remains on the menu: Longeole du val d'Arve (traditional Geneva-style sausages flavored with cumin). You can also order such delights as rack of lamb flavored with herbs of Provence.

19, Grand-Rue. ✆ 022/311-70-30. www.hdvglozu.ch. Reservations recommended. Main courses 27F–45F; fixed-price menu 47F–67F. AE, DC, MC, V. Daily 11:30am–11:30pm. Bus: 36.

Brasserie Lipp SWISS   Located on the ground floor of a modern shopping complex, this bustling restaurant is named after the famous Parisian brasserie, and when you enter, especially at lunch, you'll think you've been transported to Paris. Waiters in black jackets with long white aprons are constantly rushing about with platters of food. The menu contains a sampling of French bistro dishes. Like its Parisian namesake, the Geneva Lipp specializes in several versions of charcuterie. You can also order three kinds of *pot-au-feu* and such classic dishes as a Toulousian cassoulet with *confit de canard* (duckling). The fresh oysters are among the best in the city. These dishes will not dazzle you with subtle nuances, and service is a bit frantic, but it appeals to all lovers of the old-fashioned French brasserie.

In Confédération-Centre, 8, rue de la Confédération. ✆ 022/318-80-30. www.brasserie-lipp.com. Reservations recommended. Main courses 31F–50F; *plats du jour* 19F–37F lunch only; fixed-price menus 67F–83F. AE, DC, MC, V. Mon–Sat 7am–2am; Sun 9am–2am. Bus: 12.

Café du Centre SWISS/CONTINENTAL   This cafe is usually hysterically busy, and permeated with a kind of brusque anonymity. But despite its drawbacks, this remains very much an Old Geneva institution, established in 1871. Despite the thousands of cups of coffee and glasses of beer served here, it's more akin to a restaurant that serves drinks than a cafe that offers food. During nice weather, most of the business takes place outdoors on a terrace opening onto the square, while the rest of the year, business moves inside into a pair of street-level rooms whose nostalgic decor may remind you of an old-fashioned brasserie in Lyon. A thick, multilingual menu offers food items such as excellent versions of fresh fish as well as Wiener schnitzel, a savory version of onglet of beef, and pepper steak.

5, place du Molard. ✆ 022/311-85-86. www.cafeducentre.ch. Reservations recommended. Main courses 27F–44F; fixed-price *assiette du jour* 19F at lunch Mon–Fri only. AE, DC, MC, V. Mon 6am–midnight; Tues–Sat 9am–1am; Sun 9am–midnight. Tram: 12.

Café Metropole SWISS   Convenient and cozy, this brasserie-style restaurant and cafe attracts a young crowd for its cocktails, wine list, and good, market-fresh food. Dishes tend to be light and flavorful. You might begin with the fish soup with rouille or else a niçoise salad, perhaps one of the pâtés. Fish dishes are well prepared, especially sole from the Atlantic or red tuna. Sea bass from Mediterranean waters is another specialty, as is

Swiss beef. Even the hamburger on the menu is special here: It comes with truffles. For **329** dessert, why not try a slice of melon from Cavaillon, France? Gourmets claim they are the best in Europe.

6, rue du Prince. ℰ **022/310-06-70.** www.cafemetropole.ch. Main courses 24F–36F. AE, MC, V. Daily noon–2pm and 7–10:30pm.

La Broche SWISS/FRENCH/MIDDLE EASTERN   This restaurant turns out some of the best rotisserie platters in Geneva, especially that baby farmhouse Swiss chicken roasted on a spit. The chefs also specialize in lamb from the Limousine region, and this succulent meat is also roasted on a spit. Many of their dishes have a Middle Eastern tone, and tabbouleh is served with some courses (this is, of course, an Arabic salad with parsley, bulgur, mint, tomato, scallions, and other herbs). Main dishes are likely to include filet of half-cooked tuna in a sesame crust with ginger sauce, or else pan-fried prawns with herb butter and eggplant purée.

36, rue du Strand. ℰ **022/321-22-60.** www.restaurantlabroche.ch. Reservations recommended. Main courses 23F–39F; express menu 28F. AE, MC, V. Mon–Fri noon–2pm; Mon–Sat 7–10:30pm.

La Coupole SWISS   This is a true brasserie—far more elegant than its Parisian namesake. The place is more popular at noon, especially with shoppers and office workers, than it is at night. Fanciful and fun, it's dotted with grandfather clocks, a bronze Venus, Edwardian palms, and comfortable banquettes. The menu is limited but well selected; the *cuisine du marché* (fare with local and seasonal ingredients) is a delight, although many patrons stick to the standard old red-meat bistro specials such as the inevitable entrecôte.

116, rue du Rhône. ℰ **022/787-50-10.** www.lacoupole.ch. Reservations recommended. Main courses 32F–46F; fixed-price menu 49F. AE, DC, MC, V. Mon–Sat 11:30am–2:30pm and 7–11pm. Bus: 2, 9, or 22. Tram: 12.

La Favola ★ TUSCAN/ITALIAN   It's the best Italian restaurant in Geneva, and its most devoted habitués hail it as the best restaurant in Geneva—period. Set a few steps from the Cathédrale de St. Pierre, it contains only two cramped dining rooms. The menu is small but choice, varying with the availability of ingredients and the seasons. Look for such delightful dishes as carpaccio of beef; *vitello tonnato* (paper-thin veal with a tuna sauce); lobster salad; potato salad with cèpe mushrooms; such pastas as fresh ravioli with either eggplant or bolet mushrooms; and a luscious version of tortellini stuffed with ricotta, meat juices, red wine, and herbs. Meat and fish vary daily. Don't even think of coming here on weekends, as the place is locked tight.

15, rue Calvin. ℰ **022/311-74-37.** www.lafavola.com. Reservations required. Main courses 31F–60F. No credit cards. Mon–Fri noon–2pm and 7:15–10pm. Closed 2 weeks in July–Aug and 1 week at Christmas. Tram: 12.

Le Lyrique SWISS   Le Lyrique contains both a formal restaurant and a brasserie. The restaurant opened in 1981 but was cleverly patterned on turn-of-the-20th-century models. It bustles with urban vitality and is very tuned to the arts and business lives of Geneva. The restaurant is only open on Saturday and Sunday when there's a special presentation at the Grand Théâtre de Genève, just a short distance away. The brasserie, which has a terrace, is open all day but serves hot meals only during the hours mentioned below. In the restaurant you can try such carefully prepared dishes as filet of sea wolf with grapefruit, a roulade of rabbit with pasta maison, and tagliatelle with scampi. In the brasserie, menu items include chicken supreme with ravioli and leeks, and an *assiette Lyrique,* a meal in itself that combines four vegetarian and fish dishes—tartare of salmon, tartare of vegetables, terrine of vegetables, and eggplant "caviar."

12, bd. du Théâtre. ✆ **022/328-00-95.** www.cafe-lyrique.ch. Reservations recommended. Restaurant main courses 26F–51F; fixed-price menu 64F; brasserie main courses 21F–48F, fixed-price menu 46F–56F. AE, MC, V. Mon–Fri 7pm–midnight. Bus: 2 or 22.

Les Armures ★ (Kids) SWISS   In spite of the government-rated five-star elegance of the hotel that contains this restaurant, it is surprisingly unpretentious and affordable. Dining is possible on three different floors. This stone building is located on a cobblestone street across from a medieval arsenal in one of the most colorful neighborhoods of the Old Town. The building was constructed in the 16th century, and this place has thrived as one of the most atmospheric restaurants since its founding in 1957. The four different fondues offered are the best in Geneva. Many Swiss children make an entire meal out of *rösti* (Swiss-style hash browns). Other specialties include raclette and several pizza and pasta dishes. The winter-only sauerkraut garni is also a savory meal—made with several types of sausage and pork. Pastas and hamburgers round out the menu here, which should make any child's palate happy.

1, rue du Puits Saint-Pierre. ✆ 022/310-34-42. www.hotel-les-armures.ch. Main courses 18F–46F. AE, DC, MC, V. Mon–Fri 8am–midnight; Sat–Sun 11am–midnight. Bus: 3 or 5.

Restaurant de la Cigogne ★★ CONTINENTAL   This is one of the most appealing and best-staffed restaurants on Geneva's Left Bank. Classified as a member of the prestigious Relais & Châteaux group, it's housed within an opulently paneled ground-floor room of the also-recommended hotel (p. 321). Cosseted, discreetly elegant, and cozy, with impeccable service, it offers a full bar, a spectacular wine list, and well-groomed cuisine. At lunch the venue is a bit more businesslike and rapid, segueing into a more relaxed and leisurely venue at dinner. Menu items reflect whatever ingredients are in season at the time of your arrival, but are likely to include a superb ravioli of shrimp with a brunoise (finely diced) of vegetables and a mousseline sauce; turbot prepared *façon grand-mère;* and a delectable *cordon bleu* of veal stuffed with foie gras and truffles, served with a galette of polenta with Parmesan and asparagus.

In the Hôtel de la Cigogne, 17, place Longemalle. ✆ **022/818-40-40.** Reservations recommended. Main courses 43F–51F; fixed-price menus 65F–130F. AE, DC, MC, V. Daily noon–2pm and 7–10pm. Closed Sat–Sun during July–Aug. Bus: 6 or 9.

Restaurant Edelweiss (Kids) SWISS   This is the most famous folkloric alpine-style restaurant in Geneva. It's set within the cellar of the also-recommended Hôtel Edelweiss (p. 319), an establishment that carries the alpine chalet theme into its bedrooms, and its restaurant is the most artfully rustic within its neighborhood. Tables are lined up cozily under a high ceiling that showcases the flagstone columns, the fluegelhorns, the cowbells, and the live folkloric bands that oompah throughout the dinner hour. Rib-sticking menu items include six kinds of fondues, raclettes, roasted lamb chops with herbs, Zurich-style sliced veal in cream sauce, and several kinds of fish. If you have children, this may be a particularly worthy choice because of the folkloric distractions that add to the experience of dining here.

In the Hôtel Edelweiss, 2, place de la Navigation. ✆ **022/544-51-51.** Reservations recommended. Main courses 29F–48F; fixed-price menus 45F–55F. AE, DC, MC, V. Daily 7–11:30pm. Bus: 1.

Roberto ★ ITALIAN   One of the most appealing Italian restaurants in Geneva occupies a relatively formal-looking dining room that's sheathed with wood paneling, mirrors, and a series of contemporary paintings by the restaurant's owner, Roberto Carugati. There's more here, however, than just artwork, as the food is delectable, flavored with the kind of Mediterranean sunshine that you'd expect from a midsummer trip to Italy. Menu items include such succulent pastas as tortellini with chopped veal and a cream sauce; filets of turbot with béarnaise sauce; and scampi served with tarragon. Especially sought-after are the house versions of saltimbocca (veal with ham), *osso buco* (braised veal shanks), and *crespelle ai quattro formaggi* (Italian crepes with four kinds of cheeses).

10, rue Pierre-Fatio. © 022/311-80-33. Reservations recommended. Main courses 30F–55F. AE, MC, V. Mon–Sat noon–3:30pm; Mon–Fri 7:15–10pm. Bus: 8, 9, or 12.

Inexpensive

Au Pied de Cochon ★ LYONNAIS/SWISS   Named after a restaurant at Les Halles in Paris, this is the best place to go in Geneva for hearty Lyonnais fare, if you don't mind the smoke and the noise. The setting is *fin de siècle,* with a staff dressed entirely in black and white. The bistro maintains its Lyonnais antecedents, which every Francophile knows are the most illustrious for fine brasserie-style food. A lot of young people, artists, and local workers dine here, as well as lawyers from the Palais de Justice across the way. The cooking is as grandmother used to prepare it, provided she came from the Lyon area. Naturally, the namesake *pieds de cochon* (pigs' feet) is included on the menu, along with tender alpine lamb, grilled anguillettes, and tripe.

4, place du Bourg-de-Four. © 022/310-47-97. www.pied-de-cochon.ch. Reservations recommended. Main courses 26F–38F. AE, DC, MC, V. Daily 7:30am–2:30pm and 6:30pm–midnight. Closed Sun June–Aug. Bus: 2 or 7. Tram: 12.

Chez Ma Cousine (Value) FRENCH/SWISS   This is one of the least pretentious, and least expensive, sit-down restaurants in Geneva. What you'll find is an amiable venue of spartan-looking wooden tables and chairs, and a kitchen whose interior is open. The very limited menu lists the kind of food that French-speaking residents of Switzerland might have been nurtured on during their respective childhoods. A free salad accompanies most main courses, and the only option for potatoes is "Provençal-style." Platters include several variations of grilled chicken, the house specialty; at least two meal-sized salads of Indian-style (with curry) and Thai-style (with soy, coconut, and spicy tomato sauce) chicken; and roasted and sliced pork with a brown sauce, salad, and Provençal potatoes.

Although this branch in the rue Lissignol is the most popular, there's a second branch of Chez Ma Cousine across the river in the Old Town with the same prices and longer hours (daily 11am–11:30pm). You'll find it at 6, place du Bourg-de-Four (© 022/310-96-96).

5, rue Lissignol. © 022/731-98-98. Reservations not necessary. Main courses 15F–17F. MC, V. Mon–Fri 11:30am–2:30pm and 6:30–11:30pm. Bus: 1.

L'Aïoli FRENCH   Named after the famous garlic sauce of Provence, this popular neighborhood restaurant stands opposite Le Corbusier's Maison de Verre. Something of a local secret, it offers personalized service and some of the finest Provençal cooking in town. Among the featured dishes are lamb gigot, frogs' legs Provençal, scampi Provençal, and a delectable *pot-au-feu* of beef. Look for the daily specials, such as a savory, Provence-derived lamb stew called *gardiane camarguaise.*

6, rue Adrien-Lachenal. © 022/736-79-71. Reservations not required. Main courses 16F–36F; fixed-price dinner 33F–35F. AE, DC, MC, V. Mon–Sat 6:30pm–2am. Closed Aug. Bus: 1 or 6. Tram: 12.

Le Sumo Yakitori (Value) JAPANESE   This is a dining oddity that's well known to many cost-conscious residents of Geneva, and almost always overlooked by foreign tourists, most of whom find the culinary format of this tiny place baffling. As a Japanese restaurant, it's already an oddity in Geneva, but the fact that it doesn't serve sushi or sashimi, coupled with its claustrophobic dimensions and open-to-view galley-sized kitchen, makes it unusual. How many chargrilled beef or chicken brochettes, for example, does it take to comprise an adequate meal? (Answer: btw. five and six.) Other menu items include marinated and roasted quail, grilled shrimp, Bali-style jasmine rice, fish cakes with cheese, and all-vegetarian versions of grilled eggplant with garlic sauce.

15, rue de Monthoux. ✆ **022/731-19-50.** Reservations recommended. Brochettes 2F–5F each; platters 10F–17F; fixed-price menu 42F. AE, MC, V. Tues–Sat noon–2pm and 7–10:30pm. Bus: 1.

Nologo ★ MEDITERRANEAN/ITALIAN Surrounded by a gaggle of less creative restaurants, this is the most sophisticated, most upscale, and most "design-conscious" restaurant in the burgeoning Pâquis district, a bustling and irreverent working-class neighborhood immediately downhill from the railway station. It features the kind of high-style black and stainless steel decor you might have expected in Milan, and some of the most sophisticated and creative food in the neighborhood. Examples include veal cutlets with pesto-mint sauce, served with rosemary-roasted potatoes; sea bass with ratatouille and caponata; beefsteak with rocket and exotic mushrooms; and wide-noodle pappardelle with fresh tuna, roasted eggplant, fresh tomatoes, and mint.

11, rue de Fribourg. ✆ **022/901-0333.** www.nologo.ch. Reservations recommended Fri–Sat nights. Main courses 15F–41F. AE, DC, MC, V. Mon–Fri noon–2:30pm; Mon–Sat 7–10:30pm. Bus: 1.

Nô Sushi JAPANESE Popular, hip, and mobbed every day at lunchtime, this is a large, high-ceilinged space devoted to a labyrinth of countertops that merge into the most bemusing and whimsical Japanese restaurant in town. This is the only automated sushi bar in Switzerland, and as such, adds an eccentric and trend-conscious flair to a neighborhood that's better known for its relative conservatism. You'll know how much something costs by the color of the platter that contains it. You can pluck everything except the miso soup, which is carried to your seat by a waitress, directly from the moving conveyer belt. Hot foods remain hot thanks to a candle flickering beneath. Sushi (with rice) and sashimi (without rice) choices include mullet, calamari, octopus, salmon, and tuna. There are also teriyaki dishes, tempura, and a medley of rice and noodle dishes, any of which you can combine into a full meal.

Confédération Centre, 8, rue de la Confédération. ✆ **022/810-39-73.** Reservations not necessary. Sushi, sashimi, rolls, and small platters 22F–43F. AE, MC, V. Mon–Sat 11:30am–11pm. Bus: 12.

Sam-Lor Thai ("The Tricycle") ⓥ**alue** THAI Unpretentious and something of an insiders' secret, hip, cost-conscious Genevois have been coming here for years. It was the first Thai restaurant in the bustling Pâquis district. Inside, there's a medley of Thai and Indonesian art objects that might be appropriate in a temple, including representations of Buddha, and a pair of teakwood opium beds that were each artfully transformed into platforms for dining tables. Menu items include at least four kinds of both chicken and pork (including versions with either red or green curry, with ginger, or with white pepper and garlic); monkfish with tamarind sauce; noodles sautéed with tofu and garlic; duck meat with red curry and coconut; and vermicelli with shrimp, brought to table in an iron pot that's continually heated with a burning candle.

17, rue de Monthoux. ✆ **022/738-80-55.** Reservations recommended on Fri–Sat nights. Main courses 14F–29F. AE, DC, MC, V. Mon–Thurs noon–2pm and 7–10:30pm; Fri noon–2pm and 7:30–11pm; Sat 7:30–11pm; Sun 7–10pm. Bus: 1.

Café des Negociants ★ CONTINENTAL   This is our favorite restaurant in Carouge. There's seating on the pavement outside, as well as within two separate dining rooms, each accented with portraits of great writers from France's 19th-century literary legacy. Menu items include cream of asparagus soup; rillettes of trout and salmon in puff pastry; carpaccio of tuna with strawberries and ginger; roasted filet of sea bass with tomatoes and herbs; and a minirack of lamb with a mustard-flavored merlot sauce. Be warned in advance that despite its genuine ability to welcome its patrons, the staff has absolutely no sense of humor for anyone asking for food outside of the below-noted dining hours.

29, rue de la Filature (at the corner of rue St-Victor), in Carouge. ℂ **022/300-31-30.** www.negociants.ch. Reservations recommended. Main courses 34F–58F; fixed-price lunch 29F, dinner 66F. AE, DC, MC, V. Mon–Fri 9am–10:30pm. Tram: 12 or 13 from Geneva.

L'Olivier de Provençe ★ (Finds) FRENCH   Set in Carouge, this Provençal restaurant offers some of the best dining on Geneva's perimeter. Though open throughout the year, it's especially popular in warm weather, when patrons can dine on its tree-shaded terrace. The savory dishes include flambéed versions of *loup de mer* (sea bass), ragout of scampi, entrecôtes, *soupe de poisson,* and fresh salmon with sorrel. In autumn the restaurant is especially known for its game dishes, such as pheasant, rabbit, pigeon, and venison. A platter of guinea fowl appears in two different versions, both a supreme and a chartreuse of guinea with thighs, each served with fresh morels. In all, this is a good, bourgeois restaurant if you don't mind the slight excursion south of the city.

13, rue Jacques-Dalphin, Carouge. ℂ **022/342-04-50.** www.olivierdeprovence.ch. Reservations required. Main courses 35F–52F; fixed-price menus 19F–48F. AE, V. Mon–Fri noon–2pm; Mon–Sat 7–10:15pm. Closed Sat July–Aug. Tram: 12.

5 ATTRACTIONS

You can see most of Geneva on foot. The best way to familiarize yourself with the city, however, is by taking a walking tour, which covers all the major sights.

SUGGESTED GENEVA ITINERARIES

IF YOU HAVE 1 DAY

Begin the day by viewing the spectacular water fountain, the Jet d'Eau, and the Flower Clock in the **Jardin Anglais.** Then take a cruise of **Lake Geneva** on a steamer. Return in the early afternoon and explore the Left Bank's **Old Town.** Have dinner at a restaurant on place du Bourg-de-Four.

IF YOU HAVE 2 DAYS

Spend the first day as above. On the second day, visit some of the most important **museums** of Geneva, each

completely different. It'll take a full day of sightseeing to absorb the most important: the Musée d'Art et d'Histoire, the Musée International de la Croix-Rouge et du Croissant-Rouge (Red Cross Museum), and the Palais des Nations.

IF YOU HAVE 3 DAYS

Spend the first 2 days as outlined above. On your third day, take our walking tour of Geneva (see later in this chapter) in the morning, and in the

The Baur Collections **24**

Brunswick Monument **10**

Cathédrale de Saint-Pierre **22**

Flower Clock **12**

Fondation Martin Bodmer **29**

Hôtel-de-Ville **18**

Ile Rousseau **11**

Institut et Musée Voltaire **7**

Jardin Anglais **13**

Jardin Botanique **4**

Jet d'Eau **26**

La Perle du Lac **5**

Maison Tavel **19**

MAMCO
(Musée d'Art et Contemporain) **9**

Monument de la Réformation **16**

Musée Ariana **2**

Musée Barbier-Mueller **20**

Musée d'Art et d'Histoire **23**

Musée d'Histoire Naturelle **25**

Musée International
de la Croix-Rouge
et du Croissant-Rouge
(International Red Cross
and Red Crescent Museum) **1**

Musée Rath **14**

Palais des Nations **3**

Parc des Eaux-Vives **28**

Parc la Grange **27**

Parc Mon-Repos **6**

Patek Philippe Museum **17**

Place Neuve **15**

Temple de l'Auditoire **21**

Tour-de-l'Ile **8**

GENEVA

12

SUGGESTED GENEVA ITINERARIES

Lake Geneva

FRONTENEX

Quai Cologny

Rampe de Cologny

Route de Vandœuvres

29

PARC DES
EAUX-VIVES

28

PARC
LA GRANGE

Quai Gustave Ador

Plateau de Frontenex

Route de Frontenex

27

Avenue W. Favre

MONTCHOISY

Ch. Frank Thomas

Av. Rosemont

Woodrow Wilson

Jacquet

Rue Plantamour

Quai du Mont-Blanc

10

*Rade de
Genève*

26

Quai Gustave Ador

Rue du 31 Décembre

Rue des Eaux-Vives

Rue des Vollandes

Rue de Montchoisy

Route de Frontenex

Route de Chêne

Ch. de la Petite Boissière

Av. de l'Amandolier

Promenade Martin

Pont du-
Mont-Blanc

Pont des
Bergues

11
ILE
ROUSSEAU

12 13

JARDIN
ANGLAIS

R. de la Mairie

Av. Pictet De Rochemont

Rue Agasse

Chemin Rieu

Quai Général Guisan

RIVE
GAUCHE

Rue de la Terassière

Rue du Rhône

rd.-pt
de Rive

R. De Rive de Rive

R. Lachenal

25

RUES BASSES

les Rues Basses

VIELLE VILLE
(OLD TOWN)

la Corraterie

Grand Rue

22

19 20 21

18

R. la Fontaine

R. de l'Hôtel de Ville

Rue Hodler

Pl. Em.
Guyenot

Route de Malagnou

FLORISSANT

14
Place
Neuve

15

Dufour

R. de la Croix Rouge

16

Promenade
des Bastions

Université

R. de Candolle

Favon

Rue St. Léger

23

Bd. Jacques Dalcroze

Boulevard Helvétique

Ch. Galland

24

Bd. des Tranchées

Rue de
l'Athenée

Route de Florissant

Avenue Bertrand

PARC
A. BERTRAND

Avenue Louis Aubert

Cours ses Bastions

Philosophes

Place Ed.
Claparède

Rue de l'Athenée

Rd-pt. de
Plainpalais

PLAINE DE
PLAINPALAIS

Av. Henri Dunant

du Mail

17

Rue A. Lombard

Boulevard du Pont d'Arve

R. Prévost-Martin

R. de Carouge

Bd. de la Cluse

LA CLUSE

Avenue Peschier

Avenue de Champel

CHAMPEL

Avenue de Miremont

Av. Calas

Train Station 🛈

afternoon go on one of the organized excursions to the Alps, including **Mont Blanc,** for a panoramic view.

IF YOU HAVE 4 DAYS

Spend the first 3 days as suggested above. By now you're an old hand at finding your way around Geneva, and you can use your last days for excursions. While still based in Geneva, take a lake steamer to **Lausanne** (chapter 11). You'll have time to explore its old town and walk its lakeside quays at Ouchy before returning to Geneva in the evening.

IF YOU HAVE 5 DAYS

Spend days 1 to 4 as above. On the fifth day, take a lake steamer to **Montreux** (chapter 11). After visiting this lakeside resort, take a trip outside the town to see the **Château de Chillon,** immortalized by Lord Byron.

THE TOP ATTRACTIONS

In addition to the sites listed below, Geneva's other top attractions—all premier sights— are the **Jet d'Eau,** the famous fountain that has virtually become the city's symbol; the **Flower Clock,** in the Jardin Anglais, with 6,500 flowers (it was the world's first when it was inaugurated in the 1950s; today, it's less of a showstopper); and **Old Town,** the oldest part of the city. All these sights, and more, are detailed in our walking tour, later in this chapter.

Musée Ariana ★★   Located to the west of the Palais des Nations, this Italian Renaissance building was constructed by Gustave Revilliod, the 19th-century Genevese patron who began the collection. Today it's one of the top porcelain, glass, and pottery museums in Europe. You'll see Sèvres, Delft faience, and Meissen porcelain, as well as pieces from Japan and China. It's also the headquarters of the International Academy of Ceramics.

10, av. de la Paix. © **022/418-54-50.** www.ville-ge.ch. Free admission to the permanent collection; temporary exhibitions 5F adults, 3F students; free for children 17 and under. Wed–Mon 10am–5pm. Bus: 8 or F.

Musée d'Art et Contemporain (MAMCO) ★   Some 20 years in the making, Geneva's first modern art museum opened in 1994 in a former factory building, and immediately evoked comparisons to some of the excellent collections of modern art in Paris. This prestigious showcase displays a vast collection of European and American art covering the last 4 decades. Out of some 1,000 works of art owned by the museum, only 300 are permanently on display. This space is packed with all the big names—Frankenthaler, Stela, Segal, and others. Some 150 sq. m (1,600 sq. ft.) of space is set aside for exhibitions that change three times a year.

10, rue des Vieux-Grenadiers. © **022/320-61-22.** www.mamco.ch. Admission 8F adults, 6F students, free for children 17 and under. Tues–Fri noon–6pm; Sat–Sun 11am–6pm. Bus: 1 or 32.

Musée d'Art et d'Histoire ★★   At Geneva's most important museum, displays include prehistoric relics, Greek vases, medieval stained glass, 12th-century armor, Swiss timepieces, Flemish and Italian paintings, and Switzerland's largest collection of Egyptian art. The Etruscan pottery and medieval furniture are both impressive. A 1444 altarpiece by Konrad Witz depicts the "miraculous" draft of fishes. Many galleries also contain works by such artists as Rodin, Renoir, Hodler, Vallotton, Le Corbusier, Picasso, Chagall, Corot, Monet, and Pissarro. There's a well-managed restaurant on the premises of this place.

2, rue Charles-Galland (btw. bd. Jacques-Dalcroze and bd. Helvétique). ✆ **022/418-26-00.** www.centre.ch.
Free admission. 5F temporary exhibitions adults, 2F for children. Tues–Sun 10am–5pm. Bus: 1, 3, 5, 8, or 17.

Musée International de la Croix-Rouge et du Croissant-Rouge (International Red Cross and Red Crescent Museum) ★

Here you can experience the legendary past of the Red Cross in the city where it started; it's across from the visitors' entrance to the European headquarters of the United Nations. The dramatic story from 1863 to the present is revealed through displays of rare documents and photographs, films, multiscreen slide shows, and cycloramas. You're taken from the battlefields of Europe to the plains of Africa to see the Red Cross in action. When Henry Dunant founded the Red Cross in Geneva in 1863, he needed a recognizable symbol to suggest neutrality. The Swiss flag (a white cross on a red field), with the colors reversed, ended up providing the perfect symbol for one of the world's greatest humanitarian movements.

17, av. de la Paix. ✆ **022/748-95-25.** www.micr.org. Admission 10F adults; 5F students, seniors, and children 12–16; free for children 11 and under. Wed–Mon 10am–5pm. Bus: 8, F, V, or Z.

MORE ATTRACTIONS
Museums

The Baur Collections ★ This is Switzerland's largest collection of Far Eastern art. The collections, housed in a 19th-century mansion with a garden, constitute a private exhibit of artworks from China (dating from the 10th–19th c.) and Japan (17th–20th c.). On display are ceramics, jade, lacquer, ivories, and delicate sword fittings.

8, rue Munier-Romilly. ✆ **022/704-32-82.** www.fondation-baur.ch. Admission 10F adults, 5F students, free for children 15 and under. Tues–Sun 2–6pm. Bus: 1 or 8.

Fondation Martin Bodmer Martin Bodmer's library had long been a place for reflection and research. It was his inspiration and consultation room where he would study the work of great men and women. Upon his death in 1971, Bodmer left behind a collection of more than 160,000 books, manuscripts, autographs, and artworks depicting 3,000 years of world culture. Included in the display are early handwritten texts of Homer, illuminated manuscripts of the Bible, a manuscript of *Grimm's Fairy Tales,* and a 15th-century version of the *Nibelungenlied.* The exhibition also has the first printed versions of Cervantes's *Don Quixote,* Newton's *Principa Mathematica,* Goethe's *Faust,* Chaucer's *Canterbury Tales,* James Joyce's *Ulysses,* and works from Dante Alighieri and William Shakespeare.

19–21, rte. de Guignard, Cologny. ✆ **022/707-44-33.** www.fondationbodmer.org. Admission 15F adults, 10F for children and seniors. Tues–Sun 2–6pm. Closed 2 weeks in May. Bus: 33 or A.

Maison Tavel ★ Constructed in 1303 and partially rebuilt after a fire in 1334, this is the city's oldest house. The building underwent several transformations over the centuries before opening as a museum in 1986. The front wall is typical 17th century, with gray paint, white joints, and stone sculpted heads. The house contains a courtyard with a staircase, a 13th-century cellar, and a back garden. The museum exhibits historical collections from Geneva dating from the Middle Ages to the mid–19th century. The Magnin relief in the attic is outstanding, as is the copper-and-zinc model of Geneva in 1850, which is accompanied by a light-and-tape commentary. Objects of daily use are displayed in the old living quarters. Postcards, books, slides, and small guidebooks are available at the bookstand.

6, rue du Puits Saint-Pierre. ℭ **022/418-37-00.** www.ville-ge.ch. Free admission to permanent collection, 3F temporary expositions. Tues–Sun 10am–5pm. Bus: 3, 5, or 17.

Musée Barbier-Mueller   No one would expect a middle-class orphan, raised by a governess, to be one of the greatest art collectors of all time, but that is exactly what Josef Mueller (1887–1977) did. By the age of 31, Mueller had seven works by Cézanne, five by Matisse, five by Renoir, and a healthy assortment of Picassos and Braques, all of which are on display. However, the real heart of his collection is the gathering of primitive pieces from Africa, the East Indies, Oceania, the early Americas, tribal Asia, and the prehistoric phases of Greece, Italy, and Japan. Mueller's daughter Monique, a historian, married another art collector, Jean Paul Barbier, who added his discoveries to that of his father-in-law's, and together the pair created the Musée Barbier-Mueller.

10, rue Jean-Calvin. ℭ **022/312-02-70.** www.barbier-mueller.ch. Admission 8F adults, 5F students and seniors, free for children 11 and under. Daily 11am–5pm. Bus: 2, 7, 12, 16, or 17.

Palais des Nations ★★   The former home of the defunct League of Nations is the present headquarters of the United Nations in Europe, lying 1.6km (1 mile) north of Mont Blanc Bridge. The complex of buildings is the second largest in Europe after Versailles. Tours, conducted in English, last about an hour. They depart from the visitors' entrance opposite the Red Cross building. To join the tour, you'll need to show your passport. The monumental compound was constructed between 1929 and 1936. The highlights of the tour include the Assembly Hall, with a balcony made entirely of marble and lofty bays looking out over the Court of Honor. You are shown the Council Chamber, the home of the Conference on Disarmament with its allegorical murals by José Maria Sert, an artist from Catalonia. The Philatelic Museum offers collections of stamps relating to the League of Nations, along with a wide selection of philatelic publications from around the world, and the League of Nations Museum documents the history of the precursor to the United Nations.

Parc de l'Ariana, 14, av. de la Paix. ℭ **022/917-48-96.** www.unog.ch. Admission 10F adults, 8F students, 5F children 6–17. July–Aug daily 10am–5pm; Apr–June and Sept–Oct daily 10am–noon and 2–4pm; Nov–Mar Mon–Fri 10am–noon and 2–4pm. Bus: 5, 8, 11, 14, 18, F, V, or Z.

Patek Philippe Museum   Watch lovers flock here from all over the world to see one of the best collections of timepieces in existence. Positioned close to the larger and more visible MAMCO Museum of Modern Art, the Patek Philippe Museum contains two collections that are permanently on display here—the Antiques Collection (also known as the Archives Collection) and the Patek Philippe Collection (founded in 1839, the Patek Philippe company is one of the most venerated watchmakers in the world). The Antiques Collection contains a wide array of Genevese, Swiss, and European watches from the 16th to 19th centuries, including one worm by Empress Sissi of Austria. A good portion of the pieces are historically significant to the history of horology. An audiovisual, multilingual presentation accompanies this collection. The Patek Philippe display showcases the more than 160 years that the company has been in business.

7, rue de Vieux Grenadiers. ℭ **022/807-09-10.** www.patekmuseum.com. Admission 10F adults, 5F students and seniors, free for children 17 and under. Tues–Fri 2–6pm; Sat 10am–6pm. Bus: 1 or 4. Tram: 12 or 13.

Religious Monuments

The **Old Town** ★, or Vieille Ville, on the Left Bank, is dominated by the **Cathédrale de St. Pierre** ★, cour Saint-Pierre (ℭ **022/319-71-90;** www.saintpierre-geneve.ch), which

Frommer's Favorite Geneva Experiences

Wine Tasting in the Countryside   Winding your way through the rolling vineyards just outside Geneva makes for an enjoyable day's outing. Many of the best Swiss wines never leave the country, and grapes grow on slopes overlooking Lake Geneva and the Rhône. Pick up a brochure called *Discover Geneva and Its Vineyards* from the tourist office and set out.

Sailing Lake Geneva   The crescent-shaped lake, called Lac Léman locally, gives Geneva a resortlike ambience, stretching for 72km (45 miles). In the summer it's alive with activity: sailing, rowing, canoeing, water-skiing, and more.

Wandering Through Old Town   The gray-toned severity of Geneva's *Vieille Ville* somehow conveys some of the strict and unyielding morals of what used to be a stronghold of severely punitive Calvinism. Exploring its ancient streets brings you to art galleries, antiques shops, booksellers, and tiny bistros. Follow the Grande-Rue, where Jean-Jacques Rousseau was born, and wander back into time.

was built in the 12th and 13th centuries and partially reconstructed in the 15th century. Recent excavations have disclosed that a Christian sanctuary was here as early as A.D. 400. In 1536 the people of Geneva gathered in the cloister of St. Pierre's and voted to make the cathedral Protestant. The church, which has been heavily renovated over the years, has a modern organ with 6,000 pipes. The northern tower was reconstructed at the end of the 19th century, with a metal steeple erected between the two stone towers. If you don't mind the 145 steps, you can climb to the top of the north tower for a panoramic view of the city, its lake, the Alps, and the Jura Mountains.

To enter the St. Pierre archaeological site, called **Site Archéologique de Saint-Pierre,** go through the entrance in cour Saint-Pierre, at the right-hand corner of the cathedral steps. The underground passageway extends under the present cathedral and the High Gothic (early-15th-c.) **Chapelle des Macchabées,** which adjoins the southwestern corner of the church. The chapel was restored during World War II, after having been used as a storage room following the Reformation. Excavations of the chapel have revealed baptisteries, a crypt, the foundations of several cathedrals, the bishop's palace, 4th-century mosaics, sculptures, and geological strata.

The cathedral and the chapel are open June to September daily from 9:30am to 6:30pm; March to May and in October daily 9am to noon and 2 to 6pm; and November to February daily 10am to 5:30pm. There is no admission charge to visit the cathedral, although donations are welcome; tower admission is 4F. Sunday service is held in the cathedral at 10am, and an hour of organ music is presented on Saturday at 6pm from June to September. The archaeological site is open June to September daily from 11am to 5pm, and October to May Tuesday to Sunday from 2 to 5pm; the admission charge is 8F for adults, 4F for students and seniors. Take bus no. 2, 7, 12, or 36.

Next door to the cathedral is a Gothic church where Calvin preached, known as the **Temple de l'Auditoire,** or Calvin Auditorium. It was restored in 1959 in time for Calvin's 450th anniversary.

If you walk heading north along the quays, you'll arrive at some of the lushest parks in Geneva. **Parc Mon-Repos** ★★ is off avenue de France and **La Perle du Lac** is off rue de Lausanne. Directly to the right is the **Jardin Botanique (Botanical Garden),** which was established in 1902. It has an alpine garden, a little zoo, greenhouses, and exhibitions, and can be visited free from April to October daily from 8am to 7:30pm, and from November to March daily from 9:30am to 5pm.

You can take a boat to the other side of Lake Geneva and get off at quai Gustave-Ador. From there you can explore two more lakeside parks—**Parc la Grange,** which has the most extravagant rose garden in Switzerland (especially in June), and next to it, the **Parc des Eaux-Vives.**

When you leave the Botanical Garden on the Left Bank, you can head west, along avenue de la Paix, about 1.5km (1 mile) north from the Pont du Mont-Blanc, to the Palais des Nations in the **Parc de l'Ariana.**

Les Pâquis District ★★

One of Geneva's most animated and colorful districts, **Les Pâquis** offers a view of a workaday world that's far removed from the luxurious consumerism and (some say) indolence of better-heeled neighborhoods closer to the lake. Its main thoroughfare, the rue des Pâquis, runs parallel to the rue de Berne. To reach it, head north along quai des Bergues, which leads into quai du Mont-Blanc. On your left, at the intersection of quai du Mont-Blanc and Gare Routière, stands the **Brunswick Monument,** the tomb of Charles II of Brunswick, who died in Geneva in 1873. The duke left his fortune to the city with the provision that it build a monument to him. Geneva accepted the fortune and modeled the tomb after the Scaglieri tombs in Verona.

Les Pâquis is a sector of bistros, nightclubs, ateliers, hipster boutiques, and banks. The word *pâquis* comes from the Latin *pascuum,* meaning "pasture." The cows that grazed here are long gone, but from about A.D. 1330 the district consisted of a vast expanse of fields, pastures, and wastelands. It was far from the heart of the city and its protective ditches, and exposed to the permanent danger of invasion.

From the 14th century, as the city developed a stronger defense system, this unincorporated territory became safer, and more and more people made homes here. In the 15th century the Pâquis was home to potters and fisher folk, and eventually homes and small industries began to take root.

In 1831 the French writer Chateaubriand settled at the **Hôtel des Etrangers,** 22, rue des Pâquis. From 1851 on, development was fairly rapid, with the construction of **quai du Mont-Blanc** and of the **Rotonde,** the English church. An American church was also constructed, and in 1857 **quais Pâquis** and **Eaux-Vives** were erected. Construction on the Cornavin railway station began the following year. The **Pont du Mont-Blanc** was erected in 1862. Soon, the lake promenade, the façade des Pâquis, and quai du Mont-Blanc became fashionable.

In 1873 construction began on the **Hôtel National** (Palais Wilson); from 1925 to 1936 it would house the first secretariat of the League of Nations. The Kursaal was built between 1874 and 1879. One of the most infamous events in the history of the area was the assassination of Empress Elisabeth of Austria, in 1898, at the landing stage facing the duke of Brunswick's mausoleum.

After wandering through the district with no particular fixed itinerary, visitors may tour Lake Geneva in a lake steamer. Steamers leave from quai du Mont-Blanc.

Geneva is a city with many attractions of interest to the younger set. The following are perhaps the coolest of the cool:

Visiting the **Musée International de la Croix-Rouge et du Croissant-Rouge (Red Cross Museum)** is like attending an adventure movie, as kids are enraptured by the sweep and drama of this heroic organization, which has always been near the "core of the action."

One of the best natural-history museums of Europe, the **Musée d'Histoire Naturelle** delights children with its tropical birds, mammals, and exotic reptiles.

Jet d'Eau and the **Flower Clock** are exciting introductions for children. After viewing both of them, parents can take their kids for a tour by steamer on Lake Geneva.

For the Literary Enthusiast

At 25, rue des Délices, you'll find the house—now the **Institut et Musée Voltaire (© 022/ 344-71-33;** www.ville-ge.ch)—where Voltaire lived from 1755 to 1760 and from time to time after that up to 1765; he wrote part of *Candide* here. The museum displays furniture, manuscripts, letters, and portraits, as well as a terra-cotta model of the famous seated Voltaire by Houdon. The museum is open Monday to Saturday from 2 to 5pm, and admission is free. Take bus no. 6, 7, 11, 26, or 27.

WALKING TOUR	GENEVA'S QUAYS & OLD TOWN
START:	Jet d'Eau.
FINISH:	Place du Bourg-de-Four.
TIME:	2 hours.
BEST TIMES:	Any sunny day.
WORST TIMES:	Rush hours, Monday to Friday from 8 to 9am and 5 to 6pm.

If, like most tourists, you arrive in the summer, you may begin your discovery of the city with a long promenade **along the quays** of Geneva. The one sight you can't miss is the:

❶ Jet d'Eau

In the quai Gustave-Ador, this famous fountain is the trademark of the city. Visible for miles, from April to September it throws water 138m (453 ft.) into the air above the lake. The Genevese call the fountain the *jeddo*. It dates from 1891 but was improved in 1951. Many cities have sent engineers to Geneva to study the workings of the fountain, a version of which now throws water to a slightly higher elevation in the desert air of Jeddah, Saudi Arabia. The fountain pumps 132 gallons of water per second into the air.

Once you've seen the fountain, you'll be ready to explore the quays, with their gardens and ancient buildings. The aquatic population consists of sea gulls, ducks, and swans. A fleet of small boats, called *mouettes genevoises,* shuttles visitors from one quay to another throughout the year.

Lying directly off quai du Général-Guisan is another Geneva landmark, the:

❷ Flower Clock

In the Jardin Anglais (English Garden), the clock's face is made of carefully landscaped beds of flowers, and it keeps perfect time! The Jardin Anglais is at the foot of the Mont Blanc Bridge, which spans the river at the point where the Rhône leaves Lake Geneva. The bridge was rebuilt in 1969.

Cross Pont du Mont-Blanc and turn left (south) along quai des Bergues on the Right Bank of Geneva until you come to the next bridge, called Pont des Bergues. If you cross this bridge, you'll come to:

❸ Ile Rousseau

A statue of the philosopher, sculpted by Pradier in 1834, greets you here. The island, which was Rousseau's stomping grounds and the site of many of his reveries, is now home to ducks, swans, grebes, and other aquatic fowl. Situated in the middle of the Rhône, it was once a bulwark of Geneva's river defenses.

Return to quai des Bergues and continue to walk left along the quay until you reach place St-Gervais and the:

❹ Tour-de-l'Ile

A château was built here in 1219, although the tower is all that remains today. The château had been used as a prison and place of execution by the counts of Savoy. A wall plaque commemorates a visit by Caesar in 58 B.C. at the beginning of his Gallic Wars. Once the fortified core of the Old Town, it bears some similarities to Paris's Ile de la Cité. You can also explore the old markets, which often exhibit the works of contemporary Genevese artists.

The walking tour of the quays is particularly appropriate for children because the sights are outside and easily understandable. If the children get tired, however, you can take them to quai du Mont-Blanc, where they can board *le mini-train de Genève*. This 40-minute excursion will take them—within rubber-wheeled "trains" (a kind of urban tram, actually), which are painted in tones of green, red, and white—along the major parks and quays of Geneva. Departures from March to October are daily every 45 minutes from 9am to 10pm. Adults pay a fare of 7.90F and children are charged 4.90F.

At this point, you'll be on the doorway of Geneva's **Old Town** or Vieille Ville, set on the relatively artsy Left Bank.

After leaving the Tour-de-l'Ile, you can continue across the Rhône until you reach place Bel-Air, on the Left Bank. From here, head south for a short distance along rue de la Monnaie, which quickly becomes rue de la Cité. When that street changes its name to rue de la Tertasse, continue south along this street until you reach:

❺ Place Neuve

This is the cultural heart of Geneva. The square has a statue of General Dufour, who was a cofounder of the Red Cross. Monuments on this square include the Grand Théâtre and the Conservatory of Music *(Le Conservatoire de la Musique)*. The Grand Théâtre (opera house) was built in 1874 (see "Geneva After Dark," later in this chapter). The conservatory dates from 1858.

Also on the square is the:

❻ Musée Rath

The museum, place Neuve (✆ **022/418-33-40**; www.ville-ge.ch), has temporary exhibitions of paintings and sculpture. It's open Tuesday and Thursday to Sunday from 10am to 5pm, Wednesday from noon to 9pm; costs 10F for adults and 5F for students; and is free for children 17 and under. The museum can be reached by tram no. 12 or bus no. 3, 5, 32, or 36.

From place Neuve, continue southeast along rue de la Croix-Rouge until you come to the:

❼ Le Mur des Réformateurs (Le Monument de la Réformation)

The Reformation Monument was built in 1917 along a 16th-century rampart, beneath the walls of the Old Town on promenade des Bastions. The monument, which is 91m (298 ft.) long, represents John Knox, Calvin, Théodore de Bèze, and Guillaume Farel—the four Genevese reformers. Other statues include Cromwell, the Pilgrim Fathers, and, on either end, Luther and Zwingli.

Retrace your footsteps along rue de la Croix-Rouge until you return to place Neuve. From the square, take a sharp right and follow ramp de la Treille, which becomes rue Henri-Fazy, where you can:

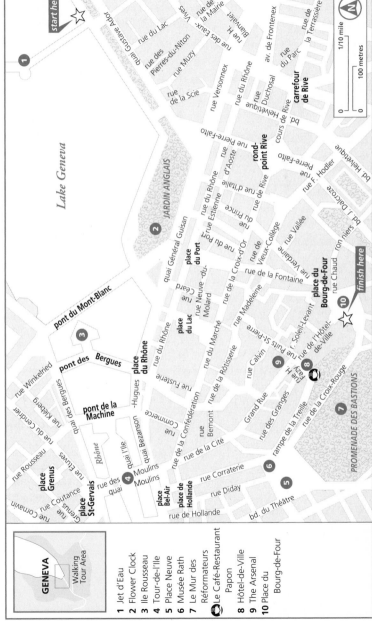

GENEVA

12

WALKING TOUR: GENEVA'S QUAYS & OLD TOWN

start here

Lake Geneva

JARDIN ANGLAIS

rond-point Rive

carrefour de Rive

pont du Mont-Blanc

pont des Bergues

pont de la Machine

place du Rhône

place du Lac

place du Port

place du Bourg-de-Four

finish here

place Grenus

place St-Gervais

place Bel-Air

place de Hollande

PROMENADE DES BASTIONS

1 Jet d'Eau
2 Flower Clock
3 Ile Rousseau
4 Tour-de-l'Ile
5 Place Neuve
6 Musée Rath
7 Le Mur des Réformateurs
Le Café-Restaurant Papon
8 Hôtel-de-Ville
9 The Arsenal
10 Place du Bourg-de-Four

GENEVA
Walking Tour Area

1/10 mile
100 metres

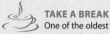

TAKE A BREAK
One of the oldest and most venerated cafes of Geneva, **Le Café-Restaurant Papon,** 1, rue Henri-Fazy (✆ **022/311-54-28**), lies near the Tour Baudet in the vicinity of the Hôtel-de-Ville. A restaurant, creperie, tearoom, and cafe, it has been entertaining drinkers and diners under its vaulted ceilings since the 17th century.

Turn right at rue de l'Hôtel-de-Ville and you'll approach the:

⑧ Hôtel-de-Ville (Town Hall)

The Hôtel-de-Ville is a short walk from the cathedral and dates from the 16th and 17th centuries. Its Baudet Tower was constructed in 1455. The building, which has a cobblestone ramp instead of a staircase, has witnessed some of the city's most important diplomatic events. The Red Cross originated here in 1864.

Across from the town hall is:

⑨ The Arsenal

This arcaded structure dates from 1634. In the courtyard of the building is a cannon that was cast in 1683.

Continue along rue de l'Hôtel-de-Ville until you reach:

⑩ Place du Bourg-de-Four

This spot was first a Roman forum and later a medieval town square. The Palais de Justice here was built in 1707, but it has housed courts of law only since 1860. While you're in this area, you'll come across a fountain, many antiquaries' shops, and art galleries.

ORGANIZED TOURS

Bus & Tram Tours

If you're new in Geneva and want an easy-to-digest breakdown of the way the city is divided into various neighborhoods and districts, consider a trolley-car tour. Departing from the south bank's Place du Rhône (Mar–Dec only), red-painted, open-sided trolley cars meander through neighborhoods that include the city's medieval center, the glossy shopping districts, and the hotel and museum-studded precincts of the river's north bank. Trams depart at 45-minute intervals every day between 10:45am and 6:45pm, last about 45 minutes, and cost 9.90F for adults and 6.90F for children. For more information, contact **STT Trains Tours S.A.,** 36, bd. St-Georges (✆ **022/781-04-04;** www.sttr.ch).

A 2-hour City Tour is operated daily all year by **Key Tours S.A.,** 7, rue des Alpes, square du Mont-Blanc (✆ **022/731-41-40;** www.keytours.ch). The tour starts from the Gare Routière, the bus station at place Dorcière, near the Key Tours office. From November to March the tour is offered only once a day at 1:30pm, but from April to October two tours leave daily at 10:30am and 1:30pm.

A bus will drive you through the city to see the monuments, landmarks, and lake promenades. In the Old Town you can take a walk down to the Bastions Park and the Reformation Wall. After a tour through the International Center, where you'll be shown the headquarters of the International Red Cross, the bus returns to its starting place. Adults pay 23F and children 4 to 12 accompanied by an adult are charged 12F, while children 3 and under go free.

Walking Tours of Carouge

Between June and September, every Saturday at 11am, 2-hour guided walking tours of Carouge depart from a point near the front entrance of Carouge's City Hall, 14, place du Marché, for a price of 8.90F per adult, 5.90F for teens aged 12 to 18, and free for children 11 and under. The expert in charge of these tours, Mme. Loredan, speaks five languages, and will tailor her dialogue to correspond to the linguistic needs of participants. For more information, click on www.carouge.ch.

The cold, clear waters of Lac Léman have attracted visitors for many generations. If you're interested in cruising on these waters (which never freeze, even in winter), at least two companies offer worthwhile tours. Your best bet involves determining how extensive you want your tour to be, and then selecting one whose duration corresponds to your schedule.

Regardless of which you select, you'll enjoy sweeping waterside views of the ringing hills, bucolic calm, and some of the most famous vineyards in Switzerland, many of which seem to roll down to the historic waters. Because of bad weather and low visibility in winter, cruises only run between April and late October, and in some cases, only between May and September.

Two separate companies offer cruises along the lake. The smaller of the two, **Mouettes Genevoises Navigation,** 8, quai du Mont-Blanc (✆ **022/732-47-47;** www.swissboat. com), specializes in small-scale boats carrying only about 100 passengers at a time. Each features some kind of prerecorded commentary, in French and English, throughout. An easy promenade that features the landscapes and bird life along the uppermost regions of the river Rhône draining the lake is the company's 2¾-hour **Tour du Rhône (Rhône River Tour).** The trip originates at quai des Moulins, adjacent to Geneva's Pont de l'Ile, and travels downstream for about 14km (9 miles) to the Barrage de Verbois (Verbois Dam) and back. From April to October, departures are Wednesday, Saturday, and Sunday at 2:15pm. It costs 17F for adults and 12F for children 4 to 12; it's free for children 3 and under.

Mouettes Genevoises Navigation's largest competitor, **CGN (Compagnie Générale de Navigation),** quai du Mont-Blanc (✆ **0848/811-848;** www.cgn.ch), offers roughly equivalent tours, in this case between May and September, that last an hour, departing six to seven times a day (depending on the season) from the company's piers along quai du Mont-Blanc. Known as Les Belles Rives Genevoises, the tours cost 16F for adults and 9F for children 6 to 16; children 5 and under ride free. Tours include prerecorded commentaries and are, frankly, about as long in duration as many short-term visitors to the city really want.

Although its hour-long cruises are popular, CGN devotes most of its time, energy, and money to hauling boatloads of commuters and sightseers between the ports that line the perimeter of the lake. They're conducted aboard larger craft that resemble seagoing ferryboats, and the experience is usually more workaday than the short cruises described above. None includes guided commentary. Despite that, many visitors appreciate the silence and the fact that CGN's larger boats each contain an attractive brasserie with uniformed waiters, starched linen, fixed-price menus at 37F each, and affordably priced *assiettes du jour* (plates of the day). You can ask the sales staff at CGN to configure almost any tour along the lake that appeals to you, incorporating half-day stopovers and/or overnights in towns like Nyon, Lausanne, Vevey, Montreux, Evian, Yvoire, and Thonon. Barring that, you can sign up for either of the prepackaged experiences (*grands et petits* tours of the lake) as described below. In most cases, CGN vessels depart from the piers beside quai du Mont-Blanc, but whenever the schedule warrants it, the departure moves 180m (590 ft.) away, to the piers in the nearby Jardin Anglais.

The most comprehensive ride requires a full day: the **Tour du Grand Lac.** It departs every morning at 9am, pulls for very brief interludes into about half a dozen ports en route, and returns to Geneva that night at 8:45pm. A 2-hour stopover in Montreux, plus a leisurely lunch onboard, are included as part of the experience. The round-trip circuit costs 67F for adults and 34F for ages 6 to 25; it's free for children 5 and under. A more recommendable, and more practical, tour is **Le Tour du Petit Lac,** which incorporates only the lower portion of the lake, including stops at Nyon (in Switzerland) and Yvoire (in France), and lasts for about half a day. It departs from quai du Mont-Blanc every afternoon at 3pm. The round-trip cost is from 27F.

CGN also offers a tour that combines a lake cruise and a visit to the Château de Chillon with a return by train back to Geneva. Between June and September, a boat leaves from the Mont Blanc pier daily at 9:15am, arriving in Chillon at 2:15pm. During July and August an additional boat departs from the Jardin Anglais pier at 10:30am, arriving in Chillon around 3:50pm. Participants can visit the castle before taking a train or bus from the small station at Chillon to Montreux, and then transfer to one of the hourly trains from Montreux back to Geneva. Some visitors opt to dally in Montreux a while, perhaps remaining for lunch or dinner. The cost for the full round-trip excursion is 54F in second class and 73F in first class. For more information, call ✆ **0848/811-848** (www.cgn.ch).

A TOUR TO MONT BLANC ★★★

If you have time, we highly recommend a Mont Blanc excursion, which is an all-day trip to Chamonix by bus and a cable-car ride to the summit of the Aiguille du Midi (3,783m/12,408 ft.). The tour leaves Geneva at 8:30am and returns at 6pm daily. Buses leave from the bus station (Gare Routière). You must take your passport with you.

Other mechanized ascents that are part of this tour are to Vallée Blanche by télécabin, an extension of the Aiguille du Midi climb, from April to October; to Mer de Glâce via electric rack railway to the edge of the glacier, from which you may descend to the ice grotto (the climb is not available in the winter); and to Le Brevent, an ascent by cable car to a rocky belvedere at 2,370m (7,774 ft.), facing the Mont Blanc range. Lunch is included.

An English-speaking guide will accompany your bus tour. **Key Tours S.A.,** 7, rue des Alpes (place du Mont-Blanc; Case Postale 1745), CH-1211 Genève (✆ **022/731-41-40;** www.keytours.ch), operator of the excursions, requires a minimum of eight people per trip. Tours start at 108F, including a ride up the mountain.

6 THE ACTIVE VACATION PLANNER

Like most cities in health-conscious Switzerland, Geneva has many sports facilities. However, locals often pursue activities outside the city. They're more interested in following their own personal sports programs than they are in spectator sports, except for soccer, which is played in various stadiums. (Matches are announced in the tourist office's monthly "List of Events.")

The big spectator event of the year, the world's most important **lake regatta** is known as the **Bol d'Or** and takes place sometime in June (the Swiss National Tourist Office abroad will provide exact dates), attracting approximately 600 sailboats and more than 3,500 competitors. The lake is virtually covered with white sails. It takes 7 hours for the luckiest to sail from one end to the other—and more than 24 hours for the unluckiest. But participants from all over the world swear it's worth trying.

BIKING Cyclists consider the Geneva countryside a paradise. What could be better than a ride through forest, vineyard, and cornfield? The most passionate bikers climb

Bernex's hill or cross the border into France (bring a passport). See "Getting Around," earlier in this chapter, for details about renting a bike.

GOLF The best course is **Golf Club de Genève,** 7, rte. de la Capite at Cologny ((_C_ **022/ 707-48-00**), which is an 18-hole course open March to December, Tuesday to Friday 8am to noon and 2 to 6pm. Greens fees are 150F for 18 holes. This is a private course, but it often allows nonmembers to play, preferably those associated with golf courses in their home countries. Always call about admission before heading here, however. There's an on-site pro shop.

HEALTH CLUB **Silhouette Health & Fitness,** 4, rue Thalberg ((_C_ **022/732-77-40**), is the most comprehensive, best-equipped, and most sociable health club in Geneva. Set very close to the grand hotels (Hôtel de la Paix, Hôtel Beau-Rivage, Le Richemond) of the Right Bank, it welcomes temporary visitors to the city for a fee of 20F to 27F, depending on the day of the week and time of day you arrive. Expect everything from aerobics to free weights, with every other kind of health and exercise machine as well. It's open Monday to Friday from 9am to 9pm, and Saturday and Sunday 10am to 5pm.

JOGGING In addition to the many trails that have been laid out in the parks, you can also jog along the quays and the lakeshore beaches. The best places for jogging are Parc Bertrand, Parc des Eaux-Vives, and Parc Mon-Repos.

SAILING This is the most popular sport in Geneva. In the summer, you'll find kiosks offering sailboats for rent all along the quays.

SKIING In the winter the people of Geneva flock to the resorts of the Haute Savoie in France, notably Chamonix and Megève. Each resort is about an hour's drive from Geneva. The smaller, lesser known French resort of Flaine is even closer to Geneva. In Switzerland itself, the place nearest Geneva where there's good skiing is the Glacier of Les Diablerets or the resort of Champéry.

SWIMMING In summer swimmers usually head for the beaches along the lake. The most popular of these is **Geneva Beach (Genève Plage),** Port Noir ((_C_ **022/736-24-82;** www.geneve-plage.ch), where you can swim mid-May to mid-September 10am to 8pm for 7F.

TENNIS Tennis somehow seems more invigorating in the sunshine and sometimes-brisk mountain air near the French Alps. An option for tennis in Geneva is the courts at **Tennis Club de Genève,** parc des Eaux-Vives ((_C_ **022/735-53-50;** www.tc-geneve.ch).

7 SHOPPING

From boutiques to department stores, Geneva is a shopper's dream come true. The city, of course, is known for its watches and jewelry, but it's also a good place to buy embroidered blouses, music boxes from the Jura region, cuckoo clocks from German Switzerland, cigars from Havana (not allowed into the United States), chocolate, Swiss Army knives, and many other items.

Geneva practically invented the wristwatch. In fact, watchmaking in the city dates from the 16th century. Be sure to avoid purchasing a Swiss watch in one of the souvenir stores. If jewelers are legitimate, they'll display a symbol of the Geneva Association of Watchmakers and Jewelers. Here, more than in any other Swiss city, you should be able to find all the best brands, including Vacheron & Constantin, Longines, Omega, and

Blancpain, to name just a few. Sometimes there are discounts on such items as cameras. Most salespeople you'll encounter speak English and are very helpful.

A shopping spree may begin at **place du Molard,** once the harbor of Geneva before the water receded. Merchants from all over Europe used to bring their wares to trade fairs here in the days before merchants migrated to the richer markets in Lyon.

If you walk along rue du Rhône and are put off by the prices, go 1 block south to rue du Marché, which in various sections becomes rue de la Croix-d'Or and rue de Rive, and is sometimes referred to by locals as "la rue du Tram" because of the many trolleys that run along its length. Don't be afraid to comparison-shop in Geneva—many stores jack up prices for visitors.

Store hours vary in Geneva. Most stores are open Monday to Friday 8am to 6:30pm and Saturday from 8am to 5pm.

ANTIQUES

Ernest Schmitt and Co. Antiquities ★   This store beautifully displays furniture in the ground-floor rooms of an 18th-century private house. Most of the furniture is from the 18th and 19th centuries, much of it English, and there's also a wide display of antique silver from the same era. Be sure to ask the owner to take you across the cobblestone courtyard to see the other showrooms. 3, rue de l'Hôtel-de-Ville. ✆ 022/310-35-40.

AUCTIONS

The city has some of the world's most famous auction houses, with sales taking place mostly in May and November. During these periods, numerous social events accompany the auctions. Moreover, the city is an important center for the world art market and hosts prominent art and antiques dealers. Details and venues of sales appear in the tourist office's monthly "List of Events."

Antiquorum ★★★   This is the largest repository of antique timepieces in the world, with a reputation that's known to connoisseurs throughout the world. Virtually all of its inventory consists of antique jewelry and antique watches. Almost everything is sold at auction, rather than over the counter. The array of watches includes some of the most historically important watches in the world. 2, rue du Mont-Blanc. ✆ 022/909-28-50. www.antiquorum.com.

Christie's ★★   Geneva has always attracted some of the wealthiest tourists in the world, and to satisfy their craving for world-class art and antiques, they often attend the showcases and auctions of Christie's Auction House. Along with its leading competitor, Sotheby's (see below), it's one of the most glamorous art and antiques emporia in Europe. 8, place de la Taconnerie. ✆ 022/319-17-66. www.christies.com.

Sotheby's ★★   If there's a rare medieval triptych for sale, or a unique collection of 18th-century silver, it's likely to be auctioned at Sotheby's. Rivaled in glamour only by the company's branches in Paris and London, the Geneva branch offers an insight into some of the most unusual art and art buyers in town. 13, quai du Mont-Blanc. ✆ 022/908-48-00. www.sothebys.com.

CHINA

Aux Arts du Feu ★   Founded in 1897, this waterside store sells fine crystal, porcelain, china, silver, and decorative objects from around the world. 18, quai du Général-Guisan. ✆ 022/311-35-21.

CHOCOLATES

Confiserie Rohr   The aroma from this chocolate store practically pulls you in off the street. Among other specialties, you'll find chocolate-covered truffles, "gold" bars with hazelnuts, and *poubelles au chocolat* (chocolate "garbage pails"). Another store is at 42, rue du Rhône. 3, place du Molard. ✆ **022/311-63-03.** www.chocolats-rohr.ch.

CLOTHING

Addison   This is the best menswear store within the sprawling, multilevel shopping mall known as the Confédération Centre. Inside, you'll find salesmen who tend to remember many of their former clients, a sense of personalized intimacy, and enough suits and blazers to outfit any of the well-tailored business meetings of Geneva. Confédération Centre, rue du Marché at place Bel-Air. ✆ **022/312-33-50.**

Anita Smaga ★   Its garments are as expensive as they are elegant, and its clientele includes some of the best-heeled women in the world. The look is grand chic couture (and haute couture), but, depending on your taste, there might be an accessory or two appealing to your sense of whimsy. 51, rue du Rhône. ✆ **022/310-26-55.**

Chanel ★★   Whatever a woman's taste in clothes, and whatever her age, there's nothing that makes her look better than Chanel. Despite the passage of time, the look can usually be identified at a glance, and remains dear to the hearts of stylishly mature women everywhere. This branch in the heart of Geneva's most glamorous shopping district keeps the tradition alive. 43, rue du Rhône. ✆ **022/311-08-62.**

DEPARTMENT STORES

Bon Genie   Located on place du Molard, this department store sells mostly high-fashion women's clothing. Its storefront windows display art objects from local museums alongside designer clothes. There's also a limited selection of men's clothing, as well as furniture, cosmetics, and perfumes. 34, rue du Marché. ✆ **022/818-11-11.** www.bongenie-grieder.ch.

Globus   This is one of the largest department stores in Geneva, with many boutique-style departments that flourish inside and a self-image that's firmly patterned after the upscale Galeries Lafayette in Paris. Expect glamour, lots of upbeat cheerfulness, and departments devoted separately to travel bureaus, an agency selling theater tickets, a hairdresser, newspaper kiosks, and a bistro and sandwich shop/cafe. 48, rue du Rhône. ✆ **022/319-50-50.** www.globus.ch.

GIFTS

Come Prima   Our favorite Geneva shop benefits from a spectacular array of gift and leather items, as organized by a hardworking entrepreneur (Myriam Krieger-Demetriadès) whose personality permeates every aspect of the place. Officially, she runs a boutique loaded with top-quality leather bags and carryalls, as well as one-of-a-kind wooden puzzles. There are also teddy bears from Germany, folk-style cushions embroidered in Hungary, hyperstylish umbrellas, and classically tasteful table decorations. 17, rue de la Cité (place Bémont). ✆ **022/310-77-79.**

JEWELRY/WATCHES

Bucherer ★   Located opposite the Mont Blanc Bridge, this chrome-and-crystal store sells deluxe watches and diamonds. The store offers such name brands as Rolex, Piaget, Ebel, Baume & Mercier, Omega, Tissot, Rado, and Swatch. The carpeted third floor is filled with relatively inexpensive watches. You'll also find a large selection of cuckoo clocks, music boxes, embroideries, and souvenirs, as well as porcelain pill boxes and other gift items. 45, rue du Rhône. ✆ 022/319-62-66. www.bucherer.com.

Gübelin Jewelers ★★ Dating from 1854, this family-run establishment is known mainly for its brand-name watches, although it also sells beautiful precious stones and jewelry in 18-karat gold. You'll see two perpetual-motion clocks in the windows, giving chronological as well as astrological time, with fanciful enamel notations of the different time zones. You can also buy reasonably priced gifts, such as pen and pencil sets. 1, place du Molard. ✆ 022/310-86-55. www.guebelin.ch.

LEATHER

Hermès ★★★ Like all Hermès boutiques, this store sells purses, leather accessories, diaries, jewelry, watches, ready-to-wear clothing, furs, and, naturally, the famous Hermès scarf and tie. Everything is beautifully handcrafted. 43, rue du Rhône. ✆ 022/819-07-19. www.hermes.ch.

PICTURE FRAMES

Pierre Berndt ★ (Finds) Never judge a picture by its frame? That's not entirely true, according to this purveyor of antique frames, any of which could suitably adorn that old-master portrait you happened to pick up on your prior trip to Geneva. The store's buyers cull the auction houses of Europe for their inventory of antique lacquered, gilded, painted, carved, or silvered frames. Most frames range in price from 2,500F to 10,000F, although some simple, unpretentious ones cost 125F. Some of the frames at this shop are new but carefully distressed to look as antique as possible, and sell for a lot less. 34–36, Grand-Rue. ✆ 022/311-74-85. www.pierreberndt.ch.

SILVER

Au Vieux Canon Its specialty is antique English silver, most of it crafted during the 19th and early 20th centuries, and much of it culled from estate sales held throughout the United Kingdom. Also look for 19th-century Viennese bronzes, depicting everything from Europe's great composers to whimsical nymphs waving garlands of flowers. Granted, you might be able to buy an equivalent item for less if you haul it back from London, but the inventory is elegant and the setting is appropriately opulent. 40, Grand-Rue. ✆ 022/310-57-58. www.vieux-canon.ch.

TOBACCO

Davidoff ★ This is the most famous tobacco store in the world, with the best cigars you'll find in Europe. This is the place where the Davidoff retail empire all began. For many years, this was the business headquarters of Zino and Marthe Davidoff, White Russian émigrés who arrived in Switzerland in 1911. When they were in their 60s, with the help of a marketing expert from Basel (Dr. Schneider), they eventually spearheaded a chain of upscale cigar stores that now extends throughout Europe and the Americas. 2, rue de Rive. ✆ 022/310-90-41. www.davidoff.com.

TOYS

Jouets Weber ★ (Kids) This member of a worldwide chain has been selling children's toys and classic games for at least 150 years from a location at the corner of rue de la Fontaine. Everything—from computer toys to simple playthings carved from wood by craftspeople in the Alps and Asia—is available. Adults appreciate such *jeux de société*

The Land of Time

August 8, 1535 The Protestant Reformation arrives in Geneva. A mob forcibly evicts the Catholic archbishop who, in his haste, forgets his watch. Today it's a prime exhibit in Geneva's watch-and-clock museum.

1541 In the wake of the Reformation, French-born Jean Calvin introduces the Protestant work ethic and welcomes exiled Protestant craftsmen from throughout Europe. Many are watchmakers and jewelers. Alas, ostentatious jewelry is outlawed in the tightly controlled new community, and jewelers' efforts must be funneled somewhere. No zealot ever claimed that a watch wasn't an essential part of any God-fearing man's wardrobe, so the ban against jewelry formed the base of what would eventually become the premier watchmaking center in the world.

1601 A watchmaker's guild enforces rules that regulate the watchmaking industry. Obligations include public prayers before each assembly of the guild, and that each watch be signed or marked as the work of a specific craftsperson.

1707 A Swiss is appointed watchmaker to the court of the Chinese emperor K'ang-Hi in Peking. Swiss compatriots fan out across the globe, creating markets in places such as the Ottoman court in Istanbul, where business booms with baubles destined for the sultan's harem.

Around 1750 Julien Le Roy, celebrated Paris-based watchmaker to the king of France, complains bitterly that the watchmakers of Geneva are flooding southern France with "their accursed watches."

1780 Most of Geneva's St. Gervais district, behind the present-day Grand Hôtel des Bergues, and 5,000 employees are devoted to the town's biggest industry, watchmaking. The town's most expensive real-estate rentals are always on the fifth and sixth floors of cramped and narrow town houses, where the light is brightest. The neighborhood's most famous child? Jean-Jacques Rousseau, whose father trained him in Plutarch and the Roman classics by night and made watches by day.

1880 Gustav Flaubert, the greatest novelist of 19th-century France, compiles a list of pithy sayings *(Idées Reçues)*. His definition of "pocket watch" was "suitable only if it was made in Geneva."

Today Thousands of technical developments and a rigorous attention to quality have made Switzerland the leading watchmaker in the world, a title it has held for more than 400 years. Although Hong Kong and Japan produce greater numbers of watches today, Switzerland produces the greatest number of upscale watches and the most complicated watches, and receives an estimated 55% of all funds worldwide spent on consumer purchases of watches. In the 1990s Switzerland produced 98 million watches and watch movements worth $5.3 billion (U.S.) at wholesale. You can buy everything from watches worth a millionaire's ransom to "fun watches," "disposal watches," watches designed for deep-sea diving or parachute jumping, all kinds of chronometers and measuring devices, and—newest of all—ecowatches crafted from recycled aluminum cans.

(parlor games) as Pictionnari, priced at 60F, which will improve both your social skills and your French-language vocabulary. 12, rue de la Croix-d'Or. ✆ **022/310-42-55.** www.fcw.ch.

SHOPPING IN CAROUGE

Shopping in Carouge is more whimsical and lighthearted than what you're likely to find in *haute Genève,* and often with garments or objects that aren't easily duplicated anywhere else. Here's a selection of some of the most intriguing—all of them centered within a relatively small area of less than 3 square blocks.

Anne-Claude Virchaux ★★ She's a one-woman show, a locally born *artiste* who designs and weaves her own textiles before cutting them into the kind of artfully "bohemian" garment that women as far away as California would fight to own. All of this occurs within a studio/sales outlet that overflows with weaving and dressmaking techniques that originated 4,000 years before the birth of Christ, although in this case with combinations of silk, cotton, linen, wool, and cashmere whose textures absolutely scream out to be touched. No other dressmaker in Switzerland crafts garments this way, or with as much innate "soul." Colors we crave that seem, at least here, perennially attractive include pumpkin, persimmon, wheat, and several heavenly shades of ocher and blue. When, one asks, will the editors at *Vogue* discover this treasure, and which female U.S. politicians would look fabulous in this kind of garment? (Clinton? Pelosi?) Garments, each completely original and one-of-a-kind, cost from 500F to 1,600F each. Anne-Claude herself is usually on-site, engagingly showcasing her craft and her looms, usually with a tape measure thrown around her neck that her fans view as a combination fashion accessory and badge of honor. 13, rue St-Joseph, in Carouge. ✆ **022/342-35-26.**

Atelier Djeihne/Atelier Mireille Donze Two independent artists display their one-of-a-kind women's dresses within this cramped but convivial boutique in the heart of Carouge. They include Djeihne (it's pronounced "Jane") Ihne and Mireille Donze. Together, their women's clothing presents a look that's anything but what you'd expect to see in *Vogue.* It's loose, boldly textured, often focusing on knits which are deliberately asymmetrical, either through placement of an off-centered pocket or the deliberately askewed garments which, alas, sometimes fail to impress. 31, rue Saint Joseph, in Carouge. ✆ **022/343-55-21.**

Atelier/Galerie Igor Siebold There are at least a dozen jewelry designers in Carouge, but this is one of the most creative of the lot. Owner/resident artist Igor fashioned an intriguing series of wrist bracelets and rings from the ball of an old-fashioned IBM Selectric typewriter. Fifty years ago, the Selectric was the most avant-garde piece of office equipment in the world: Today, its recycled parts evoke memories of ancient hieroglyphics, curiously old-fashioned yet oddly futuristic. You can buy the jewelry in its original brass alloys, or recast in some castes into gold or platinum. 8, rue St-Joseph, in Carouge. ✆ **022/301-29-55.**

Chapeaux, Atelier Circonflexe For years, fashion moguls have been lamenting the death of the milliner's art, but in Carouge, at least, the art is alive and thriving. This is the more creative and better known of Carouge's hatmakers, housed within a two-room shop crammed with more than 200 hats, each a creative statement in its own right. Fashioned from straw, silk, felt, and wool, and priced from 80F to 600F each, they're the kind of thing that Audrey Hepburn (a longtime resident of Switzerland) might have felt comfortable wearing in the 1950s. At press time, rose-fuchsia and turquoise blue were two "colors of the minute" that many women tended to look good in. 4, rue St. Joseph, in Carouge. ✆ **076/332-19-10.**

8 GENEVA AFTER DARK

Geneva has a more diverse and varied nightlife than any other city in Switzerland. At least some of the activities are centered around **place du Bourg-de-Four,** a stagecoach stop during the 19th century, and today one of the spiritual centerpieces of Geneva's Old Town. In summer, outdoor cafes, each with an almost obligatory collection of flowering shrubs and plants, seem to thrive both in the Old Town and along the banks of the river and lake.

For a listing of nightlife and cultural activities, free copies of the bilingual monthly *Genève Le Guide* (www.le-guide.ch) are distributed at hotel desks and tourist information centers.

THE PERFORMING ARTS

Geneva has always attracted the culturally sophisticated, including Byron, Jean-Baptiste Camille Corot, Victor Hugo, Balzac, George Sand, and Franz Liszt. Ernst Ansermet founded Geneva's great **Orchestre de la Suisse Romande,** whose frequent concerts entertain music lovers at **Victoria Hall.** For opera there's the 1,500-seat **Grand Théâtre,** which welcomes Béjart, the Bolshoi, and other ballet companies, in addition to having a company of its own.

For a preview of events at the time of your visit, pick up a copy of the monthly "List of Events" issued by the tourist office.

Bâtiment des Forces Motrices (Le BFM) The most startling and most centrally located theater and concert hall in Geneva, it stages an ongoing series of theater and musical concerts that are among the most controversial and iconoclastic in town. Set astride a long and narrow island in the middle of the Rhône, very close to the tramway junction at the Place du Bel-Air, it was originally inaugurated in 1886 as a hydroelectric and pumping station, moving vast quantities of water from the low-lying river to factories, fountains, and private homes up to 10km (6¼ miles) away. Abandoned during the 1960s, it was radically reconfigured in 1997, when, after changes to its acoustically sophisticated interior, it reopened as a venue for classical and rock concerts, theater pieces, fashion *defiles,* and political rallies. You'll recognize the place by its neoclassical brickwork and by the trio of gods (Neptune, Ceres, and Mercury), whose statues adorn its pediment. Locals refer to the it as "Le BFM."

2, place des Volontaires, 1204 Genève. ℂ **022/322-12-20.** www.bfm.ch. For tickets, call Resaplus 0900/552-333 or click on www.resaplus.ch. Tickets 12F–95F. Tram: 13, 15, or 16. Bus: 2, 4, 10, 19, 20, D, K, or L.

Grand Théâtre de Genève Modeled on the Paris Opéra, this building was opened in 1879. It burned down in 1951 and was subsequently rebuilt in the same style, except for the modern auditorium, which has a seating capacity of 1,488. From September to July, its resident orchestra and dance company presents eight operas and two ballets, but many other outside companies stage recitals, chamber-music concerts, and full-blown presentations of symphonies.

Place Neuve. ℂ **022/418-31-30.** www.geneveopera.ch. Tickets 31F–181F for opera, 24F–130F for ballet.

Victoria Hall ★ This 1,866-seat hall, which benefited from a radical renovation and upgrade of its entire premises during 2006, is home to the celebrated Orchestre de la Suisse Romande. This is Geneva's most famous musical institution, whose interpretations have been heard throughout the world. For 50 years it was conducted by Ernst Ansermet and, through this maestro, had close associations with Igor Stravinsky.

14, rue du Général-Dufour. © 022/418-35-00. www.osr.ch. Tickets 31F–114F.

THE CLUB & MUSIC SCENE

Au Chat Noir (Finds) In the suburb of Carouge, one of 45 independent "communes" surrounding Geneva, this is a venue for funk, rock, salsa, jazz, and some good old New Orleans blues. It's crowded on weekends but the club will take reservations. Live music is presented nightly at 9pm (10pm Fri–Sat). After a few drinks you begin to fear that the car suspended from the ceiling might fall in on you. It's open Tuesday to Thursday from 6pm to 4am, Friday 6pm to 5am, Saturday 9pm to 5am, and Sunday 8pm to 4am. 13, rue Vautier, Carouge. © 022/343-49-98. www.chatnoir.ch. Cover 16F–22F.

Griffin's Club ★ Although it's been a wee bit battered with the passage of time, Griffin's is the chic choice in Geneva. Technically it's private—you may or may not get in, depending on the mood of the management at the time of your visit. If you're "correctly dressed" and "correctly behaved," you have a good chance, more likely Monday to Thursday. The popularity of nightclubs comes and goes, but the collection of celebrities who have traipsed here reads like a who's who from the tabloids. Jackets are required for men. The decor is red and black, with lots of live plants and large paintings in the restaurant where main courses are priced at 35F to 60F. The restaurant opens nightly 8pm until at least 3 or 4am. The disco is open from 11pm to 5am. In July and August the entire premises are closed every Sunday and Monday. 36, bd. Helvétique. © 022/735-22-18. www. griffinsclub.com.

Le Dancing de la Coupole In one of the downtown area's most popular brasseries, La Coupole, this disco and dance hall focuses most intently on retro music of the 1960s. Whiskey begins at 16F, beer at 9.50F. Hours are Monday to Friday 7:30pm to 1am. 116, rue du Rhône. © 022/787-50-12. www.lacoupole.ch.

Platinum Hip and well organized, with just the slightest trace of cynicism, this is a well-known pickup bar where a gentleman who's looking for female companionship will probably find it. Security is tight, and the clientele is affluent (or at least it does a realistic imitation of appearing to be so) and international. It's open Tuesday to Sunday from 10:30pm to 5am. 18, quai du Seujet. © 022/738-90-91. www.platinum-club.ch. Cover 24F, including 1st drink.

Velvet Within its genre, this is a safe and well-recommended nightclub, especially popular with visitors, but it isn't for the timid. Unless you're an unusually brazen woman or firmly attached to an attentive male escort, it's more appropriate for men: It's very heterosexual, very permissive, and loaded with working women, some of whom might be on stage dancing, others of whom will be waiting for a visitor to buy them a drink. In most instances, its tawdrier aspects are rather artfully concealed, although that's a tall order for a place where, beginning around 11pm, as many as 32 topless international beauties begin strutting their stuff in a nonstop, informally choreographed spectacle that continues till around 5am. Despite the unadulterated promiscuity of the place, it lacks the artistic flair of Crazy Horse or Moulin Rouge in Paris. There's a restaurant and a disco on the premises, as well as a master/mistress of ceremonies who gives shape and form to the cabaret. Drinks begin at 20F, but usually average around 25F each. Velvet is open nightly 10pm to 5am. The restaurant closes on Sunday, but not the cabaret and bar.

7, rue du Jeu-de-l'Arc. © 022/735-00-00. www.velvet-club.ch. No cover Sun–Thurs, 12F Fri–Sat.

White'n Silver   This private club does allow nonmembers to enter, although men are required to wear jackets. It has become increasingly popular with people from the developing world, many of whom have settled more or less permanently in Geneva. Occasionally the club presents some top names in show business. Drinks in the club cost 19F to 27F. White'n Silver is mainly a disco, but it has a restaurant attached. The club opens daily at 11pm; the restaurant opens at 8pm. 15, Glacis-de-Rive. ℂ 022/735-15-15. www.whiten silver.ch. Cover 9F–20F.

THE BAR SCENE

Most bars in Geneva close at 1:30 or 2am.

Le Bar des Bergues ★★★   If you want to experience life in the very posh fast lane of what's probably the most consistently expensive hotel in Geneva, the suave and silky bar staff at the Hôtel des Bergues (p. 315) is ready, willing, and able to welcome you—especially if you're fetchingly dressed and nubile—into the inner sanctums of this elegant and very upscale wood-paneled bar. If you're not actually living at the hotel at the time of your appearance, you won't be alone: At least half the clients of this bar aren't residents of the hotel. Entrance is free. Whiskey-sodas begin at around 16F. In the Four Seasons Grand Hôtel des Bergues, 33, quai des Bergues. ℂ 022/908-70-00.

Le Francis Bar   This fashionable bar, which, during headier days, attracted *le tout Genève* or "cream of the crop" of Geneva, still manages to transform itself into an attractive piano bar on some evenings. Be warned: Drinks are very expensive. 8, bd. Helvétique. ℂ 022/346-32-52. www.lefrancis.ch.

The Leopard Room ★   Outfitted with the antique trunks and Grand Tour accessories that Lord Byron might have hauled with him on his poetic and revolutionary peregrinations around 19th-century Europe, it's a bit less overwhelming than the glossier and more in-the-news bar associated, say, with the also-recommended Hôtel des Bergues (p. 315). Woodsy and a bit like a library, it's in the cellar level of the Hôtel d'Angleterre. Live music from a piano begins every night except Sunday at 7pm. Tapas and sashimi cost from 15F to 32F per portion. It's open every night from 5:30pm to 1am, and if you get hungry after too many drinks, the hotel dining room, Windows (p. 323) is immediately upstairs. In the Hôtel d'Angleterre, 17, quai du Mont-Blanc. ℂ 022/906-55-55.

Mr. Pickwick Pub (Value)   This pub serves simple, English-style meals, but most patrons come here to drink. The paneled rooms are filled in the evening with a young crowd, who enjoy the dim lighting and American music. The place gets very crowded and can be fun. Irish coffee is a specialty, but most visitors order beer. Because so many United Nations employees hang out here, this pub is sometimes called the "Tower of Babble." 80, rue de Lausanne (corner of rue Rothschild). ℂ 022/731-67-97. www.mrpickwick.ch.

Nobel Bar and Restaurant Vertig'O   This section of Geneva's lakefront has other, equally posh and chic bars, but there's something a bit earthier and more fun about this place. It has to do with the willingness of the Concorde chain to play with colors and pop art in ways that defy the rigidly historic hotel that contains it. The result evokes an edgy nightclub in Paris, where Tarzan and Suzy Wong might have hung out with Coco Chanel in the palace near Timbuktu. Ceilings are high, elaborate, and formal, but the walls are painted a disconcerting shade of eggplant. Lighting manages to make everyone look good, and primitive tribal art is displayed in obvious contrast to the Beaux Arts decor that otherwise permeates the place. We recommend that you order a drink or two in the Noble Bar and, if and when hunger pangs eventually prevail, segue on to a meal in Vertig'O. The bar is open daily from 5pm till at least 1am, but the restaurant is only open Tuesday to Saturday noon to 2pm and 7:30 till 10pm. Main courses in the restaurant range from 52F to 63F, and include, among others, lamb chops with a confit of garlic, grilled dorado with a mousseline of potatoes, and slow-cooked monkfish served in a style inspired by *osso buco*. On the lobby level of the Hotel de la Paix, 11, quai du Mont-Blanc. ℂ **022/909-60-00.**

Scandale It's inevitable that the young, the restless, and the rebellious 20- and 30-somethings of Geneva would unite in a wholesale rejection of the glittering sense of posh that prevails within more upscale neighborhoods beside the city's lakefront. Many of them seem to congregate here, within the sprawling premises of Scandale, a site vaguely akin to a warehouse, which includes dining, drinking, and dancing facilities that seem to rock virtually every night it's open. Furnishings include artfully battered, hand-me-down sofas, an elongated bar where you're likely to meet hipsters from all over Europe and the Middle East, and a blend of house and electro-jazz music that keeps everybody hopping. Don't even ask about the gender preferences of the clientele here—everyone seems way beyond even attempting an easy and pat self-definition. The place is open every Tuesday to Saturday from 10am to 2am, with a DJ whose music begins in the cellar-level dance bar at 11pm and which seems to eventually permeate all aspects of the place before the joint closes. If you get hungry, a somewhat lackluster, mostly black-and-stainless-steel restaurant charges from 11F to 27F for pastas and pizzas. Artworks here change as the objects are sold, and two large plasma screens broadcast everything from sporting events to punk-rock concerts. You'll find the place within about 2 blocks from the railway station. 24, rue de Lausanne. ℂ **022/731-83-73.** www.lescandale.ch.

THE GAY & LESBIAN SCENE

Geneva's gay switchboard is **Dialogai,** 11–13, rue de la Navigation (ℂ **022/906-40-40;** www.dialogai.org). It provides multilingual information and advice to anyone who calls. On the basement level are a library, a cafe and bar, and meeting rooms for Wednesday-night dinners and Sunday-morning brunches. The organization publishes a free list of the gay bars in Geneva and French-speaking Switzerland, and is the best access to the male homosexual network of Geneva. It schedules discussion groups for gay youths and gay seniors, and it also offers support groups for people who are HIV positive.

---

9 EASY EXCURSIONS FROM GENEVA

There are many attractions in the region around Geneva. Several of the most popular places—at least around the lake—have been covered in chapter 11, "Lausanne & Lake Geneva." Refer to that chapter for highlights around the lake itself. This section will deal with the attractions that are closest to Geneva.

MONT SALEVE ★

The limestone ridge of Mont Salève (House Mountain) is 6.4km (4 miles) south of Geneva, in France. Its peak is at 1,200m (3,936 ft.), but you'll need a passport to get near it. If you have a car, you can take a road that goes up the mountain, which is popular with rock climbers. Bus no. 8 will take you to Veyrier-Douane, on the French border, where there's a passport and Customs control. A 6-minute cable-car ride will take you to

COLOGNY

Byron and Shelley both lived in the residential suburb of Cologny, where they met at the Villa Diodati in 1816. Fourteen kilometers (9 miles) northeast of Geneva, the suburb is served by both bus A and bus no. 33 from the city. The view of the lake and the city is especially good from the "Byron Stone" on chemin de Ruth (Ruth's Path) leading to the Byron fields.

The best time to go to Cologny is in the afternoon, when you can visit the **Bodmeriana Library,** 19–21, rte. du Guignard (© 022/707-44-33; www.fondationbodmer.org; Tues–Sun 2–6pm), a foundation established by a Zurich millionaire named Martin Bodmer. Get off at the Cologny-Temple stop (bus A) or the Croisée de Cologny stop (bus no. 33) and view the private collection, which contains first editions, rare manuscripts such as the most ancient St. John's Gospel, and various other forms of art (sculpture, painting, and the like). Admission is 15F for adults, 10F for students and seniors, and free for ages 15 and under.

COPPET

Located 15km (9 miles) north of Geneva in the canton of Vaud, this little town on the western shore of Lake Geneva is one of the most interesting destinations in the region.

From Geneva's main station take the train on the Lancy Pont-Rouge–Genève–Coppet line for a 20-minute ride to the Château de Coppet in Coppet. Tickets cost 16F roundtrip. If you're driving, head north from Geneva along Route 2.

Château de Coppet ★ (© 022/776-10-28; www.coppet.ch) attracted some of the greatest minds of the 18th and 19th centuries. The château, which sits on a hill beside the lake, between Lausanne and Geneva, was purchased in 1784 by Jacques Necker, the rich and powerful finance minister of Louis XVI. His daughter was Madame de Staël, a great French woman of letters, who was eventually sent into exile for her opposition to Napoleon. The château is still owned by Necker's descendants. The museum contains some mementos of Madame de Staël. From April through October, the château is open daily from 2 to 6pm (July–Aug also daily 10am–noon). Admission costs 8F for adults and 6F for students, seniors, and children 6 to 16. It's free for children 5 and under.

A noteworthy local hotel, an elegant place with only 14 units and a well-recommended restaurant, is the **Hôtel du Lac,** 51, Grand-Rue, CH-1296 Coppet (© 022/960-80-00; www.hoteldulac.ch).

Lucerne & Central Switzerland

Lucerne (Luzern in German) and its lake lie in the heart of Switzerland, where the tops of the mountains are covered with eternal snow and their sides flanked with glaciers. We're in William Tell country now, where the seeds that led to the Swiss Confederation were sown. It was near Brunnen, in the meadow of Rutli, that the Everlasting League of 1315 was created.

Despite the presence of many small resorts in the neighborhood, Lucerne, with a population of 60,000, is the district's largest and busiest city. The lake that nurtures it is the fourth largest in Switzerland, 39km (24 miles) long and (at its broadest) 3km (2 miles) wide. Geologists refer to it as the terminal basin for the nearby glaciers. The lake is known in German as Vierwaldstättersee and in French as the Lac des Quatre Cantons. Either way,

it's the lake of the four cantons: Lucerne, Uri, Unterwalden, and Schwyz (from which Switzerland derives its name).

Lucerne and its lake are among the most popular tourist destinations in all of Europe, attracting more than a million overnight visitors every year, plus countless more who stop by only for the day. Paddle steamers service the many cable cars and lidos (beaches) set at the edge of the water, providing sweeping views of mountains with names like Pilatus and Rigi along the way. The region is rich in panoramas, folklore, and sports such as tobogganing, skiing, hill climbing, ice-skating, and curling. The irregular geography of the brusquely vertical limestone and granite outcroppings make the shoreline one of the most beautiful and romantic sites in Switzerland.

1 LUCERNE ★★★

50km (31 miles) S of Zurich; 90km (56 miles) E of Bern

Lucerne is a tourist favorite partly because it embodies the storybook image of a Swiss town. Located at the north end of the lake, the city abounds in narrow cobblestone streets, slender spires and turrets, covered bridges, frescoed houses, and fountains. Its residents are quick to tell you that you're "never very far from the snow"—mounts Rigi and Pilatus form the southern gate to the city, and the snowcapped Alps loom in the distance.

Lucerne's strategic gateway to the south and the rich markets of Italy lie between Rigi and Pilatus. The city's history has always been tied to the St. Gotthard Pass. During the 13th century, the routes leading to it were simple mule paths. By 1820 the road had been widened enough to allow the easy passage of carriages. By 1882 Lucerne had a railway tunnel. Once a satellite vassal of the Habsburgs, in 1332 Lucerne became the first city to join the Swiss Confederation. Unlike Geneva and Zurich, Lucerne did not support the Reformation and has always remained a stronghold of Catholicism.

The city is a renowned cultural center. Richard Wagner spent several of his most productive years in Tribschen, on the outskirts of Lucerne (there's a Wagner museum here). Arturo Toscanini was a founder of the Lucerne Festival of Music, one of the most important musical events in Europe, which takes place annually in April, and its companion event, the Lucerne Piano Festival, an event that transpires every November.

The residents of Lucerne are a sports-oriented people. Every summer there are international rowing regattas on Rotsee. Swimmers go to the lido (lake beach) and golfers head for the 18-hole golf course on the outskirts, or to any of several others that lie within a 35-minute drive. Other sports include tennis, hiking, and mountaineering. Residents seem especially fond of horse races, and there are plenty of international horse-jumping contests.

You'll find Lucerne at its best between May and September on Tuesday and Saturday mornings, when it becomes a lively market town. The markets are sheltered by stately arcades on both banks of the Reuss River.

ESSENTIALS

GETTING THERE   Lucerne lies at the junction of four major rail lines, which connect it by fast train with every other major city in Switzerland. Travel time from Bern on one of the many express trains is 65 minutes, and from Zurich, 50 minutes. Call © **0900/ 300-300** for rail schedules.

If you're **driving** from Bern, take Route 10 north and east. From Zurich head south and west along E41, turning southwest and following the signs at the junction with N14.

VISITOR INFORMATION   The **Lucerne Tourist Office** is at Zentralstrasse 5 (© **041/ 227-17-17;** www.luzern.org). It's open April to September, Monday to Friday 8:30am to 6:30pm, and Saturday and Sunday 9am to 6:30pm. During October to March, hours are Monday to Friday 8:30am to 5:30pm, Saturday 9am to 5pm, and Sunday 9am to 1pm.

CITY LAYOUT

Most arrivals are at the railroad station, on **Bahnhofplatz,** where trains pull in from Zurich and other parts of Switzerland. This train depot is on the left (south) bank of the Reuss River.

If you cross a bridge from the station square, you'll be on the right (north) bank of the river at **Schwanenplatz (Swan Square),** which is the center of Lucerne. Also on the north bank of the Reuss is **Altstadt (Old Town),** containing many burghers' houses with oriel windows and old squares with fountains. The only way to explore this neighborhood is on foot.

Kapellgasse is a major shopping street that leads to the **Kornmarkt (Corn Market),** where you'll find the **Altes Rathaus (Old Town Hall),** dating from 1602. To the west of the Kornmarkt is the **Weinmarkt (Wine Market),** a lovely old square with a much-photographed fountain.

The Grand Casino Luzern, a casino-and-restaurant complex, stands at Kurplatz on **Nationalquai,** the major quay of Lucerne facing the lake.

From Kurplatz, Löwenstrasse leads to **Löwenplatz,** site of the Panorama, a famed canvas depicting the retreat of the French army during the Franco-Prussian War (1870–71). Nearby stands the even more famous **Löwendenkmal (Lion Monument).** Carved directly into the rocky face of a low cliff in the heart of town, it's Lucerne's second-most famous attraction, surpassed in visibility only by the Kapellbrücke, the geranium-fringed covered wooden footbridge.

Lucerne has an efficient network of local buses, one ride on which costs from 2F to 6F, depending on the distance you ride. Buy your tickets at automatic vending machines before you board. A 24-hour ticket costs 10F, and there's also a 6-day ticket selling for 50F. For more information about **bus routes** within Lucerne, call ℂ **041/369-65-65.**

Bikes can be rented at the railway station for 33F per day June to September between 7am and 7:45pm daily; October to May, hours are Monday to Saturday 7am to 7:45pm, and Sunday 9:30am to 7pm. A bike trip along the north shore of Lake Lucerne can be one of the scenic highlights of a visit to central Switzerland. This trip can easily absorb a whole day (take along a picnic lunch). The tourist office will provide a map and you can set off from the Lucerne train station heading for St. Niklausen and Kastanienbaum in the direction of Tribschen. If you have time, visit the Richard Wagner Museum. The most beautiful stretch is along the lake to Winkel-Horw beach, where you can go for a brisk lake swim if the temperature is right. The duration of this 13km (8-mile) ride, including the return to Lucerne, should take about 1½ hours.

SEEING THE SIGHTS

The best panoramas are the views from any of Lucerne's nine lookout towers, which are clustered in an orderly row within a 5-minute walk uphill and north from the center of town. Part of the old fortifications erected along the north side of the medieval sector, they were all built in a different style between 1350 and 1408. At twilight they stand in dramatic silhouette against the sky. The nine towers are known collectively as the **Museggtürme;** you can climb only three of them. Admission is free, and they're open from May until the beginning of October from noon to 8pm daily. You can also take a short walk on the old outer wall of the city.

Although our only walking tour (see below) is for the independent traveler, guided walking tours are also available; contact the tourist office (see "Visitor Information," above) for more details. These tours cost around 18F. In summer, tours depart daily at 9:45am; in winter, tours are conducted only Wednesday and Saturday at 9:45am.

SPECIAL EVENTS

The **Lucerne Festival of Music** is held from the second week of August to the second week of September. For more information, contact the Festival of Music, which also sponsors the **Festival Easter Lucerne,** another popular event (ℂ **041/226-44-00;** http://e.lucernefestival.ch). There's also the **Lucerne Piano Festival,** which focuses more on classical piano music, conducted every year during a weeklong period in November.

WALKING TOUR	LUCERNE

START:	Schwanenplatz.
FINISH:	Kurplatz.
TIME:	2½ hours.
BEST TIMES:	Any sunny day.
WORST TIMES:	Rush hours, Monday to Friday from 8 to 9am and 5 to 6pm.

The best way to see Lucerne is on foot, going along its lakeside quays, across its old squares, and through the streets of its Old Town.

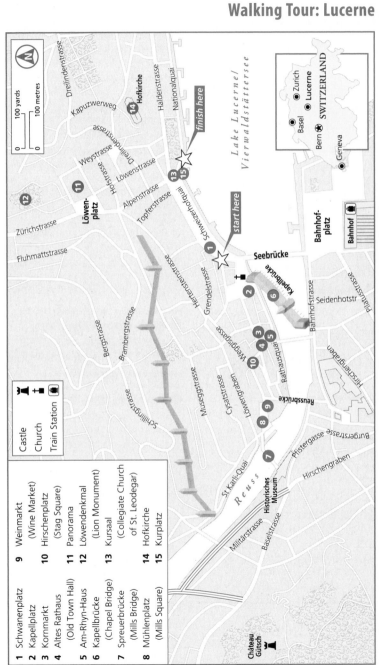

0   100 yards
0   100 metres

start here

finish here

Seebrücke

Löwen-
platz

*Lake Lucerne/
Vierwaldstättersee*

Bahnhof-
platz

Bahnhof

Reuss

Château
Gütsch

SWITZERLAND

Zurich
Lucerne
Basel
Bern
Geneva

Castle
Church
Train Station

1   Schwanenplatz
2   Kapellplatz
3   Kornmarkt
4   Altes Rathaus
    (Old Town Hall)
5   Am-Rhyn-Haus
6   Kapellbrücke
    (Chapel Bridge)
7   Spreuerbrücke
    (Mills Bridge)
8   Mühlenplatz
    (Mills Square)

9   Weinmarkt
    (Wine Market)
10 Hirschenplatz
    (Stag Square)
11 Panorama
12 Löwendenkmal
    (Lion Monument)
13 Kursaal
    (Collegiate Church
    of St. Leodegar)
14 Hofkirche
15 Kurplatz

Drillindenstrasse
Drillindenstrasse
Kapuzwerweg
Haldenstrasse
Hofkirche
Nationalquai
Weystrasse
Löwenstrasse
Hofstrasse
Drillindenstrasse
Alpenstrasse
Topferstrasse
Zürichstrasse
Fluhmattstrasse
Bergstrasse
Brambergstrasse
Museggstrasse
Schillingstrasse
Cysatstrasse
Löwengraben
Rathausquai
Kapellbrücke
Bahnhofstrasse
Seidenhotstr
Pilatusstrasse
Hirschengraben
Pfistergasse
Burgerstrasse
Hirschengraben
Militärstrasse
Baselstrasse
St Karli-Quai
Historisches
Museum
Reussbrücke
Weggisgasse
Grendelstrasse
Hertensteinstrasse
Schweizerhofquai

Start in the heart of Lucerne at:

❶ Schwanenplatz

Translated as Swan Square, it lies on the north bank of the Reuss River and is reached by crossing the bridge, the Seebrücke, from Bahnhofplatz on the south bank, site of the train station.

Adjoining the square on the west is:

❷ Kapellplatz

This is the site of St. Peter's Church. The church, the oldest in Lucerne, was built in 1178. In the center of the square is a fountain commemorating Carnival revelry in Lucerne.

From here, continue west along a major shopping street, Kapellgasse, until you reach the:

❸ Kornmarkt

This is the old Grain Exchange or Corn Market, which is today the site of the:

❹ Altes Rathaus (Old Town Hall)

A Renaissance building from 1602, the town hall has impressive masonry, a tremendous roof, and a tall rectangular tower. The tower is a good vantage point from which to survey the crowded market scene on Tuesday and Saturday mornings.

To the left of the town hall is the:

❺ Rosengart Haus

This 17th-century building houses some Picassos from the Rosengart collection (described below). The town house is entered at Furrengasse 21.

After leaving the museum, follow Rathausquai east toward Schwanenplatz again, but only to cross the:

❻ Kapellbrücke (Chapel Bridge)

The symbol of Lucerne, this covered wooden footbridge can be used to cross the Reuss River, leading to the south bank. Built in 1333, the bridge is 170m (558 ft.) long and crosses the river diagonally. It's one of the best-preserved wooden bridges in Switzerland, used originally for defense. There's also an octagonal Wasserturm (Water Tower), used variously as a prison, a torture chamber, and an archive. The bridge was always known for its 122 paintings that hung from its arched roof. Some of them were done in 1599 by Heinrich Wagmann, illustrating the daily activities and dress of the people. The bridge was damaged in a fire in 1993 and two-thirds of the original paintings were destroyed or severely damaged. Lucerne city officials directed that copies be made. After a $2.1-million reconstruction, this landmark bridge was reopened in the spring of 1994.

You emerge onto Bahnhofstrasse; you can continue right (west) until you see the next covered bridge across the Reuss, the:

❼ Spreuerbrücke (Mills Bridge)

Built in 1407 and restored in the 19th century, this wooden bridge spans an arm of the Reuss. Its gables are painted with the *Dance of Death,* a mural by Kaspar Meglinger dating from the 17th century. The mural commemorates a plague that swept through the city.

Cross the bridge and take a sharp right to reach:

❽ Mühlenplatz (Mills Square)

This square dates from the 16th century. This was the old site of Lucerne markets.

From Mühlenplatz, walk down Kramgasse (to the east) to reach the:

❾ Weinmarkt (Wine Market)

Here you'll find a lovely old square with a fountain, west of Kornmarkt. Long ago the mystery play *Confraternity of the Crown of Thorns* was performed here. Among the colorful old dwellings on the square is the Müllersche Apotheke, a "drugstore" from 1530.

Directly northeast of the Weinmarkt lies:

❿ Hirschenplatz (Stag Square)

Another landmark square of Lucerne, it's filled with restored buildings, many of them with painted facades and wrought-iron signs. In 1779 Goethe stayed at the Goldener Adler, which is located here.

From Hirschenplatz, head east along Weggisgasse, which opens eventually onto Falkenplatz. From Falkenplatz, continue east along Hertensteinstrasse until you come to Löwenplatz. This is the site of:

⑪ Panorama

Panorama is one of the largest canvases in Europe, covering 1,009 sq. m (10,861 sq. ft.) and curving in a circle around a central platform. Painted in 1889 by Edouard Castres and contained in a round building that was designed especially for it, it depicts the bloody retreat of the French army into Switzerland during the Franco-Prussian War.

The next stop on this tour is not immediately visible from Löwenplatz, but requires a brief detour north along Denkmalstrasse. Within about a block of Löwenplatz, high above your head you'll see one of the most famous statues in Switzerland, the:

⑫ Löwendenkmal (Lion Monument)

Carved in deep relief into the sandstone cliff above the town, the monument is an allegorical reference to the bravery of the Swiss Guards who died in the Tuileries of Paris in 1792 trying to save the life and honor of Marie Antoinette. During his grand tour of Europe, Mark Twain called the "Dying Lion" of Lucerne "the saddest and most poignant piece of rock in the world." Designed by the great Danish sculptor Bertel Thorvaldsen, the statue was dedicated in 1821.

Retrace your steps back to Löwenplatz, then head south along Löwenstrasse all the way to the lake and Kurplatz, a few steps east of Schwanenplatz, the site of the:

⑬ Kursaal

This spot is a casino-and-restaurant complex on Kurplatz on Nationalquai.

Above Nationalquai, view the twin towers of the Catholic:

⑭ Hofkirche (Collegiate Church of St. Leodegar)

Named after the patron saint of Lucerne, this is the most important church in the city. There was once a monastery at this site, but the present Gothic-Renaissance building dates from the 17th century. The interior has rich wrought-iron work, carvings, and a famous organ from 1640, with 4,950 pipes. Concerts are presented in the summer. The church also has a beautiful courtyard with arcades.

A good way to end the tour, you are now standing at:

⑮ Kurplatz

From here you can take in the best view of the lake from its northern rim. You can also take steamers from this area to visit various resorts along the lake. The view from here encompasses not only the lake but also the Alps from Rigi to Pilatus. The quays are lined with trees, hotels, and shops, ideal for exploring on foot. At the end of the promenade is the lido, called Lucerne's "Riviera."

OTHER ATTRACTIONS

The Bourbaki Panorama This is the world's best replica of a 19th-century blood bath that reinforced Switzerland's role as a neutral (nonaligned) power, and that provided the first testing ground for the then-fledging Red Cross. It commemorates an incident in the Franco-Prussian War (1870–71) when the defeated French forces of General Charles Bourbaki (1816–97) fled out of France into Switzerland to avoid annihilation by the Germans. In Switzerland the starving, diseased, and disorganized French forces were disarmed by the Swiss army, then welcomed into homes throughout Switzerland for rest and recuperation from the brutal winter. Today the event is hailed as one of the finest acts of humanitarian courage in Swiss history, and celebrated in the form of this circular painting, completed in 1881, of the bloody battlefield. Originally conceived as a Barnum & Bailey–style tourist attraction in the 19th century, the site was converted into an auto repair shop in 1925, and the painting was "shortened" in two separate incidents that ultimately removed about 3.6m (12 ft.) of gray sky from the top of the wraparound panorama. Between 1996 and 2003, the site was rebuilt, the painting cleaned, and the museum opened, with recorded narration, as a celebration of a genuinely bizarre but evocative interlude in European history. Be prepared for the recorded sounds of gunshots and cannons, dying men and horses, and a mournful but stirring account of wartime follies and heroism.

Löwenplatz 11. © **041/412-30-30.** www.bourbakipanorama.ch. Admission 8F adults, 7F seniors and students, 5F children 6–16, free for children 5 and under. Daily 9am–6pm. Tram: 1.

Gletschergarten (Glacier Garden)   This so-called glacier garden has 32 "potholes" that were worn into the sandstone bed of an Iron Age glacier, during the era when ice covered the surface of Lake Lucerne. Discovered and cleared of their debris in 1872, the holes measure up to 9m (30 ft.) wide, and almost as deep. A museum at the site contains a famous 18th-century relief map of the Alps, prehistoric remains of plant and animal life, and a Swiss homeland museum. A 12-minute film is also shown to visitors.

Denkmalstrasse 4. © **041/410-43-40.** www.gletschergarten.ch. Admission 12F adults, 7F children, free for children 5 and under. Apr–Oct daily 9am–6pm; Nov–Mar daily 10am–5pm. Bus: 1.

Historisches Museum Luzern (Museum of Swiss History)   Originally conceived as an arsenal for the storage of weapons in the 1560s, this building was reconfigured as a showplace for medieval and Renaissance art and sculptures in 1983. Adjacent to the surging river that flows through the center of town, this museum celebrates the arts and crafts that emerged from central Switzerland between 1600 and 1900. One of the museum's centerpieces is the Gothic-style stone monument that once dominated the Wienerplatz, in the town center. (What you'll see there today is a copy.) Thanks to the solid wooden staircase that spirals its way around it, you'll get a close-up view of the stone-carved knights and cherubs that grace its pinnacle—a view that previously was visible only to birds. Other exhibits trace the development of Lucerne beginning around 1300. The top floor of the museum is reserved for special (temporary) exhibits, such as an overview of the way 20th-century Swiss cartoons treat medieval and mystical themes.

Pfistergasse 24. © **041/228-54-24.** www.hmluzern.ch. Free admission; special exhibitions 10F adults, 8F seniors, free for children 15 and under. Tues–Sun 10am–5pm. Bus: 2.

Kunstmuseum ★★   The **Kunstmuseum (Fine Arts Museum)** and the **Neues Kunstmuseum (Modern Art Museum)** have fused into a single museum of art. The fine arts collection consists primarily of Swiss art from the Renaissance to the present, with an exceptional collection of paintings from the early and high baroque periods. Highlights of the baroque collection include works by Kaspar Meglinger and Franz Ludwig Raufft. There are also remarkable portraits by 18th-century artists such as Felix Maria Diogg and Josef Reinhard. The collection is strong in 19th-century landscape painting, including works by Alexandre Calamle, Robert Zünd, and Ferdinand Hodler. More modern and more controversial works focus on the "Zurich Concrete Artists" who flourished in the 1980s and 1990s.

The modern art collection, of course, focuses on more contemporary works, most of them avant-garde. But there is also a permanent collection of works, which are rotated. Some of these go back to the 15th century.

Europaplatz 1. © **041/226-78-00.** www.kunstmuseumluzern.ch. Admission 12F–16F adults, 10F–12F seniors, 4F–7F children 6–16. Tues and Thurs–Sun 10am–5pm; Wed 10am–8pm.

Richard Wagner Museum   Wagner lived here from 1866 to 1872 and composed several works, including *Die Meistersinger.* Located about 3km (2 miles) southeast from the city in the suburb of Tribschen, the museum contains some original scores and memorabilia, including letters and pictures. There's an exhibit of antique musical instruments in the summer. During clement weather, some hardy souls opt to walk to this museum from the center of Lucerne, following the walkways that border the edge of the lake.

Wagnerweg 27, Tribschen. ⓒ **041/360-23-70.** www.richard-wagner-museum.ch. Admission 6F adults, 3F children 6–16. Tues–Sun 10am–noon and 2–5pm. Closed Dec to mid-Mar. In summer motorboats leave every hour from in front of the railroad station (rail passes are valid for this trip). Bus: 6, 7, or 8 to Wartegg.

Sammlung Rosengart (the Rosengart Collection) and the Picasso Museum ★★   Set within what functioned since 1924 as a regional headquarters for the Swiss National Bank, this museum combines the artworks amassed by the father-daughter art collectors Siegfried and Angela Rosengart, who presented the city of Lucerne with eight masterpieces by Picasso on its 800th anniversary (one for each century). Outstanding works include *Woman and Dog Playing* (1953), *Woman Dressing Her Hair* (1954), *The Studio* (1955), *Rembrandtesque Figure and Cupid* (1969), and a sculpture, *Woman with a Hat* (1961). The collection comprises well over 200 works by 23 different classic modernist artists. These include 125 pieces of Paul Klee and some 50 by Pablo Picasso. Other artists represented include Bonnard, Braque, Cézanne, Chagall, Dufy, Kandinsky, Laurens, Léger, Marini, Matisse, Miró, Modigliani, Monet, Pissarro, Renoir, Rouault, Seurat, Signac, Soutine, Utrillo, and Vuillard.

In addition, the museum also displays some 200 of the most memorable photographs of David Douglas Duncan, one of the world's great photographers, who became famous for his combat photography of World War II for *Life* magazine. He also took countless photographs of Picasso. Be aware that during the lifetime of this edition, at least some of the Picassos within the Rosengart Collection might still be within their former home at Furrengasse 21, a short distance from the museum's new headquarters at Pilatusstrasse 10. The museum's official plan will involve moving what used to be two separate collections into the all-new headquarters on Pilatusstrasse.

Pilatusstrasse 10. ⓒ **041/220-16-60.** www.rosengart.ch. Admission 18F adults, 10F students, children 7–16. Nov–Mar daily 11am–5pm; Apr–Oct daily 10am–6pm. Bus: 1.

Verkehrshaus der Schweiz (Swiss Transport Museum) ★★★ (Kids)   This museum is the best of its kind in Europe and the most visited museum in Lucerne. It's located beyond the Haldenstrasse cable-car station, lying more than a mile northeast of the center and accessible via bus. All forms of transportation, old and new, are on display, including railway cars, airplanes, automobiles, ships, and spaceships. Also on display is the oldest steamboat in the country, the *Riga,* built in 1847. The most popular exhibition is a scale model of a Swiss railway crossing the Gotthard Pass (a dozen trains move simultaneously). Children delight in an adventure ride called the Gotthard Tunnel Show.

The Longines Planetarium is at the eastern end of the complex. Here you can experience the constellations, a solar and lunar eclipse, and simulated space travel. Also attached to the transport museum is the Hans Erni House, containing artwork by this well-known native son. The museum has an IMAX theater as well.

Lidostrasse 5. ⓒ **041/370-44-44.** www.verkehrshaus.ch. Admission 24F adults, 22F students and seniors, 12F children 7–16. IMAX/museum combo tickets 32F adults, students, and seniors; 21F children. Apr–Oct daily 10am–6pm; Nov–Mar daily 10am–5pm. Bus: 6 or 8.

13

There are dozens of half-day and full-day excursions from Lucerne—so many that we recommend you allow at least 5 days to see the city and its environs. There are several points of interest around Lake Lucerne. Most of them can be reached by paddle steamer along the lake. While en route, you can enjoy a panoramic view of the water and mountains. Lake Lucerne (Vierwaldstättersee) winds its way 39km (24 miles) into the alpine ranges of the heart of Switzerland. Many excursions can be combined with a trip to the top of a mountain by cable car or funicular. Summer is the peak season.

Schiffahrtsgesellschaft Vierwaldstättersee (Lake Lucerne Navigation Co.; © **041/ 367-67-67;** www.lakelucerne.ch) operates a flotilla of lake steamers that chug across the surface of Lake Lucerne, much to the delight of sightseers, who appreciate the steep mountains rising on all sides. Round-trip passage from Lucerne to the lake's most distant point, Flüelen (4-hr. round-trip) costs 90F in first class or 59F in second class, and departs from the quays opposite the Hauptbahnhof in Lucerne. In midsummer departures begin at 9:15am and continue every hour or so throughout the day. Wherever you decide to disembark en route, find out the departure time of the last boat back to Lucerne. Usually, the last boat from Flüelen departs before 4:20pm. All boats have a restaurant, or at least a cafeteria, onboard.

The **William Tell Express** offers an opportunity to see regions of German- and Italian-speaking Switzerland in one full-day excursion. Between May and mid-October, it transports participants, as part of a 5-hour travel experience, from Lucerne, via Lugano, to Locarno. Begin with a 3-hour boat ride from Lucerne to the lakeside hamlet of Flüelen, then hop aboard a special train for a continuation of the trip across some of the most jagged and precipitous mountain scenery in the world. Seats in the first-class compartments have wider windows and skylights, while those in the less comfortable second-class cars are slightly less panoramic. A three-course meal, served aboard the lake steamer during the first part of the journey, is included in the round-trip (Lucerne to Locarno) price of 322F. Reservations, preferably several days in advance, are vital. To make them, and get more information, call © **041/367-67-67** or visit the website at www.wilhelmtellexpress.ch.

SHOPPING

Few other cities in Switzerland rely as heavily on the tourist trade as Lucerne, so you'll be faced with a barrage of mercantilism at virtually every street corner. Most obvious of the "heavy artillery" sales involves wristwatches and folk handicrafts. The biggest jeweler in town is **Bucherer,** Schwanenplatz 5 (© **041/369-77-00**), whose sprawling displays of luxury goods are rivaled only by the showrooms of **Gübelin,** Schweizerhofquai (© **041/ 417-00-21;** www.guebelin.ch). Less consciously upscale, and more folkloric in their orientation, is the town's main outlet for handicrafts, **Casa Grande,** Kapellgasse 24 (© **041/ 418-60-60**). Embroideries and linens for dining rooms and bedrooms are the offerings at **Sturzenneger,** Buobenmatt 2 (© **041/410-19-58**). Some of the pieces come from Switzerland's embroidery center of St. Gallen, others from less evocative factories in the Far East, but many are of heirloom quality.

Souvenirs of your trip to Lucerne are a lot less expensive, and a lot more workaday, at the town's mass-market department store, **Nordmann & Co.,** Weggisgasse 5 (© **041/ 419-76-99**). The outlet sells housewares, clothing, school supplies, and anything you'd need to run a home. The store also has a limited collection of Swiss souvenirs. More upscale, and more specifically geared to clothing for men, women, and children, is **Globus,** Pilatusstrasse 4 (© **041/227-07-07**).

Hofstetter & Berney, Schweizerhofquai 6 (☎ **041/410-31-06**), features a well-rounded collection of music boxes. The staff will tell you about the differences in tones and the complexities of sounds produced by the various instruments, all of which are made in Switzerland and which contain varying numbers of musical notes. Some of them might reproduce strains from Pachelbel's *Canon,* others a replica of the *Austrian National Anthem.*

Confiserie H & M Kurmann, Bahnhofstrasse 7 (☎ **041/210-19-18;** www.art-confiserie-kurmann.ch), is the most distinguished pastry-and-chocolate shop in Lucerne. Many of the residents of Lucerne remember this shop from their childhoods, when its pastries and chocolates were likely served as part of their birthday parties. Today it's one of the few deeply entrenched big-name pastry makers in Switzerland that hasn't set up additional branches in other parts of the country. Everything is, as you'd expect, highly caloric and highly tempting.

The richly nuanced architecture of the city itself is the backdrop for the outdoor **fruit and vegetable market,** conducted during spring, summer, and autumn from both banks of the river every Tuesday and Saturday from 8am to around 1pm. Between May and October, Lucerne hosts a rowdy, somewhat disorganized **flea market** where the contents of estate sales and whatever anyone discovered in his or her grandmother's attic is displayed along either side of Untere Burgerstrasse. And the first Saturday of every month throughout the year, during daylight hours, artisans and craftspeople from throughout the region congregate at the **Weinmarkt** to display and sell their wares.

WHERE TO STAY

Lucerne is one of the most visited cities of Switzerland, with a wide range of hotels. But they're mostly expensive and moderate; there's a shortage of good budget hotels. Reservations are very important in the summer, when hordes of Europeans and North Americans pour into this town.

Very Expensive

Grand Hotel National ★★★   This is a monumental landmark and the former home base of Cesar Ritz. Although tourist officials rank it behind the Schweizerhof, we appreciate its lack of stiffness. Built "in the style of the French kings," this legend among Swiss hotels has a huge facade of gray stone, with a mansard roof and dozens of gables. Constructed in 1870, when visitors were just beginning to discover Lake Lucerne, it looks like a wing of the château at Versailles. Guests have included monarchs and diplomats from all over Europe. Between 1977 and 1980, the owner reconstructed this grand palace and installed modern conveniences. The main lobby is stately and elegant, one of the grandest in Lucerne. The predictably varied bedrooms are among the most comfortable and luxurious in the city, with thick carpets and old-fashioned charm, often with a four-poster canopied bed. Many have private balconies with a view of the lake. The bathrooms are opulent in white marble.

Haldenstrasse 4, CH-6002 Luzern. ☎ **041/419-09-09.** Fax 041/419-09-10. www.national-luzern.ch. 41 units. 370F–685F double; 710F–1,285F suite. AE, DC, MC, V. Parking 35F. Bus: 6 or 8. **Amenities:** 3 restaurants; bar; babysitting; indoor heated pool; room service; sauna. *In room:* TV, hair dryer, minibar, Wi-Fi (free).

Hotel Des Balances ★   This tranquil government-rated "four-star superior" hotel, directly on the Reuss River, also faces the most colorful square in town, an 8-minute walk from the rail station. The elaborate gray-stone building has lots of curlicue wrought-iron balconies; the interior has high ceilings and Oriental rugs. Following massive renovations to both its interior and its facade, the hotel has emerged as one of the finest in its price range in Lucerne, and frankly, as one of our favorites. Your room, likely to be decorated in high-tech Italian-derived modern style following a major renovation, with a freshly tiled bathroom, will open either onto a picture-postcard view of the river or (if in the rear) the historic Weinmarkt. If you're seeking a room in Altstadt, make it the Balances. Guests are permitted to drive to the hotel even though it lies in a pedestrian zone.

Weinmarkt, CH-6000 Luzern. (✆ **041/418-28-28.** Fax 041/418-28-38. www.balances.ch. 57 units. Apr–Oct 430F double, 630F suite; off season 350F double, 490F suite. AE, DC, MC, V. Parking 27F. Bus: 1, 6, or 8. **Amenities:** Restaurant; bar; babysitting; room service. *In room:* TV, hair dryer, minibar, Wi-Fi (free).

Schweizerhof Luzern ★ ⟨Overrated⟩ Although it has its admirers, this hotel is formal and opulent but a bit stiff. In our view, Grand Hotel National is just as elegant and a lot more appealing. Nonetheless, the Schweizerhof has remained a longtime favorite of many travelers ever since it opened in 1844. The Hauser family has owned this 19th-century palace since 1861 and reopened it again in 1999 following extensive remodeling and renovations. It has extended a welcome to such former guests as Napoleon III, Leo Tolstoy, Richard Wagner, and Mark Twain. It consists of three symmetrical white buildings connected by arched passageways lining the lake for at least 2 blocks; one of the buildings is rented as office space. The lobby has pink marble columns and pilasters and a cream-colored ceiling with plaster details. The Belle Epoque–style bedrooms are spacious and well furnished, and have well-maintained bathrooms. Try for a room, if possible, with a view of Lake Lucerne and the surrounding alpine range.

Schweizerhofquai 3, CH-6002 Luzern. (✆ **041/410-04-10.** Fax 041/410-29-71. www.schweizerhof-luzern. ch. 107 units. Apr–Oct 430F–580F double, 630F–860F suite; Nov–Mar 330F–490F double, 550F–730F suite. AE, DC, MC, V. Parking 25F in garage. Bus: 1 or 24. **Amenities:** 2 restaurants; bar; babysitting; room service. *In room:* A/C, TV, hair dryer, minibar, Wi-Fi (5F per 24 hr.).

Expensive

Art Deco Hotel Montana ★★ This is one of the best government-rated four-star hotels in central Switzerland. This neoclassical hotel was originally built in 1911 as a private villa high on a hillside overlooking the lake. In the 1960s a modern extension was added with cozy bedrooms, most of which offer views. A private funicular, departing from a point near the edge of the lake, carries clients of the hotel or its restaurants uphill to the hotel's entrance. The interior public rooms would please your Victorian great-great-grandmother, with their old-fashioned appeal of Oriental rugs, swag curtains, brocaded antique chairs and settees, and polished paneling, along with a good infusion of Art Deco styling. The bedrooms, however, are modernized, although with traditional styling, and are comfortable with firm beds and neatly kept bathrooms.

Adligenswilerstrasse 22, CH-6002 Luzern. (✆ **0800/55-23-44** in the U.S. or 041/419-00-00. Fax 041/419-00-01. www.hotel-montana.ch. 62 units. 330F–590F double; from 575F suite. Rates include buffet breakfast. AE, DC, MC, V. Free parking. Bus: 6 or 8. **Amenities:** Restaurant; bar; babysitting; room service. *In room:* TV, hair dryer, minibar, Wi-Fi (free).

The Hotel ★★★ ⟨Finds⟩ In a panoramic setting in the center of the city, this is a small-scale but particularly luxurious and trend-conscious boutique hotel, the most exclusive of its kind in Lucerne. Famed French architect Jean Nouvel designed it. Although familiar to London, this type of urban boutique hotel is new to Switzerland. Called simply "the Hotel," it is luxury personified, yet there is an artful simplicity to it. From the custom-designed furnishings in wood and steel to the luscious, avant-garde cinema scenes on the guest-room ceilings, every aspect of the hotel reflects Nouvel's unique touch. Some two dozen studios and suites are spread across the seven-story building. Preferred are five corner junior suites with park views on both sides. Other options include garden and park luxe suites with patios, and luxe studios with park views. Nouvele achieves his dream of "combining spirituality with elegance into a timeless design—not a matter of decor but of lifestyle."

Sempacherstrasse 14, CH-6002 Lucerne. 🕿 **041/226-86-86.** Fax 041/226-86-90. www.the-hotel.ch. 25 units. 370F–430F double; from 490F suite. AE, DC, MC, V. Parking 35F. **Amenities:** Restaurant; bar; babysitting; room service. *In room:* A/C, TV, hair dryer, minibar, Wi-Fi (free).

Hotel Hermitage ★ (Finds) In 1990 a run-down older hotel was demolished and in its place arose this modern lakeside building with its own private beach, some 4km (2½ miles) east of the center of town. The Hermitage's pink-painted walls contain spacious doubles and junior suites. Each unit has a lakefront view, a private balcony, and a tastefully modern design featuring rattan furniture, a minimalist decor, and parquet floors. The hotel (rated four stars by the Swiss government) has a cafe-terrace beside the water.

Seeburgstrasse 72, CH-6006 Luzern-Seeburg. 🕿 **041/375-81-81.** Fax 041/375-81-82. www.hotel-hermitage.ch. 50 units. May–Sept 390F–420F double, 450F junior suite; Oct–Apr 280F–310F double, 330F junior suite. AE, DC, MC, V. Free parking. Bus: 24. **Amenities:** 2 restaurants; bar; exercise room; room service; sauna; outdoor tennis court (lit). *In room:* TV, hair dryer, minibar, Wi-Fi (free).

Hotel Krone Despite the lushly baroque facade of this middle-bracket hotel, its bedrooms are simple, well organized, and contemporary looking. This is the result of a radical renovation in the early 1990s that ripped apart the interior of the five-story building. The Hotel Krone is solidly positioned on one of the Old Town's most charming medieval squares, in a neighborhood that shows off antique Lucerne's architectural personality. Bedrooms in back are slightly bigger than those overlooking the Weinmarkt in front, which have better views and a more intense sense of history. Each unit comes with a neatly kept private bathroom; the third floor is for nonsmoking guests. Don't expect a deeply entrenched sense of luxury, or even a particularly large or opulent-looking lobby: In this case, the space was devoted instead to accommodations.

Weinmarkt 12, CH-6004 Luzern. 🕿 **800/528-1234** in the U.S. or 041/419-44-00. Fax 041/419-44-90. www.bestwestern.ch/kroneluzern. 25 units. 310F–460F double. Rates include breakfast. AE, DC, MC, V. Parking 27F. Bus: 1 or 2. **Amenities:** Restaurant. *In room:* TV, hair dryer, minibar.

Hotel Monopol ★ Built in 1898, this grand hotel has a carved limestone facade, wrought-iron balconies, half columns, and elaborately detailed windows. Its central location is convenient for the rail station or the lake. The midsize rooms are individually furnished; some are modern and others have paneling, alcove beds, and chalet chairs. All come equipped with tidy bathrooms.

Pilatusstrasse 1, CH-6002 Luzern. 🕿 **041/226-43-43.** Fax 041/226-43-44. 73 units. Apr–Oct 360F double; Nov–Mar 290F double. Rates include buffet breakfast. AE, DC, MC, V. Bus: 1. **Amenities:** Restaurant; bar; babysitting; room service. *In room:* TV, hair dryer, minibar, Wi-Fi (free).

Moderate

Flora ★ Lying within a short walk of the Kapllebrücke, this Best Western hotel is ideally situated near the lake. It receives both business travelers and vacationers with equal efficiency, presenting a series of comfortably furnished and well-kept bedrooms. Sometimes it's the little extras that count here, including an optional child's bed, windows that can be open to take in the bracing air, cosmetic mirrors, or both cable or pay

TV. Of the bedrooms, 16 are rated deluxe. Families who need to overflow into another bedroom can sometimes rent a connecting room.

Seidenhofstrasse 5, CH-6002 Luzern. ✆ **041/227-66-66.** Fax 041/227-68-71. www.flora-hotel.ch. 161 units. 260F–305F double. AE, DC, MC, V. **Amenities:** Restaurant; bar; babysitting; concierge; room service. *In room:* TV, hair dryer, minibar, Wi-Fi (20F per 24 hr.).

Grand Hotel Europe   A neoclassical pediment graces the white facade of this 19th-century, government-rated four-star hotel lying 1.5km (1 mile) east of the center, on a hillside above the north shore of the lake. There's a row of awnings sheltering the public rooms, which face a garden. The salons contain large tapestries, Oriental rugs, and comfortable couches and chairs. Most of the rooms are spacious and well furnished, each with a firm bed and well-maintained plumbing.

Haldenstrasse 59, CH-6002 Luzern. ✆ 041/370-00-11. Fax 041/370-10-31. www.europe-luzern.ch. 174 units. 300F–400F double; 450F suite. Rates include buffet breakfast. AE, DC, MC, V. Free parking. Closed Nov–Mar. Bus: 2. **Amenities:** Restaurant; bar; babysitting; room service. *In room:* TV, hair dryer.

Hotel Astoria ★   This first-class modern hotel boasts prominent horizontal rows of windows and a desirable location in the center of Lucerne, a 5-minute walk from the lake. The hotel is often patronized by business travelers and groups drawn to its modern, streamlined, and no-nonsense atmosphere. Well maintained and well respected, this hotel was built in three separate phases: Its main core dates from 1957, and two separate enlargements were added to the hotel's (quieter and calmer) back side in the mid-1970s and again in 1998. On-site is a hugely popular and trendy club and disco on the upper floor called the Penthouse. The subdued interior of the hotel is decorated with furniture and accessories evocative of Thailand. Each of the well-furnished rooms has a firm bed and a well-maintained bathroom.

Pilatusstrasse 29, CH-6003 Luzern. ✆ **041/226-88-88.** Fax 041/210-42-62. www.astoria-luzern.ch. 180 units. 270F–400F double; 460F suite. Rates include buffet breakfast. AE, DC, MC, V. Parking 35F. **Amenities:** 3 restaurants; 2 bars; babysitting; exercise room; room service. *In room:* A/C, TV, hair dryer, Wi-Fi (free).

Hotel des Alpes   Set in Lucerne's historic core, this unpretentious, government-rated three-star hotel lies in the pedestrian zone. It was originally built around 1740 as an inn for travelers. Today, behind a tall and narrow facade with restrained baroque detailing, it continues to welcome visitors into its premises. Although the public rooms retain their old-fashioned charm, most of the midsize bedrooms have been streamlined and filled with vinyl and laminated pieces in the roadside-motel tradition. Rooms in the rear open onto Altstadt, and those on the upper floors sometimes have views over the low skyline of Lucerne.

Though parking is not available on the premises, guests can leave their cars across the river at the railway station, a 5-minute walk from the hotel.

Furrengasse 3, CH-6004 Luzern. ✆ **041/417-20-60.** Fax 041/417-20-66. www.desalpes-luzern.ch. 45 units. 201F–250F double. Rates include buffet breakfast. AE, DC, MC, V. Bus: 1, 2, 6, 7, or 8. **Amenities:** 2 restaurants; room service. *In room:* TV, hair dryer, minibar, Wi-Fi (free).

Hotel Schiller ★   Although it's surrounded by other antique buildings near the railway station, the Schiller stands out with its 19th-century details and colorful awnings above the entrance. It's favored by business travelers who want to be in the commercial center of town, close to the railway station. The interior has many fine touches, including an ample use of white marble. Each midsize room in this comfortable hotel is different; the most modern are on the fifth and sixth floors, while the more traditional fill the lower levels. The front rooms can be noisy at times. Many nonresidents patronize the hotel's drinking and eating facilities.

Pilatusstrasse 15, CH-6002 Luzern. ☎ **041/226-87-87.** Fax 041/227-87-90. www.schiller-luzern.ch. 100 units. Apr–Oct 300F–340F double, 350F suite; Nov–Mar 250F–290F double, 220F suite. Rates include buffet breakfast. AE, DC, MC, V. Bus: 1. **Amenities:** Restaurant; bar; babysitting. *In room:* A/C, TV, hair dryer.

Hotel Zum Rebstock ★ (Finds)   This is a historic landmark with many loyal fans. The foundations of this hotel date from the 12th century, when the site, west of the Hofkirche and south of the Panorama, was the setting for a monastery. Surrounded by vineyards, the half-timbered building has green shutters with a brown-tile roof. In 1443 it was the headquarters of the winegrowers' guild; later it was used as a recruitment center for the Swiss mercenaries who came from this region. The rooms are small but cozily comfortable, each outfitted in a different color and decorative motif. The inn offers two restaurants serving both Swiss regional dishes and international platters.

Sankt-Leodegar-Platz 3, CH-6004 Luzern. ☎ **041/417-18-19.** Fax 041/410-39-17. www.hereweare.ch. 30 units. 260F–295F double. Rates include buffet breakfast. AE, DC, MC, V. Parking 18F. Bus: 1, 2, or 7. **Amenities:** 3 restaurants; bar; room service. *In room:* TV, hair dryer, minibar, Wi-Fi (free).

Magic Hotel   Centrally located in Luzern, but with a venue that requires a check-in at the reception desk of the nearby Hotel Krone (see above), this hotel offers unique and often amusingly decorated bedrooms. Each room and suite is individually decorated so that no two rooms are alike and you can choose one that fits your personality and taste. The Angel Suite has a Victorian-era elegance, while the Lotus Room utilizes Asian influences and art. Some of the rooms go a little over the top with the decor, such as the tacky Egyptian Suite, which has a large mural of a pharaoh and his two servants over the bed. The Pirate Suite is over the top in a fun way, with the bed in the shape of a ship and a statue of a pirate. Kids would enjoy both rooms but adults might find them a bit garish and tawdry. Rooms with a more tasteful decor are the Swiss Chalet and the Lion-Heart Suite.

Brandgässli 1. CH-6004 Luzern. ☎ **041/417-12-20.** Fax 041/417-12-21. www.magic-hotel.ch. 13 units. 220F–310F double; 440F–460F suite. Rates include buffet breakfast. AE, DC, MC, V. *In room:* TV, hair dryer, minibar, Wi-Fi (free).

Romantik Hotel Wilden Mann ★★   This is the best choice for the nostalgia buff. Around 1900 a local entrepreneur, operating from the core of an early-16th-century tavern in the heart of the Old Town, began slowly but systematically buying up the historic real estate around him. The result you'll see today incorporates seven antique houses—the oldest dating from 1517—into a well-orchestrated whole. Inside, a confusing but charming labyrinth of hallways, many accented with exposed stone and beams, and, in some cases, with artfully old-fashioned paneling, lead to the cozy bedrooms. Here, warm colors and a sense of yesteryear combine with modern extras for winning four-star comforts.

Even if you don't stay here, consider a meal in the artfully rustic dining room (see Wilden Mann Stübe/Burgerstübe, below).

Bahnhofstrasse 30, CH-6007 Luzern. ☎ **041/210-16-66.** Fax 041/210-16-29. www.wilden-mann.ch. 50 units. 270F–425F double; 360F–490F junior suite. Rates include buffet breakfast. AE, DC, MC, V. Bus: 2. **Amenities:** 2 restaurants; babysitting; room service. *In room:* TV, hair dryer, minibar, Wi-Fi (free).

Inexpensive

Hotel Alpha   This severe-looking, white-fronted building is a 10-minute walk from the city center and rail station, near Pilatusplatz. Renovated many times since its original construction, it's one of the simplest hotels in town, offering well-scrubbed but small

LUCERNE & CENTRAL SWITZERLAND

bedrooms with few extras and modest furnishings, although the mattresses are firm. Those units containing private bathrooms are in most cases equipped with tub/shower combinations. On the premises are two lounges, each with a TV set and a collection of newspapers.

Zähringerstrasse 24, CH-6003 Luzern. ℂ **041/240-42-80.** Fax 041/240-91-31. www.hotelalpha.ch. 66 units, 10 with bathroom. 92F–98F double without bathroom, 125F–140F with bathroom; 135F–150F triple without bathroom. Rates include buffet breakfast. AE, DC, MC, V. Bus: 1 or 2 to Pilatusplatz. **Amenities:** Bikes; Internet (10F per 24 hr., in lobby). *In room:* Wi-Fi (10F per 24 hr.).

Pension Villa Maria ★ ⓕ**Finds**   Set in a charming garden near the north shore of the lake, this family-run villa was built in 1955 and is today owned by members of the Winkler family. Part of the experience is the welcome they offer in this chalet-inspired private home with comfortably cluttered public rooms decorated in shades of red, gold, and pink. The rooms—all doubles—are clean, spacious, and comfortable with excellent beds. The establishment is located about half a mile from the center of Lucerne.

Haldenstrasse 36, CH-6002 Luzern. ℂ/fax **041/370-21-19.** 14 units, 10 with bathroom. 135F–170F double without bathroom, 165F with bathroom. Additional bed in room 35F extra. Rates include buffet breakfast. AE, MC, V. Free parking. Closed Nov–Feb. Bus: 6. **Amenities:** Babysitting; room service. *In room:* Hair dryer.

Tourist Hotel   This budget hotel with a sage-green facade stands beside the river, a 10-minute walk from the train station. The hotel attracts young people and families to its rooms. Nine conventional units can accommodate up to four beds, and communal dormitory-style rooms are also available that contain between 4 and 10 beds each, usually stacked as bunk beds. The furnishings are in a basic, functional modern style. Many of the rooms open onto a view of the river and the faraway mountains of Pilatus and Titlis. Rooms with private bathrooms have clean quarters and mostly contain tub/shower combinations. All units have hot and cold running water. There's a dining room as well as a lounge on the premises. Because the hotel lies in a pedestrian zone, it's hard to find parking.

St. Karliquai 12, CH-6004 Luzern. ℂ **041/410-24-74.** Fax 041/410-84-14. www.touristhotel.ch. 40 units, 8 with bathroom; 28 dormitory beds. 88F–120F double without bathroom, 110F–220F with bathroom; 129F–144F triple without bathroom, 150F–230F with bathroom; 172F–188F quad without bathroom, 200F–260F with bathroom; 38F–45F per person dorm bed. Rates include buffet breakfast. AE, MC, V. Bus: 2 or 9. **Amenities:** Internet (free, in lobby). *In room:* TV, no phone.

WHERE TO DINE

Lucerne has some of the finest restaurants in Switzerland, in a wide range of prices, so don't confine yourself to your hotel at mealtime.

Expensive

China Restaurant Li-Tai-Pe ★ CHINESE   This long-standing Chinese restaurant was founded in 1965 by "grande dame" Margaret Chi Tsun, whose late husband was once an aide to General Chiang Kai-shek. After Chi Tsun's death in 2002, the restaurant is now run by her daughter, Greta Chi. Although fickle fame has passed on, the restaurant is still here and serving many of the same excellent dishes it always did. Located on a narrow street in the Old Town, the restaurant has two levels and is decorated with Asian artifacts and somber lighting. Many sweet-and-sour dishes are offered, such as codfish, pork, or crispy chicken. Two especially good dishes are chicken Kung Bao (made with peanuts and chili) and stewed beef with crispy rice. *Boaling* are dumplings with different fillings, a choice appetizer. You may also begin with egg-blossom soup, to be followed by beef with tomatoes or chicken with green peppers.

Des Balances ★★ SWISS/INTERNATIONAL   At this previously recommended hotel in Altstadt, opening onto the historic Weinmarkt, is one of the city's exceptional restaurants. The building housing it was the town jail back in 1369, but it was converted into a restaurant in 1519. Its terrace, with a view of the river Reuss, is one of the most hotly contested seats in town on a balmy summer night.

The decor is a stylish combination of medieval masonry, 19th-century wrought iron, and postmodern, high-tech lighting. The menu is divided into conservative and modern cuisine, both of them very successful. Modern dishes include marinated salmon with mussels and apricot chutney; fresh basil-studded ravioli with black olives, Parmesan, and pepperoni; and braised filet of zander with coconut-and-chili sauce, Asian vegetables, and roasted sesame. More conservative and traditional dishes include calves' liver with balsamic vinegar and *rösti*, grilled filets of veal with an herb-flavored cream sauce, and freshwater crabs grilled with feta cheese and marinated herbs.

In the Hotel des Balances, Weinmarkt. ✆ **041/418-28-28.** Reservations recommended. Main courses 32F–59F; fixed-price dinner 95F–125F. AE, DC, MC, V. Daily 11:30am–1:30pm and 6–10pm.

Jasper ★★★ INTERNATIONAL/SWISS   In the Hotel Palace, the most refined cuisine in Luzern is created. Against a backdrop of service and a luxurious ambience, exquisite platters arrive at your table. Market-fresh ingredients are selected with pride by the chef, who proceeds to concoct them into sublime dishes. The cuisine is sensitively prepared and imaginative, beginning with such starters as a tomato mousse with eggplant (aubergine) caviar or a tuna carpaccio marinated with poppy seeds and served with sautéed scallops. For a main, expect such light but full-flavored dishes as sautéed calves' livers with marinated cherries and Asian spices, or glazed filet of salmon with Szechuan peppers and a cucumber-and-ginger salad.

In the Hotel Palace, Holdenstrasse 10. ✆ **041/416-16-16.** www.palace-luzern.ch. Reservations required. Main courses 36F–59F. AE, DC, MC, V. Wed–Mon noon–2pm and 7–10pm.

Old Swiss House ★ SWISS/FRENCH   This half-timbered building near the Lion Monument is one of the most photographed attractions in the area. This crowd pleaser—often filled with groups—is a mandatory stopover on a dining tour of Lucerne and has been since it started attracting a horde of British visitors in 1859. To its credit, it has endured and outlasted everything else, with the food remaining good. The restaurant is decorated in 17th-century style, with porcelain and antique glass, hand-carved oak doors, wooden stairways, leaded- and stained-glass windows with heraldic panes from 1575, antique silver, and old pewter. The house has a long bar near the entry and a dining room downstairs. In fair weather you can have lunch on the terrace.

One of the dishes this place does best is an elegant version of Wiener schnitzel—a bestseller here for more than 40 years—that's pan-fried aboard a trolley that's wheeled alongside your table. Freshwater fish (fera, omble chevalier, pikeperch) from the nearby lake are excellent too, as well as turbot meunière, filet of beef stroganoff, calves' liver, roasted rack of baby lamb from Scotland, and sliced veal in cream sauce.

Löwenplatz 4. ✆ **041/410-61-71.** www.oldswisshouse.ch. Reservations recommended. Main courses 18F–58F lunch, 34F–56F dinner. AE, DC, MC, V. Tues–Sun noon–12:30am. Closed 3 weeks in Feb. Bus: 1.

Stadtkeller ★ SWISS   Although there's been an inn in the cellar of Lucerne's town hall since 1685, none of its earlier versions has placed such a heavy emphasis on Swiss folklore. In a cavernous cellar lined with antique accessories, you can enjoy hearty alpine meals whose flavors are enhanced by doses of folk music, which begins at 12:15pm at lunch and at 8pm during dinner. The most economical way to enjoy the place is simply to order a half liter of beer, with a supplemental charge that's imposed whenever music is playing. But to really get into the experience, consider the heaping platters of smoked pork with sauerkraut, pork or veal sausages with *rösti*, several kinds of schnitzel with mushrooms, or roulade of beef with new potatoes. Folk music is featured only from March to October.

Sternenplatz 3. ✆ **041/410-47-33.** www.stadtkeller.ch. Reservations recommended. Main courses 45F–50F; fixed-price lunch 57F–70F, dinner 72F–85F. Music surcharge 15F for lunch or dinner imposed on a la carte meals and drinkers only. AE, MC, V. Apr–Oct daily noon–2pm and 8–10pm; Nov–Mar Tues–Sat noon–1:30pm and 7:30–10:15pm.

Moderate

Fondue House SWISS   It's paneled, it's cozy, and the smells of melted cheese that waft onto the pavement outside is its best advertisement. Come here for raclettes, served in individual portions with a mixture of Gruyère and *vacherin* cheese, with garlic; and at least three different kinds of meat or cheese fondues, all served amidst flickering candles and a cozy kind of high-alpine claustrophobia. You'll find it on a narrow street in the heart of the Old Town, with scorch marks on some of the walls from earlier fondue parties, presumably gone bad.

Eisengasse 15. ✆ **041/412-37-37.** www.fondue-house.ch. Main courses 16F–55F. AE, DC, MC, V. Daily 11am–11pm.

Hofstube ★ SWISS/FRENCH   This flourishing restaurant is in the Hotel Zum Rebstock, next to a building used as a guildhall for Lucerne winegrowers in the Middle Ages. The 1920s-style entrance hall is filled with valuable Art Deco pieces. This is a historic Swiss-style restaurant, with two different dining rooms, both folkloric and charming. The older is the Hofstube; the slightly newer dining area is the Hofegge, which is the site of an elaborate Sunday brunch from 7am to 3pm. Beyond the dining area is a large, illuminated courtyard, where additional tables are set up on warm summer nights. The menu, a classic blend of Swiss and French traditions, usually includes an impressive array of terrines, delicious lake trout, suckling veal with spinach, filet of pork and beef in a cognac sauce, and veal and sultanas in puff pastry.

In the Hotel Zum Rebstock, Sankt-Leodegar-Platz 3. ✆ **041/410-35-81.** Reservations recommended. Main courses 19F–42F. AE, DC, MC, V. Daily 11am–midnight. Bus: 1, 2, 5, or 7.

La Bonne Cave (Finds SWISS/ITALIAN   At least some of the charm of this place involves its emphasis on wine, rather than on beer, as is the case with many of its nearby competitors. Set under the medieval stone vaulting of a building in the Old Town, directly beside the river, it offers more than 140 vintages of wine—many of them Swiss, French, or Italian, displayed on wooden racks above a cobble-covered floor. You can always select a bottle from the wine shop here, which will be uncorked in the restaurant and served without any supplemental fees, at prices less than you might expect. But if you want a broad-based exposure to as many wines as possible, consider several glasses of different vintages. Wine is king, but the kitchen also turns out plates of good food. Menu items include platters of either Italian antipasti or an assortment of Swiss cheese, shrimp marinated in olive oil, beefsteak tartare, and platters of air-dried alpine beef.

Rathausquai 1. ✆ **041/410-45-16.** Reservations not necessary. Salads 12F–19F; main courses 17F–25F; wines 7F–10F per glass. AE, MC, V. Bar and wine shop daily 10am–midnight; food daily 10am–10:30pm.

Restaurant Fritschi (Value SWISS/INTERNATIONAL   There's absolutely nothing
pretentious about this beer hall/brasserie, where clients have been soaking up suds and
enjoying filling platters of traditional food since 1602. The building that contains it has
an outrageously colorful replica of a medieval fresco on its facade, and an interior pair of
dining rooms, one of which contains a bar, and both of which are sheathed in richly
intricate marquetry. Menu items—all familiar to your Swiss great-grandmother—include
four kinds of pork schnitzel; entrecôte of beef; sliced veal with a mushroom-flavored
cream sauce; sliced veal with morels; and ostrich steak. There is also a selection of fondues, any of which seem to taste better during cold weather.

Sternenplatz 5. ℭ **041/410-16-15.** Reservations recommended. Main courses 26F–45F. AE, DC, MC, V.
Daily 11am–11pm. Bus: 1 or 2.

Wilden Mann Stübe/Burgerstübe ★ SWISS/CONTINENTAL   The Burgerstübe,
the older of the two dining rooms, dates from at least 1517. Set on the ground floor of the
Romantik Hotel, both dining rooms have carefully maintained paneling and antique
touches that include coffered ceilings painted with the coats of arms of each of Lucerne's
leading families. The restaurant is smoke-free. The food items are rich and succulent, often
inspired by the tastes of old Switzerland. Examples include Wildermann *pastete,* crafted
from filet of beef cooked in its own juices and encased in puff pastry; Küglipastete, a shank
of veal in a cream sauce with mushrooms in a puff-pastry cone with peas and carrots;
hashed Zurich-style veal served with *rösti;* and breast of veal cooked Luzern style, with a
cream-based kidney sauce. More conventional menu items include chateaubriands, steaks,
and roast rack of lamb with rosemary sauce. In midsummer, seating expands onto a flowering outdoor terrace overlooking one of the Old Town's historic squares.

In the Romantik Hotel Wilden Mann, Bahnhofstrasse 30. ℭ **041/210-16-66.** Reservations recommended. Main courses 27F–55F; 4-course fixed-price menu 82F, 5 courses 96F, 6 courses 110F. AE, DC,
MC, V. Daily 1:30–3pm and 6–11pm. Burgerstübe daily 10:30am–midnight. Closed 2 weeks in July. Bus: 2.

Inexpensive
Rathaus Brauerei Restaurant (Finds SWISS   This is one of the few establishments
in Lucerne that brews its beer on-site. They usually include at least four, whose individual
characteristics vary according to the season, but which will usually feature the most
popular brand, Rathaus Bier, a blond lager that's available year-round; a wheat beer; a
dark beer known as *dunkel;* and the heaviest, darkest, and strongest of all, *bok.* It's located
under the arcades of the riverfront promenade, close to the northern terminus of the
city's well-known covered bridge, immediately beneath the exhibitions of the Picasso
Museum. You can dine in the open air, or head inside to a series of medieval vaults that
shelter the polished copper of the fermentation vats. Menu items reflect the savory,
hearty dishes that seem to go well with beer, including schnitzels, lamb steak, Swiss
sausage (of veal or pork), and grilled chicken breast filets, as well as deep-fried pikeperch.

Unter den Egg 2. ℭ **041/410-52-57.** www.rathausbrauerei.ch. Reservations not necessary. Main courses
16F–45F; beer 4F–8F. AE, DC, MC, V. Apr–Sept daily 9am–12:30am; Oct–Mar daily 11:30am–12:30am.

Schiffrestaurant Wilhelm Tell SWISS   Built in 1908, this lake cruiser (*Schiff* is
German for "ship") sailed boatloads of happy passengers from one end of Lake Lucerne
to the other. After it was replaced by newer ships in the late 1960s, it was transformed
into a floating restaurant in 1972. Now permanently moored at one of the quays, it's
usually ringed with a colony of swans, which feed off the scraps thrown overboard.
Drinks and snacks are served on outdoor cafe tables in the bow area, where you can have

a beer or coffee throughout the day. A formal restaurant is found under the low ceiling of the aft section, where fine food is served with alert attention. The ship's engine, brightly polished and set behind glass, is on display as a work of industrial art. The well-chosen menu may include excellently prepared filets of perch or sole prepared seaman's style, chopped chicken breast with smoked ham and bits of apple in a Calvados sauce with *rösti,* and flavorful grills of succulent veal and beef.

Landungsbrücke 9. © **041/410-23-30.** www.schiffrestaurant.ch. Reservations recommended. Main courses 17F–30F. AE, MC, V. Sept–Apr Tues–Sun 11am–midnight; May–Aug daily 11am–midnight. Bus: 2.

Vinotek Opus (Finds) CONTINENTAL/MEDITERRANEAN Set within a pair of interconnected medieval buildings, one side of which opens onto views of the river, this wine bar rocks and rolls in one of the most irreverent formats in town. It's understood that you'll come here for at least one glass (and perhaps several) of the Swiss and foreign wines served. You can also order platters of Serrano-style smoked ham, Italian soft cheese marinated in olive oil with garlic, *vitello tonnato,* a tartare of smoked salmon, and gazpacho studded with smoked mussels. There are even some experimental dishes such as Asian lasagna Shanghai (with Asian vegetables, shiitake mushrooms, snow peas, tofu, and soy sprouts), or red snapper in red curry sauce, as well as more mainstream platters such as fried perch filets or roulades of rabbit filet. The cellar contains more than 650 types of wine. Sprawling and convivial, it has seating in two dining rooms, at tables beside two different bars, and on a wide terrace beside the river overlooking the Old Town.

Bahnhofstrasse 16. © **041/226-41-41.** www.restaurant-opus.ch. Reservations not necessary. Platters 22F–41F; wine 8F–16F per glass. AE, MC, V. Bars daily 8:30am–midnight; kitchen Sun–Thurs 11:30am–11:30pm, Fri–Sat 11:30am–12:30am.

Wirtshaus Galliker ★ SWISS Generous portions of unpretentious, well-prepared food are served amid a rustic decor and an often-rowdy atmosphere of fun-loving Luzerners out for a night of gluttonous drinking and smoking. The house itself was first mentioned in documents in 1681. Back then it was a private residence, but it became a restaurant in 1800 and was purchased in 1856 by the Galliker family, whose members still run it. They're especially proud of their small garden in back with space for 28 diners. The waitresses, some of whom may look like your Swiss-German grandmother if you had one, keep the suds and the regional fare flowing. The cuisine is a sort of Lucerne soul food, everything from tripe in white-wine sauce to calf's head, with sweetbreads from nearly all barnyard animals. Farm-style bratwurst seasoned with caraway seeds is consumed along with chunky bread in mass quantities.

Schützenstrasse 1. © **041/240-10-02.** Reservations required. Main courses 25F–55F. AE, DC, MC, V. Tues–Sat 9:30am–midnight. Closed last 2 weeks of July and 2 weeks in Aug. Bus: 2.

LUCERNE AFTER DARK

Flashy lights and spinning wheels of fortune are found at the **Grand Casino** (also known as **Casineum**), Haldenstrasse 6 (© **041/418-56-56;** www.grandcasinoluzern.ch). You can try your luck at 140 slot machines. Poker, roulette, and blackjack are also available.

On a more cultural note, if you speak German, you can enjoy performances at the **Stadttheater,** Theaterstrasse 2 (© **041/228-14-14;** www.luzernertheater.ch). Directly on the lake on the rail station side of town, it's the home of Luzern's major theater group. Operas in their original language are also staged here. The Allgemeine Musikgesellschaft Luzern is the local resident orchestra, presenting performances at the **KKL Congress Center** from October to June, or at the Kultur und Kongress Zentrum (see below). For more information, call © **041/210-50-50.**

In the late 1990s the city of Lucerne inaugurated one of the most dramatically modern, large-scale buildings in central Switzerland, the **Kultur und Kongress Zentrum (KKL),** Europaplatz 1 (✆ **041/226-77-77;** www.kkl-luzern.ch), as a glittering showcase to corporate conventions and the performing arts. Poised beside the railway station in starkly modern contrast to the spires and alpine architecture of the rest of Lucerne, its controversial shape may remind newcomers of an enchanted "music box" that glitters with acres of glass and metal panels in shades of forest green, dark blue, and red. It was designed with a spectacular copper-sheathed roof by noted Parisian architect Jean Nouvele. Its auditoriums have some of the best acoustics in the world, thanks to rotating panels behind the stage. Expect heavy use of this site for classical, rock, and heavy-metal concerts. (For information about the concerts that will be presented here, check out the posters in front of the building, or call the concert hall itself at ✆ **0848/800-800** or 0900/552-225.) There are also a snack bar and cafe on the premises.

If you like Swiss folkloric presentations, head for the **Stadtkeller,** Sternenplatz (✆ **041/410-47-33;** www.stadtkeller.ch), which has good food and presents a program of traditional Swiss entertainment, complete with alphorns, cowbells, national costumes, flag throwing, and yodeling. Presentations take place March to October daily from 8 to 10:30pm.

The Altstadt (Old Town) always brims with pubs and cafes. **Mr. Pickwick's Pub,** Rathausquai 6 (✆ **041/410-59-27;** www.pickwick.ch), is the most authentic looking and the most popular British pub in Lucerne, with a sudsy, woodsy-looking decor that's awash with Brits, beer, and anyone else who simply wants to toss back a pint or two from a riverfront location near the northern end of the Old Town's covered bridge. It generally stays open nightly until 1am, which is very late by the standards of Lucerne.

Many hotels have more subdued bars, especially the **National,** Haldenstrasse 4 (✆ **041/419-09-09**), which has a glossy American-type bar, and the **Palace Hotel,** Haldenstrasse 10 (✆ **041/416-16-16**), which also has one American-style bar. The most ultracool place in Lucerne is the **Lounge Bar** of the Hotel, Sempacherstrasse 14 (✆ **041/226-86-86**).

P-1 Bar, on the top floor of the Hotel Monopol, Pilatusstrasse 1 (✆ **041/220-13-15**), is our favorite nightclub in Lucerne. We say that partly because it's crowded with the kinds of hip and available people you can talk to, and partly because it boasts one of the most dramatic physical settings of any nightclub in Switzerland. To reach it, you'll wait in line on the lobby level of the hotel, a Belle Epoque beauty that sits across the plaza from the railway station. An attendant will funnel clients, in elevator-size blocks, into a lift that will haul you to a point beneath the hotel's ornate copper-sheathed cupola. Here, recently released dance music, three bars, and a pair of outdoor terraces combine to create an instant party ambience that virtually everyone finds invigorating. By all means, climb to the club's highest point for open-air views of Lucerne that are among the best in the city. Incidentally, this nightclub's name (P-1) derives from a simplification of its address (Pilatusstrasse 1).

The **Loft,** Haldenstrasse 2 (✆ **041/410-92-64;** www.theloft.ch), is a serious contender for the title of the most hip and with-it nightclub in a town that's loaded with worthy competition. Music is a sophisticated blend of whatever you might have expected in London or Los Angeles, and the crowd is young and beautiful. The decor includes at least two bar areas and a balcony that overlooks a high-tech dance floor ringed with free-standing candelabrum, whose candles seem to flicker in rhythm to the music. There is a cover charge of 10F to 15F.

The terrace of the **Penthouse Bar** at the Hotel Astoria, Pilatusstrasse 29 (© **041/226-88-88**), offers a panoramic view over the rooftops of the city and the dramatic mountainscape beyond. Large sofas are an invitation to linger. On weekends live DJs keep everybody in a party mood. Also at the same hotel is the **Pravda Dance Club,** one of the city's best venues for meeting other young people. One of the most romantic bars in Lucerne is BLUE, a lounge bar at the previously recommended Hotel Schiller, Pilatusstrasse 15 (© **041/266-87-87**), featuring the most exotic cocktails in town. Blue is the dominant theme here, but the style of the bar ranges from Asian to mock Louis XVI.

EASY EXCURSIONS FROM LUCERNE

Lake Lucerne is known for its scenery and the many old-world villages along its shores. Many poets have praised the area's beauty. You may be lucky enough to stay in a hotel room that commands a view of the lake.

Lake steamers and mountain railways can get you to most points of interest around Lake Lucerne. Boat cruises are free if you have the Swiss Card, or a Eurail or InterRail pass. Mountain railways can whisk you to elevations of 3,000m (9,840 ft.) or more in a very short time. Our first adventure will be a major mountain excursion to Mount Pilatus, a 2,100m (6,888-ft.) summit overlooking Lucerne.

Mount Pilatus ★★★

Pilatus-Kulm is located 15km (9 miles) south of Lucerne. Its German name derives from an old legend: During medieval times, it's said, the city fathers of Lucerne banned travel up the mountain because they thought that its slopes were haunted by the ghost of Pontius Pilate; they feared that Pilate would be angered by intrusive visitors and cause violent storms. For many years after the ban was finally lifted, only a few souls were brave enough to climb the mountain. Queen Victoria made the trip in 1868. Today the ascent to Pilatus is one of the most popular excursions in Switzerland.

Between May and November, weather permitting, the cog railway—the world's steepest—operates between Alpnachstad, at the edge of the lake, and the very top of Mount Pilatus. From the quays of Lucerne, take a lake steamer for a scenic 90-minute boat ride to Alpnachstad. If you have a rail pass, remember that it will be valid on this steamer.

At Alpnachstad, transfer to the electric cog railway, which runs at a 48-degree gradient—the steepest cogwheel railway in the world. Departures are every 45 minutes daily from 8:50am to 4:30pm May to September only. At Pilatus-Kulm you can get out and enjoy the view. There are two mountain hotels and a belvedere offering views of Lake Lucerne and many of the mountains around it. For the descent from Mount Pilatus, some visitors prefer to take a pair of cable cars—first a large cabin-style téléphérique, then a small gondola. The cable cars end at Kriens, a suburb of Lucerne. Here you can take bus no. 1, which will carry you into the heart of Lucerne. The round-trip fare on the cog railway and cable car is 89F, 50% off for children 15 and under.

A similar excursion to Pilatus is possible in the winter, but because the cog railway is buried in snow, you must alter your plans. You'll have to ascend and descend by cable car, which many visitors find exhilarating. From the center of Lucerne, take bus no. 1 from the Bahnhof to the outlying suburb of Kriens. At Kriens, transfer to a cable car that glides over meadows and forests to the village of Fräkmüntegg, 1,380m (4,526 ft.) above sea level. The trip takes half an hour. At Fräkmüntegg, switch to another cable car, this one much more steeply inclined than the first. A stunning feat of advanced engineering, it swings above gorges and cliffs to the very peak of Mount Pilatus (Pilatus-Kulm). Unlike the cog railways, these cable cars operate year-round. The round-trip ride by cable car from Kriens to Fräkmüntegg costs 42F. *Insider tip:* Visit Pilatus early in the day. Clouds and fog sometimes move in after the noon hour and mask the magnificent view from the top of this mountain peak. You can be fooled by a clear view at the bottom of Pilatus, only to reach the top later to be engulfed in the clouds.

For information, consult the staff at the city's tourist office or call ℰ **041/329-11-11.** They're well informed about these excursions, as are the desk personnel at most of Lucerne's hotels.

Rigi ★★★

For another panoramic view from a hilltop belvedere, go to Rigi, 24km (15 miles) east of Lucerne. The view from Rigi is different from that atop Mount Pilatus, so if you see both, you won't be replicating your experience. Pilatus offers the more panoramic vista, but the view from Rigi is more beautiful. By most accounts, Rigi (1,680m/5,510 ft.) is the most famous mountain view in the country. However, you may be disappointed if the weather's not clear. Rigi is called the "island mountain" because it appears to be surrounded by the waters of lakes Lucerne, Zug, and Lauerz. It's accessible by two cog railways and a cableway.

Adventurous visitors making the "grand tour" in the 19th century spent the night at Rigi-Kulm to see the sun rise over the Alps. Victor Hugo called it "an incredible horizon . . . that chaos of absurd exaggerations and scary diminutions." Later, Mark Twain also climbed to the top to see the sun rise across the Alps. But he was so exhausted, as he relates in *A Tramp Abroad,* that he collapsed into sleep, from which he didn't wake until sunset. Not realizing that he had slept all day, he at first recoiled in horror, believing that the sun had switched its direction and was actually rising in the west. This experience continues to be one of nature's loveliest offerings in all of Europe. For those wanting to partake of the tradition, many hotels are perched on the mountainside.

You can travel to the mountain by taking a 55-minute trip by lake steamer from Lucerne to Vitznau, a small resort on the northern shore of the lake. The rack railway from Vitznau to Rigi-Kulm was the first cog railway in Europe, built in 1871. You can also approach the mountain from Arth-Goldau, which is on the southern shore of Zug Lake. The Arth-Goldau cog railway to Rigi-Kulm opened in 1876. The maximum gradient is 21%. Both cog railways cost 65F for the round-trip. It's possible to go up one way and come down the other if you want to see both sides of the mountain. The trip from

---

Bürgenstock

The chic resort of **Bürgenstock,** lying 16km (10 miles) southeast of Lucerne, has become a virtual ghost town, except for construction crews. Audrey Hepburn, Sophia Loren, and other celebrities who used to vacation or live here temporarily are long gone, as is the resort's international reputation for glamour. That's the bad news. The good news is that the trio of hotels that existed here have shut down for major renovations, not to reopen until 2010. Upon their return, predictions are that they will be among the most elegant and luxurious hotels in all of Switzerland.

Vitznau takes 40 minutes and the trip from Arth-Goldau lasts 35 minutes. There are a dozen departures a day in season. An alternative ascent is strongly advocated by the local tourist office: Begin at the quays in Lucerne, and take a lake steamer to Vitznau. From here, after a stroll through the town, go to the top of Rigi-Kulm by cog railway and admire the view from the top. Then descend halfway down the mountain via the same cog railway, getting off midway at Rigi Kaltbad. Here you'll switch to the Rigi Seilbahn cable car, which will carry you the rest of the way downhill, a 15-minute downhill walk from the hamlet of Weggis. You can begin this trip daily between 8am and around 2pm, which is the last reasonable departure time, if you want to see the sights and return to Lucerne before dark. The tourist office or a staff member at the phone number listed below will recite the available times of departures. Many visitors, however, find that the most convenient departure time from Lucerne is at 8:32am and again at 10:32am. For more information about anything to do with ascents of Mount Rigi, call the **Lucerne Tourist office** at © **041/227-17-17.** The ascents described in this section are possible only from March to October.

Gütsch

One sweeping panorama of the region that rises immediately above the center of Lucerne (and doesn't involve a full day's excursion) is the panoramic plateau of Gütsch, 514m (1,686 ft.) above sea level. At the top is a belvedere platform that's the site of the Hotel Château Gütsch. Views from the belvedere are breathtaking. To reach this panoramic site, board bus no. 12 from the train station on Bahnhofplatz.

WHERE TO DINE

Restaurant Petit Palais ★★ SWISS/INTERNATIONAL Dining in the Hotel Château Gütsch, a castle set on a hilltop overlooking Lake Lucerne, is almost like a celebration. You can sample marvelous dishes such as poached pole-caught codfish with Italian spinach, red-wine scallions, and a porcini risotto; crispy sautéed pikeperch filet with young leeks; or small angler fish sautéed in olive oil and served with a Mediterranean potato ragout and a sweet-pepper cream sauce. Starters are prepared fresh daily, and the desserts are luscious.

Currently, this property is undergoing a conversion into a luxury boutique hotel set to open in the first half of 2012. It will contain 20 bedrooms of luxurious furnishings and exceptionally large space. Next to the castle a modern building will accommodate another 40 bedrooms and suites, plus a spa.

In the Château Gütsch, Kanonenstrasse. © **041/248-98-98.** www.chateau-guetsch.ch. Reservations required. Main courses 59F–62F; fixed-price lunch 46F, dinner 110F. AE, MC, V. Tues–Sat 11:30am–11pm; Sun 11:30am–5pm.

> ## Impressions
>
> *We were soon tramping leisurely up the leafy mulepath, and then the talk began to flow, as usual. It was twelve o'clock noon, and a breezy, cloudless day; the ascent was gradual, and the glimpses from under the curtaining boughs, of blue water, and tiny sail boats, and beetling cliffs, were as charming as glimpses of dreamland.*
>
> —Mark Twain, on "Climbing the Rigi"

Mount Titlis ★ ★

Mount Titlis, which is visited as an excursion from the little resort of Engelberg, is the highest point from which you can get a view over central Switzerland. The summit is always covered by snow and ice; there's an "ice cave," in addition to a glacier trail. The view from the belvedere, at 2,970m (9,742 ft.), takes in the Jungfrau and the Matterhorn, as well as Zurich and Basel on a clear day. There's a summer ski run with a ski lift. There are also two restaurants: the **Panorama Restaurant Titlis** (✆ **041/639-50-88**), at 3,000m (9,840 ft.), and the **Gletscher–Restaurant Stand** (✆ **041/639-50-85**), at 2,412m (7,911 ft.).

To get to the summit, you take a funicular and three cable cars. The last stage of the cable-car trip is the most spectacular, as you're taken right over the glacier. Visitors with respiratory problems may want to forgo this trip because of the thinness of the air at such elevations. The terminal at the summit (which is referred to in some timetables as Kleintitlis, or Little Titlis) has an observation lounge and a large sun terrace.

To get to Titlis from Lucerne's Bahnhof, drive or take a train to Engelberg; the round-trip costs 57F in first class, 34F in second class. Then, to reach the summit, take the cable cars that run daily beginning at 8:30am, with the last one back at 5pm. In winter skiers use this connection to get to the higher slopes. For more information and schedules, call ✆ **041/639-50-50** or 639-50-61.

2 WEGGIS ★ ★

30km (19 miles) E of Lucerne

The lakeside resort of Weggis is on the sunny side of Mount Rigi, one of three holiday centers (Vitznau and Gersau are the others) that offer the kind of mild climate found in favored parts of Italy. Weggis and the other resorts are about an hour's walk or a 5-minute drive apart. Well-tended garden promenades stretch for several miles along the lakeshore. Mark Twain stayed here in 1897.

Of the three resorts, Weggis is preferred by most. It's usually the first port of call for steamers from Lucerne and is also easily accessible from the international St. Gotthard railway line, although it's not on the main traffic route.

Many excursions are possible from early spring to late autumn. You can take the aerial cableway up to Rigi-Kaltbad (1,427m/4,681 ft.), a mountain health resort behind Weggis. This is great walking country, not only on the promenade quays but also on the slopes of the Rigi, which are planted with vines. Even some almost tropical species of vegetation grow here. In addition, mountain transport links Weggis with the Rigi Railways.

ESSENTIALS

GETTING THERE   Several **lake steamers** (✆ **041/367-67-67**) depart from the quays of Lucerne for Weggis every day, requiring about 45 minutes for the transfer. Once you reach Weggis, a local bus run by the village transports you (in the summertime only) from the lakefront to the upper reaches of the town.

Though Weggis is not directly accessible by **rail,** the railway junction of Kussnacht lies 9.6km (6 miles) from Weggis. From Kussnacht, **buses** depart for the 10- to 13-minute ride to Weggis.

If you're **driving** from Lucerne, drive east on Route 2, along the northern rim of Lake Lucerne, cutting south on Route 2b at the signposted turnoff to Weggis.

VISITOR INFORMATION The **Weggis Tourist Office,** Seestrasse 5 (✆ **041/390-11-55;** www.wvrt.ch), is open Monday to Friday from 8am to noon and 1 to 5:30pm, Saturday and Sunday 9am to 4pm. (Off season the office remains closed on weekends.) If you'd like to go biking along the banks of Lake Lucerne, you can stop in here and rent a bike for the day for 25F.

WHERE TO STAY & DINE

Hotel Albana ★ This hotel is outclassed only by the Beau-Rivage (see below). The Hotel Albana was built in the Art Nouveau style in 1896 and has been run by the Wolf family since 1910. One of the public rooms, with a grand piano and a 3m (10-ft.) Meissen ceramic stove, looks almost baronial. Heavy brass chandeliers hang from the frescoed ceiling, and large rococo mirrors reflect the wood paneling. The midsize bedrooms are modernized with excellent beds. Many have good views of the nearby lake. The best food at the resort is served in the Panorama Restaurant, which has large windows and a terrace above the lake. The decor of the hotel's Jazz Bar was inspired by Matisse; on some nights it offers live music.

CH-6353 Weggis. ✆ **041/390-21-41.** Fax 041/390-29-59. www.albana-weggis.ch. 56 units. 250F–360F double. Half board 48F–58F. Rates include buffet breakfast. AE, DC, MC, V. Closed mid-Dec to mid-Jan. **Amenities:** Restaurant; bar; babysitting; bikes; exercise room; room service; sauna. *In room:* TV, hair dryer, minibar.

Hotel Beau-Rivage ★★ One of the attractions of this 1908 hotel is its expansive, manicured lawn, which reaches down to the lake near the boat landing. The view of the mountains from here is exhilarating. The symmetrical hotel has a series of wrought-iron balconies, and the traditional and spacious rooms are comfortably furnished with wood, brass, and pastel shades. Comfortable bedrooms open onto panoramic lake and mountain views.

CH-6353 Weggis. ✆ **041/392-79-00.** Fax 041/390-19-81. www.beaurivage-weggis.ch. 41 units. 328F–550F double. Rates include half board. AE, DC, MC, V. Free parking. Closed Nov–Mar. **Amenities:** Restaurant; bar; Jacuzzi; outdoor heated pool; room service; sauna. *In room:* TV, hair dryer, minibar, Wi-Fi (15F per 24 hr.).

Hotel Central am See This old-fashioned resort hotel, built with six large gables and many smaller ones, stands on a shady peninsula with a swimming pool near the lake. Constructed in 1912, it offers an interior with traditional furniture and an elevator carrying clients to the well-maintained, rather stark bedrooms, most of which offer a view of the lake and mountains. The hotel has a greenhouse-style restaurant, the Winter Garden, overlooking the lake.

CH-6353 Weggis. ✆ **041/392-09-09.** Fax 041/392-09-00. www.central-am-see.ch. 35 units. Oct to mid-May 180F–255F double; mid-May to Sept 195F–275F double. Rates include buffet breakfast. AE, MC, V. Parking 20F. Closed mid-Nov to mid-Jan. **Amenities:** 2 restaurants; bar; babysitting; bikes; outdoor heated pool; room service. *In room:* TV, CD player, hair dryer, minibar (in some), Wi-Fi (free).

Hotel Rössli ⟨**Value**⟩ Completely renovated, this century-old hotel with elaborate shingles occupies the most desirable lakefront position at the center of the resort town, facing a tranquil square with flowers, statues, and a fountain. The hotel has ornate wood balustrades and russet-colored shutters. The interior is modern, with a decor of wrought iron, wicker chairs, and hanging lamps. The Nölly family offers pleasant midsize rooms with attractive furniture and neatly kept bathrooms. You'll also find a sidewalk cafe in front.

CH-6353 Weggis. $\mathcal{C}$ **041/392-27-27.** Fax 041/390-27-26. www.wellness-roessli.ch. 65 units. 220F–320F double. Half board 40F. Rates include buffet breakfast. AE, DC, MC, V. Parking 6F. **Amenities:** Restaurant; outdoor pool; spa. *In room:* TV, DVD (in some), hair dryer.

---

3 VITZNAU ★

26km (16 miles) E of Lucerne; 4km (2¹/₂ miles) SE of Weggis

Vitznau is located on a different bay of Lake Lucerne, at the foot of the Rigi. At 439m (1,440 ft.), it offers an alpine panorama that's mirrored in the lake. It's an hour's drive from Zurich.

Sports vacations are especially popular in Vitznau from April to October. Facilities include swimming in the lake, indoor and outdoor pools, and tennis courts. There are also many inviting hiking trails—ideal for long walks—in the meadows, woodlands, and mountains.

The Vitznau-Rigi railway starts at Vitznau along the shores of Lake Lucerne, on the south side of Mount Rigi. The railway terminates at Kulm peak, after passing through the mountain stations of Rigi-Kaltbad-First, Rigi Staffelhöehe, and Rigi Staffel. In the summer, old-fashioned steam trains travel on this stretch of electric rack-and-pinion railway. Pause to enjoy the beauty of the resort before heading up to the mountain. Departures are every 30 minutes.

ESSENTIALS

GETTING THERE The only rail line servicing Vitznau is a local alpine train connecting it to such panoramic points as Rigi-Kulm and Rigi-Kaltbad. Call $\mathcal{C}$ **0900/300-300** for **rail schedules.**

Buses depart for Vitznau from the Küssnacht railway station, which is reached from Lucerne by train every hour, requiring about 45 minutes, including a stopover in Weggis. Some of the buses continue to Gersau, where there's a connection to Brunne. For **bus schedules** and information, call $\mathcal{C}$ **041/367-67-67.**

Ferries depart for Vitznau from the quays of Lucerne every hour in summer and about every 2 hours in winter. The trip takes about 1 hour. Call $\mathcal{C}$ **041/367-67-67** for more information.

If you're **driving,** the resort is reached by first passing through Weggis (see section 2, above), then continuing along Route 2b south to Vitznau, a very short drive along the lake.

VISITOR INFORMATION The **Vitznau Tourist Board,** in the town center ($\mathcal{C}$ **041/ 398-00-35;** www.vitznau.ch), is open November to Easter, Monday to Friday from 8:30am to noon and 1 to 6:30pm, Saturday 9am to 5pm, and Sunday 9am to noon. From Easter to June and September to October, hours are Monday to Friday 8:30am to noon and 1 to 6:30pm, and Saturday 9am to noon. During July and August the office is open Monday to Friday 8:30am to 6:30pm, Saturday 9am to 5pm, and Sunday 9am to noon.

If you'd like to enjoy the pleasures of the lake itself, both paddleboats and motorboats are available for rent at **Anker Travel,** Zihlstrasse (© **041/397-17-07**). It's also possible to swim in the bay here, although the temperatures are a mite chilly for those from sunnier climes.

If you're biking down from Vitznau, you can tour the entire right bank of the lake by **Route 2,** which runs all the way to Altdorf (see section 5, below).

WHERE TO STAY & DINE

Hotel Rigi   Although the service from the staff may leave you as cold as an alpine lake, this is a clean and decent place that can be recommended for its economy. About a block from the boat-landing dock, the hotel is a century-old monument within the town center, although rooms have been kept fairly up-to-date. Units come in a variety of shapes and sizes and are comfortable, with firm beds and good maintenance. If available, opt for one of the corner bedrooms that open onto their own private balconies and a view of the lake. Don't expect many in-room amenities outside of a telephone and private bathroom.

Seestrasse, CH-6354 Vitznau. © **041/399-85-85.** Fax 041/399-85-86. www.rigi-vitznau.ch. 35 units. 120F–200F double. Rates include continental breakfast. AE, DC, MC, V. **Amenities:** Restaurant; bar; Internet (free, in lobby); room service. *In room:* TV, hair dryer, minibar (in some).

Park Hotel Vitznau ★★★   One of the most elegant waterside havens along the Lucerne Riviera, this Belle Epoque hotel offers lavish living. It was designed by architect Karl Koller and built in 1902 at the foot of Mount Rigi. A wing added in 1985 maintains the spirit of the original fairy-tale castle. Today's hotel grew out of a simple 1866 B&B that once attracted such wanderers as Mark Twain and Victor Hugo. The spacious bedrooms have been completely renovated, with marble-clad bathrooms and such thoughtful extras as heated towel racks. The bathtubs with showers have been dubbed "pharaonic." English chintz, both in draperies and upholstery, gives the rooms a summery look. Try for one of the seven or so lake-view rooms on the first floor in the older section, each of which has a sprawling lakefront terrace. Room nos. 121 and 123, with particularly large terraces, are most frequently requested. Ceilings within the hotel's public areas are particularly high and grand, each a decorative throwback to the late-19th-century age of hotel design. There's also a sun terrace with parasols.

Kantonstrasse, CH-6354 Vitznau. © **041/399-60-60.** Fax 041/399-60-70. www.parkhotel-vitznau.ch. 112 units. 540F–780F double; from 880F suite. Rates include buffet breakfast. AE, DC, MC, V. Parking 25F. Closed mid-Oct to mid-Apr. **Amenities:** 3 restaurants; bar; babysitting; bikes; concierge; exercise room; indoor heated pool; room service; spa; 2 outdoor tennis courts (lit); limited watersports equipment. *In room:* TV, hair dryer, minibar (in some), Wi-Fi (free).

Finds   An Idyllic Swimming Hole

To escape from the crowds along Lake Lucerne, we'll let you in on a secret: At the very southeastern tip of Lake Lucerne is the narrow and splendid inlet lake, the **Urnersee,** which attracts fewer visitors than the resorts along Lake Lucerne even though it's no less majestic or beautiful. In fact, this is the most remote, wildest, and loveliest part of the whole of Lake Lucerne. A natural rock obelisk, called **Schillerstein,** rises some 25m (82 ft.) out of the Urnersee, and is dedicated to Friedrich von Schiller, the author of *Wilhelm Tell.*

4 BRUNNEN ★★

45km (28 miles) SE of Lucerne

Brunnen is a popular vacation resort in the canton of Schwyz. It's located at the foot of Fronalpstock, in a beautiful inlet at the southern end of Lake Lucerne, where you find the Urnersee (or Lake Uri), one of the most beautiful lake sites in Switzerland. There's a fine view of the two lakes and the Alps from the quays. The resort is about an hour's drive from Zurich's Kloten International Airport.

ESSENTIALS

GETTING THERE   Some of the local trains running between Zurich and Lugano or Locarno in Switzerland's deep south stop in Brunnen, although others require changes in such towns as Goschenen. Call ✆ **0900/300-300** for **rail schedules.**

A mini-armada of buses commutes dozens of times every day from Schwyz to both the waterfront and the railroad station at Brunnen, requiring only about 12 minutes for the one-way passage. Other buses travel from Brunnen to the beginning of the cable car that ascends to Morschach. For **bus schedules** and information, call ✆ **041/390-11-33.**

Several **lake steamers** depart from the quays of Lucerne for Brunnen throughout the day, with more frequent service scheduled during midsummer. Travel time from Lucerne to Brunnen ranges from 2 to 2½ hours. For more information, call ✆ **041/367-67-67.**

From Lucerne, **drive** to the resorts of Weggis and Vitznau (see sections 2 and 3), then continue southeast along Route 2b until you reach Brunnen.

VISITOR INFORMATION   The **Brunnen Tourist Office,** Bahnhofstrasse 15 (✆ **041/ 825-00-41;** www.brunnentourismus.ch), is open Monday to Friday 8:30am to 6pm and Saturday and Sunday 9am to 3pm.

EXPLORING THE AREA

What you do here is walk along the shady **lakeside quays** ★★, among the country's most scenic parts, taking in views of the wild and remote lake, the Urnersee. The views of the lake from the quays are stunning, taking in the awesome Uri-Rotstock, twin peaks with a small glacier.

The area around Brunnen—so beloved by Hans Christian Andersen—is the cradle of the Confederation and abounds in reminders of the country's history, including archives in Schwyz where the Confederation documents are displayed, and the Federal Chapel in Brunnen.

This is also William Tell country. Around the year 1250, several families left Raron in the Valais and crossed the Alps to establish new homes in desolate Schächental/Uri. Records confirm that the Tell family helped found the settlement. According to folk legend, William Tell was the hero of a decisive battle in 1315 and reportedly died in 1350. Historians, however, have no proof of these events.

Nevertheless, the Swiss honor the man who shot an apple off the head of his brave young son with a bow and arrow in a test of prowess. Many visitors travel to Sisikon, just south of Brunnen, to see the **Tell Chapel,** which was restored in 1881. The chapel contains records from the early 16th century and paintings by Stückelberg.

NEARBY ATTRACTIONS   Brunnen is the starting point of **Axenstrasse,** the stunning panoramic road—a masterpiece of engineering—leading south to the St. Gotthard Pass.

13

The Legend of William Tell

One of the most famous names in Swiss history, linked with the country's struggle for liberty, concerned a William Tell, who may never have existed. But to the Swiss he's very real, the father who, with his crossbow, hit the apple that the tyrannical Austrian bailiff of Uri, Gessler, had placed on the head of his son.

When Gessler allegedly asked Tell why he had brought a second arrow, Tell told him he intended it for Gessler if he had hit his son instead of the apple. Furious, Gessler had Tell dragged to his boat at the northwestern shore of Lake Lucerne. A storm came up and Gessler released Tell from his fetters, hoping that his strong arms could save the boat party. Tell escaped and waited on the shore near Gessler's castle. When Gessler arrived, Tell hit him with an arrow straight through the heart. Or so the story goes.

First found in a ballad, the tale dates from at least before 1474. Over the years various authors have smoothed away inconsistencies and rounded out the tale. But it was Schiller's play in 1804 that gave the tale worldwide renown.

Alleged proofs of the actual existence of a William Tell break down hopelessly upon scholarly examination. For example, entries in the parish registers are forgeries. One document that alleged that 114 men in 1338 had been "personally acquainted" with Tell didn't surface until 1759—no doubt a fake.

Tellskapelle (the Tell Chapel) stands today as a monument to the legend, lying at the Lake of the Four Cantons between Sisikon and Flüelen.

It goes along the rim of Lake Uri, in and out of subterranean passageways and galleries carved out of the mountain. Brunnen is also a base for excursions by ship, mountain railway, bus, and train to points around Lake Lucerne.

WHERE TO STAY & DINE

Hotel Bellevue   Built in the 1800s and completely renovated many times since, this baroque hotel at the edge of the lake offers cozy, old-fashioned comfort. Werner Achermann and his family offer well-maintained rooms, most with carpeting and all with well-maintained bathrooms. The hotel also has a sun terrace.

Axenstrasse 2, CH-6440 Brunnen. ℭ 041/820-13-18. Fax 041/820-38-89. www.bellevue-brunnen.ch. 48 units. 160F–240F double. Half board 30F per person. Rates include buffet breakfast. AE, DC, MC, V. Free outdoor parking, 10F garage. Closed Nov to mid-Mar. **Amenities:** Restaurant. *In room:* TV, hair dryer, minibar.

Seehotel Waldstätterhof ★★   One of the few government-rated five-star hotels opening onto the lake, the Waldstätterhof offers old-style comfort. The symmetrical white building has a mansard roof and a series of balconies overlooking the lake. Plenty of modern comforts have been installed since the hotel opened in 1870. The public rooms are grand and the dining room has fanciful chandeliers. The grounds are well kept and free of traffic and include a private beach on the lake. There's also a terrace restaurant, a less formal dining room, and a rotisserie. The Lake Lucerne steamers stop nearby, and the Schiller Memorial Stone can be seen on the opposite shore of the lake. The hotel is open year-round.

Waldstätterquai 6, CH-6440 Brunnen. ℭ **041/825-06-06.** Fax 041/825-06-00. www.waldstaetterhof.ch. 104 units. 260F–430F double; 590F–710F suite. Half board 60F. Rates include buffet breakfast. AE, DC, MC, V. Free parking outside, 20F garage. **Amenities:** 2 restaurants; bar; babysitting; exercise room; room service; sauna; tennis court. *In room:* TV, hair dryer, minibar, Wi-Fi (free).

5 ALTDORF

54km (34 miles) SE of Lucerne

Altdorf is the town where the William Tell legend is said to have taken place. A statue of the Swiss national hero stands in the main square. The key to the St. Gotthard Pass, Altdorf is north of the Alps and 3km (2 miles) south of where the Reuss River flows into the Urnersee. It's the capital of the canton of Uri and the starting point of the road over the Klausen Pass. The most scenic way to get to Altdorf from Lucerne is to ride a lake steamer to Flüelen and transfer to a bus. The total trip takes about 3 hours. Call the tourist office (see below) for more information.

ESSENTIALS

GETTING THERE   Several daily trains make the 27-minute trip to Altdorf from the region's biggest railway junction, Arth-Goldau, on their way south to Chiasso and eventually Milan. Call ℭ **0900/300-300** for **rail schedules.**

The bus routes coming into Altdorf connect the town with mountain hamlets, which usually have no railway junctions of their own. In the summer a handful of buses connect it with Zurich's Hauptbahnhof, sometimes with a transfer in Flüelen. Travel time from Zurich is about 1½ hours. For **bus schedules** and information, call ℭ **0900/300-300.**

If you're **driving** from Brunnen on Lake Lucerne, continue south along N4.

VISITOR INFORMATION   The **Altdorf Tourist Office** (ℭ 041/872-04-50; www. altdorftourismus.ch) is open Monday to Saturday from 9 to 11:30am and Monday to Friday 1:30 to 5:30pm.

SEEING THE SIGHTS

The famous **William Tell statue** is in front of the early-19th-century town hall and a tower dating from the Middle Ages. The monument was created by Richard Kissling in 1895; it was this image, engraved on a postage stamp, that became familiar to people all over the globe.

Altdorf is set in a scenic area of central Switzerland that makes for good biking. You can rent a bike at the train station (ℭ **0900/300-300**). Armed with a good map from the tourist office, set out on your adventure.

NEARBY ATTRACTIONS   The road to the Klausen Pass leads to **Bürglen,** one of the oldest hamlets in Uri. Snowdrifts block the pass from October to May. Bürglen, according to legend, was the birthplace of William Tell. The **Tell Museum,** Postplatz (ℭ **041/ 870-41-55;** www.tellmuseum.ch), contains documents and mementos relating to the early history of Switzerland. The museum is in a Romanesque tower adjacent to the parish church. It's open April to June and September to October daily from 10 to 11:30am and 1:30 to 5pm; in July and August, daily hours are 10am to 5pm. Admission is 5F for adults, 1.50F for children 16 and under.

Goldener Schlüssel (Value   The best of the lot is this five-story, government-rated three-star hotel in the center of town. A historic inn dating from the 19th century, it faces a tiny medieval plaza and is distinguished by a wrought-iron sign bearing a golden key *(goldener Schlüssel).* The hotel's accessories include a handful of original paintings. The bedrooms are cozy and comfortably furnished.

The hotel's well-reputed restaurant serves a cuisine based on all-Swiss recipes and local ingredients.

Schützengasse 9, CH-6460 Altdorf. ✆ **041/871-20-02.** Fax 041/870-11-67. www.hotelschluessel.ch. 21 units, 20 with bathroom. 190F double without bathroom, 230F with bathroom. Half board 35F per person. Rates include buffet breakfast. AE, DC, MC, V. Free parking. **Amenities:** Restaurant; exercise room; Jacuzzi; room service; sauna. *In room:* TV, hair dryer, minibar.

---

6 ANDERMATT ★

50km (31 miles) SE of Lucerne

At the crossroads of the Alps, Andermatt is a sports center known for its long, sunny days in winter. It's in the Urseren Valley, at the junction of two alpine roads—the St. Gotthard highway and the road to Oberalp and Furka. Visitors flock here for the valley's scenic grandeur, best absorbed by hiking in summer or cross-country skiing in winter.

ESSENTIALS

GETTING THERE   Andermatt lies directly on a secondary rail line connecting Chur with Lucerne, where further connections can be made on express trains to the rest of Switzerland. Travel time from Lucerne is about 1¾ hours. Call ✆ **0900/300-300** for rail schedules. There is no bus service.

Three or four buses travel daily from the bus junction of Airolo to Andermatt. To Airolo, buses funnel in every day from Basel, Lucerne, Zurich, and Lugano, with connections to such other resorts as Brig and Oberwald. For **bus schedules** and information, call ✆ **081/949-20-34.**

If you're **driving** from Amsteg, continue south along N2.

VISITOR INFORMATION   The **Andermatt Tourist Office,** Gotthardstrasse 2 (✆ **041/ 888-71-00;** www.andermatt.ch), is open Monday to Saturday from 9am to noon and 2 to 5:30pm.

EXPLORING THE AREA

Andermatt is a good base for hikes across the mountain passes, including the St. Gotthard Pass and the Furka Pass. In the winter, skiers flock to Gemsstock, Natschen, Oberalp, and Winterhorn. Also in winter the town offers 10 lifts, 5 cable cars, 21km (13 miles) of cross-country trails open November to May, and 56km (35 miles) of downhill runs. Intermediate to advanced skiers are attracted to the resort. Safety devices help protect against snowdrifts and avalanches. Other sporting facilities include a Swiss Ski School, an ice-skating and curling rink, an indoor swimming pool, and squash courts. Sleigh rides are also offered.

South of Andermatt, the **St. Gotthard Pass ★,** at 2,109m (6,918 ft.), provides a link between the Grisons and the Valais Alps. It's one of the most stunning and scenic passes

in Switzerland, used by merchants and messengers as far back as the early Middle Ages.
The road through the pass was built in the 18th and 19th centuries atop a much older footpath; it's still the shortest route between the two watersheds that fall away on either side. A 15km (9-mile) railway tunnel burrows under the peak of the St. Gotthard massif; nearby, the St. Gotthard road tunnel, opened in 1980, is the longest one in the world. There's no toll along the 16km (10-mile) route, which is open year-round. (The road high above it closes during heavy snowfalls.)

If you don't have a car, you can take the postal bus over the pass or the train through the tunnel. The postal bus leaves from Andermatt and goes to Airolo daily between mid-April and mid-September. Departures from Andermatt are at 9:35am and 12:30pm. The last bus back leaves Airolo at 5pm. In winter the pass is closed and postal buses can't get through, but you could take the train to Göschenen and from there continue by train to Airolo. Trains run through the tunnel frequently, the only way for trains to cross this mountain-pass area. For train information and schedules, call ✆ **0900/300-300.**

The 32km (20-mile) **Furka Pass Road** ★★★ going from Gletsch to Andermatt takes about 2½ hours and is one of the most scenic rides in Europe. Begin the trip at Gletsch at 174m (571 ft.). As you drive along, you'll have panoramic views of the Rhone Glacier, and both the Bernese and Valais Alps. The pass at 2,392m (7,846 ft.) is the highest shelf of the towering longitudinal furrow, dividing the Swiss Alps from the rail junction at Martigny to the town of Chur. In 1982 a railway tunnel, a stunning feat of modern engineering, opened the pass between the villages of Oberwald and Realp. Going through the barren valley of Garschen and bordering the foothills of Galenstock, a mountain peak, the road comes to the severe Urseren Valley before passing through the villages of Realp, Hospental, and finally Andermatt, where you might want to spend the night.

WHERE TO STAY & DINE

Hotel Aurora   Although this hotel presents a modern and unassuming facade to the world outside, the pleasant and warmly decorated interior and the hands-on management of its owners (the Christen family) make a stay here worthwhile. Built in 1969, it's a well-managed, government-rated three-star hotel, lying at the southern edge of the village, within a 5-minute walk of the town center. Each small room has touches of pine paneling and a neatly kept bathroom.

CH-6490 Andermatt. ✆ **041/887-16-61.** Fax 041/887-00-86. www.aurora-andermatt.ch. 26 units. 190F–210F double; 240F triple. Rates include buffet breakfast. AE, MC, V. Parking 10F. Closed May and Nov. **Amenities:** Restaurant; bar; room service; sauna. *In room:* TV, hair dryer, Wi-Fi (free).

Hotel Drei Könige und Post ★   This old and fabled inn still puts up wayfarers. There has been a series of inns at this site since 1234, and Goethe spent the night at one of them in 1775. This family-run hotel has been rebuilt or renovated many times since. There's a cafe terrace in front of this white-walled chalet with buttressed eaves and brown shutters. Regional Swiss dishes are served in the hotel restaurant. The Renner family offers well-furnished paneled rooms, 10 of which have balconies. Rooms range from small to midsize, and each is comfortable with traditional furnishings.

Gotthardstrasse 69, CH-6490 Andermatt. ✆ **041/887-00-01.** Fax 041/887-16-66. www.3koenige.ch. 21 units. 160F–280F double. Half board 45F per person. AE, DC, MC, V. Free outdoor parking, 12F garage. **Amenities:** Restaurant; babysitting; exercise room; Jacuzzi; room service; sauna. *In room:* TV, hair dryer, minibar.

The Grisons

Of all the Swiss cantons, the Grisons is both the largest and the least developed. Its German name is Graubünden; to the Romansh-speaking population it's Grischun, and the Italians call it Grigioni. Grisons is the French (and English) name, although French is rarely spoken in this canton.

This sparsely settled, easternmost Swiss region is very mountainous and contains 225 sq. km (140 sq. miles) of glaciers. One-fifth of the canton's total area is covered with forests. The region contains the sources of the Rhine and Inn (*En* in Romansh) rivers, which form the major valleys of the canton. Juf, at nearly 2,100m (6,888 ft.) above sea level, is the highest permanently inhabited village in the Alps. Even the 150 or so valleys of the Grisons lie at high altitudes, between 886m and 1,969m (2,906 ft. and 6,458 ft.), and the region's highest peak, Bernina, reaches 3,986m (13,074 ft.). The alpine scenery here differs from that of other areas of Switzerland in altitude as well as topography—the air is clear and invigorating, which has led to the establishment of many health centers in the Grisons. The height makes it cooler at night, but it enjoys the extra daytime warmth of other southern cantons.

The Grisons was once a territory of Rhaetia, peopled by Celtic tribes in pre-Christian times. In 15 B.C., the Romans conquered the Rhaetians, began colonization, and built alpine roads. The Germanic Franks entered the Roman provinces in the 3rd century and established themselves along the Rhine. They and their successors, the Ostrogoths, introduced Teutonic influences into the Roman territories they seized, gradually changing the language of the inhabitants to Germanic dialects, especially in the northern regions. As a result, German is spoken today by about half the Grisons population, mainly around Davos and Chur, the capital of the canton. About a sixth of the people of the Grisons—those living in the south—speak the language of their next-door neighbor, Italy.

The people of the upper valleys of the Rhine and the Inn were isolated enough to resist Germanic influences, and today they still cling to their ancestral tongue, Romansh—the language of a third of the Swiss living in the Grisons. Both the dialect spoken in the Engadine (Ladin) and that spoken in the Vorderrhein Valley (Surveltisch) are derived from the Latin of Rhaetia. The centuries have altered it, so that today it sounds rather like Spanish spoken with a German accent. In 1938 Romansh officially became the fourth of the Swiss national languages.

The Grisons was one of the last regions of Switzerland to benefit from busy commerce with the rest of the country. Cars were forbidden on all roads until 1927, and even today it's illegal to drive cars in Arosa after nightfall. This ban on the use of roads helped to popularize the Rhaetian railway, whose narrow-gauge trains cross the region along hairpin turns and through dozens of tunnels. Today, this railway, as well as the postal buses that crisscross the district, provide panoramas of a harsh and sometimes-bleak landscape.

The peasants of this canton banded together in 1395 to form the Ligue Grise (Gray League), from which the name Grisons is derived. Two other such leagues were formed in the area to oppose

Habsburg domination. In 1803 the three leagues formed a single canton, which joined the Swiss Confederation. The belief system of the Protestant Reformation, however, was adopted by only part of the canton, and today sections of it remain staunchly Catholic.

Since the 1950s, much of the Grisons has earned its living from tourists, who visit for the skiing and the small villages, as well as the local red and "green" wines (vetliner), the exquisite embroidery, and the hand-woven linens still produced in many mountain homes.

1 CHUR ★

122km (76 miles) SE of Zurich; 59km (37 miles) W of Davos

The capital of the Grisons, Chur is the oldest town in Switzerland. According to recent excavations, the area was inhabited as early as 3000 B.C. The Romans established a settlement in 15 B.C., naming it Curia Rhaetorum. In 450 B.C. a recently Christianized Chur became the see of a bishop. The town still has a bishop, but he no longer has the power of his medieval predecessors, who ruled virtually every aspect of life in Chur until 1526.

Set at an elevation of 586m (1,922 ft.), Chur lies near the head of the Rhine Valley, surrounded by towering mountains. The Plessur River, a tributary of the Rhine, flows through the center of town. Chur is at the natural junction of several of the most important routes from Italy over the alpine passes and as a result incorporates both Italian and Rhaetian influences.

Favored by visitors, who appreciate the wilderness surrounding it, Chur is the largest mercantile center between Zurich and Milan. It's also an important rail center, a terminal for several of the most scenic railway lines in Switzerland: the narrow-gauge rail line to St. Moritz (the Rhätische Bahn), the Chur-Arosa line, the Glacier Express, the Palm Express, and the Bernina Express. You might also go to Splügen, said to have the prettiest mountain-pass village in the area.

Chur also offers a variety of sports facilities. Summer sports include hiking and mountain biking. A pair of swimming pools, both indoor and outdoor, lies within the **Sportanlagen Obere** (𝒞 **081/254-42-88**), as well as a gymnasium and health club. Access to either of the pools costs 7F for adults and 4F for children ages 6 to 15, free for children 5 and under. Access to the gym costs 15F for everyone, but entrance is restricted to persons who can present a membership card from any other gym or health club, presumably as a means of determining that the bearer is familiar with how to exercise in a nondestructive way. In the winter, skiers in and around Chur have access to the top 20 ski areas surrounding Chur, some of which reach 2,700m (8,856 ft.) and are only 1½ hours away.

Chur's Old Town is best discovered on foot. The route outlined by the city is the most scenic and most historic. You travel at your own pace, just following in the footsteps of others. In addition, the tourist office (see "Essentials," below) provides German-language guided tours that depart from the tourist office every Wednesday at 2:30pm, but only between April and October. Participation in any of the guided tours costs 8F for adults, 4F for children ages 6 to 16, free for children 5 and under.

ESSENTIALS

GETTING THERE   The town is the end of some international lines, such as the standard-gauge railway from Sargans. It's also the starting point for the narrow-gauge line to St. Moritz, known as the Rhätische Bahn. The Chur-Arosa line and the Glacier Express also start here. Chur also has frequent train connections from Zurich. Call ✆ **0900/300-300** for **rail schedules.**

Chur lies near the terminus of several bus lines, which link its railway facilities with some of the villages scattered throughout the nearby valleys. The two most prominent of these are Davos and St. Moritz, where bus connections can be made to Munich, across the German border. For **bus schedules** and information, call ✆ **081/254-40-60** for questions about buses within the city limits, and 256-31-66 for buses traveling to or from Chur from points outside the city limits.

If you're **driving,** Chur is about 90 minutes from Zurich along N3 (later N13), and easily reached by expressway.

VISITOR INFORMATION   The **tourist office** is located at Bahnhofplatz 3 (✆ **081/252-18-18;** www.churtourismus.ch) and is open Monday to Friday 7am to 8pm, Saturday and Sunday 8am to 6pm.

SEEING THE SIGHTS

You'll want to spend as much time as possible in Chur to see the legacies left by the many emperors, kings, armies, and traders who have marched through here. In the medieval sector you'll come across squares with flower-bedecked fountains and narrow streets, along with elegant houses and many towers.

The **cathedral of Chur** ★, Hof 19 (for information, call the tourist office at ✆ **081/252-18-18**), was built between 1151 and 1282 on an ancient foundation and was extensively altered in the 19th century. The last major overhaul occurred here in 2007. Inside, the high altar displays a 15th-century gilded-wood triptych in the Gothic style, the largest of its kind in Switzerland.

Near the cathedral, the baroque **Bishop's Palace,** which is not open to the public, was built in 1732 and is still the private residence of a bishop. The palace opens onto Hofplatz—site of a Roman fort.

Bündner Kunstmuseum (Fine Arts Museum)   Known as the Villa Planta, this museum, set in a park, displays paintings and sculptures by many well-known Grisons artists. Some of the works are by Giovanni, Segantini, Angelica Kauffmann, Ferdinand Hodler, and Cuno Amiet, as well as by Alberto and Augusto Giacometti. You'll also find works by Ernst Ludwig Kirchner (1880–1938), the German painter and leader of the Brücke school of expressionists.

Bahnhofstrasse 35, at Postplatz. ✆ **081/257-28-68.** www.buendner-kunstmuseum.ch. Admission 12F adults, 10F students, free for children 16 and under. Tues–Sun 10am–5pm (Thurs till 8pm).

Rätisches Museum   Loaded with memorabilia from the town's (and region's) history, this folklore museum is one of the best places in the district for an insight into the harsh climate and agrarian origins of the Grisons.

Hofstrasse 1. ✆ **081/254-16-40.** www.raetischesmuseum.gr.ch. Admission 6F adults, 4F students, free for children 15 and under. Tues–Sun 10am–5pm (until 8pm Thurs).

WHERE TO STAY

Expensive

Romantik Hotel Stern ★★   Like most members of the Romantik chain, this historic hotel is filled with authentic antiques. You know you're in for a special experience when you arrive. If notified in advance, the hotel will send a 1933 Buick to pick you up at the rail depot. The outside of the hotel looks like a giant strawberry mousse with white

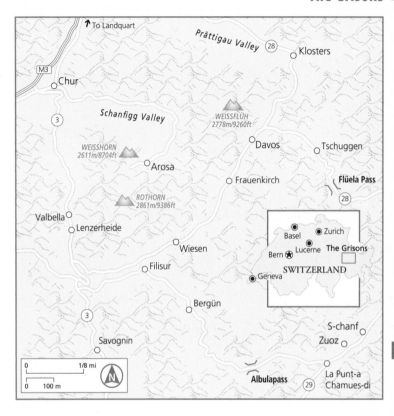

shutters. The interior has pine paneling—some of which dates from 1677—and vaulted or timbered ceilings. The modern and well-maintained bedrooms have 19th-century regional country antiques and are each fitted with a comfortable bathroom. Some have carefully preserved ceiling beams or trusses, many of them very old. In 1948 playwright Berthold Brecht lived here for 5 weeks during the midsummer production of one of his plays at a nearby theater. Special grace notes include a rooftop terrace, a lounge with a fireplace, and lots of memorabilia that evoke rustic and alpine Switzerland.

Reichsgasse 11, CH-7000 Chur. ℭ **081/258-57-57.** Fax 081/258-57-58. www.stern-chur.ch. 58 units. 290F double. Rates include buffet breakfast. Half board 40F per person. AE, DC, MC, V. Free parking outdoors, 16F inside. **Amenities:** Restaurant; room service. *In room:* TV, minibar (in some), Wi-Fi (free).

Moderate

Hotel Chur The Chur lies in the center of town near the Old Town and about a 10-minute walk from the rail station. This imposing neoclassical building with arched windows and fifth-floor gables contains two different dining areas with old-fashioned (but frequently renovated) charm, and comfortable, well-furnished bedrooms, each with a medium-size bathroom.

Welschdörfli 2, CH-7000 Chur. ✆ **081/254-34-00.** Fax 081/254-34-10. www.hotelchur.ch. 54 units. 160F–180F double. Rates include buffet breakfast. AE, DC, MC, V. Free parking. **Amenities:** 5 different dining areas; bar; room service. *In room:* TV, hair dryer, minibar.

Hotel Freieck   Originally built in 1575 and rising seven imposing, fresco-covered stories, this is an old favorite. It has been renovated countless times. Clinging stubbornly to tradition, the hotel, in the center of town, boasts a facade decorated with drawings of grapevines, a sundial, and two lions. The renovated, well-scrubbed, and midsize bedrooms contain simple furniture and comfortable bathrooms. The owners place a lot of emphasis on its dining rooms, which include stucco rooms with massive beams and vaulting as well as a more contemporary-looking, richly paneled modern area.

Reichsgasse 44/50, CH-7002 Chur. ✆ **081/255-15-15.** Fax 081/255-15-16. www.freieck.ch. 37 units. 150F–230F double. Rates include buffet breakfast. AE, DC, MC, V. Free parking 7pm–8am. **Amenities:** Bar; room service. *In room:* TV, hair dryer, minibar.

Inexpensive
Hotel Drei Könige ★   This historic hotel is at the entrance to the Old Town. The building's foundation dates from at least the 14th century. Excavations in the hotel cellar unearthed a collapsed tunnel that had led to the bishop's palace at the opposite end of the old city. Over the years the hotel has welcomed royalty, high-ranking politicians, and world-famous artists. The Drei Könige Hall on the premises used to be part of a monastery and, later, the seat of government.

Except for a handful of budget accommodations without private bathrooms, the well-scrubbed midsize rooms have comfortable furniture, including good beds, and the standard amenities such as up-to-date plumbing. The hotel has one of the most popular restaurants in town (see "Where to Dine," below).

Reichsgasse 18, CH-7000 Chur. ✆ **081/354-90-90.** Fax 081/354-90-91. www.dreikoenige.ch. 40 units, 28 with bathroom. 124F–130F double without bathroom, 158F–168F with bathroom. Rates include continental breakfast. AE, DC, MC, V. Parking 15F. **Amenities:** Restaurant; bar; room service. *In room:* TV, hair dryer, minibar.

Hotel Zunfthaus Rebleüten ★★   In its way, thanks to a sophisticated blend of Scottish and Swiss ownership, this is one of the most appealing and hip hotels in town. The venue is a meticulously restored guildhall dating from the 1470s, artfully positioned behind a bubbling fountain on one of the Old Town's most evocative squares. Graced with frescoes and blue-painted shutters on its facade, and staffed inside by a crew of great warmth and humor, it offers clean, well-maintained, and not particularly ostentatious bedrooms, each with simple but well-planned comforts. The coziest of the bedrooms (including nos. 5, 6, 7, 8, and 9) lie on the building's uppermost floor, beneath the sloping eaves. Here, architectural features include views of massive exposed beams and panoramas out over the Old Town.

Pfisterplatz 1, CH-7000 Chur. ✆ **081/255-11-44.** Fax 081/255-11-45. www.rebleuten.ch. 10 units. 140F double. Rates include buffet breakfast. AE, MC, V. **Amenities:** Restaurant w/2 outdoor terraces; bar. *In room:* TV.

WHERE TO DINE
Moderate
Hotel Stern Restaurant ★ SWISS/REGIONAL   This previously recommended hotel is known for serving some of the most authentic Grisons-inspired recipes in eastern Switzerland. At this historic 1677 hotel, the restaurant is wrapped in timeworn *arvenholz*, a rich wood paneling. Regional wine is served in pewter pitchers and waiters are in folk costumes. This may sound corny, but somehow it works.

When we call the cuisine traditional, we're referring to great-grandmother style. For example, begin with barley soup or air-dried beef on a wooden plate. The rye bread from Puschlav that accompanies most dishes is scented with anise and butter. Lake trout is poached and flavored with Riesling, and vegetarian meals are also prepared. *Bizochels sursilvans* are country-style flour dumplings with bacon and potato pieces, onions, cheese, and melted butter. Dessert may be walnut ice cream with damsons.

Reichsgasse 11. ✆ **081/258-57-57.** Reservations recommended. Main courses 19F–38F; fixed-price lunch 19F–75F, dinner 24F–80F. AE, MC, V. Daily 11:30am–1:30pm and 6–9:30pm.

Zunfthaus Rebleüten ★★ FRENCH/ITALIAN/SWISS Originally built as a guildhall in the 1400s, this is one of the most enduring, charming, and historic restaurants in Chur. Within a trio of rooms that date from 1483, amid 200-year-old tables and chairs, an antique clock, fireplaces, and ceiling frescoes that evoke alpine Switzerland of long ago, you can benefit from the skill and hard work of the Law family, a Scottish and Swiss managerial team that seems to handle all guests, and all venues, with heroic style. Consider the filets of sole with wild rice; tomato mousse with shrimp; a mixed platter of air-dried beef with mountain sausages; filets of flounder in a potato crust, or roasted breast of goose in a cabbage-and-kirsch sauce. A particularly appealing appetizer is the stuffed trout in a saffron sauce. During clement weather the establishment offers two separate outdoor terraces, each with views out over the town's historic core.

Pfisterplatz. ✆ **081/255-11-44.** Reservations recommended. Main courses 21F–44F. AE, DC, MC, V. Mon-Sat 7:30am–midnight; Sun 7:30am–6pm.

Inexpensive

The Weinstube in the Hotel Drei Könige SWISS Cozy and evocative, this popular dining room, set on the first floor of the previously recommended hotel, is covered with worn paneling, whose nicks and scratches only add to the character of the room. Don't expect haute cuisine here. Instead you get soul-satisfying mountain-style food prepared with honest ingredients handled in an efficient and straightforward manner. Meals are served amid hunting trophies, collections of medals, and old photographs.

The Weinstube welcomes some of Chur's most prominent citizens. Sometimes the chef prepares a double entrecôte *marchand de vin* or a chateaubriand Henri-IV. You can also order more standard fare, such as *pot-au-feu* (meat stew) and polenta with cheese.

Reichsgasse 18. ✆ **081/354-90-90.** Main courses 19F–28F. AE, DC, MC, V. Daily 10am–2pm and 5–10pm (last order).

CHUR AFTER DARK

The hot spot in town is **Giger Bar,** Comercialstrasse 23 (✆ **081/253-75-06**). The Oscar-winning H. R. Giger, a native of Chur and set designer on the movie *Alien,* was responsible for creating this 1980 bar and disco with its starship *Enterprise* aura.

---

2 AROSA ★★★

30km (19 miles) E of Chur

Arosa, one of the highest of the alpine resorts (1,800m/5,904 ft. above sea level), lies in a sheltered basin above the Schanfigg Valley. The most popular resort in the Grisons after Davos and St. Moritz, it basically consists of one main street (Poststrasse) lined with hotels and shops. Though parts of the village date from the 14th century, the resort has a modern and contemporary look. If St. Moritz is too ultrachic for you, Arosa may be your answer. Both visitors and the hotels that house them tend to be low-key and family-oriented, often favoring ski jackets over dinner jackets. Arosa lures the family trade through such attractions as kindergartens for children.

ESSENTIALS

GETTING THERE   Trains connect Chur and Arosa at the rate of one per hour during the day (trip time: 1 hr.). Trains from Zurich take 3 hours to reach Arosa. Call ✆ **0900/ 300-300** for **rail information** and schedules. Zurich is the nearest airport to Arosa.

If you're **driving** the 31km (19-mile) drive from Chur in good weather, allow at least an hour, as the road is steep, with hairpin curves. Don't make the drive in icy weather. Instead, take the narrow-gauge railway, which has been in operation since World War I.

VISITOR INFORMATION   Poststrasse is the main traffic artery through the center of town; visitors can follow hotel and restaurant directional signs. The **tourist office** is on Poststrasse (✆ **081/378-70-20;** www.arosa.ch), and is open Monday to Friday 8am to noon and 1:30 to 6pm, Saturday 9am to 1pm and 2 to 6pm, and Sunday 9am to noon.

GETTING AROUND   Every night in Arosa, between midnight and 6am, most cars are forbidden from moving within the resort's center, with the exception of taxis and Night Express buses (see below), which make scheduled runs through the town center, stopping at the parking areas that flank the periphery of the resort. The most consistent of the night buses operates only in wintertime. Known as the **"Night Express"** (call the tourist office for information), it's a minivan service that runs continually from 8pm to 2am between December and April, charging 8F per person per ride anywhere along its trajectory. The vehicles are marked NIGHT EXPRESS and can be stopped for boarding or getting off anywhere along the way.

FUN IN THE GREAT OUTDOORS

Skiing is the big attraction in Arosa, but summer activities and other winter sports, such as tobogganing and horse-drawn sleigh rides on the Arlenwald road, are also popular. Tennis, squash, bowling, and golf can all be played year-round at indoor facilities. Walks can be taken over 60km (37 miles) of easy and varied trails kept open in the winter. In addition, guided walks are conducted from June to October, both in the morning and in the afternoon. The tourist office (see above) will supply details and trail maps. Visits are possible to a chapel from the 1400s, a cheese maker, and a local museum.

Arosa draws an international crowd to its ski slopes, offering 64km (40 miles) of the best ski runs in the Grisons. It also has the Swiss Ski School, which, with 100 instructors, is one of the best ski schools in Switzerland.

Skiing is popular in the Obersee area at the eastern edge of the resort, whose focal point—reached by cable car—is the **Weisshorn** ★★ (2,611m/8,564 ft.). During the day, cable cars leave for the Weisshorn at the rate of one every 20 minutes. You first make the ascent to the middle station, Larn Mittle, at 1,992m (6,534 ft.), from which there are panoramas of Arosa. From the top station is one of the grandest views in eastern Switzerland, taking in a vast panorama of the Grison Alps. Even Chur can be viewed to the northwest, at the foothills of the Calanda mountain peak.

To the west, skiers take the Hörnli gondola, reaching Hörnligrat (2,454m/8,049 ft.) in about 16 minutes. Drag lifts at Hörnligrat fan out, taking skiers to the top of several different ski slopes.

The **Swiss Ski and Snowboard School** (© 081/378-75-00; www.sssk.ch) provides skiing lessons for both adults and children, and private ski instruction is available from the **Grison Association of Private Ski Instructors Arosa** (© 081/377-14-07).

Intermediate, advanced, and professional skiers come to Arosa because of its proximity to the slopes on either side of the valley formed by the Weisshorn and the Hörnli mountains. Access to the 76km (47 miles) of marked downhill runs on either side of the valley is made possible by at least 16 cable cars, some chairlifts, and a network of buses that make frequent runs up and down the valley floor. A ski pass that provides access to all of this costs 113F for 2 days, 240F for 5 days, and 295F for 7 days. The cost for children is 38F for 2 days, 80F for 5 days, and 98F for 7 days. Other passes that allow access to the ski slopes as far away as Davos, Klosters, Flims, and Lax are available, as well as some of the slopes in the Engadine, but only in increments of 90 days at a time.

Arosa offers some of the best horseback riding in eastern Switzerland. Visit the stables at **Fuhrhalterei,** Wierhof (© 081/377-41-96), which are open throughout the year. The Ritsch family usually has a dozen or so horses on hand, each willing to carry you across scenic local trails for around 32F per hour. You must call them at least a day in advance to make arrangements. The stables lie just outside the center adjacent to a local campground.

SHOPPING

The best way to get an overview of the diversity of Arosa's shops is to stroll up and down its main street, Poststrasse. If you're looking for equipment or clothing that will keep you competitive in this sports-conscious town, head for **Sprecher Sports,** Poststrasse (© 081/377-12-06); **Carmenna Sport,** Poststrasse (© 081/377-12-05); or **Schatz Sport,** Poststrasse (© 081/377-18-14), near the Hotel Kulm. If it's Grisons souvenirs you're looking for, head for **Vital,** Poststrasse (© 081/377-12-77). The best bet for a winning mixture of books (mostly in German, but with some in English and French) and Grisons-inspired souvenirs and gift items is **Banker,** Oberseeplatz (© 081/377-16-90). Other than that, your best bet is to simply wander along either side of the street.

WHERE TO STAY

Most of Arosa's hotels are modern and expensive. In the peak winter season, reservations are imperative. Most hotels in Arosa demand a minimum stay of 7 to 10 days over the Christmas holidays. In the summer, it's much easier to find accommodations. Some hotels are on a street plan; others are not. Those that aren't are clearly signposted from the center of town.

Very Expensive

Arosa Kulm Hotel ★★★ (Kids) This government-rated five-star hotel, built in the 1970s on the site of a simple guesthouse from 1882, is one of the two leading hotels here, surpassed only by the Tschuggen Grand Hotel (see below). Surrounded by rushing streams and close to the departure point of one of the cable cars rising into the surrounding mountains, the hotel is large, glamorous, and contemporary, with well-insulated, spacious, and exceedingly comfortable bedrooms plus deluxe bathrooms. The decor combines warm tones with pine-wood paneling. Almost everyone stays here on half board (which is, for the most part, required). At Christmastime prices go even higher than those mentioned below.

CH-7050 Arosa. ✆ **081/378-88-88.** Fax 081/378-88-89. www.arosakulm.ch. 137 units. Winter 490F– 1,060F double, from 940F suite for 2; off season 430F–520F double, from 680F suite for 2. Rates include half board. Parking 20F extra per night. AE, DC, MC, V. Closed mid-Apr to mid-June and mid-Sept to Dec. **Amenities:** 4 restaurants; 3 bars; babysitting; children's center; exercise room; indoor heated pool; room service; spa. *In room:* TV, hair dryer, minibar, Wi-Fi (free).

BelArosa ★ (**Kids**) This hotel is a pioneer in the trend away from big government-rated five-star hotels. It's an informal, family-style suite inn. The service is highly attentive, the accommodations are of good quality, and there's plenty of atmosphere here as well. Each suite is spacious, containing a generous living room with a tile stove—kitchenettes in some. Most of the accommodations also open onto a balcony with a view.

Prätschilstrasse, CH-7050 Arosa. ✆ **081/378-89-99.** Fax 081/378-89-89. www.belarosa.ch. 22 units. Winter 400F–680F suite; summer 240F–370F suite. Rates include buffet breakfast. AE, DC, MC, V. **Amenities:** Bar; babysitting; exercise room; Jacuzzi; sauna. *In room:* TV, fridge, kitchenette (in some), Wi-Fi (45F per 24 hr.).

Tschuggen Grand Hotel ★★★ (**Kids**) With its potted palms, distressed tortoiseshell wallpaper, and brass-framed mirrors, this modern high-rise could be in the pages of *Architectural Digest.* It's one of the most glamorous hotels in the Swiss Alps. The hotel looks down over Arosa from a hillside position that emphasizes its modern, rectangular design. No attempts were made to duplicate traditional chalet architecture, and the interior is richly outfitted with some of the most opulent accessories in Arosa. The spacious rooms are handsomely decorated and beautifully kept. Each week there are two *soirées élégantes,* for which evening dress is compulsory. The hotel opens every year around the first of December, with Arosa's traditional ski weeks, and continues until early April.

Sonnenbergstrasse, CH-7050 Arosa. ✆ **081/378-99-99.** Fax 081/378-99-90. www.tschuggen.ch. 129 units. 395F–880F double; from 820F suite for 2. Rates include buffet breakfast. AE, DC, MC, V. Parking 30F. Half board 40F per person. Closed mid-Apr to mid-June. **Amenities:** 4 restaurants; bar; children's programs; exercise room; 2 heated pools (1 indoor); room service; spa. *In room:* TV/DVD, CD player, hair dryer, minibar, Wi-Fi (45F per 24 hr.).

Expensive

Golfhotel Hof Maran ★ Set high in an alpine meadow, about 1.6km (a mile) from the center of Arosa, this impressive-looking wood-sided mountain chalet is rustically decorated with beamed ceilings, lots of pine-wood paneling, carpeting in autumnal colors, and comfortable armchairs. Many of the handsomely furnished midsize bedrooms have balconies for year-round tanning. Accommodations come in varied styles although the overall effect is exceedingly comfortable alpine traditional.

In Maran, Nord CH-7050 Arosa. ✆ **081/378-51-51.** Fax 081/378-51-00. www.hofmaran.ch. 53 units. Winter 390F–530F double; summer 220F–380F double. Rates include buffet breakfast. AE, DC, MC, V. Closed mid-Apr to mid-June and mid-Sept to mid-Dec. **Amenities:** 2 restaurants; bar; babysitting; exercise room; room service; sauna; Wi-Fi (free, in lobby). *In room:* TV, hair dryer, minibar.

Waldhotel-National Hotel ★★★ This sylvan retreat, although not as elegant as the Tschuggen Grand or the Arosa Kulm, is the most tranquil and isolated retreat at the resort. Set in a forest, this generously proportioned building was designed with symmetrical wings extending from a central core. Originally the Waldhotel was a sanatorium and later became a military hospital, and it still promotes its role as a center for "Fitness and Wellness." In the public rooms, accessories include apricot-colored stencils decorating the arched ceilings, a beautifully carved and embellished booth resembling a church pulpit, and decorative ovens sheathed in ceramic tiles. The midsize to spacious bedrooms

are comfortably and attractively furnished, with price level determined by the view.
Rooms facing south open onto a view of Arosa, and those looking north open onto a vast
woodland.

CH-7050 Arosa. ✆ **081/378-55-55.** Fax 081/378-55-99. www.waldhotel.ch. 93 units. Winter 390F–560F
double, 650F–990F suite for 2; summer 260F–320F double, 410F–540F suite for 2. Rates include half
board. AE, DC, MC, V. Closed mid-Apr to mid-June and mid-Sept to Dec. **Amenities:** Restaurant; exercise
room; indoor heated pool; room service; sauna. *In room:* TV, hair dryer, minibar, Wi-Fi (20F per 24 hr.).

Moderate

Hotel Cresta (Value) It's true the hotel is rather functional, but it's far from basic. The
bedrooms are bright and spacious, each well furnished with a tiled bathroom. The heated
indoor swimming pool comes as a pleasant surprise, as do the terrace and a garden. Rolf
and Romy Jäggi are your hosts with the most. The central location and the affordable
prices have made the hotel a favorite among families traveling together. All rooms are
twin bedded and handsomely maintained, and the best accommodations are those facing
south with their own private balconies. Some of the best accommodations have a sitting
area with a third bed for that additional family member.

Talstrasse 57, CH-7050 Arosa. ✆ **081/417-16-16.** Fax 081/417-16-85. www.cresta-hotels.ch. 40 units.
Winter 160F–240F per person double; summer 115F–135F per person double. Rates include buffet breakfast. AE, DC, MC, V. Free parking. **Amenities:** Restaurant; indoor heated pool; sauna. *In room:* TV, minibar.

Hotel Eden ★ (Kids) The restored Eden, in the center of Arosa, is surrounded by pine
trees, near the cable car and ski lift. It has five floors of weathered balconies and sun-
streaked planking over white walls. The hotel interior is brightly colored, whimsical, and
very comfortable. This is an aggressively marketed hotel with a flair for entertaining non-
Swiss clients with or without their children, and a sense of urbanized, big-city hipness.
The public rooms have marble floors, Oriental rugs, hanging lamps, and wall-to-wall
carpeting. Each of the spacious and comfortably furnished bedrooms has a private bathroom. The rooms with southern exposures have balconies. Some of the staff members
remain as rude as ever.

CH-7050 Arosa. ✆ **081/378-71-00.** Fax 081/378-71-01. www.edenarosa.ch. 80 units. 143F–258F per
person standard double; 178F–268F per person designer double. Rates include buffet breakfast. AE, DC,
MC, V. Parking 15F per night. Closed Apr–Dec. **Amenities:** 3 restaurants (including a sushi bar); bar;
babysitting; children's center; exercise room; Jacuzzi; room service; sauna. *In room:* TV, CD player, hair
dryer, minibar.

Hotel Streiff (Value) A government-rated three-star hotel, this establishment is set at
the edge of a forest, a short distance uphill and away from the center of Arosa. Although
there's ample use of varnished pine both inside and out, very little attempt was made to
duplicate the look or feel of a traditional chalet. Trails, cable cars, and chair and ski lifts
are all nearby. All of the small to midsize rooms have a well-organized private bathroom.
The bedrooms are sensibly but somewhat sparsely furnished with angular modern pieces,
a bit bland but comfortable and clean.

CH-7050 Arosa. ✆ **081/378-71-71.** Fax 081/378-71-78. www.streiff.ch. 41 units. Winter 168F–188F per
person double, 198F junior suite; summer 118F–130F per person double, 138F per person junior suite.
Rates include half board. AE, MC, V. Closed mid-Apr to July and Sept to mid-Dec. **Amenities:** Restaurant;
children's center; room service. *In room:* TV, hair dryer, Wi-Fi (free).

Inexpensive

Arve Central Originally built about a century ago and remodeled many times since
then, this hotel is set back from the main street but still very much in the center of the

action. It's located only a short walk from the train station. Some of the pleasant bed-rooms have balconies crafted from weathered wood and are attractively furnished with a collection of upholstered settees and wooden chalet chairs. The rooms in the rear, how-ever, have no balcony and don't open onto a view. Overall, it provides unpretentious comfort but not a lot of glamour.

Hubelstrasse, CH-7050 Arosa. ✆ **081/378-52-52.** Fax 081/378-52-50. www.arve-central.ch. 48 units. 111F–197F double; 144F–250F suite. Rates include half board. AE, DC, MC, V. Parking 7F–14F. Closed May. **Amenities:** Restaurant; exercise room; Jacuzzi; room service; sauna. *In room:* TV, hair dryer, minibar.

Hotel Alpina ★ (**Finds**)   Finally we've found a hotel in Arosa that looks like the type of old-fashioned chalet that's always associated with Switzerland. The balconies have hand-carved railings and trim. There's a terraced garden, and near the entrance a Swiss flag flaps in the mountain breeze. Our favorite rooms are up under the eaves. All of the accommodations have been renovated without losing any of their alpine charm, and each comes with a private bathroom. Many have exposed beams whose massive dimensions testify to the antique age of the building. The public rooms are filled with furniture painted in alpine designs, baroque clocks, and traditional chairs and couches.

CH-7050 Arosa. ✆ **081/377-16-58.** Fax 081/377-37-52. www.alpina-arosa.ch. 35 units. Winter 235F per person double; summer 100F–120F per person double. Rates include buffet breakfast. AE, DC, MC, V. Free parking outdoors, 12F indoors. Closed late Apr to mid-June and mid-Nov to Dec 6. **Amenities:** Bar. *In room:* TV.

Vetter (**Value**)   Centrally located a few steps from the railroad station and the Tschug-gen cable car, this boxy-looking, flat-roofed hotel offers glassed-in verandas, open porches, and wooden balconies. The interior is a mix of wrought iron and wood beams, enlivened by pithy bits of wisdom stenciled in German above a masonry fireplace. Every-thing is well maintained and comfortable. Furnishings are generally ragtag unless you get one of the time-mellowed antique rooms in wood paneling. Some units open onto views of woodlands; others face the busy street and town center.

CH-7050 Arosa. ✆ **081/378-80-00.** Fax 081/378-80-08. www.hotel-vetter.ch. 28 units. 120F–300F dou-ble. Rates include buffet breakfast. No credit cards. Parking 8F. Closed May–July. **Amenities:** Restaurant; bar; children's center; room service. *In room:* TV, minibar, Wi-Fi (free).

WHERE TO DINE

Most guests book into the Arosa resort hotels on a board basis. Nearly all the major restaurants are in hotels—hence the shortage of well-known independent dining spots. However, if you can break away from your hotel for a main meal, you may want to try one of the places below.

Cuculouche MEXICAN/SPANISH   Since it was established in the late 1990s, this Mexican/Latino restaurant has captured the hearts and imaginations of many of the young and fun-loving night owls of Arosa. The setting looks less Mexican than you might have expected, with fewer folkloric and rustic implements than, say, in a Tex-Mex empo-rium in San Antonio. Instead, you'll find walls painted in vivid tones of red, blue, and yellow, some Cuban and South America–derived paintings, and a bar that busily dis-penses tequila-based drinks whose party-colored hues might remind you of a sunset in the Yucatán. Menu items include tacos, tortillas, burritos, fajitas, an excellent version of spareribs, and chili. Overall, this place is a welcome antidote from too constant (and too dour) a dose of the Alps, especially during the midwinter chill.

Unterseestrasse. ✆ **081/377-55-05.** Reservations not necessary. Main courses 23F–39F. AE, DC, MC, V. Daily 6–10:30pm. Closed early Oct to Nov and mid-Apr to late June.

Kachelofa Stübli ★ SWISS   In the Waldhotel National, this restaurant is imbued
with a cozy ambience and has a kitchen that is rather passionate about its cuisine. At
lunch expect regular but tasty *Bündner* fare (mountain cookery). In the evening when the
lamps go on, the place becomes fancier, as does the always-changing menu based on the
best of seasonal ingredients. In winter fondue is a specialty, but year-round the repertoire
of dishes is completely natural and unfussy.

In the Waldhotel National, Tomelistrasse. © 081/378-55-55. www.waldhotel.ch. Reservations required.
Main courses 25F–42F. Fixed-price lunch 42F, dinner 135F. AE, DC, MC, V. Daily noon–2:30pm and
7–10pm. Closed mid-Apr to mid-June and mid-Sept to Dec.

Osteria Poltera ITALIAN   At this little rustic trattoria, with outside tables in summer, the best Italian cuisine is presented via a series of Mediterranean specialties that are
both tasty and affordable. These regional recipes from south of the border are presented
with a certain flair and are full of flavor, including, for example, a simple spaghetti al ragu
A homemade soup is always offered daily, but it's most often minestrone. You can also
order a series of freshly made salads. The chefs are also skilled at making various risottos,
and veal cutlets are prepared just right. There is no great pretense at originality here. The
place is popular because the products are fresh and skillfully handled, even if the dish is
only vine-ripened tomatoes, freshly harvested, with mozzarella and fresh basil leaves.

Poststrasse 794. © 081/377-21-15. www.arosa.com/osteria. Reservations recommended. Main courses
20F–43F. MC, V. Tues–Sun noon–2pm and 6–10pm.

AROSA AFTER DARK

Don't be confused by the presence of a building known as the Spielcasino, within the
Kursaal, on Poststrasse. Despite the implications of its name, there's no casino inside—it
functions as a somewhat desultory and low-key venue for some shops, restaurants, and
bars, having closed its gambling facilities several years ago. One of its highlights is its
disco, **Nuts** (© 081/377-39-40; www.disconuts.ch), a glossily modern haven for drinkers and dancers that's open every day in midsummer and midwinter between 9:30pm and
at least 3am. Entrance costs around 10F per person. Expect a crowd of seasonal visitors
ages 18 to 55, some energetic dancing, and a lot of voyeuristic ogling of the attractive
and fit bodies that venture onto the dance floor.

Another amusing after-dark choice is the **Kitchen Klub** of the Hotel Eden (© 081/
378-71-06), in the center of Arosa. This dance club is inside what functioned, at the turn
of the 20th century, as an actual kitchen. The old pots and pans are still there. This place
starts to fill up after dinner, and the DJ, sitting on top of old refrigerators, keeps the
music lively. Entrance costs 10F per person. It's open every night from 7:30pm, but only
in winter, between December and early April. The **Hotel Obersee,** Aussere Poststrasse
(© 081/377-12-16), has an attractive restaurant and a warm and convivial bar that from
time to time focuses on the music produced by live bands, but because their schedules
are erratic, it's best to phone before you head over there.

The Post Hotel, on Poststrasse, offers a handful of stubes, a pizzeria, and the **Crazy
Club** (© 081/377-13-13), where drinks flow and a cabaret act features attractive
women who strip in ways that tease and titillate but rarely get really down and dirty. The
club is in the same building as the Hotel Eden but under separate management. A sometime competitor, offering cabaret only during midwinter's high season, most nights
between 9pm and 3am, is an area known as "the Lounge" in the **Hotel Seehof** (© 081/
377-15-41), which is otherwise just a quiet and rather conventional bar. Entrance to
both sites is free.

Finally, you can drop in to the bar of the previously recommended restaurant, **Cucu-louche,** on Unterseestrasse (*©* **081/377-55-05**), for a sunset-colored cocktail whose ingredients include tequila, mango, strawberries, and more.

---

3 KLOSTERS ★★

13km (8 miles) N of Davos; 43km (27 miles) E of Chur; 29km (18 miles) E of Landquart

Life at this 1,200m (3,936-ft.) village in the Prattigau Valley has changed greatly from 1222, when a cloister was founded here. Many visitors prefer the intimacy and hospitality of Klosters to the carnival-like atmosphere of Davos. Unlike some of its neighbors (most notably St. Moritz), Klosters has few unattractive structures. All its buildings are constructed in the chalet style, giving the town a pleasing architectural harmony. Local residents claim that the sport of tobogganing originated here.

The main road to Davos runs through Klosters, and the two resorts have been known to compete aggressively for the tourist franc. Famous past visitors include Sir Arthur Conan Doyle and Robert Louis Stevenson. In the heyday of tax benefits, Klosters became known as "Hollywood on the Rocks." It still attracts an international crowd of movie people. It has also been given a royal seal of approval by the king and queen of Sweden, who visit regularly; but invariably generating more publicity were Prince Charles and the late Princess Diana, who for many years considered it one of their favorite Swiss resorts.

ESSENTIALS

GETTING THERE   There are frequent express trains between Zurich and the railway junction at Landquart. From Landquart, connecting trains depart about once an hour for Klosters on secondary rail lines. Call *©* **0900/300-300** for **rail information** and schedules.

If you're **driving** from Zurich, head south on the N3 expressway until you reach Landquart, at which point you cut southeast along Route 28.

VISITOR INFORMATION   Some roads in the center have street names, others outside the town don't, but establishments can easily be found by following directional signs. The **Klosters Tourist Board,** in the center of town at Alte Bahnhofstrasse 6 (*©* **081/410-20-20;** www.klosters.ch), is open in the winter Monday to Saturday 8:30am to noon and 4 to 6pm, and Sunday 9:30 to 11:30am and 3:30 to 6:30pm; and in the summer Monday to Friday 8:30am to noon and 2:30 to 6pm, and Saturday 8:30am to noon and 2:30 to 4pm.

GETTING AROUND   A city bus, known locally as either the "Ortsbus" or the "Klosters-Serneus" bus, makes frequent runs from Klosters-Dorf (the railroad station) to the base of the town's ski lifts, passing virtually every building in town along the way. Access to the bus is free for anyone in possession of a "guest card" (which proves your residency within a local hotel or guesthouse) or a ski pass. Otherwise, a ride on the bus costs from 1F to 3F, depending on how far within the town you ride.

SKIING & OTHER OUTDOOR FUN

Some of the finest downhill skiing in the world is here, with slopes for beginners as well as for the most advanced skiers. A kindergarten will look after the very young while you hit the slopes. The most populous part of Klosters, centered around the railway station, is called **Klosters-Platz (Klosters Square).** A smaller, less populated neighborhood—site of the resort's excellent ski school—lies about a mile to the north and at a slightly lower altitude. Set near the departure point for the Madrisa cable cars, it's known as **Klosters-Dorf (Klosters Village).**

The region contains two principal areas for skiing or hiking, the more popular of which is the **Gotschna-Parsenn.** To reach it, board the Gotschnagrat cableway in Klosters-Platz; the cable car carries more than 50 skiers up to the 2,263m (7,423-ft.) Gotschnagrat elevation. In the peak season, especially around February, expect lines. A series of cableways, a chairlift, and 18 ski lifts hook up with the Davos-Parsenn skiing areas, where your highest point will be Weissflühgipfel (2,778m/9,112 ft.). The Parsenn area is world-renowned and has some of the longest runs in Europe. It offers more than 14 different cable ways and ski lifts, plus more than 137km (85 miles) of well-kept runs.

The other major area, **Madrisa,** dates from the 1960s. To reach it, you go to Dorf via a bus, which leaves from Klosters-Platz every 10 to 30 minutes, depending on the season. From Dorf, the Klosters-Albeina gondola, a conveyance that's suitable for between one and four occupants at a time, will take you to a height of 1,897m (6,222 ft.). Then, by drag lift, known as the Schaffüggli, you rise to 2,355m (7,724 ft.).

Nontransferable R.E.G.A. (season) tickets are priced according to the number of days you plan to ski. For ski passes for the whole area, see "The Active Vacation Planner" in section 4 on Davos, later.

Horse sleighing, curling, and skating are popular sports for those who don't ski. Ask at the tourist office (see "Essentials," above) about the various venues for these activities.

In the summer Klosters is in the center of fine hiking grounds. The Madrisa and Gotschna-Parsenn cable cars will carry you to starting points on both sides of the valley for hikes on well-marked trails through woods and alpine meadows. In Klosters you can also enjoy tennis, squash, mountain biking, and swimming in a heated pool.

SHOPPING

Most of the shops are sports oriented. One of the best is **Grischa-Sport,** Bahnhofstrasse 12C (𝄞 **081/422-18-55**). Galleries abound but the one that seems the most genuinely devoted to various works of Graubünden artists is **Alexis Art Gallerie,** Talstrasse 1 (𝄞 **081/ 422-36-37**). For local paintings and Grisons-style souvenirs, visit **Déjà-Vue,** Bahnhofstrasse 7, in Klosters-Platz (𝄞 **081/422-56-54**).

WHERE TO STAY

Some hotels in Klosters are not on street plans, but directional signs point the way from the center.

Very Expensive

Hotel Pardenn ★★★   A posh and luxurious resort complex, often host to the rich and famous, this government-rated four-star deluxe hotel offers tradition, comfort, atmosphere, conservatism, and a feeling of graciousness—a winning combination for which you'll pay plenty. The terrace overlooks the well-landscaped lawn. Inside you'll find such architectural touches as a monumental, green-marble, circular staircase, masses of flowers, lots of wooden paneling, and oil paintings. Many of the small to midsize accommodations have pine paneling, while others contain flowery carpets and Louis XV–style armchairs. The rooms are well accessorized although the bathrooms are often small. Try for a room with a balcony facing south.

Monbielerstrasse 18, CH-7250 Klosters. ☎ **081/423-20-20.** Fax 081/423-20-21. www.pardenn.ch. 64 units. 295F–505F double; 445F–545F junior suite. Rates include half board. AE, DC, MC, V. Free parking outside, 15F in a garage. Closed mid-Mar to mid-Dec. **Amenities:** 3 restaurants; exercise room; indoor heated pool; room service; sauna. *In room:* TV, hair dryer, minibar, Wi-Fi (30F per 24 hr.).

Hotel Vereina ★★★   Ultrachic and elegant, this landmark hotel, launched in 1890, has made an amazing comeback in the 21st century, even knocking the Pardenn off its pedestal as the number-one choice in Klosters. The location is a short drive from the village center, the ice-skating rink, and a 9-hole golf course. Guests come here to ski in winter; in summer they can be found sunbathing in the large and well-maintained garden. The two-story hotel is small and offers the most personalized service at the resort. There are more suites than double rooms, each with bathrooms lined in Italian marble. Bedrooms are spacious, each supplied with elegant furnishings, plus your robe and pair of slippers laid out at night. The choice of restaurants guarantees a wide choice of food from the kitchen brigade—in fact, cuisine is one of the reasons for booking here. In winter you'll find us in the cozy bar around the piano. The on-site spa is state of the art.

Landstrasse 179, CH-7520 Klosters. ☎ **081/410-27-27.** Fax 081/410-27-28. www.vereinahotel.ch. 25 units. Winter 410F–620F double; 800F–1,440F suite; summer 280F–420F double, 450F–920F suite. Rates include buffet breakfast. AE, DC, MC, V. Free parking. **Amenities:** 3 restaurants; bar; babysitting; exercise room; indoor heated pool; room service; spa. *In room:* TV, minibar.

Expensive

Alpina ★   Near the Bahnhof (train station), the Alpina is not the most glamorous hotel at the resort, but in many ways it's the most dependable and reliable, with solid comfort, good rooms, and some of the best local cooking in Klosters. Rated four-star superior by the government, it lies close to the cable car taking you to the ski slopes. The bedrooms are midsize and furnished with rustic yet modern furniture; most rooms open onto a balcony with a view. Some of the most recently renovated bedrooms have Samina beds, an orthopedic sleeping system. There is also an array of facilities such as a sauna, steam bath, solarium, and beauty center.

Bahnhofstrasse, CH-7250 Klosters. ☎ **081/410-24-24.** Fax 081/410-24-25. www.alpina-klosters.ch. 36 units. Winter 280F–428F double; summer 240F–316F double. Rates include buffet breakfast. AE, MC, V. Parking 10F. Closed mid-Oct to mid-Nov. **Amenities:** Restaurant; bar; health center and spa; pool (indoor); room service. *In room:* TV, hair dryer, minibar.

Hotel Bad Serneus (**Value**)   This well-managed and cozy government-rated three-star hotel is one of the most visible buildings in Klosters' suburb of Bad Serneus, 6km (3½ miles) north (and downhill) from Klosters. Consequently—despite the fact that the rooms are cozy, well maintained, and comfortable—prices are somewhat lower than in the heart of Klosters. When snowfalls are deep, clients can ski here from Klosters; they'll have to take a short bus ride, with their equipment, for access to the resort's ski lifts. Older (it originated as a private farmhouse more than 200 years ago, but with many subsequent enlargements) and solidly built of heavy slabs of wood painted yellow with black shutters, the hotel was enlarged and upgraded in 1987 and contains public rooms with wooden beams, regional-style stenciling, and blazing fireplaces. In summer guests can stroll in nearby flower-filled meadows.

Bad Serneus, CH-7250 Klosters. ☎ **081/422-14-44.** Fax 081/422-22-51. www.badserneus.ch. 52 units. Winter 330F–370F double; summer 220F–330F double. Rates include half board. AE, MC, V. Closed mid-Mar to mid-May and mid-Oct to Dec. **Amenities:** Restaurant; indoor heated pool; spa. *In room:* TV, hair dryer.

Chesa Grischuna ★★★ This historic *landgasthof* (country inn) in the center of Klosters is the most celebrated of its kind in the whole resort area. Set behind a lavishly decorated facade and rebuilt in 1938 on the foundation of a farmhouse and guesthouse from the 1860s, this six-story hotel has hosted some of the most illustrious personalities of Europe. Since this hotel is on the see-and-be-seen circuit, it can command, and get, a lot of francs. The small to midsize rooms are for the most part paneled in local pine and fir, and are both elegant and cozy. The overflow from the main house is lodged in a comfortable annex nearby where the rooms are more spacious. The hotel is famous for its chic restaurant.

Bahnhofstrasse 12, CH-7250 Klosters. © **081/422-22-22.** Fax 081/422-22-25. www.chesagrischuna.ch. 25 units. Winter 329F–489F double; summer 229F–290F double. Rates include buffet breakfast. Half board 45F per person. AE, DC, MC, V. Parking 15F. Closed Easter to early July and mid-Oct to mid-Dec. **Amenities:** Restaurant; bar; babysitting; room service. *In room:* TV, hair dryer, Wi-Fi (free).

Silvretta Park Hotel ★ Opened in 1990 as a reconstruction of a well-respected hotel that had been in business since the 1870s, this government-rated four-star hotel lies opposite Silvretta Park with its cross-country ski runs and ice rink for skating, hockey, and curling. It's within walking distance of the Gotschna lift connecting the Parsenn skiing area with Klosters. Designed in a stylishly updated evolution and enlargement of a Swiss chalet, with lots of varnished pine and sophisticated styling, it offers comfortably modern and midsize rooms in a countrified style, each containing an elegant bathroom. Facilities include a balcony or terrace.

Landstrasse 190, CH-7250 Klosters. © **081/423-34-35.** Fax 081/423-34-50. www.silvretta.ch. 101 units. Winter 125F–355F per person double, 205F–445F per person suite for 2; summer 110F–185F per person double, 185F–210F per person suite for 2. Rates include half board. AE, DC, MC, V. Free parking outdoors, 7.50F in garage. Closed Easter to early July and mid-Oct to mid-Dec. **Amenities:** 3 restaurants; bar; babysitting; health club and spa; indoor heated pool; room service. *In room:* TV, hair dryer, minibar, Wi-Fi (free).

Moderate

Hotel-Pension Büel Built in stages between 1967 and 1986, this is a simple and completely unpretentious government-rated three-star hotel with stucco walls, brown trim, and balconies. Inside, it's clean, well scrubbed, and rustic, with blazing midwinter fireplaces and, in most cases, flagstone floors and knotty-pine ceilings. Rooms are small and basic, yet cozily comfortable with tasteful furniture and tidy maintenance.

Büel-Weg 1, CH-7252 Klosters-Dorf. © **081/422-26-69.** Fax 081/422-49-41. www.hotelbuel.ch. 18 units. Winter 224F–254F double; summer 175F double. Rates include half board. AE, MC, V. Parking 4F–8F. Closed May and Nov. **Amenities:** Restaurant. *In room:* TV.

Rustico Hotel ★ (**Value**) If you have a dream of a small inn in the mountains, make it this aptly named retreat. It's small but choice. Bedrooms are stylishly furnished with mirrors, flowers, artwork, and tasteful accessories. The Thony family run the hotel, and we consider them the most hospitable in the area (the patriarch, Al, is quite wonderful). He's outfitted his hotel in a rather lavish regional style, inspired by the Prattinger Tal (the valley in which Klosters lies). The reception is one floor above street level. Even though categorized by the government as three stars, the four-story building is quite luxurious. For dining, see recommendations below. On winter nights the lounge area, with its fireplace, is a gathering point, but in summer a terrace, dominated by a Buddha statue, is the draw.

Landstrasse 194, CH-7250 Klosters-Platz. © **081/410-22-88.** Fax 081/410-22-80. www.rusticohotel.com. 259F–385F double. AE, MC, V. Closed mid-Apr to mid-June. **Amenities:** Restaurant; bar; sauna. *In room:* TV, hair dryer, minibar, Wi-Fi (free).

Bündnerstube ★ SWISS   At this restaurant, in the previously recommended Hotel Alpina, the chef creates original cuisine, happily pulling off culinary surprises along the way. One of the special features is an Amuse Bouche Menu, consisting of 6, 8, or 10 different small courses, each one special. We recommend your whole table order this, but you can choose from regular set menus as well. For starters, launch yourself with a crème brûlée of gooseliver, glazed quail breast, and a clear quail soup, or else red tuna in pepper crust with South African scampi. For a main course, opt for the saltimbocca of angler fish or the grilled filet of veal with artichokes and fennel.

In the Hotel Alpina, Bahnhofstrasse 1. ☏ **081/410-24-25.** www.alpina-klosters.ch. Main courses 56F–68F; fixed-price menus 79F for 3 courses, 89F for 4 courses, 102F for 5 courses; Amuse Bouche Menus 65F for 6 courses, 75F for 8 courses, 85F for 10 courses. AE, DC, MC, V. Daily 6:30–9pm. Closed mid-Apr to mid-June and mid-Oct to mid-Nov.

Chesa Grischuna ★★★ INTERNATIONAL   This restaurant is so popular that celebrities often book tables a year in advance. The restaurant has attractively decorated alpine walls and a scattering of unusual portraits. Part of the reason for its persistent popularity is the warm welcome from the Guler family, and, of course, the food. Specialties prepared with the freshest and best of ingredients include a crepe *suédoise* (Swedish) stuffed with shrimp, chicken livers in puff pastry on a bed of leeks, grilled salmon with white butter and tomato sauce, and rack of lamb. In the summer you can eat outside.

Bahnhofstrasse 12. ☏ **081/422-22-22.** www.chesagrischuna.ch. Reservations required in winter. Main courses 25F–49F. AE, DC, MC, V. Winter daily 7am–midnight; off season daily 11:30am–2pm and 6:30–10pm. Closed Easter to early July and mid-Oct to mid-Dec.

Prättinger Huschi SWISS   Built in 1779, this is a local landmark of alpine charm, and it's the number-one choice for those seeking conviviality and mountain nostalgia—very charming, very down-home (that is, if you live in the Alps). Attached to the previously recommended Rustico Hotel (see above), it specializes in four kinds of fondues, and is *tres populaire* with winter skiers. In fact, it is open only in winter.

In the Rustico Hotel. Landstrasse 194. ☏ **081/410-22-88.** Reservations required. Fondues 12F–30F per person. AE, MC, V. Dec to early Apr daily 6–11pm. Closed mid-Apr to mid-June.

The Rustico Hotel Restaurant ★ SWISS/ASIAN   On-site at this previously recommended hotel, is this cozy restaurant, surprisingly superior for such a small mountain inn. The international menus contain many Asia-inspired specialties but also don't neglect Swiss dishes. In winter fondue and raclette are specialties. The wine cellar contains 80 of the top wines of the Grisons, plus vintages from other countries.

In the Rustico Hotel, Landstrasse 194. ☏ **081/410-22-88.** www.rusticohotel.ch. Reservations recommended. Main courses 40F–80F. Daily noon–2pm and 6–11pm. AE, MC, V. Closed mid-Apr to mid-June.

Walserstube ★★★ SWISS   The Walserstube's Beat Bolliger entertains everybody from celebrities such as Prince Andrew to regular folks, and has been doing so since 1981. The timeworn and alpine-seasoned building materials came in part from an old Grisons farmhouse, and the restaurant and cafe are paneled with this wood. Art objects and antiques are used discreetly throughout. The location is right on the main street of town, with often-heavy traffic in the peak summer and winter seasons. His cuisine is a winning combination of fresh ingredients and the best culinary skills. As you sit under the restaurant's massive wood beams and alpine carvings, you might begin with a duckling foie gras or a yogurt mousse with seasonal fruit. In season, asparagus is featured and

prepared in a variety of elegant ways. The fish is special here, including salmon with
onions, a fricassee of lobster, ravioli stuffed with crayfish, and trout grilled and served
with ratatouille. You can also order excellent meat dishes, among them Scottish lamb
seasoned with thyme.

Although acclaimed as the leading restaurant of Klosters, the Walserhof also offers 14
elegant accommodations. In winter, with breakfast included, charges range from 300F to
400F in a double. In summer doubles are 300F to 320F.

In the Walserhof Hotel, Landstrasse 141, CH-7250 Klosters-Platz. 𝄢 **081/410-29-29.** Fax 081/410-29-39.
www.walserhof.ch. Reservations required in peak season. Main courses 48F–69F; fixed-price menus
125F–175F. AE, DC, MC, V. Daily 11:30am–2pm and 6:30–10pm. Closed late Apr to mid-June and late Oct
to early Dec.

KLOSTERS AFTER DARK

One of the most consistently popular nightclubs in Klosters is the **Casa Antica,** Landstrasse 176 (𝄢 **081/422-16-21;** www.casaantica-klosters.ch). Set on the resort's main
street, directly across from the Alexis Gallery, it's a rustically (some say indestructibly)
decorated bar and disco whose clientele ranges from 18 to 65. Open nightly during both
midsummer and midwinter (with less frequent openings, depending on business, in
shoulder seasons), it charges a 10F to 17F per-person entrance fee, which includes the
first drink.

4 DAVOS ★★★

24km (15 miles) E of Chur; 11km (7 miles) S of Klosters

Along with St. Moritz and Zermatt, Davos has some of the finest sports facilities in the
world, as well as a diversified choice of après-ski entertainment. The variety of activities
makes it a favorite vacation spot for the chic and wealthy as well as for the hundreds of
ordinary folk just out to have a good time in the mountains.

The name Davos (first Tavauns, later Dafaas) entered written history in 1160 in a
document in the Episcopal archives of Chur. In 1289 a group of families from the Valais
established homes here. In 1649 the town bought its freedom from Austria.

The two sections, Davos-Platz and Davos-Dorf, were once separate entities, but in the
past 25 years or so, construction on the land between the two has served to join them,
making Davos today somewhat larger than St. Moritz.

The canton of Davos is the second largest in Switzerland. The high valley that contains
it is surrounded by forest-covered mountains that shelter it from rough winds. Thus the
area has a bracing climate, which has proven ideal for a summer-and-winter resort. Davos
first entered the world limelight as a health resort in the 19th century, when Dr. Alexander Spengler prescribed mountain air for his tuberculosis patients. He brought the first
summer visitors here in 1860 and the first winter ones 5 years later. There are still several
sanatoriums in the area.

Thomas Mann used Davos, at the foot of the Zauberberg (Magic Mountain), as the
setting for his famous novel *The Magic Mountain.* He visited the resort when his wife
went there briefly in 1913 for her health, seeing it as a symbol of the general malaise that
afflicted Europe on the eve of World War I. Robert Louis Stevenson wrote the last seven
chapters of *Treasure Island* here between 1881 and 1882, as he, too, tended his consump-
tive wife. Another writer, Sir Arthur Conan Doyle, engaged in a daring run on skis over

Kirchner: The Tormented Genius

Ernst Ludwig Kirchner was born in Aschaffenburg, Germany, in 1880. He studied architecture in Dresden and in 1905 was a cofounder of an expressionist group, Die Brücke, which was disbanded in 1913. The artist moved to Berlin in 1911, and it was there that his body of work reached its zenith. His highly personal paintings were noted for their sharp, vivid colors, their eroticism, and their psychological tension.

Physically and mentally scarred by his confrontation with Berlin and his experiences in military service, he tried several sanatoriums before deciding on Davos in 1917. First on the Stafelalp, later in the house In den Lärchen, and finally on the Wildboden, he produced a unique body of work. In Nazi Germany in 1936, his paintings were withdrawn from museums and labeled "degenerate art." As a result of the defamation of his character and his oeuvre, he fell into a deep depression that ended in suicide in 1938. His grave and that of his longtime companion, Erna, are located in the Davos forest cemetery.

For a look at this artist and his work, visit the **Davos Kirchner Museum,** Ernst Ludwig Kirchner Platz (© **081/413-22-02;** www.kirchnermuseum.ch). Entrance to the museum is 12F for adults, 10F for seniors, and 5F for children. From Christmas to Easter and mid-July to September, it's open Tuesday to Sunday 10am to 6pm; the rest of the year, Tuesday to Sunday 2 to 6pm.

the Furka Pass to Arosa. Unfortunately, the much-celebrated villa-hotel where all three writers stayed, Am Stein, contains only private apartments and cannot be visited.

The German painter Ernst Ludwig Kirchner (1880–1938) lived at Davos from 1917 until his death. He was a leading exponent of the expressionist movement.

In addition to being a well-known summer-and-winter vacation resort, Davos is also a health spa, a sports center, and an important venue for international meetings. Whether you're a hiker, mountain biker, downhill or cross-country skier, hang-glider, or ice-sports fan, Davos is an ideal place, and many nonathletes visit just for the relaxation. There's a wide choice of hotels, restaurants, bars, and discos, plus museums and concert and theater performances.

ESSENTIALS

GETTING THERE   Trains from Zurich usually require a transfer in the provincial railway junction of either Landquart or Filisur, where secondary rail lines continue on to Davos. Throughout the day, trains travel to Davos from both these towns every hour. The nearest airport is Zurich's Kloten, but the trip involves three different trains and two transfers. For information about **train schedules,** call © **0900/300-300.**

Bus lines connect Chur with Munich, stopping at Davos and several other mountain towns along the way, but they usually require transfers. Call the tourist office (see below) for more information.

If you're **driving,** proceed to Klosters (see section 3, earlier in this chapter), then continue south on Route 28 to Davos.

415-21-21; www.davos.ch), and is open Monday to Friday from 8:30am to 6:30pm, with telephone service until 7pm; on Saturday it's open from 9am to 5pm, and on Sunday from 10am to noon and from 3 to 5:30pm.

CITY LAYOUT The town's two sections, Davos-Platz (1,535m/5,035 ft.) and Davos-Dorf (1,538m/5,045 ft.), are linked by a boulevard flanked by boutiques, shops, hotels, and cafes. This thoroughfare is the famous Promenade, which takes the one-way traffic flow from Dorf to Platz (beware, however, if you're driving, as buses go in both directions). The lower artery, Talstrasse, runs along the railroad tracks, linking the train station in Davos-Platz with the station in Davos-Dorf.

Not all roads in Davos have street names, but there are signs pointing the way to all the hotels and restaurants. Public children's **playgrounds** are found in the Kurpark in Davos-Platz and opposite the lower terminal station of the Parsenn funicular at Davos-Dorf.

GETTING AROUND Silver-sided buses, many of them plastered with advertisements from seemingly every store in town, run along the major arteries from Davos-Dorf to Davos-Platz, making scheduled stops near all the main hotels and restaurants. In winter the buses depart daily every 10 minutes from 7am to 11:20pm; in summer departures are every 20 minutes. A single ride costs 2.90F, but rides are free for anyone who displays a guest card (they're available to anyone staying in one of Davos's hotels or guesthouses).

The postal bus leaves from the Davos-Platz railroad station. Organized excursions are available on the postal buses; for information, go to the nearest post office.

SEEING THE SIGHTS

Among the old buildings to be seen in Davos-Platz are the parish Church of St. John the Baptist, with a nave dating from 1280 to 1285. The church, now restored, was completed in 1481. It stands east of the train station along Talstrasse. A window in the choir is by Augusto Giacometti. The adjoining Rathaus (town hall) has been extensively restored. Its paneled Grosse Stube (Great Chamber) dates from 1564.

In Davos-Dorf you can visit the 14th-century **Church of St. Theodulus.** At Museumstrasse 1 is the **Altes Pfründhaus (Old Prebend House),** the town's only surviving example of a medieval burgher's domicile, now sheltering a minor local museum, the **Heimatmuseum** (© **081/**

> (Tips **A Free Ride**
>
> Any resident of a hotel or guesthouse in Davos showing proof of that occupancy and having paid the room tax can ride on town buses for free.

416-26-66; www.heimatmuseum-davos.ch), which traces the history of the resort town through a collection of objects and documents relating to its past. It's open January to April and June to October on Wednesday, Friday, and Sunday from 3 to 5pm, although special tours can be arranged in other months by contacting the museum or the tourist office. Guided tours cost 100F. Adult admission is 5F; children are charged 2F.

THE ACTIVE VACATION PLANNER

SKIING Recreational skiing began here in 1888, but Davos first appeared on the world sports stage in 1899, when a large ice rink was opened for the world figure-skating and the European speed-skating championship competitions. In the same year the Davos-Schatzalp funicular and the Schatzalp toboggan run were inaugurated. Now Davos is one of the best ski regions in the world.

On both sides of the valley, you're faced with five large ski areas, of which the most noted is the **Parsenn-Weissflüh.** Some experts say that this is the finest ski area in Europe. To reach it, take the Parsennbahn (railway) from Davos-Dorf to **Weissflühjoch** (2,622m/8,600 ft.), the gateway to the major ski area, with a huge number of runs in every category; there are a few downhill ski runs leading back to Davos that are suitable for only the most skilled skiers.

From Weissflühjoch, where there's a restaurant, take the cableway to **Weissflühgipfel** ★★ (2,778m/9,112 ft.). It takes about 30 minutes transit, via a trio of cable-car stages, from Davos-Dorf. From there you can reach the celebrated Küblis run to the north.

Davos shares its snow with nearby Klosters, where you can also ski, but cable cars and T-bar lift service may keep you happy with the ski opportunities nearer to Davos. Beginners are advised to stick to Rinerhorn or perhaps Pischa, where, if you're graded "intermediate" by your ski-school instructor, you may be directed to the somewhat more challenging slopes at Jakobshorn.

The ski facilities around Davos aren't the most widespread and far-flung in Switzerland, but they nonetheless incorporate enough challenges to keep intermediate and expert skiers engrossed. Most visitors opt for the **RegionPass,** which includes access to five different ski regions around Klosters and Davos. Together, they incorporate 322km (200 miles) of marked ski runs, and access to three funiculars, 10 cable cars, four gondolas, and 39 other mechanical conveyances designed to haul you and your equipment uphill. It also includes free rides on the railway cars from Küblis, a nearby hamlet surrounded by snowfields, back uphill to Davos. Adults pay 129F for a 2-day pass, 223F for a 4-day pass, and 300F for a 6-day pass. Children 6 to 12 are granted reductions of around 70% off those rates, and children 5 and under ride free.

OTHER SPORTS   Several winter sports besides skiing are offered here as well. For information on curling, contact the **Davos Curling Club/Davos-Village Curling Club,** Hintere Gasse 4B, Davos-Platz (② **081/420-27-00**). Two hours of curling, including instruction, cost 40F to 45F per person.

If you're interested in ice-skating on the **Natureisbahn,** Davos-Platz, the largest natural ice rink in Europe, phone the Davos-Dorf Tourist Office (see "Essentials," above), which manages the rink. Admission costs 6F for adults, 4F for children. Prices are 1F less for holders of the Guest Card, which is presented to all hotel guests. The rink is usually open from December to late February, depending on weather conditions. Davos-Platz also has a huge artificial ice rink, and both are open daily from 10am to 4pm, with additional openings every Thursday and Saturday from 8 to 10pm. In addition to this natural ice-skating rink midway between Davos-Platz and Davos-Dorf, there are at least two other ice-skating venues. For any information about ice-skating, contact the tourist office (see above) or www.davos-skating.ch.

Many Davos sports facilities can be used in both the winter and the summer. It has first-class tennis courts, sailing and windsurfing on Lake Davos, swimming, and horseback riding. There's an 18-hole golf course, **Golf Club Davis** (② **081/416-56-34;** www.golfdavos.ch), with a weekday greens fee of 87F that includes a golf cart; on weekends the fee goes up to 100F. If you're staying in accommodations at Davos, there's a 10F discount. Golf clubs can be rented for an additional 45F a day. There's also a large indoor ice rink if you want to keep your skills and your skates sharp during the summer months.

Davos has an impressive **Tennis & Squash Center,** on Clavadelerstrasse 2 in Davos-Platz (© **081/413-31-31;** www.indoor-sport.ch), which is open daily from 8am to 10pm. Prices depend on when you play, day or night. Court rental from 5:30 to 10:30pm is 28F for an indoor or outdoor court in summer or between 35F and 45F in winter.

Want to go swimming? Call **Hallenbad,** Promenade 99, next to the Kongress (© **081/413-64-63**), for information on either indoor swimming in winter or outdoor swimming in the summer. Adults pay 9F and children 6 to 15 are charged 5F, all of which includes changing-room facilities. With use of the mixed sauna included, adults pay 26F.

HIKING & WALKING   Well-marked and -maintained footpaths and mountain trails give access to meadows, pastures, woods, and mountains both close to and far away from Davos. A 451km (280-mile) network of pathways follows brooks, crosses alpine meadows, and leads to remote hamlets, allowing you to explore the side valleys of Sertig, Dischma, and Flüela. Davos mountain railways provide access to five different walking areas and to the most rewarding vantage points around Davos. The tourist office (see "Essentials," above) will supply more details.

(Finds) Hiking Without Luggage

Three Grisons vacation resorts—Arosa, Lenzerheide-Valbella, and Davos—have joined forces to create a "Hiking without Luggage" program. It's intended for hikers who enjoy walking from one resort to another but don't want to be bothered by luggage. Instead, your luggage is delivered to your next hotel for you, an arrangement made by various hotels. Either a 3-night/4-day or a 6-night/7-day program can be booked. The most popular departure point for this program is Davos, although, if the idea appeals to you, you can hike in the opposite direction from, say, Lenzerheide-Valbella into Davos.

There are two hiking routes between Arosa and Davos to choose from. The easier one is via the Sapün, and the more challenging and loftier route is via the Tritt. Both paths lead to the Strela Pass. You can either take the Schatzalp/Strela mountain railway to get to Davos or continue on foot. The 4-day program, including 3 nights' accommodations with half board included, is available for 405F to 570F per person. The 7-day program, including 6 nights' accommodations, with half-pension included, costs 625F to 945F per person. Children from 12 to 16 years old are eligible for a 30% discount, children from 6 to 11 get a 50% discount, and children 5 and under stay for free. Included in the price is breakfast, luggage transfer, one ascent or descent in a mountain railway for each day's hike, the relevant maps and route descriptions, and box lunches for most of the days you'll be hiking. The program is available only during the warm-weather months.

For more information, call the **Davos Tourist Office** (© **081/415-21-21**).

Davos is not obsessed with Swiss folklore, but you'll find lots of emphasis on cutting-edge sports equipment and clothing. Check out **Ettinger Sport,** Promenade 153, Davos-Dorf (② **081/410-12-12**), or its less comprehensive counterpart at the opposite end of the resort, **Angerer Intersport,** Promenade 49, Davos-Platz (② **081/410-60-60**).

Souvenirs of your stay in the Grisons are most conveniently acquired at **Pfister Holzladen,** Promenade 121A, Davos-Dorf (② **081/416-40-60**). **Benetton** sells casual men's and women's clothes at Promenade 62, in Davos-Platz (② **081/413-49-50**). If you're looking for etchings, oil paintings, watercolors, or lithographs created by artists from the region, head for any of the oft-changing exhibitions at either of the resort's most noteworthy art galleries, **Galerie Iris-Wazzau,** Promenade 72, Davos-Platz (② **081/413-31-06**), or **Galerie Eule Art,** Promenade 41, Davos-Platz (② **081/413-15-00**).

WHERE TO STAY
In Davos-Platz
Very Expensive
Morosani Posthotel ★   Set at the gateway to the Promenade in Davos-Platz, this is a landmark that has been efficiently run for more than a century by the Morosani family. The hotel consists of three buildings connected by a rustically decorated underground tunnel. The cozy lobby has an open fireplace, and bedrooms are spacious. The hotel has a winter-only nightclub open Thursday to Saturday nights.

Promenade 42, CH-7270 Davos-Platz. ② **081/415-45-00.** Fax 081/415-45-01. www.posthotel-davos.ch. 90 units. Winter 430F–650F double, 590F–730F junior suite; summer 340F–390F double, 410F junior suite. Rates include half board. AE, DC, MC, V. Free parking outdoors, 15F in garage. Closed mid-Mar to mid-May and mid-Oct to Dec. Davos bus to stop 9. **Amenities:** Restaurant; bar; babysitting; concierge; indoor heated pool; room service; sauna. *In room:* TV, CD player, hair dryer, minibar, Wi-Fi.

Steigenberger Belvédère ★★★   This, the most famous and prestigious hotel in Davos, occupies a light-gray neoclassical building on the main road of Davos-Platz. Originally built around 1875, it was purchased in the 1980s by the Germany-based Steigenberger chain and lavishly upgraded to some of the highest standards in Switzerland. The carefully groomed interior has a series of intricately carved fireplaces, ornate ceilings, a well-polished bar, and both contemporary and Victorian armchairs. Guests have a choice of modern, Belle Epoque, or regionally decorated rooms, many with furniture crafted from a local wood called arvenholz. A few, however, are rather standard in decor. It's worth visiting the pool for the murals even if you don't swim: a Tahitian lagoon with flamingos and lifelike jungle plants that sway in the imaginary breeze and seem to grow right out of the pool.

Promenade 89, CH-4270 Davos-Platz. ② **800/223-5652** in the U.S. and Canada or 081/415-60-00. Fax 081/415-60-01. www.davos.steigenberger.ch. 131 units. Winter 480F–740F double, 685F–2,100F suite for 2; summer 330F–378F double, 415F–559F suite for 2. Rates include buffet breakfast. Half board 56F per person. AE, DC, MC, V. Indoor parking 25F, free outdoor parking. Closed mid-Apr to mid-June. **Amenities:** 3 restaurants; bar; babysitting; concierge; indoor heated pool; room service; sauna. *In room:* TV, hair dryer, minibar, Wi-Fi (30F per 24 hr.).

Expensive
Hotel Europe ★   This longtime favorite is near the tourist office and the Schatzalp-Strela funicular. Right in the heart of Davos-Platz, the hotel lies just a few steps from the lifts, a few yards from the ice rink, and only 5 minutes from the golf greens. It was built

in 1868, and is thus the oldest of the resort's big hotels. The present building is a flat- roofed, white stucco structure whose exterior detailing has been restored. The formal interior is decorated with Oriental rugs and hunting trophies. Rooms are not at all lavish, with laminated furniture, but they are well equipped with double glazing, tiled bathrooms, and twin beds. Try for a unit with a balcony facing south.

Promenade 63, CH-7270 Davos-Platz. © 081/415-41-41. Fax 081/415-41-11. www.europe-davos.ch. 64 units. Winter 326F–500F double; 832F–1,120F junior suite for 2; off season 230F–260F double, 600F junior suite for 2. Rates include buffet breakfast. AE, DC, MC, V. Indoor parking 15F, outdoor parking free. Davos bus to stop 10. **Amenities:** 2 restaurants; bar; babysitting; concierge; exercise room; indoor heated pool; room service; sauna; Wi-Fi (30F per 24 hr., in lobby). *In room:* TV, hair dryer, minibar.

Kongress Hotel Davos ★   Well-designed and efficient, this first-class hotel lies midway between Davos-Dorf and Davos-Platz, about .8km (½ mile) from each. From its premises, you'll enjoy a view of the Landwasser River and snowfields in winter or green Davos mountains in summer. The hotel, which opened in 1982, lies immediately adjacent to the Convention Center, and it's next to the indoor swimming pool complex. Virtually all the sports facilities of Davos are close by. In addition, a public bus stops in front of the hotel for frequent rides to the ski runs. The midsize bedrooms are smartly furnished.

Promenade 94, CH-7270 Davos-Platz. © 081/417-11-22. Fax 081/417-11-23. www.hotelkongress.ch. 80 units. Winter 370F–480F double; off season 300F–350F double. Rates include buffet breakfast. Half board 30F per person. AE, DC, MC, V. Free parking outdoors, 17F in garage. Closed mid-Apr to mid-May. Davos bus to stop 10. **Amenities:** Restaurant; bar; room service; sauna. *In room:* TV, hair dryer, minibar, Wi-Fi (30F per 24 hr.).

In Davos-Dorf
Very Expensive
Flüela Hotel ★   More than 150 years after its opening, this thick-walled, solidly built hotel is still managed by the Gredig family, who focus entirely on winter (not summer) lodgings for their guests. Its unadorned beige facade conceals an elegantly rustic and cozy interior with comfortable and well-furnished bedrooms, each fitted with cozy appointments and state-of-the-art plumbing. Most of the bedrooms are renovated, and substantial improvements have been made to the health club and exercise areas. Overall, it's a cozy, well-managed choice in Davos.

Bahnhofstrasse 5, CH-7260 Davos-Dorf. © 081/410-17-17. Fax 081/410-17-18. www.fluela.ch. 73 units. 470F–860F double; 710F–1,740F suite. Rates include half board. AE, DC, MC, V. Parking 15F. Closed late Apr to late Nov. **Amenities:** 2 restaurants; bar; babysitting; exercise room; Jacuzzi; indoor heated pool; room service; sauna. *In room:* TV, hair dryer, minibar, Wi-Fi (30F per 24 hr.).

Moderate
Hotel Dischma (**Value**   This is a well-recommended government-rated three-star hotel with modern amenities and a location in the heart of Davos-Dorf, near the Parsenn funicular; the Pischa bus stop is about a 5-minute walk away. The small to midsize bedrooms are renovated although still rustic; you don't check in here for style but for value. Nonetheless, there is much comfort, including well-maintained plumbing.

Promenade 128, CH-7260 Davos-Dorf. © 081/410-12-50. Fax 081/416-32-88. 27 units. Winter 270F–360F double; summer 216F–230F double. Rates include buffet breakfast. Supplement for half board 25F–35F extra per person. AE, DC, MC, V. Free parking. Bus to stop 5. **Amenities:** 2 restaurants; 2 bars; room service; sauna. *In room:* TV, hair dryer, minibar.

Hotel Bûnda   Modern and well maintained, and set within a short walk from the Davos-Dorf railway station and the lake, this hotel consists of two buildings connected via an underground passageway. Built in 1964 and 1995, they contain cozy, relatively spacious bedrooms, with those in the newer annex looking somewhat more contemporary than their old-fashioned counterparts in the other building. Each unit contains a private shower-only bathroom. Many of the rooms have rustic-looking beamed ceilings, and many open onto private balconies. During clement weather the in-house restaurant expands onto a wooden deck whose view stretches out over the other houses in the neighborhood.

Museumstrasse 4, CH-7260 Davos-Dorf. ✆ **081/417-18-19.** Fax 081/417-18-20. www.buenda.ch. 31 units. Winter 240F–360F double; summer 174F–236F double. Half board 30F per person. AE, DC, MC, V. Garage parking 14F. Closed mid-Apr to early June. **Amenities:** 2 restaurants (1 reserved for hotel residents); bar; exercise room; sauna. *In room:* TV, hair dryer, minibar.

Parsenn Sporthotel   In the heart of Davos-Dorf, across the road from the Parsennbahn, this is a large and substantial Grisons chalet whose facade is covered in intricate stencils. Built in 1907 and enlarged in 1972, it sits beside a large parking lot and near a cluster of gas stations, not far from the base of several ski lifts. The ceilings of the public rooms are beamed or vaulted, sheltering a mountain-rustic decor with few frills but with a sense of genuine old-fashioned charm. The midsize bedrooms are comfortable—some are newer than others—furnished in a pine-wood chalet style.

Promenade 152, CH-7260 Davos-Dorf. ✆ **081/416-32-32.** Fax 081/416-38-67. www.hotelparsenn.ch. 40 units. Winter 170F–260F double; 190F–300F junior suite for 2; summer 170F double, 190F junior suite. Rates include buffet breakfast. Half board available for an additional 25F per person per day. AE, MC, V. **Amenities:** Restaurant; bar. *In room:* TV, hair dryer.

WHERE TO DINE
Expensive

Bündnerstübli ★ SWISS   The walls and the ceiling of this cozy place are covered with local pine, giving it a rustic look. The menu, however, is a lot more sophisticated, and the venue is a lot more worldly, than its mountain veneer would have you believe. Within an undeniably cozy ambience that lies within a 5-minute walk downhill from the center of Davos-Dorf, you can enjoy such glamorous food as smoked carpaccio of venison with duck liver, South African shrimp in a vegetable-flavored vinaigrette, rack of veal stuffed with shrimp, and braised filets of turbot on a bed of truffled leeks.

Dischmastrasse 8, Davos-Dorf. ✆ **081/416-33-93.** Reservations required. Main courses 35F–60F. AE, DC, MC, V. Thurs–Tues 11:30am–2pm and 5–11pm. Closed Easter to late June and Nov.

Restaurant Pöstli ★ SWISS   In winter this elegant room usually offers live music from 5 to 5:30pm and from 8:30pm until closing time. In summer, live music begins at 6pm and lasts until closing. The restaurant has a bar as well as a more formal seating area. Your choice in tasty platters is extensive—a different fresh fish daily or something classic, such as *Tafelspitz* (boiled beef Viennese style). Other selections are veal liver with polenta, venison in a hunter's sauce, filet of U.S. beef with mushrooms, and rack of lamb with braised cabbage. Overall, it's a well-managed, cozy restaurant with lots of ambience and flavorful food.

In the Morosani Posthotel, Promenade 42 at Postplatz, Davos-Platz. ✆ **081/413-74-74.** Reservations required. Main courses 36F–55F; fixed-price menu 99F. AE, DC, MC, V. Daily 11:30am–2pm and 6–10pm. Closed mid-Mar to mid-May, mid-Oct to Dec, and Sun–Mon in summer.

Moderate

Bistro Gentiana SWISS   Housed in a gold-colored building opposite the Hotel Sch-weizerhof in the center of town, this restaurant is known for its 10 different types of fondue dishes, as well as for its unusual list of dishes prepared with snails. Unpretentious and bustling, and within a cozy alpine environment, the establishment serves ample portions of air-dried beef and ham, as well as inexpensive daily specials. Its selection of desserts includes local pears in cinnamon syrup, honey-flavored ice cream, and chocolate mousse. Wines are sold by the carafe. Don't overlook the somewhat more formal pair of upstairs dining rooms, whose focal point is a blue-toned painting by the German artist Ernst Ludwig Kirchner, a former resident of Davos.

Promenade 53, Davos-Platz. (C) **081/413-56-49.** www.gentiana.ch. Reservations required. Main courses 34F–45F; meat and cheese fondues 26F–47F. AE, DC, MC, V. Daily year-round 11am–11pm. Closed Wed in summer.

DAVOS AFTER DARK

Everybody's favorite late-night den, bar, and disco is the **Bar Rotliechtli,** which somewhat provocatively translates as "Red Light Bar." It's also known as Cava Grischi, near Postplatz, just off the main street of Davos-Platz ((C) **081/414-94-43;** www.rotliechtli.ch). Warm, cozy, cramped, and convivial, it offers a rustic-looking decor of varnished pine and masonry, free entrance, and a bar that caters to all ages and all types of personalities, provided that they're late-nighters looking for interaction with like-minded extroverts. It's open nightly from 8pm till around 3am. Beers cost from 8F each.

THE GRISONS

14

DAVOS

The Engadine

The Valley of the Inn (or En, as the locals call it in Romansh) stretches for 97km (60 miles), from the Maloja Plateau (1,786m/5,858 ft.) to Finstermünz. All of the villages here except Sils lie at a higher altitude than the plateau. The highest is St. Moritz, at 1,811m (5,940 ft.).

The Engadine is enclosed by great mountain ranges with meadows and forests on the steep hillsides. The villages are built of stone, originally as a protection against the fires that swept the narrow windy valleys. The whitewashed houses in the villages, known for their larders, often have sgraffito decorations (designs in plasterwork), with mottoes and heraldic devices. The population is of Rhaeto-Romanic heritage and is mostly Protestant.

From the Maloja Pass, the road runs northeast through the Upper Engadine, where the clear mountain skies and dry, light breezes make the area popular in both summer and winter. Since the 19th century, when the Upper Engadine became fashionable for its "air cure," it has developed into a winter-sports resort, highlighted by St. Moritz.

The two major attractions of the Lower Engadine, where the valley is narrower and more heavily forested, are the mineral springs of Scuol and the Swiss National Park, an 89km (55-mile) wildlife sanctuary.

St. Moritz is the major **rail** terminus for the valley. For information and schedules, call ✆ **0900/300-300.** From here you can make bus or rail links to other villages of the Engadine.

1 ESSENTIALS

EXPLORING THE REGION BY CAR

The Lower Engadine is reached from Davos over the Flüela Pass (2,345m/7,692 ft.) and the Ofen Pass (2,115m/6,937 ft.). Four major passes lead into the Upper Engadine: Maloja (1,786m/5,858 ft.), Julier (2,248m/7,373 ft.), Albula (2,275m/7,462 ft.), and Bernina (2,286m/7,498 ft.). The upper valley contains several lakes, including that of St. Moritz.

If you have time to drive only one of these passes, and weather conditions are right, make it the **Bernina Pass** ★★, a 2-hour, 55km (34-mile) drive between St. Moritz and Tirano in Italy. This pass is one of the most spectacular in Europe, and is most often blocked by snow from October to May. Since the pass is not cleared at night, it's best to start out in daytime.

Leaving St. Moritz, on the way toward Pontresina, you'll pass **Muottas Muragl,** from which you can take a funicular to an altitude of 2,414m (7,918 ft.), where you'll be rewarded with the most stunning view of the Upper Engadine Gap. The panorama also takes in a chain of lakes lying between St. Moritz and Maloja. From the top of the station, you can take some of the most dramatic mountain walks in eastern Switzerland, enjoying the alpine flora and fauna.

The road passes by Pontresina, a resort, and continues until the **Chünetta Belvedere** at 2,050m (6,724 ft.). You cannot drive all the way to the top of the belvedere; you'll have

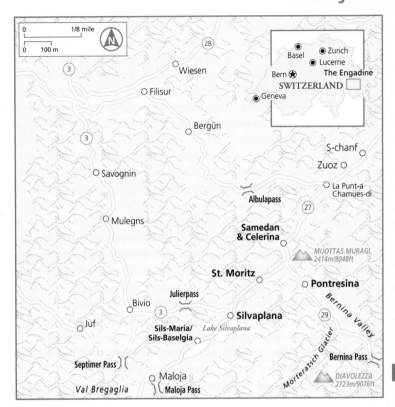

to go 1 hour on foot. At the belvedere, the spectacular peaks of the Bernina Massif, including Piz Bernina and Piz Morteratsch, lie before you.

As you continue along, you'll pass another sign, directing you to the **Diavolezza,** another spectacular belvedere at 2,723m (8,931 ft.) that includes a 15-minute journey by cable car. Diavolezza is the starting point of one of the most famous glacier runs in the world. See "Pontresina," section 4, later in this chapter, for more information.

After crossing the Bernina Pass, where there are clear views of the Piz Cambrena and its glacier, you come to **Alp Grüm** at 2,058m (6,750 ft.), overlooking the Palü Glacier and the Poschiavo Valley. Going through the resort of Poschiavo you arrive finally at **Tirano** on the downward slope, passing through tobacco fields and vineyards. At Tirano you will have arrived on Italian soil.

THE ENGADINE OUTDOORS

You don't come to this rugged part of Switzerland to stay in your hotel room all day, not with a wilderness out there to explore. After leaving the chic resorts such as St. Moritz, you enter wild, untamed scenery.

Great Express Trains

From Zurich, the **Glacier Express** climbs over the Alps from St. Moritz to Zermatt in the Valais. The **Engadine Express** also goes from Chur through the Swiss National Park into the Lower Engadine. The **Palm Express** from St. Moritz to Lugano is one of the great train rides in the area, going from the snowy alpine peaks and mountain lakes of the Upper Engadine to the subtropical atmosphere of the Lake District near Italy. The scenery along the way is some of the most panoramic in Switzerland. You have a choice of a 1- or 2-day itinerary, the latter involving a hotel night en route. For information and seasonal availability, call Rail Europe at ✆ **877/272-RAIL** (272-7245).

For hikers, the **Swiss National Park Service,** Schweizerischer National Park (✆ **081/ 856-12-82;** www.nationalpark.ch) maps out a group of panoramic half- or full-day adventures into the choicest and most scenic of its wilderness landholdings. Many of these take you along rugged and often steep mountain trails, so you should be in good shape. All major villages and resorts in the Engadine also offer signposted and well-maintained hiking trails and footpaths. Visit local or regional tourist offices to learn more.

For one of the **great walks** in the Engadine, you can take in vistas of four highland lakes at 1,771m (5,809 ft.) above sea level. Even at this high altitude the walk is like traversing the floor of a valley. The walk begins at Maloja and goes for 14km (8½ miles) to the resort of Silvaplana. Allow some 3 to 3½ hours for this alpine stroll. From Maloja, traverse the eastern or southern tier of Lej da Segl. The route is well marked leading you to Segl-Maria, one of the most charming old Romansh villages. Eventually you reach the resort of Silvaplana. As you walk along you'll be following in the footsteps of Nietzsche, who lived in this area and often took this walk "to think."

For serious **mountaineering,** the **Bergsteigerschule La Margna** at Pontresina has a mountaineering school with guided tours. One day of instruction for beginners costs 500F. Call ✆ **081/838-83-33** to arrange for an appointment and to get prices and listings of scheduled climbing trips.

White-water expeditions are possible on the River En, but only between June and September. A half-day's outing, where you'll shoot the rapids in a rubber-sided raft, is priced at 110F, but cost can vary depending on the options you select. A full day's excursion goes for 180F. For more information about this, contact **Swissraft Engadine** (✆ **081/ 911-52-50;** www.swissraft.ch), in Scuol, or any local tourist office within the Engadine.

It's also possible to go **horseback riding** in the Engadine. The best stables are in St. Moritz (see section 3, below).

The Engadine is known for its steep, river-eroded canyons, the sides of which rise vertiginously upward on either side. An outfit that can help direct you through some of the steepest of these is **St. Moritz Experience,** via Suot Chesas, CH-7512 Champfèr (✆ **081/833-77-14;** www.stmoritz-experience.ch). For 180F per day from 9am to 5pm, they'll include transportation, use of all equipment, and instruction on how to navigate up and down the edges of canyons and valleys whose microclimates are softer and gentler than those on the wind-swept upper regions nearby. The same outfit will take you on an 8-hour glacier-and-rock hike for around 120F per person.

3km (2 miles) NE of St. Moritz; 5km (3 miles) NW of Pontresina

These twin resorts are virtually at the doorstep of St. Moritz and are sometimes referred to as suburbs of St. Moritz. But that's a somewhat demeaning label, as Samedan and Celerina have individual characters.

Samedan, originally a Roman settlement, survived to become a principal village of the Upper Engadine. Over the years many well-known Swiss families have made their homes here. Seek out the Planta House and note its large roof and impressive library of Romansh works.

Celerina, a hamlet on the Inn River, has long been overshadowed by its more cele-brated neighbors. But for those in search of local color, Celerina (Schlarigna in Romansh) is an ideal choice as a winter or summer resort. Known for its charming Engadine houses, this little village on a sunny plain is sheltered from bitter winds.

ESSENTIALS

GETTING THERE Almost 20 trains depart from St. Moritz every day, stopping 4 minutes later in Celerina and 7 minutes later in Samedan. Trains also run from Chur to Samedan. For information, call ✆ **0900/300-300.**

Buses running from St. Moritz to Lugano are not scheduled to stop at Celerina and Samedan; usually, however, if you let the driver know that you'd like to get off at either point, he'll stop for you. Buses running between Pontresina and St. Moritz (there are two to five buses a day, depending on the season) stop regularly at Samedan.

If you're driving from St. Moritz, head northeast along Route 27.

VISITOR INFORMATION The **Celerina Tourist Office** (✆ **081/830-00-11**), in the center, is open Monday to Friday from 8:30am to noon and 2 to 6:30pm and Saturday from 10am to noon and 3 to 5pm. It is closed Saturday from October to December and mid-April to mid-June. In the center of Samedan, the **Samedan Tourist Office** (✆ **081/851-00-60**) is open Monday to Saturday 8am to noon and 2:30 to 6pm.

EXPLORING THE AREA

In Samedan

The village (1,548m/5,077 ft.) has its own ski lift and ice-skating rink, plus a ski school. In the summer it's ideal for mountain walks and for climbing. The tourist office will provide maps. Visitors can fish or play tennis and golf. When there's snow, it's possible to take a horse-drawn sleigh to St. Moritz in less than an hour, and all mountain trans-portation can be reached in a short time.

In Celerina

Celerina has an old Romanesque church, **St. John's (San Gian),** with a painted ceiling dating from 1478.

The Cresta run, a mecca for bobsledders, starts from St. Moritz and terminates near Celerina. The village also has ice rinks for curling and skating, a toboggan run, and a ski school. Winter packages for skiing, cross-country, and curling are offered, as well as sum-mer guided mountain-bike tours with a picnic included.

Several interesting **conducted tours** are offered in the summer through the tourist office. An experienced guide will take you on an explorative tour through the Swiss

National Park, or you can join a botanical excursion to see alpine flowers in bloom. Strenuous geological and mineralogical tours are also offered, and you can make an exciting journey from the Diavolezza over the glacier to Morteratsch. The latter tour is offered only in the spring and summer.

Celerina (1,702m/5,583 ft.) is known for its belvederes and panoramic views. One such view is of **Piz Nair,** at 3,251m (10,663 ft.). To reach it, you can take a cable car from St. Moritz, departing every 20 minutes daily from 8:30am to 5pm. You'll ride from St. Moritz to Corviglia. At Corviglia you board another cable car between Corviglia and Piz Nair. The round-trip passage for this ride is 71F for adults and 47F for children 5 to 15. The circular panorama takes in the Bernina summits. For information, call ✆ **081/839-80-15.**

You can also visit **Muottas Muragl** (2,412m/7,911 ft.). From the lower station at Punt Muragle, funicular departures are about every 30 minutes. The round-trip fare is 30F for adults and 20F for children 5 to 16. You'll have views of the Upper Engadine Gap, and in the distance you can see the peaks of the Bernina massif. You'll probably see ibex and marmots as you take mountain walks. For information, call ✆ **081/842-83-08.**

WHERE TO STAY
In Samedan
Donatz   This is a good, solid, reliable inn, known for its affordable rooms and fine mountain cooking. For more than 4 decades, the Donatz family has welcomed visitors from all over the world into their cozy abode. From the copious breakfast buffet served here to the relaxing Jacuzzi lounge under the open sky, this hotel offers much comfort. Bedrooms are traditionally furnished and well maintained. If you're not staying here, consider a meal in their La Padella restaurant, known for its traditional dishes, of which flambé platters are a specialty.

Plazzet 15, CH-7503 Samedan. ✆ **081/852-4677.** Fax 081/852-5451. www.hoteldonatz.ch. 25 units. Winter 190F–230F; summer 190F–200F. Rates include breakfast. MC, V. Parking 15F. **Amenities:** Restaurant; bar; room service. *In room:* TV, hair dryer, Wi-Fi (free).

Hotel Quadratscha ★   This hotel was established in 1975 on the site of an Engadine-style private home that was built in the 1870s. During the most recent renovation, the lobby was enlarged, the health and sports facilities were improved, and the in-house restaurant, U3 (see below), was rebuilt using antique paneling and architectural accessories. The bedrooms are outfitted in a cozy alpine style, each with comfortable furnishings and a mountain view.

Via Quadratscha, CH-7503 Samedan. ✆ **081/851-15-15.** Fax 081/851-15-16. www.quadratscha.ch. 26 units. Winter 220F–330F double, 310F–410F suite; summer 210F–280F double, 280F–360F suite. Rates include breakfast. Half board 39F–50F per person, depending on the season. AE, DC, MC, V. Outdoor parking free, indoor parking 10F. Closed mid-Apr to mid-June and mid-Oct to mid-Dec. **Amenities:** Restaurant; bar; Internet (free, in lobby); exercise room; pool (indoor); room service. *In room:* TV, hair dryer, minibar.

In Celerina
Cresta Palace Hotel ★★ (Kids)   Set within a 5-minute walk from the railway station and the center of Celerina, within a stately looking white-stucco building with green shutters and a pedigree dating to around 1910, this is the most extravagant, most opulent, and most prestigious hotel in town. It's also the highest rated, granted four stars by the local tourist authorities. Each of the bedrooms was radically upgraded and renovated

with contemporary styling and lots of varnished hardwood, plus they offer sweeping views over the mountains nearby. Most contain bright colors; rustic pine-wood furnishings; tiled, good-size bathrooms; and a sense of well-ordered coziness. Many clients here are repeat visitors, known to the staff and to each other.

Hauptstrasse, CH-7505 Celerina. ✆ **081/836-56-56.** Fax 081/836-56-57. www.crestapalace.ch. 98 units. Winter 444F–752F double, 1,480F–1,820F suite; summer 299F–495F double, 508F–741F suite. Rates include buffet breakfast. Half board 60F per person. AE, DC, MC, V. Parking 15F in winter, 10F in summer. Closed Easter to mid-June and mid-Oct to Dec. **Amenities:** 3 restaurants; bar; children's center; Internet (free, in lobby); health club and spa; pool (indoor); room service; 2 tennis courts (lit). *In room:* TV, hair dryer, minibar.

Hotel Misani ⟨**Value**⟩ This is a cost-conscious and solid hotel that's set behind an ocher-colored facade on the near perimeter of Celerina, a 4-minute walk from the center. Rated three-and-a-half stars by the local government, it was built before 1900 but was radically renovated and frequently renewed since. Originally established 120 years ago, it was enlarged with an annex in the 1970s, then rebuilt to include the annex behind a single, carefully orchestrated facade that incorporated its various elements and outbuildings into a coherent, ocher-fronted whole. Bedrooms are warm, cozy, and contemporary-looking. The hotel's restaurant, the Ustaria, is well recommended and well run.

Hauptstrasse, CH-7505 Celerina. ✆ **081/839-89-89.** Fax 081/831-89-90. www.hotelmisani.ch. 38 units. Summer 170F–310F double, from 360F suite; winter 170F–350F double, from 520F suite. Rates include buffet breakfast. AE, DC, MC, V. Parking 8F–10F outdoors, 10F–20F indoors. Closed Apr and mid-Oct to late Nov. **Amenities:** 2 restaurants; babysitting. *In room:* TV in some, no phone in some.

WHERE TO DINE

U3 ★ ITALIAN This restaurant's paneling and elaborate architectural detailing are remnants of a villa that originally stood on this site in the 1870s. Today a polite staff serves a wide array of well-prepared Italian dishes, most cooked in health-conscious ways with olive oil and an emphasis on fresh vegetables and Mediterranean flavors. You may opt for any of several freshly made pastas, salads, a "turban" of sole with shrimp, a platter containing three different filet mignons, several kinds of grilled fish and meat, and—in season—venison or quail with truffles. Cuisine is well conceived, flavorful, and well suited to the bracing climate.

In the Hotel Quadratscha, Samedan. ✆ **081/851-15-15.** Reservations recommended. Main courses 28F–50F. AE, DC, MC, V. Daily 7–10pm. Closed mid-Apr to mid-June and mid-Oct to mid-Dec.

---

3 ST. MORITZ ★★★

80km (50 miles) S of Davos; 74km (46 miles) SE of Chur; 202km (126 miles) SE of Zurich

St. Moritz is the ne plus ultra of winter glamour—a haven for German and Italian aristocracy and the jet-setters who come in February and March. Long a favorite of movie stars, it also attracts internationally prominent people in politics, the world of finance, and the arts. St. Moritz may well be the most fashionable resort in the world.

Not all its visitors, however, are prestigious. The author Peter Viertel wrote that St. Moritz attracts "the hangers-on of the rich . . . the jewel thieves, the professional backgammon players and general layabouts, as well as the high-class ladies of doubtful virtue (if such a thing still exists)."

The Glacier Express

The most famous of Switzerland's railway lines, the **Glacier Express** ★★★ connects the highest peaks and glaciers of the southeastern Alps with those of the southwestern Alps. When the train link opened in 1928, the danger of winter blizzards and snowdrifts required that many of the most isolated mountain bridges be dismantled every October and then reassembled the following May. As a result, in the winter trains were rerouted on a lengthy detour through Zurich and northern Switzerland. In 1982 a 13km (8-mile) tunnel was drilled beneath the Furka mountain, and today trains run uninterrupted across the mountains all year long. The route is one of the most spectacular in the world, with 91 viaducts and tunnels and 291 bridges along the way. There's one daily train that runs between the regions in the winter; in summer, with its longer hours of sunlight, there are two and, in rare cases, three trains per day.

The one-way trip from Zermatt to St. Moritz takes 7½ hours and costs 221F in first class and 133F in second class. En route, many travelers opt to disembark in the medieval trading city of Chur to spend the night. From Chur, convenient connections can be arranged to Davos and all points east, including many towns in the alpine regions of Austria.

Advance seat reservations are required for the comfortably upholstered coaches with restaurant cars. Note that the Swiss Pass covers the full fare on the Glacier Express, but because part of the route is administered by a different organization from the rest of the Swiss Rail network, holders of any travel pass in the Eurailpass family, including Youthpass and Flexipasses, are charged about half the total fare. For more information about fares, call ℂ **877/272-RAIL** (272-7245).

For more general information about the journey, contact any Switzerland Tourism, or the **Swiss Center,** 608 Fifth Ave., Ste. 202, New York, NY 10020 (ℂ **212/757-5944**).

On the southern side of the Alps in the Upper Engadine, at an altitude of 1,800m (5,904 ft.), St. Moritz (San Murezza in Romansh) was originally known for its mineral springs, which were discovered, probably by the Celts, some 3,000 years ago. From Roman times through the Middle Ages, visitors came here in the summer to experience the curative powers of the spring waters. The hamlet first appears in written history in an official document referring to the sale of the Upper Engadine by a count to the bishop of Chur in 1138. It was first referred to as a spring by the Swiss-born alchemist and physician known as Paracelsus.

Use of the spring waters was a summer pursuit. It was not until 1834 that the first winter guest stayed in the area. The earliest skiers appeared on the Upper Engadine scene in 1859 (the natives thought they were nutty), and in 1864 a pension owner, Johannes Badrutt, brought a group of English people to St. Moritz to spend the winter, starting what has grown into a flood of tourism.

ESSENTIALS

GETTING THERE   St. Moritz is linked by rail (through a complicated series of tunnels) to the rest of Switzerland via Chur, with other links to such non-Swiss population centers as Milan and Munich. Travel time by train from Chur is 2 hours. St. Moritz is also the endpoint of the world-famous Glacier Express, which links Zermatt, in the southwest, with St. Moritz, in the southeast. For **rail information** and schedules, call ✆ **0900/300-300.**

St. Moritz is linked by **bus** to Chur, Lugano, and Pontresina, each of which is easily reachable via bus connections from Munich. Call the tourist office (see below) for further information.

By **car** from Zurich, take N3 (later N13) to Chur and, once there, head southwest along Route 3.

VISITOR INFORMATION   The St. Moritz tourist office, via Maistra 12 (✆ **081/837-33-33;** www.stmoritz.ch), will answer many of the questions a visitor might have. It's open in midsummer and midwinter, Monday to Friday from 9am to 6:30pm, Saturday 9am to 6pm, and Sunday from 4 to 6pm; off-season hours are Monday to Friday from 9am to noon and 2 to 6pm, and Saturday from 9am to noon.

SEEING THE SIGHTS

Engadine Museum ★   This museum offers a glimpse of the history of St. Moritz and the Engadine. You'll learn about the sgraffito on Engadine buildings and local styles of architecture, and see a collection of Engadine antiques and regional furniture. The elegantly decorated stateroom shows how nobility in the area lived. Artifacts from the Bronze Age, when Druids lived in the land, are also on display, including the 3,000-year-old encasement of the spring of Mauritius. St. Moritz stands on a former "mystic place" of the Druids.

Via dal Bagn 39. ✆ **081/833-43-33.** Admission 5F adults, 2.50F children 6–16. June–Oct Mon–Fri 9:30am–noon and 2–5pm, Sun 10am–noon; Dec–Apr Sun–Fri 10am–noon, Mon–Fri 2–5pm. Bus: 1.

Segantini Museum   Housed here are works by the artist Giovanni Segantini (1858–99), who lived in the Engadine (Maloja) during the last years of his life. The artist is known for his technique termed divisionism; his most important work is a triptych called *Birth, Life, Death,* which is exhibited at the museum, among other notable pictures.

Via Somplaz 30. ✆ **081/833-44-54.** www.segantini-museum.ch. Admission 10F adults, 7F students, 3F children 6–16. Tues–Sun 10am–noon and 3–6pm. Closed mid-Oct to mid-Dec and mid-Apr to mid-May. Bus: 1.

THE ACTIVE VACATION PLANNER

The tourist office has complete details about the various activities in the area. Although skiing is the premier sport, other winter-sports activities, including curling, ice-skating, tobogganing, bobsledding, and an early form of ice hockey, have been enjoyed by winter visitors here since the latter half of the 19th century.

Skiing

The world's oldest ski school is at Moritz-Dorf, founded in 1927. A total of five ski complexes encircle St. Moritz, the nearest being Corviglia-Piz Nair, which has some challenging, 1.6km (1-mile) runs back to the base. There's an abundance of snow in winter on 402km (250 miles) of downhill ski runs, 161km (100 miles) of cross-country ski trails, and the Olympic ski-jumping hill.

THE ENGADINE

15

ST. MORITZ

Corvatsch, at 1,740m (5,707 ft.), is known for its bowl skiing. **Corviglia** has broad runs attracting fledgling and intermediate skiers and is the base for skiing **Piz Nair ★★**, the highest skiable mountain at 3,251m (10,663 ft.), with a vertical drop of 1,424m (4,671 ft.). Nearby, in Pontresina, a neighbor resort (see section 4), are the steep **Piz Legalb** and **Diavolezza,** with skiing for all levels of experience, including a run over the Morteratsch Glacier. All five mountains can be skied on one lift pass.

The Upper Engadine region, of which St. Moritz plays the pivotal role, has 54 mechanical ski lifts, 349km (216 miles) of marked ski slopes, seven ski schools, and an estimated 700 ski instructors who come and go semi-nomadically from season to season. A general ski pass valid for 1 day costs 58F to 71F for adults, 39F to 48F for children 13 to 17, and 20F to 24F for children 12 and under. Various other ski passes are also sold, including a popular 6-day pass, which costs 297F to 373F for adults, 208F to 250F for those ages 13 to 17, and 119F to 127F for children 12 and under. These rates include unlimited use of all ski lifts and slopes in the Engadine region. Telephone **Engadine Information Center** at © **0900/558-040** for more information about cable cars and ski lifts in the Engadine region.

The groomed and tracked cross-country runs in the Upper Engadine valley include a tame 1.6km (1-mile) loop near the cross-country center; trails are laid out between the valley resorts. A 1.6km (1-mile) segment is lit for night skiing. The Engadine cross-country ski marathon—a 42km (26-mile) run conducted in mid-March every year, is a major event. Instruction in cross-country skiing, available in groups on Monday, Tuesday, and Wednesday from 11am to 1pm, costs 55F for nine 2-hour lessons, and 125F for three half-day lessons. A full day's cross-country excursion, as part of a large group, costs 70F. For more information, contact the **Schweizer Langlaufschule St. Moritz** (© **081/833-62-33**).

Other Winter Sports

Horse racing on the frozen lake of St. Moritz is popular, or you can take rides on the natural-ice bobsled run. There are 30 curling rinks, winter golf played on the frozen lake, and tobogganing on the Cresta run. You can also play tennis and squash indoors.

If you're interested in **curling** but don't know how to do it, you can have a first training session free (40 min.). Individual **curling lessons** thereafter cost 80F for 45 minutes. Call © **796/58-02-76** for details. The curling rink is the A1 Parc rink on via Maistra.

A bobsled ride costs 250F, but you get your picture taken, a drink, and a certificate in addition to the ride. Bobsled rides occur at the town's **Olympic Bobsled Run** on via Maistra (© **081/830-02-00;** www.olympia-bobrun.ch). Advance reservations are required.

Summer Sports

Windsurfing at St. Moritz and on the lakes of nearby resorts, especially Silvaplana, has boomed in popularity. If you're already experienced, rental of equipment for 2 hours costs 80F. If you're a beginner, or if you just want to brush up on your technique, private lessons are available, costing 300F for 10 lessons. Call **Water Sports Center** in Silvaplana (© **081/828-92-29**) for information. Sailing on the area's 25 lakes is also possible.

The closest golf course lies in Samedan, 7km (4½ miles) down the valley. This is a 6,587-yard par-72 course. Greens fees for a full day are 120F and club rental is 50F a day. Golfing is available from the end of May to the beginning of October daily from 7am

until 7pm, depending on the weather. In July and August the course often stays open
later. Call **Golf Engadine St. Moritz** (✆ **081/851-04-66**) for more information. There's
also a 9-hole course that's part of the Kulm Hotel (✆ **081/836-80-00**).

For tennis and squash information, consult the **Corviglia Tennis Center** in St.
Moritz-Bad (✆ **081/833-15-00**). Rates for tennis are 33F per hour outdoors and 37F
per hour indoors during the summer, or 37F to 59F per hour for winter indoor tennis.
Rental of one racquet and balls is 3F, and two racquets and balls rent for 5.50F. Squash
courts run 20F for 45 minutes in summer and 20F to 30F for the same period of time
in winter. The center is open daily from 9am to 8pm or 11pm depending on the season.

Fishing, in season between May 15 and September 15, requires the purchase of a fishing license, available only to interested parties age 16 or older. A passport and another
form of picture identification are required to get a fishing license, which costs 50F for
1 day or 100F for 1 week. Equipment and bait are also available. For more information
about **fishing** in the area, call ✆ **081/833-67-52.**

SPAS

The spa section of this resort town is called **St. Moritz-Bad,** where you can take mud
and carbon-dioxide mineral-water baths, physical therapy, and physiotherapy while you
enjoy the stimulating alpine climate in a modern **Health Spa Center (Heilbad
Zentrum),** Plaza Paracelsus (✆ **081/833-30-62**; www.heilbad-stmoritz.ch), next to the
Kempinski Grand Hotel. The spa opened in 1976. Since Roman times, "taking the
waters" has been a popular pursuit for those seeking natural curative treatment for relief
from pain and stress. The charge for every treatment at the spa is lower for residents of
any of the town's hotels or apartments. Treatments cost 98F for a 50-minute massage and
35F for an hour-long soak within a mineral-rich "carbonic bath."

SHOPPING

Most of St. Moritz's shops line either side of the steeply inclined **via Maistra,** and most
of the horrendously upscale ones vie with one another for proximity to the town's most
spectacularly expensive hotel, **Badrutt's Palace** (✆ **081/837-10-00**), near the corner of
via Serlas. On its premises you'll find boutiques for Versace, Prada, Jil Sander, Bulgari,
and Louis Vuitton, as well as enough upscale shops for watches and jewelry to outfit a
prosperous royal court. But if it's well-designed sports equipment you're looking for, or
relatively durable clothing that will shelter you from the fierce Engadine weather, head
for any of the following shops: **Boom Sports,** via Tegiatscha 5 (✆ **081/832-22-22;** www.
boom-sport.ch); **Corviglia Sports,** via Maistra 21 (✆ **081/833-44-77;** www.corviglia-
sport.ch); and **Ender Sport,** via Maistra 26 (✆ **081/833-35-36;** www.endersport.com).

The region produces lots of folkloric crafts that could commemorate your stay in the
Engadine. The town's main outlet for all sorts of woodcarvings, including depictions of
gnarled native Engadiners in Swiss costumes and some handcrafted furniture, is **Ettlin,**
via Rosatsch 7 (✆ **081/832-17-07;** www.ursettlin.ch). More broad-based in its folkloric
inventories, with ceramics, glassware, textiles, and wrought iron, is the souvenir-and-
artifacts shop **Lüthi,** via dal Bagn 54 (✆ **081/833-42-36**).

The town's largest jeweler, and the one that saturates the high-season market with
more advertising campaigns than any other in town, is **Bucherer,** via Maistra 17 (✆ **081/
833-31-03**). Finally, the town's largest emporium for chocolates is **Merkur,** via Serlas 26
(✆ **081/833-57-26**).

St. Moritz offers several different types of accommodations, with dozens of hotels, boardinghouses, and chalet-style apartments. But because it's expensive, you may prefer one of several neighboring resorts, such as Pontresina, Silvaplana, Samedan, or Celerina, all of which are covered in this chapter. The following hotels are in the heart of St. Moritz.

Very Expensive

Badrutt's Palace Hotel ★★★   This architectural hodgepodge of mock Gothic has been at the center of St. Moritz society for decades. Society isn't what it was, but today's glitzy and ritzy still fill its vast precincts—that is, if they can afford the lethal tariffs. However, for those on the winter see-and-be-seen circuit, this flamboyant edifice remains an enduring symbol of wealth, prestige, and conspicuous consumption. Set in the center of town behind a chiseled stone facade and a series of mock-fortified towers, the Palace was built at the turn of the 20th century by Caspar Badrutt. Over the years the chic and famous have come through the doors of the Palace. The hotel's Great Hall soars in Gothic dimensions above twin black-marble fireplaces, clusters of antique furniture, and massive bouquets of flowers. Except for some special suites and spacious doubles, most of the rooms are fairly standardized and "international" in styling. You're paying more for the address than the room if you lodge here.

Via Serlas 27, CH-7500 St. Moritz. ✆ **800/223-6800** in the U.S. and Canada or 081/837-10-00. Fax 081/837-29-99. www.badruttspalace.com. 159 units. Winter 460F–2,270F double, 1,665F–12,500F suite; summer 365F–860F double, 970F–3,700F suite. Rates include breakfast. AE, DC, MC, V. Free parking outdoors, 14F indoors. Closed early Apr to late June and mid-Sept to early Dec. Bus: 1. **Amenities:** 7 restaurants; 4 bars; babysitting; children's center; concierge; health club and spa; 2 heated pools (1 indoor); room service; 4 outdoor tennis courts (lit). *In room:* TV, hair dryer, minibar, Wi-Fi (free).

Carlton Hotel ★★★   Owned by the Grand Hotel Tschuggen of Arosa, this is an elaborate, ocher-colored château that was originally built for Nicholas II, the last tsar of Russia, in 1913. With a view of the lake and the mountains, it's one of the loveliest hotels in St. Moritz—luxurious, but without the glitzy consumption of Badrutt's Palace. The hotel reopened in 2007 after a wholesale renovation that retained its traditional architecture but made it completely up-to-date in modern technology. One particularly spectacular sitting room has tall, narrow columns with neoclassical designs and a pair of matching fireplaces. The bedrooms are elegantly furnished and spacious with white marble bathrooms.

Via Badrutt 11, Dorf, CH-7500 St. Moritz. ✆ **081/836-70-00.** Fax 081/836-70-01. www.carlton-stmoritz.ch. 60 suites. 950F–2,600F junior suite; 1,700F–3,000F deluxe suite. AE, DC, MC, V. Parking 30F in winter, 15F in summer. Closed mid-Apr to mid-June and late Sept to mid-Dec. Bus: 1. **Amenities:** 2 restaurants; 2 bars; babysitting; children's center; concierge; state-of-the-art health club and spa; pool (indoor); room service. *In room:* TV, hair dryer, minibar, Wi-Fi (free).

Hotel Waldhaus am See ★★ (Finds)   Built in 1880 as a tavern, this building was later expanded into a private home by a Swiss industrialist and now resembles a castle. Today it's one of the few buildings in St. Moritz to remain open all year. You can dine in one of three lovely rooms, the largest of which has access to a sheltered sun terrace and views over the lake. Helen and Claudio Bernasconi-Mettier, the hosts, offer comfortably conservative midsize rooms with firm beds and good plumbing. The most desirable accommodations have views of the lake.

Via Dimlej 6, CH-7500 St. Moritz. ✆ **081/836-60-00.** Fax 081/836-60-60. www.waldhaus-am-see.ch. 54 units. Winter 1,290F–1,550F double; summer 680F–1,250F double. Rates include half board. AE, DC, MC, V. Free parking outside, 18F in garage. **Amenities:** 3 restaurants; bar; sauna. *In room:* TV/DVD, CD player, hair dryer, minibar, Wi-Fi (free).

Kempinski Grand Hotel des Bains ★★★ (Kids) This hotel originated in 1896 as the Grand Hotel des Bains. Sometime in the 1950s, it was reorganized as the Kurthaus Park Hotel, but since 2002, after being ripped apart and rebuilt by Kempinski, it's the Kempinski Grand Hotel des Bains. Set at the eastern entrance to St. Moritz, adjacent to the ski slopes and ski lifts, it has welcomed the Sultan of Brunei. The decor is very grand hotel with lots of mahogany, brown marble from Sardinia, and local granite from the Engadine. This was the first of only two Kempinskis in Switzerland (the other, newer one, is near Montreux). In contrast to the Kulm Hotel and the Suvretta House (both of which have a distinct and aged clientele, and a passion about formality), it caters to a young-ish, hip, and urban clientele ages 30 to 50. The deluxe citadel offers sumptuous accommodations and living on a very grand scale. It has a casino, two state-of-the-art restaurants, and the best health, fitness, and beauty facilities in the area. Bedrooms are spacious and stylish, each thoughtfully designed and laid out for ultimate comfort, and each coming with a deluxe bathroom with heated floors in winter. The most luxurious living of all is in the glamorous spa suites or the tower suites.

Via Mezdi 27, CH-7500 St. Moritz. ✆ **800/426-3135** in the U.S. and Canada or 081/838-38-38. Fax 081/838-30-00. www.kempinski-stmoritz.com. 184 units. Winter 720F–1,380F double, 1,300F–4,641F suite; summer 435F–515F double, 625F–3,130F suite. Rates include buffet breakfast. Parking 25F outdoors, 35F indoors. AE, DC, MC, V. Closed mid-Apr to mid-June and mid-Oct to Nov. **Amenities:** 3 restaurants; 3 bars; babysitting; bikes; children's center; concierge; health club and spa; pool (indoor); room service; Wi-Fi (free, in lobby). *In room:* TV/DVD, hair dryer, minibar.

Kulm Hotel ★★★ We prefer this tranquil bastion of luxury even to the Palace itself. These three elegant buildings, the oldest of which was erected in 1760, were taken over in 1856 by Johannes Badrutt, who was the first to encourage British vacationers to come to the Alps and who went on to establish Badrutt's Palace. In 1878 it became the first building in Switzerland to have electricity, and it was the center of the Olympic Games in 1928 and 1948. Over the years the Kulm has hosted royalty from all over the world, including the kings and queens of industry and entertainment. It still draws a sedate clientele, those who deliberately shun the more ostentatious Badrutt's Palace. The public rooms are beautifully paneled, with vaulted ceilings. The spacious bedrooms are grand classics, with traditional furnishings, generous closet space, and luxury beds; tiled bathrooms have dual marble basins, heated towel racks, and robes. A large part of the city's world-famous bobsled run, the Crest run, and the curling rinks of St. Moritz are on hotel property.

Via Veglia 18, Dorf, CH-7500 St. Moritz. ✆ **800/223-1230** in the U.S. and Canada or 081/836-80-00. Fax 081/836-80-01. www.kulmhotel-stmoritz.ch. 173 units. Winter 540F–1,550F double, 1,140F–2,310F suite; summer 520F–905F double, 855F–1,140F suite. Rates include half board. AE, DC, MC, V. Parking 15F in garage in summer, 25F in winter. Closed mid-Apr to June and mid-Sept to early Dec. Bus: 1. **Amenities:** 3 restaurants; 2 bars; babysitting; children's center; concierge; 9-hole golf course; room service; 3 outdoor tennis courts (lit). *In room:* TV, hair dryer, minibar, Wi-Fi (free).

Expensive

Hotel Crystal ★ A short walk from the Corviglia cogwheel train, this large white-painted building looks oddly futuristic compared to the 19th-century structures around it. The interior combines comfortable alpine rusticity of knotty-pine Engadine-style cabinets and ceiling beams with wall-to-wall carpeting and informal furniture. All the midsize bedrooms are accented with either Swiss pine or walnut paneling. A cavernous 350-sq.-m (3,767-sq.-ft.) fitness center was added in the basement of the hotel. The lobby and some of the rooms have also been enlarged, although the rustic alpine decor is still intact.

Via Traunter Plazzas 1, CH-7500 St. Moritz. 📞 **888/989-1768** in the U.S. or 081/836-26-26. Fax 081/836-26-27. www.crystalhotel.ch. 73 units. Winter 340F–590F double, 500F–900F junior suite; summer 300F–320F double, 430F–480F junior suite. Rates include buffet breakfast. Half board 50F per person in summer, 65F per person in winter. AE, DC, MC, V. Parking 20F. Closed Apr to mid-May and Oct 5–Nov. Bus: 1. **Amenities:** Restaurant; bar; babysitting; exercise room; room service; sauna. *In room:* TV, hair dryer, minibar, Wi-Fi (free).

Hotel Schweizerhof ★★

This government-rated four-star establishment is still owned by the von Gugelberg-Hoehemer family, and has been since it was built in 1896. In 1906 the German Kaiser Wilhelm II celebrated his 48th birthday party inside this hotel in a lavish ceremony draped with flowers. Staid and traditional, it's well maintained and continues in its upscale tradition. It's a favorite of many clients who prefer its somewhat-dated Victorian overlay to the more obvious five-star hotels in town. It's also one of the few hotels of its size and stature remaining open year-round. The best units are on the fifth floor, which dates from the 1970s. This is where all the suites and the best doubles have views to the south. The least expensive accommodations are those facing north, which also lack tubs. What makes this hotel exceptional is its personal service, along with its array of drinking and dining choices.

Via dal Bagn 54, Dorf, CH-7500 St. Moritz. 📞 **081/837-07-07.** Fax 081/837-07-00. www.schweizerhof stmoritz.ch. 84 units. Winter 370F–710F double, 600F–840F suite; summer 270F–430F double, 450F–480F suite. Rates include half board in winter. AE, DC, MC, V. Free parking outdoors, 21F in garage. Bus: 1. **Amenities:** 2 restaurants; 4 bars; babysitting; bikes; children's center; Internet (free, in lobby); room service; sauna. *In room:* TV, hair dryer, minibar, Wi-Fi (30F per 24 hr.).

Monopol ★★

Set above a busy street, this 3-decades-old stucco building offers elegant public rooms furnished with French pieces, oil paintings, and well-polished wood detailing. Half of the usually spacious bedrooms are designed around Louis XV and Louis XVI or rustic furniture, while the other half have been renovated in a modern Swiss style, with lots of wood and updated bathroom fixtures.

Via Maistra 17, Dorf, CH-7500 St. Moritz. 📞 **081/837-04-04.** Fax 081/837-04-05. www.monopol.ch. 66 units. Winter 410F–640F double, 550F–2,210F suite; summer 360F–410F double, 440F–1,550F suite. Rates include buffet breakfast. Half board 40F per person per day. AE, DC, MC, V. Closed mid-Apr to mid-May and mid-Oct to Dec 10. Bus: 1. **Amenities:** Restaurant; 2 bars; health club and spa; pool (indoor); room service. *In room:* TV, hair dryer, minibar, Wi-Fi (19F per 4 hr.).

Suvretta House ★★

Set about 1.5km (1 mile) from the resort town, this five-star government-rated hotel is a citadel of subdued elegance and conservative charm. It attracts an established clientele with its grand decor and understated elegance and is slightly more luxurious than Badrutt's Palace, though it doesn't quite reach the lofty peaks of Kulm. The place is so formal that it's off-putting to some visitors. It was built in 1912 on a plateau surrounded by mountains and lakes. Its Edwardian facade has two neomedieval towers and a baroque central gable that has become the hotel's trademark. Except for areas of richly grained oak paneling and Engadine sgraffito, the interior is covered with plaster and pierced with an endless series of vaulted arches. The spacious guest rooms in traditional or alpine style are luxurious without being glitzy. The roomy bathrooms are tiled. It's surrounded with more land than any other hotel in St. Moritz and offers a private ski lift about 90m (295 ft.) from the hotel.

Via Chasellas 1, CH-7500 St. Moritz. 📞 **081/836-36-36.** Fax 081/836-37-37. www.suvrettahouse.ch. 210 units. Winter 385F–840F per person double, 1,550F–3,610F suite; summer 290F–570F per person double, 1,210F–2,480F suite. Rates include half board. AE, DC, MC, V. Parking 30F in winter, 20F in summer. Closed mid-Apr to mid-June and mid-Sept to mid-Dec. **Amenities:** 2 restaurants; 3 bars; babysitting;

Moderate

Hotel Eden ★   A pleasant hotel whose architecture evokes a Tuscan villa, this establishment was built more than a century ago and has been in the Degiacomi family for some 40 years. It doesn't cost as much as either of its more glamorous neighbors, the Kulm and Badrutt's Palace. The Eden, which opens onto a tiny but charming plaza in the center of town, is filled with pine-wood paneling and family antiques. Each of the simple and modernized midsize bedrooms has tasteful, conservative furniture, and all units come with a midsize private bathroom. The hotel dining room is only open to hotel guests.

Via Veglia 12, Dorf, CH-7500 St. Moritz. ⓒ **081/830-81-00.** Fax 081/830-81-01. www.edenstmoritz.ch. 36 units. Winter 304F–454F double; summer 208F–332F double. Rates include buffet breakfast. AE, MC, V. Free parking. Closed mid-Apr to mid-June and mid-Oct to mid-Dec. Bus: 1. **Amenities:** Restaurant; babysitting; room service. *In room:* TV, hair dryer, Wi-Fi (free).

Hotel Languard ★★   Built more than a century ago as the private home of the owner of the nearby Kulm Hotel, this much-enlarged and -altered property lies just off the main street of town. It's run by a conservative Swiss staff and the Trivella family, who display their family's ski awards (one of their brothers, Roberto, was a champion in 1978) in a glass case by the reception desk. The hotel's pine-paneled interior is well maintained and very inviting, with a breakfast room that overlooks the valley and the lake. Some of the small to midsize rooms have private balconies, and all have private bathrooms.

Via Veglia 14, CH-7500 St. Moritz. ⓒ **081/833-31-37.** Fax 081/833-45-46. www.languard-stmoritz.ch. 22 units. Winter 245F–520F double; summer 195F–280F double. Rates include buffet breakfast. AE, DC, MC, V. Free parking. Closed May and Nov. Bus: 1. *In room:* TV, hair dryer.

Inexpensive

Bellaval ⟨**Value**⟩   This is the best choice for train travelers, as it stands at the rail station. But trains don't run at night so you won't be kept awake. Rooms in front open onto the station; those in back face Lake St. Moritz. The century-old building is kept up-to-date, its rooms comfortable and well maintained, though simply furnished. Some of the bedrooms have private balconies. Free Internet access is provided for guests in the lobby. On-site is a country restaurant specializing in homemade fondue dinners and other Swiss specialties. The hotel, originally called the Bahnhof, was once run by an alcohol-free women's club. Those days are now gone, and the on-site RHBar is installed in an old Rhätibahn railcar.

Via Grevas, 55, CH-7500 St. Moritz-Dorf. ⓒ **081/833-32-45.** Fax 081/833-04-06. www.bellaval-stmoritz. ch. 23 units, 18 with bathroom. 130F–150F double without bathroom, 160F–190F with bathroom. AE, DC, MC, V. Free parking. **Amenities:** Restaurant; bar; Internet (free, in lobby). *In room:* TV.

Corvatsch   Bleak on the outside, this family-run hotel in the center of St. Moritz-Bad has more of an intimate, down-home feel once you go inside. The bedrooms are decorated in a cozy, Engadine style, each with a well-kept private bathroom with shower. The views open onto traffic, but at least the location is central. The handcrafted wooden furniture adds to the intimate atmosphere. Many nonguests patronize its Italian/Swiss restaurant that specializes in barbecued meats. The grilled specialties emerge from a charcoal furnace. Fresh trout is an especially good fish, and the chefs also make fondues. Marc and Daniela Aerni-Bonetti are your warm and welcoming hosts.

THE ENGADINE

15

ST. MORITZ

Via Tegiatschal, CH-7500 St. Moritz. ☎ **081/837-57-57.** Fax 081/837-57-58. www.hotel-corvatsch.ch. 27 units. Winter 130F–195F per person double; summer 100F–140F per person double. MC, V. Parking 15F. **Amenities:** Restaurant; bar. *In room:* TV, minibar.

WHERE TO DINE

Although meals may be included in the cost of your hotel room, you may want to sample the selections at other hotels and restaurants. There are also dozens of fashionable *konditoreien* (coffeehouses).

Very Expensive

Chadafo Grill, in the Chesa Veglia ★★ FRENCH   This is one of the most upscale restaurants in a resort that's loaded with almost-comparable equivalents. Owned and operated by the also-recommended Badrutt's Palace Hotel, whose mock-fortified bulk rises a short walk away, it's housed within one of the most historic buildings in St. Moritz, the Engadine-style *Chesa Veglia.* Originally built in 1658 of stone, stucco, and now deeply weathered wood, this antique *chesa* (house) retains much of its original paneling and carving, and a monumental arched entranceway that's often depicted as part of the press and PR for St. Moritz itself. Within its sprawling interior is a labyrinth of rooms (and three separate restaurants) whose decor is entirely composed of architectural remnants from older, since-demolished, houses.

Despite competition from two in-house establishments (see below), the culinary and atmospheric star of this place is the **Chadafo Grill,** where impeccable service blends with an antique decor of high-alpine charm and top-notch cuisine. Expect a whiff of the glamour of faraway Paris, and odors wafting in from the kitchen. Specialities change with the season, but are likely to include chateaubriand, roasted rack of lamb with alpine herbs, shrimp with Pernod sauce, trout meunière, chicken Kiev, terrines of foie gras, and garnishes that include dollops of, among others, caviar.

The same building contains the two other restaurants, including the middle-bracket **Patrizier-Stube,** a casual dining spot serving Swiss and French food daily from 11am to 11pm. Main courses cost from 42F to 65F each. Less appealing is a simple pizzeria, **Heuboden,** which serves pizzas, pastas, and grills, but only at dinnertime, winter and summer alike, every day from 6:30 to 11pm. Main courses in Heuboden cost from 26F to 45F. Overall, we emphasize that the star of the entire complex is the Chadafo Grill.

In the Chesa Veglia, via Veglia 2, Dorf. ☎ **081/837-28-00.** Reservations required. Main courses 40F–65F. AE, DC, MC, V. Daily 11:30am–3pm and 6:30pm–midnight. Closed mid-Apr to late June and early Sept to Nov.

Jöhri's Talvo ★★★ FRENCH   Established in 1992 inside the solid pine-sheathed walls of a 350-year-old Engadine house, this restaurant is St. Moritz's most upscale dining option. It lies in the center of the satellite village of Champfèr, a 10-minute walk from the western periphery of St. Moritz. The much-praised cuisine manages to blend regional recipes (as filtered by the owner's French training) with the skillful preparation of upscale ingredients. For example, the menu lists different preparations of North Atlantic lobsters and scallops in wine sauce. Our personal favorite is a whole turbot cooked in a salt crust, which is broken open at table side and then served with an array of garnishes and dressings.

Better suited to the cold, high-altitude climate, however, are a range of regional dishes derived from time-honored Engadine traditions. These include *capuns* (spinach-flavored pasta cooked with cold-weather greens in consommé and served with truffles); *puschlav* ("poor man's soup," prepared with consommé and enriched with flour); and lamb raised in nearby meadows prepared with mustard sauce, mountain herbs, and sautéed potatoes.

Via Gunels 15, Champfèr. ☏ **081/833-44-55.** www.talvo.ch. Reservations recommended. Main courses **431** 46F–88F; fixed-price lunch 148F–178F, dinner 230F–265F, fish menu from 230F. AE, DC, MC, V. Tues–Sun 11am–11pm (closed Tues in summer). Closed Easter to mid-June and mid-Oct to mid-Dec.

Nobu JAPANESE This addition to the St. Moritz culinary scene is another outlet of a restaurant that gained fame in Manhattan, where it's still known for incorporating new ingredients into old dishes or retooling traditional recipes. Internationally renowned chef Nobuyuki "Nobu" Matsuhisa has crossed the Atlantic and opened what quickly became the trendiest, and most difficult, reservation in town.

So what does one of the world's greatest sushi chefs have in store for you? Excellent starters include New Zealand mussels with your choice of Matsuhisa sauces, Toro tartar, tuna *takati* with Panzu, and squid "pasta" in a garlic sauce. For a main dish we recommend the filet of salmon with teriyaki or Anti-Cucho sauce. Those who can't decide what they want should try the tempura, sashimi, or sushi dinners, which offer a variety of the type of fare they've chosen. Other than the dinners, sushi and tempura are served by the piece, so diners can try each variety on the menu or stick to their favorites. Reservations can be backed up for months at a time in peak season and for weeks in low season, so call far in advance.

In the Badrutt's Palace Hotel. ☏ **081/837-10-00.** Reservations required. Main courses 60F–120F; sushi and tempura 4F–15F per piece. AE, DC, MC, V. Dec to mid-Apr daily 7:30–11pm. Closed mid-Apr to Nov.

Expensive

La Marmite ★★ SWISS/INTERNATIONAL This woodsy lunch establishment is the best high-altitude restaurant in the Grisons. It can be reached only by the Corviglia funicular. The Mathis family offers excellent service and a varied menu. There's also a less expensive cafeteria on the premises that in midwinter is usually crowded with skiers. The region's choicest ingredients turn up in such dishes as venison with polenta in a truffle reduction; tuna sashimi with black truffles and salmon caviar; or a 16-ounce black Angus steak with thick Parmesan shavings and arugula.

Corviglia Bergstation. ☏ **081/833-63-55.** Reservations recommended. Main courses 33F–79F. AE, MC, V. Daily 8am–5pm. Closed mid-Apr to mid-Dec.

Landgasthof Meierei ★★ SWISS Built a century ago as a relay station for the Swiss postal service, today it houses four dining rooms, which have in days of yore served playboys, princes, and kings. Those heady glory days are now relegated to local legend, though, as the place has become solidly bourgeois. Considering the glamorous clientele that the place has attracted, it serves an earthy and simple menu, ranging from fried pork steak with celeriac and zucchini to slices of salmon with an orange-laced fennel ragout. Also try the Wiener schnitzel and goulash dishes.

No diner is allowed to drive a car along the difficult-to-navigate service roads that reach the restaurant. You can hire a taxi costing up to 100F for four passengers. Our recommendation is that you park your car in the public parking lot near the edge of the lake, just below the Hotel Waldhaus am See, and walk the 20-minute lakeside promenade to the restaurant. The footpath has been carefully paved, and there are only a few slopes to negotiate. Before you set out, it's advisable to phone the restaurant to confirm that it's open.

There are nine cozy alpine rooms rented here costing from 250F to 320F for a double or from 350F to 450F for a suite, including breakfast.

Via Dim Lej 52. ☏ **081/833-20-60.** Reservations required. Main courses 25F–48F. AE, MC, V. Tues–Sun 10am–2:30pm and 6:30–9:30pm. Closed mid-Apr to mid-June and Oct to mid-Dec.

Rôtisserie des Chevaliers ★ FRENCH   This exquisitely paneled grillroom, in one of the most historic hotels in St. Moritz, offers a cozy ambience that's especially suited to cold weather. The delectable menu is likely to include terrine and gooseliver, grilled sea bass flambé, baby turbot prepared Marseille style, and a unique stuffed Veal a la Hotel Kulm. Dishes are most often based on the freshest and best produce available in any given season.

In the Hotel Kulm, via Veglia 18, Dorf. ✆ **081/836-80-00.** Reservations required. Main courses 55F–72F. AE, MC, V. Daily 7pm–midnight. Closed mid-Mar to mid-Dec. Bus: 1.

Moderate

Lapin Bleu SWISS/FRENCH/ITALIAN   Half-board guests of the hotel usually dine upstairs in the elegant grillroom, but in many ways we prefer the warm, wood-lined decor and the polite service of the street-level tavern. Specialties from the hearty alpine kitchen include veal sausage with *rösti;* grilled rump steak with herb butter, and grilled veal liver with green beans. Liver, pork, and several preparations of veal, pasta, and seafood, including lobster, are also served. Many residents of St. Moritz come here to dine, a good sign.

In the Hotel Steffani, Sonnenplatz 1. ✆ **081/836-96-96.** Reservations required in winter. Main courses 21F–54F. AE, DC, MC, V. Daily 11:30am–1:45pm and 7–9:30pm.

Restaurant Acla ★ (Finds) SWISS/INTERNATIONAL   Situated in the Hotel Schweizerhof, this "little house on the mountain"—as its name is translated from Romansh—serves Swiss specialties and international dishes in a rustically appealing and rather formal ambience. In summer, during clement lunch hours, the venue moves onto a flowering outdoor terrace called Il Restaurant Giardino. Prices in Il Giardino are slightly lower than those in Acla. Summer specialties include filet of perch with tomato crust and olive-oil sauce with grilled zucchini; sautéed guinea fowl breast with summer vegetables and semolina-mushroom slices; and filet of veal with basil-cream sauce, leaf spinach, and fine noodles. In winter main courses include salmon with strips of celery, morels, and truffle sauce, served with early potatoes; cereal risotto with asparagus; grilled zucchini and tomato ragout; or chateaubriand with béarnaise sauce. You can also order classic dishes such as Wiener schnitzel or the famous *Tafelspitz* (the boiled beef of Vienna) served with apple-horseradish and chive sauce, or blinis with caviar and smoked salmon. Trout is from the Inn River.

In the Hotel Schweizerhof, via del Bagn 54, Dorf. ✆ **081/837-07-07.** Reservations recommended. Main courses 37F–54F. AE, DC, MC, V. Daily noon–2pm and 6:30–11pm.

Restaurant Engadina (Value) SWISS   In the direct center of St. Moritz-Dorf, across the street from the town hall, is this old-fashioned family dining room that's uncharacteristic for St. Moritz. You get good value for your money here. Pleasant, comfortable, and simple, it consists of two hunter-style rooms filled with trophies and alpine accents, such as pine-wood tables and paneling. There's even an outdoor wooden deck for drinking and dining if the weather is right. Selections include carpaccio, *petite marmite* (a famous Parisian soup made with lean pieces of meat and vegetable stock), fondues (with cheese or champagne), grilled steaks, goulash, and snails in garlic butter. The food is robust and hearty. No one ever accused the chefs of being too imaginative, but this is the type of chow the locals love.

Piazza da Scoula 2. ✆ **081/833-32-65.** www.restaurant-engiadina.ch. Reservations recommended. Cheese fondue 38F per person; main courses 29F–47F. AE, DC, MC, V. Winter Mon–Sat 10am–10pm; summer Mon–Sat noon–2pm and 6:30–9:30pm.

Veltliner-Keller SWISS/ITALIAN   It's a cafe and tavern by day, but this venue is at its best for evening dining, when the rustically informal premises welcome many of the town's professional ski-and-see crowd. The menu includes mushroom salads, trout with mushrooms, spaghetti, and a wide selection of meats and fish, along with a savory risotto and many kinds of pasta. Desserts include just about every in-season fruit in Europe. This is a very simple and very ethnic Swiss place, the quintessential village tavern preferred by many of the locals, some of whom are hotel workers.

Via dal Bagn 11. ℂ **081/833-40-09.** Reservations required for dinner. Main courses 24F–46F. AE, DC, MC, V. Daily noon–3pm and 6–11:30pm.

Inexpensive

Hanselmann   Originally established in the mid-1800s, this tavern and tearoom has grown to occupy a much-embellished building decorated with sgraffito. Today it's one of the best and most inexpensive places in town for breakfast or lunch. It's owned by Fritz Mutschler, grandson of the original founder. From the German-language breakfast menu, you may choose an omelet, an egg-and-cheese dish, or a country platter piled high with Black Forest ham and Valais rye rolls. Other dishes include Welsh rarebit and smoked salmon with buttered toast. The upstairs restaurant opens at 11:30am. The place is also popular with the après-ski crowd.

Via Maistra 8. ℂ **081/833-38-64.** www.hanselmann.ch. Reservations accepted only for lunch. Main courses 22F–45F; breakfast 10F–22F; fixed-price breakfast 15F, lunch 32F. MC, V. Dec 25–Feb and July–Aug daily 7:30am–7pm; Mar–June and Sept–Dec 24 Wed–Mon 7:30am–7pm.

Trattoria Bellaval ⟨**Value**⟩ ITALIAN/SWISS   This is one of our preferred low-cost restaurants in St. Moritz. Set within a century-old hotel near the town center, within a woodsy-looking dining room, it focuses on grilled schnitzels and steaks (both beef and pork) and a dazzling range of pastas that you'll build yourself based on whatever combination of sauce and toppings (16 different kinds), noodles (5 different kinds), and sizes (medium, large, and *grande*) you designate. Some of the best antipasto in town is served here, and all the salads are delicious fare and freshly made. You may also check out the daily specials, and vegetarians will take delight in the vegetable lasagna.

In the Hotel Bellaval, via Grevas 55. ℂ **81/833-32-45.** Reservations not necessary. Main courses 11F–32F; fixed-price 2-course menu 15F. AE, DC, MC, V. Daily 11:30am–midnight.

ST. MORITZ AFTER DARK

Few other resorts are as depressing off season as St. Moritz, where very few of the local entrepreneurs even pretend to be interested in doing business. But as the midwinter and midsummer seasons get underway, you'll find lots of warm cubbyholes in St. Moritz, often in hotels whose bars are inspired by the Romansh sgraffito that's so prevalent in the region. Many are eminently appropriate for a quiet and cozy drink, and some, as noted below, make special efforts to attract drinking, and sometimes dancing, clients from other hotels.

One of the best examples of this is the **Hotel Schweizerhof,** via dal Bagn 54 (ℂ **081/837-07-07;** see earlier), where three separate bars provide a labyrinth of nightlife options that range from the subdued to the rowdy. They include the **Muli Bar** (only open in winter), with North American–style country-western music; the **Stübli** (open year-round), which divides its energies between cozy folkloric platters, a resident musician, and foaming steins of beer; and the **Piano Bar** (closed May–June and Oct–Nov), where melodies are tinkled out by visiting pianists from throughout Europe.

434 **Bobby's Pub,** in the Caspar Badrutt Shopping Gallery, via dal Bagn 50a (© 081/834-42-83), is everybody's favorite English-style pub, replete with faux Victoriana and beers from throughout Europe, including merry old England. A well-entrenched staple on the nightlife circuit is **Vivai's Disco,** in the Hotel Steffani, via Somplazt 1 (© 081/836-96-96). Here, despite an antique-looking entrance etched in Engadine-style line drawings, the music is contemporary and the decor is intimately lit and modern. Depending on whether there's live music, entrance costs 30F, which usually includes the first drink.

More expensive, and much more posh, are the disco and bar facilities in **Badrutt's Palace Hotel,** via Serlas 27 (© 081/837-10-00). Most visible of these is the **King's Club Disco,** where outsiders can mingle with the rich and famous, or more likely the wannabes, in a mock-medieval decor that reverberates with the sound of recently released dance music. Jackets and ties for men aren't required. Cover is from 35F to 45F, depending on the season and night of the week, and includes the first drink. In winter it's open every night from 10:30pm to 3am. In summer it's open only Friday and Saturday from 10:30pm to 3am. Quieter, somewhat less manic bars and watering holes, all of them relentlessly upscale, are scattered throughout other parts of the hotel as well.

4 PONTRESINA ★★

6km (4 miles) E of St. Moritz; 85km (53 miles) SE of Chur; 208km (130 miles) SE of Zurich

Pontresina (1,775m/5,822 ft.) doesn't have the fame of St. Moritz, but it offers some of the best hiking and mountaineering in the Engadine. Its long hours of sunshine in the winter, and its access to all the noted ski sites in the greater St. Moritz area, make Pontresina an attractive alternative to the more expensive town. Situated in the Upper Engadine on the road to the Bernina Pass, at the mouth of the Bernina Valley, it's surrounded by larches, stone pines, and the Alps. From Pontresina, you also have views of what's called the "glacier amphitheater" of the Roseg Mountains.

Originally a 19th-century summer resort, Pontresina has become a leading ski resort, known for its famous ski runs, cross-country skiing tracks, and a family-friendly venue that's less expensive and less forbidding than more glamorous St. Moritz. The village today is filled with hotels and shops and has much old Engadine architecture.

ESSENTIALS

GETTING THERE From Zurich, via Chur, a **train** arrives in Pontresina every hour throughout the day until 9pm (until 10pm Fri–Sun). There's also a train arriving every hour from St. Moritz. For train schedules, call © 0900/300-300.

In the winter a "sportbus" runs between St. Moritz and Pontresina every 25 minutes daily from 7:30am to midnight (until 2am Fri–Sat). Tickets can be purchased at the post office or directly on the bus. Each way costs 15F; for information call the **bus station** in St. Moritz (© 081/834-90-90).

If you're **driving** from St. Moritz, head northeast along Route 27, then cut southeast at the junction with Route 29.

VISITOR INFORMATION In lieu of street names, follow hotel or restaurant directional signs. The **Pontresina Tourist Office** (© 081/838-83-20; www.pontresina.com) is open Monday to Friday from 8:30am to noon and 2 to 6pm. During high season it is also open Saturday 9am to noon and 3 to 6pm, and Sunday 2 to 6pm.

The Engadine provides a wealth of hiking tours that combine rides on cable cars or gondolas with sometimes-strenuous hikes across rocky or, in some cases, glacial terrain. The most spectacular of these is the **Diavolezza tour** ★, which reaches a maximum height of 2,723m (8,931 ft.), and which includes views of—and if you opt for it, hikes over—as many as two separate glaciers. To access it, travel by road 7km (4½ miles) south of Pontresina, following the signs to the Bernina Pass until you reach the lowest station of the Diavolezza cable car, and climb aboard for a head-spinning 15-minute ascent to the top. One-way transit costs 24F for adults and 8F for children ages 6 to 12; the round-trip cost for adults is 33F and 11F for children. If it's winter, you can ski back down to the valley, or—more precariously (and this is only for experts)—you can negotiate down the face of the glacier to the hamlet of Morteratsch. The better bet occurs in summer, when you can take a guided hike along the surface of the glacier as part of a 4- to 5-hour tour that's recommended only for the fit and hardy. (Don't even consider this without the proper equipment, including sturdy boots with rubber treads, sunglasses, sunscreen, and protection against the rain and sometimes howling winds, even during midsummer.) A guide waits for participants every day, from May to September, at the top of the Diavolezza cable car, at noon. Participation in the walking tour costs 40F for adults, and 20F for children 11 and under. For more information about the Diavolezza hiking tour, contact the tourist offices of any of the surrounding towns and villages, including St. Moritz, Silvaplana, and Pontresina, or the **Pontresina Mountaineering School** (Bergsteigerschule Pontresina; ✆ **081/838-83-33**).

Another of the region's panoramic aeries, in this case one that's more conveniently reached than the above-recommended Diavolezza, is **Alp Languard,** whose chairlifts will carry you to a height of 2,550m (8,364 ft.). You'll access it from a hillside above the rest of the town that's within walking distance. A one-way ticket costs 15F for adults and 5F for children 6 to 12, and a round-trip ticket costs 22F for adults and 9F for children 6 to 12. Ascents are continuous during daylight hours throughout the year. For more information, contact **Sesselbahn Languard** at ✆ **081/842-62-55**.

The area's chief attraction is **Muottas Muragl** ★★★, a mountain whose peak is reached by funicular. The excursion begins in Pontresina, where you board a bus that travels 3km (2 miles) downhill in the direction of Samedan, to a final destination at the base of the funicular, Punt Muragl. The funicular ride takes 15 minutes to reach a platform set at 2,414m (7,918 ft.) above sea level. From it you'll see the Upper Engadine Gap, with the mountain ranges of Piz Julier and Piz Rosatsch on either side. If the day is clear, you can also see the lakes between Maloja and St. Moritz. The excursion, including bus rides, costs 30F round-trip, but a one-way ticket is available as well, for 21F depending on the season. For information in Pontresina, call the tourist information center or inquire at the reception desk of your hotel. For information about the funicular, contact **Standseilbahn Muottas Muragle** at ✆ **081/842-83-08**.

WHERE TO STAY
Very Expensive
Grand Hotel Kronenhof ★★★ (Kids) This is the grandest hotel in town and has been run by the same family since the 1850s. In spite of its age, it's completely modern, having undergone a massive renovation in 2007. Set in the center of the Pontresina, behind iron gates and a circular driveway, the Kronenhof is decorated with Corinthian

columns and vaulted, frescoed ceilings. Its oldest section dates from 1848; the impressive details are from 1898 and include such baroque accessories as gilt, baby-pink cherubs, alluring nymphs, dark-wood pine, restored murals, and even the original parquet floors. The midsize to spacious bedrooms are individually decorated with traditional pieces; others are in soothing pastels. One of the most spectacular renovations is an elegant spa, among the best in the Engadine. Children are especially welcome here; there's even a kiddie restaurant for them, plus other activities.

CH-7504 Pontresina. ☎ **081/830-30-30.** Fax 081/830-30-31. www.kronenhof.com. 125 units. Winter 520F–930F double, 830F–1,790F suite; summer 440F–620F double, 680F–1,120F suite. Half board 70F extra per person. AE, DC, MC, V. Parking 25F. Closed Apr to mid-May and mid-Oct to Dec. **Amenities:** 2 restaurants; bar; babysitting; bikes; children's center; concierge; health club and spa; 2 heated pools (1 indoor); room service; 2 outdoor tennis courts (lit). *In room:* TV, hair dryer, minibar, Wi-Fi (30F per 24 hr.).

Walther ★★★ (Kids)   With its updated decor and better facilities, the Grand Hotel Kronenhof is the premier address. But the Walther is the more tranquil, and in some ways the more charming, choice. The spacious bedrooms are not only comfortable but also handsomely decorated with wood furnishings in knotty pine, larch, or cherry. This is a cozy retreat, with each room having a private balcony or terrace. If you want to pay more, you'll get a junior suite or a larger and more elegant suite, perhaps the best accommodations at this resort. The sunniest units face south and east. A large park surrounds the hotel, containing a terrace with restaurant and a sunbathing lawn with gardens. There's also a playground in the park. The hotel has a first-class restaurant, serving both international dishes and Swiss specialties.

Via Maistra, CH-7504 Pontresina. ☎ **081/839-36-36.** Fax 081/839-36-37. www.hotelwalther.ch. 70 units. Winter 460F–740F double, from 890F suite; summer 410F–610F double, from 770F suite. Rates include half board. AE, DC, MC, V. Parking 18F. **Amenities:** Restaurant; bar; Internet (free, in lobby); indoor heated pool; room service; spa; 3 outdoor tennis courts (lit). *In room:* TV, hair dryer, minibar, Wi-Fi (35F per 24 hr.).

Expensive

Hotel La Collina & Soldanella ★   This establishment is composed of two connected hotels, one built just after the turn of the 20th century (the government-rated three-star Soldanella) and the other during the 1970s (the four-star La Collina). Many loyal clients deliberately opt for rooms in the Soldanella, knowing that the facilities of the better-rated La Collina are at their disposal, including La Collina's elegant dining room. Clients for either property register in the lobby of La Collina before heading through a network of hallways and covered passageways to their respective buildings. Regardless of which of the areas you select, bedrooms are comfortable, and the public rooms are cozy and elegant, with Oriental carpets and a scattering of regional antiques.

CH-7504 Pontresina. ☎ **081/838-85-85.** Fax 081/838-85-00. www.collina.ch. 46 units (28 in La Collina, 18 in Soldanella). La Collina: winter 220F–320F double, summer 210F–290F double. Soldanella: winter 170F–250F double, summer 180F–220F double. Rates include buffet breakfast. AE, DC, MC, V. Free parking outdoors. Closed Apr–May and mid-Oct to mid-Dec. **Amenities:** 2 restaurants; room service. *In room:* TV, hair dryer, minibar, Wi-Fi (free).

Hotel Schweizerhof ★   The Schweizerhof dates from 1910, but it was so drastically modernized in 1975 that old-time visitors hardly recognize it; much of its roofline (including the towers and turrets) was removed. Yet it remains a huge, comfortable hotel. The midsize rooms are well furnished and comfortable, and the corner bay-windowed doubles open onto views to the southwest. All the bathrooms are neatly maintained.

Winter 340F–540F double; summer 200F–330F double. Rates include buffet breakfast. Half board 35F per person. AE, DC, MC, V. Parking 15F. Closed mid-Apr to June. **Amenities:** Restaurant; bar; exercise room; Jacuzzi; sauna. *In room:* TV, hair dryer, minibar, Wi-Fi (30F per 24 hr.).

Moderate

Hotel Bernina (**Value**)   This hotel is not particularly historic, but it offers good value and cozy comfort in an often-forbidding landscape. Tiled midsize bathrooms, pine-wood furnishings, and flower prints made the bedrooms inviting after renovation. The most panoramic views are from the corner doubles with private balconies. All rooms have been renovated, each with wood paneling and lots of folkloric touches. The dining room is decorated with panels of local wood, and the hotel's popular restaurant has excellent a la carte specialties. It's a place where the locals from the ski school meet in the winter.

CH-7504 Pontresina. ⓒ **081/838-86-86.** Fax 081/838-86-87. www.hotelbernina.ch. 43 units. Summer 200F–260F double; winter 210F–280F double. Rates include buffet breakfast. Half board 30F per person. AE, DC, MC, V. Parking free outdoors, 10F in garage. Closed mid-Apr to mid-June and mid-Sept to mid-Dec. **Amenities:** 2 restaurants; bar; sauna. *In room:* TV, hair dryer, minibar.

Hotel Garni Chesa Mulin   The staff goes out of its way to make guests feel welcome in this quiet, centrally located hotel originally built in 1983. The public rooms are filled with plants, which serve to accentuate the wood paneling. The large, airy bedrooms have comfortable furnishings.

CH-7504 Pontresina. ⓒ **081/838-82-00.** Fax 081/838-82-30. www.chesa-mulin.ch. 30 units. Winter 208F–268F double; summer 198F–232F double. Rates include buffet breakfast. AE, DC, MC, V. Free parking outside, 15F in garage nearby. Closed May and Nov. *In room:* TV, hair dryer, minibar.

WHERE TO DINE

Expensive

Hof Restaurant ★ ITALIAN/SWISS   One of the most reliable dining rooms in town occupies a stone-floored room whose walls are accented with reproductions of medieval-looking sgraffito and big windows that overlook surrounding landscapes. The menu, geared for the high-altitude, hearty climate outside, features generous portions of regional recipes that reflect the local traditions of both Switzerland and nearby Austria and Italy. Examples include pork filets with lemon sauce; lamb cutlets with balsamic vinegar sauce; carpaccio of veal or beef; air-dried *bündnerfleisch* (a type of beef); different preparations of salmon and trout; and the classic dish of Vienna, *Tafelspitz,* the boiled beef with horseradish sauce. Dessert may include rich chocolate cake or flambéed raspberries with cream.

In the Hotel Schweizerhof. ⓒ **081/842-01-31.** Reservations recommended. Main courses 26F–48F. AE, DC, MC, V. Daily 11am–11pm. Closed mid-Apr to June.

Kronenstübli ★★ SWISS/FRENCH/ITALIAN   The restaurant at the Grand Hotel Kronenhof is one of the most popular spots in town, serving the finest cuisine. It's filled with valuable pieces of brass and pewter; the wood paneling is from the mid–19th century. The dishes are fresh-flavored, inventive, and prepared with time-tested skill. You may enjoy a "variation of tomatoes with cheese" served with a dollop of basil-flavored sorbet; a medley of marinated salmon and tuna served with mango-flavored vinaigrette and strips of roasted duck meat; and filets of pikeperch in a potato crust, served with cheese sauce and fresh chanterelles. Veal mignon with a foie gras mousse is especially delightful, or perhaps a supreme of turbot with saffron.

In the Grand Hotel Kronenhof. ℂ **081/830-30-30.** Reservations required. Main courses 53F–59F; 5-course menu 148F. AE, DC, MC, V. Tues–Sat 7–10pm. Closed Apr to mid-May and mid-Oct to Dec.

Moderate

Stüvetta SWISS/CONTINENTAL This restaurant provides intimate, vaulted rooms, where guests gather on snowy nights for classic raclette and fondues. Of course, other good-tasting fare, such as pastas, fresh trout, steaks, and various schnitzels, is also offered. The service is efficient.

In the Hotel Bernina. ℂ **081/852-12-12.** Reservations recommended. Main courses 23F–35F. AE, DC, MC, V. Daily 11am–midnight. Closed mid-Apr to June and Oct to mid-Dec.

5 SILVAPLANA ★

6km (4 miles) SW of St. Moritz

Situated on Lake Silvaplana, in sight of Lake Champfèr, within a 10-minute drive of St. Moritz, the little village of Silvaplana (1,770m/5,806 ft.) is at the foot of Piz Corvatsch (3,401m/11,155 ft.), at the beginning of the Julier Pass.

Built around a late Gothic parish church, whose stone walls were completed in 1491, the hamlet of Silvaplana is one of the most unspoiled resort towns in the Engadine.

ESSENTIALS

GETTING THERE Silvaplana is not serviced by any railroad. Local residents usually take the bus or drive to the railway station at St. Moritz for most of their transportation needs.

A flotilla of blue-sided Engadine buses makes runs every 15 minutes in winter, and every 30 minutes in summer, from the St. Moritz railroad station to the center of Silvaplana at a cost of 4F each way. The yellow-sided Palm Express bus also travels through Silvaplana as part of its twice-per-day route from Lugano to St. Moritz. One-way transit from Lugano to St. Moritz costs 71F. For information on the Engadine buses, contact **Engadine Buses** in St. Moritz at ℂ **081/834-91-00.** For the Palm Express, contact **Post Auto Schweitz** at ℂ **081/833-94-40.**

If you're **driving** from St. Moritz, head southwest along Route 27 for 10 minutes.

VISITOR INFORMATION The **Silvaplana Tourist Office** (ℂ **081/838-60-00;** www. silvaplana.ch) is open year-round Monday to Friday from 8:30am to noon and 1:30 to 6:30pm, and Saturday from 9am to noon and 4 to 6pm.

EXPLORING THE AREA

Swimming, hill climbing, horseback riding, fishing, and even windsurfing on Lake Silvaplana are options in the summer. A range of cross-country trails and hiking paths are situated around the lake of Silvaplana.

Whether you're a skier, a mountaineer, a nature lover, or just a sightseer, you may want to visit **Corvatsch.** From Silvaplana, go across the narrow neck of water where Lake Champfèr and Lake Silvaplana join and take an aerial cable car at Surlej. In just 15 minutes you'll reach the mountain station, from which you have a view of the lakes, meadows, forests, and villages of the Upper Engadine. From the lookout terrace, you take in a panorama of what appears to be an infinity of mountain peaks, with the giant glacier of the Bernina group seemingly close enough to touch.

From December to May, skiers are presented with nearly 80km (50 miles) of ski runs covered with deep, powdery snow, while in the summer you can ski on the granular ice of the glacier. Ski lifts, the most visible of which is the **Corvatsch Bergbahn** (𝄢 081/ 838-73-73; www.corvatsch.ch), carry skiers to the glacier throughout the year. It charges round-trip fares of 40F for adults and 20F for children.

The town's ski school, **Skischule Corvatsch** (𝄢 081/828-86-84), which is open only from December to May, charges 90F per hour for private lessons, or 50F per person for group lessons that last for a full day.

WHERE TO STAY

Hotel Albana ★★ This year-round hotel, a government-rated four-star choice and the best at the small resort town, stands on medieval foundations. Designed with beamed ceilings and a stone fireplace, it also has half-timbered walls and regional stenciling throughout. The midsize bedrooms are modern and inviting. The best accommodations are those with private balconies facing south.

CH-7513 Silvaplana. 𝄢 **081/838-78-78.** Fax 081/838-78-79. www.albana-silvaplana.ch. 39 units. Winter 340F–550F double; summer 220F–280F double. Rates include buffet breakfast. AE, DC, MC, V. Parking 18F in garage in winter, 10F in summer. Closed May and mid-Oct to mid-Nov. **Amenities:** Restaurant; exercise room; Jacuzzi; indoor heated pool; room service; sauna; Wi-Fi (free, in lobby). *In room:* TV, hair dryer, minibar.

Hotel Julier Palace In the heart of Silvaplana, this hotel consists of a red-fronted, turn-of-the-20th-century chalet (the Hotel Julier) connected to a smaller, yellow-fronted annex that was added in the 1980s. The bedrooms in the annex are a bit larger than those in the Julier and more modern in their decor. The hotel is family operated, with a good knowledge of foreign languages and customs. Most rooms are outfitted with warm colors and often some genuine charm.

CH-7513 Silvaplana. 𝄢 **081/828-96-44.** Fax 081/834-30-03. 35 units. www.julierpalace.com. 80F–200F per person double; 200F–400F per person suite. Rates include buffet breakfast. AE, DC, MC, V. Free parking outdoors, 15F in garage. **Amenities:** Restaurant; bar. *In room:* TV, hair dryer.

St. Moritz-Chesa Silva A modern chalet-style structure, this small inn is designed and furnished in a typically Engadine style fashion. It opens onto beautiful views of Silvaplana Lake and the distant Alps. It's located 4km (2½ miles) from St. Moritz at the foot of the Julier Pass, facing the Corvatsch mountains. Bedrooms are simply furnished with functional styling, but they're comfortable. The hotel serves breakfast but no other meals. Apartments are available for long-term rentals.

Via Munterots, CH-7513 Silvaplana. 𝄢 **081/838-61-00.** Fax 081/838-61-99. www.chesasilva.ch. 12 units. 110F–160F double. Rates include buffet breakfast. AE, DC, MC, V. **Amenities:** Bar; sauna. *In room:* TV.

WHERE TO DINE

Le Gourmet ★ SWISS The dining room in the Hotel Albana is the best choice in Silvaplana. It has a richly appealing decor of wrought iron, heavy timbers, and striped fabrics. The chef prepares such tempting specialties as medallions of pork with grapes and nuts, sweetbreads in an artichoke sauce with a purée of asparagus, filet of lamb with black truffles, and filet of red mullet with saffron and fresh morels.

The hotel also maintains a less glamorous second-floor dining room, the Spunta Grischun, which offers Engadine dishes costing 35F to 52F.

In the Hotel Albana. 𝄢 **081/828-92-92.** Reservations recommended. Main courses 46F–56F; 7-course menu 169F. AE, DC, MC, V. Daily noon–1:30pm and 7:30–10pm. Closed May and mid-Oct to mid-Nov.

16

Lugano, Locarno & the Ticino

If you don't normally think of palm trees in Switzerland, you haven't seen the Ticino. Also called the Tessin, it's the Swiss Riviera—the retirement fantasy of thousands of Swiss living in the northern cantons. Although Italian is the major language, German and French (as well as English) are also widely spoken.

A visitor could spend at least 2 weeks just touring the valleys of the Ticino. Officially, the canton begins at Airolo (the southern exit of the St. Gotthard Tunnel), but most visitors head for the district's major resorts of Locarno, Lugano, and fast-rising Ascona. Lugano and Locarno share the shores of lakes Lugano and Maggiore with Italy. Relations between Switzerland and Italy, however, weren't always peaceful. The Ticino was basically carved out of the Duchy of Milan by Swiss soldiers and staunchly defended in several bloody battles.

The name of the canton is taken from the Ticino River, a tributary of northern Italy's Po River. The balmy climate produces subtropical vegetation, which thrives in gardens famous throughout Switzerland. The district's weather is almost addictive between March and November, but the rest of the year can be cold and damp.

The proximity of Italy manifests itself in the Ticino's architecture and cuisine. Many buildings are made of stone and are proportioned like structures in Lombardy or Tuscany. Also, in many cases, a trattoria will be owned by a Swiss-German husband and a Swiss-Italian wife, so their cuisine ends up being a concession to each other's culinary traditions.

Sometimes getting to the Ticino is part of the fun. One of the most dramatic ways to arrive is over the **Simplon Pass** ★★, a journey that stretches from the German-speaking town of Brig in Switzerland and, after crossing the pass, descends to the Italian border town of Domodossola, a distance of some 64km (40 miles). The pass owes its origins to Napoleon, who demanded a low-altitude pass 1,950m (6,396 ft.) above sea level through which artillery could be transported. This pass is often closed between December and early May because of bad road conditions. At those times automobiles are transported onto flatbed trains, which are carried through one of the longest railway tunnels in the world, the Simplon Tunnel. The tunnel stretches for 20km (12 miles). But when the pass is open, it affords one of the most panoramic mountain views in Europe.

Rail passengers can also arrive dramatically by taking the **Bernina Express** ★★★, a 4-hour trip that begins in Chur and ends in Tirano, Italy. As you near the town of Chur you will be awed by the rugged peaks around you, but before the end of the journey, as you near the Italian border town of Tirano, you'll see palm-lined lakefronts. This is the only express train that crosses the Alps with no tunnels, and, as such, it is one of the steepest railway lines in the world. At Tirano, the end of the rail run from Zurich, you can make easy bus connections on to Lugano. For more information about the Bernina Express, call **Rail Europe** at ⓒ **877/272-RAIL** (7245).

1 BELLINZONA

22km (14 miles) E of Locarno; 35km (22 miles) N of Lugano; 192km (119 miles) S of Zurich; 416km (258 miles) W of Geneva

The opening of the St. Gotthard Tunnel made this once-remote Swiss town on Italy's side of the Alps very accessible. Bellinzona is known for the beauty of its old city and the nearby hills, as well as for the hospitality of its inhabitants.

Because of its location astride the best of the ancient military and trade routes between Rome and its colonies in the north, the town is believed to be of Roman origin. It was later occupied, along with the rest of the Ticino, by both the Celts and the Ligurians. Records of the town date from A.D. 590. As the strategic key to the passes of St. Gotthard, San Bernardino, and Lucomagno, Bellinzona loomed large in the history of Lombardy. In the 8th century it was owned outright by the bishop of Como, and ownership went back and forth between Como and Milan in the 13th and 14th centuries. By 1798 it had become the capital of its own canton, Bellinzona, in the Swiss Confederation. Five years later it was incorporated into the newly formed canton of the Ticino, where it has remained ever since, serving as the canton's capital.

Saturday morning is a good time to visit here to see the lively outdoor market, between 7am and noon. Peddlers, vendors, country people, artisans, and townsfolk converse in Italian over the wares.

ESSENTIALS

GETTING THERE Bellinzona is the easiest destination to reach in the Ticino. Every train from the north of Switzerland stops here, as Bellinzona lies on the Brussels-Basel-Zurich-Milan international line. Indeed, every day regional and international trains stop here about once every 30 minutes. For **rail information** and schedules, call ✆ **0900/300-300.**

The nearest **airport** is at Lugano-Agno, 30 minutes from Bellinzona by train.

If you're **driving** from Zurich, continue along the N2 expressway through the St. Gotthard Tunnel into the Ticino. N2 continues southeast to Bellinzona.

VISITOR INFORMATION The **Bellinzona Tourist Bureau,** Palazzo Civico at Piazza Nosetto (✆ **091/825-21-31;** www.bellinzonaturismo.ch), is open Sunday to Friday 9am to 6pm and Saturday 9am to 1pm.

EXPLORING THE AREA

Bellinzona has three castles dating from the 13th to the 15th centuries: the Schwyz, the Unterwald, and the Uri.

Castle of Uri ★ (Castelgrande, or San Michele in Italian; ✆ **091/825-81-45**), built in 1280, is the most ancient and the largest castle in town. To reach the castle, take an elevator from piazza del Sole in the town center. In addition to the elevator, there are signposted paths from piazza Collegiata and piazza Nosetto for those who'd like to take one of the most scenic walks in the area. The castle was restored in 1991 with a historical section and a small numismatic museum. The castle contains a restaurant (see the Castelgrande review below), a banquet room, and a congress hall. It's open daily from 10am to 6pm. Admission is 5F for adults; 2.50F for children, students, and seniors 65 or over.

The most outstanding of the three medieval fortifications is the **Schwyz Castle** ★★ (Castello di Montebello; ✆ **091/825-13-42**). It has a 13th-century château with a courtyard,

(Finds) **Bellinzona Blues**

In late July hordes from throughout Switzerland gather in Bellinzona for the annual **Blues Festival,** where free concerts are staged in squares. Some of the biggest names in blues, such as Buddy Guy and Son Seals, have appeared here, and the tourist office (see "Essentials," above) will supply the details, which change every year.

as well as several 15th-century additions. Today it's a minor museum of history and archaeology. To get here by car, start from viale Stazione and follow the steep ramp up to this huge citadel. It's open daily from 8am to 8pm, and admission is 5F for adults; 2.50F for children, students, and seniors 65 or over.

Castle of Unterwald ★ (Castello di Sasso Corbaro; ✆ **091/825-59-06**) was built in 1479. It can be reached by the same road that goes up to the Schwyz (see above). The view from the terrace here is the finest in Bellinzona. You'll see not only the lower valley of the Ticino but Lake Maggiore as well. The castle hosts temporary exhibitions. Open only April to October daily from 10am to 6pm, the castle's admission price is 5F for adults and 2.50F for children, students, and seniors, depending on the exhibit. A combination ticket to all three castles costs 13F and 9F for children.

Also worth visiting is the collegiate **Church of Sts. Peter and Stephen,** dating from the 16th century. It's a fine Renaissance structure, with a richly embellished baroque interior. The location is across from Castelgrande.

Guided walking tours of Bellinzona, its Old Town, and its castles are available upon request at the tourist office (see "Essentials," above).

SHOPPING

Pick up a map from the tourist office in the center of the Old Town. A look at the map will direct you to **Villa dei Cedri** (✆ **091/821-85-20;** www.villacedri.ch), Bellinzona's municipally owned art gallery, founded in 1985. The gallery contains private art donated to the city but also mounts temporary exhibitions. In back is an enclosed garden and grounds where the townsfolk grow their own small crop of local merlot, bottles of which are offered for sale in the gallery. It's open Tuesday to Friday from 2 to 6pm, and Saturday and Sunday from 11am to 6pm. Admission is 8F for adults, and 5.50F for students, children, and seniors 65 or over.

WHERE TO STAY

Albergo Unione   The best hotel in town is a plain-looking white building with a pink-marble extension with balconies. It's surrounded by gardens, some with fountains. The government-rated three-star hotel offers modernized, midsize rooms with flowered carpets, tiles, firm beds, and up-to-date plumbing.

Via Général Guisan 1, CH-6500 Bellinzona. ✆ **091/825-55-77.** Fax 091/825-94-60. www.hotel-unione.ch. 33 units. 220F–240F double; 260F triple. Rates include breakfast. AE, DC, MC, V. Closed mid-Dec to mid-Jan. **Amenities:** Restaurant; bar; concierge; room service. *In room:* TV, hair dryer, minibar, Wi-Fi (10F per hour).

WHERE TO DINE

Castelgrande ★ TICINESE/ITALIAN   Located in the largest and most ancient castle in Bellinzona (see "Exploring the Area," above), this restaurant might be predictably

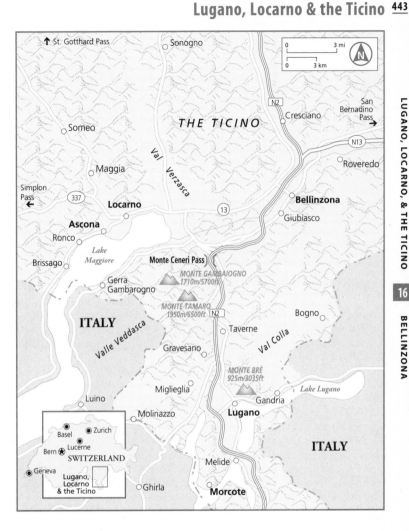

overrun with camera-toting tourists getting off tour buses. But unlike restaurants installed in most European castles, the upstairs dining room here is decidedly upmarket. Downstairs, there's an informal grotto with terrace, which serves less expensive Ticino and Italian dishes, while the more formal upstairs room features gourmet specialties. When dining in this second-level room, men are advised to wear a jacket.

The restaurant is not only the most luxurious in town, it also serves the best food. The cuisine combines that of the Ticino region with dishes inspired by sunny Italy. Game is a feature, and the wine list is particularly extensive. Try such dishes as pigeon with onions in a sweet-and-sour sauce, or if it's autumn, perfectly cooked quail with porcini mushrooms. The chef's imagination is reflected in such dishes as gooseliver accompanied by blueberries. Guests can ask for a table in the cavelike interior or, if the weather is right, for one on the large terrace.

Salita al Castello. ☎ **091/826-23-53.** www.castelgrande.ch. Reservations recommended. Main courses 19F–54F. AE, DC, MC, V. Tues–Sun noon–2:30pm and 6:30–10pm.

Locanda Orico ★★★ ITALIAN/FRENCH   This is one of the best restaurants in the Ticino, serving a refined cuisine based on market-fresh ingredients. The inn lies in a stately town house at the foot of Castelgrande in the center of Bellinzona. The chef, Lorenzo Albrici, was once a student of Frédy Girardet, hailed as one of the greatest chefs of Europe. The fixed-price lunch menu (45F) is the town's great dining bargain. An array of warm and cold appetizers is there to tempt you, ranging from house-marinated salmon in a sweet-and-sour sauce to carpaccio of duck liver flavored with sea salt. Baked shrimp are also a starter, floating in an Andalusian gazpacho. Main courses, which are especially delightful, include filet of freshwater lake perch stuffed with green leafy vegetables and filet of roasted veal with rosemary-flavored butter.

Via Orico 13. ☎ **091/825-15-18.** www.locandaorico.ch. Reservations recommended. Main courses 38F–50F; 6-course menu degustation 110F. AE, DC, MC, V. Tues–Sat 11:30am–2pm and 6:30–11pm.

2 LOCARNO ★★

22km (14 miles) W of Bellinzona; 40km (25 miles) N of Lugano

This ancient town at the north end of **Lake Maggiore** ★★★ is a vacation resort known for its mild climate. The rich Mediterranean vegetation includes camellias, magnolias, mimosa, wisteria, azaleas, and oleander in the spring. Olives, figs, and pomegranates also flourish in this climate.

Locarno entered world history in 1925, when an international conference held here resulted in a series of agreements known collectively as the Locarno Pact. It was in Locarno that the former enemies of World War I, seeking to reorder the affairs of Europe, committed themselves to a peaceful coexistence. Locarno was chosen over Lucerne, reportedly, because the mistress of the French representative wanted the meeting to be held on Lake Maggiore. The "spirit of Locarno," however, did not last long; within a decade the participants were again arming for war.

If you take the electric railway between Locarno and the Simplon Pass, you'll pass through the Centovalli, named for the hundred valleys that slope toward the river. There are many charming villages on the banks of this river. At Carnedo, in Italy, the railway climbs up to the plateau of Santa Maria Maggiore, a wide, barren, and solitary district that stretches for about 10km (6 miles) at 840m (2,755 ft.) above sea level. A steep descent leads down to the railway junction of Domodossola. This international railway serves as a link between the Gotthard and the Simplon lines. The bridges are technological wonders.

ESSENTIALS

GETTING THERE   The nearest **airport** is at Lugano (see section 4, later in this chapter), 45 minutes away by train.

The Locarno-Domodossola electric railway links Locarno with the Italian town of Domodossola. From here, you can continue to Brig in the Rhône Valley, through the Simplon Tunnel. Railway lines connect Brig with Lake Geneva and Bern through the

Lotschberg Tunnel. Direct trains from Lausanne or Bern take 4 hours to reach Locarno. From the other direction, through the St. Gotthard Tunnel, Locarno is 23km (14 miles) west of Bellinzona by rail. For **rail information** and schedules, call ✆ **0900/300-300.**

Locarno sits atop the **bus** routes that connect Ascona with Lugano, and they continue on to many different mountain villages to the northeast, eventually arriving at Chur. For more details about bus transportation, call the tourist bureau (see below).

After **driving** through the St. Gotthard Tunnel and reaching Bellinzona on the N2 expressway, take Route 13 west to reach Locarno.

VISITOR INFORMATION The **Locarno Tourist Bureau,** on largo Zorzi 1 (✆ **091/ 791-00-91;** www.maggiore.ch), is open March to October Monday to Friday 9am to 6pm, Saturday 10am to 6pm, and Sunday 10am to 1:30pm and 2:30 to 5pm; November to February, hours are Monday to Friday 9am to 12:30pm and 2 to 6pm.

SEEING THE SIGHTS

Start your walk around town at **piazza Grande,** the main square. On the north side the arcades are filled with shops. You can find antiques, art, Swiss and Italian handicrafts, and high fashion from Milan.

From piazza Grande, follow the curvy via Francesco Rusca to the Old Town. Along the way, you can visit the **Castello Visconteo,** piazza Castello 2 (✆ **091/756-31-80**). This structure is all that survives from a late-medieval castle in which the dukes of Milan lived. It was severely damaged in 1518. Today the castle contains the Museum Civico, which displays many Roman artifacts excavated in the area. It's open April to October, Tuesday to Sunday from 10am to 5pm. Admission is 7F.

The most important sight in Locarno is the **Santuario della Madonna del Sasso** ★ (✆ **091/743-62-65**), on a wooded crag above the resort in the hamlet of Orselina. Hearty visitors and devout pilgrims can climb to the church, at an elevation of 350m (1,148 ft.). However, we recommend the funicular, which leaves every 15 minutes from 7am to 11pm. The round-trip fare is 6.60F for adults, 3.30F for children. The church was founded in 1480 after a friar, Bartolomeo da Ivrea, reportedly saw a vision of the Virgin. It was reconstructed in 1616. The basilica contains much artwork, including Bramantino's *Flight into Egypt* (1520). In a museum next door to the basilica hang masterpieces by such artists as Raphael. Another masterpiece, painted in 1870, is *Christ Carried to the Sepulcher,* by Antonio Ciseri. This procession scene is most often described as "Caravaggiesque." The stunning **panoramic view** ★ can be taken in from the loggia, opening onto the rooftops of Locarno with Lake Maggiore in the distance. The grounds are open March to October daily 7am to 6:45pm. Today the general public is not admitted at will, but arrangements can be made with the friars by calling in advance and booking a reservation to visit.

One of our favorite pastimes is to go biking along the way. At the train station (Piazza Stazione; ✆ **091/743-65-64**) you can rent bikes for 33F per day. Bikes can be rented daily 8am to 7pm.

Fleeing the city (not that you would want to), you can take a postal bus (no. 630) to the village of **Sonogno** in just 1 hour. At the end of the ride, you'll be in the midst of towering peaks in one of the Ticino's most scenic valleys, **Val Verzasca.** After getting off the bus, take the first left and let the yellow signs direct you to **Lavertezzo,** across shaded glens and riverbeds through perfect and bucolic valley scenery. Allow about 3½ hours to go from Sonogno to Lavertezzo. Should you tire at any time, you can take one of the postal buses that run through the valley.

THE GAMBAROGNO RIVIERA ★★★

The Gambarogno Riviera, with its characteristic Ticinese villages, spreads along Lake Maggiore's left shore for about 11km (6½ miles) to the Italian border. It begins at Contone, at the foot of the Monte Ceneri, and includes part of the Piano di Magadino (plain of Magadino) as well as a wildlife refuge, Bolle di Magadino, in a delta formed by the Ticino River.

The lush vegetation, the green chestnut forests, and the iridescent colors of the lake—ranging from azure to emerald green—give a uniqueness to this well-preserved region. Thanks to its Mediterranean climate, the annual temperatures average 59°F (15°C). In summer the weather is ideal for all aquatic sports. The Riviera isn't just a lakeshore, but also a steep mountain sloping up from the lake. On one side it's crowned by Monte Tamaro, at 1,950m (6,396 ft.) above sea level, and on the other by Monte Gambarogno, at 1,710m (5,609 ft.). It's this latter mountain that gives its name to the region. There's a panorama of the Alps from Monte Rosa on the west to the chain of Ticinese Alps on the north.

The region is riddled with some 201km (125 miles) of **footpaths.** The Locarno Tourist Bureau (see "Essentials," above) distributes a map indicating every trail; this map also outlines various itineraries with the time that it takes to cover them.

One path indicated on the map provides access to the whole area, from the mouth of the Ticino River to the village of Magadino, from which the biological cycles of local species can be observed. More than 300 different kinds of birds alone live and nest in this tangle of vegetation. **Ente Turistico del Gambarogno,** via Cantonale, CH-6574 Vira (✆ **091/ 795-18-66**), arranges guided tours of the area in a rowboat, but only on Thursdays.

SHOPPING

Most of the merchandise that's for sale in Locarno is practical instead of glittery. There's a cluster of fashionable boutiques along piazza Grande, the centerpiece of the town's shopping district, but overall, shoppers are usually better off wandering through the sprawling spaces of the town's three department stores. These are **Globus,** Largo Zorzi (✆ **091/756-39-39**), where a worthy collection of local handicrafts and Swiss souvenirs is for sale; the somewhat less upscale but just as comprehensive **Manor,** Piazza Grande (✆ **091/756-86-99**); and **Migros,** via Franchini 31 (✆ **091/756-88-11**). In other corners of Switzerland Migros is known only as an American-style grocery-store chain, but in Locarno the store sells Italian and Swiss food, wine, and specialty goods such as prosciutto, as well as hardware, clothing, souvenirs of the region, and virtually everything else you'd expect in a major department store.

Does your proximity to Italy make you thirsty for the fruit of the grape? Two family-run vineyards lie within 3km (2 miles) of Locarno, and both sell bottles of their products. They are **Delea,** signposted in the hamlet of Losone, a short drive north of Locarno (✆ **091/791-08-17**), and **Matasci,** signposted in the hamlet of Tenero (✆ **091/735-60-11;** www.matasci-vini.ch). Each produces both white and red wines, all of which are for sale.

WHERE TO STAY

Locarno has many good hotels that accommodate travelers on their way to or from Italy. You can also spend a pleasant vacation along the lake here.

Expensive

Hotel Orselina ★★★ Guests enjoy a dramatic view from this peaceful five-story oasis in a suburb north of town, accessible by funicular from Orselina. Situated on a hillside, it resembles a Spanish parador. Its sloping lawns, shaded loggias, and many-tiered subtropical gardens may cause you to linger for a month at this tranquil retreat. It's got everything but a lakeside location (though the lake is visible in the distance). The midsize to spacious rooms are well furnished and comfortable, each with a firm French bed and a balcony facing south. Those in the newer wing are more up-to-date, although all the rooms are warmly inviting.

Via Santuario 10, CH-6600 Orselina-Locarno. ✆ **091/735-73-50.** Fax 091/735-73-51. www.orselina.com. 74 units. 380F–500F double; 550F–700F suite. Rates include half board. MC, V. Outdoor parking 10F, garage parking 12F. Closed Dec to mid-Feb. **Amenities:** Restaurant; bar; children's center; exercise room; Jacuzzi; 2 heated pools (1 indoor); room service; sauna; outdoor tennis court (lit). *In room:* TV, hair dryer, minibar.

Moderate

Hotel Belvedere ★★ (Finds) Set on a steep hillside in the upper heights of Locarno, this ocher-colored neoclassical hotel is a beautifully landscaped retreat. It was built in 1910 on the foundations of a 300-year-old house. Reopened in 1990 after 4 years of total restoration, it offers modernized comforts and sweeping views of the lake from each of its streamlined and contemporary bedrooms. All but three of its bedrooms have a private balcony.

Via ai Monti della Trinità 44, CH-6600 Locarno. ✆ **091/751-03-63.** Fax 091/751-52-39. www.belvedere-locarno.ch. 81 units. 320F–440F double; 430F–520F suite. Rates include buffet breakfast. AE, DC, MC, V. Parking 13F. Take Locarno's only funicular, departing from via Ramogna near the lakefront, to its 2nd stop (Belvedere), a few steps from the hotel. **Amenities:** 3 restaurants; bar; exercise room; Jacuzzi; 2 pools (1 saltwater heated indoor); room service; sauna. *In room:* TV, hair dryer, minibar, Wi-Fi (10F per hour).

Millennium (Value) Built at the turn of the 21st century, this hotel is named for the new millennium. Lying in Locarno's Old Town, it's a cozy nest of comfort and convenience and was planned from the start to take advantage of the technology of the new century. Each of the small to midsize bedrooms is tastefully decorated, coming with a small bathroom. The building was originally an old Customs house before its conversion to a hotel. Local artists and photographers have contributed some of their works to decorate the public areas. Bedrooms are soundproof and are equipped with such conveniences as a working desk and orthopedic mattresses.

Via Dogana Nuova 2, CH-6600 Locarno. ✆ **091/759-67-67.** Fax 091/759-67-68. www.millennium-hotel. ch. 11 units. 140F–290F. AE, MC, V. Free parking. *In room:* A/C, TV, hair dryer, minibar, Wi-Fi (free).

Ramada La Palma au Lac ★ Dating from the mid-1950s (and looking it), this balconied hotel of six- and seven-story buildings faces the lake and is a particular favorite of clients who were young when Queen Elizabeth was. Sun chairs and chaise longues are set up on the terrace. The updated public rooms are decorated with oil paintings and tapestries and retain their 19th-century grace. The elegantly furnished and spacious bedrooms have an Italian flair, and units with private balconies overlook the lake.

Viale Verbano 29, CH-6600 Locarno-Muralto. ✆ **091/735-36-36.** Fax 091/735-36-16. www.ramada.com. 68 units. 280F–420F double; 460F–520F suite. Rates include buffet breakfast. AE, DC, MC, V. Free parking outside. **Amenities:** 2 restaurants; bar; room service; sauna. *In room:* TV, hair dryer, minibar, Wi-Fi (25F per 24 hr.).

Remorino Hotel-Garni ★ (Finds) In a secluded residential area a short walk from the center of town, this hotel lies only 2 minutes from the lakeside promenade. For almost 3 decades it has been owned by the Kirchlechner-Qualizza family, which now personally directs the management. All the bedrooms have modern furnishings along with immaculately maintained bathrooms. Try for a bedroom facing the lake. The garden is especially inviting, with its Mediterranean plants such as camellia, magnolia, and olive and palm trees.

Via Verbano 29, CH-6648 Minusio-Locarno. ✆ **091/743-10-33.** Fax 091/743-74-29. www.remorino.ch. 25 units. 182F–344F double. Rates include buffet breakfast. AE, V. Free parking outdoors, 15F in garage. Closed Nov–Feb. **Amenities:** Bikes; outdoor heated pool. *In room:* A/C (in some), TV, hair dryer, minibar, Wi-Fi (free).

Rosa Seegarten (Value)
For good value in Locarno, try this old-fashioned, cream-colored hotel on the lake, a 3-minute walk from the train station. Half board is encouraged. Meals are served on a lakeside terrace under a grape arbor. This is the largest terrace in town, capable of seating between 150 and 200 people. Rooms are comfortable but functionally furnished.

Viale Verbano 25, CH-6600 Locarno. ✆ **091/743-87-31.** Fax 091/743-50-02. www.rosa-seegarten.ch. 37 units. 220F–330F double. Rates include buffet breakfast. Half board 35F per person. AE, DC, MC, V. Free parking. Closed Nov–Feb. **Amenities:** Restaurant; room service. *In room:* TV, minibar (in some), hair dryer (in some).

Inexpensive

Camelia
Surrounded by a sumptuous garden, this hotel in the Muralto section of Locarno is family run and inviting. Its charm lies in its romantic architecture of the early 20th century. The modern bedrooms are comfortable and well maintained. The food is another good reason to stay here, especially if you like Italian specialties. The staff is also most helpful, arranging bungee jumping, rock climbing, canyoning, and other activities (such as helping you rent motorbikes). The hotel also shuttles guests to and from the local train station and the airport.

Via G.G. Nessi 9, CH-6600 Muralto-Locarno. ✆ **091/743-00-21.** Fax 091/743-00-22. www.camelia.ch. 41 units. 178F–236F double. AE, DC, MC, V. Free parking. Closed Nov–Feb. **Amenities:** Restaurant; bar; Wi-Fi (free, in lobby). *In room:* TV.

Hotel dell'Angelo (Finds)
In the center of the action, this hotel at the end of piazza Grande is a winning choice even if you disregard its low rates. Reconstructed in 1976, it grew up over the ruins of a building from the late 17th century. Arches on the ground floor and balconies trimmed in iron grace its facade. As with many bargain rooms, the furnishings are sparse—with much use of Formica—but they're clean and comfortable nevertheless. Freshly starched linens and immaculately scrubbed tile bathrooms complete with bidets make the rooms more appealing. In contrast to the bedrooms, some of the public lounges are more enticing, with paintings and antiques adding a grace note. The hotel's terrace features views of the town.

Piazza Grande 1, CH-6600 Locarno. ✆ **091/751-81-75.** Fax 091/751-82-56. www.hotel-dell-angelo.ch. 55 units. 110F–240F double. Rates include buffet breakfast. AE, DC, MC, V. Parking 7F. **Amenities:** Restaurant; bar. *In room:* TV, hair dryer.

Piccolo (Value)
One of the town's smallest hotels is also one of its most affordable. Lying only a 5-minute walk from the city center, it's convenient for jaunts down to the lake and the train station. Rooms are small but comfortable and handsomely decorated with flowery draperies, duvets, and cane-backed chairs. Each room comes with a tiny but adequate private bathroom.

Via Buetti 11, CH-6600 Locarno-Muralto. ✆ **091/743-02-12.** Fax 091/743-21-98. www.piccolo-hotel.ch. 21 units. 160F–200F double. AE, DC, MC, V. Closed Nov to mid-Mar. **Amenities:** Bar. *In room:* TV, minibar.

Expensive

Restaurant Cittadella ★ MEDITERRANEAN Located in the center of the Old Town, this restaurant complex is separated from the narrow cobblestone street by a granite arcade draped with vines. The downstairs trattoria has timbered ceilings, stucco walls, and an informal ambience. Upstairs is a chic enclave of *cuisine moderne* deftly and imaginatively prepared. Specialties include a gooseliver terrine and a salad of large shrimp with nuts and mango. A mixed grill with saltwater and freshwater fish is delicious.

If you don't object to the often-noisy streets of the historic Old Town, you'll find 10 simply furnished bedrooms upstairs renting for 140F to 170F for a double, including a buffet breakfast.

Via Cittadella 18. © 091/751-58-85. Fax 091/751-77-59. www.cittadella.ch. Reservations required. Restaurant (upstairs) main courses 45F–80F, fixed-price gourmet menu 90F; trattoria (downstairs) main courses 35F–50F, pizzas 15F–20F. AE, DC, MC, V. Tues–Sun noon–2pm and 7–11pm.

Moderate

Osteria del Centenario ★★★ ITALIAN There is no finer dining in Locarno than that found here, not even in the restaurants of the most deluxe hotels. The dining room, with austere white walls and straight-back chairs, has a simplicity that contrasts with the colorful creations of Gérard Perriard. The menu is based on fresh ingredients from the market. Seasonal specialties—and delightful ones at that—include sea bass with fennel, foie gras of duck with salad, lobster salad in mango sauce, and stuffed lamb in asparagus sauce. For an unusual first course, ask for a cold consommé of quail eggs garnished with caviar.

Lungolago 17, Muralto. © 091/743-82-22. www.osteriacentenario.ch. Reservations required. Main courses 20F–47F. AE, MC, V. Mon–Sat 11:30am–2pm and 6:30–9:30pm. Closed 2 weeks in Feb and 2 weeks in Nov.

Restaurant La Carbonara SWISS/ITALIAN There's a well-stocked bar near the entrance of this restaurant, separated from the dining room by a glass partition. The stucco walls are decorated with original paintings and copper pots. Patrons are regaled with perfectly prepared, full-flavored dishes. Specialties include veal kidney with grappa and mushrooms, saltimbocca (veal with ham), and a large pasta menu, featuring macaroni with four different types of cheese. Other dishes include gnocchi in a Gorgonzola sauce and grilled filets of lamb with aromatic herbs, grilled shrimp, and 15 types of pizza.

Piazza Stazione. © 091/743-67-14. Reservations not required. Main courses 22F–35F. AE, DC, MC, V. Daily 11:30am–midnight.

LOCARNO AFTER DARK

Nightlife in Locarno may not impress you, as it's a lot quieter here than in larger, and more extroverted, Ticino cities such as Lugano. So either haul yourself off to Lugano for the night, or drag out your dinner and then have a nightcap in the bar at your hotel. If this idea doesn't particularly appeal to you, you may opt for a stroll along the lakefront, stopping perhaps at the **Café Debarcadero,** Lungolago G. Motta (© **091/751-05-55**), which stays open every night till midnight. Debarcadero also offers pizzas and pastas for 12F to 18F. Another option is the cozy bar in the **Hotel Arcadia,** Lungolago G. Motta (© **091/756-18-18**), where potted palms, rattan furniture, and black-and-pink marble flooring evoke a Caribbean hideaway. Piano music sometimes accompanies the liquor.

There's a congenial bar tucked away next to the dining room of the previously recommended **Ristorante La Carbonara** (✆ **091/743-67-14**).

One of the best piano bars is the **Palm'Arte** at the Hotel La Palma au Lac, viale Verbano 29, Locarno-Muralto (✆ **091/735-36-36**).

If you're intrigued with gambling, you may decide to spin the small-stakes wheel of fortune at the town's obscure and rather dull casino, the **Kursaal Locarno,** largo Zorzi (✆ **091/756-30-30;** www.casinolocarno.ch). Open every day of the year but Christmas from noon to 3am Monday to Thursday and noon to 4am Friday to Sunday, it offers a small bar area, lots of noisy slot machines, and croupiers at blackjack and roulette tables.

3 ASCONA ★

4km (2¹/₂ miles) SW of Locarno; 42km (26 miles) NW of Lugano

Once a tiny fishing port, Ascona has swiftly developed into a resort to rival nearby Locarno. Located snugly on Lake Maggiore, it has long been a popular rendezvous point for painters, writers, and celebrities. Lenin found the place ideal, as did Isadora Duncan and Carl Jung. Rudolf Steiner, Hermann Hesse, and Paul Klee also lived here. Today, Ascona is one of the most popular destinations in the Ticino.

New developments have obscured much of the Old Town cherished by these famous people, but the heart of Ascona is still worth exploring—although you'll use up a lot of shoe leather. It has colorful little shops, art galleries (some good, some of the souvenir variety), and antiques stores.

Because of its mild climate, Ascona has subtropical vegetation. Flowers bloom year-round. Facilities include a golf course, a lido (beach), and a *Kursaal* (casino).

ESSENTIALS

GETTING THERE Ascona has no railway station of its own, so most train passengers disembark at nearby Locarno and transfer to a bus or taxi for the short ride to Ascona. Locarno has good connections to the region's major railway junction of Bellinzona, which has frequent express train connections from Milan and Zurich. For rail information and schedules, call ✆ **0900/300-300.**

A handful of buses connects Ascona with the railroad junction of Locarno, a short distance to the northeast. The bus ride takes 15 minutes, and departures are every 15 minutes and cost 3F one-way. For bus information, call Locarno's tourist office (see "Essentials" in section 2, earlier in this chapter).

If you're driving, continue west from Locarno along Route 13.

VISITOR INFORMATION The **Ascona Tourist Board,** via B. Papio 5 (✆ **091/791-00-91;** www.ascona.ch), is open mid-March to late October, Monday to Friday 9am to 6pm, Saturday 10am to 6pm, and Sunday 2:30 to 5pm.

SEEING THE SIGHTS

Collegio Pontificio Papio, off via Cappelle, has one of the most beautiful Renaissance courtyards in Switzerland. Dating from 1584, the building has two-story Italianate loggias. The **Chiesa Santa Maria della Misericordia** is part of the cloisters of the Collegio Pontificio Papio. Built at the end of the 14th century, it contains one of the largest late-Gothic frescoes in Switzerland.

Casa Serodine (also called Casa Borrani), which lies off piazza G. Motta, was built in 1620 and has one of the most richly embellished facades of any secular structure in the country.

Museo Comunale d'Arte Moderna, via Borgo 34 (© **091/759-81-40;** www.museo ascona.ch), has both changing exhibitions of modern art and a permanent collection, the latter including works by Klee and Utrillo. It's open March to December, Tuesday to Saturday from 10am to noon and 3 to 6pm, and Sunday 4 to 6pm, charging adults 7F and students, seniors, and children 5F.

Near the town, **Isole di Brissago** ★, off the shore of Lake Maggiore, contains a botanical garden of Mediterranean and subtropical flora. The gardens can be reached by boat from the center of Ascona as well as from other lakeside locales, including Locarno. Boats depart Ascona daily at 9:30am and run throughout the day, with the last departure from the island back to Ascona at 6pm. The ride takes 10 minutes and costs 3.80F. Admission to the botanical park is an additional 8F.

You can also visit the little village of **Ronco** ★★ along the corniche road west, an 18km (11-mile) trip. This very Mediterranean-type village is on a slope in one of the most charming settings in all of the Ticino. Erich Maria Remarque, the German author of *All Quiet on the Western Front,* lived here and is buried in the cemetery of the little church.

SHOPPING

Ascona doesn't place much emphasis on the sale of cutesy souvenirs, so you'll have to look hard for shops selling only handicrafts. You'll find postcards and a limited array of smaller, less impressive items imported directly from Italy at newsstands and kiosks in the town's pedestrian zone, which is centered around via Borgo and its offshoots. More prevalent, however, are stylish shops selling luxury goods, such as crystal at **Baccarat,** Carrà dei Nasi 22 (© **091/791-21-38**). For upscale, Milan-inspired clothing for women, the best shop is **Jiuditta,** in the Galleria della Carrà (© **091/791-20-19**). More intriguing are any of the town's roster of antiques dealers and art galleries. The town's most appealing antiques store, **Monna Lisa,** via Collegio 6 (© **091/791-45-52**), is managed by Hans-Peter Lehmann and his English/Irish wife, Liz. Inside, you'll find a worthy collection of china, silver, paintings, and furniture.

WHERE TO STAY

Bus no. 31 from Locarno services the hotels listed below.

Very Expensive

Albergo Casa Berno ★★ (Finds) Built into a hillside on a forest road above the town, this deluxe hotel, with several balconied wings, is a gem of a retreat. Its good-size rooms are comfortably furnished—some of them with elegant Louis XVI–style chairs. Each room has a concrete balcony with a southern exposure, and all are equipped with beautifully maintained bathrooms. The view extends from Bellinzona (see section 1, earlier in this chapter) to the Islands of Brissago.

Via G. Madonna, CH-6612 Ascona. © **091/791-32-32.** Fax 091/792-11-14. www.casaberno.ch. 62 units. 442F–524F double; 604F junior suite. Rates include half board. AE, DC, MC, V. Free parking. Closed late Oct to Mar. **Amenities:** Restaurant; bar; babysitting; bikes; outdoor heated pool; room service; sauna. *In room:* TV, hair dryer, minibar, Wi-Fi (free).

Castello del Sole ★★★ The grandest hotel in Ascona is surrounded by an 8-hectare (20-acre) park and green meadows. This peaceful haven is near the Maggia River, at the point where it flows into Lake Maggiore. It has the atmosphere of a private estate,

2km (1½ miles) from the center of town. There's an antique palazzo with many court-yards. The spacious public rooms have vaulted ceilings, granite columns, and marble terraces, with one room available for those with limited mobility. The rooms, which come in various shapes and sizes, have balconies and beautiful furniture, along with deluxe bathrooms. The suites are in a building east of the main hotel. Located nearby is the 18-hole golf course Locarno.

Via Muraccio 142, CH-6612 Ascona. ℂ **091/791-02-02.** Fax 091/792-11-18. www.castellodelsole.com. 85 units. 630F–820F double; 910F–970F junior suite; 1,510F deluxe suite. Rates include continental break-fast. Half board 70F per person. AE, DC, MC, V. Parking 25F. Closed mid-Oct to Apr. **Amenities:** 2 restau-rants; babysitting; exercise room; 2 pools (1 heated indoor); room service; spa; 6 tennis courts (lit). *In room:* A/C, TV, hair dryer, minibar, Wi-Fi (30F per 24 hr.).

Hotel Ascolago ★   This is a large concrete-block hotel with an angular facade and a roofline inspired by a Chinese pagoda. It's ideally located in the center of town, in a park with flowers and sculpture. A portico by the entrance looks as if it was designed by Le Corbusier. Many of the spacious bedrooms have been upgraded and are fairly stylish, decorated with subtle pastels and rosewood pieces, while others linger in the stuffy, fussy mode. Each room, however, is comfortable, with rows of awning-shaded balconies open-ing onto views of the garden and the lake.

Via Albarelle, CH-6612 Ascona. ℂ **091/785-82-00.** Fax 091/791-42-26. www.ascolago.ch. 18 units. Sum-mer 380F–480F double; winter 280F–360F double. MC, V. Free parking. Closed mid-Nov to mid-Dec. **Amenities:** Restaurant; bar; 2 heated pools (1 indoor); room service; sauna; limited watersports equip-ment/rental. *In room:* TV, hair dryer, minibar.

Relais & Châteaux Hotel Giardino ★★★   Although this atmospheric Mediter-ranean villa is one of four government-rated five-star hotels in Ascona, it's the most romantically appealing. Set about .4km (¼ mile) from the heart of town, connected by an antique shuttle bus that makes hourly runs back and forth, this glamorous, Mediter-ranean-style villa was built on a large plot of land in 1986. Today its structure incorpo-rates Portuguese and Italian tile work, Veronese marble, antique Swiss panels imported from very old *Weinstubes* in Zurich, and some of the most sophisticated interior decor in the region. The spacious bedrooms are cozy and plushly accessorized. Most alluring of all is the lavish garden *(il giardino),* whose illuminated lily pond is covered with a movable stage for the entertainment, which is sometimes provided after 8pm.

Via Segnale 10, CH-6612 Ascona. ℂ **091/785-88-88.** Fax 091/785-88-99. www.giardino.ch. 77 units. 625F–870F double; 1,085F–1,255F suite. Rates include half board. AE, DC, MC, V. Free parking. Closed mid-Nov to Mar. **Amenities:** 2 restaurants; bar; babysitting; exercise room; indoor heated pool; room service; spa. *In room:* TV, hair dryer, minibar, Wi-Fi (5F per 30 min.).

Expensive

Hotel Sasso Boretto ★   The entire balconied structure of this hotel seems to be set on top of concrete columns. Glass windows frame the ground floor, which is surrounded by redbrick terraces and Mediterranean trees. Most of the bedrooms (20 are nonsmok-ing) are decorated in warm, monochromatic tones of brown and beige. The larger ones show Italian flair; the smaller ones are less dramatic but cozy and comfortable nonethe-less, with well-maintained bathrooms.

Via Locarno 45, CH-6612 Ascona. ℂ **091/791-71-15.** Fax 091/786-99-00. www.sassoboretto.com. 50 units. 220F–360F double. Rates include continental breakfast. Half board 40F per person. AE, DC, MC, V. Parking 18F. Closed mid-Jan to mid-Mar. **Amenities:** 2 restaurants; bar; babysitting; exercise room; indoor heated pool; room service; sauna. *In room:* A/C (in some), TV, hair dryer, minibar, Wi-Fi (5F per 30 min.).

Seeschloss-Castello ★★ (Finds) This gem will appeal to romantics. The tower was 453 built in 1250 by a countess of Milan from the Ghiriglioni family. It served as the fortified dwelling of the family, which eventually controlled most of the navigation on the lake. Today palms and palmettos surround the flagstone terrace leading to the stone entryway. Pull the wrought-iron bell handle for assistance. The lobby is filled with antiques, and the spacious rooms are well maintained and comfortable, with private bathrooms. The best rooms—certainly the most romantic—are those in the tower. These are ideal for both honeymooners and off-the-record weekenders.

Piazza G. Motta, CH-6612 Ascona. (C) 091/791-01-61. Fax 091/791-18-04. www.castello-seeschloss.ch. 46 units. 248F–448F double; 528F–648F double in the tower. Rates include buffet breakfast. Half board 38F per person. AE, DC, MC, V. Free parking outdoors, 21F in garage. Closed Nov to mid-Mar. **Amenities:** Restaurant; bar; outdoor heated pool; room service. *In room:* TV, hair dryer, minibar, Wi-Fi (25F per 24 hr.).

Moderate

Albergo Elvezia au Lac This hotel lies in the heart of the resort town with a cobblestone terrace facing the lake and an indoor dining room just behind it. The upper-story terrace is ringed with vines. Each room, ranging from small to medium, is priced according to its panorama over the lake and whether it has a balcony or terrace looking inward to the city.

Piazza G. Motta 15, CH-6612 Ascona. (C) 091/791-15-14. Fax 091/791-00-03. www.hotel-elvezia.ch. 20 units. 206F–266F double. Rates include continental breakfast. AE, DC, MC, V. Parking 12F. Closed Nov–Feb. **Amenities:** Restaurant; room service. *In room:* TV, minibar.

Hotel la Perla This white-walled hotel is located in a residential area away from the lake. Its small rooms have balconies with a good view of the mountains, and each comes with a private bathroom. Note that there are three extra double rooms separated from the hotel with private bathrooms, but without balconies, costing 220F.

Via Collina 14, CH-6612 Ascona. (C) 091/791-35-77. Fax 091/791-79-62. www.laperla.ch. 50 units. 220F–260F double. Rates include buffet breakfast. AE, DC, MC, V. Parking 8F. **Amenities:** Restaurant; outdoor heated pool; room service. *In room:* TV, minibar.

Riposo ★ (Value) The most tranquil hotel in Ascona is a rather romantic and traditional structure standing in a quiet corner of the Old Town, a 3-minute walk to the lake. It's in a part of Ascona filled with narrow alleys, art galleries, and fashion boutiques. Each bedroom is individually designed and furnished, each with its own color, art objects, and furnishings; most of them have a private terrace or balcony overlooking Old Town and the lake itself. Breakfast is served in the courtyard or on the roof terrace, and the serving table is filled with homemade jams, Swiss cheese from the Ticino, Italian salami, farm-raised ham, and a variety of freshly baked organic breads and Swiss muesli. The on-site restaurant is worth a visit even if you don't stay here. It serves a creative regional cuisine with many other specialties from the Mediterranean kitchen. The roof terrace is the major allure of this hotel; it's decorated with subtropical plants and has a heated pool surrounded by natural rocks.

Scalinata della Ruga 4, CH-6612, Ascona. (C) 091/791-31-64. Fax 091/791-46-63. www.hotelriposo.ch. 32 units. 180F–320F double. Rates include breakfast buffet. MC, V. Parking 17F. Closed mid-Oct to mid-Mar. **Amenities:** Restaurant; bar; bikes; outdoor pool; room service. *In room:* TV.

Tamaro du Lac ★ (Finds) A welcome is painted in Latin above the huge arch leading into the flagstone reception hall of the original core of this gracious lakefront hotel, which was formerly an abbey. Farther on is a sky-lit central courtyard, with vines growing over the massive vaults of the arcade surrounding it. In the early 1990s a comfortable, very quiet annex was added a few steps from the main building. The owners have decorated the interior with antiques and some romantic artifacts. The bedrooms, although lacking great style, are comfortably furnished and well maintained.

Piazza G. Motta 35, CH-6612 Ascona. ✆ **091/785-48-48.** Fax 091/791-29-28. www.hotel-tamaro.ch. 51 units, 41 with bathroom, in main building; 10 units, all with bathroom, in annex. 180F–290F double with bathroom, 130F–150F without bathroom. Rates include breakfast. Half board 33F per person. AE, DC, MC, V. Parking 11F in private garage, 9F in private parking outside. Closed Dec–Mar. **Amenities:** Restaurant; room service. *In room:* A/C, TV, hair dryer, minibar.

WHERE TO DINE

The harbor of Ascona is lined with many restaurants. Most guests dine outside during the summer, by the lake. There are also many fine restaurants on the cobblestone streets of the Old Town.

Expensive

Al Pontile ITALIAN/FRENCH   Many of the restaurants along the quays look alike and have similar menus, but the decor here, with a darkly rustic interior and hanging straw lamps, seems a little warmer and more intimate than elsewhere. The food is better, too. The menu might include quail with risotto, *osso buco,* and saltimbocca (veal with ham), in addition to a variety of good pasta dishes. Fish dishes include scampi, sole, and salmon. For dessert, we recommend one of the homemade pies.

Longalago G. Motta 31. ✆ **091/791-46-04.** Reservations not required. Main courses 35F–45F. AE, DC, MC, V. Daily noon–2:30pm and 6–9:30pm.

Aphrodite ECCO ★★★ FRENCH/ITALIAN   These two restaurants are in the most desirable deluxe hotel in Ascona, about .4km (¼ mile) from the center of town. Aphrodite, the more elegant and formal, requests that men wear jackets and ties for meals served on a flowering terrace within view of a water garden and plenty of greenery. Menu specialties change every week, but include perfectly prepared modern choices such as tea-smoked duck breast, wild sea bass with a saffron tomato risotto, or marinated fresh uncooked tuna in lime oil with sautéed vegetables. The chef prepares 16 different fixed-price menus whose composition changes daily, based on the seasonal ingredients available.

ECCO is in a cozy environment reminiscent of a mountain hideaway, with old-fashioned menu items similar to what your Italian-Swiss grandmother might have prepared for you when you were a child. Portions are copious.

In the Relais & Châteaux Hotel Giardino, via Segnale. ✆ **091/785-88-88.** Reservations recommended. Aphrodite main courses 40F–70F; ECCO main courses 35F–56F. AE, DC, MC, V. Aphrodite daily 12:30–2pm and 7–9:30pm. ECCO Wed–Sun 7–9:30pm. Closed mid-Nov to mid-Mar.

Navegna ★ SWISS/REGIONAL   This is one of the best restaurants in Locarno, both for aesthetic and gastronomic reasons. If the weather permits, we highly recommend that you sit on the beautiful terrace overlooking the lake. The white tablecloths with lace edges add to the delight. If you must sit inside, the sophisticated dining room, with its deep browns and soft creams, has a lovely view as well—just try to get a seat next to a window. Almost all of the food here is fresh, going from owner Enrico Ravelli's farm straight to chef Marco Meneganti's kitchen. The homemade pasta is delicious, as are the poultry dishes.

Albergo Navegna, which houses Restaurant Navegna, is also a charming hotel, although it is secondary to the restaurant. Double rooms range from 160F–270F and have televisions, telephones, minibars (in some), hair dryers (in some), and balconies (in some). Try to get one of the south-facing rooms if you decide to stay here, as they have views of the lake.

Via alla Riva 2. ☎ 091/743-22-22. www.navegna.ch. Reservations recommended. Main courses 34F–50F. MC, V. Daily noon–2pm and 7–9pm. Closed Tues in Sept.

Moderate

Al Torchio ITALIAN   The first room of this rambling restaurant offers a rustic decor, red candles, and designs painted on the plaster walls. On a warm night you may continue past the American-style salad bar in the back and turn left into the vine-covered courtyard. The well-prepared menu may include rabbit with leeks in beer sauce, filet of lamb, a divine risotto with porcini mushrooms, a winter fondue, and a succulent spaghetti with clams. An especially delectable dish is homemade tagliolini stuffed with pulverized fish and shrimp and served with a tomato sauce flavored with olive oil and fresh herbs. For dessert, try the *gelato misto* (a mixed selection of ice cream) or a sorbet with vodka. There's a garden-style piano bar in a summery courtyard.

Contrada Maggiore 1. ☎ 091/791-71-26. Reservations recommended. Main courses 18F–38F. AE, DC, MC, V. Daily noon–2pm and 6–10pm. Closed Tues in winter.

Ristorante Borromeo ★ SWISS/ITALIAN   Dating from around 1350, this former monastery and Catholic school is one of the most popular restaurants in the region, noted for its outdoor terrace. Local residents flock to its three rustic rooms with high ceilings. The kitchen staff is versatile, knowing how to prepare the best of both the Italian and Swiss kitchens. They use very fresh ingredients and don't oversauce. The menu may include risotto Milanese with saffron, a mixed grill, piccata Marsala, trout, scampi, and an especially good *osso buco*. On our recent rounds, we especially enjoyed saltimbocca (veal with ham), served with a potato-based gnocchi.

Via Collegio 16. ☎ 091/791-92-81. Reservations recommended. Main courses 25F–46F. AE, DC, MC, V. Daily noon–2pm and 6–10pm. Closed Mon July–Aug.

Inexpensive

Osteria Nostrana ⟨Value⟩ PIZZA/PASTA   This is one of the most active harborfront restaurants in Ascona, with sidewalk tables overlooking the lake and its fashionable promenade. The rustically comfortable dining room serves the town's best and most reasonably priced pastas and pizzas. They also feature daily specials, sometimes as many as 15 per day, depending on the season and what's good at the market. The best pasta is the spaghetti *alla carbonara* (with meat sauce), although the linguine *ai fruitti di mare* (with shellfish) is a close runner-up, as is the fusili with heavy cream and ham. For a superb pizza, opt for the Siciliana with anchovies and black olives or the *prosciutto e funghi* (ham and mushrooms).

Piazza Giuseppe Motta. ☎ 091/791-51-58. www.osteria-nostrana.ch. Reservations not necessary. Pasta and pizzas 15F–25F. AE, DC, MC, V. Summer daily 9am–1am; winter daily 9am–midnight.

ASCONA AFTER DARK

Ascona is quiet and calm, with not nearly as energetic a night scene as, say, nearby Lugano. A likable bar favored by those seeking live music is **Piper,** via Aerodromo 3 (☎ 091/791-13-74). Finally, an establishment noted for its ability to provide feminine companionship for unaccompanied men is **Happyville,** via Borgo (☎ **091/791-49-22**), where a tiny dance floor is a lot less important than the seductively lit stage. Strip shows are usually presented nightly beginning around 11:30pm.

16

4 LUGANO ★★★

32km (20 miles) S of Bellinzona; 229km (143 miles) S of Zurich

Lugano is a Swiss town with an Italian flavor. The Italian influence is evident in the city's cafes, sunny piazzas, cobblestone streets, and arcades. It's a city designed for walking. You can wander at leisure, exploring its historic old streets.

Lugano is built along the shore of **Lake Lugano** ★★★, which the Italians call Lake Ceresio. The peaks of San Salvatore and Monte Brè loom on opposite sides of town. The low mountains protect it from cold alpine winds, and the climate is ideal from March to November. As the cultural center of the Ticino, Lugano has attracted many artists and casual visitors.

ESSENTIALS

GETTING THERE   The airline **Swiss,** Aeroporto Lugano (☎ **0848/700-700**), provides air links between Lugano and Zurich. Taxis await visitors at the Lugano airport for the 10-minute ride to the center of Lugano.

Lugano is a major stop along the rail lines that connect Milan with Zurich. As such, trains from all parts of Switzerland arrive throughout the day and night. For **rail information** and schedules, call ☎ **0900/300-300.** Rail passengers arrive at the Lugano railroad station, piazzale della Stazione, which is in the center of the city, west of piazza Indipendenza. If your luggage is light, you can walk to many of the hotels; if not, you can take one of the taxis waiting outside the station.

Lugano is linked by **bus** to dozens of hamlets in the Ticino that lack rail connections. There are also long-range trains that come from Italian cities: Como (trip time: 45 min.), Venice (trip time: 5 hr.), and Milan (trip time: 90 min.).

If you're **driving,** pass through the St. Gotthard Tunnel and continue south along N2, via Bellinzona, all the way to Lugano.

GETTING AROUND   An explanation of fares and ticket machines can be found in a brochure distributed by the tourist office and the Public Transport Board, **Trasporti Pubblici Luganesi,** via Carducci (☎ **058/866-72-24**; www.tplsa.ch).

You must purchase a ticket before boarding a bus or a train. If you're caught without one, you may have to pay a 55F fine. You can purchase a 1-day ticket from automatic ticket machines for 5F. This ticket allows you unlimited travel for 24 hours from the moment you purchase it. It includes the Funicular Lugano–Main Street SBBM, but not line 12, Lugano-Brè.

For **taxi service,** call ☎ **091/922-88-33.**

The town of Lugano and the lakefront itself are ideal for bikers. You can rent a **bike** at the railway station in Lugano (☎ **051/221-56-42**), at ticket window no. 1. Prices begin at 33F per day, depending on the type of bicycle.

VISITOR INFORMATION   The **Lugano Tourist Office** is at riva Albertolli 5 (☎ **091/913-32-32;** www.lugano-tourism.ch). From April to October hours are Monday to Friday 9am to 7pm, Saturday 9am to 5:30pm, and Sunday 10am to 5pm. November to

March, it's open Monday to Friday 9am to noon and 2 to 5:30pm, and Saturday 10am to 12:30pm and 1:30 to 5pm.

CITY LAYOUT The center of town is **piazza Riforma,** dominated by a neoclassical city hall constructed in 1844. From here you can explore the ancient streets of the Old Town on foot.

Lugano is built along several lakeside quays, of which **riva Albertolli, riva Vincenzo Vela,** and **riva Antonio Caccia** are the most important. They are ideal for long, leisurely walks. They run from piazza Cassarate to piazza Paradiso.

Other major squares of Lugano, also by the lake, are **piazza Riziero Rezzonico** and **piazza Alessandro Manzioni,** the latter with gardens.

The biggest park of Lugano, also opening onto the lake, is the **Parco Civico,** site of the casino, the Palazzo dei Congressi, and the town's large swimming pool.

Directly east of the center is **Castagnola,** a suburb and site of the Villa Favorita, with its celebrated collection of art.

Towering over Lugano are two hills, **Monte San Salvatore,** at 898m (2,945 ft.), and **Monte Brè,** at 918m (3,011 ft.). They're ideal for full- or half-day excursions.

SEEING THE SIGHTS

The city tourist office (see "Essentials," above) offers a **walking tour** with a guide on Mondays at 9:30am, April to October. These free tours depart from the Palazzo Civico at the Piazza Riforma.

In Town

Parco Civico ★★ is the city park along Lake Lugano. It contains the Palazzo dei Congressi (the convention center), the casino, and the Villa Ciani art museum. Outdoor concerts are presented in the summer.

Cattedrale di San Lorenzo (St. Lawrence), via Cattedrale, in the Old Town, was originally a Romanesque church. It was reconstructed in the 13th and 14th centuries and overhauled in the 17th and 18th centuries. It has three outstanding Renaissance doorways and a baroque interior. Look for the 16th-century tabernacle at the end of the south aisle; it was designed by the Rodari brothers of Maroggia.

The major church is the **Chiesa di Santa Maria degli Angeli (Church of St. Mary of the Angels),** piazza Luini, located on the south side of the resort. This church was built at the end of the 15th century and is known throughout the Ticino for its **frescoes** ★★ by Bernardino Luini, the Lombard painter. His huge fresco *The Crucifixion* dates from 1529. Many critics have compared the beauty of his work to that of Leonardo da Vinci. Art critic John Ruskin found an "unstudied sweetness" in Luini's work. The church was occupied by Franciscans until 1848.

Nearby Attractions

The best way to discover the small lakeside villages around Lugano is to rent a bike at the railway station (see above) and set off to explore. Arm yourself with a good map from the tourist office and head for the **nature reserve** of Origlio Lake, proceeding to Ponte Capriasca, where you can visit a **parish church** with a copy of Leonardo da Vinci's *The Last Supper.* From here you can continue to the villages of **Tesserete** and **Colla** along the left valley side of Cassarate, going through the woods with a marked trail to **Sonvico.** On your way back to Lugano, you'll pass through the idyllic villages of **Dino, Ponte di Valle,** and finally Lugano. In all, the trip takes in about 37km (23 miles) and can be done in about 4 hours.

Swiss Miniature Village (**Kids**) Small replicas of the major buildings in Switzerland are displayed along a labyrinth of asphalt paths. There's also a miniature of the twin castles in Sion. You can purchase an official guidebook for detailed explanations. This attraction is especially popular with children.

Via Cantonale, Melide-Lugano. ✆ **091/640-10-60.** www.swissminiatur.ch. Admission 15F adults, 10F children 15 and under. Daily 9am–6pm. Closed Nov to mid-Mar. Take a train from Lugano Village.

Villa Heleneum Lying 4km (2½ miles) northwest of Lugano, this landmark building is along the much-frequented walk to Gandria. It contains the Museum of Extra-European Cultures, which exhibits objects from Oceania, Indonesia, and Africa. The collection was donated by Serge Brignoni, an exponent of the surrealist movement. There's also a center for ethnographic studies, as well as a library annexed to the museum.

Via Cortivo 24, Lugano-Castagnola. ✆ **058/866-69-60.** Free admission. Wed–Sun 10am–5pm. Bus: 1.

THE ACTIVE VACATION PLANNER

Watersports are popular in Lugano; you can also bike or play golf and tennis.

BOATING You can rent rowboats and motorboats along the lakefront.

SAILING Go to **Circolo Velico,** Lago di Lugano, Foce Cassarate (✆ **091/971-09-75;** www.cvll.ch), which charges 15F to 20F per hour or 55F to 100F for a half-day, depending on the size of the boat.

SCUBA Try **Lugano-Sub,** Riva Paradiso 23 (✆ **091/994-37-40;** www.luganosub.ch).

SWIMMING The **Lido** (✆ **091/971-40-41**) is a sandy stretch of beach along the lake. You can also relax on the lawn or eat at the cafeteria on the terrace. Admission to the Lido is 10F for adults, 5F for children 9 to 20, and 3F for children 8 and under. Rental of a cabana costs another 20F, plus a 10F deposit. The beach is open in the summer daily from 9am to 7:30pm. In addition, many hotels have heated pools, some with salt water.

WATER-SKIING The **Club Nautico-Lugano,** via Calloni 9 (✆ **091/649-61-39**), between Lugano and Melide, charges 150F per hour, instruction included.

WINDSURFING You can windsurf on the lake at **Club Nautico-Lugano,** via Calloni 9 (✆ **091/649-61-39**), between Lugano and Melide. The cost is 18F per hour.

SHOPPING

Its role as capital of Italian-speaking Switzerland almost guarantees that Lugano's selection of merchandise will include a cosmopolitan blend of Teutonic and Mediterranean merchandise. Most of it can be viewed along either side of the resort's main shopping street, **via Nassa.**

You'll find five floors of department-store shopping at everybody's favorite large store, **Manor,** piazza Dante (✆ **091/912-76-99**). A roughly equivalent department store, with some gift items and more of an emphasis on foodstuffs, groceries, hardware, and housewares, is **Migros,** via Pretorio 15 (✆ **091/913-72-13**). If you're looking for chocolates and pastries, head for a bakery that many locals remember from their childhood, **Münger,** via Luvini 4 (✆ **091/985-69-43**).

WHERE TO STAY

Lugano has hotels in all price categories. Many are located in the suburbs of Paradiso, Cassarate, and Castagnola.

Hotel Splendide Royal ★★★

The splendor of the 19th century is evident in the elegant architecture of this mansard-roofed hotel. Built in 1888, the Splendide Royal has welcomed many famous people (and even a few infamous ones). Maria, queen of Romania; Vittorio Emanuele di Savoia; George H. W. Bush; and Sophia Loren have stayed here. The public rooms are decorated with columns, crystal-and-gilt chandeliers, Venetian furniture, and Oriental rugs. Guests have a choice of bedrooms, either in the flowery rooms of the original landmark wing, where some rooms contain ceiling frescoes, or in the 1983 modern wing, where the decoration is in soft colors and the furnishings in a streamlined beech. The swimming pool is shaped like an oyster, and there's a rock garden.

Riva A. Caccia 7, CH-6900 Lugano. ✆ **091/985-77-11.** Fax 091/985-77-22. www.splendide.ch. 96 units. Apr–Oct 460F–660F double, 1,330F suite; Nov–Mar 360F–510F double, 970F suite. Rates include buffet breakfast. Half board 85F per person. AE, DC, MC, V. Free parking outdoors, 30F in garage. Bus: 1. **Amenities:** Restaurant; bar; babysitting; concierge; exercise room; indoor heated pool; room service; sauna. *In room:* A/C, TV, hair dryer, minibar, Wi-Fi (25F per 24 hr.).

Principe Leopoldo & Residence ★★★

This extravagant mansion lies on a panoramic hill site, Collina d'Oro (Golden Hill), in an exclusive neighborhood overlooking the lake. The villa was built in 1868 as the home of Prince Leopold, of Austria's von Hohenzollerns. After World War I it was sold to a Swiss industrialist. In 1986 the villa was transformed into the Ticino's smallest luxury hotel, with an understated Italian style. Today it's our favorite hotel in Lugano. There's a modern addition with a two-story atrium and a cascade of illuminated water. The suites have beige travertine trim, and each spacious room has a terrace overlooking the lake and the suburb of Paradiso. The hotel has more amenities and services than any other in the Ticino, including deluxe toiletries, well-lit vanity mirrors, pressing facilities, and even complimentary shoeshines. The hotel restaurant is one of the finest and most elegant in the Ticino (see below).

Via Montalbano 5, CH-6900 Lugano. ✆ **091/985-88-55.** Fax 091/985-88-25. www.leopoldohotel.com. 77 units. 400F–740F double; from 1,150F suite. Rates include buffet breakfast. Children 11 and under stay free in parent's room. AE, DC, MC, V. Parking 25F. **Amenities:** 2 restaurants; bar; airport transfers; babysitting; concierge; exercise room; 2 outdoor heated pools; room service; spa; 2 outdoor tennis courts (lit). *In room:* A/C, TV, hair dryer, minibar, Wi-Fi (2F per 30 min.).

Expensive

Grand Hotel Villa Castagnola au Lac ★★★

The beauty of this ocher, Mediterranean-style villa across the street from the lake is enhanced by its exotic trees and plants—even banana trees, no less. The public rooms contain marble or parquet floors; some have large fireplaces in consonance with their baronial decor. Each spacious bedroom is uniquely and luxuriously furnished, decorated tastefully in Mediterranean styling. The manager has instructed his staff to pay attention to even the smallest detail to make guests feel at home. All rooms open onto views of the lake and the subtropical park.

Viale Castagnola 31, CH-6906 Lugano. ✆ **091/973-25-55.** Fax 091/973-25-50. www.villacastagnola.com. 93 units. 340F–565F double; from 750F suite. Rates include buffet breakfast. Half board 70F per person. AE, DC, MC, V. Free parking outdoors, 15F in garage. Bus: 1. **Amenities:** 2 restaurants; bar; exercise room; indoor heated pool; room service; spa; 2 outdoor tennis courts (lit); limited watersports rentals. *In room:* A/C (in most units), TV, fridge, hair dryer, Wi-Fi (10F per hour).

Moderate

Delfino

As modern as tomorrow, this hotel in the Paradiso section of town lies close to the lakeshore next to a pedestrian area that leads into the heart of town. Its rooms open onto balconies. Bedrooms are streamlined, sleekly furnished, and most comfortable. Most of the standard rooms offer twin beds but some have queen-sized beds. The star attraction here is the swimming pool opening onto a wide sun terrace.

Via Casserinette 6, CH-6900 Lugano. © **091/985-9999.** Fax 091/985-9900. www.delfinolugano.ch. 49 units. 199F–280F double. Rates include breakfast buffet. AE, DC, MC, V. Parking 15F. **Amenities:** Restaurant; bar; pool (outdoor); room service. *In room:* A/C, TV, hair dryer, Internet (free), minibar.

Holiday Inn Lugano Centre   This first-class chain hotel was built in 1975 out of concrete and glass and is today one of the finest hotels on the outskirts of Lugano. The seven-story high-rise is near the Lugano-Sud exit from the main highway. Many of the public rooms have red leather accents and wood trim. The showplace salon has French-style armchairs, Oriental rugs, and large windows with a view of the garden. The bedrooms are quite comfortable and well equipped.

Via Geretta 15, CH-6902 Lugano-Paradiso. © **091/986-38-38.** Fax 091/986-38-39. www.holiday-inn.com/luganocentre. 92 units. 239F–320F double. Half board 48F per person. AE, DC, MC, V. Free parking outdoors, 20F in garage. Bus: 1 or 9. **Amenities:** Restaurant; bar; concierge; exercise room; 2 heated pools (1 indoor); room service; sauna. *In room:* A/C, TV, fridge, hair dryer, minibar, Wi-Fi (12F per hour).

Hotel du Lac (Value)   Architecturally bandboxy and lacking style, this hotel nonetheless offers much comfort and value. Owned by the Kneschaurek family since 1920, it was reconstructed in the early 1960s. Renovated and improved over the years, it enjoys a lakefront location with its own private swimming area in front. All the midsize to spacious bedrooms have been updated with the installation of improved plumbing. All open onto lakeside vistas; the most desirable accommodations—and the most tranquil—are on the sixth floor.

Riva Paradiso 3, CH-6902 Lugano-Paradiso. © **091/986-47-47.** Fax 091/986-47-48. www.dulac.ch. 53 units. 236F–424F double; 460F–540F suite. Rates include buffet breakfast. AE, DC, MC, V. Parking 10F. **Amenities:** Restaurant; babysitting; exercise room; Jacuzzi; outdoor heated pool; room service; sauna. *In room:* TV, hair dryer, minibar, Wi-Fi (free).

Lugano Dante   In the heart of town, only a short walk from the lake, this moderately priced hotel opens onto the Piazza Cioccaro in a pedestrian zone. It is one of the best and most well-run hotels in its category. Five different sets of accommodations are offered, ranging from standard doubles and executive rooms to junior suites and luxurious suites. Rooms are soundproof, and the hotel is especially proud of its deluxe mattresses. The breakfast buffet is one of the best in town.

Piazza Cioccaro 5, CH-6900 Lugano. © **091/910/5700.** Fax 091/910-5777. www.hotel-luganodante.com. 83 units. 270F–300F double; 340F executive room; 390F junior suite; 460F suite. AE, DC, MC, V. Parking 30F. **Amenities:** Bar; access to nearby gym; Internet in lobby (9F). *In room:* A/C, TV/DVD, CD player, hair dryer, Wi-Fi (free in executive units and suites).

Inexpensive

Carlton Hotel Villa Moritz ★★ (Finds)   Peace and quiet are assured at this hotel, as it's located in a park a good distance from the main road. The Wernli-Sigrist family manages several 19th-century buildings clustered near a swimming pool surrounded by flagstones. The hotel also benefits from being on the sunny side of Mount Brè. The bedrooms are comfortably furnished with traditional styling. The public rooms are modern, with stone accents around the bar. Public buses transport guests to the center of Lugano in 10 minutes.

Via Cortivo 9, CH-6976 Lugano-Castagnola. ℂ **091/971-38-12.** Fax 091/971-38-14. www.carlton-villa-moritz.ch. 55 units. 210F–270F double. Rates include buffet breakfast. AE, MC, V. Parking 14F. Closed late Oct to late Mar. Bus: 1. **Amenities:** Restaurant; bar; outdoor heated pool; room service. *In room:* TV.

San Carlo Garni   Modern decor, fully renovated rooms, and low rates have made this a popular spot with visitors. Via Nassa is a great shopping street, located in the heart of the city, so it is easy to get to just about anywhere in Lugano from the hotel. The lakefront is only a block away. The rooms are very small, but they have all the basics and more. The staff is friendly and attentive, happily giving tips about the best places to see and go. There is a breakfast room, but there are only a few tables, so either get up early or have your meal delivered to your room.

Via Nassa 28, CH-6900 Lugano. ℂ **091/922-71-07.** Fax 091/922-80-22. 44 units. 110F–170F double. AE, DC, MC, V. Parking 25F. **Amenities:** Room service. *In room:* TV.

Zurigo   Located nearby to several points of interest, such as parks and the waterfront promenade, this value hotel has become a popular spot in Lugano. Midsize to spacious rooms are modern and brightly furnished. Refurbishing has upgraded the hotel to a new level in spite of the linoleum floors. If you're going when the weather will be warm, know that the more spacious superior accommodations are the only ones equipped with air-conditioning. Any other part of the year, however, standard rooms are just as comfortable. For those looking for some rest and relaxation, the north-facing rooms are quieter most of the time.

Corso Pestalozzi 13, Old Town, CH-6900 Lugano. ℂ **091/923-43-43.** Fax 091/923-92-68. www.hotel zurigo.ch. 40 units. 170F–200F double. AE, DC, MC, V. Parking 10F. *In room:* A/C (in some), TV, minibar (in some), Wi-Fi (free).

WHERE TO DINE

Expensive

Principe Leopoldo ★★★ INTERNATIONAL   Excellent regional and international cuisine is combined with a luxury setting in three rooms to make award-winning meals. The chef creates memorable dishes here, especially his divine risottos, one made with Gorgonzola and pears, another a green risotto with lobster and fresh herbs. The chef will dazzle you with his steamed sea bass filet with fresh tomatoes or his roasted turbot with Mediterranean "perfumes." We also like his beef sautéed with duck livers and morels. Some dishes, such as roasted Scottish lamb with fine herbs, are prepared only for two. Hors d'oeuvres are the finest at the resort, everything from a quail salad with peaches and walnuts to lobster medallions on a carpaccio of fennel and oranges. Although the menu is international, it is strongest on Ticinese and Mediterranean dishes. Each tantalizing course comes with superb wines in perfect condition.

In the Villa Principe Leopoldo & Residence, via Montalbano 5. ℂ **091/985-88-55.** Reservations required. Main courses 29F–39F. AE, DC, MC, V. Daily noon–2:30pm and 7–9:30pm.

Ristorante al Portone ★ SWISS/ITALIAN   If you enjoy Italian-style modern cuisine, head for this sophisticated restaurant managed by chef Roberto and Doris Galizzi. As with all *cuisine moderne,* many of the combinations sound bizarre, but the taste is usually sensational. Large scampi with curry and mango and the sole are veritable palate pleasers. If you order the most expensive fixed-price menu, you can *lascia fare à Roberto*— leave it up to Roberto, the chef. You'll rarely be disappointed: Roberto is known for putting his own culinary spin on even the most traditional of Italian dishes. The desserts are also exceptional.

Viale Cassarate 3. ✆ **091/923-55-11.** www.ristorantealportone.ch. Reservations required. Main courses 46F–58F. AE, DC, MC, V. Tues–Sat noon–2pm and 7:30–9:30pm. Closed Jan 1–10 and mid-July to mid-Aug.

Ristorante Orologio ITALIAN/INTERNATIONAL   The Orologio occupies the ground floor of a buff-colored building with restrained detailing and leaded-glass windows. The restaurant has 19th-century French-provincial chairs and an ice chest displaying salads and condiments. Amusing illustrations advertise the dishes—a mermaid draws your attention to the fish courses, although the menu features more meat courses. In September and October there's an emphasis on game and mushroom dishes, such as the filet of venison with porcini mushrooms or the platter of venison for two. Pheasant dishes are also well prepared. Of all the restaurants we've recommended in Lugano, this one draws the most mixed reaction. Some locals swear by it and some foreign visitors sound its praise.

Via Nizzola 2. ✆ **091/923-23-38.** www.ristorante-orologio.ch. Reservations recommended. Main courses 32F–58F. AE, DC, MC, V. Mon–Fri 11am–3pm and 7–10:30pm. Closed Aug. Bus: 1 or 2.

Ristorante Santabbondio ★ (Finds) MEDITERRANEAN   Its amiable, hardworking staff refers to the restaurant as a much-renovated, century-old grotto, but they're using the word to describe a rustic farmhouse (ca. 1862) rather than a cave. It's less than a mile south of Lugano, midway between the town center and the airport. Menu choices are based on a solid and well-intentioned respect for *cuisine du marché,* incorporating a roster of market-fresh specialties that changes every day. In a setting suitable for up to 50 diners at a time, outfitted in Tuscan-made terra-cotta tiles and tones of green and white, you'll enjoy some of the most sophisticated cuisine in the district. Examples include tartare of salmon served with a parfait of tomatoes and shrimp, Scottish grouse roasted in aged balsamic vinegar, scallops in a ginger-flavored orange-and-basil sauce, grilled filets of turbot with capers, and medallions of goat with wine sauce. Martin Dalsass is the well-rehearsed chef.

Via Fomelino 10. ✆ **091/993-23-88.** www.ristorante-santabbondio.ch. Reservations recommended. Main courses 42F–72F; fixed-price menus 138F–158F. AE, DC, MC, V. Tues–Fri noon–2:30pm and 7:30–10:30pm; Sat 7:30–11pm. Closed 1st 2 weeks in Jan.

Moderate

Note: The following restaurants can be expensive if you order the two or three highest-priced dishes, but most of the main courses are priced at the lower end of the scale.

Locanda del Boschetto ★ (Value) SWISS/ITALIAN   The place doesn't spend much money on decor, other than some rustic alpine wood, and no one puts on airs here. Service is direct in the sort of no-frills trattoria style. Guests can watch the chef cook beef and fish over the glowing coals. He produces a simple but flavor-filled cuisine, which includes a mixed grill of local fish, spaghetti with clam sauce, grilled calves' liver, and several succulent beef dishes. The well-known restaurant is in a wooded area near the highway.

Via Boschetto 8. ✆ **091/994-24-93.** Reservations recommended. Main courses 20F–51F. AE, DC, MC, V. Tues–Sun noon–2pm and 7–10pm. Closed 2 weeks in Aug. Bus: 1 or 2.

Mövenpick Ristorante Parco Ciani MEDITERRANEAN/INTERNATIONAL   Guests select from two distinct dining areas, decorated in soft pastel tones with a bright atmosphere. One of the dining rooms has bentwood armchairs, while the other contains reproductions of Empire-style antiques. Located at the edge of a city park, the concrete block structure has irregular balconies and large windows. The menu is one of the largest in the center of town. The cooking is internationally acceptable rather than creatively innovative. Begin with a minestrone soup made with fresh vegetables, or sample carpaccio. Many guests, particularly those from south of the border (in Italy) prefer to begin their meal with one of the many pasta dishes, including tagliatelle, spaghetti, pappardelle, tortellini, and even a risotto. One risotto served with artichokes is delectable. The chef wisely allows you to order three different sizes of pasta, depending on your appetite. A salad buffet is offered, and every night at least three vegetarian main courses are featured. Many dishes are made with curry, the fish of the day is often grilled, and for the carnivore, there's an ample selection ranging from veal T-bones to U.S. Angus entrecôtes.

In the Palazzo dei Congressi, piazza Indipendenza. 🕿 **091/923-86-56.** Reservations recommended. Main courses 20F–49F. AE, DC, MC, V. Daily 9am–midnight. Bus: 1, 8, or 9.

Osteria Calprino ★ (Finds) SWISS/NORTHERN ITALIAN In the suburb of Paradiso, about 1.5km (1 mile) from the center of Lugano, this is one of the best trattorias in the area. Decorated in a rustic provincial style, the restaurant is unpretentious with wooden furniture and a terra-cotta floor. The typical regional cuisine uses market-fresh ingredients, as well as tried-and-true recipes from grandmother's pantry. Start with the pumpkin soup or freshly made minestrone. An old-fashioned dish (not for modern dieters) is a savory bean stew with pork rinds. Try also the grilled shrimp with fresh vegetables or else grilled beefsteak with polenta. A house specialty is fresh porcini mushrooms stir-fried with garlic and parsley and served with polenta on the side. Yet another specialty is roast suckling pig.

Via Carona 18. 🕿 **091/994-1480.** Reservations recommended. Main courses 18F–25F; fixed-price 3-course menu 42F. MC, V. Thurs–Tues noon–2:30pm and 7–10:30pm. Closed Aug.

Inexpensive

La Tinera ★ (Value) SWISS/ITALIAN A familiar array of Italian specialties are served at budget prices in this basement trattoria in the center of the historic Old Town. No one bothers to dress up here, as families, often Italian, mingle with visitors for the day, each "tucking in" plenty of the regional fare served in generous portions. Fresh pasta dishes, risotto, and a robust selection of grilled meats are cooked the same as in grandmother's day—and no one would want to change a thing. Regional wine is served in ceramic carafes.

Via dei Gorini 2 (off piazza Riforma). 🕿 **091/923-52-19.** Reservations not accepted. Main courses 18F–25F. AE, MC, V. Mon–Sat 11:30am–3pm and 5:30–11pm. Closed last week of July and 1st 3 weeks of Aug. Bus: 1 or 2. Or walk down via Pessina.

Nearby Dining & Lodging

Motto del Gallo ★★ (Finds) MEDITERRANEAN For a visual treat, visit this baroque house practically bursting with atmosphere. There's a collection of antiques and the tables are covered with lace. The restaurant is in a 15th-century hamlet that alone is worth the trip—13km (8 miles) from Lugano on the road to Bellinzona. The excellent menu features a selection of homemade pastas, including green tagliolini with scampi. Two types of risotto are offered, one of them cooked delectably in champagne. Fresh fish looms large on the menu, including a selection of gratinée with zabaglione. Main meat dishes are likely to include a veal mignon, veal kidneys cooked with sherry, a mixed medley of meats, or perhaps alpine-style lamb roasted aromatically with fresh herbs. Instead of dessert, such as one of the cold soufflés, many diners prefer to end their meal with a regional cheese of the Ticino. The wine list includes some 500 wines from all over the world.

If you're looking for a romantic place to spend the night, there are three well-maintained suites here, which cost 235F for two, including breakfast.

CH-6807 Taverne. ✆ **091/945-28-71.** Fax 091/945-27-23. www.mottodelgallo.ch. Reservations required. Main courses 29F–49F; *menu dégustazione* 72F; 8-course menu 146F. AE, DC, V. Tues–Sat noon–2pm; Mon–Sat 7–10pm. Take the unnumbered bus or local train marked TAVERNE.

LUGANO AFTER DARK

Lugano reigns as the center of the Ticino's nightlife circuit, with options that attract local residents from quieter towns throughout the district. The most obvious options involve visits to either of the two casinos described below.

Casinos

Casino Lugano   This casino features 350 slots, 26 table games, 2 elegant restaurants, and 5 bars. Games of chance include American roulette, blackjack, French roulette, Caribbean stud poker, punto banco, poker, and wheel of fortune. Entrance is free but visitors must show a passport. It's open Sunday to Thursday noon to 4am, and Friday and Saturday noon to 5am. Via Stauffacher 1. ✆ **091/973-71-11.** www.casinolugano.ch.

Casino Municipale   This casino lies on Italian soil, across the lake from Lugano, only 20 minutes away by ferry. The casino is a glittering establishment, filled with an international clientele and such games as blackjack and chemin de fer, along with the inevitable slot machines. Here, in Italy, gambling stakes are unlimited. Oddly, however, despite the casino's location, the currency is Swiss. Patrons must show a passport and men must have a jacket, tie, and shirt on—a policy that's strictly enforced.

The casino is in the village of Campione, which, because of the vagaries of 19th- and 20th-century politics and because of the rugged terrain around it, is completely surrounded by Switzerland. Even its telephone area code is the same as Lugano's. Long ago, the imperial fiefdom of Campione was presented to a Milanese monastery and it has remained Italian ever since. The men of Campione were famous for their stonework, and many buildings in Milan are a testament to their skill. Take a moment to admire their handiwork in some of the local buildings. ID is required for admission. Hours are Sunday to Thursday 10:30pm to 5am, and Friday and Saturday 10:30pm to 6am. Piazzale Milano 1, Campione, Italy. ✆ **091/640-11-11.** No cover. www.casinocampione.it.

Other Nightlife Offerings

Other than gambling, you'll find a dense roster of bars and cafes, many of them lining the edges of the historic center's most famous square, piazza Riforma. One of the most interesting is the **Café Olimpia** (✆ **091/922-74-88**), an elegant stone building with hundreds of chairs set out in front and a focus on live music some evenings. A few steps away is the **Café Tango** (✆ **091/922-27-01**), more like a bar than a traditional cafe, where an Argentine motif (and recorded music) often attracts clients from everywhere in Europe. If you ever wondered about South American expatriates and where they happened to live in Switzerland, head no farther than the **Mango Club,** piazza Dante 8 (✆ **091/922-94-38**). Here, almost everybody will know how to salsa and merengue, probably better than you, and with a more convincing grasp of *Español* as it's spoken in Colombia and the Dominican Republic. Originally established in 1995 and now a fixture on the nightlife circuit of the Ticino, it's open every night beginning at 10pm, with many of the guests arriving after 12:30am. Cover, which includes the first drink, costs 15F.

If striptease *artistes* are your thing, consider **Dancing Cécil,** Via Guisan 3, in the nearby suburb of Lugarno-Paradiso (✆ **091/994-97-24**). It's open daily from 10pm.

5 MORCOTE ★★

11km (7 miles) S of Lugano; 40km (25 miles) S of Bellinzona

Morcote is one of the most idyllic villages of Switzerland. Its arcaded houses and old streets are built on the southern slopes of Monte Arbostora, at 826m (2,709 ft.). Cypresses and vineyards grow on the mountain.

ESSENTIALS

GETTING THERE Several **buses** depart from Lugano every day for Morcote (trip time: 30 min.).

Throughout the summer about a dozen **boats** make the trip every day from Lugano to Morcote, with many intermediary stops along the way. Depending on the schedule, trip time is between 50 minutes and 2 hours. The round-trip boat fare is 31F. In the winter boats continue to run, but on a less frequent schedule.

For bus and boat schedules and information, contact the tourist office (see below).

If you're **driving** from Lugano, head south along Route A4.

VISITOR INFORMATION Morcote now has its own tourist information office in the center (✆ **091/996-11-20;** www.promorcote.ch). Office hours are Tuesday to Friday from 1 to 5pm.

SEEING THE SIGHTS

Chiesa di Madonna del Sasso dates from the 15th century; it was reconstructed later, however, and given a baroque overlay. It has some memorable 16th-century frescoes. A staircase with more than 400 steps leads down to the village and the lake, and the cemetery contains the remains of many famous people.

Scherrer Park (✆ **091/996-21-25**) contains typical Ticino trees and plants, as well as sculpture and architecture. Some of the sculpture is from the Far East. Admission is 7F for adults, 6F students and seniors, 2F children 16 and under. It's open March to October daily from 10am to 5pm.

WHERE TO STAY

Carina Carlton ★★ This hotel has an Italian-style facade, with pink-and-cream trim and lime-green shutters. Such lighthearted contrast of colors also marks the lobby, which is decorated with Oriental rugs. The hotel's several terraces are filled with potted plants and small tables. A structure of whimsical design, it was once owned by the architect Gaspare Fossati (1809–83), a native of Morcote, who was known for his renovations of Saint Sophia in Constantinople (present-day Istanbul). Some of the awards he received from the Ottoman sultan are displayed in the lobby. The Carina Carlton offers midsize bedrooms filled with provincial furniture (some of it antique).

Via Cantonale, CH-6922 Morcote. ✆ **091/996-11-31.** Fax 091/996-19-29. www.carina-morcote.ch. 22 units. 205F–280F double; 300F–340F suite. Rates include continental breakfast. Half board 50F per person. AE, DC, MC, V. Closed mid-Oct to mid-Mar. **Amenities:** Restaurant; outdoor heated pool; room service. *In room:* TV, hair dryer, minibar.

Swiss Diamond Hotel ★★★ The best and most elegant hotel lies outside Morcote in the village of Vico, 4km (2½ miles) to the northeast on the shores of Lake Lugano. This hotel is elegantly modern and very deluxe, among the finest in all the Ticino. A personalized welcome awaits you, along with a sublime decor that takes in crystal chandeliers, marble floors, and columns in Sicilian travertine. Bedrooms are beautifully furnished and equipped with modern technology, and each comes with a cozy sitting area. The most desirable units face south with sliding windows overlooking the lake and the village. From the goose-feather duvets to the oversized bath towels, everything here focuses on *la dolce vita*.

One of the reasons to stay here is the cuisine, which is classic and international but also lighter in sections for more modern tastes. For a romantic evening near the lake, the Lago Restaurant, with its Mediterranean specialties, is recommended. More formal dining can be found at the Panorama, with its seasonally adjusted menu. A private boat takes guests on a tour of the lake. The Wellness Centre, an elegant spa decorated like an ancient Roman thermal bath, is one of the finest in the Ticino.

Via Cantonale, CH-6921 Vico-Morcote. ℂ **091/735-00-00.** Fax 091/735-00-99. www.swissdiamondhotel. com. 74 units. 295F–565F double; 500F–650F junior suite, from 805F suite. AE, DC, MC, V. Free parking. **Amenities:** 2 restaurants; exercise room; 2 pools (1 heated indoor); room service; spa. *In room:* A/C, TV, hair dryer, minibar, Wi-Fi (10F per hour).

WHERE TO DINE

Dellago ★ SEAFOOD   Directly on the lake with a terrace, this is a favorite of both locals and visitors. This restaurant and its 50-room hotel lie in the village of Melide outside Lugano. Delicious dishes—classic but with creative touches—are prepared, the cooking based on the sublime products of the Ticino. The chefs have a talent for sauces and combining flavors. Start with such delights as spicy Thai prawns on a lemon-grass skewer served with a mango and pineapple chutney, or a salad of green asparagus and papaya served with Ticino goat cheese and a hot rhubarb and walnut dressing. Among the main dishes, we savor the crispy pan-fried filet of salmon trout with an orange- and basil-laced pesto or the organic beef filet steak with a honey and coriander sauce. Desserts are advertised as sinful but they are also delightful, especially the chilled green-apple soup with a walnut-stuffed "cigar" and coconut ice cream, and the creamy poppy seed mousse with dates laced with a caramel and orange sauce.

The restaurant also rents individually furnished bedrooms, with such extras as "massage showers" and a hot tub on the roof. Other surprising extras include an espresso machine and a free minibar. Each room comes with a safe and a small but modern bathroom with shower. Rates for a double range from 190F to 430F.

Lago di Lugano, CH-6815 Melide, 10km (6 miles) south of Lugano. ℂ **091/649-70-41.** Fax 091/649-89-15. www.hotel-dellago.ch. Main courses 33F–47F. AE, DC, MC, V. Daily noon–2pm and 6:30–11pm.

Ristorante della Posta SWISS/ITALIAN   Established in 1863, this restaurant features two terraces staggered back from each other overlooking the lake. It operates from the center of Morcote. Waiters scurry with food-laden trays from the kitchen across the street. The setting is charming, but the traffic makes it somewhat hectic. Delectable specialties include risotto with mushrooms, *osso buco* with polenta, fresh lake fish, and real Italian pizza. Fresh fish is the chef's specialty, and it's most often served grilled. There are also several different preparations of fresh mushrooms offered nightly, and the veal cutlet Milanese is always reliable.

In the Albergo della Posta, via Cantonale. ℂ **091/996-11-27.** www.hotelmorcote.com. Main courses 27F–48F; pizza 14F–21F. AE, DC, MC, V. Daily 8am–midnight. Closed Nov to mid-Mar.

17

Liechtenstein

With a history dating from the 14th century, Liechtenstein is a wonderful land of fairy-tale castles (one inhabited by the reigning prince), chalets decorated with geraniums, Rhine meadows, and small villages high in the Alps.

Separated from Switzerland by the Rhine River, it's one of the smallest independent sovereign states of Europe, along with San Marino in Italy and Andorra in the Pyrenees. The entire country is only about 26km (16 miles) long and 6km (4 miles) wide.

Liechtenstein is famous for its finely engraved postage stamps, which are treasured by collectors the world over. The stamps illustrate the country's religion (predominantly Roman Catholic), monarchy, art, history, landscape, nature, and leisure activities. Stamps provide 25% of the government's income, and new series are introduced all the time. There's a postal museum in Vaduz, the capital of the principality.

Although commonly regarded as remote, Liechtenstein is actually very accessible from eastern Switzerland. A number of good roads link the two countries, and there are no border formalities or Customs stops. There are guards at the Austrian border, but they rarely stamp visitors' passports.

The ideal way to explore Liechtenstein is to wander around. Every village has a network of hiking and walking routes, which the locals themselves put to good use. Marked hiking routes cover 150km (93 miles) in the alpine area and 119km (74 miles) in the valley, which, considering the country's size, takes up a huge chunk of the land space.

Malbun and Steg are ideal starting points for mountain tours, and Gaflei and Planken (the tiniest hamlet in the country) are departure points for the Drei Schwestern area. The tourist office (see "Information" in "Fast Facts: Liechtenstein," below) has a pamphlet outlining the best hiking trails throughout the Unterland (Lower Country), the Oberland (Upper Country), and the alpine region.

Guided half- or full-day tours are arranged every Thursday in summer by the **Liechtenstein Alpine Association.** Routes depend on weather conditions and are published on the Saturday preceding the tour in local newspapers under a column headed "Wanderungen des Liechtensteiner Alpenvereins." For information and registration, contact the guide given in the announcement.

1 ABOUT LIECHTENSTEIN

ORIENTATION

GEOGRAPHY The Rhine River forms Liechtenstein's western boundary; the Swiss canton of St. Gallen is on the other bank. To the east is the Austrian province of Vorarlberg, and to the south are the Grisons of Switzerland. Liechtenstein is cradled by the **Drei Schwestern (Three Sisters)** mountains.

PEOPLE About 35,000 citizens live in 11 communes (comparable to Switzerland's cantons). Most—more than 80%—are Roman Catholic and of German ancestry. They

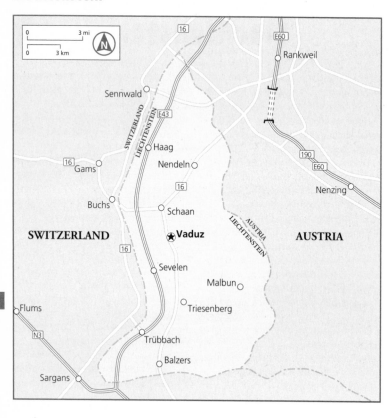

enjoy one of the highest standards of living in the world and pay very little in taxes. Unemployment is rare.

The country's prosperity, however, is a relatively recent development. Many old-timers remember the hardships of World War I, when the country was virtually cut off from food supplies because of blockades. The social and economic growth since the end of World War II has exceeded that of any other Western nation. Today, Liechtenstein is one of the most highly industrialized countries in Europe. The industry is hardly noticeable, however, because the factories and workshops are dispersed among orchards, meadows, and woodlands. There are no smokestacks, with their pollution from fumes. One of the industrial specialties is the production of false teeth.

Liechtenstein has a rich cultural life, supported by royal patrons and the cooperation of neighboring countries. Though open to foreign influences, through commerce and cultural exchanges as well as through tourism, Liechtenstein maintains its unique national identity by severely restricting citizenship. Any foreigner wishing to become a citizen must first be approved by a majority of the commune he or she intends to live in; then his/her application must be approved by parliament, and then by the monarch. The process is obviously meant to discourage immigration.

LANGUAGE   Most residents of Liechtenstein, who are largely of Austrian origin, speak a German dialect. English is also understood throughout the country.

GOVERNMENT   The Principality of Liechtenstein is a constitutional hereditary monarchy with a unicameral parliament (Diet). The state power is vested in the prince and the people. The prince's powers are passed on through hereditary succession to the throne and are independent of the will of the people. The people also have political power and must work together with the prince, according to the constitution.

Members of the parliament are chosen for 4 years by general elections. The right to vote is universal (women received the right to vote in 1984), secret, and direct. Public referendum is an important right of all citizens. Any law passed by the Diet that is not declared urgent may be put to referendum. The constitution also assures freedom of speech, freedom of the press, and freedom of assembly.

Liechtenstein has a prime minister and four councilors, appointed by the prince for a 4-year term. They act as a link between the prince and the Diet.

Liechtenstein made world headlines in 2003 when its prince, Hans-Adam II, demanded and got sweeping powers in a nationwide referendum. If he weren't granted these powers, he had threatened to move to Austria. Desperate to hold onto their prince, 64.3% of the electorate voted to give him such rights as the power to dismiss governments and approve judicial nominees. The revised constitution also allows the prince to veto laws simply by refusing to sign them within a 6-month period. The prince likened the opposition to "World War II traitors." One supporter, Adriana Dill, told the press: "The country should be exactly the way the prince wants to have it. It's his country. It has his name on it." Former prime minister Mario Frick said otherwise, claiming the referendum made Liechtenstein "an international laughingstock."

ESSENTIALS

GETTING THERE   The nearest airport is **Kloten International Airport** outside Zurich, about 130km (80 miles) to the west of Vaduz. There is both train and bus transportation into Liechtenstein from Zurich.

Many express trains pass through Liechtenstein, but none stop there. You can take a train from Zurich to Sargans or to Buchs in nearby Switzerland. Call ℂ **0900/300-300** for **rail schedules.** At both Sargans and Buchs, you'll find good bus connections to Vaduz and other communes in Liechtenstein.

If you're **driving** from Zurich, head southwest along N3 until you reach the junction with N1, and then take N1 north to the turnoff for Vaduz.

ⒻFast Facts   Liechtenstein

Currency   The Swiss franc is legal tender in Liechtenstein; the exchange rate is the same as in Switzerland (see "Money & Costs" in chapter 3).

Documents Required   All travel documents recognized by Swiss authorities are valid in Liechtenstein. However, you'll encounter the formalities of any western European border crossing if you enter through Austria.

Holidays   Public holidays are January 1 (New Year's Day), January 6 (Epiphany), February 28 (Mardi Gras), Good Friday, Easter Monday, May 1 (Labor Day), May 25 (Feast of the Ascension), June 5 (Whit Monday), June 15 (Corpus Christi), August

15 (Feast of the Assumption), September 8 (Nativity of Our Lady), November 1 (All Saints' Day), December 8 (Feast of the Immaculate Conception), December 25 (Christmas), and December 26 (Boxing Day).

Information For further information about the principality, contact the **Liechtenstein National Tourist Office,** Städtle 37 (P.O. Box 139), FL-9490 Vaduz, Liechtenstein (© **00423/239-63-00;** www.tourismus.li). The office is open daily 9am to 5pm.

Mail The postage rates are the same as in Switzerland (see "Fast Facts: Switzerland," in chapter 18). But you must, of course, use Liechtenstein stamps.

Medical Needs Doctors and dentists take turns handling emergency calls (the names of those currently available are published in the Sat and Sun newspapers). Your hotel will put you in touch with an English-speaking doctor or dentist. Phone © **144** for an ambulance.

Telephone To call Liechtenstein from the U.S., dial your international prefix (usually **011**), followed by Liechtenstein's country code **00423,** followed by the seven-digit local number. To call Liechtenstein from anywhere in Switzerland or anywhere else in the world, dial whatever international prefix is required at the phone you happen to be using, followed by the country code for Liechtenstein (00423), followed by the seven-digit local number.

2 VADUZ ★

130km (80 miles) E of Zurich; 38km (24 miles) E of Chur

Vaduz (pronounced Va-*dootz*) is the capital of the Principality of Liechtenstein. Vineyards surround this little town (pop. about 5,000) at the foot of the royal family's castle. The rural commune, known for its good wines, is also very hospitable and sociable to visitors. The capital is most often visited on a brief stopover—just time enough to buy some of the famous postage stamps and record the visit to this tiny country in your passport. But as the capital of one of the last vestiges of the Holy Roman Empire and the seat of the only German-speaking monarchy in the world, Vaduz merits a closer look—at least to walk its streets and visit some of its museums.

ESSENTIALS

GETTING THERE See "Essentials" in "About Liechtenstein," above.

VISITOR INFORMATION See "Information" in "Fast Facts: Liechtenstein," above.

SEEING THE SIGHTS

Traffic is allowed one-way on the main street, **Städtle.** Also at the center of Vaduz is the **Rathaus (town hall).** The post office is across the street. Vaduz offers a wide range of sports and entertainment. Facilities include a miniature golf course, tennis courts, and a large swimming pool.

One of the best ways to get around Vaduz—and other parts of the country—is to rent a bike or a small motorcycle. Rentals are possible at **Bike Garage,** Landstrasse 323 (© **00423/390-03-90;** www.bikegarage.li). The cost is 35F per day for the average bike.

The prince's castle, **Schloss Vaduz,** dates from the 12th century. The oldest parts are the keep and the buildings on the east side. The castle was burned down by Swiss troops in 1499 and rebuilt at the beginning of the 16th century. It has round bastions at the northeast and southwest corners. Once a bleak and gloomy fortress, the castle is much improved. The interior—not open to the public—contains lavish furnishings, antiques, and priceless artwork. The exterior of the fortress is surely worth seeing. The climb along the wooded footpath takes 20 minutes and starts between the Hotel Real and the Hotel Engel. There's a sweeping vista from the grounds of the castle.

In the upper village, on the road to the castle, is the **Red House.** This was the seat of the vassals of the counts of Werdenberg during the Middle Ages. The house was acquired along with the vineyard by the Monastery of St. Johann in the Toggenburg.

Briefmarkenmuseum (Stamp Museum)   Philatelists and other admirers come from all over the world to see the Liechtenstein stamps. The collection includes the stamps of the Universal Postal Union, printing plates, and postal documents. Liechtenstein's first stamp dates from 1912. The museum was opened in 1930.

Städtle 37. ✆ **00423/236-61-05.** Free admission. Daily 10am–noon and 1–5pm.

Kunstmuseum Liechtenstein ★★   Regrettably, some of the greatest art treasures amassed by the princes of Liechtenstein have been transferred to the Palais Liechtenstein in Vienna. However, there is much left of the works of Old Masters at this modern museum, along with a constantly changing exhibition of contemporary art. Most of the collection is from the 1800s to the present day. It is so up-to-date that there are even works from the 21st century. You can also dine on sushi at the restaurant. The location is in the center of Vaduz between the pedestrian zone (Städtl) and the Aulestrasse.

Städtle 32. ✆ **00423/235-03-00.** www.kunstmuseum.li. Admission 12F adults; 8F students, seniors, and children 6–16; free for children 5 and under. Tues–Sun 10am–5pm (Thurs until 8pm).

SHOPPING

If there's any flash and glitter in Liechtenstein at all, it appears only in very subdued form. You may notice this during your shopping excursions, which are best limited to central Vaduz, a neighborhood that can never really escape the sense of being a somewhat overgrown village. An outlet that sells gift items from Liechtenstein, Austria, Italy, and Switzerland is **L'Atelier,** Städtle 36 (✆ **00423/232-46-88**). Its merchandise, as selected by the outfit's longtime owner, Hélène de Marchi, includes lamps, dolls, hand-painted silks, stoneware, pewter, and other handmade objects.

Liechtenstein has been famous since the turn of the 20th century for its rustic and durable pottery, produced in natural-looking colors such as blue, beige, and yellow, in factories that lie within a 10-minute drive of Vaduz. The larger of the principality's two factories for stoneware is **Schaedler Keramik A.G.,** which straddles Churer Strasse (✆ **00423/373-14-14**), the main street of the hamlet of Nendeln, 8km (5 miles) north of Vaduz.

The principality's premier outlet for wines produced by vineyards belonging to the prince is the **Hofkellerei des Fürsten Liechtenstein,** Feldstrasse, Vaduz (✆ **00423/232-10-18**). Set in a solid, not particularly imaginative-looking building that's owned by the prince, it stockpiles the fruit of his family's vineyards, most of which are either in the principality or in Lower Austria (Niederösterreich) just across the border. Look for both whites and reds—and a somewhat heavy-handed emphasis on the organization's royal connections.

When shopping, don't overlook the Liechtenstinian postal service, which produces more stamps than are ever used to actually mail letters. One of the busiest emporiums in the principality is the bureaucratic-looking kiosk in the main post office, **Postwert Zeichenstelle der Regierung,** Städtle, FL-9490 Vaduz (✆ **00423/236-64-44**). Here stamps that commemorate Liechtenstein's history, botany, zoology, and achievements are sold to avid collectors, and even to folk who never thought they were collectors.

WHERE TO STAY

Most of Liechtenstein's hotels are in the capital.

Very Expensive

Park Hotel Sonnenhof ★★★ The finest hotel in the principality (a Relais & Châteaux) is also among the finest in Europe. Diplomatic receptions are held here frequently. Built in the late 1800s, the hotel has been modernized into a streamlined chalet, with balconies and awnings. The garden is beautiful, and the spacious, elegant rooms are handsomely decorated and furnished with luxury beds and state-of-the-art plumbing.

Mareestrasse 29, FL-9490 Vaduz, Liechtenstein. ✆ **00423/239-02-02.** Fax 00423/239-02-03. www.sonnenhof.li. 29 units. 390F–630F double; 540F–710F junior suite. Rates include buffet breakfast. AE, DC, MC, V. Free parking outdoors, 15F in garage. **Amenities:** Restaurant; indoor heated pool; room service; sauna. *In room:* TV, hair dryer, minibar, Wi-Fi (free).

Moderate

Gasthof Löwen ★ Set on the highway within a pleasant and well-cultivated garden, this is the oldest inn (established in 1380) in Liechtenstein. Few others evoke old-fashioned alpine life as effectively as this one, thanks to its antique rooms outfitted with furniture that was originally crafted around 1920, and a clear, clean color scheme of stark white offset with varnished paneling. Bedrooms come in a variety of sizes and shapes, but all are comfortably Middle Europa, with dowdy furniture, soft beds, crisp linens, and plumbing that still works (though often noisily).

Herrengasse 35, FL-9490 Vaduz, Liechtenstein. ✆ **00423/238-11-44.** Fax 00423/238-11-45. www.hotelloewen.li. 7 units. 299F–349F double. Rates include buffet breakfast. AE, DC, MC, V. From Vaduz, take the bus marked FELDKIRCH. **Amenities:** Restaurant; room service. *In room:* TV, hair dryer, minibar.

Hotel Real ★★ Rich in tradition, this well-maintained hotel is on the main street, below the wooded bluff on which the palace of the prince is built. Although known primarily for its restaurant, it's a superlative choice for its luxurious bedrooms as well. The facade is decorated with flower boxes in the summer. The spacious rooms are well maintained and comfortable and have been renovated in a modern style, with deluxe mattresses and beautifully maintained private bathrooms. The hotel restaurant serves the best food in the principality (see review below).

Städtle 21, FL-9490 Vaduz, Liechtenstein. ✆ **00423/232-22-22.** Fax 00423/232-08-91. www.hotel-real.li. 13 units. 250F–270F double; 370F–430F suite. Rates include buffet breakfast. AE, DC, MC, V. Parking 8F. **Amenities:** Restaurant; bar; room service. *In room:* TV, hair dryer, minibar.

Residence ★ In the heart of the pedestrian zone of Vaduz, below the castle, this hotel is the most modern in the principality. It hardly lives up to the romantic, traditional atmosphere of Liechtenstein, but for those seeking the latest in comfort, it's superb. The decor is almost Japanese in concept, with rice paper screens and related artifacts. The hotel is sleek and commercial, with the latest technology. Bedrooms contain custom-designed wood furniture, and each comes with a work desk and computer. The hotel also

operates one of the country's best restaurants, serving market-fresh ingredients deftly
prepared.

Städtle 23, FL-9490 Vaduz, Liechtenstein. © **00423/239-20-20.** Fax 00423/239-20-22. www.residence.li.
24 units. 300F–320F double; 400F–500F suite. Rates include buffet breakfast. AE, DC, MC, V. **Amenities:**
Restaurant; bar; room service. *In room:* A/C (in some), TV, hair dryer, minibar, Wi-Fi (free).

Inexpensive

Landhaus am Giessen   Located a 5-minute walk east from the town center, this
structure dates from 1917, when it was built as the home of a prosperous conservative
burgher. Today it retains the solid and well-grounded aura of its original function. The
public areas are covered with flagstone floors, while the small bedrooms have wall-to-wall
carpeting and durable, reliable country-style furnishings, including private bathrooms.

Zollstrasse 16, FL-9490 Nendeln, Liechtenstein. © **00423/235-00-35.** Fax 00423/235-00-36. www.giessen.
li. 22 units. 150F–160F double. Rates include buffet breakfast. MC, V. Free parking. Closed Oct–Mar. **Amenities:** Jacuzzi; indoor heated pool; sauna. *In room:* TV, hair dryer, minibar, Wi-Fi (free).

WHERE TO DINE

Residence Restaurant ★ SWISS/INTERNATIONAL   In this previously recommended hotel lies one of the finest dining rooms in the principality. A wide range of
regional flavors and international specialties are served in a first-class setting. In the summer months tables are placed on a flower-filled terrace. One of the most skilled som-
meliers in Vaduz will guide you through the extensive wine *carte.* The cuisine is seriously
classical but the chef manages to hit a few contemporary and personal notes. For starters,
consider such dishes as a mixed salad of fried chicken strips, mushrooms, and fresh
tomatoes, or else the salad of sautéed garlic prawns. A selection of vegetarian dishes is also
offered, or else you can enjoy such delights as a caramelized filet of salmon in a curry-
and–lemon grass sauce, or else truffled breast of guinea fowl with polenta and a grappa
sauce.

Städtle 23. © **00423/239-8787.** Reservations recommended. Main courses 22F–43F. AE, MC, V. Daily
8am–10pm.

Restaurant Real ★★★ CONTINENTAL   Members of the royal family are frequent guests here—their castle looms above the restaurant, which is on the main street
of Vaduz. Cafe tables and chairs are outside. The dining rooms have paneling and lighting fixtures shaped like grape garlands. You'll appreciate the well-polished ambience of
understated prosperity. The chefs are the finest in the principality, working with the very
best ingredients, which they fashion into delectable platters with razor-sharp techniques.
There is a certain charm and fragrance connected with every dish. The menu may
include bouillabaisse, scampi ravioli, a gratin of seafood, *Tafelspitz* (boiled beef), veal
piccata, or perhaps a perfectly done Wiener schnitzel.

Städtle 21. © **00423/232-22-22.** Reservations required. Main courses 42F–61F; fixed-price 5-course
meal 135F. AE, DC, MC, V. Daily noon–2pm and 6–10pm.

Restaurant Torkel ★ (Finds FRENCH   The prince owns this charming country inn
on the site of an old wine press. It's in the royal vineyards on the outskirts of town; park
your car and follow the signs a short distance to a low-lying building. The cuisine,
though never accused of being overly imaginative, is satisfying and most filling, and a
true regional flavor of central Europe. Seasonal specialties are likely to include veal dishes,
filet goulash Stroganoff, and freshwater fish in Riesling sauce, as well as *rösti* dishes. Wine

is available from the royal cellars, including a house variety of the local sparkling wine *(sekt)*. The menu changes every day, offering only what is fresh at the market.

Hintergasse 9. © **00423/232-44-10.** www.torkel.li. Reservations recommended. Main courses 32F–59F. AE, DC, MC, V. Mon–Fri 11:30am–2:30pm; Mon–Sat 6:30–11:30pm.

VADUZ AFTER DARK

Conservative—and according to its critics, drab—Liechtenstein can't even begin to compete with the nightlife options of larger cities in Switzerland. Your best bet will probably involve retiring early after a nightcap at either your hotel bar or one of the spots mentioned below. Discos aren't really a factor here. Noteworthy bars, however, include the **Vanini Bar,** a youthful, high-energy meeting place in the Hotel Adler, Herrengasse (© **00423/232-21-31**), and the **Apero-Bar,** a site associated with the Restaurant Wolf, Städtle (© **00423/232-23-21**).

3 THE UNTERLAND

Formed by the Rhine Valley, Liechtenstein's Unterland (Lower Country) is at the foot of the Drei Schwestern (Three Sisters) mountains. It contains eight villages along the slopes of the Eschnerberg and five parishes. The landscape is a rugged mix of wooded hills, meadows, and clean brooks. Agricultural and industrial development has not been allowed to damage the environment.

The **Eschnerberg Historical Trail** is an extensive network of footpaths. The Eschnerberg hills were a refuge for prehistoric settlers, offering an islandlike setting in the marshy Rhine Valley. The marshes have since been drained. A hike here is pleasant and informative. You'll learn the history of the people who have lived in this region.

All the villages recommended below are on the postal-bus route from Vaduz. The Vaduz tourist office will provide a map outlining the various routings and transportation connections possible.

SCHELLENBERG

This second-smallest parish in the principality (pop. 577) also has the smallest surface area. It was already settled when the New Stone Age began. Some of the Iron Age artifacts displayed in the National Museum in Vaduz were unearthed here. The Herren (nobles) von Schellenberg built two castles here in the Middle Ages. One of the castles, the **Obere Burg Schellenberg,** has been restored and offers a good view. Schellenberg is a starting point for the Eschnerberg Historical Trail.

MAUREN-SCHAANWALD

These two villages are a mile apart, in a parish covering only 5 sq. km (3 sq. miles). Mauren is one of the most beautiful sights in Liechtenstein. It was called Muron in 1178 and today is known as the "Village of the Seven Hillocks." The remains of Roman baths and a 2nd-century farmhouse or outbuilding have been excavated here. The village is also known for its fine church, dating from 1787. The meadows and woodlands between Mauren and Schaanwald have been designated a bird sanctuary. The preserve contains a conservation pond and a nature trail. The villages are on the Schaan-Feldkirch road leading to Austria.

GAMPRIN-BENDERN

This small parish along the Rhine has picture-postcard charm. The two hamlets on the west spur of Eschnerberg are rich in archaeological discoveries. Excavations have shown that the area was inhabited continuously from about 2500 B.C. to the Roman era. Discoveries around Gamprin have yielded many clues about the culture of the New Stone Age. The remains of a farm and a small church dating from A.D. 55 have been found on the hill on which the **Bendern church** stands today. This church belonged to the Convent of Schanis (St. Gallen) from 809 to 1177 and to the Monastery of St. Luzi (Chur) from 1200 to 1816. After the Reformation, the St. Luzi monks built a larger structure, which included the abbot's quarters.

It was at Bendern's **Kirchhügel** that the men of the lowlands swore loyalty to the prince of Liechtenstein in 1699. It's very scenic and includes a fitness track, a history trail, and a campground. The **Mariengrotte (Mary's Grotto)** at Bendern is the only shrine of its kind in the country.

ESCHEN-NENDELN

Eschen was first mentioned in the Carolingian land registry in 850 under the name Essane, derived from the Celtic word *esca,* meaning "by the water." The water refers to the Esche, a nearby brook. Flint artifacts from the Middle Stone Age, about 5000 B.C., have been found here, and New Stone Age settlements have been excavated at Malanser and Schneller. The upper part of Eschen, **Schönbühl,** is one of the country's most attractive residential areas.

The parish includes the village of **Nendeln,** in which the foundation of a Roman villa and a prehistoric settlement have been discovered. Nendeln lies 5km (3 miles) northeast of Schaan, on Route 16.

Several buildings in the area are worth a visit. The **Pfründhaus** is a prebend structure, where the clergy lived. **Holy Cross Chapel,** on the Rofenberg, was formerly a place of public assembly. The restored **church at Eschen** has the original walls of the old church laid bare. Other churches include **St. Sebastian's Chapel** and the **Rochus Chapel.** Liechtenstein's first industrial enterprise was a **tile factory** founded at Nendeln in 1836. For a century, it was the only industrial plant in the Unterland.

There's a pool in Eschen and a health trail in Nendeln. You can also enjoy the peaceful mountain footpaths of the Eschnerberg trail.

Where to Stay & Dine

Hotel Engel   This is one of two hotels with the same name in Liechtenstein, a fact that causes lots of confusion to visitors arriving in the principality for the first time. A 10-minute drive north from Vaduz, near the principality's biggest ceramic factories (recommended separately in "Shopping" in section 2), the hotel has a dark, modern facade and a large, antique wine press in the yard. Seasonal flowers and plants add freshness to the public areas, a fact that appeals to some local residents, who like to congregate in the hotel on Sunday mornings. The midsize bedrooms are simple, durable, and very clean; 10 have a phone and TV.

Churer Strasse 1, FL-9485 Nendeln, Liechtenstein. ℂ **00423/373-31-31.** Fax 00423/373-12-60. 17 units. 170F–210F double. Rates include breakfast. AE, DC, MC, V. **Amenities:** Breakfast room. *In room:* TV (in some), phone (in some).

4 THE OBERLAND

The Oberland (Upper Country) of Liechtenstein was the former estate of the count of Vaduz. It consists of Vaduz and five parishes or communes: Planken, Schaan, Triesen, Triesenberg, and Balzers. Although the area is in the south of Liechtenstein, it's still known as the Upper Country because of topography. The Unterland (Lower Country), to the north, is filled with meadows and hills gently rising from the Rhine Valley, while the Oberland, from Planken on south, consists of higher country, reaching up to the Liechtenstein Alps.

In the shadow of the Drei Schwestern mountains, the Oberland abounds in woodlands and mountain trails, alpine flowers, and protected animal species. Settlements founded by Swiss immigrants some 700 years ago still retain their ancient traditions. There are plenty of opportunities for recreation throughout the region, but the alpine portion is the best place for winter sports.

All the villages and hamlets discussed below are reached by postal bus from Vaduz. Pick up a map at the tourist office in Vaduz (see "Essentials," earlier in this chapter), where you can also learn about possible routings and schedules.

Planken is the starting point for excursions to the **Drei Schwestern (Three Sisters)** area. From here, you'll have an outstanding panoramic view of the Rhine Valley and the Swiss mountains extending from Pizol to Lake Constance. A chapel here dedicated to St. Joseph contains copies of old masters and a bronze cross by Georg Malin.

SCHAAN

Located on the Arlberg railway line, at the foot of the Drei Schwestern, 3km (2 miles) west of Vaduz, Schaan is the country's main communications center. The Carolingian land registry (ca. A.D. 831) lists Liechtenstein's second-largest parish under the name Scana. Archaeologists have discovered the remains of a Roman fort, two Roman legionnaires' helmets from the 1st century A.D., and an Alemannic decorative shield from the 6th or 7th century. The 12th-century **Romanesque church** is worth a visit.

There's a **sports center** (© 00423/233-35-25) near a forest, offering tennis courts, a health center, an indoor swimming pool, public baths, and a children's playground. You can also hike in the mountains.

Theater a Kirchplatz (© 00423/237-59-69; www.tak.li) is one of the important cultural centers of the region. It presents international artists.

Where to Stay & Dine

Dux Hotel This Iberian-style country house is a superior tourist-class hotel. Built in 1924, it has a large sun terrace and long wrought-iron balconies. The rugged mountains loom in the background, and there are several old oak trees on the lawn. The comfortable, midsize rooms have wood ceilings and modern amenities, including well-maintained private bathrooms.

Duxweg 31, FL-9494 Schaan, Liechtenstein. © **00423/232-17-27.** Fax 00423/232-48-78. 10 units. 120F–144F double. Rates include buffet breakfast. MC, V. Free parking. Closed Feb and the 1st 3 weeks of Sept. **Amenities:** 3 restaurants; room service; sauna. *In room:* TV, minibar.

Hotel Linde (Value) This is the town's hotel bargain. The semibaroque facade has a single ornate gable and a pumpkin-colored extension. Well-pruned hedges shield the sun

terrace from street traffic. The clean and comfortable, but small, rooms are functionally
furnished. The hotel's restaurant (closed on Sun) serves a very limited but reasonably
priced menu.

Feldkircherstrasse 1, FL-9494 Schaan, Liechtenstein. ℂ **00423/232-17-04.** Fax 00423/232-09-29. www.
hotel-linde.li. 23 units. 150F–170F double. Rates include continental breakfast. AE, MC, V. Free parking.
Amenities: Restaurant. *In room:* TV, hair dryer, minibar.

Hotel Sylva im Sax ★ **Finds** This little chalet in the woods is so inviting that you
may want to anchor here for the night and make the easy commute to Vaduz. It's about
a block above the main road. A mother and daughter, Friederecke and Sylva Eberle, offer
well-furnished rooms and a sauna. The largest room is laid out for business travelers and
includes a fax machine and a second telephone. The restaurant serves some of the best
food in the area.

Saxgasse 6, FL-9494 Schaan, Liechtenstein. ℂ **00423/232-39-42.** Fax 00423/232-82-47. www.hotel-
sylva.li. 12 units. 174F–196F double. Rates include buffet breakfast. MC, V. Free parking. **Amenities:** Restaurant; bar; sauna. *In room:* TV, hair dryer, minibar.

Schaanerhof This is a modern hotel with a pink-and-white facade and balconies on
several sides. The interior is comfortable and warm, and the bedrooms are well furnished
and maintained. The main dining room serves Italian, Austrian, and Asian dishes, with
a revolving monthly menu featuring different cuisines of the world.

In der Ballota 3, FL-9494 Schaan, Liechtenstein. ℂ **00423/232-18-77.** Fax 00423/233-16-27. www.
schaanerhof.li. 28 units. 336F–440F double. Rates include buffet breakfast. AE, DC, V. Free parking. Closed
mid-Dec to mid-Jan. **Amenities:** Restaurant; bar; exercise room; Jacuzzi; sauna. *In room:* TV, hair dryer,
minibar.

TRIESENBERG

The largest parish of Liechtenstein has stretches of woodland, scrub, farmland, and pasture. High above the Rhine Valley is the village Triesenberg, containing about 2,000
inhabitants, reached by taking a hill road out of Vaduz. The road is filled with steep
bends but offers extensive views. The farming community is developing into a center for
light industry and tourism.

Triesenberg, like Planken, was settled in the late 13th century by Swiss immigrants
from the Valais. Many of the parish residents wear colorful regional garb. Modern materials and methods are used to build the houses, but the style dates from the early 14th
century. The influence of the Valais is evident. The restored town hall is elegant.

You can visit the **Heimatmuseum (Valais Heritage Museum),** which traces the culture of these immigrants. Artifacts, including tools, crafts, and furnishings, depict their
life, that and a 20-minute slide show in English. The museum (ℂ **00423/262-19-26**)
lies at Dorfzentrum, charging an admission of 2F. It's open Tuesday to Friday 1:30 to
5:30pm and Saturday 1:30 to 5pm; additionallly, from June to August the museum is
open Sunday 2 to 5pm.

At 780m (2,558 ft.), Triesenberg is a good base for excursions to the Liechtenstein
Alps. Excellent highways and well-tended hiking trails lead from Triesenberg to the
alpine resorts: Masescha (1,230m/4,034 ft.), Silum (1,500m/4,920 ft.), Gaflei
(1,500m/4,920 ft.), Malbun (1,575m/5,166 ft.), and Steg (1,380m/4,526 ft.). Steg is on
the way to Malbun and features the Valuna-Lopp cross-country skiing center and a ski
lift. The .8km (½-mile) Gnalp-Steg tunnel connects the valley with the alpine area.

Hotel Kulm   Spring blossoms cascade down the balconies of this centrally located hotel with a pink and light-grained wood facade. It offers a wide view of the valley, with a sidewalk cafe in front. The interior is a mix of rustic and modern styles. The furniture is comfortable in the well-maintained bedrooms, each with a private bathroom.

Dorfzentrum, FL-9497 Triesenberg, Liechtenstein. ℂ **00423/237-79-79.** Fax 00423/237-79-78. www. hotelkulm.li. 20 units. 70F–90F per person double. Rates include buffet breakfast. Half board 44F per person. AE, DC, MC, V. Free parking. **Amenities:** Restaurant; bar. In room: TV, hair dryer, Wi-Fi (free).

Hotel Restaurant Steg   This well-kept hotel, run by the Lamperts, is north of Triesenberg on the road to Steg. The building is more than 200 years old and has been renovated frequently. It's a rather underpublicized and unpretentious choice. The small rooms are simple but generally adequate. In addition to the regular doubles, there are two dormitories, one for 10 occupants, another for 5 occupants. Corridor bathrooms are well maintained and uncrowded.

Steg 274, FL-9497 Steg/Triesenberg, Liechtenstein. ℂ **00423/263-21-46.** Fax 00423/263-21-47. 11 units, none with bathroom; 7 dorm beds. 90F double; 25F dorm bed. Rates include buffet breakfast. Half board 25F. MC, V. Free parking. Closed mid-Apr to mid-May and mid-Nov to mid-Dec. **Amenities:** Restaurant. In room: No phone.

MASESCHA

Hikers and mountaineers prefer this small resort village 3km (2 miles) north of Triesenberg. The hamlet is perched high above the Rhine Valley. You can admire the cliffs, woods, lush meadows, and clear mountain brooks of this alpine world. In the village you should see **Theodul's Chapel,** a restored medieval church.

MALBUN

Fast rising as a winter ski area, Malbun, 15km (9 miles) north of Vaduz, is the center of winter sports in Liechtenstein, with ski lifts, chairlifts, a ski school, and hotels with indoor swimming pools. You can take the chairlift up to the **Bettlerjoch Peak,** at 2,070m (6,790 ft.). The Prince of Wales and Princess Anne learned to ski here many winters ago. In the summer this is an ideal starting point for mountain walks.

Where to Stay & Dine

Alpenhotel ★ (Finds   This is one of the oldest hotels in Malbun, in the same family since 1908. It's filled with charming details, such as chandeliers made from deer antlers. The wooden ceilings are painted with alpine floral designs and the heavy timbers are carved with regional reliefs. Jacob and Elsa Vögeli-Schroth are eager to please. There is a modern annex and a covered swimming pool. The attractive restaurant serves savory food.

Malbun, FL-9497 Triesenberg, Liechtenstein. ℂ **00423/263-11-81.** Fax 00423/263-96-46. www.alpen hotel.li. 23 units. 100F–210F double. Rates include buffet breakfast. Half board 25F per person. AE, DC, MC, V. Free parking. Closed mid-Apr to mid-May and Nov to mid-Dec. **Amenities:** Restaurant; indoor heated pool; room service. In room: TV, minibar.

Gorfion-Malbun ★ (Kids   This government-rated four-star chalet—the best in town—is near the ski lifts. The timbered lounge has a fireplace and stucco walls decorated with farm implements. The small to midsize rooms are comfortable and well furnished in a modern, but not stylish, way. The restaurant serves excellent meals in a homelike atmosphere. Note that in winter a junior suite costs the same price for anywhere from two to four guests.

Malbun, FL-9497 Triesenberg, Liechtenstein. ✆ **00423/263-29-44.** Fax 00423/263-95-61. www.s-hotels.
com. 64 units. Winter 248F–426F double, 328F–506F junior suite for 2–4; summer 214F–242F double, 294F–322F junior suite for 2, 314F–342F junior suite for 4. Rates include buffet breakfast in summer, half board in winter. AE, DC, MC, V. Free parking. Closed mid-Apr to mid-May and mid-Oct to mid-Dec. **Amenities:** Restaurant; bar; indoor heated pool; room service; sauna. *In room:* TV, hair dryer, minibar, Wi-Fi (free).

18

Fast Facts

1 FAST FACTS: SWITZERLAND

BUSINESS HOURS **Banks** are usually open Monday through Friday from 8:30am to 4:30pm (closed on legal holidays). Foreign currency may be exchanged at major railroad stations and airports daily from 8am to 10pm. Most **business offices** are open Monday to Friday 8am to noon and 2 to 6pm. **Shops** are usually open Monday to Friday 8am to 12:15pm and 1:30 to 6:30pm, and on Saturday 9am to 4pm. In most major cities, shops and supermarkets in the main train station are open on Sundays—generally between 11am and 4pm. In large cities most shops don't close during the lunch hour, although many do close on Monday morning.

DRINKING LAWS The official drinking age is 16. As in many European countries, the application of laws governing drinking is flexible and enforced only if a problem develops or if decorum is broken. Driving while intoxicated, particularly if it results in damage to property or persons, brings swift and severe punishment involving sizable fines and possible imprisonment.

DRUG LAWS *A word of warning:* Penalties for illegal drug possession are more severe in Switzerland than they are in the United States and Canada. You could go to jail or be deported immediately.

DRIVING RULES See "Getting There & Getting Around," p. 41.

ELECTRICITY Switzerland's electricity is 220 volts, 50 cycles, AC. Some international hotels are specially wired to allow North Americans to plug in their appliances, but you'll usually need a transformer for your electric razor, hair dryer, or soft-contact-lens sterilizer. You'll also need an adapter plug to channel the electricity from the Swiss system to the flat-pronged American system. Don't plug anything into the house current in Switzerland without being certain the systems are compatible.

EMBASSIES & CONSULATES Most embassies are located in the national capital, Bern; some nations maintain consulates in other cities such as Geneva. There's an **Australian consulate** in Geneva at 2, Chemins des Fins (✆ **022/799-91-00;** www.geneva.mission.gov.au). The **Canadian embassy** is at Kirchenfeldstrasse 88, Bern (✆ **031/357-32-00**). The embassy of the **United Kingdom** is at Thunstrasse 50, Bern (✆ **031/359-77-00**), and there is a British consulate in Geneva at 58, av. Louis Casaï, Cointrin (✆ **022/918-24-00**). The embassy of the **United States** is located at Jubiläumsstrasse 93, Bern (✆ **031/357-70-11**), with consulates in Zurich at Dufourstrasse 101 (✆ **043/499-29-60**) and in Geneva at 7, rue Versonnex (✆ **022/840-51-60**).

EMERGENCIES Dial ✆ **117** for the police (emergencies only) and ✆ **118** to report a fire.

GASOLINE (PETROL) See "Getting There & Getting Around," p. 41.

HOLIDAYS The legal holidays in Switzerland are New Year's (Jan 1–2), Good

Friday, Easter Monday, Ascension Day, Whit Monday, Bundesfeier (the Swiss National Holiday, Aug 1), and Christmas (Dec 25–26).

For more information on holidays, see "Switzerland Calendar of Events," in chapter 3.

HOSPITALS A prime location for medical aid is the **Geneva University Hospital,** 24, rue Micheli-du-Crest, CH-1211 Genève (✆ **022/372-60-19;** www.hug-ge.ch). Most physicians speak English and German.

INSURANCE For information on traveler's insurance, trip cancellation insurance, and medical insurance while traveling, please visit www.frommers.com/planning.

Travel Insurance Since Switzerland for most of us is far from home, and a number of things could go wrong—lost luggage, trip cancellation, a medical emergency—consider the following types of insurance.

Check your existing insurance policies and credit card coverage before you buy travel insurance. You may already be covered for lost luggage, canceled tickets, and/or medical expenses. The cost of travel insurance varies widely, depending on the cost and length of your trip, your age, health, and the type of trip you're taking, but expect to pay between 5% and 8% of the vacation itself.

You can get estimates from various providers through **InsureMyTrip.com.** Enter your trip cost and dates, your age, and other information, for prices from more than a dozen companies.

U.K. citizens and their families who make more than one trip abroad per year may find an annual travel insurance policy works out cheaper. Check **www.money supermarket.com**, which compares prices across a wide range of providers for single- and multitrip policies.

Most big travel agents offer their own insurance and will probably try to sell you their package when you book a holiday. Think before you sign. **Britain's Consumers' Association** recommends that you insist on seeing the policy and reading the fine print before buying travel insurance. The **Association of British Insurers** (✆ **020/7600-3333;** www.abi.org.uk) gives advice by phone and publishes *Holiday Insurance,* a free guide to policy provisions and prices. You might also shop around for better deals: Try **Columbus Direct** (✆ 0870/033-9988; www.columbusdirect.net).

Trip-Cancellation Insurance Trip-cancellation insurance will help retrieve your money if you have to back out of a trip or depart early, or if your travel supplier goes bankrupt. Trip cancellation traditionally covers such events as sickness, natural disasters, and State Department advisories. The latest news in trip-cancellation insurance is the availability of **expanded hurricane coverage** and the **"any-reason"** cancellation coverage—which costs more but covers cancellations made for any reason. You won't get back 100% of your prepaid trip cost, but you'll be refunded a substantial portion. **TravelSafe** (✆ **888/ 885-7233;** www.travelsafe.com) offers both types of coverage. Expedia also offers any-reason cancellation coverage for its air-hotel packages.

For details, contact one of the following recommended insurers: **Access America** (✆ 800/729-6021; www.accessamerica.com); **Travel Guard International** (✆ 800/ 826-4919; www.travelguard.com); **Travel Insured International** (✆ 800/243-3174; www.travelinsured.com); and **Travelex Insurance Services** (✆ 800/228-9792; www.travelex-insurance.com).

Medical Insurance For travel overseas, most U.S. health plans (including Medicare and Medicaid) do not provide coverage, and the ones that do often require you to pay for services upfront and reimburse you only after you return home.

As a safety net, you may want to buy travel medical insurance, particularly if you're traveling to a remote or high-risk area where emergency evacuation might be necessary. If you require additional medical insurance, try **MEDEX Assistance** (© 800/732-5309; www.medex assist.com) or **Travel Assistance International** (© 800/821-2828; www.travel assistance.com; for general information on services, call the company's **Worldwide Assistance Services, Inc.,** at © 800/777-8710; www.worldwideassistance.com).

Canadians should check with their provincial health plan offices or call **Health Canada** (© 866/225-0709; www. hc-sc.gc.ca) to find out the extent of their coverage and what documentation and receipts they must take home in case they are treated overseas.

On international flights (including U.S. portions of international trips), baggage coverage is limited to approximately $9.07 per pound, up to approximately $635 per checked bag. If you plan to check items more valuable than what's covered by the standard liability, see if your homeowner's policy covers your valuables, or get baggage insurance as part of your comprehensive travel-insurance package.

Lost-Luggage Insurance If your luggage is lost, immediately file a lost-luggage claim at the airport, detailing the luggage contents. Most airlines require that you report delayed, damaged, or lost baggage within 4 hours of arrival. The airlines are required to deliver luggage, once found, directly to your house or destination free.

LANGUAGE The three major languages are German, French, and Italian, although most people in the tourist industry speak English.

LEGAL AID This may be hard to come by in Switzerland. The government advises foreigners to consult their embassy or consulate (see "Embassies & Consulates," above) in case of a dire emergency, such as an arrest. Even if your embassy or consulate declines to offer financial or legal help, it will generally offer advice on how to obtain help locally.

MAIL Post offices in large cities are open Monday to Friday 7:30am to noon and 2 to 6:30pm, and on Saturday 7:30 to 11am. If you have letters forwarded to a post office to be collected after you arrive, you'll need a passport for identification. The words POSTE RESTANTE must be clearly written on the envelope. Letters not collected within 30 days are returned to the sender. Letters are either first class, meaning air mail, or surface mail, rated second class.

NEWSPAPERS & MAGAZINES Swiss papers are published in German, French, or Italian (depending on the region). Most news kiosks in major cities stock the British dailies, plus the latest editions of the *International Herald Tribune,* which, although edited in Paris, is printed in Zurich. *USA Today,* the latest copies of *Time* and *Newsweek,* and other U.S. and British magazines are also widely available.

PASSPORTS See www.frommers.com/planning for information on how to obtain a passport. For other information, please contact the following agencies:

For Residents of Australia Contact the **Australian Passport Information Service** at © 131-232, or visit the government website at www.passports.gov.au.

For Residents of Canada Contact the central **Passport Office,** Department of Foreign Affairs and International Trade, Ottawa, ON K1A 0G3 (© 800/567-6868; www.ppt.gc.ca).

For Residents of Ireland Contact the **Passport Office,** Setanta Centre, Molesworth Street, Dublin 2 (© **01/671-1633;** www.irlgov.ie/iveagh).

For Residents of New Zealand Contact the **Passports Office** at © **0800/225-050** in New Zealand or 04/474-8100, or log on to www.passports.govt.nz.

For Residents of the United Kingdom Visit your nearest passport office, major post office, or travel agency or contact the **United Kingdom Passport Service** at © **0870/521-0410** or search its website at www.ukpa.gov.uk.

For Residents of the United States To find your regional passport office, either check the U.S. State Department website or call the **National Passport Information Center** toll-free number (© **877/ 487-2778**) for automated information.

POLICE Dial © **117** for emergencies.

SMOKING Switzerland remains one of the last havens in western Europe for the smoker, and many restaurants and hotel lobbies want to keep it that way. Six out of 26 cantons have introduced laws to curb passive smoking. So far, only the Ticino and Geneva have outlawed public smoking. Since the law is in a state of flux, one should inquire before lighting up in a public place.

TAXES A value-added tax (VAT) of 7.6% is added to bills. In addition, drivers entering Switzerland are required by law to purchase a windshield sticker for 40F, valid for travel on Swiss roads for 1 year. Stickers are sold at all Customs posts upon entering Switzerland.

TIME Switzerland's clocks are usually 6 hours ahead of Eastern Standard Time in the United States, and 1 hour ahead of Greenwich Mean Time. However, because Switzerland and the United States switch their clocks every spring and fall during different weeks, the time difference is sometimes only 5 hours.

TIPPING A 15% service charge is included in all hotel and restaurant bills, although some people leave an additional tip for exceptional service. For taxis, a tip is usually included in the charges (a notice will be posted in the cab).

TOILETS Most public restrooms are clean and modernized. However, in this multilingual country you have to know what you are looking for. Depending on the part of Switzerland, public restrooms may be WC (water closet), *Toiletten, toilettes,* or *gabinetti.* Women's rooms may be identified as DAMEN or FRAUEN, SIGNORE or DONNE, FEMMES or DAMES, and men's rooms may be labeled HERREN or MÄNNER, SIGNORI or UOMINI, HOMMES or MESSIEURS. Public restrooms can be found at bus stations, railway terminals, and cable-car platforms. If these aren't handy, use the restrooms in cafes. Most public lavatories are not free, usually costing 1F for standing, 2F for sitting. You can sometimes find free toilets in train stations.

VISITOR INFORMATION You can get the latest tourist information before leaving home from the nearest branch of the Swiss tourism office. In the **United States** the center has an office at 608 Fifth Ave., New York, NY 10020 (© **877/794-8037;** www.myswitzerland.com).

In **Great Britain,** visit 30 Bedford St., London WC2E 9ED (© **020/7845-7680**).

WEATHER American Express Travel Related Service Company provides hourly reports on current weather conditions and 3-day forecasts for more than 900 cities in Europe. For Switzerland, dial © **900/ WEATHER** (900/932-8437; there's a 95¢ per-minute charge for the call) and press the first three letters of the desired city: BAS (Basel), BER (Bern), GEN (Geneva), LUC (Lucerne), STM (St. Moritz), or VAD (Vaduz, Liechtenstein).

2 AIRLINE, HOTEL & CAR-RENTAL WEBSITES

MAJOR AIRLINES

Air Canada
www.aircanada.com

Adria
www.adria.si

Aeroflot
www.aeroflot.ru

Air France
www.airfrance.com

Alitalia
www.alitalia.com

American Airlines
www.aa.com

British Airways
www.british-airways.com

Continental Airlines
www.continental.com

Delta Air Lines
www.delta.com

EgyptAir
www.egyptair.com

El Al Airlines
www.el.co.il

Emirates Airlines
www.emirates.com

Finnair
www.finnair.com

Fly Niki
www.flyniki.com

Germanwings Airlines
www.germanwings.com

Iberia Airlines
www.iberia.com

Lufthansa
www.lufthansa.com

North American Airlines
www.flynaa.com

Northwest Airlines
www.nwa.com

Norwegian Airlines
www.norwegian.no

Qatar Airlines
www.qatarairways.com

Royal Dutch Airlines
www.klm.com

Scandinavian Airlines
www.flysas.com

Singapore Airlines
www.singaporeair.com

South African Airways
www.flysaa.com

Spanair
www.spanair.com

Swiss International Airlines
www.swiss.com

Thai Airways International
www.thaiair.com

Tunisair
www.tunisair.com

Turkish Airlines
www.thy.com

United Airlines
www.united.com

US Airways
www.usairways.com

Virgin America
www.virginamerica.com

Virgin Atlantic Airways
www.virgin-atlantic.com

BUDGET AIRLINES

Aer Lingus
www.aerlingus.com

Air Berlin
www.airberlin.com

Austrian Airlines
www.aua.com

Avolar
www.avolar.com.mx

Baboo Airlines
www.flybaboo.com

Blue Islands Air
www.blueislands.com

BMI Baby
www.bmibaby.com

Brussels Airlines
www.brusselsairlines.com

Cirrus Airlines
www.cirrusairlines.de

Condor
www.condor.com

Croatia Airlines
www.croatiaairlines.com

Czech Airlines
www.czechairlines.com

Darwin Airline
www.darwinairline.com

easyJet
www.easyjet.com

Frontier Airlines
www.frontierairlines.com

LOT
www.lot.com

Malèv Airlines
www.malev.com

Ryanair
www.ryanair.com

Tap Airlines
www.flytap.com

Ted (part of United Airlines)
www.flyted.com

Tuifly Airlines
www.tuifly.com

MAJOR HOTEL & MOTEL CHAINS

Best Western International
www.bestwestern.com

Clarion Hotels
www.choicehotels.com

Comfort Inns
www.comfortinn.com

Concorde Hotels & Resorts
www.concorde-hotels.fr

Courtyard by Marriott
www.marriott.com/courtyard

Econo Lodges
www.choicehotels.com

Epoque Hotels
www.epoquehotels.com

Etap Hotel
www.etaphotel.com

Europa Wander Hotels
www.wanderhotels.com

Four Seasons
www.fourseasons.com

Hilton Hotels
www1.hilton.com

Hyatt
www.hyatt.com

Hotel Formula 1
www.hotelformule1.com

Ibis Hotels
www.ibishotel.com

InterContinental Hotels & Resorts
www.ichotelsgroup.com

Kempinski Hotels
www.kempinski.com

Leading Hotels of the World
www.lhw.com

Marriott
www.marriott.com

Mercure Hotels
www.mercure.com

MinOtels
www.minotel.com

Mövenpick Hotel Group
http://group.moevenpick.com

Novotel Hotels
www.novotel.com

Preferred Hotels & Resorts
www.preferredhotels.com

Private Selection Hotels
www.alpineclassics.ch

Quality
www.qualityinn.choicehotels.com

Radisson Hotels & Resorts
www.radisson.com

Relais & Châteaux Hotels
www.relaischateaux.com

Ramada Worldwide
www.ramada.com

Renaissance
www.renaissancehotels.com

Residence Inn by Marriott
www.marriott.com/residenceinn

The Rezidor Hotel Group
www.rezidorparkinn.com

Romantik Hotels
www.romantikhotels.ch

Sheraton Hotels & Resorts
www.starwoodhotels.com/sheraton

Silence Hotel
www.relaisdusilence.com

Small Luxury Hotels of the World
www.slh.com

Sol Melia Hotels & Resorts
www.solmelia.com

Swiss International Hotels
www.sih.ch

Wellness Plus Hotels
www.wellnessplus.ch

Westin Hotels & Resorts
www.starwoodhotels.com/westin

CAR-RENTAL AGENCIES

Advantage
www.advantage.com

Alamo
www.alamo.com

Auto Europe
www.autoeurope.com

Avis
www.avis.com

Budget
www.budget.com

Dollar
www.dollar.com

Enterprise
www.enterprise.com

Hertz
www.hertz.com

Kemwel (KHA)
www.kemwel.com

National
www.nationalcar.com

Payless
www.paylesscarrental.com

Rent-A-Wreck
www.rentawreck.com

Thrifty
www.thrifty.com

INDEX

See also Accommodations and Restaurant indexes, below.

RESTAURANTS

500